SOCIAL CRITIQUE AND COMMITMENT

Essays in Honor of Henry Rosenfeld

Edited by

Majid Al-Haj
Michael Saltman
Zvi Sobel

University Press of America,® Inc.
Lanham · Boulder · New York · Toronto · Oxford

**Copyright © 2005 by
University Press of America,® Inc.**
4501 Forbes Boulevard
Suite 200
Lanham, Maryland 20706
UPA Acquisitions Department (301) 459-3366

PO Box 317
Oxford
OX2 9RU, UK

Library of Congress Control Number: 2005921316
ISBN 0-7618-3149-5 (paperback : alk. ppr.)

For Henry Rosenfeld
A just soul and teacher of soft power

Contents

Acknowledgments

We are thankful for the encouragement and support this undertaking has enjoyed from a wide variety of friends and colleagues of Henry Rosenfeld. Various bodies within The University of Haifa have shown a particularly high level of support including the Office of the Rector, the Research Authority, the Faculty of Social Sciences, the Sociology and Anthropology Department and the Center for Multiculturalism and Educational Research.

Additionally, we wish to thank Ms. Claudia Goodich-Avram, a doctoral candidate in The Department of Sociology and Anthropology, who acted as project assistant from the project's inception.

We also wish to acknowledge with thanks permission to reprint the following:

- 1967 as a Political – Economic Turning Point by Shlomo Swirsky which is reprinted from Avi Bareli, Tuvia Friling, Daniel Gutwein (eds.), *Society and Economy in Israel: Historical and Contemporary Aspects*, the Ben Gurion Research Institute for the Study of Israel & Zionism, Sede Boker, Israel, 2005.
- Suicide Terrorism and America's Mission Impossible by Scott Atran which was previously published as Trends in Suicide Terrorism: Sense and Nonsense in the *Science and Culture series, International Seminar on Nuclear War – 31st session of May 2004.*
- Map of Roads in the West Bank which appears in the article by Maya Rosenfeld adapted with permission from B'tselem.

Introduction

The initial letter that was sent out to the contributors to this volume requested that the papers should strive to relate, in the broadest of terms, either to the ethnographic region of the Middle East or to a critical assessment of social and cultural issues. A combination of both would, of course, be ideal. For these are the matters that have characterized Henry Rosenfeld's professional career for over half a century and these are the matters that have consistently entered both the academic and social discourse between Henry and his colleagues and his students. The same should be said for Henry's wife, Shula, who has also been his research partner during this long period of academic activity.

If Zvi Sobel's biographic interview of Henry tells us much of the man himself, the contributions to this *festschrift* can tell us something about the impact that Henry may have had on us, the contributors. If the interview with Henry represents and clarifies Henry's world view and the theoretical perspectives that are consistent with that world view, this introduction will confine itself to addressing the essays of the contributors and their conformity to the parameters we set out in our initial letter. It is certainly not our aim to discuss the conformity of the papers to Henry's anthropological framework of reference. We have, indeed, intentionally left the interview with Henry as the last chapter, and the reader, if he is so inclined, can satisfy his/her academic curiosity by measuring up the different papers against the yardstick of Henry's thinking. But the volume, in addition to being a celebratory *festschrift* to Henry makes its own academic statement in terms of the subject matter and contentions of each and every paper.

Most of the papers have focused on Israel, not only in terms of its difficulties and inequities, but also in terms of some of its prevalent beliefs as well as some of the consequences of its existence for the region as a whole. In this last category it is possible to place Kimmerling's paper. On face value, there is absolutely no connection between Baruch Kimmerling's paper on the plight of the Crimean Tatars and the State of Israel. Had the paper been written as a journal article or as a contribution to any other book, it is a piece of ethno-historical research that deals exclusively with the political and cultural status of the Tatars in Crimea. But since it was written for this book, it has an allegorical standing that highlights the equivalent plight of indigenous Palestinians. An Israeli reader might be appalled at the shabby treatment meted out by the Russian and Ukrainian authorities to Tatar refugees, their political disenfranchisement and their ethnic-cultural impoverishment. But many of them would also not be prepared to recognize that much of what Kimmerling has written in his paper entitled *The Dispersal, Ethnic Cleansing and Return of the Tatar People* is implicitly relevant and applicable to the plight of the Palestinians closer to home.

Ethnic Cleansing is a blanket term that covers a pathological problem that ranges in severity from deliberate mass murder, as in former Yugoslavia or

Ruanda and Burundi, to its minor expression in the hostile control over the educational system of an ethnic minority in a sovereign state. Majid Al Haj's paper, *Education among the Palestinians in Israel: Born under Control*, describes this latter process. He contends that despite the quantitative expansion of educational facilities for Israeli Arabs, the Israeli educational system has not furthered social and cultural change, but has rather hampered development in the Israeli Arab community. It is a system not based on the liberalism of a multicultural ideology but is rather geared to the political interests of the State, which, to a degree, also holds true for education in the Jewish sector. Al Haj attributes the failures of the Arab sector's educational system to the government's deliberate policy of control over both the personnel and the content of the school system. He cites as examples the vetting of teachers by the Israeli security services that gives greater emphasis to political reliability than professional competence. He draws several comparisons between Jewish and Arab schools that demonstrate not only inequality but also outright discrimination against Arabs. The policy is clearly delineated in his analysis of the development of the history curriculum during different historical periods and the asymmetrical teaching of languages, Hebrew and Arabic, which are totally different both in aim and content.

A second paper that examines Israeli policy-making towards its Arab citizens focuses on urban planning. In most western societies, it is understood that villages are small traditional communities, originally based on an agricultural economy, whereas towns are large impersonal conglomerates based on multi-faceted non-agricultural economic activity. Somewhere in between is the anomalous phenomenon of suburbia. Rassem Khamaisi's paper, *Between Town and Village: Continuity and Change in Arab Localities in Israel*, demonstrates a historical and culturally specific process, exclusively relevant for the Arab citizens of the State of Israel. The crux of the Israeli-Palestinian conflict is land, not only in terms of national sovereignty, but also in terms of physical control over land in an objective sense. The aims of the Israeli planners have been directed towards limiting the expansion of villages and to encourage the Arabs to adopt the residential and occupational patterns of urbanization. The overall idea is to concentrate and contain the growing Arab population in compact, densely-populated areas, rather than enabling the spatial growth of rural areas. Large-scale sequestration of Arab lands had already left the Arabs with diminished reserves of land to accommodate the population expansion, which has grown from 156,000 in 1948 to over a million in 2002. From the standpoint of the Israeli planners the ideology of segregation has not enabled Arabs to be absorbed in the Jewish cities and towns and even in the traditionally "mixed" cities there are specifically recognized Arab neighbourhoods. But the "urbanization" of Arab villages has been based on incomplete planning, leading to a lack of infrastructure, housing shortage and the consequential illegal building of houses for the ever-growing population. Furthermore, the transfer of economic activity from agriculture to industry and the services has placed the Arab population into a state of even greater dependency on the government. But Khamaisi stresses that despite all these pressures, most Arab Israelis have stubbornly remained "villagers", even though their locale is technically defined as a town. The elites are still based on the rural structure and its associated values and there is a strong sense of socio-cultural belonging to that rural context. Despite the clear aims of the planners to exercise control over the Arab sector, Israeli Arabs have demonstrated a remarkable resilience in adapting to this process. In at least one sense this same resilience is reflected in Maya Rosenfeld's paper in this volume by her use of the concept of *sumud.*

Referring back to Al Haj's paper, it is not surprising then that some of the consequences of the Israeli educational system find their way into the perceptions of students vis-a-vis the concept of ethnicity. Yuval Yonay's paper, *Why it's so Hard to Teach Radical Ideas: Some Reflections on the Sociology of (Radical)(Sociology) Teaching* demonstrates this precisely. He focuses on the attitudes of graduate students in the Sociology and Anthropology Department at the University of Haifa. Ethnicity is, of course, a fundamental issue in Israeli Sociology. As a generalized conclusion he finds that students resist the idea of ethnic gaps, since it goes against their preconceptions of the need for solidarity. He found that students of oriental parentage have greater anxieties as regards their origins than students of Ashkenazi (European) parentage. The former have developed a strong "Israeli" identity expressed in the idea of Jewish solidarity against Arabs, this solidarity serving to reduce their own self-denigration within Israeli society. Yonay's "fieldwork site" was, primarily, his own course on the *Sociology of the Occupation.* His findings are a series of propositions that are inductively drawn from his observations in class. For example, scientific theories cannot overcome emotional convictions. When he presented the students with evidence of atrocities perpetrated against Arabs, the students initially argued that these were committed out of necessity, but in the end they lost interest in arguing with him on the grounds that his radical thinking had tainted his scientific sociology. The students created a binary opposition by pitting a desire to avoid issues against the demand to return to "academic matters". So a further proposition is that that radical speakers are partisan and unreliable as contrasted with neutral speakers. Yonay found that Jewish students did not change their views as a result of this course. Equally interesting is that the Israeli Palestinian students did everything to avoid discussing politics in the public discourse. On a pragmatic level, they were the representatives of their families who were funding their studies and that economic investment should not be endangered by political activity. Only by being distanced from the problem, does the problem become heightened and clarified. In essence, this links to Kimmerling's paper, for one might assume that Yonay's students would find the issue of the Crimean Tatars, a legitimate "academic" matter without understanding the significance of Kimmerling's irony.

Maya Rosenfeld's paper *"Pleasures of Duty" of the Occupiers, "Duty of Sumud" of the Besieged:The Israeli Imposed Closure Regime in the Occupied West Bank,* could be described as an Ethnography of the Occupation. The strength of this paper does not lie in any abstract theoretical propositions, but rather in the powerful description of a situation by means of a classic participant-observational technique. A group of volunteer women, ideologically committed to human rights, opposed to the Occupation, stand vigil at Israeli Army roadblocks in the West Bank. They observe the behaviour of the soldiers who are sent to man the roadblocks and the behaviour of the Palestinians who, for various mundane reasons, have to pass through these roadblocks, more often than not without success. On occasions the women intervene on behalf of the Palestinians on extreme humanitarian grounds. The observations are stark and disturbing. The phenomenon of the roadblock is presented as a process, in its evolvement over a time sequence, the ethnographic present being a strange, almost ritualized confrontation between the soldiers and the Palestinians, whom Rosenfeld describes as the "besieged". Some of the soldiers approach their task with pleasure, on occasions sadistic pleasure, legitimized by seeing what they are doing as protecting the State against the Palestinians, who are cognitively dehumanized in the soldiers' perceptions of reality. The other side of the coin is the persistence of the Palestinians who present themselves passively day after day at the humiliating roadblocks. For them, the duty of the persistence, of the *sumud* is to clearly sound a message to the Israelis and to the soldiers that the Palestinians are here to stay. The paper is somewhat reminiscent of the ethnographic style of Colin Turnbull who described the horrors of the reality of the Ik, giving his readers a startling "slice of life" of reality.

The catastrophe of the Palestinian/Israeli conflict was exacerbated by the 1967 war, the consequences not only being the body count over the past 34 years, but also the countless accumulated suffering by both peoples including the economic deprivation that is the logical outcome of prolonged conflict. Shlomo Swirski's essay is a sweeping survey of many of the ills that have befallen Israel since the capture of the West Bank and Gaza in 1967. These are above and beyond the phenomenon of an international dispute and constitute a set of far-reaching consequences for the economic, social and ethnic composition of Israel. The key causative factor has been Israel's illegal settlement of the conquered territories. Hundreds of thousands of settlers have been systematically diverting enormous sums of money into the settlements, distorting Israel's economy from what was once a broad-based welfare state ideology to a narrow capitalist model of supply-side economics. Add to this the losses incurred through additional wars, the *intifadas* and economic mismanagement throughout different periods, Israel's economy has become the antithesis to any state effort to remedy the society's social ills. In fact it has aggravated the gaps that had already existed in Israeli society from the outset. Israel has produced one of the world's leading military-industrial complexes, with all of its concomitant spin-offs into the high technology industry. The money invested and the money earned in these latter enterprises stand in excessively sharp contrast to the investment in and earnings of the traditional industries, usually of a labour intensive nature and usually to be found in the socio-geographic periphery of the society. What clearly emerges from Swirski's paper is the fact that the socio-economic structure of Israel has in large part been determined by Israel's expansionist policy of illegal settlement on the West Bank and Gaza. This policy has been one of the impediments to peace in the

Middle East and has skewed the inequities of the economy in the direction described by Swirski.

Alex Weingrod's paper, *What Went Wrong?*, is an overview of the processes through which Israel has passed leading to a contemporary state of widespread malaise. Weingrod chooses to demonstrate this by reviewing two books that take a broad view on Israeli society. The first is Baruch Kimmerling's, *The Invention and Decline of Israeliness* and the second is Shafir and Peled's work, *Being Israeli: The Dynamics of Multiple Citizenship*. As claimed in several other papers in this volume, Israel's major watershed is the Six Day War and its aftermath. New elites have emerged to challenge the old hegemony. One of the values that motivates some of these elites is their "Jewishness", which in turn raises the question of the incompatibility between "Jewish" and "Democratic" as political concepts, a point also noted by Saltman in his paper. "Jewishness" and Security has segregated and marginalized the Arabs within Israeli society. Kimmerling's book is a gloomy assessment, which Weingrod sums up cogently by saying that nothing went wrong, since, according to Kimmerling, nothing was ever right. The second book, addressed by Weingrod, follows some of the paths taken by Kimmerling. Its main message, however, does not focus so much on Israeliness, but rather on the inequities of Israeli civil society throughout its history. The argument stems more from the point of departure of Liberal Democracy, which supposedly represents the values of contemporary Israeli society. If Kimmerling emphasizes Militarism as a dominant value underlying the Israeli ethos, Shafir and Peled single out the Jewish settlement of the West Bank and the Gaza Strip as Israel's Achilles heel. Not accepting either approach *in toto*, Weingrod nevertheless leans more to the Shafir-Peled approach, for embedded within it are the seeds of hope. For a civil society cannot live endlessly under the conditions, described as "what went wrong" and Weingrod views Israeli society as a civil society.

Not all the papers are critical in their orientation, but indicate processes that have occurred as a consequence of Israel's presence in the region. Emmanuel Marx examines the concept of "stranger" as applied to the traders who traded with the Beduin of South Sinai. He employs Simmel's idea of every individual becoming a stranger in this modern cosmopolitan world. In the indigenous world of Beduin trading, the Beduin themselves were the traders. Trading and traders were an integral part of their normative existence. But the effects of the Israeli occupation of Sinai had their non-intended effects. New labour opportunities were created and villages achieved a greater degree of permanency. The changes in economic activity brought in turn changes in patterns of consumption, and traders became the lifeline between the Beduin and the external world. But the Israeli authorities regarded the traders with much suspicion, for these were now strangers and strangers are not easily regulated. Despite these suspicions, the traders of El Arish still flourished and the 1973 war created an even greater dependence of the Beduin on these traders. Even though the nomads view traders unfavourably, as exploiters, they cannot survive without them. The trader is an ambiguous entity, familiar with the community within which he lives, but also a stranger to that community. He serves a function, as does the Leopard

Skin Chief among the Nuer, who is also a "stranger" in the community where he resides. Anyone, beyond the immediate circle of intimate relationships becomes a "stranger". Relations towards the traders of El Arish are based on mutual commercial interests and not on the informal ties of friendship. These traders are part of the social reality, but do not belong to it.

Two papers address themselves to predominantly internal issues within Israeli society that only have implicit connections to Israel's relationship to the outside world. Daphna and Yoram Carmeli's paper, entitled *Donor Insemination in Israel: Demography, Politics and the Natural Family*, reveals a strong cultural bias by Israelis to opt for artificial insemination, when required by the IVF rather than by the DI technique. The second paper, *The Political Culture of the Separation of Powers in Israel*, by Michael Saltman, examines a mythical relationship of checks and balances between the three branches of government in Israel—the Legislature, executive and Judiciary.

The Carmelis argue that biotechnological technologies affect the relationship of the body to both culture and nature. Reproduction in Israel is seen as a policy aim for Jewish collective national interests in the maintenance of a Jewish majority in Israel. Since 1953 there have been monetary incentives for large families, well-funded fertility treatments and impediments placed in the way of abortions. While no discrimination has been made against Muslim women, the latter have made little use of these services and neither have they been encouraged to do so. Jews accord a very high value to the idea of a "natural family" and the preferred biotechnological technique is IVF, which although more complex, more intrusive, more unpleasant and not free of medical accidents is still the technique closest to the ideal family. Orthodox Jews tend to reject the alternative donor insemination (DI) technique, for precisely that stated familial value. When DI is the technique of choice in Israel, the demands at the screening stage are to realize a phenotype that most resembles the physical attributes of the parents themselves, again in the attempt to achieve the "natural family" ideal. DI recipients tend to be secretive about the treatment itself, male partners even more so than females. But where "openness" is allowed for, there are some clear preferences for stated phenotypes, for example, "tallness" which probably originates in the influence of mass-culture. Also Ashkenazi donors are the preferred type, this reflecting a statement about Israel's socio-economic and political structure and cultural preferences. The family emerges from this study as being of utmost importance both on the plane of power relations, as well as at the level of the making of Israel's collective and national definitions.

Saltman's paper examines the problematic relationship between the polity and the judiciary in democracies and the nature of the checks and balances in the separation of powers that enables the political system, as a whole, to function. In Israel's case, there are a number of culture-specific issues that affect this relationship. The first factor is the incompatibility between the very concept of Democracy and the claim that is laid to Israel being a Jewish State. Democracies, in their modern form, only emerged as a function of the breakdown of the hegemony of the religious authorities over state institutions. This has not happened in Israel. The second factor was the historical particularism of Israel's formative years, during which Ben Gurion coined and imposed the concept of "mamlachtiut" (statism) on Israeli society. This was a concept that elevated state interests, as defined by the polity, to a level above and beyond basic individual rights and their associated values, even when reflected in legal norms. The third factor is the cultural phenomenon of "illegalism". This is cultural, because Israel has not yet fully escaped from the "shtetl" (East European Jewish village/township) mentality, where "cutting legal corners" was an adaptive survival mechanism in a hostile political environment. The fourth factor is that the lawyers who established Israel's judicial institutions, were mostly of German origin and German legal training that reflected the liberal and scientific legal tradition of the *Rechtsstaat*, a concept, analagous in some respects to the Anglo-American idea of Rule of Law. These German lawyers and the East European politicians found themselves together in a relationship of strong mutual antipathy that characterized the relationship between the polity and the judiciary. The pejorative barb of being a "judicial elite" is still thrown at the Supreme Court Justices by the politicians of 2004.

Three papers deal with global issues, and as such, have their implications also for Israel. Hart and Atran's papers are overtly critical in their intent. Lewis paper is implicitly critical, if that is what the reader wants to read into the paper. *The Globalization of Spirit Possession* deals with the growth of the belief in the supernatural in the modern world in general and in Israel in particular. If the nineteenth century evolutionists envisaged the ultimate triumph of science over animism, they might be unpleasantly surprised by some of the contemporary global trends that have returned to animism. Believers in oracular spirit possession claim that the spirits have direct powers over people's lives or special information about the supernatural powers that have such powers. The spirits themselves can act for both good and bad. In equating saint worship in Israel to the phenomenon of oracular spirit possession, Lewis is really looking at the more generalized phenomenon of belief in the supernatural as it spreads throughout the modern world. He seeks explanations that ultimately relate to deprivation in one way or another, claiming, at least in the Israeli case, that the irrational movements that emerge are the reactions of people to the unremitting crises of Israeli society. These explanations, when applied to the specific case studies, are the classical structural-functional, neo-evolutionary or Marxist that look for the root causes of a phenomenon in the system. But Lewis is interested in the world-wide phenomenon of movements that seek answers for questions, when it is clear that the people are convinced of both the reality and efficacy of these supernatural agents, when they turn to them. Lewis opts for a theory based on diffusionism, the arch enemy of the nineteenth century evolutionists. He points out that that it is ironic that the diffusionist forces supposedly allowing for the triumph of science over animism are the very same forces that are spreading supernatural belief systems throughout the contemporary world. The mass media spread the news of various belief systems to huge receptive audiences, which cuts across ethnic, class and rural/urban divisions. Lewis points out the irony of alternative medicine being sponsored by established medical institutions.

Scott Atran's paper, *Suicide Terrorism and America's Mission Impossible*, demonstrates America's lack of understanding of the root causes of suicide terrorism. The United States administration and media misconceive suicide bombers as evil, deluded, homicidal misfits who thrive on poverty, ignorance and anarchy. It also emphasizes that military responses to suicide terrorism as practiced by America, Israel, Russia and other States have little more than tactical value at any given point of time, and as such, have little potential for finding a strategic solution for the problem. To date, counter-terrorist policies have done little more than achieve the breakdown of terrorist organizations into small decentralized transnational cells that are even more dangerous than the identifiable terrorist groups. He argues that American or other major power support for oppressive regimes engenders terrorism. If the aim is to dry up support for the terrorists, then one must address the basic grievances of those who lend their support to terrorism. But what is happening, in fact, is that Muslim sentiment against America is progressively radicalizing, even though the people who support the suicide bombers look favourably on American freedom rights, but, at the same time, despise the American foreign policy that support corrupt states and abuse human rights. Many corrupt Arab governments have delegated social welfare functions to radical Islamic groups that engage in terrorism. Ethnicity is the general parameter for recruitment purposes, but, for example, the Palestinians use religious sentiments more than do the Bosnian Muslims. On the whole recruitment is more ideologically based than grievance based, even though the two are not mutually exclusive. Atran argues that in the war against terror, the first step is to identify the values in the culture in order to learn how to prevent these values from endangering societies. America cannot expect to impose its own economic and political values on these societies. Instead one should attempt to understand how religious fundamentalists want to desecularize modernity.

Keith Hart's paper, *Some Reflections on Anthropology and Political Economy*, is a critical overview of the processes underlying the development of the concept, The Economy. After millennia of the economy being nothing more than household management, it is now an issue, which we call Economics. Hart demonstrates that the original Greek concept of household management had nothing to do with markets, money and a wider notion of society. But Adam Smith transformed the emphasis from the narrow scope of the domestic order to the concept of a political economy. Capitalists were motivated by growth as an economic aim. At the same time States became interested in furthering their national interests by means of their involvement in the economy. Both these factors have brought about an historical shift from self-sufficient rural households to dependence on urban, national and global markets. One of the consequences of this has been the growth of inequality. On occasions, inequality is legitimized and institutionalized within the phenomenon of Apartheid. But even without such institutionalization, inequality is intrinsic to the functioning of all modern economies within modern political systems. At this point, Hart's paper neatly links up with Swirski's paper which describes how the political intervention of the Israeli government has created an inequality discriminating in favour of a small number of settlers in the occupied territories. This in turn discriminates against the true social and geographical periphery of the Israeli economy. The contemporary Economy is even further removed from reality and much of its activity has become virtual. More money is made today in playing the stock markets, than by the classical economic activities of production and consumption. Hart claims that there has been a shift of emphasis from material production to competition over knowledge, a phenomenon predicted by Daniel Bell some decades ago. The internet extension of reality cannot be easily regulated by sovereign states, which are having diminishing influence over international money markets. But there is no doubt as to where Hart's critique is pointed, for the global economy is being run by American and other western corporations and has become totally dehumanized in the process.

Nira Reiss' paper, *Rhetoric of the Destruction of the Israeli Welfare State*, describes the death throes of the dying values of social justice, accelerated by the policies of the Sharon government of 2003-2004. It is the culmination of a long process, during which successive governments, of parties ostensibly laying claim to different socio-economic ideologies, have all eroded the social welfare components of Israeli society as well as the rights of workers. The current Finance Minister, Netanyahu, is totally committed ideologically to the letter and spirit of the neo-liberal aims of the global capital economy. Reiss' paper, based on the Israeli case study, spells out in some detail some of the more generalized points made by Hart in his contribution to this volume. Reiss is an anthropologist with strong disciplinary leanings towards socio-linguistics and in this present paper she highlights the metaphors employed by Israel's current economic leadership to convince all sectors of the public to accept and internalize the "rightness" of the economic policy, despite the highly visible social damage it creates in its wake. The metaphors manipulatively raise both transparent "professional" and "common sense" images. For example, she cites the invention of the concept of "growth engines" that transform the economy into an idealized future of economic prosperity for all sectors of the society. Netanyahu, the demagogue, is a past master in manipulating language and creating verbal images to further his aims. In his vicious attack on the public sector, he uses the metaphor of the "fat man" (the parasitic public sector) riding on the back of the "thin man" (the supposedly productive, private business and manufacturing sectors) The images are powerful and are designed to lull the senses of those who ultimately will pay the price of these policies. Reiss' conclusions are grim, for if the public at large accepts the rhetoric, it becomes helpless and apathetic in struggling against the discriminatory consequences of the economic policy, which are cynically directed against that same public.

The contributors have written their papers in honour of Henry. The writers present their own views, interests and orientations without specifically tailoring their papers to the positions held by Henry or for that matter, those of the editors. Tailoring of this nature should not be the aim of a *festschrift*. The book has been organized and edited by three friends and colleagues of Henry Rosenfeld. Each of us approaches our discipline in different ways and indeed represents different areas of specialization within these disciplines. But in addition each of us maintains a different view with respect to how we understand matters of pressing concern to us as citizens of a particular country and participants in a very troubled and highly fragmented society. Thus, we do not share among ourselves a unified understanding of "the situation" as we so often refer to the miasma of what appears to be the highly disintegrative reality which we confront on a daily basis . In the current parlance or political discourse prevalent in Israel we three run the gamut from radical to relatively centrist resulting in a wide divergence with regard to how we view the positions assumed in the various papers comprising this volume. Were this not a book celebrating the life and work of a particular person who holds to a very definite and definable world view much disagreement could have arisen among the editors with regard to various positions propounded in some of the papers. But it was quickly and effortlessly decided at the earliest stages of planning and organization that this book was not to be about this or that fearsomely maintained position of the projects progenitors but was rather a tribute to Henry Rosenfeld. This made for a spirit of inclusivity which, we feel, is as it should be.

Majid Al-Haj
Michael Saltman
Zvi Sobel

November, 2004

1967 as a Political-Economic Turning Point

Shlomo Swirski

Introduction

In September 2001, the height of the "second Intifada," the Sharon government introduced the first of a series of consecutive budget cuts, resulting in severe strains on the operation of the state school and health systems, the state-run social safety net, and a variety of other state functions. The fiscal cuts were supplemented by wage reductions in the public sector, by attempts to constrain the activities of labor unions, and by continued privatization of government corporations and administrative units. There is wide agreement that the consequences for Israeli society have been dramatic—and unprecedented.

The immediate rationale for the various steps taken was the economic downturn that followed in the wake of the Intifada. At the same time, both political leaders and government officials overtly described those steps as part of an agenda aimed at creating a full market economy, in which the state would play no more than a minimal role. The severity of the measures undertaken by the Sharon government, accentuated by the articulation of a neo-liberal ideology, has aroused an interest in the origins of policies associated with Margaret Thatcher and Ronald Reagan, or with agendas like the Washington Consensus.

In the search for origins, the obvious way is to look for previous events or processes that could be seen as attempts to change the balance between the main actors in the political economy—capital, labor and state, in favor of capital. Such a search would lead us to several significant signposts. The most recent one would be the 1985 emergency economic stabilization plan, which introduced into Israel such elements of the Washington Consensus as liberalization of the movement of capital, down-sizing the state by reducing government expenditures as a ratio of GDP, weakening the labor unions and cutting the cost of labor. The 1985 stabilization plan was for many years considered a success story, mainly due to the fact that it put an end to runaway inflation that had reached alarming proportions (Ben Bassat, 2001). Analyses that present a more critical view are less known (see, for instance, Alexander, 1990: Ch. 9).

Going further back in time, some analysts cite the tax reform of 1975, described by Bichler and Nitzan as a clear attempt on the part of the then ruling Labor party to side with the rising middle class (Bichler and Nitzan, 2001: 278); and to 1965, when a previous Labor government engineered a recession designed to restrain wage demands after several years of full employment (Michael Shalev, 1992).

The years 1985, 1975 and 1965 mark significant changes in the previously existing balance between state, labor and capital. A different kind of change—one in the very structure of Israeli capital, as well as a change in the agenda of the state-led development effort, occurred after the 1967 war. This change resulted in the marginalization of the emerging industrial working class, itself largely a product of the two previous decades of industrialization. At the same time, the old managerial and entrepreneurial class was catapulted into a new and more powerful position. It was this position that enabled them to lead the 1985 official rupture with the "socialist" traditions of Israel. Over the last three years (2001-2003), this is the class that played a crucial role in the promotion of a neoliberal agenda. The watershed of 1967 is the focus of this paper.

1967 As A Turning Point I:
A New Road to Industrialization Displaces A Slightly Older One

Following the Six Day War in 1967, Israel's geopolitical status changed: it became a regional power. This state of affairs was reflected in three areas. First of all, its stunning victory made Israel a desirable partner for the United States, at the time engaged in a race for global domination with its rival, the Soviet Union. Within a short time, Israel became a strategic anchor of the United States in the Middle East. To this end the US was prepared to invest in strengthening Israel's military power through generous financial and military assistance. US assistance enabled Israel to expand its defense capabilities to world-class dimensions.

Secondly, four months after the war, Israel's leadership decided to retain the territories that had been conquered in the Six Day War, and to consolidate its control of them, inter alia through settlement activities. A week after the war, the Israeli government decided to offer Syria and Egypt the return of the territories conquered from them in exchange for peace treaties; in October of 1967 the government retracted its position, as a result, among other things, of the resolutions adopted by the Arab leaders at Khartoum, which rejected negotiations of any kind with Israel (Pedatsur, 1996: 57). As for the Palestinian territories, the Israel government decided immediately after the war to maintain full de facto military control, by declaring the Jordan River Israel's defense border. In addition, it decided on "border corrections," foremost among them the annexation of East Jerusalem (ibid: 44-46; 120). Control over the entire historical area of Eretz Israel/Palestine meant that Israel came to dominate most of the Palestinian people. As a result, a new stage was inaugurated in the history of relationships between Jews and Palestinians. Most of the Jews, who until 1948 had been a minority in Eretz Israel/Palestine, and for most of the period until that year had also been the weaker side, had viewed the United Nations decision to partition Eretz Israel/Palestine and to give the Jews one of its parts—the smaller one—as a great achievement. The leadership now aspired to control the entire area, subjugating the Palestinian people to Israeli rule and erasing the memory of the very idea of partition.

Thirdly, as part of its revamped self-definition as a regional power, Israel's leadership embarked upon a new project: the development of its own large-scale military industry—a distinctly "great power" measure, undertaken by very few countries. Although the development of a military industry is generally perceived as constituting part of a country's defense sector, in fact, it is just as much part of its economy—one that can be discussed in the framework of an analysis of the socio-economic development strategy of the country. Thus, the choice to develop a large-scale military industry had a profound impact on Israel's social structure.

Highlighting the importance of the turnaround that took place in the wake of the Six Day War is not tantamount to arguing that it was this war that "created" the Israeli policy grounded in the military option. The emergence of such a policy orientation did not begin in 1967. Shulamit Carmi and Henry Rosenfeld, for example, ascribe the birth of the power-based policy—they speak of militarism—to the decision taken immediately after the 1948 war, not to allow the return of the Palestinian refugees (Carmi and Rosenfeld, 1993:285). Uri Ben Eliezer, who has analyzed the growth of the "military option" in Israeli policy, situates its genesis somewhere in the 1930s (Ben Eliezer, 1995). Avishai Ehrlich recommends viewing the violent Jewish-Palestinian struggle as an integral part of any and every discussion in Israel society, and argues that this must be done from the very first stage of the conflict, i.e. from the moment the earliest Zionists came to Palestine (Ehrlich, 1993).

Nevertheless, there is a broad consensus to the effect that the 1967 war constitutes a significant turning point in all matters relating to the centrality of the military component in Israeli policy. Avishai Ehrlich contends that this war marked a new stage in the conflict, transforming it from a local struggle to an international or inter-power conflict, as a result of the involvement of the great powers, each siding with one of the local parties. This transition compelled Israel to increase its military infrastructure, and here it received aid from the United States Administration (Ehrlich, 1993:257). Carmi and Rosenfeld also saw 1967 as a turning point: they have called this a transition from "low-level militarism" to "high-level militarism" (Carmi and Rosenfeld, 1993:293).

The Military-Industrial Complex

The primary financial expression of the fact that the leadership of Israel initiated and pursued a new national project is to be found in the exceptional growth of its defense budget. In the case of the two previous wars in which Israel had been involved—1948 and 1956—its defense spending decreased once the fighting was over. Between 1948 and 1949, there was a 35% drop in defense expenditures (Kochav and Lifschitz, 1973: Table 1, p. 258); a few years later, in 1952, there was a similar drop (op. cit: ibid.), after Ben-Gurion initiated cutbacks that led, among other things, to the resignation of the Chief of General Staff, Yigal Yadin. At the time of the 1956 Suez War, defense spending increased once again, but again dropped following the end of hostilities.

In contrast, after 1967 not only did the defense budget not shrink: it actually experienced significant growth. In the first years after the war, practically half of every additional *lira* in the government's expenditure went to the defense budget (Kochav and Lifshitz, 1973:256). The defense budget expanded further after the 1973 war (Lifshitz, 2000:157). Defense spending, which in the years preceding the Six Day War (1962-1966) constituted 10.1 per cent of GDP, shot up after the war to 21.7 per cent of Israel's GDP (1968-1973) and later to 27.8 per cent of GDP (1974-1980) (Berglass, 1989: 216). In the first half of the 1970s, defense spending constituted some 40 per cent of Israel's national budget, declining slightly in the second half of the decade to one third (Lifshitz, 2000:175). The defense budget began to shrink only after the signing of the peace agreement with Egypt in 1980. It continued to decline further in the wake of the emergency plan to stabilize the economy initiated in 1985.

A significant proportion of the expanded defense budget went toward greatly expanding the military research and industrial infrastructure—whose origins go back to the pre-1948 era (Evron, 1980)—so that Israel was able to independently produce main-line weapons systems. The immediate catalyst for this decision was the embargo imposed by the French government on exporting arms to Israel. For about a decade prior to the Six Day War, France had been Israel's main supplier. In 1970s and the early 80s, between 20% and 33% of Israel's defense budget was allocated to its defense industries (Steinberg, 1983:286-287; for a similar assessment, see Halperin, 1987:997).

The State's massive investment in the defense industry relied on two financial sources: Israel's own resources, and US aid, part of which was earmarked for the military-industrial complex (Razin, 1984:48-49; Blumenthal, 1985:133). This assistance was the tangible expression of the key role that the US saw Israel playing in the regional balance of power.

The vital importance that the US attached to Israel's new position is attested to by the fact that, about one quarter of annual American foreign aid went to Israel in the early 1980s (Razin, 1984:348). Unlike other aid recipients, Israel was authorized to convert a considerable proportion of its loans into grants. It also received *"permission to use the aid for developing sophisticated weaponry with export capability"* (my emphasis) (Razin, 1984: 48-49; also see Blumenthal, 1984:133; and Toren, 2002). American aid enabled Israel to increase its defense budget, while at the same time maintaining and even improving its standard of living (Razin, 1984:52; see also Mintz, 1984:71).

For the first time, Israel's defense industry gave it an economic sector with the ability to compete on global markets. Decision-makers had indeed foreseen such a result (see, for example, Steinberg 1983:281; 285-286). Until the 1967 war, local economic activities had been relatively limited in scope, with exports largely comprising agricultural produce and polished diamonds (Halevy and Klinov-Maloul,1972:121-127; CBS, 1998: Table I, p. 7). The decision to expand Israel's military industry completely changed the picture: as early as 1970-1974, industrial exports outstripped agricultural and diamond exports combined (CBS 1998: ibid.). In the 1970s, military industrial products constituted around 25% of Israel's total exports. This represented the highest proportion in the world

(Mintz, 1983:112; Berglass, 1989:213-214). The proportion of the workforce employed in the defense sector rose accordingly: in 1980, around half of all industrial personnel were engaged on defense-related projects (Mintz,1983:111). The defense industry grew more rapidly than other sectors of the economy, and became a force impacting on the entire economy (Lifshitz, 2000:363). It is noteworthy that these achievements by the country's military industry occurred at a time of maximum slowdown in Israel's overall growth (see the articles in Ben-Porath, 1989).

The process of developing a military-industrial capacity on a world class level brought together different camps within Israel's political leadership, such as Shimon Peres and top executives in the military industry, who advocated developing a local military-industrial capacity, and Yitzhak Rabin, who for his part advocated acquiring ready-made arms from abroad. Rabin, who was Israel's ambassador to the United States immediately after the 1967 war, worked to consolidate the strategic cooperation with the US, based on a mindset that required Israel to be the strongest power in its part of the world, just as the United States had to be the stronger of the two Great Powers (Rabin, 1979: Section Five, Chapters 1 and 2). This strategic cooperation gave rise to an unprecedented increase in American aid to Israel during Rabin's term as ambassador (ibid: 395). Part of this, as indicated above, was used to develop Israel's defense industry.

In Israel it was the State that initiated, financed, and implemented the development of the military-industrial complex. As Lifshitz puts it, "the government influenced the defense industry, as it continues to do, because it is the body that delineates and operates both national defense policy and macro-economic policy—as a major customer, as the owner of the largest defense companies, as the export-license granting authority, and more" (Lifshitz, 2000:372). The State also encouraged the establishment of numerous private companies specializing in the manufacture of various components for weapons and armaments systems (Kochav and Lifshitz, 1973:264). Some of Israel's largest financial and industrial corporations managed to gain a foothold in this space created by the State, including Discount Investments, Clal Industries, and Koor Industries. These corporations grew and amassed considerable power, becoming players in the global economic arena thanks to their investments in and the services they provided for the defense industries. Military industrial production contributed to the strengthening of what Bichler and Nitzan call "the great economy," enabling a select number of sizeable corporations to acquire more and more control over the accumulation of capital in Israel (Bichler and Nitzan, 2001:190).

The State's decisive role, whether as owner or financier of private companies, is noteworthy, given the present domination of Israeli political-economic discourse by the neo-liberal ideology. That massive state effort would seem to run counter to present-day shibboleths, such as the one presented by Benjamin Netanyahu, the Finance Minister at the time of this writing (2004): Netanyahu declared that he would like to put an end to the situation whereby the thin man (the private sector) has to carry the fat man (the public sector) on his narrow shoulders . A state-led industrialization initiative is, of course, anathema to contemporary neo-liberals; yet, as we will see, ideology aside, military-industrial complexes enjoy massive support by the state even in the most liberally-oriented economies, such as those of the US and Britain. Of course, this does not stop them from preaching neo-liberal ideologies to other countries.

Neo-liberalism made its public entrance to Israel in 1985, in the framework of the emergency economic stabilization program. It was a scant five years after the assumption of power by Margaret Thatcher in England and by Ronald Reagan in the US. Adoption of the 1985 emergency stabilization program occurred against the background of economic crisis and galloping inflation, which were in part the result of the vast amounts of money disbursed on the army and on military production. However, the emergency stabilization plan was not limited to just stamping out inflation: it proposed what the International Monetary Fund likes to call "structural adjustment" of Israel's entire socio-economic system, in a way similar to that proposed by that body for other countries, and particularly those in Latin America, Eastern Europe, and Southeast Asia.

By 1985, when restructuring was first undertaken, large-scale state investment in the military-industrial complex had already brought about the emergence and enrichment of a stratum of wealthy bankers, executives, exporters, retired major generals, accountants, attorneys, and others. Between 1967 and 1985, the members of this stratum had acquired self-awareness and self-confidence. As a result of weapons diplomacy and arms dealing, they became acquainted with many of their counterparts in similar circles, both in the West and in Third World countries, absorbing the neo-liberal atmosphere that permeated the corridors of government and financial institutions in the countries of the West, particularly in the patron state, the US. By 1985, after having grown strong thanks to massive state support, that stratum felt confident enough to embrace an ideology calling for the reduction of that very same support—among other things through cuts in corporate and payroll taxes that finance state programs for the benefit all sectors of society. Shai Talmon, a former chief financial officer of the Israel Finance Ministry, described the day that the 1985 emergency stabilization plan was adopted as "Israel's economic independence day" (*Haaretz*, October 17, 1999). It would be no less accurate to call it "the independence day of the new grand bourgeoisie of Israel."

The first significant public expression of this stratum was the emergence of the Dash Party, founded in order to run in the 1977 national elections. Although the party itself rose and fell rapidly, its conduct during its short-lived existence marked the revolution brought about by the Israeli "great power" project, with its focus on the military-industrial complex. The men who set up the Dash Party included some of the most prominent heads of the military-industrial complex— CEOs of industrial corporations and banks, as well as ex-senior military figures, together with individuals from the legal, academic, and media worlds. They included people from Rafi, the splinter-party that David Ben-Gurion had founded in 1965 in the wake of the Lavon Affair, and which, under the leadership of Moshe Dayan and Shimon Peres, criticized the Histadrut and the left parties even before the 1967 war. The Dash leadership included people who wanted to replace the representative machinery of the existing parties with "a party of the good hundred ('the Centurions')—the good ones, the non-corrupt..." (Urieli and Barzilai, 1982:35). Dash was the first of a long list of Israeli political parties to express the desire of the middle and upper classes, strengthened by the flourishing of the military-industrial complex, to curtail the representation of those parts of society that had fared less well under the new economic regime, and to catapult to office CEOs and ex-army officers described as "having no vested interests," so that they could run the country "in the spirit of western countries" (Urieli and Barzilai, 1982:35).

Dash did not replace Mapai at the helm of the state; rather it was the Likud that came into power. By taking votes away from Mapai, Dash was instrumental in disrupting the unbroken continuity of Mapai's political dominance. Moreover, through Dash the heads of the military-industrial complex gave legitimacy to right-wing rule. The leaders of Dash, most of them people who had been groomed in Mapai institutions, saw no obstacle to joining Menahem Begin's Likud government, following a path blazed by the symbol of Israeli "securitism," Moshe Dayan, whom Begin personally invited to serve as his foreign minister. When Dash disintegrated, most of its leaders did not bother to try their luck elsewhere on Israel's political party map. This did not mean, however, that they abandoned all possibilities of bringing influence to bear on Israeli social and economic policy. Their short service in government had taught them that it was possible to influence economic and social policy without having an organizational framework of their own. Thus, what Dash did was to lay the groundwork for a new cross-partisan elite—a position of strength that made it possible to influence political and social developments irrespective of the party actually in power.

High-Road Development, Low-Road Development

What were the economic and social implications of the massive State investment in the military-industrial complex? The answer can be found in a discussion about the historical role of similar complexes in the United States and Britain. David Coates (Coates, 2000) recently highlighted the fact that in the United States and Britain, the defense industry has played a vital role in these countries' economic development policies (see also Dunne, 1990). According to Coates, the way the United States and Britain operate in the military industrial field brings to mind development policies of countries in which the state has traditionally played a central role in economic matters—rather than the neo-liberal model with which they are so identified. This aspect of public policy in the United States and Britain has not received the consideration it deserves, mainly because when it comes to the defense industry, the "control seat" of the "developmental state" is located in the defense ministry, and not where it might be expected, in the "economic" ministries. Once attention is focused on the defense ministry, the picture is very different from the conventional image of these two countries. As Coates puts it, in the post-WWII period, the military industries of the United States played the role of catalyst, similar to that of the textile industry in England during the period of the Industrial Revolution, or of the railroad industry in the US and Germany during the drive for industrialization in the nineteenth century (Coates, 2000:205). The defense industries conferred a leading role on the United States in the aviation and electronics industries (ibid: 204). The Pentagon has basically functioned—as it still does—as a powerful ministry of industry. The situation in Britain is similar: Britain has the largest military-industrial-scientific complex in Western Europe, and it is the second largest exporter of weapons in the world. The British Ministry of Defense, like its American counterpart, operates in all respects as a ministry of industry, and even Prime Minister Margaret Thatcher, that champion of free market economics, played an extremely active role in marketing the output of the British military-industrial complex (ibid: 196).

Coates' arguments about the United States and Britain are also applicable to Israel. Firstly, there is a similarity when it comes to the key role played by the State, through the defense ministry, in determining economic development policy. As in the US and Britain, in Israel, too, neo-liberal ideology came to a halt at the entrance gate of the military-industrial complex, since in all three countries it was created not as a result of private initiatives, but as a result of central State planning. As Lifshitz puts it, "some people see the industrial-defense base as a factor that confers legitimacy on a form of industrial planning that was acceptable in market economies only because it was accompanied by arguments of national security, and on the whole its adoption led to positive macro-economic results" (Lifshitz, 2000:313).

Secondly, in Israel as in Britain and the United States, the defense industry was the catalyst for an advanced technological development. Central State-level planning in the industrial-defense sphere gave rise to high-value returns for private capitalists in related areas, primarily hitech industries. When the defense industry experienced crisis in the second half of the 1980s, thousands of its employees went out looking for jobs—"a vast workforce that had received high-value, albeit largely informal, vocational training in the defense sector, particularly the hitech and communications sectors" (Yustman, 2001:574). This was the background to the spectacular takeoff of the hitech sector. The result was a "flood of hitech industrial activities, in part based on the intangible technological assets of the defense industry that underwent a spontaneous process of civilianization" (ibid: 568). It turned out that government investment in the defense industry gave rise to very enjoyable and lasting fruits for a whole stratum; as Yustman puts it, "one can argue about the extent of social justice of this process, which made public assets—albeit intangible ones—available for commercial use by individuals without anything being given in return, but it is difficult to argue about their effectiveness: the market value of the new companies that have come about in this way considerably outstrips the worth of the entire public defense industry" (ibid: 568).

This point leads us to one of the primary social ramifications of placing the military-industrial complex at the center of Israeli development policy. The complex fitted in with what economists call high-road economic development, which is based on the manufacture of products with high added value, intended for "high" market segments, involving small-series production tailored to the clients' requirements and based on a cutting-edge workforce that enjoys high remuneration levels (Betcherman,1996:261).

Let us now go back to the argument about 1967 being a turning point. Until the Six Day War, it was the Ministry of Trade and Industry, under the baton of Pinhas Sapir, who orchestrated the industrialization of Israel's economy. The representative branch of this journey towards industrialization was the textile industry, which had been a pioneer in England's Industrial Revolution and which some considered an obligatory first stage through which any country desirous of achieving modern industry had to pass. Unlike the post-Fordist defense and hitech industries, the industry of the 1950s and '60s was distinctly Fordist in nature, involving mass production lines producing mass consumer products. Moreover, it suited what the economists call low-road development— mass production of low value added products using a large, low-skilled, low-waged labor force.

Looking back, the decision to invest in a sector like textiles might be considered somewhat anachronistic, since even at the time this industry, with its large and cheap workforce, was considered an unlikely candidate to lead the economy in a drive for overall industrial development. It must be added, however, that the decision to industrialize, whose first step involved the textile industry, was guided at least partially by an inclusionary socio-political vision, designed to involve wide sectors of society in the development effort. While one of the pressing reasons for embarking upon rapid industrialization was the need to tackle the problem of unemployment, especially among new immigrants, industrialization itself was viewed at that time as part of the process of nation-building. The main candidates for work in the new industries were the hundreds of thousands of recently arrived Jewish immigrants, especially those who had come from Arab and Muslim countries of the Middle East and many of whom had been settled in the outlying development towns. Israeli Palestinians were left out of those development plans; in fact, Palestinian Israelis were hardly ever considered part of the universe in any of the state-led development projects (Lustick, 1980), to this day. While the politicians viewed industrialization as a means of acquiring the trust—and the votes—of the new Jewish immigrants and their leaders, the sociologists and economists, in particular those who, subscribing to the modernization theory, saw this as a corridor through which the Jewish immigrants could be channeled towards the mainstream of Israeli society (for a critique of this approach see Swirski and Bernstein, 1980; and Swirski, 1981).

While the industries of the Fifties were established on the basis of a Jewish inclusionary, albeit anachronistic, vision of economic development, the military-industrial complex was perceived as an opportunity to join high-road development on a world level through an exclusive and exclusionary approach. The new complex was largely based on a small proportion of the Israeli labor force: the core development focused on no more than a few thousand engineers and scientists, plus technicians and computer people, army officers, graduates of certain units in the military, and skilled personnel from small-scale production lines. A not particularly wide-ranging network of business services—financial, legal, accounting, advertising and others—grew up around it and were fed by the complex.

Most Israelis found it difficult to gain access to this new club. Male and female blue-collar workers, most of them Mizrahim, who in the 1960s had been recruited to work on textile production lines, remained outside the gates. On the whole, the only contact between these workers and the new complex was in the military sewing shops set up in Israel's development towns. From this point of view, working on textile factory production lines did not give them a springboard for entering the modern industrial world, because it failed to provide them with the tools that would enable them to access the new R&D centers. Arab citizens of Israel were another group that failed to gain admission to the complex, "for security reasons"—but then neither had they been included in the industrialization of the 1950s and '60s. Israeli women were similarly excluded, since the new club was a predominantly male bastion.

The military-industrial complex took a relatively select social stratum and launched it into high-road development, leaving behind a broader social stratum that for 10 or 15 years had constituted the focus of the previous wave of industrial development.

There Was an Option to Develop Differently

The military-industrial complex did not grow out of the industrial infrastructure whose establishment had begun a decade and a half earlier. Rather, it marked a new beginning (here the word "new" refers to the extent of the investment, not to the actual production of weapons, since this also took place earlier, albeit without dimensions befitting a "regional power" [Evron, 1980]). The new start ignored the previous start, which was still fairly fresh. Against this background it may be asked whether the investment in this complex, which promoted specific industrial sectors, did not block the development of other sectors, such as the industries that produced consumer goods (for a comparison between government investments in the defense industries and government investment in other sectors, see Steinberg, 1983:289). Referring to the British situation, David Coates argues that the government preference for the defense industries was one of the reasons for the lag of the "old" industries (Coates, 2000:196). Similarly, in his discussion of the United States, he argues that its fostering of the defense industries is one of the reasons for the United States' relative disadvantage in the area of consumer goods industries (ibid: 206).

Similar arguments have been advanced in Israel. Economist Ariel Halperin viewed the massive investment in the defense industry as a possible explanation for the decline in growth rates. "It could have been anticipated," he wrote, "that the rise of the new wave of advanced industry would bring accelerated growth in its wake. This is not what happened, however. Between 1968 and 1972, the annual growth rate for industrial goods was 15%. Between 1973 and 1979, it dropped to under 5%, and to 2.5% between 1979 and 1984. The annual rate of increase in productivity, which was 7% for the 1968-1972 period, dropped to 0% in the 1980s" (Halperin, 1988:3). Halperin recounts that many people tried to establish a link between this standstill in growth—which the economists later dubbed "the lost decade" (see Ben Porath, 1989)—and the oil crisis, as well as other factors, such as the halt in immigration to Israel and in the import of capital to the country. Halperin disagrees: he notes that "because of the limited resources available to the country, resources invested in military technology are lost to other technological domains" (Halperin, 1988:4). As he puts it, "the massive drain of technological manpower to the defense sector halted the development of conventional industry before the optimum was reached" (Halperin, 1987:1002). Halperin goes on to note that in Israel, some 60% of national research and development is invested in the defense field—compared to up to 20%-30% in western countries. Investment in civilian R&D is lower in Israel than in its western counterparts (Halperin, 1988:5-6). The same picture applies to all aspects of the workforce: of an estimated 20,000-22,000 engineers and scientists in Israel, 55%-60% were employed in the new complex (Halperin, 1987:1000). Halperin attributed these figures to "a certain defense doctrine," and noted that "an alternative national policy, emphasizing diversified and advanced civilian industry, [could] bring about significant change in the growth process of industry and the economy" (Halperin, 1988:9).

Yaacov Arnon, director-general of the Israeli Finance Ministry under Pinhas Sapir, wrote in an article entitled "A Fool's Paradise," that "one must look disapprovingly on. . .the ability of the Israeli economy to adjust to a situation in which a considerable proportion of the country's economic efforts are directed at defense, with the requisite resources coming from other economies" (Arnon, 1984: 157). Countering those who justified investment in the defense industry by calling it a step that enabled Israel to enter the modern production era, Arnon argued that the same outcome could have been achieved by different means. As examples he cited Germany and Japan, which after World War II "made practically no investment in the defense area (they were prohibited from doing so under the arrangements signed after the war), but managed to streamline their production processes so much that other countries were unable to compete with them" (ibid: 158; for a similar argument see Peri and Neubach 1985:36). Arnon also asserted that "the only responses to the disastrous policy pursued since 1967—a policy that is threatening to destroy our independence, first economic and then political, impacting on every aspect of our lives—would be a return to pre-Six-Day-War Israel and achieving peace with the Arab world" (Arnon, 1984:160).

These two industrial starts, each of which was based on a different theory of development, different forms of production, different products, different markets, a different group of workers, and different pay and working conditions, incorporate a number of the key problems of contemporary Israeli society. It is true that the development of the military-industrial complex helped to promote

Israel's admission to the relatively exclusive club of countries with a high per capita GDP; however, if we disaggregate GDP down into its components we will find that only a small proportion of Israel's population really belong to the high income club.

One demonstration of this "split personality" can be found in the area of salaries. Workers in the defense industries—and later on in the hitech industries—have enjoyed relatively high levels of remuneration, while those employed in what came to be known as "the traditional industries," such as food processing and textiles, have received relatively low wages. Moreover, these two levels of pay have grown further and further apart. This can be seen from the growth in wage disparities between those with a college education and those with lower qualifications: while the salaries of workers with 16 years of education and more (men employed in the business sector) grew from 153% of the average wage (in 1980-1982) to 171% of the average wage (in 1995-1997), the pay of those with eight years of schooling or less dropped from 64% of the average wage at the beginning of the period to 59% of the average wage at the end of the period (Muallem and Frisch, 1999:1; see also Ruth Klinov , 1999: 1; and Dahan, 2001, Part II). Another disparity concerns employees' abilities to bargain over wages and fringe benefits: the labor organizations in the defense industries have always been among the strongest trade unions in Israel, while the power of the workers in the "traditional" industries has always been weak.

The erosion of income and of the organized power of laborers at the lower end of the salary scale was also fed, of course, by yet another consequence of the 1967 war, one not dealt with in this paper—namely, the entrance into the Israeli labor market of tens of thousands of Palestinians from the occupied territories, into specific niches of the low road economic track. This was compounded later on, in the 1990s, by the recruitment of hundreds of thousands of migrant workers from South East Asia, Africa and Eastern Europe, to replace the Palestinians whose entry was curtailed during the first Intifada.

Welfare in Lieu of Income

One of the ways in which the State chose to cope with increasing wage disparities was to speed up the development of a social safety net. The same two decades that saw the development of the military-industrial complex also saw the introduction of some of the basic elements of the social security system, as we know it today. Unemployment benefits were introduced in 1973; 1975 marked the introduction of universal child allowances (although the Arabs were discriminated against in the form of a special allowance earmarked for the children of parents who had served in the army, until 1994); most of the disability and mobility allowances were introduced between 1974 and 1981; income support was introduced in 1982; and a nursing benefit was inaugurated in 1988 (National Insurance Institute, 2002). The development of the social safety net was made possible, among other things, by the fact that Israel's population did not need to finance the full cost of the military-industrial complex from its own resources, since it was in receipt of American assistance.

The purpose of a social safety net is to serve as a supplement, not a replacement, to the wage system. In Israel, the net helped to soften the blow of being elbowed out of the mainstream economy and marginalized—which is what happened to the "first" proletariat, that of the 1950s and '60s, i.e., the primarily Mizrahi proletariat in the development towns. However, it could not enable them to enter the ranks of the middle classes. It certainly contained nothing that could enable those on the fringes to become part of the mainstream.

Despite the numerous cuts it has suffered in recent years, the present-day Israeli social safety net is comprehensive and universal, and in this it resembles the Western European systems (more than the American system)—only it is far less generous. In Israel, benefit levels are so low that the people who have no other sources of income live at poverty level. Compared to most developed countries, overall expenditure on social security in Israel is modest (Doron, 1999:441). Although expenditure on National Insurance Institute benefits rose from 6.09% of GDP in 1980 to 8.71% in 1999 (National Insurance Institute, 2000:10), in Europe most countries spend between 60% and 90% more than Israel (Doron, 1999:442).

The main weakness of the social safety net, of course, is the fact that it depends heavily on the goodwill of the State as well as that of persons of means. In Israel, for a number of years we have witnessed a no-holds-barred ideological and practical campaign being waged against the social safety net by the political leadership and the spokespersons of the upper-middle classes. It is argued that the safety net has led to the growth of "a generation of scroungers gorging themselves at the State's expense." Consequently the war cry is "get a job"— ignoring the fact that the development policy pursued by none other than the political leadership of the country since 1967 has left Israel's socio-economic "periphery" on the margins of the push towards economic development, utterly lacking in adequate, stable sources of employment.

In the 1980s, and especially post-1985, a significant reduction took place in the national budget in general and in the defense budget in particular. Slashing the defense budget was viewed as an obligatory part of Israel's restructuring process. The weight of the defense budget in the country's national budget returned to 1950s proportions. At the beginning of the 1990s, with the arrival of the large-scale wave of immigration from the countries of the former Soviet Union, it dropped to even lower levels (Lifshitz, 2000:175). Nevertheless, even today the defense industry is still a key component of Israeli industry in general and of Israeli industrial exports in particular: according to figures supplied by the defense ministry's director-general, Amos Yaron, Israel was one of the world's largest arms exporters in 2002, ranking fifth with a market share of 8-10 per cent (Yaron, 2002; for different figures, see Ackerman in the same book; for some present-day figures on the military industries see Bank of Israel, 2002: 56-57). Moreover, the defense industry spawned business activities, which no longer required massive government support, especially in the hitech sphere.

Referring to the 1950s, Henry Rosenfeld and Shulamit Carmi have written that during this period, the state budgets contributed to the emergence of what they called "a state-made middle class" (Rosenfeld and Carmi, 1979). In the same vein it can be said that in the 1970s and '80s, the State's regional power project helped to empower parts of this middle class, turning them into a defense industrial and financial elite, marked by domestic political power and the ability to bargain in the global corridors of power.

1967 as a Turning Point II:
A New Road to Settlements Displaces a Slightly Older One

Just as the military-industrial complex overtook the textile industry to assume the lead in Israel's economy, society, and politics, springboarding a narrow segment of Israeli society, in the same manner, settlements in the occupied territories have overtaken the development towns and *moshavim* of the 1950s and '60s. Their inhabitants now raced ahead into the ranks of the middle and sometimes the upper-middle classes, thanks to the state-led settlement project.

The settlements were set up in all the territories that came under Israeli control in the Six Day War. Israel remained in possession of the Sinai Peninsula for more than a decade. As former defense minister Moshe Dayan was wont to say, it was better to have Sharm el-Sheikh without peace than peace without Sharm el-Sheikh. Still, Sinai was eventually evacuated in the wake of the peace treaty signed with Egypt, and the Israeli settlements there were dismantled. The Golan Heights, the great majority of whose Syrian inhabitants were expelled in the Six Day War (leaving four Druze villages), were quickly settled, with Israel applying Israeli law to the area in 1981. Later, in the 1990s, both right and left wing Israeli governments expressed willingness to return the greater part of the Golan Heights to Syria in the framework of a peace agreement. Israel's greatest ideological and political commitment is to the territories that were occupied in the historical area of Eretz Israel/Palestine. A large part of the Palestinian people live in the territories of the West Bank, which were under Jordanian control until 1967, and in the Gaza Strip, which was previously under Egyptian control. In these territories, particularly in the West Bank, Israel has made major efforts to consolidate its long-term domination.

The settlement project in the Palestinian territories began, on a small scale, shortly after the Six Day War. In the first ten years following the war, when the Labor Party (formerly the Ma'arach) was in power, twenty settlements were founded, the majority in two areas: the Jordan Valley, which the Labor Party saw as the location of Israel's "security border," and the Etzion Bloc, whose Jewish residents had been expelled in 1948, so that settling there was viewed as a legitimate return of Jewish territory taken by force. Out of line with these two settlement areas was Kiryat Arba, established next to Hebrom. Most of these settlements were small: in 1977 their residents numbered under 6,000 (all figures are taken from Goldberg, 1993).

A significant turning point was 1977, when the right-wing Likud party came to power. What the Likud did was to make the settlements—and in effect permanent control of the Palestinian territories—its own unique national project. The signal for large-scale settlement was given when the Begin government declared 40% of the West Bank "State lands" (Goldberg, 1993: 21). This brought about the channeling to these areas of generous government allocations, accompanied by the extravagant benefits enjoyed by settlers, then as today (ibid: 14); benefits were lowered somewhat only during the 1992-1995 Rabin government. During the period of the first Begin government, from 1977 to 1981, 35 settlements were founded, mainly in densely populated areas in Samaria and the Binyamin region, and the number of settlers rose to 17,000. Under the second Begin government and the Shamir government (1981-1984), 43 more settlements were founded, most of them in Samaria and the Binyamin region, but also in the Jordan Valley and the Gaza Strip, and the number of settlers rose to 46,000.

The 1985 emergency plan for stabilizing the economy did not slow down or halt the settlements project. During the period of the national unity government (1984-1988), the same government that had adopted the economic emergency plan, 32 new settlements were set up, most of them in Samaria and the Binyamin region. The settlers' numbers practically doubled.

Finally, during the second Shamir government (1988-1992), another seven settlements were established, and the number of settlers rose to 107,000 (Goldberg, 1993:13). During the lifetime of this government, in which Ariel Sharon served as housing and construction minister (1990-1992), a grandiose plan was worked out with the goal of greatly increasing the number of settlements and settlers (see below), and generous benefits were given to people purchasing apartments in the occupied territories. During these years, residential building starts did indeed shoot up (Swirski, Konor-Attias and Etkin, 2002:50). The Rabin government, which took power in 1992, put an end to this acceleration, froze part of the construction plans, and revoked some of the decisions (Goldberg, 1993:14). From the signing of the Oslo Accords to the end of 2000, just three new settlements were established. However, the total settler population swelled—especially at the beginning of the decade, under the Shamir government—and at its end, under the Barak and Netanyahu governments (1996-1999 and 1999-2001, respectively. By the end of the decade the number of settlers had reached some 200,000 (Swirski, Konor-Attias and Etkin, 2002:23).

Even though the aura of the settlements is connected with the settlers— individuals or groups, foremost among them the right wing religious Gush Emunim movement—the taking over of the occupied territories was in fact a straightforward state project. In the first decade following the Six Day War, it was Ma'arach (former Mapai) governments that initiated and financed the settlement operations in the Rafiah seaside plain, the Golan Heights, and the Jordan Valley, while in the second decade after the war it was Likud governments and the national unity government that initiated and financed the settlement drives in the heart of the Palestinian territories in the West Bank and the Gaza Strip. Gush Emunim leaders founded settlements at specific locations, but the most grandiose plans for controlling the Palestinian territories were undertaken by government circles. The settlements in the Jordan valley, along the border with the Kingdom of Jordan, were initiated by Yigal Alon, Minister of Labor in the Golda Meir cabinet, soon after the Six Day War. Golda Meir's Minister of Defense, Moshe Dayan, initiated the stationing of Israel Defense Forces bases along the ridge of West Bank mountains, and pushed for the building of Israeli towns next to those bases; the bases were duly erected, but not the towns (Pedatsur, 1996: ch. 7). In 1983, the Zionist Federation's Rural Settlement Division, in conjunction with the Agricultural Ministry, drew up a master plan (known as the "Drobles Plan"), which anticipated 800,000 Jews in the West Bank by 2010. At the beginning of the 1990s, when Ariel Sharon was housing and construction minister in the second Shamir government, a start was made on preparing a master plan for settling 2.6 million Jews in the West Bank and Gaza Strip (Goldberg, 1993:21). The plan was intended to drastically transform the demographic picture in the occupied territories, by creating a very large Jewish minority, amounting to some 40% of the total population of the West Bank (ibid: 23). These grandiose plans came to an end when Yitzhak Rabin came to power and the Oslo Agreement was signed.

Following the 1973 Yom Kippur War, Gush Emunim and other groups played a key role in expanding the settler movement, by spurring on the government to seize territories, and by stimulating public legitimacy for settlement activities; nevertheless, most of the Jews who went to live in the occupied territories did so as a result of government housing campaigns in areas near the big cities, whether Jerusalem or the cities of central Israel. Their main motive in moving to the territories was to obtain a higher standard of living at lower cost—while retaining their sources of income within the Green Line (Goldberg, 1993:16, 19). Most of the time, "ideological" settlers were in the minority: in 1992, at the end of the development drive conducted by the Likud, the settlements of Amana, Gush Emunim's settlement movement, had 20,000 residents—19% of the total settler body (Goldberg, 1993:18).

The settlement drive in the occupied territories was not the first government campaign in Israel to establish and populate communities in new locales. In fact, the settlement project was set in motion just a few years after the end—or the failure to complete—a far larger government relocation and construction project, the project to house more than a million Jews who came to Israel in the first decade following the establishment of the State. Between 1948 and the early 1960s, some 300 villages for new immigrants were established (Swirski, 1981: 22; Swirski and Shoshan, 1985:5; Lifshitz, G., 1997). To this must be added the construction of dozens of new neighborhoods in towns and cities throughout the country, to replace the transit camps (ma'abarot) that originally housed new immigrants.

A comparison of the relocation and housing campaigns of the years of mass immigration with the settlement campaigns in the territories occupied in 1967 also points to an important turn-about in policy, as does the comparison between the early wave of industrialization and the establishment of the military-industrial complex. Firstly, the settlement and housing campaigns of the 1950s and '60s were carried out under more arduous conditions: a bigger population had to be housed—it was in fact larger than the aggregate population present in Israeli territory immediately after the 1948 war—while at any given moment, the settlers were a small minority of Israel's population. Secondly, in the 1950s, the new immigrants arrived in large, frequent waves, and the process of housing them was carried out under pressure, while the construction of the settlements took place with a far more relaxed timetable. Thirdly, the resources available to the State after 1967 were far greater than those available in the 1950s.

Most of the villages and development towns established for new immigrants in the 1950s were located in border areas, as part of government efforts to put Israel's claim to the 1948 borders on a solid footing, as the international community had not recognized these borders as permanent. It was also part of the policy to settle Jews in areas which up to1948 had been inhabited by Palestinians. A geographically peripheral location soon became peripheral from a social, economic, and political point of view as well. Under the pressure of events, new communities were established before any infrastructure could be developed for economic activities and sources of employment. Moreover, the resources allocated to the *moshavim* and development towns were inferior to those provided to established locales during the same period; they were also inferior compared with the resources allocated to the post-1967 settlements. New immigrants' moshavim, where in principle a start could have been made fairly quickly, were given smaller plots of land and smaller production quotas than those of veteran moshavim and kibbutzim. The development towns, intended to serve as urban centers for the farming communities in their hinterland, found it difficult to compete with their neighbors from the veteran kibbutzim and moshavim, which had excellent ties with the political and economic center. Instead of the veteran communities utilizing the services of the development towns, in practice the latter utilized the services of the former. Throughout most of the 1950s, the immigrants' moshavim and development towns suffered high unemployment levels, and the public works projects for the unemployed did not compensate for the residents' hardships, since they were sporadic and the wages paid to those employed on them were low (Swirski, 1981: Chapter 2).

Housing disparities became a key component of Israel's emerging class-based inequality. In the development towns, apartments were relatively small, and their low-cost construction was inferior in terms of specifications and finish. Maintenance standards were also low (Law-Yone and Kalush, 1995: 33-32). A comparison between the quality of public construction, most of which was intended for new immigrants, and private building, earmarked primarily for old-timers, reveals significant differences. Privately constructed housing was worth more, and the apartments themselves were larger: in 1955 the average public housing apartment measured 45 square meters; in 1960 the equivalent figure was 57 sq.m., and in 1985, 61 sq.m., while the equivalent figures for privately constructed apartments were 75 sq.m., 81 sq.m., and 92 sq.m. respectively (Haber, cited from Swirski 1981:30). Public housing apartments, it must be said, were not given to immigrants for free: 65% of the financing of public housing came from their residents. In addition, the people who were accommodated in these new housing complexes bore the burden of a considerable proportion of the development costs, a state of affairs which led a Housing Ministry director-general to wonder at the time "whether there is any justification for the inhabitants of development areas, who are playing a pioneering role by building up parts of the country and new towns and are living in relatively difficult conditions, having to also shoulder the development costs" (cited in Swirski, 1981:32).

Those locales that became known as "development towns" found it difficult to develop. Many of the new factories erected during the industrialization drive of the 1950s and 1960s ran into trouble. After 1967, as resources were diverted to the military-industrial complex and to the settlements, the development towns entered a protracted period of declining investments and economic stalemate. Frequently, the not-so-old factories depended for their very survival on the political goodwill of the government, which would intervene from time to time in order to prevent their closure; that is, those factories became industrial welfare cases (Swirski and Shoshan, 1985:1).

In addition, in the mid-Sixties the number of new immigrants coming to Israel fell off sharply, and population growth in the development towns came to an abrupt halt. The towns' migration balance became negative: for a long time, the numbers of those leaving outweighed those coming to live there. Between the 1960s and the end of the 1980s, most of the development towns lost inhabitants, while some barely managed to balance their figures; only a few places such as Arad, Carmiel, Eilat and Ashdod experienced growth (Lifshitz, G., 1997:11). The economic standstill and negative migration continued until the large-scale immigration from the former Soviet Union, which began in 1989. Only then did the populations of the development towns start to grow again (Lifshitz, G., 1997:12, 37).

Let us now go back to the 1967 war. Following the war, the resources available to the State grew considerably, as did its expenditures. Had the latter been allocated to the development towns, moshavim and underprivileged neighborhoods, it might have helped to renovate and upgrade housing stocks, diversify sources of employment, expand vehicular and rail transport networks, and improve education levels and vocational training standards. In other words, the new resources could have been used to successfully complete the settlement process of the 1950s and '60s and to bring their residents to the high road. Instead, the new resources were earmarked for the regional power project— expanding the army, increasing the military-industrial complex, and settling the occupied territories. The State of Israel, which in 1967 was very far from successfully "digesting" the areas and population groups that had come under its control some 20 years earlier, now wanted to digest new areas and new groups taken over in 1967. Just as the State acted in the area of economic development, when it invested its new resources in the military-industrial complex, displacing and marginalizing the industries of the Fifties and Sixties, so it invested its new resources in the occupied territories, abandoning the development towns to their peripheral status. The settlements "overtook" the development towns—exactly as the military-industrial complex "overtook" the industries of the Fifties and Sixties.

How the Settlements "Overtook" the Development Towns

First of all, from 1977 onwards at least, the settlements became Israel's national project, designed so as to enable the Likud to have its name inscribed in the history of gaining Jewish control over the historical Land of Israel, Eretz Israel. Menahem Begin promised in the 1977 election campaign that "there will be many Eilon Morehs"—a settlement that was established in 1974 near Nablus by Gush Emunim and was only approved by the Rabin government after protracted wavering. Following this undertaking by Menahem Begin, two individuals—David Levy, who hailed from the development town of Beit Shean and was the minister of construction and housing in the Begin government, Shamir government, and national unity government, and Moshe Katsav—the present President of Israel—from the development town of Kiryat Malachi, who was the deputy minister of construction and housing in the Begin and Shamir governments—found themselves presiding over a campaign to build settlements. At a time when the settlements project was helping to position Gush Emunim and its supporters at a strategic reference point in the power networks of Israel politics, David Levy and Moshe Katsav, together with other local-level Mizrahi politicians, were achieving what appeared to be important political positions through the infiltration of a favored few, aspiring to turn themselves and the hundreds of thousands of their former neighbors (who had elevated scores of go-getters like them to the ranks of local government, and put the Likud Party into national office) into a significant political force capable of preventing the marginalization of the Mizrahi proletariat and slowing down the rise of a new stratum of CEOs and settlers. Such a political force emerged somewhat later in the form of the orthodox Mizrahi party Shas. However, from the very outset, Shas took socio-economic marginalization of many Mizrahim as a given, choosing to carry on its struggle in the domain of the social safety net rather than the area of the labor market.

The settlements in the occupied territories were built to the standards of the middle classes in the 1970s—single-storey houses surrounded by green areas dotted with spacious public structures (Rubinstein, 1982:9). At the same time, the compensation that the Likud offered Mizrahi voters, who swelled its constituency dramatically in the 1970s, was far less generous: Project Renewal, designed to spruce up neighborhoods in the cities and development towns which by the Six Day War had already become run down. While the settlements were funded by the State budget, Project Renewal was based on donations given by Jewish communities overseas (Swirski, 1981:344). As the years passed, funds for Project Renewal tended to dry up (Swirski, B., and Swirski S., 2003), while funding for the settlements remained generous and constant to this day. While the State funds that were channeled to the settlements helped to strengthen and empower settler organizations and to make them a highly influential political force, from its inception to its demise Project Renewal was run by political hacks, and neighborhood residents enjoyed only minimal representation (Swirski, 1981:344). The settlements succeeded in empowering a distinct social group and elevating it to the ranks of the middle and the upper-middle class; in contrast, Project Renewal involved nothing that could alter the class position of most of the residents of the neighborhoods and development towns.

Another reason for the ascendance of the settlements was that the settler leadership was viewed by many of the country's leaders, and particularly those who espoused the idea of "Greater Israel," as "new pioneers," as the modern standard-bearers of Zionist appropriation of the lands of historic Eretz Israel. The settlers' leaders were no strangers to the political leadership: they came from the ranks of the National Religious Party (NRP)—a veteran European Zionist political party that had been part of the power apparatus of pre-State institutions, as well as of most post-1948 governments. However, by the time that Gush Emunim was founded, NRP youngsters had been relegated to the sidelines of Zionist history: during the heroic period, it was the youngsters of the Labor movement who had occupied front stage, as pioneers and fighters, and on the eve of the 1948 war they were joined by the fighters of the IZL (Irgun Zvai Leumi) and Lehi (Lohamei Herut Israel). The Gush Emunim settlement operations placed the NRP's youngsters on center stage, turning them into legitimate contenders for the Zionist crown (Rubinstein, 1982:13, 127). The settlers received paternal pats on the head from the leaders of the then governing Labor movement (ibid:3)—this shortly after Golda Meir had rejected the Black Panther leaders, the spokespersons of the young people who had grown up in the Mizrahi neighborhoods and development towns, referring to them distastefully as "not nice."

The settlements were also aided by the fact that they were founded in a period when the country had more resources available to it than in earlier periods, and these resources were channeled into the settlements with largesse—more generously than to the development towns, which had also been for years on the various lists of "national priorities." An examination of the municipal budgets of the Jewish settlements in Judea and Samaria for the year 1983/84 revealed that the budget intended to finance social services—education, culture, health, welfare, religious services (in the framework of the regular budget)—was significantly larger than that of locales of similar size within Israel (Dehter, 1987). The data available on municipal budgets in the 1990s enable us to undertake a more methodical and comprehensive analysis. Thus a study by the Adva Center reveals that in the 1990s, the municipal budgets (regular budget) of the settlements in Judea, Samaria and the Golan, calculated per capita, were 30% higher than the average budget of the aggregate of all local authorities in Israel, and 24% higher than the average development town budget (Swirski, Konor-Attias and Etkin, 2002:7). The lion's share of the municipal budgets comes from the government, and here the settlements had an even greater edge: the municipal income that the localities in Judea, Samaria and the Golan Heights received from the government (calculated on a per capita basis, in the regular budget) was 60% higher than the figure for all the local authorities in Israel, and 37% higher than that for the development towns (ibid: 8).

It should of course be noted that the government financing of municipal budgets (through the Interior Ministry) is only part of the government financing that has been channeled into the settlements over the years: to it must be added expenditure in the framework of the defense budget and the Agriculture Ministry's rural settlement division budget, the development budgets of the Housing and Construction Ministry, the preferential treatment under the housing aid budgets of the Housing Ministry and the special assistance budget of the Education Ministry, as well as the benefits enjoyed by settlers (together with residents of other communities defined as "national priority areas," including some development towns) on a personal and family level—for example, income tax credits and exemptions from pre-nursery school fees.

Fourthly, while it is true that the settlements were set up in close proximity to—frequently even within—a hostile Palestinian population, unlike the development towns, they did not turn into a "periphery." Most of them were established near Israel's two central metropolitan areas, Jerusalem and Tel Aviv, making it easier for the settlers in terms of livelihood and even enabling them to bring home high wages commensurate with the country's central area. Moreover, the State has made a point of paving special roads that by-pass Palestinian towns and villages, greatly shortening travel times between settlement centers and Jerusalem and Tel Aviv; and this at a time when the transport system to the development towns makes it impossible to combine living in the Negev and the Galilee with working in Israel's central region. These two factors have attracted middle-class families to the settlements (see Rubinstein, 1982:12) or alternatively have enabled families from lower classes to achieve socio-economic mobility: National Insurance Institute figures about average salaries by locale reveal that the residents of the settlements in the Judea and Samaria District rank third in terms of pay levels in Israel, high above both the southern and northern districts, which have many development towns, particularly the southern district (Etkin, 2003:4).

Conclusion

Victory in the 1967 war turned the heads of Israel's political and economic leadership—with a few exceptions—and tempted them to swallow more than Israel could chew. Because of the regional power project, Israel's best human and economic resources were concentrated on maintaining an outsized army and a large-scale military industry, as well as using force to dominate all the territories of historical Palestine/Eretz Israel. Some of the many resources required to implement the regional power project did indeed come from the United States, but this was a gift that cost its recipients dearly, since they were recruited into promoting the global hegemony of the United States. The advantages accruing to this recruitment were not one-sided, of course: as a result, Israel acquired the status of a regional military and economic power, removing, to a large extent, fears about the survival that had been prevalent prior to 1967. On the other hand, the "regional power" project could not but contribute to the constant confrontation between Israel and its neighbors, as the military option—now greatly strengthened—became a key component of any contact with them.

It could be said that the regional power project distorted Israeli society, in the same way that anabolic steroids distort athletes' bodies: certain parts of society became stronger and richer, like those bulging muscles that become over-developed, while other parts of society were marginalized, analogous to those muscles and parts of the body that waste away as a result of under use (I have borrowed this image from Arundhati Roy, 1999:84).

In economists' terms, the military industry was supposed to act as a locomotive that would pull the entire Israeli economy along in its wake. As we have seen, this industry did indeed provide the infrastructure for the growth of the Israeli hitech industry—but both of these employed and enriched just a small part of society, and neither of them was strong enough to pull the whole Israeli economy after it.

Had the project of making Israel into a regional power been primarily financed by Israel's own resources, it is reasonable to assume that at a fairly early stage it would have led to an economic crash, similar to the one that occurred in the Soviet Union, which for years invested too many resources on too grand a scale to maintain a large army and to finance expensive military projects like nuclear weaponry, inter-continental ballistic missiles, and a space program, at the expense of investments in consumer products, infrastructure, and improving the standard of living of the general population. The difference, however, is that Israel enjoyed—and continues to enjoy—generous American aid. The aid Israel receives is more generous than that given to any other country that receives US support. However, even if it prevents Israel's economic collapse, this assistance is not able to prevent Israeli society from developing in a distorted fashion.

The settlements are not an inevitable result of the project to make Israel a regional power: Israel could have controlled the territories occupied in 1967 even without the settlements. On the other hand, the settlements could not have existed without Israel's military control of the territories. It is this control that made possible the development of another distortion in Israeli society: the channeling of large-scale official resources—greater, in relative terms, than the funds that were allocated to the development towns and Arab locales—to the settlement of the occupied territories. On the one hand, the settlement project catapulted some social groups into the ranks of the elite, and on the other hand, it also placed Israel in a situation of unending confrontation with the Palestinians.

Investment in the military-industrial complex has wider-ranging and longer-term socio-economic implications than investment in the settlements. The military-industrial project was a strategic course of political action that reshaped and greatly strengthened some of the key players in the Israeli economy, enabling them to become a focal point of non-partisan political-economic power with great influence. At the same time, investing in the military-industrial complex helped to render marginal—and later on, in many instances even superfluous—the proletariat (particularly of Mizrahi origin) which had begun to emerge around the industries of the first wave of industrialization.

The "regional power" policy prepared the way for the great ideological transformation that took place in 1985, when the emergency economic stabilization plan was implemented, giving Israeli capital freedom of maneuver and action in the spirit of the Washington Consensus. One instance of the new power and legitimation can be found in the attempts made throughout the 1990s and up to the time of writing, to impose a tax on capital gains. The first attempt was made during the Rabin government, but strong pressure applied at the last moment on Rabin by some of Israel's senior business people killed the idea. A second attempt was made under Barak's administration, but was again turned down. The third attempt was made during Sharon's government, and this time it passed—but the tax was fixed at a relatively low level; in addition, the government implemented a cut in income tax, structured in such a way as to primarily benefit people with large salaries. The main argument used to justify the income tax break was the need to prevent the emigration from Israel of the hitech industry workforce—which, as explained above, had developed out of the military-industrial complex.

While the structural implications of the settlement project are more limited than those of the military-industrial complex, they are far from insignificant. First of all, the settlement project helped to complete the marginalization of the development towns—and the Arab locales in Israel—by enabling many of the settlers to consolidate their middle or upper middle class position. Secondly, the steady expansion of the settler population, after the Oslo Accords, was one of the main reasons for the outbreak of the second Intifada, which in turn led to an acute economic crisis in Israel. Thirdly, since the settlements project required massive civil and military expenditure, it hampered the State's ability to balance the results of the economic crisis precipitated by the Intifada by maintaining the previous level of social services.

There is no better way to conclude this article than with the quotation from Yaacov Arnon, director-general of the Israeli Finance Ministry under Pinhas Sapir: "The only responses to the disastrous policy pursued since 1967—a policy that is threatening to destroy our independence, first economic and then political, impacting on every single aspect of our lives—would be a return to pre-Six-Day-War Israel and achieving peace with the Arab world" (Arnon, 1984:160).

This citation should not be interpreted as expressing a desire to return to the "good old days" prior to the Six Day War. Simply looking at what I have written about those times will show that this is not how I see them. The desire being expressed is for the adoption of an inclusionary—fully inclusionary, this time—development policy, one that takes into account not only the growth in GDP but also its distribution. Such a policy should not be based on the assumption of inevitable and everlasting confrontation with our neighbors, but rather on the possibilities of cooperating and joining hands with them.

Bibliography

Ackerman, Yosi. 2002. Policy from the Perspective of The Mixed Public-Private Industry. In Tov, Imry (ed.), *Security and the National Economy: Challenges and Answers in the Military Production Policy.* Tel Aviv: Tel Aviv University, the Yaffe Center for Strategic Studies (in Hebrew).

Alexander, Esther. 1990. *The Power of Equality in the Economy: The Israeli Economy in the 1980s.* Tel Aviv: HaKibbutz HaMeuchad (in Hebrew).

Arnon, Yaacov. 1984. A Fool's Paradise. In Ofer, Zvi, and Avi Kober (Eds.), *The Price of Power.* Tel Aviv: Maarakhot (in Hebrew).

Bank of Israel. 2002. *Annual Report, 2002.* Jerusalem (in Hebrew).

Ben-Bassat, Avi (ed.). 2001. *From Governmental Intervention to a Market Economy: The Israeli Economy, 1985-1998.* Tel Aviv: Am Oved (in Hebrew).

Ben-Eliezer, Uri. 1995. *Through the Rifle-Sight: The Formation of Israeli Militarism, 1936-1956.* Tel Aviv: Dvir (in Hebrew).

Ben-Porath, Yoram (ed.). 1989. *The Israeli Economy: Maturing through Crises.* Tel Aviv: Am Oved (in Hebrew).

Berglass, Eitan. 1989. Defense Expenses and the Israeli Economy. In Ben-Porath, Yoram (ed.). 1989. *The Israeli Economy: Maturing through Crises.* Tel Aviv: Am Oved (in Hebrew).

Betcherman, Gordon. 1996. Globalization, Labor Markets and Public Policy. In Boyer, Robert, and Daniel Drache (Eds.), *States against Markets: The Limits of Globalization.* London and New York: Routledge.

Bichler, Shimshon, and Yehonatan Nitzan. 2001. *From War Profits to Peace Dividends.* Jerusalem: Carmel (in Hebrew).

Blumenthal, Naftali. 1985. The Impact of Investments in the Military Industries on the Israeli Economy. In Laneer, Zvi (ed.). *Defense and the Israeli Economy in the 1980s.* Tel Aviv: Ministry of Defense (in Hebrew).

Boaz, David. 2002. The Economic Consequences of the Increase in Foreign Defense Aid to Israel. In Tov, Imry (ed.), *Security and the National Economy: Challenges and Answers in the Military Production Policy.* Tel Aviv: Tel Aviv University, the Yaffe Center for Strategic Studies (in Hebrew).

Carmi, Shulamit, and Henry Rosenfeld. 1993. The Political Economy of Israeli Militaristic Nationalism. In Uri Ram (ed.), *Israeli Society: Critical Points of View.* Tel Aviv: Breirot (in Hebrew).

Coates, David. 2000. Models of Capitalism: Growth and Stagnation in the Modern Era. Cambridge, U.K.: Polity Press.

Dehter, Aaron. 1987. How Expensive are West Bank Settlements? A Comparative Analysis of the Financing of Social Services. Jerusalem: The West Bank Data Base Project.

Doron, Avraham. 1999. Welfare Policy in Israel in the 1980s and 1990s. In Nachmias, David, and Gila Menachem (Eds.), *Public Policy in Israel.* Jerusalem: The Israel Democracy Institute (in Hebrew).

Dunne, J.P. 1990. The Political Economy of Military Expenditure: an Introduction. *Cambridge Journal of Economics*, 14.

Erlich, Avishai. 1993. A Society at War: The National Conflict and the Social Structure. In Uri Ram (ed.), *Israeli Society: Critical Points of View.* Tel Aviv: Breirot (in Hebrew).

Etkin, Alon. 2003. *Place of Residence and Income Level in Israel, 1993-2000.* Tel Aviv: Adva Center (in Hebrew).

Goldberg, Esther. 1993. *The Settlements in the West Bank and the Gaza Strip—1992.* Tel Aviv: The Center for Peace (in Hebrew).

Dahan, Momi. 2000. The Rise in Economic Inequality. In Ben-Bassat, Avi (ed.). 2001. *From Governmental Intervention to a Market Economy: The Israeli Economy, 1985-1998.* Tel Aviv: Am Oved (in Hebrew).

Haaretz. Hebrew daily.

Halevy, Nadav, and Ruth Klinov-Malul. 1968. *Israel's Economic Development.* Jerusalem: Akademon (in Hebrew).

Halperin, Ariel. 1987. The Construction of Military Strength and Economic Growth. *Economic Quarterly, 27*(131) (February) (in Hebrew).

Halperin, Ariel. 1988. *The Defense Industry and Economic Growth.* Jerusalem: The Jerusalem Institute for the Study of Israel (in Hebrew).

Israel Central Bureau of Statistics. 1998. *Israel Statistical Yearbook.* Jerusalem (in Hebrew).

Israel National Insurance Institute. 2000. *Yearly Report, 1998/99.* Jerusalem (in Hebrew).

Israel National Insurance Institute. 2002. The Israeli National Insurance System. Jerusalem (in Hebrew).

Kleiman, Aharon. 1992. *A Double-Edged Sword: Israel's Military Exports and the World Armaments Market.* Tel Aviv: Am Oved (in Hebrew).

Klinov, Ruth. 1999. *Changes in the Structure of Wages, 1970-1997.* Tel Aviv: Histadrut—The Institute for Economic and Social Research (in Hebrew).

Kochav, David, and Yaakov Lifschitz. 1973. The Impact of Defense Expenditures on the National Economy and Industry. *Economic Quarterly, 20*(78-79) (in Hebrew).

Law-Yone, Hubert, and Rachel Kalush. 1995. Housing in Israel. *Israel Equality Monitor, 4.* Tel Aviv: Adva Center (in Hebrew).

Lifschitz, Gabriel. 1997. *Immigrant Absorption in Development Towns, 1990-1995.* Jerusalem: Jerusalem Institute for the Study of Israel (in Hebrew).

Lifschitz, Yaakov. 2000. Defense Economics. Jerusalem: Ministry of Defense and Jerusalem Institute for the Study of Israel (in Hebrew).

Lustick, Ian. 1980. *Arabs in the Jewish State: Israel's Control of a National Minority.* Austin, Texas: Texas University Press.

Mintz, Alex. 1983. The Military-Industrial Complex: The Israeli Case. The Journal of Strategic Studies, Vol. 6, No. 3 (September).

Mintz, Alex. 1984. Budgeting Defense: the Chicken and the Egg. In Ofer, Zvi, and Avi Kober (Eds.), *The Price of Power.* Tel Aviv: Maarakhot (in Hebrew).

Muallem, Yosi, and Roni Frisch. 1999. *The Rise in Return to Education in Israel, 1976-1997.* Jerusalem: Bank of Israel, Research Department (in Hebrew).

Peace Now. December 3, 2000. *The Settlements and the Occupation since the Signing of the Oslo Agreements.*

Pedatsur, Reuven. 1995. The Closing of the Circle: Back to the Palestinian Option. *Medina, Memshal VeYechassim Bein-Leumiin, 40* (Summer).

Pedatsur, Reuven. 1996. *The Triumph of Embarrassment: Israel and the Territories after the Six-Say War.* Tel Aviv: Bitan (in Hebrew).

Peri, Yoram, and Amnon Neubach. 1985. *The Military Industrial Complex in Israel: A Pilot Study.* Tel Aviv: The International Center for Peace in the Middle East.

Rabin, Yitzhak (with Dov Goldstein). *Pinkas Sherut* (Autobiography). Tel Aviv: Maariv.

Razin, Assaf. 1984. Al Hadvash veal Haoketz: The Implications of the US Aid. In Ofer, Zvi, and Avi Kober (Eds.), *The Price of Power.* Tel Aviv: Maarakhot (in Hebrew).

Rosenfeld, Henry, and Shulamit Carmi. 1979. The Appropriation of Public Means and the State-Made Middle Class. Haifa: *Makhbarot LeMehkar Ulebikoret*, No. 2 (in Hebrew).

Roy, Arundhati. 1999. *The Cost of Living.* London: Flamingo.

Rubinstein, Danny. 1982: *Gush Emunim.* Tel Aviv: HaKibbutz HaMeuchad (in Hebrew).

Shalev, Michael. 1984. The Recession: A Political-Economic Analysis of Unemployment in Israel. Haifa: *Makhbarot LeMehkar Ulebikoret*, No. 9 (in Hebrew).

Shalev, Michael. 1992. *Labor and the Political Economy of Israel*. London: Oxford University Press.

Steinberg, Gerald. 1983. Israel. *In* Ball, Nicole, and Milton Leitenberg (Eds.), *The Structure of the Defense Industry*. New York: St. Martin's Press.

Swirski, Shlomo, and Deborah Bernstein. 1980. Who Worked at What, for Whom and in Return for What: Israel's Economic Development and the Emergence of the Ethnic Division of Labor. *Makhbarot LeMehkar Ulebikoret, 4,* Haifa (in Hebrew).

Swirski, Shlomo. 1989. Israel: *The Ethnic Division of Labor*. Haifa: Makhbarot LeMehkar Ulebikoret (in Hebrew).

Swirski, Shlomo, and Menachem Shoshan. 1985: *The Development Towns—Towards and New Tomorrow*. Haifa: Yated (in Hebrew).

Swirski, Shlomo, Etty Konor-Attias and Alon Etkin. 2002. *Government Funding of Israel Settlements in the West Bank, the Gaza Strip and the Golan Heights in the 1990s: Municipal Budgets, Construction for Housing and Road Construction*. Tel Aviv: Adva Center (in Hebrew).

Swirski, Shlomo, and Barbara Swirski. 2003. *Changing Values in State Policy: Budgetary Erosion in Long Standing Support for Low Income Groups*. Tel Aviv: Adva Center (in Hebrew).

Toren, Yaacov. 2002. The Effect of the Military Foreign Aid on Industrial Policy. In Tov, Imry (ed.), *Security and the National Economy: Challenges and Answers in the Military Production Policy*. Tel Aviv: Tel Aviv University, the Yaffe Center for Strategic Studies (in Hebrew).

Urieli, Nachman, and Amnon Barzilay. 1982. *The Rise and Fall of Dash*. Tel Aviv: Reshafim (in Hebrew).

Yaron, Amos. 2002. The Industrial Policy of the Defense System. In Tov, Imry (ed.), *Security and the National Economy: Challenges and Answers in the Military Production Policy*. Tel Aviv: Tel Aviv University, the Yaffe Center for Strategic Studies (in Hebrew).

Yiftachel, Oren, and Erez Tzfadia. 1999. *Policy and Identity in the Development Towns*. Beer Sheba: Ben-Gurion University, the Negev Center for Regional Development (in Hebrew).

Yustman, Moshe. 2001. Branch Changes in the Israeli Economy. In Ben-Bassat, Avi (ed.). 2001. *From Governmental Intervention to a Market Economy: The Israeli Economy, 1985-1998*. Tel Aviv: Am Oved (in Hebrew).

The Political Culture of the Separation of Powers in Israel

Michael Saltman

Underlying the classic concept of the "separation of powers", there is an assumption that a set of checks and balances stabilizes the relationships between, and the activities of, the three major branches of government. Arian has written, "One of the most important myths of Israeli political life is that checks and balances exist within the system. This is simply not so" (1989:173). In Israel, the history of the relationships between the executive and the legislature, on the one hand and the judiciary on the other, has been marked by a constant power struggle, always latent, but on occasions, open. As in all power struggles, the megalomania of the power seekers is involved in their efforts not to share power. This paper, however, addresses itself to the cultural milieu within which the power-seekers operate

The High Court of Justice in Israel is a unique institution among international judicial bodies. Dotan in a paper, that highlights the judicial *hyperactivism* of the Israeli court, writes that the "HJC is probably the only Supreme Court in the world that can influence any state action *while it is taking place and in real time*.....since the Court serves as a first (and last) instance of judicial review, it preserves full discretion to intervene immediately in *any* public issue that is brought before it" (2002:99). Despite the fact that Israel has no Constitution, the Supreme Court (usually in its capacity of the High Court of Justice) has always exercised a degree of judicial review over the actions of the Executive. In the formative and early years of the State, the frequency of judicial intervention was characterized by self-restraint. It was applied on a limited basis to protect individual rights against arbitrary administrative excesses. Over time the court developed a series of principles that served as mechanisms of judicial review in the absence of any formal constitutionally recognized framework of judicial review.

The Passage of two Basic Laws in 1992 (in partial lieu of the Constitution that never materialized)—the Freedom of Occupation Law and the Human Dignity and Liberty Law—now provided the Court with an additional and statutory mechanism to review not only the actions of the Executive, but also to evaluate the legal validity of laws passed by the Legislature. The current Chief Justice, Aharon Barak, laid the ground for open conflict with the Legislature, when he claimed that "everything is justiciable". This ideology of his was expressed even earlier in a case before the Court in 1986

> any action is susceptible to determination by a legal norm, and there is no action regarding which there is no legal norm in its determination. There is no 'legal vacuum', in which actions are taken without the law having anything to say about them. The law encompasses any action...the fact that an issue is 'strictly

political' does not change the fact that such an issue is also a 'legal issue'.

(*Piskei Din* 910/86 477)

In recent years, both in plenary and committee sessions of the Knesset, the Supreme Court has been under attack. The sources, from which the attacks have been made, appear to be consistently spearheaded by members of the religious parties or by some members of nationalistically-oriented parties. MK Rivlin, the current Speaker of the House, made the following point, "The Knesset when legislating the Basic Laws, never considered during the process of legislation...that it was functioning as a "constitutive authority" and that the Basic Laws would be transformed into a special legal status that would in the future influence not only the Basic Laws themselves, but also any future legislation and even the very authority of the Legislative Branch to legislate as it sees fit" (*Divrei Haknesset* 24.1.2000)

A number of strategies have been employed on various occasions in an attempt to curtail the power of the court. One such attempt is to change the procedure in the appointment of Supreme Court justices by changing the composition of the Appointments' Committee. As presently constituted, the committee has a higher representation of the legal profession in its membership, thus ensuring in practical terms that the selection of judges would effectively be made by the judges of the Supreme Court themselves. This was originally legislated specifically in order to ensure the independence of the judiciary from the other two branches. The opponents, both past and present, of the Supreme Court's degree of independence have attempted to increase the number of political representatives on the appointments' committee. This strategy has so far not met with much success. But a more recent strategy whereby the number of judges to the court has been increased has served to reduce the input of the justices themselves in manipulating the actual appointments.

A third strategy has been the attempt to establish a special court that would deal with matters that have political ramifications. A debate took place in the Knesset's Constitution, Law and Justice Committee discussing a proposal to establish a special Court for Constitutional Affairs that would be more amenable to the sovereign demands of the Legislature. The proposal was raised by MK Eliezer Cohen of the right-wing National Unity party and supported by all the committee members representing the religious parties. MK Dan Meridor, at different times associated with the Likud and Centrist parties, was openly critical of the proposal, exposing what he considered was its true motivation, "...the truth is that the proposals here were designed for absolutely one purpose, not the establishment of a Court for Constitutional Affairs and not to solve problems of representation...but to damage the Supreme Court and its authority" (*Divrei Haknesset* 2.7.2001)

The onslaught against the judicial activism of the Supreme Court continues into 2003. One of the foremost antagonists of the Supreme Court is MK Michael Eitan, of the Likud party. In the same abovementioned committee, he stated,

they use a whip against us, wielded by the Supreme Court and its President, Aharon Barak, whose policy, his policy of judicial activism and whose steps are taken in order to enact a Constitution. The President of the Supreme Court waits for nobody, he legislates a Constitution, he writes the Constitution and he decides what should and what should not be in it. And we reach a situation, whereby a judge in a Magistrate's Court decides not to accept a determination made by the Knesset, because, in his opinion, it conflicts with one of the Basic Laws.

(Divrei Haknesset 18.5.2003)

Much has been written of the conflict of issues between the branches and of the issues themselves, but little has been written on the cultural milieu that defines the nature of the protagonists. This paper, then, becomes an essay in Political Anthropology that seeks a relationship between aspects of the political culture of Israel and the ongoing power struggle, primarily between the legislature and the judiciary in Israel.

The cultural parameters, to which this paper will address itself, are those that are historically particular to Israel. This in no way contradicts the universalistic aspects of the issue that are reflected in the power struggles between the branches of government in other contemporary, modern, political systems. The variables, isolated for discussion, are, first, the incompatibility between Judaism and Democracy, oft-stated in the notion of a Jewish and Democratic State. Second, the utilitarian notion of Statism, which was developed by Ben Gurion and Mapai in the early formative years of the state, has had a long-term impact on the relationship between the judiciary and the legislature. A third, influential factor, suggested here, was the mutual antipathy and dissonance in values between the politicians of Eastern European origin and the jurists, very many of whom had been educated in German universities and who formed the bulk of the judges at the Supreme Court level at the time of Israel's independence. Oz-Salzberger has written, in reference to Pinchas Rosen, the first Minister of Justice in Israel, "...that he had preferred German Jews in the legal establishment, because they were, in his words, 'honest and law abiding'. This statement can be understood not only as praise for the German Jewish immigrants, but also as an intimation of Rosen's view of the ethical stature of the personnel of Israel's other branches of government, most of whom were born east of the River Oder" (2000: 83). A final factor, more tenuous, but if valid, then more pervasive, is the high value placed on consensual thinking in Israeli society. Such thinking bolsters the already cited factor of majoritarianism as a characteristic of Israeli political thinking. In part this is an offshoot of the mentality of a "garrison state" that further reinforces the attitudes of statism. At the same time, it is also a function of the centralization of the educational system. The authoritarianism, that pervades this system from top to bottom, demands conformity with the thinking underlying educational programmes, and correspondingly accords a negative value to individualistic and critical thinking.

A Jewish and Democratic State ?

There are a number of reasons why the idea of a *Jewish Democratic State* is a contradiction in terms. The concept "Jewish" cannot be equated accurately with the sovereign-territorial basis of British, French, and Ugandan etc. Halpern states that Western nationalism, and by the same token, Western liberalism could only emerge from the collapse of a religiously-ordered social system:

> Occidental Christendom had to be displaced, or gradually made to yield its hegemonic sway, in order for the essentially secular, technical, and, eventually, *democratic* (my italics) order of Western civilization to emerge. Together with the rise of national territories, national languages, literatures and histories superceded the culture and hierarchy of religion as the formative principles of the European political system...wherever religious boundaries still served to define political units, these were regarded as an obstacle to the complete realization of the liberal nationalist vision.   (1979:313)

According to Graetz, if other monotheistic religions have emphasized past events in their histories as their major defining characteristics, the cultural specificity of Judaism compacts past, present and future into a single framework of reference. It can do this, because the Bible is a mythical text, which enables, what Eliade has termed an "escape from time". "One 'escapes' from historical and personal time and is submerged in a time that is fabulous and trans-historical" (1963:192). Particularly in Judaism ritual serves to transcend time by re-enacting the myth in the present as well as into an unforeseen future. This linkage between myth and ritual has been extensively dealt with by Leach (1965). Graetz, almost prophetically, concludes from his monumental analysis of the History of Jews some of the political realities of the contemporary State of Israel.

> The fusion of the religious and the political, the union of a transcendent God-idea with a political life must become, in Judaism, a reality, even though both these forces in another sphere might give rise to constant friction and struggle or even to appear to be irreconcilable. . .the vision of a political life conducted within the framework of Jewish institutions remains the distant ideal of Judaism
>
> (1975:65)

"Jewish" means, first and foremost, an organized religion, a way of life, supernaturally ordained for a specific group of people and, correspondingly, exclusive of other peoples. For centuries, the legal system of the majority of Jews in the Diaspora was based primarily on a rabbinical authority, an authority that could interpret divine texts and apply those interpretations to determine the rules of everyday life situations. The debate over these interpretations is confined to those sufficiently qualified and learned in the law, and these men acquired their legitimacy in their capacity of being the qualified exponents of the supernatural word. The religious establishment, then, is oligarchic rather than democratic. Rabbis convert legal decisions into decrees, which are ultimately sanctioned supernaturally, but also by a number of coercive sanctions, expulsion from the community being the most severe. But this, too has to be balanced by the fact that the system could only work, when those governed consensually agreed to be governed by this system. Dowty has written,

> But even at the peak of *kahal* (lit. community) powers, enforcement did not depend in the end on formal sanctions as much as on the reputation of the rabbis issuing decrees, on public opinion and pressure, and on shared values and interests. . .in a very real sense, it was government by consent of the governed.
>
> (1998:27)

The seeds of majoritarian political thinking were strongly embedded in this period and survive to the present day. But the institutional polity of the *kahal* was essentially eroded by the Enlightenment, the Emancipation and ultimately by political Zionism (Avineri, 1981: 219). But in that same text, Avineri devotes a chapter to Rabbi Kook: The Dialectics of Redemption. In this chapter we learn of the religious atavism that Kook predicted for the Zionist State. "But what Jewish secular nationalists want they do not themselves know: the spirit of Israel is so closely linked to the Spirit of God, that a Jewish nationalist, no matter how secularist his intention may be, is, despite himself, imbued with the divine spirit even against his own will" (ibid, 1981:193). This atavism is consistently reflected in the inability or unwillingness of successive Governments in Israel to achieve a separation between Church and State.

It is also perhaps curious to note that Aharon Barak, the President of the Supreme Court, who on face value represents a liberal and secular world view, cannot entirely escape Kook's generalization. For what Barak does is to translate humanistic values into Jewish values, by abstracting from the latter. Maybe it is just lip-service, but at all events a brilliant piece of politically correct casuistry, when he states,

> The foundational values of Judaism are the foundational values of the state. I mean the values of love of mankind, the sanctity of life, social justice, "doing what is good and right", the protection of human dignity, the rule of law over the legislature, etc—the values that Judaism has bequeathed to the world at large.
>
> (1992:30-31)

None of this is consistent with the democratic idea, where competing ideologies, interests and motivations vie for the legitimacy of public approval. Given, then, the contradiction between the notions of a Jewish and a Democratic State, the achieved compromise between the poles within the Israeli polity has been known as the *status quo*, whereby a number of religious laws are secularly sanctioned, even though the majority does not have a religious-ideological commitment to them, nor any vested interest in them. In exchange, the religious minority has its ideology and interests partially protected by the secular establishment, and agree not to press for additional religious legislation. The original accord for the *status* quo was in the form of a letter, dated 19/6/47 and sent by Ben Gurion to the political leadership of the Agudat Yisrael ultra-orthodox party. It essentially recognized in law that the Jewish Sabbath is the official day of rest in Israel; that religious dietary laws would be enforced within governmental institutions; that religious schools will be funded out of state funds and that the jurisdiction over marriage and divorce would be the prerogative of the rabbinical authorities. The *status quo* is a tenuous line that is constantly being probed by both the religious and the secular in order to improve positions, and on many occasions the Judiciary is called upon to act as a referee between the protagonists. It is, therefore, important who these judges are, as well as what their world views may be.

Within the religious establishment, which is not a monolithic institution, there are different conceptualizations of what constitutes a Jewish State, ranging from a state governed by halachic rabbinical law to a state based on Jewish law, adapted to the changing conditions of modern society. But from the inception of the State, the factions of the political religious establishment have consistently attempted to create legal norms in accordance with its value system. When it appraised the situation that a Constitution would not reflect its aspirations, it ensured, together with other elements in the polity, which had no interest in a Constitution, that a Constitution would not be enacted.

Israel's failure to adopt a secular constitution was not only a consequence of the manifest opposition of the religious political parties, but also due in part to the latent political considerations of the ruling party (to be discussed below). The Knesset debates over the proposed constitution give some credence to the contentions of Graetz and Kook, as cited above. A speech by MK Zerach Warhaftig of the United Religious Front illustrates Graetz's contention vis-à-vis the conceptual time frame of Judaism as compared to the other major religions,

> We fear that such a Constitution will not strengthen the link with our own rich past, but will sever the connection......Egypt, Greece and Rome still exist today. People returned there, built states and began their lives anew. But they are neither the heirs nor the continuity of the original peoples. They are new peoples, who have abandoned their ancient law and adopted new constitutions. And these new constitutions are not the heirs of their great past cultures.
>
> (*Divrei Haknesset* 7.2.1950, p. 732).

The atavism, alluded to by Kook (above) achieves its expression more subtly than the direct and outspoken demands of the religious politicians. Ben Gurion's speech in that same debate, also standing firm against the demands of the religious parties, has sixteen references to different verses in the Bible. Only the truly socialist parties, the Communists and Mapam rejected the discourse that entertained the idea of a Jewish polity.

Over the years the religious bloc has consistently lobbied for the appointment of *dayanim* (Rabbinical judges) to the Supreme Court. The debate is ongoing, endless and recurs each time an act of legislation is considered that has consequences for the judiciary. The inconsistency between *Jewish* and *Democratic*, the potential conflict between them is recognized even by those contemporary lawyers, religious protagonists who advocate the merging of Jewish religious law within the existing corpus of secular law. Rakover, one of the more prolific writers in that group, recognizes the contradiction between *Jewish* and *Democratic* and pointedly asks, "what is the significance of the terms "Jewish State" and "Democratic State", and how will the court balance between these values, when it appears that they clash with each other?" (1998:31)

In terms of the morality of law, this "balancing act" in untenable. Joseph Raz has argued against the idea of Israel being a Jewish State. He attacks what he sees as the lack of morality in a section of the preamble to the Basic Law: Human Dignity and Liberty, which states..."the purpose of this basic law is to protect human dignity and liberty so as to anchor in a basic law the values of the state of Israel as a Jewish and democratic state". If many of Israel's jurists lay claim to the fact the morality of Israel's law lies, not in the acceptance of Jewish law, but rather on ·a vaguer concept of Jewish values, Raz retorts to the proponents of this idea that "morality is universal and so are values generally. Ethnic or national values are false values of self-aggrandizement and chauvinism" (2000:510) The bottom line of Raz's argument is that,

> Morally speaking, a state is the home of all its inhabitants, and none are second-class; none of them belong to protected minorities. The law of most Western countries is consistent with this view. So far as I know, Israel and Germany are the only ones that define themselves as the state of an ethnic group, a definition which is symbolic but which in both countries has practical consequences. In both of them this blemish on their law cultivates racism, hatred, and the inability of part of their population to regard themselves as equal citizens in their homeland.   (ibid: 514)

Statism

A second cultural-specific factor that has influenced the attitudes and relationships of politicians towards the judiciary is to be seen in the Zionist movement's attitude to the concept of the "rule of law". Ben Gurion and the "classic" Mapai ideology of "Statism" (mamlachtiut) accorded higher value to state interests than to the rule of law. If state interests demanded the subordination of human rights to the political interests that safeguarded the security of the state, it was those interests that won the day. The lack of a Constitution and the minimalist application of judicial review served the interests of the government, which curbed judicial interference in the pursuit of policies that often entered the grey area between legality and illegality. For pragmatic reasons the government could side with the religious parties in their opposition to a Constitution.

It was not an ideological confrontation of one party against another in terms of attitudes to the rule of law. It was the party in power that did not want judicial interference in the implementation of policies, and correspondingly, the parties in opposition that wished to strengthen the role of the judiciary. The right wing parties, which constituted the opposition until 1977, were the champions of liberal ideologies and defenders of the independence of the High Court of Justice until they assumed power. After empowerment, they no longer backed these positions with the same fervour.

Ben Gurion's concept of *mamlachtiut* was not a clearly defined one. It was certainly not an expression of the fascist ideal type of the state "above all", but in reality it was a policy that concentrated enormous powers within the state's institutions. It was perhaps more a Benthamite ideology, as seen in phrases used by Ben-Gurion to the effect that *mamlachtiut* directs the citizenry "to the good of the whole", "to the public interest", "to the good of the citizen" and "to the service of the state" (1954:90). Medding has written that Ben Gurion's approach also "incorporated strong party government to provide the state with its values and policies. The state framework's content and the direction of its activity were of necessity fixed by a political party"(1990:137). But above and beyond the political direction, *mamlachtiut* is predicated on a required consensus, a majoritarian approach towards political thinking, which would ultimately have its effects on the thinking of the Supreme Court.

In the sterile debate over the Constitution that never came into being, Ben Gurion ruled out the autonomy of the court by defining the role of the judge, "The judge does not make the Law, the judge does not invalidate laws, for the judge, like any other citizen in the state is subject to the law. The judge just interprets the law and applies it to the specific situations brought before him" (*Divrei Haknesset* 20.2.1950 p.818). He continues by defining the limitations of the judiciary in his version of what constitutes the separation of powers, "....in a state where the Law rules, there is total separation between the authority of the legislator, the *chosen* representative of the people and the *appointed* body of judges, independent of the executive after their appointment "(op.cit.) (my italics). This is a truly strange sentence. The independence of the court stands vis-à-vis the executive, but does not equally apply in respect of the legislature. Ben Gurion then spells out his majoritarian, *mamlachtiut*, concept of democracy, which leaves no place for judicial review over the legislature. He declaimed,

> The Americans accepted with love—and that not always— when the Supreme Court invalidated a law that stood in contradiction to the Constitution. Will the public (here) accept this with the same facility? Will this not bring about, amongst us, a strong sense of contempt towards our judges ? And the two things are equally dangerous for the State—disrespect for the Law and distrust of the judge.   (ibid., p.818)

For Ben Gurion, the "public" was identified ideally as no more than the consensual attitudes of the majority.

Griffith, in his study of the politics of the judiciary in the British context, criticizes the consensual approach,

> It has long been argued that the concept of the whole society suggests a homogeneity of interest among the different classes within that society, which is false. And that this concept is used to persuade the governed that not the Government, but the "State" is the highest organization and transcends conflicts in society. It is a short step to say that it is the State which makes the laws, thus enabling those in political power to promote their own interests in the name of the whole abstracted society.   (1977:204)

Griffith continues and argues that

> the maintenance of authoritarian structures in all public institutions is wholly in

the interests of Governments....whenever governments or their agencies are acting to preserve that stability.....judges will not be over-concerned if to do so, requires the invasion of individual liberty.   (ibid., 209)

If, in the formative years of the state, the right wing and liberal elements of the opposition were the strongest protagonists in favour of a Constitution and a strong judiciary, today the right-wing elements and the liberals hold power and are hostile to the judiciary. And the reverse is true, for the classic Mapai in its contemporary form is now the supporter of judicial activism, together with the true "left" which has never held significant power in the Israeli polity and has consistently supported the judiciary. Apparently, it is not an ideological confrontation between the political ideologies of opposing parties, but rather a manipulative issue between the political "haves" and "have-nots".

Illegalism

A third issue is the manner in which the population at large regards the concept of the "rule of law". As already stated above, the rabbinical authorities in the diaspora were, inter alia, the effective political and judicial institutions of the Jewish community. The community, however, lived in the wider jurisdiction of the host country, which had a secular law applicable to all citizens of that country. This law of the land was often at odds with the law of the Jewish community. When the civil laws of the host nation conflicted with the interests of the community, creative adaptive mechanisms were sought in order to "bend" the law. Zborowski and Herzog's ethnographic study of the *shtetl* states quite bluntly that "bribery has come to be a routine part of dealings with their official representatives. In this respect the shtetl merely accepts the prevailing pattern of Eastern Europe where the 'good official' is the one who can be bribed" (1952: 232-3). Many of the countries of origin of the founders of the "yishuv", and ultimately, the State of Israel, were not liberal democracies with strong traditional values of non-coerced respect for the rule of law. Sprinzak claims that,

> even though the vast majority of the pioneers, who established the Zionist polity in Israel, rebelled against the *shtetl* and all that it represented in the scope of religion, society and culture....and even if the negation of the Diaspora was also the negation of the *shtetl*, one cannot underestimate the influence of the 'little township' on their patterns of behaviour. With this they grew up, underwent their initial socialization process, in the framework of which they internalized the long tradition of Jewish life and behaviour patterns within the Diaspora. This growth and internalization was to have a profound effect on the formation of the legal norms of the Zionist enterprise in Israel.   (1987:30)

Similarly, many of the new immigrants, who came from Islamic countries, after the founding of the state, were totally ignorant of the values embedded in the democratic ideal. Sprinzak has noted exactly the same syndrome of bribery, as an adaptive mechanism to the external polity, in these communities.

Zborowski and Herzog were followers of the Culture and Personality School of Anthropology at Columbia University. As a theoretical framework of reference this school is outmoded in its explanatory capacity. But in a descriptive ethnographic capacity, it designates individual "cultural types" within a society. They singled out two political intermediaries in the *shtetl*, which are still functional within the Israeli polity today. The first is the *makher* (a "fixer") who is little more than a shady profiteer working on a limited scale and meriting low social status for his activity. The second is the *shtadlan* (roughly translatable as a "lobbyist") who works on behalf of others, on a large scale and enjoys a measure of esteem and prestige within the community (1952: 234-5). There are, of course, other networks functioning as intermediaries in Israeli society, as in other societies. But the two above mentioned cultural types possess the same normative quality that was so characteristic of their status and function in *shtetl* society.

Israeli civic norms are more tolerant of corruption than in many Western democracies. Throughout the country's brief history only a handful of high-level politicians have been convicted and sentenced for acts of corruption. The decision to bring corruption charges against politicians is based on more stringent evidential grounds than what is required for non-politicians. Legal decision-making is differential, when some non-legal or utilitarian principle is cited in justification. Expediency has a higher value in Israeli society than respect for the letter of the law. Sprinzak writes that illegalism in Israeli society is the "orientation that regards respect for the law and the respect for the rule of law not as a basic value, but as a specific mode of behaviour that one may or may not follow according to considerations of expediency"(ibid, p.30). The courts in Israel have adjusted themselves to this reality.

Judicial Professionalism as Opposed to the Non-Professionalism of the Legislature

Within the three branches of government, the judiciary constitutes the most highly professionalized element, reflecting an almost guild-like status. In the executive branch there are other professionals, too, but they are not a branch of the government by virtue of their professions. They do not have the same traditional corporateness that is the mark of the legal profession. Furthermore, these other professionals are not necessarily directly involved in the political decision-making process, as is the judiciary. Of the three branches of government, the least professional in its composition is the legislature. On those occasions when rifts occur between the legislature and the judiciary, the latter is often accused by the former of elitism while the legislature at the same time promotes its own self-image as being representative of the "people". The interstices between which these conflicts were played out were the majoritarianism of *mamlachtiut* and the flawed socialism of Mapai on the one hand, and the court's professional commitment to protect minoritarian and individual rights. An illustrative example can be taken from the debate on the Judge's Law 1953. MK Ephraim Taburi of Mapai made the following remarks,

> We constructed our State on the basis of the separation of powers, but not in order to deny the Supreme Order or our period. The judge educates the people....I shall take a risk and bring an example, that of the lack of total war against black marketeering and economic crimes at this time. This is anti-national, anti-Zionist and is against the people. Justice is supposed to assist in this war and not to remain indifferent to it...the judges are the people's judges and not judges who sit on Olympus and judge by the dead letter of the law...even the simplest of men can be judges, not only jurists...we are transforming these professionals into a caste   (*Divrei Haknesset* pp. 438-9, 5.1.1953)

This may hold true as prevailing attitudes in all democratic societies, but the cultural specificity of the Israeli example is reinforced by the ethnic composition of the Israeli population viewed in its historical context. Many of the pioneer founding fathers of the country came from East European countries. Their perceptions were influenced by several ideological streams—nineteenth century ideas of anarchism, the altruism of Tolstoy, the socialism of the First Russian revolution. They were proletarian in their own social self-awareness, but were also well-read as a consequence of auto-didactism. They were also going to constitute the first generation of politicians in the State of Israel. On the other hand, the lawyers, who were going to constitute the first generation of the senior judiciary in Israel, came from a different background. They came in a late wave of immigration, mainly in the 1930's, after the East European pioneers had established their political veterancy. They came from Central Europe, mainly Germany, or were Eastern Europeans who had studied in Germany. These Germans (*yekkes*) were in many respects the social and cultural antithesis of the East Europeans who had preceded them. They came from a bourgeois background, they were formally educated and viewed their own cultural background, ethnocentrically, as being vastly superior to that of the East Europeans. The held themselves aloof from the mainstream of accepted cultural patterns, spoke German among themselves and attempted to maintain their own cultural niche. All this did not endear them to the *apparatchniks* of the political system. Furthermore, their legal education, during the Weimar period, would not necessarily prove to be consistent with the interests and demands of the polity during the formative years of the state.

Fania Oz-Salzberger and Eli Salzberger (2000) have shown how the juridical concept of *Rechtsstaat*, a central concept in the legal studies of law students in the Weimar Republic was transplanted into the Israeli legal system by the first generation of Supreme Court justices, who had obtained their legal education in German Universities. *Rechtsstaat* was born out of nineteenth century liberalism. On the one hand it was a positivist, almost scientific approach to law, but also, in its substantive aspect, it reflected the collective will on an "enlightened public". In the original European context—both in time and place-, the enlightened public was of course the propertied bourgeoisie. But concepts such as these get partially lost in translation, linguistically, culturally and socially.

Rechtsstaat ultimately becomes a narrower version of the Anglo American idea of "Rule of Law" and clearly the "enlightened public" of Israel in the 1950's was a far cry from the original European concept. Oz-Salzberger has summed up the German legal transplant quite succinctly,

> the Israeli Supreme Court, in other words, uncritically adopted a German conceptual tradition, which is humanist and liberal, yet elitist and socially conservative...they took for granted the statist and authoritative notion of *medinat chok* (a state ruled by law)and the cultural, ethnic and social exclusiveness of the *tzibur ha-naor* (the enlightened public) (200:117). . .it appears that the struggles on the political form and style of the young State of Israel were played out, to some degree, in accordance with the participants' countries and cultures of origin. The legislative and executive parts of the Israeli government harked back to an East European political legacy, which was socialist in ideology and centralist in style. . .the judiciary, on the other hand, attracted graduates of German universities, who were sometimes faced with the challenge of coaxing or forcing the Russian-born and Polish-born politicians into liberal constitutional norms.   (200:120)

"Holy Cows" and Security Considerations

The Judiciary is a sub-system within the overall political system and as such will on occasion find itself in conflict with the other sub-systems. The context, in which this usually occurs and on which this paper is focused, is when the Judiciary declares illegal the actions of the Executive branch, or invalidates a law adopted by the Legislative Branch. In many cases these conflicts take the form, whereby the rights of an individual, as defined by law or by concepts of natural justice, are pitted against the utilitarian interests of the state as defined by the other two sub-systems. On this particular issue, Israel has a number of specific "holy cows", which place the judiciary in an awkward situation.

Even prior to the establishment of the state, and certainly after its establishment, security issues, real or imagined, have been in the forefront of Israeli consciousness. This consciousness is buttressed by a collective historical remembrance of persecution that is both real and constantly reified in order that it not be forgotten. Thus, the security forces, in a reality of constant insecurity, are, in the eyes of the majority, not only beyond reproach but also an object of adulation in a militaristic society such as Israel and militarism is an essential ingredient in Israeli cultural life. (Carmi and Rosenfeld, 1989). The Judiciary, when reviewing the legality of the actions of the security forces, is fully aware of public opinion and the potential that the other branches have in mustering public opinion against the courts if necessary.

Whatever the reasons, Israel has had a security problem from its outset and even prior to its establishment as a state. Wars, border skirmishes, terror attacks, counter attacks against Arabs, military occupation and rule have been the major features characterizing Israeli history. Security considerations are high on the agenda of Israeli politicians and foremost in the perceptions of the Israeli public, particularly as an election issue. This factor tends to exacerbate the friction between the politicians and the judiciary, the former claiming that they represent the Public Interest, while the latter lay claim to being the guardians of the Rule of Law. Saltman and Rosenfeld (1990) have shown that when Public Interest is pitted against the Rule of Law, the intermediating variable of Security Considerations has often been used by the legislative and executive branches of government to force the hand of the judiciary and oblige it to "cooperate". Only in few instances has the judiciary balked at this heavy-handedness. The most effective procedure employed by successive governments, in order to reduce intervention by the court, has been the use of draconian Emergency Laws, described by Saltman (1982).

The powerful impact of security considerations on public awareness is a weapon in the hands of the politicians. The court realizes that its standing is dependent, to a degree, on the favourable public opinion towards it. The court has in fact enjoyed a high standard of approval by the public over the years. It takes this into account when it hands down "balanced" judgments. On one of the rare occasions when the court found against the government on a security issue, prior to the period of its judicial *hyperactivism*, the Chief Justice at the time, Landau made the following statement,

> But there is still considerable apprehension that the court will be seen as having abandoned its proper station and having descended into the public debate, and that its decision will be received by one section of the public with applause and by another section with total emotional rejection. In this sense, I see myself as someone, whose responsibility is to judge by the law any matter that is rightfully brought before this court, in a burdensome position. For I know full well, and in advance, that the public at large will not pay attention to the legal argumentation but solely to the final conclusion, and the proper status of the court, as an institution will be damaged over the differences that divide the public.
> (*Piskei Din* 390/79)

In the above mentioned Saltman and Rosenfeld paper, the issue under discussion was the 300 Bus case that occurred in 1984. Two captured Arab bus hijackers were murdered by members of the General Security Service. This was followed by a series of Commissions of Inquiry, before which those suspected of the murders and their lawyers lied in their evidence. When it became clear to the politicians that the Attorney-General was about to embark on a criminal prosecution of those involved, they made every effort to thwart his intention.

> They insisted on the need for a fully protected General Security Service, irrespective of its actions. They claimed that any exposure would seriously damage the service, that the nation's security was at stake and that different ethical criteria operated differentially in the civilian and military branches of the security services.   (1990:11)

When a watered-down case eventually reached the Supreme Court, the majority opinion opted to protect the security services. Shamgar accepted the primacy of security considerations. Ben Porath "was satisfied that vital state security considerations were at stake and that it was also necessary to put an end to the public hue and cry" (1990:13). As against this, Aharon Barak, the judicial activist and "red rag" to the politicians, neatly twisted the importance of security considerations in his minority opinion,

> Security considerations do not require a different result; there is no security without law. The Rule of Law is a component of national security. . .the strength of the service is in the public's confidence in it. Its strength lies in the court's confidence in it. If security considerations turn the scales, neither the public nor the courts will have confidence in the security service and in the legality of its investigations. Without this confidence the systems of government cannot function.   (1990:15)

Another related characteristic of Israeli political thinking is that of the almost infallible rightness of the majority that justifies the occasional curbing of the rights of the minority and the individual who may represent that minority in the arena of the court. The "holy cow" of the majority's infallibility is fostered by the demand for conformism to basic societal values, not only as a function of the security situation, but also as a result of the educational system.

The Israeli educational system is a centralized system controlled by the Ministry of Education. It is as much geared to imparting nationalistic values to the pupils in the system as it is to developing their intellectual skills. The values change subtly in accordance with the political ideology of the incumbent Minister of Education.

Resnik, in describing, the social and cultural values inculcated into children by the state educational system since the inception of the state, has reached the following conclusion,

> The picture that emerges from this description is a gloomy one from the standpoint of democracy and the rule of law. The idea of a civil society in the construction of the national subject is mere flotsam in the sea of Jewish-religious particularism.   (1999:507)

The Ministry determines text books to be used in schools, formulates curricula and is the examining body that grants matriculation status. It is an authoritarian system that encourages conformism not only in the acceptance of basic values, but also in the development of intellectual abilities. In a normative sense, it is a system whereby teachers teach the "material" and pupils are expected to learn that material exactly as it is taught. There is little or no room for critical analysis, either of the text or the teacher's interpretation of it. In other words, the system appears to be geared towards achieving a high degree of conformism, and correspondingly, to discouraging non-conformist and critical thought. Such thinking serves the interests of the majority.

The authoritarianism that underlies the educational system may well have its roots in the traditions of Jewish religious education. This was a system within which there was no room for doubts or skepticism. It was a closed paranoid world in which the creativity of non-conformist thinking had no place. The word of the teacher was paramount. The words of the text only interpreted within acceptable rigid frameworks of reference. The axioms of the original text are unquestionable, only the inferences from the Biblical text could be argued. But the supposition that the traditional forms of Jewish education have any role as a variable in the formation of the current Israeli educational system has not been researched as an anthropological issue and thus has no standing beyond that of a supposition.

Discussion

The "Separation of Powers" concept, as taught in school Civics courses, is little more than a myth by virtue of its over-simplicity. In all democratic political systems there are grey areas in which the branches of government may overlap each other and, as a consequence, tensions may arise between them. The specific political culture of a society characterizes the nature of these interactions.

This paper has attempted to focus on those aspects of Israeli culture and history that have affected the relationships between the three branches of government. The major overall problem is that of the contradictory terms of a "Jewish" and "Democratic" state. It is this problem, more than any other that has aggravated the tensions between the legislature and the judiciary. The incompatibility between "Jewish" and "Democratic" is first and foremost to be seen in the fact that a sizeable minority of the population is non-Jewish, which in addition, has a serious conflict of interest with the majority. In addition to this is a second factor that pits a potential theocracy, based on *halakhik* law against the secular ideals and procedures of a Democracy. Here an interesting paradox occurs, for the court has to both reflect majoritarian values, while also being under an obligation to protect minority groups against the tyranny of the majority.

The question arises as to what actually constitutes a majority. The government, as an elected representative majority, presumably represents the will of the people. But Israeli governments have invariably been coalition governments, in which minority religious parties have been the key elements in holding the coalition together. This has augmented the power of these small key parties far beyond their proportional representation within the society at large. These parties have, throughout their history, attempted to enact Jewish religious legislation, promote and protect Jewish religious institutions and to oppose the country's growing secularization. The Supreme Court then finds itself interceding between the parliamentary majority—the government, which submits to the demands of the religious minority elements in its coalition—and the real majority of Israel's largely secular majority. The court then finds itself between two majoritarian poles, virtual and ideal—the "virtual" majoritarian government that enacts laws on behalf of small key coalition partners, laws that curtail the rights of the "real" demographic majority.

The classic role of a Supreme Court in most democracies is counter-majoritarian. It protects the fundamental rights of individuals and minorities against the excesses of the majority. In 1969 the government decreed that the

Israeli Broadcasting Authority should not operate the television service during the hours of the Sabbath. A petition to the Supreme Court upheld, by means of an interim order, the IBA's right to air television broadcasts on the Sabbath, or more to the point, the public's right to view television on the Sabbath. The court's activism, based on various legal techniques, grew incrementally until the passage of the Basic Laws in 1992, after which its activism increased significantly on the basis of the new tools afforded by the Basic Laws. It applied itself not only to protecting the rights of the "real" demographic majority against the "virtual" majority of the coalition, but also protected minority groups, such as non-orthodox Jews in the Conservative and Reform movements, non-Jewish immigrants who could not legally intermarry in Israel and the recognition of the rights of homosexuals. All these issues created tension between the legislature and the judiciary. The court, in effect, threatened the power base of the legislature which lay in its coalition arrangements. Ben Gurion's *mamlachtiut* was one of the prime causes of the anomaly, a consequence of which was that the court had, on occasions, to protect the interests of the majority against its own government. Ben Gurion, in order to achieve the widest possible consensus in the pursuit of state interests, traded off basic rights of the public in order to gain the support of coalition partners, even though he had a majority without them. He achieved the dominance of the executive in the management of state affairs, even above the sovereign power of the Knesset itself.

The Executive branch, to this very day, has behaved with little restraint in the security domain. By the same token, the court's liberal record on security issues has been less impressive than on other civic matters. The real and imaginary security threats facing Israel have given rise to innumerable infringements of basic rights and relatively few landmark cases or other restitutive measures by the courts. In this sense the Supreme Court is sensitive to the conformity of public opinion on security issues, namely that security considerations outweigh all other considerations. The Court is fully aware that its prestigious standing in the public regard is due in large measure to the court's reflecting majoritarian opinions in its decision making over security matters. In the power struggle with the politicians the Supreme Court Justices require positive public opinion ratings, no less than the politicians themselves, and they cannot jeopardize the court's standing by adopting a policy of overt "counter-security" decisions, even at the expense of the infringement of civil liberties by the executive.

In conclusion, the achievement of a separation of powers in a democracy is little more than a Weberian ideal type and invariably falls short of the ideal. The social-institutional variables in accounting for the gap are insufficient by themselves to give this account. Each specific case, for subsequent comparative analysis at a later stage, should be initially analyzed within its specific cultural context and the particular historical circumstances that have given rise to that context. While the separation of powers in other democracies falls short of the ideal, the nature and substance of the shortfall will clearly be different from what has been described here above.

References

Arian, A. 1989. *Politics in Israel: The Second Generation*. London: Chatham House.
Avineri, S. 1981. *The Making of Modern Zionism: The Intellectual Origins of the Jewish State*. London: Weidenfeld and Nicolson.
Barak, A. 1992. Law and Government in Israel. *Mishpat U'Mimshal, 1* (in Hebrew).
Ben-Gurion, D. 1951-57. *Hazon V'Derech* Tel-Aviv: Mapai 5 Volumes (in Hebrew).
Carmi, S. and H. Rosenfeld. 1989. The Emergence of Militaristic Nationalism in Israel. *International Journal of Politics, Culture and Society 3*(1): 5-49.
Divrei Haknesset (The Official Record of Speeches Delivered in the Knesset.) Jerusalem (in Hebrew)
Dotan, Y. 2002. Judicial Accountability in Israel: The High Court of Justice and the Phenomenon of Judicial Hyperactivism. *In* Maor, M. (ed.) *Developments in Israeli Public Administration*. London: Frank Cass
Dowty, A. 1998. *The Jewish State: A Century Later*. Berkeley: University of California Press.
Eliade, M. 1963. *Myth and Reality*. New York: Harper and Row.
Graetz, H. 1975. *The Structure of Jewish History* (I. Schorsch, trans., ed.) New York: Jewish Theological Seminary of America
Griffith, J.A.G. 1977. *The Politics of the Judiciary*. Manchester: Manchester University Press.
Halpern, B. 1979. Jewish Nationalism: Self-Determination as a Human Right. *In* Sidorsky, D. *Essays on Human Rights: Contemporary Issues and Jewish Perspectives*. Philadelphia: The Jewish Publication Society of America.
Leach, E.R. 1954. *Political Systems of Highland Burma*. Cambridge, Mass: Harvard University Press.
Medding, P.Y. 1990. *The Founding of Israeli Democracy 1948-1967*. Oxford: OUP
Oz-Salzberger, F and E.M. Salzberger. 2000. *The Hidden German Sources of the Israeli Supreme Court*. Tel-Aviv: University Studies in Law, Vol.15
PD. Piskei Din, Law Reports of the Supreme Court. Jerusalem: Ministry of Justice (in Hebrew).
Rakover, N. 1998. *Jewish Law and Israeli Law: On the Process of Integration*. Jerusalem: The Jewish Legal Heritage Society (in Hebrew)
Raz, J. 2000. Commentary. Against the Idea of a Jewish State. *In* Walzer, M. et al. (eds.) *The Jewish Political Tradition*, Vol I, Authority. New Haven: Yale University Press
Resnik, J. 1999. Particularistic vs. Universalistic Content in the Israeli Education System. *Curriculum Inquiry, 29*(4). The Ontario Institute for Studies in Education.
Saltman, M. 1982. The Use of the Mandatory Emergency Laws by the Israeli Government. *International Journal of the Sociology of Law, 10*.
Saltman, M. and H. Rosenfeld. 1990. Rule of Law Versus Political Interest. *Contemporary Crises, 14*.
Sprinzak, E. 1987. *Every Man Whatsoever is Right in His Own Eyes: Illegalism in Israeli Society*. Tel-Aviv Sifriat Poalim Publishing House Ltd. (in Hebrew)
Zborowski, M. and E. Herzog. 1952. *Life is with People: The Jewish Little-Town of Eastern Europe*. New York: International Universities Press, Inc.

Demography, Politics, and the 'Natural Family': Donor insemination in Israel

Daphna Birenbaum-Carmeli
Yoram S. Carmeli

Procreative technologies have always been exceptionally popular In Israel. In this paper we examine the application of one such technology—donor insemination (DI). We take the application of this technology as a vantage point for a critical observation of local constitutive narratives and for the politics of their construction in Israel. The protagonists in our discussion are Israeli health-policy makers, practicing doctors, a large number of Jewish Israeli recipients of DI, and the unseen participants behind the curtain—the sperm donors. At stake are not only sperm donations and the children to-be-born, but—as we found—the concepts of Jewish nationality, as well as power relations in the domains of gender and ethnicity. These relations are generated and reproduced through the regulation and practice of DI: the power of the state vs. constituencies, practitioners vs. recipients, men vs. women, a Jewish dominant majority vs. the Israeli Palestinians, who are practically absent from the DI scene in Israel. The Israeli cultural and political scene—so richly observed from a variety of perspectives—will be explored here from this relatively new and provoking perspective.

In the past several decades, technological innovations have become the ordinary state of affairs in medicine. Still, certain biotechnologies—among them those that pertain to human reproduction—stand out as being more revolutionary than others, triggering a qualitative shift in foundational cultural concepts (Webster, 2002). Through their development and availability to large clienteles, these biotechnologies, as depicted by several social theoreticians, challenge and reconfigure the culturally established spatial and temporal boundaries of the human body and, more generally, the deep structure of the relations between culture and nature (Strathern, 1992; Luhmann, 1985, Webster, 2002). By explicating "facts otherwise assumed to be foundational. . .[procreative technologies] set off an irreversible process. The implicit can never be recovered, and there is no return to old assumptions" (Strathern, 1995b, p. 347). Alongside this outlook, which emphasizes technological intervention as a source of ontological crisis, a somewhat more 'optimistic' approach views the 'post-modern condition' in general as primarily liberating. When applied to nature and the new biotechnologies, this latter approach is implied in the discourse of the body as an object to be displayed, a project to be accomplished (Featherstone, 1991:187; Shilling, 1999). The human body, its displays and its 'molding' through new reproductive technologies, may be conceived, from this alternative approach, as a further extension of the realm of choice and modern consumer freedom (on consumption and freedom, see Friedman, 1994; Miller, 1995;

Slater, 1997). Tested contextually, in Israel or in any other social and cultural setting, both these general outlooks inspire an understanding of modern biotechnologies as being in the midst of the social process and, as such, as being at the core of power relations and politics.

A major reason underpinning the heightened political significance of such biotechnologies is the prevailing perception of the body as essentially objective and 'naturally' given. Hence, the centrality of the body and of body metaphors and practices in the legitimization of the social order and in the naturalization of power relations (e.g., Foucault, Barthes, Bourdieu, Bell 1992). The destabilization of the naturalness of the body through the application of new biotechnologies—whether shattering or liberating—unveils the constructed quality and the politics of the 'given' body and the naturalized order. As such, it inspires critiques of culture, state and medical intervention in the private sphere, and of the political shaping of the morally acceptable and the physically normal. In some social contexts, these processes also touch upon the making of societal categories and broader collectivities. The application of biotechnologies introduces, then, a new dimension into modern cosmologies while disclosing the politics of its fabricated web.

Looking at the Israeli context through the application of DI may shed light on some aspects of the politics of its primordial foundations and on the place of body and Nature in negotiating and cementing individuals, families and collectivity; myths and social hierarchies.

We start our analysis of the Israeli case by outlining main characteristics of the state's reproductive policy and zoom in on the policy regarding procreative technologies. We then look at the state-dictated DI regulations and their application by doctors, who control recipients' bodies through daily practice. The last section explores recipients' approaches to DI: taking individuals as agents who actively influence the shaping of their own lives, we consider recipients' approaches as central to an understanding of the operation of bodily control by means of procreative technologies.

Our study identified a consistent movement: policy makers, practitioners, as well as recipients, all exhibited a preference for reproductive processes that led to the creation of 'natural families'. This preference is understood to be part of Israel's politics of grounding the 'natural givenness' of kinship at the heart of Jewish Israel's collective identity, thus bestowing a family-like quality on individuals' ties to the collectivity. We also point to the ways in which the 'natural family' is endorsed so as to support existing power structures in the spheres of gender, ethnicity and professional authority.

The paper is based on policy analysis, interviews with sperm bank managers and on questionnaires delivered to recipients in DI clinics.

Families and Childbearing in Israel

Israel is a highly familial society. Despite some erosion of the traditional family in the past few decades, more Jewish Israelis of all ethnic and class identities marry than do their North American counterparts; they do so at an earlier age, have fewer births out of wedlock, and have lower rates of divorce (Friedlander and Feldmann,1993; Fogiel-Bijaoui, 1999). Moreover, although Israel resembles European countries in levels of women's education and labor-market participation, the total fertility rate of Israeli women is about 50 percent higher than that of North American and European women (Table 1). Whereas recent total fertility rates in Canada, the UK and Italy were 1.5, 1.65 and 1.2, respectively, Israel recorded a figure that was still as high as 2.89 in 2001, though down from 3.07 in 1989 and 3.8 in 1964. Among Jewish women, the respective figures were, 2.59, 2.79 and 3.39. (At least part of the recent decline may be attributed to the arrival of immigrants from the Former Soviet Union, whose families are substantially smaller.) In the Muslim community, fertility rates have also declined, but have stabilized at 4.7 since 1989. While the high fertility rates among Muslim women are accounted for in terms of religious and patriarchal dictates, the relatively high figures among Jewish women are facilitated also by state intervention in the form of a pronatalist policy. Although offered to the entire Israeli citizenry, Israeli Palestinians—as will be illustrated later—make less use of these services.

Israel's Reproductive Policy

In any country, social policies perpetuate and legitimize local attitudes towards key issues, such as social order and the family. In addition, they also advance state interests and various types of power relations. Gradually, measures that were initially imposed from the outside influence people's subjectivities, their social perceptions and norms of conduct, so that the people themselves contribute, though not necessarily consciously, to a government's model of social order. Of major importance in enabling this dynamic is the effectiveness of policies as vehicles for disguising the goals that policy-makers seek to advance (Shore and Wright, 1997: 5-6, 11).

In the particular case of Israel, the local reproductive policy also mobilizes the body and reproduction for and through the collective, national goal of securing Jewish continuity. Reproduction then becomes a vehicle for steeping Jewish Israelis with collective national interests. As for the country's Palestinian citizens—although Israel's reproductive policy applies to the entire citizenry, various indications suggest that the pronatalist goal is directed primarily at the Jewish population: Some conditions of eligibility for allowances (e.g., military service), the spatial distribution of expert clinics (e.g., the relative rarity in areas populated primarily by Palestinians), as well as users' demography, are among the indicators of the partiality of the civil, contractual basis of the policy. (The political underpinnings of this absence are beyond the present discussion). Owing to the negligible use that Israeli Palestinians make of DI, the present paper focuses on the Jewish sector.

Forged and implemented by the state's Jewish majority, Israel's reproductive policy is couched in the pronatalist Jewish tradition. The biblical commandment

Table 1: Total Fertility Rates by sector and country

	1964	1989	2001
Israel—general	3.80[1]	3.07	2.89
Jewish women	3.39	2.79	2.59
ırthodox Jewish Women	5.60	4.57[2]	7.20
Muslim Women	9.23	4.70	4.71
Christian Women	4.68	2.49	2.46
Druze Women	7.49	4.19	3.02
Canada	3.50[3]	1.61[4]	1.50[5]
UK	3.00[6]	1.65[7]	1.65[8]
Italy	2.50[9]	1.25[10]	1.20[11]

[1] Unless indicated otherwise, figures are adapted from Central Bureau of Statistics Israel, 2003, p. 3.12.

[2] In the early 1980s; Source: Berman, E. (1999) Subsidized sacrifice: state support of religion in Israel, Contemporary Jewry, 20.

[3] http://www.vs.gov.bc.ca/stats/annual/1998/tab03.html

[4] http://www.vs.gov.bc.ca/stats/annual/1998/tab03.html

[5] http://www.statcan.ca/Daily/English/031222/d031222c.htm

[6] http://www.gro-scotland.gov.uk/grosweb/grosweb.nsf/pages/01sect3

[7] http://www.gro-scotland.gov.uk/grosweb/grosweb.nsf/pages/01sect3

[8] http://www.statistics.gov.uk/STATBASE/Expodata/Spreadsheets/D5797.xls

[9] http://www.un.org/esa/population/publications/migration/italy.pdf

[10] http://www.un.org/esa/agenda21/natlinfo/countr/italy/social.htm#demo

[11] http://www.un.org/esa/population/publications/migration/italy.pdf

of 'Be fruitful and multiply' has been historically constituted as both a major moral goal in one's life and a collective mission to be accomplished (Gold, 1988:23-27; Safir, 1991). In the Diaspora era, the political converged with the private to equate individual procreation with community survival (Katz, 1971:29; Swirski, 1976:129-130). In more recent years, the Holocaust trauma and the nationalist Zionist ideology have coincided to nurture an emphasis on regeneration as a means to ensure a Jewish majority within the evolving state of Israel. In line with this ideology, childbearing was constituted as a contribution to the nation-building effort and explicitly praised as such (Shuval, 1992:66).

State officials have translated the demographic interest into a pronatalist policy. Historically a pioneer in the domain of women's rights, Israel's policy now lags behind many industrialized countries. Maternity benefits were the first social benefits to be distributed (since 1953), preceding old-age pensions by three years (Barkai, 1998: 44,36,63). Maternity facilities in hospitals have also been free since this early period; and as of 1968, every woman who delivers a baby in a recognized hospital receives a one-time fixed Birth Grant. Child allowance, which was legislated in 1959 as a scheme for families with more than four children, has gradually universalized. The allowance increases proportionately with the number of children. In 1996, the Embryo Carrying Agreement Law was passed, making Israel the first country in the world to legalize surrogate-mother agreements (Shalev & Lev, 1999).

A pronatalist interest also seems to underpin the protection of women's participation in the paid labor market. Laws restrict the possibilities of firing a pregnant woman or a woman on maternity leave (since 1954), and allow absence from work for birth-related reasons (e.g., pregnancy, miscarriage, breast-feeding, adoption). Since 1990, fertility treatments, too, qualify employees for sick leave. A 'Mother Position'—anchored in law—entitles mothers to full payment for reduced working hours. Employed mothers also benefit from various tax exemptions. While securing women's position in the labor market, these laws also constitute Israeli women as 'secondary breadwinners', thereby suggesting the primacy of their familial role.

A different aspect of pronatalism is that of the hurdles associated with obtaining abortion and contraceptives through the public health-care system, and with the lingering inadequacy of sex education (Portuguese, 1998, 129–132).

At the same time, fertility treatments are exceptionally well funded. This 'generous' policy, like any other policy regarding procreative technologies, reflects the complex social and political consequences arising from these technologies. Openly counted by politicians as a method to increase the country's Jewish population (Birenbaum-Carmeli, forthcoming, SHI), practically unrestricted fertility treatments are offered free of charge to women of all ages, family statuses and sexual preferences, including mothers of children (up to two) with one's present partner. In December 2003, parliamentary discussions of cuts in health services nevertheless reconfirmed IVF funding for the second child once again.) Israel holds the world's record for IVF (In Vitro Fertilization) usage and is in the forefront of related research. Donor insemination, too, is available for an affordable sum to any woman, including singles and lesbians, as part of the public health-care system. Israeli courts and religious authorities have also been favorable towards procreative technologies and have supported potentially controversial issues, such as embryo transfer after divorce and post-mortem sperm aspiration (Kahn, 1998; 2000; Shalev, 1998). Treatment is as freely available to non-Jewish Israelis. Yet, in practice, owing to cultural and religious restrictions and possibly also because they are less ardently encouraged to do so, Muslim women make but little use of these services.

The availability of procreative technologies to all women removes the concern regarding economically-based differences in access. However, in the context of the surrounding myths and history, the scope of the public investment in this domain contributes to the establishment of motherhood, legally and morally, as the primary goal in women's lives. Infertility is thus endowed with heightened gravity as a personal bodily impairment and an injury to the collective well-being. It is within this social climate that we need to consider the politics behind Jewish-Israeli women's readiness to subordinate their bodies to prolonged invasive treatments. The consistent marginalization of the potential health hazards of the reproductive body is another aspect of the political construction of the reproductive body in Israel.

State-Dictated DI Regulations

For many years, DI has been provided unofficially in private gynecological clinics in Israel. In 1979, sperm banks started to operate in hospitals, under the inspection of the Ministry of Health. Today, 15 hospital-based sperm banks are the main providers of DI in Israel; serving from a few dozen to 200-300 cases annually.

On November 13, 1992, the Director-General of Israel's Ministry of Health published obligatory DI regulations. The document required that sperm banks operated exclusively in established hospitals, be headed by fully licensed gynecologists, and be subject to the Director-General's inspection. Private DI was deemed illegal. Beyond the centralization of DI control by the state, the contents of the regulations are instructive. First, the regulations allowed treatment only after establishing 'the woman's inability to conceive through conventional therapies by her husband or partner's sperm exclusively has been established'. Beyond the gendered language, which located the problem in the woman's body, this requirement obliged the woman to subject her body—in most cases, a healthy fertile body—to intrusive IVF treatments as a prerequisite for addressing her partner's impairment. This state-dictated course of action, which interfered with couples' fertility strategies, also drew 'in and through the activity itself, a privileged distinction between ways of acting' (Bell, 1992:90). In other words, it established an official preference for 'natural families' to those formed by DI. Given the obvious advantage of DI over IVF in terms of women's health, resulting pregnancy rates and cost-effectiveness, the relegation of DI to the end of the treatments-list highlighted the political interest that apparently underlay its state-sponsored inferiorization.

The devaluation of DI also ran through the dictates regarding the actual treatment technicalities. Here, the requirement for full and permanent secrecy was the main vehicle for endowing DI with a dubious moral character and for reasserting the superiority of the natural family. We may start with the self-imposed limitation that state control of sperm banks 'will not include any inspection of the donor's registry'. Later on in the document, the protection of the natural family was hinted at by a denial of the donor's personhood through consistent reference to 'the sperm' and through conferring the responsibility for sperm matching on 'the doctor alone, without any involvement of the couple and without their knowing. Donor, recipient and resulting child must remain anonymous forever; information about the donor, the woman and the sperm kept in separate files; and the donor's file placed in a safe, accessible only to the sperm-bank manager. Thus, the state endowed gynecologists, who lacked any training in psychology or related fields,[1] with a monopoly in this sensitive domain, and—in the name of privacy and discreteness—exempted them from supervision and deprived them of guidance. Eventually, the obfuscation was extended to the donor's contribution itself in a requirement that 'whenever possible, the husband's sperm should be mixed with that of the donor'. As fertilization by the husband's sperm in this way was most unlikely, the instruction seemed to aim primarily at clouding the very intervention. Apparently, the more denied the donor, the more 'natural' is the family and the greater is the treatment's success.

Finally, the consent form that was appended to the regulations established not only the physician's monopoly over donor matching, but also the recipients' disavowal of all donor-related information; it waived their right to pursue any treatment-related complaint. This was probably the clearest manifestation of the power relations that the state induced through DI. As dictated by the regulations—signed by the Minister of Health and the Ministry's Director-General, both physicians—Israeli doctors are mandated to maintain all the relevant information, and the recipients to be left in total ignorance.

This strictly medicalized version of DI through its confinement to hospitals and medical experts, as well as the state-dictated secrecy, contrasts with current trends in many industrialized countries. In Western Europe and North America, DI is not as centrally monitored, and governments are not as involved in its implementation. In Sweden, as of 1985, a law grants DI children the right to receive identifying details about the donor, and medical data about donors are to be kept by service providers for 70 years in order to secure access to genetic information. In the United States, more and more sperm banks provide donor-related information to clients (sometimes, though, in proportion to the fees paid). Some clinics sell donor sperm for home administration, also via the Internet. The differences revealed by these comparative references might serve to further highlight the cultural-political influences that underpin Israel's mode of DI application.

The state-sanctioned concealment of DI from the public, as well as from the protagonists themselves, bears cultural and political consequences. By symbolically reducing the participants to generic 'donor', 'woman', 'child', the state's policy undermines the emergence of alternatives to the hegemonic 'natural family' discourse. It nurtures a shameful image of DI and disables any coherent meaning to the treatment outside the medical discourse. By subordinating their bodies to abide by the state policy, Israelis—both practitioners and recipients—are compelled to subscribe to the traditional, exclusive embeddedness of the 'family' in 'nature'.

From a wider historical perspective, the centralized state-protection of the natural family concept may be traced to Jewish tradition and some of its communal codes. In the Diaspora, the governing institutions, primarily the Rabbis, were considered to be in charge of ensuring the continuity of the community as a whole (e.g., Swirski, 1976). Present-day intrusion of social institutions into one's private life, as dictated by the DI regulations, might therefore be viewed as part of the responsibility that the State of Israel has assumed for the reproduction of the Jewish nation. The control of what is perceived as a potential moral threat to the 'natural family' conjures up the desirable character of this social entity: a biologically related network of extended kin. Procreative technologies that enhance this character—e.g., IVF—are therefore promoted over others. Following from this socio-religious logic is the subordination of individual bodies to a policy that defines the normal body through its contribution to the collectivity. The healthy body is that which fulfills its role in terms of the collective well-being. The political quality of this definition is made all the more evident when we recall the omission from the public discourse of the subject of the health hazards that fertility treatments may entail.

Doctors' Practice of DI

Our study of DI in Israel went beyond the state's policy to explore the actual practice of this last-resort treatment. This aspect of DI in Israel was studied by semi-structured interviews conducted individually with the heads of six hospital-based sperm banks. As is typical of the Israeli gynecology scene, the doctors were all Jewish males, in their mid-40s to mid-50s, married with children. (At the time of our study, all sperm-bank managers in Israel were males.) All but one were of Ashkenazi origin. The interviews, which lasted between one and four hours each, took place in the clinics (Birenbaum-Carmeli and Carmeli, 2000).

As dictated by the DI regulations, gynecologists were the primary executors of the state policy. Generally speaking, in contributing their professional authority to legitimize an unfavorable approach to DI, the doctors seemed supportive of the state's political interests.

Secrecy already shrouded the signs on the clinics' doors, which read: 'Fertility Research Institute' or 'Fertility Laboratory'. In his rural hospital, Dr. Pinski[2] linked the elusiveness to recipients' wish to conceal the treatment, should they meet an acquaintance. The professionals, themselves, too, seemed to view DI as morally dubious: relying on the state regulations, all six doctors tended to refer married couples to additional IVF cycles. This preference for a treatment that was less effective, more taxing on the woman's health and financially dearer probably echoed gender-power relations, as well as the doctors' conviction in regard to the 'natural family'.

Owing to the dictates of the regulations, doctors had great freedom in the implementation of DI. At the donor-screening stage, they tended to add to the physical and mental health criteria some personal considerations that accommodated their own sensitivities: Dr. Perlman rejected 'ugly-looking donors' as 'there are enough troubles as it is'; Dr. Monet refrained from exceptionally talented donors, because 'geniuses have disturbed children'; Dr. Aljam stated no particular guidelines, but an analysis of the donor registry in his clinic revealed a bias towards men who were more educated, more Ashkenazi, taller and slimmer than the average Israeli man (Table 2). Either because the gate-keeping professionals approached and selected such men more than others or because such men were more responsive to the clinic's invitation, this particular social-physiological profile—with its ethnic political significance—was being reproduced in Israeli sperm banks.

Further on in the medical procedure, doctors faced the critical stage of donor-recipient matching. Appearing impressively confident—though they never asked the recipients—the doctors we interviewed unanimously assumed that 'all the recipients care about are health, body resemblance and education. The uneducated, too, want an educated donor, a student' (Dr. Poliker). Dr. Pinski claimed that recipients' wishes were 'always the same, looking for health and body similarity to the husband'. Dr. Perlman claimed that his monopolistic acquaintance with both donor and recipients was crucial for the ability to create a 'natural family' appearance: 'This is crucial, as there are all kinds of blonds

Table 2: Physical features of donors compared to Average Israeli men

	Average Israeli man	Average donor (N=34)
Height (cm)	174.70[1] (175.81[2])	178.19
Weight (kg)	80.10 (77.72)	72.81
BMI	26.39 (25.17)	22.20

[1] Ministry of Health Survey, 2001
[2] Figures in parentheses represent the respective figure for Israeli men aged 25-35.

with blue eyes; some have wide eyes and others have narrow eyes'. Dr. Katz endorsed the 'natural family' concept to the extent that it allowed him to trivialize his matchings by relaying familial semblance to the eyes of the beholder:

We look for similarity, so we find it. It takes a Yemenite baby born to a Swedish mother to draw our attention. In normal families, too, the similarity is not perfect. I, for instance, have two red-headed children. [He is dark haired.]

More than his colleagues, the compassionate Dr. Monet saw himself responsible for the long-term consequences of his matching. He traced his sensitivity to the case of an oriental, dark-skinned couple that had undergone five unsuccessful DI cycles. Consequently, the doctor offered them a blond, blue-eyed donor, who was more fertile than others. The woman indeed conceived after a single treatment, but the couple seemed uncomfortable with the fair-skinned baby that was born. When, in the context of Israel's class system, passers-by once referred to the mother as the child's nanny and were surprised to hear she was his mother, the woman was extremely anguished. The couple did not return for additional children. Dr. Monet assumed responsibility for what he considered a total failure of mine, because when a couple comes for treatment, they want a child and will agree to anything; they can always find a blond cousin and a grandmother with blue eyes. It's only later on, when the baby is born, that they regain their senses. And often, this is the time difficulties arise. I consider it my role to protect them from doing something stupid. I must convince them.

Dr. Monet thus exemplified the pain that deviation from the external appearance of the social parents might inflict in the Israeli setting. Such stories served not only to reaffirm body resemblance and the natural family paradigm as the basis for matching. They also revalidated the conviction that 'the doctor knows best', thereby legitimizing recipients' exclusion as the 'right' mode of operation.

Somewhat different, yet eventually similar, was Dr. Aljam's approach. In his newer sperm bank, recipients were allowed to participate in the matching process. (Dr. Aljam was surprised to learn, during the interview, that this was a breach of the state regulations, and then dismissed the clause as obsolete.)

However, in cases of married recipients, he would enforce the natural family paradigm by presenting the couple only with donors that matched the partners' blood types, rationalizing that 'they wouldn't want to be exposed in case the child needed a blood transfusion'.

The view of the natural family as superior to DI-assisted families re-emerged in the different doctors' approaches to the issue of additional DI children. Five of the doctors allowed recipients to reserve sperm from the same donor for additional children, claiming that this option rendered the family more 'normal'. Dr. Monet, however, supported the natural family guise through an opposite strategy: banning sperm reserving. His argument was that a natural 'ghost father' might become a significant if abstract presence that might jeopardize the spouses' bond. Therefore, even when he did use the same donor, he would say nothing to the recipients, or—if asked—denied that this was the case.

The broader political relevance of the natural family discourse was made evident in Dr. Perlman's statement regarding an additional matching principle that guided him: 'I would never give the sperm of a Jew to an Arab or vice versa', he declared. In the light of the negligible use that Israeli Palestinians have made of DI as either donors or recipients, this statement essentially revealed the view of the sperm-bank manager regarding the place of DI in the reproduction of the Jewish collectivity.

A world is thus created through the medical practice of DI, in which actions become the proof of their own premises; in which the subordination of individual reproductive bodies to the state interest in reproducing a biologically related Jewish collectivity is promoted by doctors, who invest their professional authority to subtly impose the 'natural family' on recipients.

In line with this state interest and the power it granted them, and probably also out of sincere ideological conviction, doctors rejected altogether the idea of opening up DI. Claiming that disclosure would drive out all donors—an assertion that is only partially supported by the Swedish experience—they encouraged recipients to conceal the treatment from their social surrounding. Dr. Poliker contended that disclosure was a pointless complication of the children's lives and that couples managed the lifetime secret 'very very well'. The gynecologist was apparently unaware of the literature showing the detrimental effects that secrecy and deception have on some DI families (Lasker, 1993; Landau, 1998), of the requirement to inform DI children of their genetic origins and of the increasing unacceptability of a doctor-parent conspiracy (Karow, 1982; Landau, 1998; Lauritzen, 1993; Nachtigall, 1993). Indeed, professionals who once supported the secrecy policy (Haimes, 1993) now compare DI to adoption (Triseliotis, 1993) and encourage greater openness. A slightly more open view was expressed by Dr. Perlman, who admitted that the natural family guise might be relaxed when intelligent parents could tell a mature intelligent child that 'these are not my genes, but all the rest remains the same'. However, he dismissed this scenario as only rarely applicable.

Eventually, the natural family guise unfolded as a denial towards the recipients themselves. One may recall the state instruction that the donor's sperm should be mixed with the male partner's whenever possible. The doctors—some more so than others—seemed happy to nurture the illusion. Dr. Monet provided recipients with a quasi-scientific explanation about the increased likelihood of fertilization by the husband's sperm owing to the presence of the donor's more 'energetic' sperm. He further cultivated a sense of body similarity when , in his routine post-partum visits with DI parents, he joked: 'Your husband fooled me. I thought the baby is from the sperm I gave you, and here you are and the baby is his!' Dr. Monet admitted that despite the humorous tone, he consciously 'offered a fantasy, and I think such fantasies are good. I think they should be encouraged'.

In this evasive ethical climate, a doctor would sometimes go a step further. Dr. Poliker openly described how he had collaborated with women whose partners refused to undertake DI. When approached with a query by the partner of a woman who 'had arranged her own donation', he proudly stated that he had always used his professional authority to reassure the husband that it was medically possible that his wife had conceived from him. 'Why should I spoil their happiness: she loves him and wants to go on living with him, but he wouldn't have DI. Should we be the one to tell him the truth?'

That such circumstances evolved in the first place and that a doctor was the person approached is of course, the result of the a state policy that constructed DI as strictly medical and that overlooked the serious extra-medical aspects of this seemingly simple bio-technology. In a sense, the powerful, collaborative doctor was himself caught in the web of state interests.

Returning to the theoretical questions presented at the outset of this paper, the technologically assisted creation of the natural family, controlled by state and professionals, was largely guided by the Natural Family concept. At the same time, the state and the doctors operated within the bio-medical cosmology, in which the givenness of the body and the natural family were being challenged and deconstructed. The production of 'DI families' thus entangled policy-makers as well as practitioners in actions that were consciously aimed at patching up a somewhat false facade. In other words, the 'natural family' was now apprehended as requiring active tailoring, rather than as being strictly natural. In this respect, the production and performance of the natural family through DI became not only a response to contemporary destabilizing social order, it also became a component of its making. This ambiguity, which imbued some doctors' concerns, also surfaced in our study of the recipients' behavior.

Recipients' Responses to DI

The recipients, though subject to tight control, still retained a degree of agency and self-direction in the DI process. This part of our study, which complements the analysis of the state policy and doctors' practice, was conducted by means of questionnaires administered in four hospital-based sperm banks between 1996 and 1998.

The sample consisted of 285 respondents, 213 of whom were married, cohabiting or single women (Table 3). In terms of nationality, the respondent population included only 4 (0.19%) Palestinian women and no men. Owing to this small figure, we decided not to include the Palestinian respondents in the analysis. In regard to ethnicity, 80.8% of the respondents were native Israelis. On the basis of paternal grandfather's country of birth, we found that the percentages of Ashkenazi and Oriental recipients were nearly equal among the married respondents. Among the singles, the respective ratio was roughly 5:3. As for age, the single recipients were significantly older than the married and cohabiting ones. The recipient population was relatively educated. Whereas the National average of mean years of education was 9.6. (http://www.nationmaster. com/ country/is/Education), the respective figure was 13.8 years among married women, and 14.8 years among the single recipients. However, with 10% of all respondents and 11.4% of the singles having had less than a high school education, DI might be said to have reached Israeli women of all educational categories, even if to different degrees. A clear distinction was observed in relation to religiosity. While no single recipient described herself as 'religious' and a mere 19.3% considered themselves 'traditional', the respective figures among married women were 8.3% and 31.4%. The secular respondents comprised 80.7% of the singles and 60.3% of the married recipients. This last set of figures indicates a clear over-representation of this sector, which consists of a mere 21.0% of the general Jewish Israeli population (Levi, Levinson and Katz, 1993). Altogether, the data covered about 70% of the user population at the time. The newer sperm bank, which allowed recipient's input in the donor-matching process, was studied in 2000.

Of the range of issues through which we explored attitudes and practices of DI recipients, two clusters of data will be presented here: the first tackled recipients' patterns of secrecy and disclosure regarding fertility-related information, including DI. The second cluster questioned recipients' preferences in regard to a donor's bodily characteristics.

Generally speaking, married Israelis tended to conceal the third-party intervention in the creation of their family. As shown in Table 4, the male-factor was more concealed within the generally secretive sphere of infertility than was the existence of the fertility problem, and DI was the most private aspect. Less than a quarter of the married women and as few as a tenth of the men confided to anyone about the DI treatment. Partners to the secret seemed to be carefully selected, primarily from the family circle. As shown in Table 5, friends were consistently less confided in than was kin so long as the general scale of discreteness persisted (i.e., infertility > male factor > DI). Consistency was also found regarding the gender factor, with men being less than half as likely to share DI information than women, and to the total exclusion of friends from this constricted circle of confidants. Beyond the threat of symbolic contamination of the matrimonial relationship in the traditional Israeli familial context, DI possibly also entails a blow to masculinity, of which the man is the main sufferer. The sharing of private information only with kin further attests to Israelis' general view of reproduction as bearing relevance that goes beyond the nuclear family.

The second cluster of questions explored the recipients' attitudes towards the natural family through their preferences in regard to the similarity of the donor's

Table 3: Demographic characteristics of recipients by family status

		Married (N=128) %	Single (N=85) %
Nationality	Jewish	59.80	40.00
	Palestinian	0.19	0.00
Recipients Aged 35+		39.20	90.50[1]
Childless Recipients aged 34+		23.08	90.90
Ethnic origin	Ashkenazi	45·70	59·80
	Oriental	49·20	36·60
Education (Mean Years)[2]		13.80	14.80
Religiosity	Religious	8·30	0.00
	Traditional	31·40	19·30
	Secular[3]	60·30	80·70

[1] National percentage of single women aged over 35 = 12·9% (Source: Central Bureau of Statistics, 2001).

[2] National Average of years of education = 9.6 (Source: http://www.nationmaster.com/country/is/Education)

[3] National percentage of self-defined secular Israelis = 21% (Levi, Levinson and Katz, 1993)

Table 4: Disclosure Patterns by Gender*

	Men		Women		Total	
	%	N	%	N	%	N
Fertility problem	57.6	(38)	64.8	(79)	62.2	(117)
Man's problem	47.0	(31)	45.9	(56)	46.3	(87)
DI treatment	10.6	(7)	22.1	(27)	18.1	(34)

* Since some respondents listed more than one category, total percentages exceed 100%

Table 5: Disclosure Patterns by gender and confidant

	Men		Women		Total	
	%	N	%	N	%	N
Told Own Family about infertility	50.0	(33)	51.6	(63)	51.1	(96)
Told Own Family about male impairment	37.9	(25)	36.9	(45)	37.2	(70)
Told Own Family about DI	7.6	(5)	17.2	(21)	13.8	(26)
Told friends about infertility	19.7	(13)	33.6	(41)	28.7	(54)
Told friends about male impairment	13.6	(9)	14.8	(18)	14.4	(27)
Told friends about DI	0.0	(0)	4.9	(6)	3.2	(6)

body to the male partner's. Having been transferred from the givenness of the parents' bodily nature to the spheres of exchange value and commodification, the child's body image becomes negotiable in DI. A preference for similar features was considered similar to seeking a natural family appearance. Departure from the male partner's bodily features was considered as availing oneself of the choice that the technology enabled and that was possible in a world in which body givenness was itself being deconstructed. The recipients' preferences were hypothetical, as the state excluded them from the donor-matching process. Nevertheless, these preferences would hint at the extent to which DI recipients accorded with the state-supported natural family by trying to reproduce the man's body image in the child, or diverted from it in favor of an appearance that was more socially valued.

Recipients' physiognomic preferences were tackled by questions regarding the height, eye color and skin color of the woman, her partner, if existing, and of the preferred donor. We will illustrate the general trend by means of the data about the donor's height.

Eighteen of the male respondents were 1.70 m tall or shorter (Table 6). When presented with a choice, only 5 of their partners wished to reproduce these heights. The others preferred a taller donor (n=5) or expressed indifference to the donor's height (n=8, 44%). It is noteworthy that among women whose partners were 1.80 m tall or more, the percentage of indifference was substantially lower—11% (Figure 1). We read this discrepancy as indicating that the partners of short men were not as keen to reproduce their partners' height as were the wives of taller men, for whom the existing partner's tallness was an important feature to be sustained. In fact, 1.80m appeared to be the height of

Table 6: Women's (hypothetical) preferences of donor's height by partner's height

Spouse's Height	No Preference	Preferred Donor's height								Total (N)
		<1.66	1.67-69	1.70-73	1.74-76	1.77-78	1.79-80	1.81-85	1.86+	
<1.66	3	1	-	-	-	-	1	-	-	5
1.67-69	-	-	-	2	1	-	-	-	-	3
1.70-73	9	-	-	2	2	-	4	-	-	17
1.74-76	3	-	-	1	7	1	1	2	-	15
1.77-78	1	-	-	-	5	-	4	1	-	11
1.79-80	2	-	-	-	1	-	12	-	1	16
1.81-85	1	-	-	-	-	-	3	6	1	11
1.86+	1	-	-	-	-	-	2	5	2	10
Total (N)	20	1	0	5	16	1	27	14	4	88

Figure 1:
Recipients' preferences for a taller donor by men's height

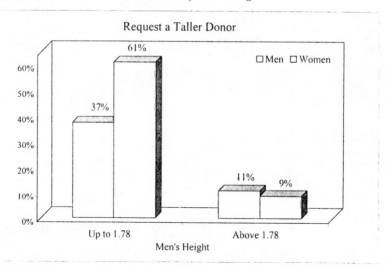

cultural choice: it turned out to be the Mode among both married female and male recipients, as well as among single women (Table 8), for whom the natural family paradigm did not apply. It was also the height above which very few married recipients requested taller donors (Fig. 1). Given the fact that the average height of Jewish-Israeli men is 1.74m (Ministry of Health Survey, 2000), the preference for 1.80m tall donors probably reflects the influence of international mass culture, in which this height is constituted as the ideal: American male models and shop-window models tend to be roughly this height, and American DI recipients, as well as people placing personal dating advertisements, also tend to prefer it over others. Altogether, about 60% of the married women prioritized social desirability over a precise replication of their male partner's body. Male recipients (Table 7) were even more willing to deviate from the natural family paradigm in favor of taller donors. Our findings thus suggest that married recipients would have departed from the natural family guise up to a certain degree in order to shape a child's appearance in the spirit of prevailing consumer-culture ideals.

Table 7: Men's (hypothetical) preferences of donor's height by their own height

Own Height	No Preference	Preferred Donor's Height								Total (N)
		<1.66	1.67-69	1.70-73	1.74-76	1.77-78	1.79-80	1.81-85	1.86+	
<1.66	1	-	-	-	1	-	1	-	-	3
1.67-69	-	-	-	-	1	-	-	-	-	1
1.70-73	4	-	-	2	2	-	1	-	-	9
1.74-76	1	-	-	-	2	1	2	-	-	6
1.77-78	-	-	-	-	-	-	4	-	-	4
1.79-80	5	-	-	-	1	-	5	1	-	12
1.81-85	-	-	-	-	-	-	1	4	-	5
1.86+	1	-	-	-	1	-	-	1	3	6
Total (N)	12	0	0	2	8	1	14	6	3	46

Table 8: Single women's (hypothetical) preference of donor's height (in numbers)

No Preference	Requested Height						Total (N)
	1.64-5	1.70-3	1.75-6	1.78-80	1.83-5	1.88-90	
7	1	8	12	30	11	3	72

Having said that, the wish for attractive children seemed to be secondary to the quest of married recipients for a 'natural family' guise, as their readiness to deviate from the male partner's height went only so far, remaining within the limits of 'natural' resemblance. (The mean deviation for women was 1 cm, and for men 2 cm.) Judging by this data, recipients themselves largely endorsed the natural family paradigm, which was partially imposed on them by the state policy and through the professionals' practice.

Two years after we had completed this study, we approached the newer sperm bank, in which recipients were incorporated into the donor-matching process. In this more open setting, recipients' actual choices, rather than their hypothetical preferences, could be probed. We obtained data on choices of donor height, weight, body-mass index (BMI), eye color, skin color, hair color, hair type, ethnic origin and education. We will continue to illustrate the general trend by looking at the variable of height.

Like the previous data, the figures obtained from this sperm bank revealed recipients' preference for taller-than-average donors (Table 9). While the average height of the Israeli man is 1.75m and that of younger men aged 25-35 is 1.76m, married recipients' choices were on the average for a height of 1.77m. Among single recipients, the average height of the popular donors was 1.83m. This pattern suggests, firstly, that all recipients preferred taller donors. Secondly, that married recipients were concerned with putting on a natural family appearance and, therefore, did not depart as much from the national average.

At this point, we need to recall that the average height of the donors in this clinic was higher than that of Israeli men in general. In other words, doctors' apparent preference for taller donors made the recipients' selection of such men more probable. However, it is interesting that the average height of married recipients' donors of choice was lower than the clinic's average (Table 9). This pattern further supports the argument on behalf of the importance of a natural family appearance for married DI recipients.

That putting on a natural family appearance was indeed a concern for the married recipients could also be gathered from their above-mentioned tendency to conceal the DI intervention from their social surrounding (Tables 4, 5). The fact that the male factor was more secretive than the existence of fertility treatment implies the threat to masculinity that the latter entails. That DI was an even more closely guarded secret indicates that the protection of the image of family naturalness and normalcy was still more crucial.

Table 9: The most popular donors vs. Average Israeli men

	Height (cm)	Weight (kg)	BMI	Eye color	Skin color	Hair color	Hair type	Ethnic origin	Field of study
National Average Man[1]	174.70 (7.62)	80.10 (13.89)	26.39 (4.11)	---	---	---	---	Ashken: Oriental = 1.1	
National Average Man 25-35*	175.81 (7.02)	77.72 (14.50)	25.17 (4.02)	---	---	---	---		
Donors' Average	178.19 (6.68)	72.81 (8.80)	22.20 (1.61)	---		---	---	8:1 (5 of mixed origin)	
Married recipients' choices (N=79)	177.15 (5.55)	70.01 (8.44)	22.22 (1.6)	3 brown 1 hazel 1 blue	3 fair-skinned 2 swarthy	3 light-brown 1 brown 1 black	4 Straight-Haired 1 wavy	2 Mixed 2 Ashken. 1 Oriental	All soldiers
Single recipients' choices N=125	83.05 (3.15)	74.58 (4.90)	22.31 (1.70)	2 brown 3 blue	All fair-skinned	3 light-brown 1 brown 1 black	All straight-haired	4 Ashken. 1 mixed	3 students 2 soldiers

As for the single recipients—here the most popular donor type was a fair-skinned, tall (1.83m) Ashkenazi, with straight, light brown hair, and light-colored eyes (Birenbaum-Carmeli and Carmeli, 2003). This bodily appearance, which deviated considerably from the features of the average Israeli man, might be attributed to these women's freedom from any constraints of resemblance to a male partner. The singles could therefore refer more openly to international mass media images and make choices in their light. This finding can be interpreted in the spirit of the more optimistic consumption theories that consider choice—even if conducted within the limitations of hegemonized contexts—to be 'the privileged site of autonomy, meaning, subjectivity. . .and freedom' (Slater, 1997:31).

On the other hand, we could emphasize the impact of the cultural-political contexts within which human images—beauty included—are being consumed. As a system of signs, physiognomy conjures up social, ethnic and class significances (Bordo, 1993; Grogan, 1999: 117–65). Viewed from the hegemony perspective, human desiderata, the politics of choice and the choice of physiological features are all linked to power relations. Dominant groups influence the conditions and social climate in which people make presumably autonomous decisions (Mouffe, 1979). Having their origins in hegemony—'the powerful is beautiful'—images of beauty enhance the naturalization of power relations, thus rendering hegemony transparent. Cultivating a popular will to emulate the bodily appearance of the powerful is one case within this category. This technology of power, which may also entail a demeaning of alternatives, anchors existing power relations in nature, thereby legitimizing and rendering them self-evident, and hence unchangeable (Mills, 1997; Skelton, 1993). Within this framework, singles' choices of donors may be considered as being guided by and supportive of the 'naturalness' of prevailing power relations in Israel. In other words, alongside the influences of global power relations, as disseminated by the media, the preference for Ashkenazi donors appears to reflect the local ethnic hierarchy, in which Ashkenazi Jews have generally been more privileged economically, socially and politically (Smooha, 1998; Shohat, 1999). In the discrete, isolated world that the state of Israel has forged for DI, the professionals, as gatekeepers, exerted—so they in fact stated—a crucial impact on recipients' decisions. The popularity of this type of donors, then, might be an additional reflection of the professionals' social-ethnic preferences.

However, single women, too, were not indifferent to the natural family paradigm. As mentioned, single recipients were relatively older: more than 90% were over 35 years old and more than half were 39 or older. This distribution suggests that rather than positively preferring single parenthood, many single Israeli women approached DI under the pressure of the 'biological clock', when establishing a traditional family seemed less likely. At this stage, conception out of wedlock was apparently interpreted as a determination to become a mother, rather than as an act of defiance. Probably, in Israel's pronatalist climate, the pressure on women to bear children rendered DI a conformist option for singles, especially as they grew somewhat older. The data suggested that this acceptance of DI was to be found—at least to some extent—also in more traditional circles of Oriental or less educated women. Orthodox Jews, however, rejected DI.

On the whole, then, DI in Israel's familistic context emerges as not unproblematic, since it may challenge the 'natural family' concept in both its contractual (marriage) and natural (blood relations) senses. This challenge becomes most evident when the 'family' is sanctioned through a religious code. However, when the 'natural family' notion tolerates somewhat greater autonomy and variability, as well as inevitable gaps between dreams and reality, DI is welcomed by Israelis of all walks of life.

Discussion

In this paper we probed Israeli society through the DI view point and identified several domains of power/cosmology that are negotiated through it. We started with the sphere in which the operation of power is the most evident—policy making. Coping with the so-called 'demographic problem'— i.e., the high natural growth of the Palestinian population in Israel—and with the very perpetuation of the Jewish people, are explicit goals of Jewish-Israeli policy makers. Taking advantage of their privileged position, they forged such regulations that advance Jewish fertility, a strategy that is accepted as legitimate by nearly all Jewish Israelis. The policy-makers and the state at large thus reinforced the state's legitimacy amongst its Jewish constituency. They also reproduced Jewish domination vis-a-vis the state's non-Jewish citizens. This politics of demography was worked out within the traditional 'natural family' paradigm. In other words, though the state is receptive of DI, it dictated a silenced and concealed mode of operation for this biotechnology, thus preserving the 'natural family' cosmology intact.

The medical clinic is where doctors' professional power and identity (vs. the state and the DI recipients) were negotiated. The state's policy, which aimed at camouflaging DI families as natural, has granted physicians a monopoly in donor screening and matching and in the application of the procedure. Israeli gynecologists, men who have been trained exclusively in the life sciences, were thus both entitled and required to perform—without guidance or supervision— extra-medical functions bearing far-reaching personal consequences. In this secretive medicalized version of DI, gynecologists became highly empowered vs. the recipients. Devoid of alternatives and of any knowledge, recipients could not but entirely depend on the doctors. The latter' authoritative mode of operation indeed reflected their position, and was often abided by recipients (Carmeli and Birenbaum-Carmeli, 2000).

A more general domain of power/cosmology that was negotiated in the context of DI was that of gender relations. In the clinic, this negotiation could be observed in the doctors' (male) paternalism towards the female recipients. Beyond the clinic's walls, at the level of the recipients' spousal dyad, the male partner's shortcomings might become highlighted in the application of DI technology, his macho image potentially threatened. Indeed, choice, as enabled by DI, might render the male partner somewhat substitutable, devalued by a fertile donor of a socially more desirable profile. At the same time, the woman—the traditional carrier of the infertility stigma—might be partially relieved. She might also be empowered by acquiring an unprecedented option to influence the future of her offspring by modifying their appearance. For her, unlike her partner, DI should not threaten the bond with the pregnancy and future children. In the Israeli scene, this 'dispensibility' was epitomized by the availability of the service to single and lesbian women.

However, our study of the DI regulations, practice and of recipients' approaches has not revealed any significant destabilization in gender hierarchy. At the policy level, we pointed to the requirement of establishing the woman's inability to conceive from her partner's sperm. In practice, doctors applied this requirement by routinely referring healthy, fertile women to difficult medical treatments. In the realm of the spousal dialogue, as inscribed in recipients' preferences, the limits that married female Israelis imposed on their departures from the male partner's physiognomy might be understood as choosing/ complying to remain within the confines of the 'natural family' model. Both sets of data might echo not only the 'natural family' but a social ethos of male domination. In this context, the state's policy coincided with the doctors' practices, so as to perpetuate gender hierarchies through 'the natural family' paradigm.

Yet another layer of power negotiated through DI in Israel was that of ethnic class hierarchy and the hegemony of the Ashkenazi middle class that has prevailed in Israel over the past few decades (Smooha, 1998). As mentioned, on the 'demand' side, recipients tended to prefer Ashkenazi donors. Our data suggested that Israelis preferred their children to have a more 'Western', Ashkenazi look. On the 'supply' side, the professionals themselves mostly belonged to this social sector and seemed to identify with its ideals and interests. Hence, their own proclivity for this type of man, as expressed in the over-representation of tall Ashkenazi men in the donor registry and in the promotion of such donors. This was true also for our one non-Ashkenazi doctor.

The professionals' implicit preference for 'the Ashkenazi', which was obviously not stated and most likely not consciously intended, might be viewed as illustrating the 'sophistication and intensification of the means of regulation and surveillance, what some … call "governing by culture"' (Hall, 1997: 215). From this perspective, through their selection of donors, the doctors promoted hegemonic images. In so doing, they enhanced the general tendency of hegemonic groups—to which they themselves belonged—to generalize their own external features into the privileged standard of beauty (Etcoff, 2000: 130). Being constituted as natural (and denying the intensive effort that is invested in their creation), the promotion of these features further ritualizes the 'Natural Family', while also contributing to the naturalization of Ashkenazi hegemony.

True, in a somewhat paradoxical manner, commodification and reproductive choice undermine the naturalization of hegemony, as everyone can choose the dominant appearance. The rational-scientific framework of the practice of DI, the availability of the sperm in 'banks', the choice and valuation of sperm, all bestow a commodity-like quality on nature. The naturalness of the 'natural'—the source of nature's strength as a basis for ontological grounding—is itself deflated through this scientific deconstruction and through commodification. However, the preference for one 'appropriate' look, which naturalized hegemony of the powerful, revalidates the natural metaphor. Nature, as a foundation, even if not 'natural', is not entirely abandoned.

Beyond these various domains of power and identities that shape and are being shaped through the application of DI in Israel, one needs to consider the hegemony of familism as entrenched in Jewish-Israeli social fabrics. The demographic data that was presented above concerning marriage, divorce and childbirth in Israel, alongside the proliferation of reproductive technologies, are all symptoms of an underlying structure that is being constantly shaped through politics of myth and history and through various daily practices. Furthermore, on the symbolic level is the broader politics of privileging the 'natural family' as a key metaphor in the making of the Jewish collectivity. This is evident in the definition of the Jewish people through a familial/tribal idiom, e.g., through ancestral myths of 'the Patriarchs and the Matriarchs', or through Zionist/nationalist notions like 'our forefathers' land' (eretz avotaynoo) or 'Sons of Israel' (Bnei Yisrael). In traditional discourses the family is constructed as a foundational space for participation in this broader collectivity, a space realized within a collective whole ('a home [family] in Israel'; bayit be'Yisrael), as well as a space that contains the whole ('a Jewish home'; [bayit Yehudi]) or is itself being generalized as the whole ('the home=people of Israel'; Beit Yisrael).

In the context of this pervasive Family ethos, neither expert-practitioners nor their recipients appeared to perceive of DI as deconstructing nature, or as a modern alchemy, concocting 'nature' through secrecy and camouflage. Rather, they perceived the state-dictated regulations and the practice of DI as part of an established social-cosmological order, a mode of relocating individuals and couples at the heart of a Jewish and Jewish-Israeli cosmos. The doctors' own privileged position, as Ashkenazi males, doctors, patrons, delegates of the state and of tradition, could thus be perceived not only as a medical but also as a 'redemptive' quest.

Recalling the different theories regarding the consequences of 'post-modern' biotechnologies as alluded to at the outset of this paper, one can now reaffirm a common knowledge about the importance of contexts: as illustrated in our Israeli case study, while cautiously saving and fabricating 'nature', Jewish-Israelis' experience of its shattering, that is emphasized in some central anthropological theories, is apparently moderate. Though potentially endangering the traditional cosmology, the technology of DI as applied in the Israeli context, is in fact largely contained within the traditional cosmology. In a sense, its practices and procedures even ritualize 'nature' and the 'natural family'.

At the level of Israeli society, the particularities of the Jewish Israeli mode of DI application are both contextualized by our discussion of the family and further elucidate its very significance. At a theoretical level, the place of the family among Jewish Israelis as expounded in our paper, suggests the significance of the Family in the making of macro-social textures. Being often analyzed as secondary to major economic and political domains, the family emerges from the present study as being of prime importance on the plane of power relations, as well as at the level of the making of Israel's collective and national definitions. In a 'post-modern' world, where biotechnologies travel globally, the family may emerge not only as potentially pertinent to the 'traditional' and the 'local', but also as a vehicle for accommodating the 'innovative' and the 'global', into a modified yet taken-for-granted order of things.

Notes

[1] With one exception, the curricula of medical schools in Israel do not contain any training in this or other related fields of the social sciences; see Shuval, 1992, pp. 104-105; Mirvis, 1993, p. 18.
[2] All names have been changed.

References

Barkai, H. 1998. *The Evolution of Israels Social Security System: Structure, Time Pattern and Macroeconomic Impact.* Aldershot: Ashgate.

Barthes, R. 1994. *Mythologies.* London: Grant and Cutler.

Bell C. 1992. *Ritual theory, ritual practice.* Oxford: Oxford University Press.

Birenbaum-Carmeli, D. (Forthcoming). Cheaper than a Newcomer: On the political economy of IVF in Israel. *The Sociology of Health and Illness.*

Birenbaum-Carmeli, D. and Y. S. Carmeli,. (2002). Hegemony and homogeneity: Donor Preferences of recipients of donor insemination. *The Journal of Material Culture,* 7(1): 73-94.

Bordo, S. (1993). *Unbearable weight: Feminism, western culture, and the body.* Berkeley: University of California Press.

Bourdieu, P. 1984. *Distinctions.* Boston, MA: Harvard University Press.

Carmeli, Y. S. and Birenbaum-Carmeli, D. (2000). Ritualizing the Natural Family: Secrecy in Israeli Donor Insemination. *Science as Culture,* 9(3): 301-325.

Central Bureau of Statistics, Israel. 2003. *Statistical Abstract of Israel.*

Etcoff, Nancy L. 1999. *Survival of the prettiest: the science of beauty.* New York: Doubleday.

Featherstone, M. (1991) The Body in Consumer Culture, in M. Featherstone, M. Hepworth and B.S. Turner (eds.) *The Body: Social Processes and Cultural Theory,* pp. 170–96. London: Sage.

Fogiel-Bijaoui, S. 1999. Families in Israel: Between familism and post modernism. *In* Friedman, A. (ed.), *Sex, Gender, Politics: Women in Israel.* Tel Aviv: Hakibbutz Hameuchad. [Hebrew].

Foucault, M. 1980. *Power/Knowledge: Selected Interviews and Other Writings, 1972-1977.* New York: Pantheon Books.

Friedlander D. and C. Feldman 1993. The modern shift to below-replacement fertility: Has Israels population joined the process? *Population Studies,* 47: 295-306.

Friedman, J. (1994) Introduction, in J. Friedman (ed.) *Consumption and Identity.* Chur, Switzerland: Harwood Academic Publishers.

Gold, M. 1988. *And Hannah Wept: Infertility, Adoption and the Jewish Couple*. Philadelphia: The Jewish Publication Society.

Grogan, S. (1999). *Body Image: Understanding body dissatisfaction in men, women and children*. London: Routledge.

Haimes, E. (1993). Secrecy and Openness in Donor Insemination: A Sociological Comment on Daniels and Taylor. *Politics and the Life Sciences*, *12*(2):178-79.

Hall, S. (1997) The Centrality of Culture: Notes on the Cultural Revolution of our Time. *In* Kenneth Thompson (ed.) *Media, and Cultural Regulation*, pp. 207–38. Milton Keynes: The Open University Press.

Kahn, S. M. 2000. *Reproducing Jews: A cultural account of assisted conception in Israel*. Durham and London: Duke University Press.

Karow, A.M. Jr. (1982). Family Secrets: Who Is to Know about AID? *New England Journal of Medicine, 306*: 372.

Katz, J. (1971). *Tradition and Crisis: Jewish Society at the End of the Middle Ages*. New York: Schoken Books.

Landau, R. (1998). Secrecy, Anonymity, and Deception in Donor Insemination: A Genetic, Psycho-social and Ethical Critique. *Social Work in Health Care 28*(1):75-89.

Lasker, J.N. (1993). Doctors and Donors: A Comment on Secrecy and Openness in Donor Insemination. *Politics and the Life Sciences 12*(2):186-88.

Lauritzen, P. (1993). DIs Dirty Little Secret. *Politics and the Life Sciences 12*(2):188-9.

Luhmann, N. 1985. *A Sociological Theory of Law*, translated by E. King and M. Albrow, M. Albrow (ed.), Boston and London: Routledge and Kegan Paul.

Miller, D. (1995) Consumption and Commodities, *Annual Review of Anthropology, 24*: 141–61.

Mills, Martin (1997) Football, Desire and the Social Organization of Masculinity, *Social Alternatives 16*(1): 10–13.

Mouffe C. (1979) Hegemony and Ideology in Gramsci. *In* C. Mouffe (ed.) *Gramsci and Marxist Theory*, pp. 168–204. London: Routledge and Kegan Paul.

Nachtigall, R.D. (1993). Secrecy: An Unresolved Issue in the Practice of Donor Insemination. *American Journal of Obstetrics and Gynecology 168*(6 Pt 1):1841-51.

Portuguese, J. (1998) *Fertility Policy in Israel: The Politics of Religion, Gender and Nation*. Westport, CT: Praeger.

Safir, M. 1991. Religion, Tradition and Public Policy Give Family First Priority. *In* Swirski, B. and M.P. Safir (eds.) *Calling the Equality Bluff*, New York: Pergamon. pp. 57-65.

Shalev, Carmel. 1998. *Halakha* and Patriarchal Motherhood: An Anatomy of the Israeli Surrogacy Law. *Israel Law Review, 32* (1).

Shalev, C. and B. Lev. (1999). Public Funding for IVF in Israel—Ethical Aspects, working paper.

Shilling, C. 1999 The Body. *In* G. Browning, A. Halcli and F. Webster (eds.), *Understanding Contemporary Society: Theories of the Present*, pp. 415-31, London: Sage.

Shohat, E. 1999. The invention of the Mizrahim, *Journal of Palestine Studies 29*(1): 5-20.

Shore, Cris and Susan Wright. 1997. Policy: A new field of anthropology. *In* Shore, Cris and Susan Wright (eds.) *Anthropology of Policy: Critical perspectives on governance and power*, London: Routledge.

Shuval, J. T. 1992. *Social Dimensions of Health: The Israeli Experience*. Westport, CN: Praeger.

Skelton, A. 1993. On Becoming a Male Physical Education Teacher: The Informal Culture of Students and the construction of Hegemonic Masculinity. *Gender and Education 5*(3): 289–303.

Slater, D. 1997. *Consumer Culture and Modernity*. Cambridge: Polity Press.

Smooha, S. 1998. The Implication of the Transition to Peace for Israeli Society, *Annals of the American Academy 555*: 26-45.

Strathern, M. 1992. *After Nature: English Kinship in the Late 20th Century*. Cambridge: Cambridge University Press.

Strathern, 1995b, p. 347

Swirski, S. 1976. Community and the Meaning of the Modern State: The Case of Israel, *The Jewish Journal of Sociology*, *18*: 123-40.

Swirski, S., E. Konor-Attias, B. Swirski, Y. Yecheskel. 2001. *Women in the Labor Force of the Israeli Welfare State*, Tel-Aviv: Adva Center [Hebrew].

Triseliotis, J. (1993). Donor Insemination and the Child. *Politics and the Life Sciences 12*(2):195-96.

Webster, A. 2002. Innovative Health Technologies and the Social: Redefining Health, Medicine and the Body, *Current Sociology*, *50*(3), 443-458.

Rhetoric of the Destruction of the Israeli Welfare State

Nira Reiss

Introduction: Destruction of the Israeli Welfare State

Henry Rosenfeld's anthropology is Marxist in both the materialist and the humanistic aspects, focusing on the class consequences of state formations while striving for political and social justice. Writing in 2002 on the potential of the Arab citizens of Israel to resist the state's structures of discrimination, Rosenfeld looks hopefully as always at the possibility of struggling against state and ruling class control and oppression. He takes heart from two aspects of Israeli society which allow for some optimism, namely parliamentary democracy which provides an arena for struggle and the welfare state which has offered economic protection to minorities:

> the results could have been much worse if there had not been a safety net of welfare rights such as unemployment compensation, minimum wage, supplementary income, old age pension, health insurance, children's allowance, free education, and citizens' rights...this is common ground provided by the Israeli welfare state. (Rosenfeld 2002; 1091)

In 2003-2004 all of these components of the safety net, as well as parliamentary democracy, have been subjected to concerted attempts at demolition by the right-wing government headed by Ariel Sharon with former Prime Minister Netanyhu in charge of the Ministry of the Treasury. The Knesset is increasingly bypassed by the Executive Branch, its legislation often ignored. A series of Treasury-initiated and government- approved radical budget cuts, affecting first the poor and more widely all workers, have led to what have been called dark years in Israel (Swirski and Konor-Atias 2003).

Successful attacks on the right of workers to secure employment and a minimum wage, as well as processes of attrition in social rights with consequences of increasing gaps in health care and education, have been going on for more than a decade. Assaults on the welfare state and in particular on its universalistic aspects are not unique to Israel, or for that matter characteristic only of the political right (Doron 1995, 2003, Katan 2000, Kopp 2003). Israel's post-labor 'Labor Alignment Party' participated in the weakening of institutions of the labor-state such as the Histadrut general labor union and its comprehensive sick fund. What distinguishes the present political administration's wholesale attempt to quickly turn Israel into an American-style "residual" welfare state, which recognizes only the most helpless of its citizens as possible recipients of what is conceived as state charity, is its Thatcherist enthusiasm, ferocity and swift successes in this matter (Yishuvi 2004).

This destruction takes place under the processes described and analyzed by Carmi and Rosenfeld as definitive of the trajectory of Israel's political economy. The labor union, health and education structures created during the pre-state socialist hegemony were expanded during the first three decades of the state under the 'labor etatist' regime, and a national insurance/social security system was put in place. What made welfare state affluence possible was American support based on Israeli militarism. The 'socialist potential' preceding the state was replaced by stratification directed by the state, whose selective privatization of public means brought into being a state-created middle class and resulted in widening gaps between affluent and deprived, Jews and Arabs (Rosenfeld and Carmi 1976, 1992a). Since 1967 ideologies of national superiority and separatism have flourished in consequence of militarism (Carmi and Rosenfeld 1989, 1992b).

The Likkud in 1977 proposed "to convert the combination of socialism, capitalism and anarchy to a private market, free and competitive." The political and economic approaches of the various governments (headed by the Likkud, by post-Labor variants, and by both jointly) which have ruled since the Labor Party lost its hegemony in 1977 have been aligned in congruence with the growing dependency on the US's global military and economic policies (e.g. Chomsky 2003) . At the same time they have been in tune with the military and economic consequences of Israeli occupation of Palestinian lands. Privatization, social Darwinism and gaps between rich and poor have intensified.

There are no major differences in policy in either the political or the economic approaches of the alternating and supposedly different recent governments headed by Peres, Barak, Netanyahu or Sharon, although the first two voiced a 'social democratic' ideology, and the next two a 'neo-liberal' one. When there is divergence it is in degree more than in kind, less in the attempted policies themselves than around their rhetoric and the appearances of their application. Both have continued the military occupation—a situation entailing some risk for investors. Both attempt to reduce such risk through oppressive wall building and 'separation' from the Palestinians rather than through putting an end to the occupation. Both have privileged Israeli settlers in the Occupied Territories with government investments in infrastructure and in other require- ments of well being increasingly withdrawn from Israelis within the Green Line. Both propose structural changes consistent with global capitalism, to better serve the local and international oligarchy under the umbrella of creating economic growth (absent since 1996; Yediot 13/2/04). These changes include: Accelerated favoritism toward private capital investors; insistence on a small budgetary deficit (or none) entailing decreased government responsibility for investing in means of employment; tax cuts presented as 'incentives for participating in the circle of work' implying curtailment of education, health care and welfare rights; 'reforms' in the labor market and unemployment benefits meaning a cheapening of labor and an increase of its precariousness. All of these aim at making the world safe for large-scale investors. Some of these policies are cited as well in the Labor Party's Economic Plan in 2003.

Netanyahu announces at a 'meeting with the IMF' that "the government is committed to the market economy and to moving to cut its expenses" (Haaretz 3/12/03). Labor's economic expert and candidate for Treasury Minister Ben-Shahar announces his "support [of] Netanyahu's policies" (Haaretz 6/2/04). Former Minister of the Treasury and PM and perennial Labor candidate Peres proposes no-end of plans for placing Israel in the globalized arena for international capital. Huge U.S. Loan guarantees supplied to Israel under Sharon in 2003 in accompaniment to the U.S.'s invasion of Iraq are no longer designated for maintaining even a semblance of a serious welfare state, but rather for explicitly promoting 'economic growth' on terms consistent with those of the IMF and the World Bank. There is no reason to think this would be significantly otherwise in a government headed by or including what is left of the [Labor] Alignment, if such were a possibility.

Given the continuation of state influence and historicity under conditions of globalization (Rosenfeld 2002), the resultant form of state hegemony which followed the regime of 'labor etatism' in Israel, in which the state 's control of the military and economic arenas is still determinative with regard to its subjects though not with regard to global military and economic power and in which etatist ideological terms of reference persist, might accordingly be called 'global-capital statism'. Capitalism is hardly statism's opposite: On the contrary, a so-called 'free market' economy requires a centralized state in order to strengthen owners and weaken workers. Global capitalism therefore promotes increase in the power of states.

Displacement of the value of labor (the alienation of workers from labor itself, not only from its products) by the primacy of capital investment, appropriation and accumulation, resulting in socioeconomic polarization, is a world-wide phenomenon. In Israel these processes have been enhanced by the state's accelerated garage-sale of public means to enrich favored investors, and by its policy of 'separation' from Palestinian lands whose military occupation it has no intention to end. Palestinian laborers were first employed to cheaply replace Arab Israeli laborers, then made expendable and prevented from working in Israel, to be replaced by even cheaper and equally expendable Eastern European, Asian and African foreign workers, who are in turn being deported or caused to leave in order to make menial jobs nominally available to Israeli citizens, Jewish and Arab, most of whom will in fact stay unemployed.

Through preference of capital and through anti-labor policies such as slashing health and education and welfare budgets and erasing the hard-won achievements of national insurance (Gal 2002) while allowing high rates of unemployment, the state takes the major role in determining the extent and the direction of enrichment and pauperization. Pro-business policies such as 'liberalization', 'deregulation' and 'privatization', designed to make the world safe for investors, do not in spite of their semantics represent a weakening of the state in its directive aspect, but rather slough off its responsibilities to the majority of its citizens for the benefit of the ruling class which politicians depend on, serve and often join.

What follows in this paper is a discussion of how the work of hegemony of Israel's 'global-capital statism', and in particular the work of attempting to gain public consent for the destruction of the welfare state, is done through the rhetorical strategies used by Israeli state leaders (Gramsci 1971 {1929-1935}). I focus in the following mainly on current right-wing rhetorical practice in Israel since it is more explicit in its expression of the capitalist disposition and more insistent in liquidating ideological as well as institutional expressions of Israel's earlier labor orientation, including those relating to the (other than residual) welfare state which had served as a major means of political recruitment and control in the previous state regime (Reiss 1991). Most of the examples used in this paper are from newspaper quotes of the speech of government ministers in 2003-2004.

Metaphors to Rule by: 'Mechanical' Promise (A) and 'Organic' Threat (B)

In the rhetoric now used to achieve neo-liberal hegemony in the Israeli global-capital state, 'mechanical' and 'organic' metaphors are employed to justify economic policies ('reforms') and to convince citizens to consent to them. The 'mechanical' metaphor works as an attempt to achieve a unifying consensus between potential constituencies through offering them unwarranted hope for what is presented as an inevitably produced universal personal prosperity which will thrive upon the replacement of the welfare state by free-market principles. At the same time, an 'organic' metaphor stressing some citizens' weakness and fallibility is used to sectorialize these constituencies and to get the consent of a majority to right-wing rule through stigmatizing, weakening and threatening some groups associated with the labor-state's welfare program, while setting others against them (Pepper 1942, Reiss 1990, G. Lakoff and Johnson 1980, R. Lakoff 2000).

Verbal 'Growth Engines' Generate Good News

As neo-liberal discourse replaces labor-statist discourse in Israel, 'the economy' is the capital-statist preferred idiom of national solidarity, replacing 'the state' as the term which expresses the main source of good for all citizens. The Israeli economy is said to be in catastrophic trouble caused by the welfare state, and exhibits no 'economic growth'. Minister of the Treasury Netanyahu's stated goal is to bring about such growth through private investments together with government budget-cuts, in accordance with the economics textbooks he relies on. Calling for patience in the face of delays in the improvements the Israeli public expects all-the-more since it has paid through budget-cuts and received nothing in return, he asks: "If the car is stuck in the mud are we going to call it quits, or do we give it another push?" In this metaphor, down-to-earth mechanical language concretizes an abstract 'economy' in terms popularly understood and includes all citizens as partners in its trouble and in its rescue, even though 'another push' (more firing, more budget cuts and less public services) will actually be at the expense of working people and the unemployed. Finally, the use of this metaphor indexes its speaker as the master-mechanic/engineer who can get the economy free and running.

The Minister of the Treasury began the practice of employing an army of public relations experts to assist him in convincing the Israeli public to support his set of 'economic reforms'. This is an unsurprising expense of ruling, since achieving consent to these policies is doing the work of hegemony. Netanyahu proudly claims that he has 'changed the diskette' of the Israeli public, i.e. eliminated previous ideas of the welfare state and re-programmed the public to think in terms of a 'free market' economy. Such an exchange would be a triumph of hegemonic succession, a true mass conversion.

The terms of text-book economics which make up the neo-liberal program are mechanical no less than a car, but refer to a more abstract mega-machine. Not only is understanding the operation of this machine beyond the ability of anyone but specialist experts—even its terminology is made up of figures of speech whose references are not tangible parts but are abstractions, both mechanical principles (e.g. 'lowering taxes promotes economic growth and employment') and statistical expressions of outcomes (e.g. 'standard of living', 'unemployment' and 'growth'). This machine's mechanical 'growth engines' are so capable of transforming economies that the Ministry of the Treasury's Comptroller is able to make the following announcement, which has the sound of instrumental magic (his boss at the Ministry is popularly called, only half in praise, 'the magician'):

"We are now putting into operation very powerful growth engines so that 2005 will be the year of the great leap, a leap in the standard of living, in the level of employment, in investment, in business. A new era in the economy of the state of Israel has begun. I am only surprised that not everyone has yet realized the great meaning of this turn" (Yediot 29/6/04).

What typifies the use of the mechanical metaphor by the economic leadership of the present administration is the use of a language of rationality expressing the supposedly infallible workings of the economic machine, together with a language of irrational magical power supposedly given to its expert-operators to overcome any uncertainties and doubt. This combination makes for an economic rhetoric which replaces the social solidarity and personal security of the welfare state's safety net with the excitement and jugglery of the figurative free market casino.

It goes without saying that Netanyahu and his Treasury crew (whom he calls 'my people') speak not only public relations idioms but also the language of capital investment, where projections of profit carry the day (until the bottom line has its own say). The 'turn' the Comptroller refers to might be that of the stock-market's roulette wheel, a gambling machine which generates an outcome that is generally and mechanically absolutely and inevitably sure, and yet specifically and statistically contingent and uncertain: A few will win and many will lose. Since the Minister of the Treasury aims to convince a majority of the losers they've won, his rhetorical efforts focus on those aspects of the economic model which make its theoretical outcomes appear to be inevitably and encompassingly beneficial. When doubt remains in public opinion, this will be supplemented by magic.

The basic metaphor of the economy as a national machine serves the goal of unifying the audience. In addition, the esoteric character of the theoretical definitions of parts of the economics model, and in particular the fact that its terms have a different meaning in everyday usage, is worked to this end, through a 'rhetoric of objectivity', particularly citing numbers, which experts use to show their unique hold on reality (Roeh 1994). To people who share the theory's values and semantics 'economic growth' means statistics indicating increase in profits, not necessarily based on production, 'Employment' is an expense and a classical economic indicator for growth, although an increasingly unimportant one, and 'unemployment' is a technically defined statistical variable. To those not literate in economics theory, whether of the working class or the employed middle class, 'growth' means increased tangible employment and prosperity, while 'unemployment' means not having an all-important job that pays. This polysemy makes for two different and often opposite senses conveyed by each message addressed by neo-liberal leaders to the public.

The Treasury speakers, including the Minister, consistently speak a technocratic disciplinary language consistent with the neo-liberal text. However, when the message is positive, a 'non-literate' or 'economics-naive' audience addressed by an authoritative politician may assume it is hearing popular speech, and may make sense of the message in an ego-centric way favorable to its own interests, unaware of the extent to which the economy's designers/operators have 'fixed' or tilted the machine. In other words, through its semantically forked tongue one prong of which lets audiences believe that an interpretation on their own terms is legitimate, this rhetoric encourages false belief in the machine and a false consciousness among the structurally-determined losers in the capitalist casino.

The announcement cited above appears to articulate a promise by politicians (or their assistants) for a better future, already here. Promises, after all, make up a major slice of political speech, while a parallel slice consists of the politician's *post-hoc* explanation of why these promises were not carried out. As speech acts, promises imply the speaker's responsibility for doing something in the future (Austin 1962, Searle 1969, 1979, Reiss 1984, 1989).

Prime Minister Sharon, for example, has adeptly developed the art of skirting a promise, choreographing formulations which keep his verbal skates from cutting the ice of committing himself to any future actions. These include the following:

I would like to cancel children's allowances for children of the top 20% [in income], but I find it difficult to see this happening soon.

(*Maariv* 16/2/04)

[The government is instructed] to rank the social problems of old people, of girls in distress and of new immigrants as issues which require care-taking in government budgets in the next years.   (*Yediot* 21/6/04).

I see with special worry the situation of children at risk from the weaker social strata. This week I decided that we have to push more quickly for a long school day, and in its center a feeding plan for every child.

(5/1/04 quoted in *Haaretz* 21/1.04).

So fuzzy is the last utterance that Sharon's actual vote against a long school day two days later does not even contradict it.

Verbal circumspection and avoidance are not Netanyahu's strategy. He and his assistants flood the media with constant announcements of economic plans to be attempted, budgets and legislation proposed, local translations of the neo-liberal/neo-conservative program. The plans themselves are hardly original, having been collated during the term in office of the previous Minister of the Treasury Shalom, and having been at hand during both Likkud and post-Labor administrations since 1977. What is new is the fact of taking them as a set out of bureau-drawers, placing them on the government's immediate agenda, and packaging, advertising and broadcasting them intensively in the media as good news for the Israeli public.

Such announced plans do not necessarily commit those proposing them to carrying them out, since that requires the government's agreement. They are a model, a wish-list and an agenda, a promise to try. But behind them there does stand one basic, original promise. That promise, which dates to the election of the Likkud and in particular to the appointment of Netanyahu as Minister of the Treasury, is that the 'free market' economic model to be enacted is efficacious; that its 'growth engines' can effect 'the great leap'; and that what previous Ministers and candidates for the job carried out only partially, fearing to fight institutional interests and voters' resistance to 'reforms', will this time be done. The promise is that the equipment which works in theory works in practice, and will be put to work. Its invitation to the majority of voters is: We have opened the doors to the free- market hall where Israel as an economy and you as its citizen shall win. This casino promises equal access and equal chances for enrichment; its machinery works for you.

Beyond this, promises are hardly needed. An utterance such as the Comptroller's above is not in itself a promise to do anything in the future, but rather an assurance that machinery has been put into motion whose consequences are a sure thing—so much so that not having universal recognition of its as yet unseen universal benefits is a great surprise. The words convey a sense of the economic model as omnipotent and of the Treasury's technocracy as having the power to turn its wheels. Theirs is not a promise to act in the future, but a claim of success achieved.

Similar speech acts are typical of the fashion of speaking about economics current in this administration. As indicated by the following examples, Netanyahu and his people specialize in euphoric and self-confident utterances of two kinds: Those in future tense, which critics ordinarily interpret as promises or inflated predictions, and those in present tense, which critics rush to point out as exaggerations or lies. Often, as in the Comptrollers' utterance, past, present and future are indistinguishable, tied by a grammar of inevitability. The word 'spin'—rooted in both 'yarn' and 'rotation' and meaning a media interpretation aiming to sway public opinion—is sometimes applied in the media to Netanyahu's characteristic way of public speaking. This derogatory application is based on the interpretation of his utterances as insincere promises and untrue statements. However, this misses out on the performative character of the spin, and in particular on the linguistic/pragmatic intentional significance of the typical speech acts which constitute it.

These speech acts are neither promises undertaken nor descriptions of a present or predicted future, but rather self-congratulations, expressions of pride in the good news presented by the speaker as self evident outcomes of his policies.

Netanyahu's good news spoken in the present tense does not necessarily match the world as seen by others, but neither is it necessarily intended to: "Israel has the fastest rate of reform in the world and is an excellent target for investment", he said when foreign investors are dissuaded by the continuing war against the Palestinians, and when 'reforms' encounter considerable resistance. "Seventy thousand jobs have been added in one year to the private sector...Israelis are going back to work" (*Yediot* 8/7/04), he said when unemployment shows no sign of decline. "The Israeli economy which was at the edge of an abyss is now on its way up. The slowdown is over and I am sure the economy has entered a process of growth" (*Yediot* 19/11/03). One day later this is countered by Dunn and Bradstreet's experts in Israel who claimed that there has been "an aggravation of the state of the economy, a slowdown in the productive sector" (*Yediot* 20/11/03).

The fact that alternative facts contradict them does not mean that Netanyahu's utterances are lies. His speech has typically transcended the obstacles mentioned in these contradicting descriptions and occurs in a fantasized linguistic space—present or future—far beyond them, a place where planned reforms have already and inevitably come true.

The same is true with regard to the avalanche of good tidings spoken by the Minister of the Treasury with unfailing certainty in the future tense: "Unemployment will go down in 2005 at an accelerated rate" (*Haaretz* 1.7.04). "Within a year the maximum income tax will be 49%" (*Yediot* 9/12/ 03). The first of these is good news delivered with differential meanings to investors on the one hand and to the insecurely employed and the unemployed on the other. The second is good news for the rich, aiming also at middle class voters. It is not good news for the poor—but neither is it addressed to them.

Frequent personalized and concretized examples of good things that will happen when the neo-liberal agenda is realized are of the same pattern. "Each citizen will receive bank options at half price" (when the banks are privatized; *Yediot* 25/12/2003). "Newly married couples will be able to buy electrical appliances" (when the sales tax is reduced by 1%) "(*Yediot* 12/2/04).

There is a reverberating aspect to this self-congratulatory mode of speaking on the sides of other ministers. An example is Minister of Education Livnat's enthusiasm while announcing the publication of a report which she sponsored (the *Dovrat Report*) planning reforms in the system of education: "This is a revolution in education....Israel will be Number One in the field of education."

This is of course contingent on the Treasury's funding, so that when the revolution is diverted and there is no gold medal, Livnat herself, carrying no responsibility since she is expressing joy rather than pledging to do something in the future, will not have to account for her words as one does for a promise. At most, she can later announce some bad news.

With a verbal sleight of hand, before the economy has produced any material results fortunate for the voting public, its operators' self congratulations imply that it did. Projected self confidence is used to sustain a positive atmosphere of great expectations through huckstering. While there is no positive turn-around of the state's indicators of economic growth, even according to neo-liberal intentions and semantics, congratulation upon presumed success is hocus-pocus intended to maintain the illusion that the machine's benefits are forthcoming. Such premature expressions present the economy as absolutely reliable yet temporarily slowed down, like a car stuck in the mud.

At the same time, beginning as self-praise these speech acts continue as operators' exhortations to the machine, constituting a show of conjuring to speed it along. Whether uttered in present or future tense, all the Ministry of the Treasury's sayings cited above should therefore be seen not only as Expressive speech acts showing pride and happiness, but at the same time perform the Declarative (or Bringing-about) speech acts of blessing the economy. This category of speech acts is, when successful, performatively instant: It creates new reality by mere enunciation, and is usually indicative of power—divine, magical or institutional. In this case, these utterances are incantations to the economic machine, intended to make a show of how operators turn its wheel while showing the public that the economy is not only trustworthy but also exhortable, subject to the Treasury's influential magic and by extension to the public's wishes.

This is a gesture familiar from gambling, a rubbing of hands and envisioning the win to stimulate it before turning the wheel. With it, the public's irrational/magical attitude to the machine is encouraged. This is what political consent, if it is to be achieved, has to be based on since the public's beliefs, rational and irrational, are challenged by the actual outcomes. In this kind of verbal juggling the sorcerer and his assistants throw blessings at the ceiling with hope that they fly, at the same time modeling for the public the magical thinking required to maintain belief in a positive outcome. Meanwhile, the economically privileged don't need this show: The chips piling up at their side of the table are convincing enough. The problem with the economy is not that it isn't rational, dependable and beneficial for some, but that it is materially tilted.

The promise of a profitable change for working people with the change of the economic model is not instantly fulfilled because it is unfulfillable: In this kind of economy there have to be many more losers than winners. For the poor, heavy losses are immediate; to the majority as time goes by cumulative losses become apparent as a result of the change in hegemony and the resultant exchange: The remainder, in Israel, of relative equality and of the 'safety net' of government responsibility for most citizens' basic routine economic security, for the temptation of playing an exciting game and the illusion of personal freedom and control.

The economic 'growth engines' mobilized by this administration promote an accumulation of capital resources at the top and a growth in socioeconomic gaps, in middle-class and working class economic hardship and in the state-dependent poor's unprotected despair. Rhetorical 'growth engines', such as the mechanical metaphor and its pragmatic expression in official speech acts, are used to hide the class division behind the unifying claim made by capital statism that the economy serves everyone, and to maintain an illusion, typical of a speculative economy, of a chance at winning which hides the reality of loss. By the time frustration has grown to disappointment, all that citizens can do is to count their growing losses.

Fat, Thin, and Dieting

Who's on whose back?

Soon after he became Minister of the Treasury in 2003, Benjamin Netanyahu declared war on the public (government) sector which he saw as unproductive, inefficient and wasteful. He spoke of the public sector as a "fat man riding on the back of the thin man". The 'thin man' stood for the private (business) sector, perceived as productive and described as about to collapse under the 'fat man''s burden, taking down the economy as a whole.

The image of one man carrying another on his back points to an assumed metaphorical background of two soldiers in a military battlefield, one of them taking on the burden of getting both out of danger, while the other is only a dead weight hindrance. Under such circumstances the thin, fit man is responsible and brave, while the unfit fat man is irresponsible, parasitic and immoral. By implication, the Minister of the Treasury is the army commander assigned to deploy the troops in a way that will save the economy.

The labeling of 'fat' and 'thin' is consistent with the current demonizing of fat characteristic of the hegemonic cultural formulations of affluent Western societies, in which fat is a class issue, but blame is individualistic. In fact most of the obese in these societies are the urban and suburban working class poor who suffer from stress, inexpensive foods and snacking, and from the lack of time and incentive to exercise; the privileged are most often thin and worry, along with the middle classes, about the public health cost to themselves of what they prefer to see as bad habits of members of the underclass.

Culturally 'fat' has become so much of a stigma and 'thin' is so much seen as virtue that members of every category like to think of themselves as thin whether mainly in association with attractiveness, health and efficiency, or of relative deprivation and under-privilege. The ideological 'other' is labeled 'fat'.

Netanyahu's figure of speech used the fat/thin terms of reference from current American and globalized-Israeli discourse, broadcast in the mass media and increasingly current in Israeli culture, to make a neo-liberal ideological claim: The private sector, the economy and the citizens whom it is presumed to serve are all victims of the public sector's indolence and waste.

This was a powerful opening to a public relations campaign for neo-liberal policies. As Minister of the Treasury Netanyahu, who has the public reputation of a "communications wizard', employed in 2003-2004, at a tremendous cost to the taxpayer, eight different concurrent communications advisers, five of them within the Ministry and three from private public relations firms. He has made the ambitious declaration : "I intend to change the social discourse in Israel" (*Yediot* 5/7/04).

In using a metaphor in which a basic militaristic frame of reference reinforced an ideal self-image of business organizations as inherently streamlined, efficient and virtuous, Netanyahu made clear to the multinational and Israeli business community that he spoke their language and that he was setting out on a road which would serve their interests, freeing them from tax baggage and promoting their unencumbered growth.

Under the biological metaphor used to represent the two sectors, members of both carry a moral valence. With regard to the social meanings of thin and fat, within the Israeli public Netanyahu addresses there are a number of significations which are different from his hegemonic figuration. Decoding this metaphor is an ideological process of interpretation. It is an indication of Netanyahu's marketing genius that in such a short formulation he is able to present the view of his backers and offers a shiny business image to those of them who might resist his metaphor for reasons of personal self-image (4), reverses, opposes and derogates the social references used by his socialist ideological enemies and organized labor (1), excludes the Israeli-Palestinian working class (6) stigmatizes the government-dependent poor (7), and creates one figurative master-key which fits the variant identifications of the different groups of voters to whom he aims to appeal (2, 3 and 5).

1. For the socialist left whose cultural hegemony has been replaced by social democratic and neo liberal views, and for organized labor, thin is a positive signifier of labor while fat ordinarily signifies decadent over-privilege. On these terms, a fat man riding on the back of the thin man would represent the private sector riding on the back of workers everywhere. Clearly Netanyahu's metonymy reverses this order; as is to be expected, ideological warfare takes the form of denouncing organized labor and the welfare state.
2. For middle class social democrats whose connections lie in both public and private sectors, fat would be immoderate and thin is seemly. Excess is unattractive: "Labor Party" leader Shimon Peres has called Netanyahu's policies 'piggish capitalism.' This implies that capitalism is fine as long as it does not flaunt its biases. On these terms, a fat man riding on the back of a thin man would be a picture of capitalists greedy enough to ride over everyone else. But there is no reason middle class social democrats cannot share in Netanyahu's metaphor, given their drive toward liberalizing the economy and their willingness to curb public expenditure (with reservations, of course).

3. For middle class liberals and conservatives, including small businessmen and the independently employed, as well as some in the state-created middle class whose identifications with organized labor had dissolved along with their economic rise, the image of socialist government bureaucracy as a fat strongman riding on the back of thin entrepreneurs struggling to succeed is easy to accept.

4. For the business elite represented by Netanyahu, fat is the over-demanding and exploitative public sector, thin is the commendable and altruistic private sector. But not all parts of the Israeli oligarchy have necessarily bought into the new business imagery. As infatuated as Israelis are with all things American, the profile of Israel's political economy as a whole and of many in its elite is East European before it is East Coast. For example, many of the most visible members of the Israeli business oligarchy as well as ministers in Prime Minister's Sharon's Likud coalition, including first and foremost Sharon (and not excluding Netanyahu himself), present to their own mirrors, to others of their class and to the Israeli public a living corporeal reminder and *ad hominem* challenge to the metaphorical figures in Netanyahu's elitist signification. The self image they are familiar with is that fat stands for political/business power; thin means weak. Netanyahu's referring to fat men pejoratively in this environment might score negative points, although it does set his educated economist's gloss against the less than physically sleek political figure he is offering to succeed and replace. But the ideological image has the potential power to supersede the previous associations and their correlate body image, since the interpretation afforded in his metaphor presents to his cronies an attractively packaged new physical and moral image of their business selves.

5. For members of the Jewish working class who may be called 'weak labor', 'fat' signifies the higher standard of living available to those who have socially arrived and are economically thriving, i.e. those who have found their way into high levels of job security and income through strong organized labor or have been inducted into the middle class through privileged state-bureaucracy and other remunerative public sector employment. In this ethno-class system, the fat man riding on the back of a thin one is most likely to be figured as privileged 'ashkenazi' riding over the underprivileged 'mizrahi'.

The most politically interesting working of Netanyahu's metaphor vis-à-vis the different groups is in its designated appeal to members of this category. By rhetorically structuring a dichotomy between sectors, as opposed to between classes, it conceals class differences in a way which capsulizes neo-liberal ideology, presuming sectorial identity and solidarity between employers and employees whether subsumed in the 'thin' private sector or in the 'fat' public sector. Netanyahu's equation thus assimilates 'weak labor' and their private sector employers into the same 'thin' side, in opposition to organized labor which is seen as allied with the 'fat' government/public employer. This figurative key works well, for the same reasons which have made this category's historical voting allegiance to Herut/Likkud exasperating to the members of the Israeli Left who ask: How can they ignore the conflict of interest between workers and capitalists? How can they think and act against their class interest? The answer usually given is that nationalistic identifications mystify class. Both questions and answer assume an abstract working class solidarity which contradicts the practical reality of competition and indifference in the stratified working class, and ignores the difference between small local entrepreneurs and and the increasingly globalized corporate fat-cats. It is on these structural differences that Netanyahu's metaphor plays, amplifying working class divisions in order to maximize 'weak labor's class envy toward other employees, and minimizing distinctions between businessmen in order to position them all on one side.

'Weak labor' workers are excluded from the higher echelons of private industry which require higher education and technological skills, and are generally excluded from large government plants and offices, except in menial jobs. In the central towns they mostly work for small private employers as unskilled and semi-skilled service-workers such as cooks, waiters, vendors, etc. Many of these employees and their small-business employers are more similar than different in background and life-style. They share intense economic insecurity. Classifying them as 'thin' poses no problem.

In the 'development towns' in the periphery, low-paid blue and pink collar and menial workers of the local municipalities' bureaucracies and services are increasingly unemployed (not to mention illegally unpaid). In the private sector in the 'development towns', as in the more central towns, there is not much difference between (the limited number of) small local entrepreneurs and their employees. But 'weak labor' is also employed in the few larger privately owned industrial plants which are labor-intensive: These have been floundering as their owners take their investments to global markets. These rich corporate owners have over the years profited greatly from government subsidies, tax benefits and grants bestowed on them by the state. It's Netanyahu's distortion to present these favorites of all Israeli governments as 'thin' allies of 'weak labor'. In the context of meaning salient to 'weak labor', this signifies under-privilege vis-à-vis the 'fat' public sector, whereas in fact large-business owners have been the state's economic partners and beneficiaries.

As 'weak labor''s resentment is directed toward the state as a macro-employer which for many years excluded it, maintained a too-low minimum wage, and allowed others to achieve preferred status, class envy is directed mainly toward public sector employees, especially the privileged labor elite and members of the middle class. Many of the more educated white collar public state or municipal employees in the service professions are ordinarily considered part of the middle class although they earn not much more than a minimum wage. Their major achievement— job tenure—is under fierce attack, as are all the rights won by organized labor. Netanyahu's identifying of employees such as teachers, social workers, state and municipal bureaucrats, etc. as over-privileged 'fat' fits well with the neo-liberal attempt to achieve a radical downward levelling which would actually reduce relative deprivation by breaking labor security at all levels and by radically reducing the middle class (perhaps this is what Netanyahu means when he claims that his policies are reducing social gaps). Netanyahu's dichotomy hides the presently besieged majority of public sector employees under the rhetorical camouflage of 'fat' over-privilege, separating 'weak labor' from organized labor in opposing categories as a means of discouraging labor solidarity.

6. For the Israeli-Palestinian working class, thin and fat would stand respectively for poor vs. well-off, that is to say in general for Arabs vs. Jews. Both public and private sectors, owned and controlled by the Jewish establishment can be assumed to be envisioned as fat men riding on Arabs' back; but with regard to Netanyahu's metaphor, this population cannot be expected to agree with its attack on the system of public expenditures which has denied them their equal rights, when they are trying to get this system to give them some of its fat.

7. For the government-dependent poor, who may have not necessarily internalized the newly dominant cultural lingo about fat and thin (even when it reflects historical processes which adversely affect their health and wellbeing), thin men can stand only for the poor on whose backs fat men ride. But since in Netanyahu's metaphor the "fat man"'s over-weight is constituted (in part) by the state-provided benefits which sustain the poor (employed, unemployed, or unable to work), there's no escape from seeing how its blame-the-victim implications clearly stigmatize them as parasitic overload.

In sum, Netanyahu, a facile ad-man, effectively uses a metaphor whose ideological intention and sense are clear but whose referential meaning and place in a system of signification polysemous and poly-indexical between various ideologies and social/political categories. He uses the metonymous "fat" and "thin" within a figurative 'rhetorical pliers' representing the ideologically valuated relation between the two terms in neo-liberal thinking. Manipulating this instrument he is able to tactically latch into the systems of meaning and reference of the oligarchy and of the two major segments of the political spectrum he needs to recruit: The middle class (whatever its ideological variants) on the one side, and on the other the traditional Jewish (mainly mizrahi) working class constituency of the Likkud.

The whole cow or only the milk?

At the end of the year of his first year in office, Netanyahu uses an even more vulgar metaphor to jab at the public sector: Escalating to a more pejorative although less personal epithet than 'fat man' he labels the public sector a 'fat government cow'. One may speculate that one of the reasons for this figurative switch is that Netanyahu is taking extreme care to step around an idiomatic land-mine by avoiding all semblance of a personal conflict with fat-man Sharon. A sufficient reason is that the new utterance addressing 'the Israeli citizen' evokes an ostensibly unified more widely appealing signification untouched by the pragmatic polysemy of the previous one, so that it has fewer audience resistances to overcome. In fact, the Israeli citizen is conceived as a masculine paterfamilias, moved by rational self-concern and by the responsibility of efficiently managing his family's expenditures. The conversation is to take place between men:

> I will come to the Israeli citizen and present him with the choice: Do you want to receive another 200 I.S. In tax reduction as an addition to your free income, or do you prefer that your 200 be swallowed-up within the government apparatus and feed it? Do you want to feed the fat government cow or do you want to buy milk for you and for your family?
>
> (*Yediot* 5/7/04)

The 'fat government cow' wastes the citizen's resources; instead of unwisely investing in her, he would be smart to buy only what he needs from the efficient private sector (unmarked, unmentioned, but a hidden masculine marketer who is *not* called a 'thin private sector cow'). Netanyahu's misogynist figure of speech reproduces the old saw regarding sex without commitment: 'You don't have to buy a cow in order to drink milk'. The private sector will sell the citizen whatever he wants at a fair price. The public sector just wants to exploit him, extracting an avoidable investment. Man to man, Netanyahu advises the citizen not to let her.

Getting rid of the fat

Several days later the meaning is modified: "The public sector is like a fat cow: It's possible to get thin without losing production of milk" (*Yediot* 8/7/04) Since the efficient producer of milk is the private sector, it's possible to let the public cow starve.

Beyond showing himself as the economist who can get the economy fixed, the commander who can get the soldiers in fighting shape and the mechanic who can get the Israeli car out of the mud, Netanyahu's can-do stance makes him into a healer who can get Israel to be healthy and fit. His get-well plan for the Israeli economy prescribes a radical diet for shrinking the public sector inspired by Ronald Reagan, who in 1981 recommended to 'stop feeding' and 'change the diet' of a 'too fat' American government. Netanyahu's weight- loss program is to be effected through radical budget cuts involving drastic curtailment of unemployment benefits, National Insurance pensions and welfare payments (low as compared with Europe), the firing of masses of public employees— especially those who have achieved decent terms of employment, and a lowering of wages and social benefits beginning at the lowest level and pulling down the rest.

The image the Minister of the Treasury projects as a thin-making physician-nutritionist is supplemented by a fantasy of being a ministerial Robin Hood engaged in bringing about social justice by taking from the fat to give to the thin:

> No-one helps the weak in society more than my people and myself...[I]t is not true that economic growth is beneficial only to the strong. On the contrary, it's primarily beneficial to the weak. In 2004 unbelievably 100% of the jobs added to the economy were directed to the private sector with no additions at all to the public sector. . .70 thousand jobs have been added in one year to the private sector. . .Israelis are going back to work.   (*Yediot* 8/7/04)

Here Netanyahu is responding to criticism which demonstrates that 'economic growth' increases socio-economic gaps and inequality by benefiting the rich (strong) and not helping the poor (weak). He fantastically creates on paper an unbelievable number of 70,000 new jobs in one year, a quantitative estimate evidently referring to the temporary and underpaid positions in home care, construction and agriculture vacated by 70,000 foreign workers reported earlier to 'have left Israel this year', whose jobs have in theory become available to Israelis willing to work under conditions of deprivation. This is an accounting which has everything to do with market -economics theory, and nothing to do with socioeconomic reality. Moreover, considering that according to this statement these 70,000 positions are *all* of the jobs added to the economy in this year, there is no cause for celebration. Nevertheless accentuating the positive, Netanyahu's claim leaves out and makes invisible these non-Israeli workers, now gone. Having been subject to near-slavery conditions, police raids and sudden deportation, they have been cut. Elsewhere Netanyahu reports that within a year jobs vacated by 150, 000 foreign workers who will leave Israel will be available to Israelis (Yediot 9.12.03). More 'economic growth' is in sight.

In addition, Netanyahu's reply manages to switch in mid-air, so to speak, the meaning of 'strong' and 'weak' intended by his critics—a rhetorical somersault which lands private business and their projected employees again on the same 'thin' side, in line with the ideologically based alliance of private employers and employees discussed above. 'Helping the weak', then, means letting the private sector employ the unemployed under conditions more exploitative than Israelis have generally been willing to work for until now. To complete the picture, new legislation is currently proposed to allow government contracts to also allow the public sector employment of personnel under the same conditions.

For those political leaders less positive-thinking than Netanyahu, yet eager to show their expertise at diet-making efficiency, talk of wholesale firing of Israelis is a favorite recommendation for slashing off weight. Minister of Defense Mofaz, recommending the benefits of the wall being built to effect 'separation', is pleased to say that it will result in financial saving since"8000 security guards will be fired." Minister of Education Livnat promises that "We will fire 15,000 (teachers; September 2003, revised to 10,000 in December *Haaretz* 18/12/03)". S. Dovrat, the head of a public committee she appointed to delineate 'reforms' in the system of education adds: "There are too many teachers, (and they are) not good, not the best. 20,000 will become superannuated" *Haaretz* 17/5/04).

The committee recommends and Livnat and Netanyahu agree, that far-reaching changes be made to make the system more efficient. For example new young teachers will be hired to work much longer hours for a somewhat higher starting salary, their employment subject to principals' whims (Livnat in Ynet 20/5/04). Dovrat announces that "the raise in teachers salaries and the improvement in their working conditions will be achieved by cuts achieved by the firing of senior teachers" (*Haaretz* 17/5/04). These senior teachers seen as grist for the mill are mostly women, union members who have achieved job-security and a relatively higher salary over the years.

Leaders who are true believers in laissez-faire go beyond cuts to annulment. Thus 'Minister in the Treasury Bureau' Shitrit: "There is one way to cause people to go out to work, and it is to cancel completely all the allowances... of those who do not work, and live at the expense of the state" (*Maariv* 19/12/03). The Good Doctor Shitrit promises that although such actions may hurt they are all for the patient's own good: "I determine here that because of all the allowances that we pay to those who do not work, poverty increases. My worry about the weak is expressed in the fact that I am trying to cancel these superfluous allowances" (*Yediot* 20/1/04).

The various budgets presented by this administration as the way to bring health to the Israeli economy actually offer different diets based on an ideological and socioeconomic Body Mass Index: Middle level and low level 'fat' public sector employees will be given a starvation diet based on being fired or on not being paid a salary for months at a time (as has been done to local authority employees in 2004) or will be made so insecure and pliant that they will accept any terms of employment and eat what they can get. Already average middle class income has gone down over the last two years (Swirski and Konor Atias 2004). Higher level public sector employees—executives, directors and such—will lose nothing. The 'thin' unemployed and poor will be given a near-starvation diet of fictive promises of inferior employment and a starvation diet of stressful unemployment, with cotton candy prizes once in a while. The 'thin' private sector will be given the means (cheaper labor, tax cuts) to eat whatever they like.

Over the socioeconomic capitalist rainbow there is the prospect of an interminable restricted maintenance diet for both poor and middle class, which will no longer require supervision since it is to take effect after the radical efforts are done, and after corporate and income taxes (mostly of the rich) and sales taxes (disproportionately of the poor) are cut. Physicians of cosmopolitan/capitalist medicine ordinarily blame the victim for bad health-risk behavior, applying individualistic morality so as to ignore the historical class bases of suffering. In this case, the politician-healers of Israel promise that weaning citizen/patients from the state's nurturing will be better for them, since without public support and public services nutrition will be healthy. Middle class persons can stay trim through the effort of paying for what they need, and the poor—who need to be regulated most—will know not to be tempted by what they cannot afford. Whether it's about food or sex, moralistic restriction with regard to the poor is always in order. Minister of the Interior Poraz put it in a salient context: "People who cannot afford children shouldn't have them" (Yediot 29/12/04). If health care, nutritional security and education are beyond their means, the poor will just have to die sick, hungry and stupid.

Poraz's saying is an accusation, an insult and a threat to the poor, especially the orthodox and Arab citizens of Israel. So is his following, zeroing-in on the Arabs:

> The government cannot be responsible for all the local authorities. . . [A]mong the Arabs there is a norm of not paying local taxes . When water is disconnected they connect themselves to the water pipe and steal. There are fictive municipal workers...[T]he norms in the Arab sector have to be changed; but on the other hand if that's the way they want to live, OK   (Maariv 20/5/04).

The weakest of the Jewish state-supported poor (single unemployed mothers, the disabled) are also easy targets to stigmatize, through 'culture of poverty' or 'poverty trap' attributions of immorality (e.g. Valentine 1968). Humiliating them is one of the methods of reinforcing anxiety about unemployment at all levels of labor above them in the process of making 'the labor market' more 'flexible' and submissive (e.g. Piven and Cloward 1971). Minister of Welfare Orlev, expressing a preference for state-subsidized meals for poor children in school instead of a National Insurance children's allowance says: "We don't know where the money goes" (Maariv 30/11/03). In the same vein, Prime Minister Sharon, defending a proposed cut in children's allowances, adds: [We have to] "do everything so that the money does not go to drinking and to drugs for the parents" (Maariv 29/12/03). This goes on: Netanyahu: "If they can walk 200 kilometers., they can work" (Yediot 7/03/04) he said of the unemployed single mothers who undertook a march to protest radical cuts in their National Insurance benefits. Shitrit: "Whoever doesn't show up at the unemployment office will not get an allowance. But don't worry, for money they will run" (Yediot 4/3/04). "If they are dead, let them come out of the grave and we'll pay them", said of supposed welfare cheats, and he widens the stigmatized circle: "They're either dead or they're Arabs. They don't belong here" (Yediot 11/3/04).

The organic metaphor consistently used by this administration symbolizes citizens' vulnerability, as creatures with physiological weaknesses and moral failings, to the ruling power of the state. The prototypical speech acts in which this metaphor is embedded in the governments' right wing rhetoric are Expressive accusatory insults like 'fat', and Commissive threats like the proposed 'diets' of the public sector , which constitute the negative counterpart of promising, and thus committing powerful speakers to undertake punishment of their subjects in the future. The budget cuts themselves, when passed along with other harsh edicts, are institutional Declaratives, the secular equivalent of curses, which bring about an instantaneous deterioration in the legal and material status of the citizens affected. They too make up the threatening and intimidating atmosphere which forms the setting for the neo-liberal destruction of the welfare state.

If the mechanical metaphor is used to bring about a blinding-white magic of fake unity and false expectation, the organic metaphor is employed to effect a black magic of explicit division and destruction. Through attempting to persuade constituencies to consent to the state's power on the basis of fantasized hopes or internalized fears, both metaphors serve hegemony's work of political subjectification (e.g. Butler 1997).

Conclusion

As an account of ruling, the discourse of 'global capital statism' identifies nationhood with the externally-dependent military and civilian functions of 'national security' and 'the economy', while obviating the internally-oriented claims of promoting social equality and solidarity which originated in socialism. these were politically utilized by 'labor etatism', and are continued as rhetoric by current social-democratic successors.

As the second of the two bulls attempting to plow-under any survivals of Israel's national and international socialist potential, Netanyahu in his role of Minister of the Treasury speaks of solidarity and equality in a market-economic rather than in a social way. Sectorially, he appeals to a solidarity of the private sector. Individualistically, he appeals to each citizen: Everyone should do their part to get the economic car out of the mud. Everyone will benefit from economic growth. Every citizen will receive a free share when government-owned banks are privatized. Poor ('weak') people will be able (each of them) to buy a DVD when the sales tax is reduced (*Yediot* 13/2/04).

Sharon's expressions of solidarity between Israelis are focused on national security and military goals, as were Netanyahu's when he was Prime Minister. Against the ubiquitous war-talk and national security discourse which makes for the explosive buzz in the foreground of life in Israel, economic talk comes in a close second. As has been shown above, an affinity to the instantaneous 'magical' aspect of speech acts is a defining feature of this administration's economic rhetoric. The power-bound preference for the brutally instant, which is not only rhetorical but characterizes the Likkud's execution of its economic policies, is congruent with Israel's increasingly violent and brutal military behavior.

With regard to economics this brutality includes attempts at legislation abolishing the right to strike; success at instituting almost-unilateral legislation of government budgets instead of permitting open discussion and mutual negotiation vis a vis the public, the Knesset, and to some degree even government Ministries other than the Treasury; unilateral withholding, for many months, of the salaries of municipal workers; and of course the anti-labor, anti-poor and anti-Arab contents of these legislations as well as the creation of two new police forces to enforce edicts against 'illegal' foreign workers and welfare payment recipients (*Yediot* 26/2/04, *Haaretz* 23/6/04)..

While the policy trends, military and economic, of neo-liberals and post-labor democrats in Israel have been parallel, there are differences between the

Likkud and the Labor Party in their execution and in the accompanying rhetoric. For example, for both the concept of solidarity, before it is social or economic, is applied to a national/religious Jewish identification. Both speak of separating from the Palestinians and support the oppressive Wall, but Social Democrats maintain the rhetoric of 'making peace' with the Palestinians even when their actions preclude its possibility.

During their attempts since 1977 to recapture hegemony, the post-labor regimes headed by Rabin, Peres, and Barak projected a social democratic civilian rhetoric. This rhetoric's main feature is the expression of interest in social solidarity through purported social equality and inclusion. Arab citizens of Israel, excluded by Netanyahu's right wing demagoguery as ' a demographic problem dangerous to the state" (*Haaretz* 18/2/03), are included in the span of social democratic discourse, although not necessarily as equals. The poor as a category are socially included while patronized. Even Ehud Barak's notorious call as Prime Minister to affluent residents of the Tel Aviv suburb of Ramat Hasharon to "open your refrigerators" in order to donate food to the hungry poor may be seen in this light. While calling in effect for voluntarism to make up for the abnegation of the state's responsibility, Barak at least thought that the haves should make a gesture of participating in providing for the have-nots' basic needs. This may be considered solidary compared with present Minister of Education Livnat's haughty royalism as to children of poor families for whom there will be no subsidized lunches at school: "The Ministry of Education is not responsible for social gaps... Let them eat sandwiches" (*Yediot* 3/9/04).

In rethinking the Labor Party's Shimon Peres's reference to Netanyahu's economic policies (and one may add rhetoric) as 'piggish capitalism', one may contrastively call post-labor policies and rhetoric 'capitalism with a mouthwash'. The Labor Party today is hardly a viable opposition to Likkud rule, nor does one exist in the current parliamentary scene. A last line of resistance to neo-liberal policies is now formed by the stronger targets under siege: Organized labor, and some middle class employees vested in the welfare state's institutions. So far, they have almost held their own—when it comes to themselves only.

The possibility of successful resistance against state and ruling class control and oppression have been greatly diminished with the ongoing attacks and effectiveness of the current government in breaking down the two aspects of Israeli society which elicited Rosenfeld's optimism in the article cited at the beginning of this paper, parliamentary democracy and the welfare state. To sustain optimism until more effective socialist opposition to the state's oppressive policies can come about, one may only hope that what remains of the welfare state and of parliamentary democracy, together with the ideals of social solidarity and equality even if presently expressed mainly in rhetoric, can water the grass-roots of a struggle to realize them more fully.

References Cited

Austin J.L. 1962. *How to Do Things with Words*. Cambridge: Harvard University Press.
Butler J. 1997 *The Psychic Life of Power: Theories in Subjection.* Stanford: Stanford University Press.
Carmi Sh. and H. Rosenfeld 1989. The emergence of militaristic nationalism in Israel. *International Journal of Politics, Culture and Society* 3(1) Fall, 5-49.
_____ 1992a. Israel's political economy and the widening class gap between its two national groups, *Asian and African Studies* 26(1) March, 15-62
_____ 1992b. Political and economic transformations leading to the ascendancy of militaristic-nationalism in Israel, *Studies in Third World Societies* 4, June 191-249
Chomsky N. 2003. *Hegemony or Survival? America's Quest for Global Dominance*, New York: Henry Holt.
Doron A. 1995. *In Favor of Universality: The Challenges of Social Policy in Israel.* Jerusalem: Magnes Press (Hebrew).
_____ 2003. The welfare state in an era of cutbacks: A view from the beginning of the 21st century, *Hevra u-Revaha 23*(3), 275-294 (Hebrew)
Gal J. 2002. *A Burden by Choice? Policy toward the Unemployed in Pre-State Palestine and Israel 1920-1995*, The Ben Gurion Research Center: Ben Gurion University Press (Hebrew)
Gramsci A. 1971 (1929-1935). *Selections from Prison Notebooks*. London: Lawrence and Wishart.
Katan Y. 2000. *The Welfare State on the Eve of a New Century*, The Henrietta Szold Institute. Jerusalem: National Institute for Research in the Behavioral Sciences, (Hebrew)
Kopp, J. 2003. *Allocation of Resources for Social Services: Annual Report*, The Center for the Study of Social Policy in Israel, Jerusalem
Lakoff G.and M. Johnson 1980. *Metaphors We Live By.* Chicago: University of Chicago.
Lakoff R. 2000. *The Language War.* Berkeley: University of California Press.
Pepper S. 1942 *World Hypotheses: A Study in Evidence.* Berkeley: University of California.
Piven F. and R. Cloward 1971. *Regulating the Poor*. New York: Pantheon.
Reiss N. 1984. *Speech Act Taxonomy as a Tool for Ethnographic Description.* Amsterdam: John Benjamins.
_____ 1989. Speech Act Taxonomy, Chimpanzee Communication, and the Evolutionary Basis of Language. *In* J. Wind, E. Pulleybank, E. de Grolier, and B. Bichakjian, eds. *Studies in Language Origins* Vol.I, pp. 283-304. Amsterdam: John Benjamins.
_____ 1990. The Emics/Etic Distinction as Applied to Language, in Th. Headland, K. Pike and M. Harris, eds, *Emics and Etics :The Insider/Outsider Debate, Frontiers of Anthropology*, volume 7, pp. 168-183. Newbury Park: Sage.
_____ 1991. *Health Care to the Arab Population of Israel*, Westview Press, Boulder.
Roeh Y. 1994 *Otherwise about Communication*. Even Yehuda: Reches (Hebrew).
Rosenfeld H. and Sh. Carmi 1976 The privatization of public means: The state-made middle class and the realization of family value in Israel, *Kinship and Modernization in Mediterranean Society*, pp. 131-159. Rome: Center for Mediterranean Studies, American Universities Field Staff.
Rosenfeld H. 2002 The idea is to change the state, not the 'conceptual' terminology, *Ethnic and Racial Studies, 25*(6), (November 1), 1083-1095
Searle J. 1969 *Speech Acts.* Cambridge: Cambridge University Press.
_____ 1979 *Expressions and Meanings*. Cambridge: Cambridge University Press.
Swirski, Sh. and E. Konor-Atias 11/2003. *Black years*. Tel Aviv: Adva Center (Hebrew).

_____ 6/2004. *Reduction of the middle class in Israel 1988-2002.* Tel Aviv: Adva Center (Hebrew)

Valentine Ch. 1968. *Culture and Poverty.* Chicago: University of Chicago.

Yishuvi N. 2004. *Annual Report: The Condition of Human Rights in Israel 2003.* Jerusalem: The Association for Civil Rights in Israel (Hebrew).

Education, Social Change, and Control: The Case of the Palestinians in Israel

Majid Al-Haj

Background

Education is considered the foremost issue among the Palestinians in Israel. This is the result of the dramatic shift in the status of this community as a result of the 1948 Arab-Israel war and their transformation from a majority (66% of the population of mandatory Palestine in 1947) into an involuntary minority in an ethno-national state. After this war, only 156,000 Palestinians (or 13% of the total Israeli population) remained within the "Green Line" and became Israeli citizens. They were a weak and isolated group, cut off from their kin, including the intellectual and political elites and the bulk of the urban Arab middle and upper class—merchants, professionals, and the clergy—who had become refugees in the Arab countries (Al-Haj and Rosenfeld 1990: 24). Only 6% of the 200,000 Arab city-dwellers remained after the war (Lustick 1980). Some 20% of the Arab population of Israel were "internal refugees," forced to relocate to new communities when their original villages were destroyed during and immediately after the war (Al-Haj 1988). Furthermore, most Arab-owned land was confiscated by the state, leaving their former occupants totally dependent on the Jewish-controlled economy.

Consequently, the Palestinian community sought to invest in their human capital through education, in order to reconstruct their social capital, rebuild their leadership, and pursue the struggle for civil equality within Israel. As in other developing societies, the educated elite among the Palestinians in Israel are agents of social change who fulfil an important mission in directing the collective and leading the struggle to improve the status of its members (Al-Haj 2004). In addition, the motivation for education among the Palestinians as a whole, and among those in Israel in particular, has been enhanced by the loss of their land. In this sense, education has replaced land as a source of dignity and as a reliable way to secure a livelihood and achieve socioeconomic mobility (Tahir 1985: 36).

Several questions may be raised: What are the main quantitative and qualitative changes that have taken place in education among the Arabs in Israel over time? What role does education play in the process of social change among a developing national minority that has little or no access to the opportunity structure but has achieved an advanced stage of individual "modernization"? Is education a source of empowerment for the Palestinian community? Or is it a control mechanism employed by the state in order to perpetuate the cultural and ideological dominance of the Jewish majority?

We shall try to answer these questions below. First we shall consider the main developments in preschool, elementary, and secondary education. Then we shall discuss the main barriers that have interfered with education's ability to serve as a catalyst for social change. The school curricula in history and language will be presented from a comparison of Arab and Jewish schools.

Elementary and Secondary Education

The dismantling of the Palestinian community as a result of the 1948 Israel-Arab war produced a parallel dismantling of its educational system. This system, which had experienced considerable development since the 1920s, totally collapsed (for a discussion of the Palestinian education system in the Mandatory period, see Tibawi 1956). The damage affected mainly the private schools that constituted the backbone of Palestinian educational and cultural institutions. These schools included Muslim schools, foreign-run Christian schools, and locally run Christian schools. In the late 1940s, more than a third of all Arab students studied in such schools (ibid.; Badran 1969).

At the start of the 1948/49 school year, there were only 45 Arab elementary schools in the entire country, plus one secondary school (in Nazareth). Of the total Arab enrollment of 11,129 pupils, only 8% attended private schools (Al-Haj 1995).

Since then, there has been a considerable expansion of the educational system among the Palestinians in Israel. Today there are 650 Arab schools, including 171 at the secondary level. The increase in the number of educational institutions coincided with a concomitant increase in the number of pupils. In 2003, there were 387,866 Arab preschool, elementary, and secondary students—a thirty-fold increase from 1948 and four times the increase in the size of the Arab population (*SAI* 2003, p. 24). (See Table 1.)

Table 1: Pupils in Arab Educational Institutions, Over Time

	1948/49	1959/60	1969/70	1979/80	1990/91	2002/03
Preschool	1,124	7,274	14,211	17,344	22,500	67,000
Elementary schools	9,991	36,729	85,449	121,985	140,776	204,897
Junior high schools	-	-	2,457	14,803	31,293	56,226
High schools	14	1,956	8,050	22,473	40,271	56,514
Post-secondary non-university institutions	-	121	370	621	717	3,227
Total	11,129	46,080	110,537	177,226	235,557	387,866

Source: *SAI* 1989, Table 22/10, p. 610; *SAI* 1991, p. 615; *SAI* 2003 Table 8/22, p.27.

The expansion of the education system is an outcome of the Palestinians' growing awareness of education as an existential need. It has been facilitated by Israeli laws that guarantee (at least formally) all children's right to an education (including the Compulsory Education Law 1949, the State Education Law 1953, and the Free Education Law 1978). In addition, because of the age structure of the Palestinian population (about 50% below age of 18), one of every three Arabs in Israel is a student at some level (*SAI* 2003, Table 8/22, p. 27).

Despite the expansion of the educational system, however, there is still a wide gap between Arabs and Jews, starting at the preschool level. In 1999/2000, only 39.6% of Arab children attended preschools, as compared to 83.3 % of Jewish children (*SAI* 2001: 8-26).

The Arab school dropout rate is also higher. According to the Ministry of Education statistics for 2001, the high-school dropout rate of Arab students was twice that of Jewish students (10% and 4.5%, respectively) (Ministry of Education 2003: 87).

Despite the improvement over time, there has always been a gap between the scholastic achievements of Arab and Jewish pupils, in favor of the latter. Success in the matriculation exams *(bagrut)* is the main criterion for evaluating achievement, since it largely determines the likelihood of acquiring higher education (a matriculation certificate is a prerequisite for admission to Israeli universities). In 1998, the percentage of twelfth-grade students entitled to a matriculation certificate was 39.6% among Arab and 51.4% among Jewish students (*SAI* 2001: 8-36). The gap is even wider if measured in terms of the entire age cohort, given the higher Arab dropout rate.

Education—Social Change vs. Control

While the expansion of the education system is considered to be one of the main achievements of the Palestinians in Israel, the return on education, measured in terms of their socioeconomic mobility, has been limited. In addition, formal education has not spearheaded social change and cultural competence among this community. On the contrary, the educational system has served as a conservative factor that has retarded the development of a national and cultural identity among the Arabs in Israeli (see Mari 1978; Al-Haj 1995; Amarah and Mari 1999). At the same time, formal education has failed to create a genuine civil identity, based on diversity and multicultural ideology, common to Jewish and Arab students (see Al-Haj 2003).

The main factor behind this failure has been its use by the Israeli authorities as a mechanism to control the Palestinian citizens of Israel. This policy was facilitated by a comprehensive system that includes administration, resources, teachers, and curriculum.

Administration

Already in the 1950s, there was a serious discussion among policymakers about the administration of the Arab school system. The main debate focused on two models: assimilation and segregation. Blum, an inspector of Arab schools, pushed for "assimilation" rather than emphasizing the distinctiveness of Arab culture. In an undated document addressed to the minister of education, and classified at the time as "confidential," he delineated his idea as follows:

> I have already expressed my conception regarding the Arab problem and how it should be handled in the field of education. I said that in my opinion it is conceivable that by abolishing or minimizing the differences between us and them (the Arabs) we can also decrease the contradictions that originate in different orientations, so that the prospects for a quiet and peaceful life would increase. In the field of education this might be reflected by giving Arab schools the same structure as exists in the Hebrew schools, as far as possible, the same methods, the same class hours, the same atmosphere, and if possible also a similar curriculum. ... In this way we can hope not only to bring our Arabs closer to us but also to take them away from the Arab world that surrounds us.
>
> (State Archives, 145/1733/G).

The group that advocated the control-and-segregation strategy realized that it would be extremely difficult to educate Arabs as Israelis, in the absence of a general secular Israeli civic identity. The one adopted was strongly interwoven with Jewish-Zionist symbols, which naturally exclude Arabs. In addition, they came to the conclusion that such a strategy would exact a high price, because it would entail equal rights for the Arab minority. Nor was it certain that the Arabs would accept such assimilation (see Ben-Or 1957).

Eventually, the assimilation option was abandoned in favor of a strategy that may be termed "controlled segregation" (ibid.), based on administrative and sectarian segregation of the two educational systems. In fact, this segregation suits the orientations of both groups, which favor maintaining their cultural distinctiveness (see Smooha 1990). It has enabled Arabs to use Arabic as the language of instruction in their schools and thus to retain their own culture (Al-Haj 1996). This "cultural territorialization" has not been accompanied by cultural autonomy, however, in the sense of giving the Arabs administrative control of their schools and the right to determine their curriculum. Instead, the Arab educational system has been subjected to Jewish control of its management, personnel, resources, and, most important of all, curriculum (see Mari 1978; Mazawi 1994; Amareh and Mari 1999). Its main objective has been legitimizing the Jewish-Zionist state, enhancing loyalty to it, maintaining order and stability, and educating for a Jewish-Arab co-existence in which Arabs accept their inferior status (Peres et al. 1968; Mari 1978; Al-Haj 1994).

It should be noted that the Arabs' lack of cultural autonomy has been accompanied by a minimal role they have been allowed in managing their own education. The Arab educational system has been Jewish-dominated in terms of its administration and curricula. For decades, the Arab education unit in the Ministry of Education was headed by a Jewish bureaucrat. Only in 1987 was an Arab appointed the "official in charge of Arab Education." In fact, by then the position had been stripped of its meaning. Its incumbent is no longer involved in the allocation of resources, planning, or setting priorities. His main activity is confined to the curricula and textbooks used in the various levels of education. Even in this matter his authority is restricted by a rigid bureaucratic hierarchy: the Pedagogical Secretary, the Curricula Department, the director general of the

Ministry of Education, and the minister, in addition to the district commissioners. In fact, real power has been held by the official's deputy, who is a Jewish civil servant affiliated with the Israeli intelligence service (Saa'r, 2001). The latter controls one of the most important functions in the educational system—the hiring of teachers and appointment of school principals and superintendents (ibid).

Control of Resources

The administrative structure of the Arab educational system, described above, has given the authorities tight control over resources, both material (funding and services) and human (teachers, principals, and inspectors). On top of this, the general discrimination against Arab localities in terms of budgets and services has been reflected in the school system as well.

One of the perpetual physical problems facing Arab education is the shortage of adequate buildings. Today, about 20% of Arab classrooms are located in substandard buildings that do not meet minimal educational conditions. Some of these are rented rooms in private houses and naturally are not designed for educational purposes.

While Arab schools have been striving to achieve decent physical conditions, the gap between them and Jewish schools has continued to widen in other spheres. Many services taken for granted in Jewish schools are still lacking in Arab schools; some are even beyond the imagination of Arab pupils. Basic support services found in almost every Jewish school (such as counselors, psychologists, physicians, dentists, nurses, and social workers) were first introduced to Arab schools—and even then to only a small number of them—in the late 1980s (see Al-Haj 1995). Whereas the Jewish educational system provides a wide range of subsidized cultural, social, and educational activities for its pupils, Arab pupils are confined to the monotonous activity included in the regular curricula.

The problems are especially severe among the Bedouin population in southern Israel, especially in "non-recognized villages." Since these villages do not exist, as far as the authorities are concerned, they lack any infrastructure, educational, or cultural services. According to different estimates about 50% of 140,000 Bedouins who live in the Negev reside in 45 villages, which are considered by the government as "non-recognized" and "temporary" (see Abu-Saad 2001). Since the ultimate aim of the government is to abolish the "non recognized" villages and move their residents elsewhere, there is a continuing official effort to prevent any sort of development in these villages.

Control of Teachers

Control of Arab teachers is doubly important for the state authorities. On the one hand, by controlling teachers' behavior the authorities secure the implementation of official goals and maintain stability in the educational system. On the other hand, teachers' compliance with official policy "buys" the Arab elite's cooperation, because of its total dependence on the Jewish sector for white-collar jobs (Lustick 1980, 2000).

The security establishment's oversight of Arab teachers decreased considerably but did not vanish entirely even after the abolition of the military government in 1966. "Security classification" has been used as an efficient instrument for controlling Arab teachers and through them of the Arab educational system. Teachers who do not fit in with the authorities' approved political consensus are excluded from the system (Wergift 1989).

Despite the opposition of Arabs and democratic elements among officials in the Ministry of Education to the security establishment's interference in the hiring of teachers and principals over time, this phenomenon continues to be one of the hallmarks of Arab education (Saa'r, 2001).

Unlike the situation in elementary schools, the Ministry of Education does not have full control of the employment of secondary-school teachers. Here the local authority plays a major role. Towards the end of every school year the head of the local council publishes the faculty requirements of the local secondary school for the coming year. A committee composed of representatives of the municipality and the Ministry of Education (and sometimes of the parents) interviews the candidates and chooses those found suitable. Even so, the committee's decisions must be sent to the Ministry of Education for ratification.

It should be noted that the Arab local authorities' involvement in teacher hiring for secondary schools and the appointment of principles provides an additional source of control that impedes the functioning of the educational system. In many cases, local clan considerations are introduced to the selection process and candidates related to or politically affiliated with the council head are chosen to vacant posts, regardless of their educational qualifications.

For a long time the Education Ministry barred Arab teachers from discussing with their pupils any political issue defined as "sensitive," such as national identity, civil discrimination against Arabs, or current events related to the Arab-Israel conflict.

In the aftermath of the Israeli invasion of Lebanon (1982), and in particular the Sabra and Shatila massacre, various officials of the Education Ministry, including the minister, the director general, the director of the Arab Education division, and Arab inspectors and teachers, decided, convinced that something had to be done in the framework of the educational system to deal with the "increasing wave of extremism among Arab pupils" (*Al Hamishmar*, January 28, 1983). In a director general's bulletin to the Arab schools, issued later that year, Arab teachers were told to discuss political topics and bring up current problems (Ministry of Education and Culture, *Director General's Bulletin*, 1983). However, the absence of clear instructions from the Ministry of Education in this regard and the lack of a pertinent curriculum and goals increased Arab teachers' confusion. Meanwhile, Arab schools continued to be confronted by topical issues without knowing how to deal with them or how to face the questions raised by pupils.

The official permission to deal with controversial issues has not eliminated the years of fear, which created a "culture of silence" among Arab teachers. This is manifested in a recent survey on the status of Arab teachers in Israel, conducted by the author in March 2004 (Al-Haj, forthcoming). This survey, which addressed a representative sample of teachers at all levels (elementary, junior high, and high school), posed a series of questions on political education in Arab schools. The findings revealed that only 17% of teachers discuss current political issues with their pupils very often. Only 16% reported discussing the Palestinian-Israel conflict with the pupils very often; 23% reported discussing the events of October 2000 (when 13 Arab citizens were killed by Israeli police) with their classes. When teachers who did conduct political discussions were asked who had initiated it, 40% said they themselves, 32% said the pupils, 10% said the principal, and the rest said someone else (ibid.).

Policy, Goals and Curricula

One of the main elements of the policy of control has involved control of curricula. For decades the stated goals of education in Israel did not take the cultural and national distinctiveness of the Arab minority into consideration. According to the State Education Law 1953, its goal was

> to base elementary education in the State of Israel upon the values of Jewish culture and scientific achievements, upon love of the homeland and loyalty to the state and to the people of Israel, upon belief in agriculture and labor, upon pioneer training, and the aspiration towards a society built on freedom, equality, tolerance, mutual assistance, and love for one's fellow man.
> Educators and public figures criticized this omission, asking questions about the social and political repercussions of evading the national aspect of Arab education. (see Peres et al. 1968).

However, this does not mean that no goals were defined for Arab education. The official policy towards Arab education was an integral part of a wider policy concerning the Arab minority in Israel, with the active participation of the Prime Minister's advisor for Arab affairs and other Arabists in various ministries (see Al-Haj 1995, 1996). This policy was driven by the perception of Arabs as a security risk and as a potential source of unrest and instability. The means adopted to lessen this danger were control, on the one hand, and improvement of the conditions of the Arab population, on the other. These means were not always complementary. In many cases, in fact, they proved to be rather contradictory.

Restating Goals and Curricula

In 1975, the director general of the Education Ministry established the Peled Committee to reformulate the goals of education in Israel (see Smooha 1989;

Nakhleh 1977). Its report suggested as follows:

> *Arabs:* The goal of state education in the Arab sector in Israel is to base education on the foundations of Arab culture; on the achievements of science; on the aspiration for peace between Israel and its neighbors; on love of the country shared by all citizens and loyalty to the state of Israel, through an emphasis on their common interests and by encouraging the uniqueness of Israeli Arabs; on knowledge of Jewish culture; on respect for creative work and on an aspiration for a society built on freedom, equality, mutual assistance, and love of mankind.
>
> *Jews:* To help the young form a full personality as a Jew who identifies himself with the heritage and destiny of his nation; is keenly aware of his uniqueness as a Jew; is keenly aware of the ties between the People of Israel and the Land of Israel, between the People of Israel and their State and the Jewish People in the Diaspora; and who has a sense of the common destiny and responsibility for his nation. To inculcate the values of Jewish culture by the practical and academic acquisition of this heritage, as it was crystallized in all the ethnic groups of the People of Israel until recent generations in their homeland and in the Diaspora. At the same time they should be exposed to the best cultural heritages of other nations and become familiar with the culture of the Arab minority.

The suggested goals for Arab education were repeatedly criticized by Arab and Jewish scholars. One of the main points of the criticism was that they gave no recognition, implicit or explicit, to the fact that the Arabs in Israel are a national minority and an integral part of the Palestinian people. Whereas the inculcation of national identity is the core of Jewish education, "Arab culture" and the "uniqueness of Israeli Arabs" form the basis of Arab education. The goals envision Arab pupils' aspiring to peace between Israel and its neighbors and to love of the homeland common to all citizens of the state; but these ideas are not found in the goals for Jewish pupils (Sarsour 1981).

It should be noted that after the Peled Committee report was published, the Minister of Education rephrased the suggested goals for Arab education, replacing "love of the country shared by all its citizens" with "love of the country" (Ministry of Education 1977). This was a retreat to the spirit of the former goals, according to which Arab pupils are educated to love the country as the homeland of the Jewish people and not as their own. By contrast, the proposed goals for the Jewish sector were promulgated without change. So while Arab pupils are not allowed to be educated to be genuine partners in the State of Israel, Jewish pupils are educated to love Israel as their homeland and as the state of the Jewish people everywhere. Nevertheless, the report of the Peled Committee served as a starting point for reformulating the curricula for the Arab schools (*Hinnukh mevugarim be-yisrael*, August 1977: 6). But the changes that have taken place in this context still fall far short of meeting the needs of the Arab schools.

Aims of the Curricula

The asymmetric goals for Arab and Jewish education are reflected in the specific aims for various subjects, including history, language, civics, and religion. Below we shall briefly analyze the goals and content of history and language study in Arab and Jewish schools, because these subjects are most oriented to shaping pupils' identity and orientation. The following conclusions, which have been published elsewhere, are based on a comprehensive longitudinal analysis of the history curriculum over the span of fifty years.

In the above-mentioned articles we have presented an overview of the evolution of the history curriculum in Arab and Jewish schools in Israel. We have divided the main trends into three periods: 1950–1969, 1970–1989, and 1990 to the present.

A comparison of the goals of teaching history in Arab and Jewish schools reveals a clear alignment with the official goals mentioned earlier. In the latter, the emphasis is on the Jewish national content; but this topic is totally neglected in the Arab curricula. Arab pupils are taught that the "culture of mankind is the result of the combined efforts of the nations of the world," while Jewish pupils learn that the Jewish people have played a central role in shaping this culture of mankind. The value of Jewish-Arab co-existence, though with the Jews in the dominant role, is inculcated in Arab pupils by repeated emphasis on the common role played by Jews and Arabs in history and the shared destiny of the two peoples. Co-existence is totally ignored for Jewish pupils and the Arabs are conflated with the other nations. Moreover, Arab pupils are supposed to learn about the importance of the State of Israel for the Jewish people, not for both Jews and Arabs. These facts are translated in the division of the history curriculum.

A comparison of the successive editions of the curricula reveals a number of changes in both the general and the specific goals, especially in Arab schools: a curriculum with absolutely no Arab national content in the 1950s, one that refers to fostering identification with the Arab nation in the 1970s, and finally identification with the Arab nation and Palestinian people in the 1990s. Of course these goals are presented in a balanced fashion that emphasizes in the same breath the goal of fostering identification with the State of Israel and its citizens, with no reference to the nature of the state.

The Arab-Israeli and Israeli-Palestinian conflict, which stands at the center of the curriculum for Jewish schools, is presented in a one-sided fashion that corresponds to the Jewish-Zionist narrative, with no expression of the Palestinian or pan-Arab narrative. By contrast, the history curriculum for Arab schools refers to the conflict in a balanced fashion, offering a dry presentation of the historical facts from the perspectives of both the Jewish people and the Palestinian Arab people.

It should be indicated that a new history curriculum in history has been introduced to both Jewish and Arab schools in the late 1990s, in the wake of the Israel-Palestinian Oslo agreement. We have analyzed this curriculum in a series of publications, which have been published elsewhere (see Al-Haj, 1995, 1998, 2001). Hereafter we will briefly present the main conclusions.

A careful analysis of the goals and history textbooks in Jewish and Arab schools reveals some changes in the values presented to students. The declared aims refer to very important educational values, such as fostering judgment of historical events on the basis of humane and ethical values and fostering understanding and tolerance of the feelings, traditions, and ways of life of other peoples and nations (Ministry of Education, 1998:10). But after stating these liberal generalities the curriculum in practice fails to relate to a cardinal point— the form in which the Arab-Israeli and Israel-Palestinian conflict and the various and contradictory narratives about this conflict are to be considered. In fact, the only innovation with regard to values is in the goals for Arab schools: "Fostering a sense of affiliation with the Palestinian Arab people and the Arab people on one hand, and with the State of Israel and its citizens on the other" (Ministry of Education, 1999: 8–9).

However, that "fostering a sense of affiliation with the Palestinian Arab people" is accompanied by fostering a sense of affiliation "with the State of Israel and its citizens," with no reference to the nature of the State of Israel and the status of its Arab citizens (Ministry of Education, 1999: 8-9). Consciously or unconsciously, then, Arab students are called on to "enhance the sense of belonging to the state of Israel and its Israeli citizens" as a Jewish state and not as a bi-national state, a state of all its citizens or a multicultural democracy.

What is more, one of the key goals in the curriculum for Jewish schools is "recognition of the role of the state in the life of society and fostering a desire for active participation in shaping its destiny" (Ministry of Education 1998: 12). This section, which is missing from the curriculum for Arab schools, aims at perpetuating the status quo that internalizes Jewish students' perception that Israel is a Jewish state, not a civil state shared by Jews and Arabs. Unlike Jewish students, Arab students are not called upon to participate actively in shaping the destiny of the state and to feel full members thereof (see Al-Haj, 2001).

Language

The asymmetric goals and contents of the history curriculum in Arab and Hebrew schools are also to be found in the Hebrew and Arabic language curricula. In Arab schools, Hebrew is a mandatory subject from third grade till the end of high school. Both the linguistic and cultural aspects are taught—to some extent in even more depth than Arabic is taught. The aims of teaching Hebrew in Arab schools emphasize the exposure of Arab students to the culture and heritage of the Jewish people: "To open the way for the Arab pupil to become acquainted with Jewish culture and its values, past and present; to facilitate his understanding of the cultural and social life of the Jewish population in Israel" (Al-Haj 1995: 131).

As with history, there is also a great asymmetry in the teaching of language and literature, in both official goals and content. In Jewish schools, teaching Hebrew is used as a vehicle for national revival, reinforcement of national identity, and fostering of Jewish dignity, while the goal of teaching Arabic in Arab schools is purely technical, focusing on literacy, and devoid of national content. Perhaps more striking is that, although Hebrew is taught in Arab schools as a second language, the goals of the curriculum are not technical.

Hebrew language and literature are rather used to "open the way for the Arab pupil to become acquainted with Jewish culture and its values, past and present; to facilitate his understanding of the culture and social life of the Jewish population in Israel." In other words, the Hebrew language occupies a more central role in Arab schools than Arabic does itself (see Al-Haj 1995, 1998).

While the teaching of Hebrew in Arab schools is oriented mainly to deepen bicultural and bilingual education, the aim of teaching Arabic in Hebrew schools is mainly technical—to provide students with a basic knowledge of the Arabic language in order to satisfy instrumental needs (Al-Haj, 1998). The aims for the teaching of the Arabic language in the Hebrew schools are stated as follows:

1. Learning Arabic as a living language
2. Acquiring an instrument for communicating with Arabic speakers
3. Basic familiarity with Arabic newspapers and literature.
4. Acquiring basic ideas about the life of Arabs and their culture.

(Ministry of Education, 1975: 2).

The comparison between how Hebrew is taught to Arab students and how Arabic is taught to Jewish students is even more striking when it comes to the methods used in Arab and Jewish schools. In Arab schools, pupils learn Hebrew through the Bible, the Mishna, and Aggada, and by systematic study of classical and modern Hebrew literature. All this is clearly oriented to reinforce the positive image of the Hebrew language and culture and to inculcate in Arab pupils the Jewish right to Eretz Israel. In contrast, Jewish pupils learn Arabic mainly through the media and "street language" (Al-Haj 1996). Intentionally or unintentionally, this may reinforce the negative image that most Jewish pupils already have of Arabs.

It should be noted that the teaching of Arabic in the Jewish schools has been oriented from the very beginning toward "security needs" with a central aim to preparing the new generation of intelligent forces and liaisons in the Israeli military forces with the Arab population (Al-Haj, 1998).

In 1994, a new curriculum was introduced for Arabic in Hebrew schools. The stated aim of this curriculum was mainly technical: "create a change in the methods of teaching Arabic in the senior high classes of Hebrew schools and to contribute to promoting the prestige and the professional level of those involved in it." (Ministry of Education, 1994: 6). According to the new curriculum, students first study classic Arabic and then spoken Arabic, while in the senior classes of the high school both classic and spoken Arabic are combined (ibid).

The specific goals of the new curriculum just reiterate the technical-instrumental approach of the Ministry of Education in teaching Arabic in the Hebrew schools. Among the seven goals, only one relates to providing students with a knowledge of the Arabs' history and culture and of the Muslim religion. The other six sections emphasize the knowledge of Arabic as an instrument for communication in order to enable students to read Arabic newspapers and understand radio and TV broadcasting in Arabic (Ministry of Education, 1994: 7). Unlike Hebrew curriculum for Arab schools, which aims at strengthening the appreciation of the Arab pupil for the Hebrew heritage and culture, in the Arabic curriculum for Hebrew schools there is no mentioning of such a goal.

Conclusions

In this paper an attempt has been made to analyze formal education among the Palestinians in Israel. We have traced the main quantitative and qualitative developments in this regard and, we have also addressed the barriers that retard the role of education as a catalyst for social change.

Our analysis shows that there has been a considerable expansion of the participation of the Palestinians in the education system over time at the different levels. Also, education has served to bridge the gap between various social groups within the Palestinians themselves, mainly between men and women.

However, there is still a wide gap between expectations and the real situation. Our analysis highlighted the contradictory expectations of the Palestinian community and the Israeli establishment as to the role of the education system. While Palestinians have seen education as a source of empowerment, the Israeli establishment has utilized the education system as a mechanism of social control. In this sense, education has been used as an "adaptive system," through which the ruling group aimed at controlling the entire population and maintaining traditional structures and patterns of interaction. Given this state of contradictory expectations between official policy and the Palestinian community, the development of any national consciousness among the latter has been perceived as threatening to the interests of the dominant group and leading toward instability. Moreover, the Israeli establishment has attempted to delegitimize Arab and Palestinian nationalism and to use the education system as an instrument for legitimizing the official-Zionist ideology of the state of Israel, alongside the transmission of vague universal values.

At the same time, the strengthening of the national ethos occupies a major place in the school curricula among the Jewish majority. In addition, the Arab-Israeli and Israeli-Palestinian conflict that stands at the center of the curriculum for Jewish schools is presented in a one-way fashion that corresponds to the Jewish-Zionist narrative, with no expression of the Palestinian or pan-Arab narrative.

We may conclude, therefore, that the education system in Israel reflects the asymmetric nature of Jewish-Arab relations and the ethno-national political culture of the state. In this sense, policy toward Arab education reflects the general policy toward Arabs, which is affected by the contradictory elements in the character of the state being democratic and ethno-national at the same time and strongly affected by security considerations and militaristic culture. Such policy has been based on a tight system of control of administration, resources, teachers and curricula of the education system among Arabs. A comparison between curriculum in Jewish and Arab schools shows that educational contents in Israel have never been based on a genuine holistic multicultural ideology. It has rather been oriented to furnish one- sided "co-existence", based on the superiority of the majority and the internalizing by the minority of its inferior status.

References

Abu-Saad, Ismael. 2001. Education as a Tool for Control vs. Development among Indigenous People: The Case of Bedouin Arabs in Israel. *Hagar: International Social Science Review*, 2(2): 241-259.

Al-Haj, Majid. (1995). *Education, Empowerment and Control: The Case of the Arabs in Israel*. New York: SUNY.

Al-Haj, Majid. (1996). *Education of Arabs in Israel, Control and Social Change* (Hebrew). Jerusalem: Magnes Press.

Al-Haj, Majid (1998). Multicultural Education in Israel in Light of the Peace Process. *In* Menachim Mautner, Avi Sagi and Ronin Shamir (eds.), *Multiculturalism in a Democratic and Jewish State*, pp. 703-713. Tel-Aviv University: Ramut (Hebrew).

Al-Haj, Majid. (2002). Multiculturalism in deeply divided societies: The Israeli Case. *International Journal of Intercultural Relations 26*: 169-183.

Al-Haj, Majid and Henry Rosenfeld. 1990. *Arab local government in Israel*. Boulder, San Francisco and London: Westview Press.

Amara, Muhammad, and Abd al-Rahman Mari. 1999. *Issues in Linguistic Education Policy in Arab Schools in Israel*. Givat Haviva: Institute for Peace Studies (Hebrew).

Badran, Nabil. 1969. Education and Modernization in Palestine 1918-1948. Palestine Monograph, No. 63. Beirut: Palestine Liberation Organization Research Center.

Benor, J.L. 1951. The Arab Education in Israel. *Hamizrach Hehadash, 3*, 1(9): 1-8 (Hebrew).

Hinukh Mevogarim Biesrael, August 1977, p. 6 (Hebrew).

Lewin-Epstein, Noah. (1990). The Arab Economy in Israel: Growing Population, Jobs Mismatch, Discussion Paper No. 14:90. Tel Aviv: The Pinhas Sapir Center for Development, Tel Aviv University

Lewin-Epstein, Noah, Majid Al-Haj, and Moshe Semyonov. (1994). *Arabs in Israel in the Work Market* (Heb.). Jerusalem, Floersheimer Institute for Policy Studies.

Lustick, Ian S. 1980. *Arabs in the Jewish State: Israel's control of a national minority.* Austin, Texas: University of Texas Press.

Mari, Sami. 1978. *Arab Education in Israel*. Syracuse, N.Y.: Syracuse University Press.

Mazawi, Andre. 1994. Palestinian Arabs in Israel: Educational Expansion, Social Mobility and Political Control. *Compare 24*(3): 277–284.

Ministry of Education and Culture. 1998. History Curriculum for Grades Seven to Nine in the State Stream. Second revised edition. Jerusalem: Ministry of Education and Culture, Pedagogic Secretariat (Hebrew).

Ministry of Education and Culture. 1999. The History Curriculum for Arab High Schools. Jerusalem: Ministry of Education and Culture, Pedagogic Secretariat (Hebrew).

Nakhleh, Khalil. 1977. The Goals of Education for Arabs in Israel. *New Outlook* (April-May): 29-35.

Peres, Yochanan, Avishai Ehrlich and Nira Yuval-Davis. 1968. National Education for Arab Youth in Israel: A Comparative Analysis of Curricula. *Megamot 17*, 1: 26-36 (Hebrew). Also in *The Jewish Journal of Sociology, 12*, 2 (December, 1970): 147-164.

Statistical Abstract of Israel. (1972) (No. 23); (1977) (No. 28): (1982) (No. 33): (1990) (No. 41): (1991) (No. 42): (1995)(No. 46); 1996 (No. 47); 2000 (No. 51). 2001 (No. 52); 2003 (No. 54).

Smooha, S. 1990. Minority Status in an Ethnic Democracy: The Status of the Arab Minority in Israel. *Ethnic and Racial Studies 13*(3): 389–413.

Tahir, Jamil. (1985). An Assessment of Palestinian Human Resources: Higher Education and Manpower. *Journal of Palestine Studies 14*(53): 32–53.

Wergift, Nurit. 1989. A School for Discrimination. *Kul Hair.* Jerusalem. June 2, 1989 (Hebrew).

Between Town and Village: Continuity and Change in Arab Localities in Israel

Rassem Khamaisi

Introduction

If you were to ask an Arab in Israel, "Where do you live?", a common response may be, "I live in a village called…". The term "village" will most likely be prefixed to the name of the locality. An average visitor to such a locality however, would more likely call it a "town", based, for example, on its size and appearance. Whether to call an area a town or a village is both a practical and theoretical question, and is posed globally. The criteria for making such a distinction range from individuals' behaviour to community relations, functional activities, or means of livelihood. Urbanization as a physical process takes place sometimes with and sometimes without an increase in *urbanism*, or urban culture (as defined by Palen, 1981).

This paper discusses the phenomenon of urbanization with *ruralism* (rural culture), using the example of Arab localities in Israel. A question raised in the paper, for example, is why Arabs in Israel usually refer to themselves as villagers, although most lead (or wish to lead) urban lives. To understand this phenomenon, this paper examines the process of urbanization in Arab localities, and concludes that various factors led to a preference of ruralism over urbanism.

The paper begins with a general theoretical framework on rural-urban definitions. Following this is a discussion of urbanization among the Arabs in Israel. This deals with limitations on migration, and with planning policies to increase urbanization in Arab localities. The third part of the paper addresses the question of why ruralism prevails in urbanized areas. Finally, the paper concludes with the implications of this phenomenon.

The paper is based upon a literature review, interviews with 30 local government representatives, and the experience of preparing Master Plans for 20 localities. Preparation of Master Plans was a participatory process and involved 15 meetings of 10-15 people each.

Theoretical Framework

Classical geography and sociology literature clearly distinguishes between villages and towns according to numerous variables, including population, land use, political and administrative centrality, community relations, individual behavior, and social, economic and cultural activities. A village, for example, is traditionally defined as a small community, based partly on kinship, primarily involved in agriculture and following a traditional way of life. The classical definition of a town refers to a large area containing numerous communities, with various ways of life, and primarily dependent on non-agricultural activities such as services, handcrafts and industry. The archetypical town functions as a center for several villages, receiving agricultural products while providing services, markets, and an administrative center.

In contrast to such clear-cut definitions, recent literature gives more attention to processes resulting in hybrid localities, such as suburbanization (Gonen, 1995), in which rural communities are formed on the basis of non-agricultural economic activities. The mid-1900s saw the growth not only of the suburb but also other kinds of localities, such as the hamlet, metropolis and megalopolis. Recent literature, therefore, now defines a spectrum of localities, and provides a range of topology and morphology, dealing with localities' characteristics, roles and functions. The industrial revolution, population growth, and the recent revolution in information and communication technology have all played a part in blurring the definition between village and town (Allen and You, 2002).

Small localities, including villages, are formed in three ways, through population growth, urban-rural migration (suburbanization), or geopolitical planning. Most villages are formed through population growth. Suburbs develop when town-dwellers search in rural areas for an improved standard of living, improved residential conditions (large house, large plot of land, low population density), and a small community (Connel, 1974). These suburbs, or "community localities" (*yeshve khelaty* in Hebrew) (Applebaum and Newman, 1989) are populated mainly by urban dwellers, dependent on nearby towns and cities for employment, services and cultural activities. Residents commute to towns and cities (Gonen, 1995). The third and final way of forming small localities is through spatial planning. National policy goals may, for example, seek to disperse the population, implement a project of internal colonialism, utilize land resources for agricultural activities, limit migration between localities, and organize localities' spatial distribution within the state. Localities formed through these two latter processes, suburbanization and state planning, both look like "villages", despite being populated by urban residents, and being formed in ways contradictory to natural village formation—in which a small agricultural community develops self-sufficiently, and in which migration is rural-urban, not urban-rural.

Town formation can also be either organic or planned. Organic processes involve a village growing in population until it becomes a town, or the integration of several villages to become a larger locality (village urbanization). Planned processes involve establishing and building new towns, as part of national spatial planning and development policy (Khamaisi, 1996).

Urbanization involves changes in population size and area, economic activities, and the built environment. It may also involve urbanism, that is, cultural changes in community relations, individuals' behaviour, and production and consumption patterns. Urban characteristics include individualism, ambition, consumer culture, and non-agricultural forms of income. Yet "urban" individuals may reside in rural areas, and vice versa, and each rural or urban area is unique, with its own "spirit".

While (cultural) urbanism is usually associated with (physical) urbanization, urbanism can also be found in rural areas. This is increasingly the case globally, where factors such as the rise in information and communication technology have reduced the dichotomy between rural and urban culture. While these global trends can be found in Arab localities in Israel, these localities also possess qualities unique to their situation, discussed in the following sections of this paper.

Arab Localities in Israel: Truncated Urbanization

Urbanization in Palestine began long before the British Mandate period (1923-1948), but increased rapidly in this period. During the Mandate period, administrative services, employment opportunities and socio-cultural activities were concentrated in urban areas. Rural-urban migration increased and the middle class expanded. In 1945, about one third of the Arab population lived in cities and towns. Overall, the Arabs in Palestine lived in about 963 villages and towns, and the network of settlements was diversifying. Palestinians had the freedom to live in the kind of locality they wished. Urbanization patterns matched those in other Middle Eastern societies and in the world in general. Palestinian cities and towns with a history of natural urbanization included Jaffa, Jerusalem, Jericho, Nablus, Acre, and others.

A clear distinction between village and town existed, as in other parts of the world. Urban areas housed the upper and middle classes, and functioned as service and market centers for the surrounding villages. Unlike other parts of the world, urbanization took place without industrialization. Villagers migrated to cities and towns, which absorbed them and consequently grew in size and area. Population growth was limited initially (Persson, 1990), but grew at the beginning of the twentieth century. Villages grew slowly; their built up areas were compact, introverted, clustered and layered; villages continued a traditional way of life.

The 1948 war ended rural-urban migration. Arab towns were converted to Jewish towns; urban Arab populations were evicted and Arab majorities became Arab minorities. The United Nations partition plan of 1947 (Resolution 181) had placed many Arab villages inside the proposed "Arab state"; the war of 1948 resulted in these villages being located on the inside periphery of the 1949 Rhodes Armistice line (the "Green Line"). Rural-urban migration was halted, and village populations grew over time. The Arab urban population was largely expelled, resulting in a loss of the upper and middle classes and a disproportionately high level of absenteeism. Thus, the result was a mostly rural Arab population on the peripheries of the new state, and a loss of urban centers—a truncated urbanization process (Gonen and Khamaisi, 1992).

Why Did Rural-Urban Migration End?

At present, urbanisation in Arab localities is primarily due to population growth, estimated at 3-4% from the 1950s to 1990s (CBC, 2003). Palestinians remaining after the 1948 war numbered 156,000; they now number one million people (excluding those in East Jerusalem; statistics from 2002) (CBC, 2003). Yet despite changes in population size, no changes have occurred in population distribution. The geographic patterns created by the war of 1948 have remained intact until today, with only small and localized changes. This freezing of movement is a result of governmental spatial policy, which aimed to concentrate the Arabs in as little territory as possible—best illustrated in the case of the "Bedouin" in northern and southern Israel. Arabs are now concentrated in three peripheral regions—the Galilee, the "small Triangle", and the northeast Negev desert—as well as in five towns (once Arab, now mixed): Jaffa, Haifa, Acre, Lydd and Ramla. Rural-urban migration is very limited. The little migration that does occur is due to inter-village marriage, internal refugees joining their relatives, and forced migration of the Bedouin according to governmental orders. All this gives rise to the question: why did rural-urban migration end? Several explanations exist (Mear-Brodneis, 1983), some of which are presented below.

A. **1948-1966 enclosure period:** After the war of 1948, the first Israeli government divided the Arab population into five regions, and imposed on each a military governor (Jiryis, 1966). Until 1966, the military governor was an effective instrument of the state to spatially control the Arab population: concentrating the population and forbidding movement without possession of an Israeli-issued permit. Although restrictions lightened somewhat in the mid-1950s, the effects remained profound. Today, movement is extremely limited among Arab localities and between Arab and Jewish localities. These restrictions accelerated Arab urbanization, particularly among the "Bedouin", who faced a policy of re-settlement into planned urban localities (Falah, 1989).

B. **Ideology of segregation:** The military nature of the Zionist movement since the early 1880s created an atmosphere of antagonism that has remained until the present, embodied in slogans such as "We are here, and the Other, there". Although Arabs and Jews may work in the same spaces and live in the same towns, they continue to reside in segregated neighborhoods.

C. **Communal support:** Kinship ties in a *hamula,* or extended family, provide social, economic and political support. Village hamulas are especially important where feelings of belonging to the central government are weak, and civil society is limited. Hamula importance has also increased since the establishment of local governments in Arab rural localities, and the replacement of the traditional leader, *Mukhtar,* with an elected mayor and council members (Rosenfild and Al-Haj, 1990). In general, villagers prefer to remain in rural areas among their hamula, rather than migrate to urban areas where family networks are cut off.

D. **Insecure land tenure:** Within five years of its establishment, the Israeli state had confiscated large portions of Arab land through military, political and "legal" maneuvers (Jiryis, 1966, Lustick, 1980, Kretzmer, 2002, Khamaisi, 2003). Currently, therefore, Arabs are reluctant to migrate for fear of land confiscations and inheritance loss. Given the instability of non-agricultural economic activities, land and agriculture remain crucial sources of income.

E. **Migrant labour:** Arabs living in rural areas often commute to work in Jewish localities. They provide labour for construction, industry and services. The commute to Jewish localities may be shorter from rural than urban areas; and the village—as mentioned above—offers a social support network.

F. **Economic constraints:** The social support network above also provides economic security, and rural living costs are lower than those in urban areas.

G. **Discrimination and minority status:** Life in urban areas was controlled by the military until the mid-1950s (as mentioned above, Arabs were forcibly kept in enclosed areas). The Arabs remaining in urban areas after 1948 were made minorities, and suffered difficult housing conditions. They were mostly lower class urban residents, joined by refugees from surrounding villages. Today, urban "mixed" areas continue to be internally segregated into Arab and Jewish neighborhoods. In the aftermath of the war, Arab migration to Jewish towns was unthinkable; now, Jewish opposition prevents Arab in-migration to those towns.

H. **Forced migration into villages / Social barriers to intra-rural migration:** Between 1948 and the present, very little migration has taken place between Arab localities. The limited migration that has occurred has mainly been forced migration, specifically, Israel's internment and resettlement of internal refugees into villages (Al-Haj, 1988). Unforced migration, however, has hardly occurred. Nazareth and Shefar'am, for example, were defined by the Ottoman Empire as towns, and in 1948 absorbed refugees and Bedouins—yet they never grew into large towns. One of the reasons for limited migration between Arab localities is the difficulty in gaining social acceptance in a new location. Standards of living are roughly equal between localities, yet newcomers have a somewhat lower standing compared to longstanding resident families.

For the reasons explained above, out-migration from Arab localities is still very limited despite improvements in standards of living and ongoing urbanization. Population growth and urbanization are due to natural increase, not immigration. In 2002, 24 of the 116 Arab localities had populations over 10,000—in all 24 localities, the emigration balance was low (see Table 1).

Table 1 shows that little migration is occurring within the main Arab localities in Israel. The only movement taking place is mainly from internal refugees and Bedouins, marriages among localities, movement of land "absentees" from villages in order to rent or purchase apartments in Jewish towns, and changes of address. Nazareth, which according to its size and area would be expected to absorb in-migration, performs the opposite function—its population migrates out to surrounding localities, such as Reine, Yafi, Shefar'am and upper Nazareth (Khamaisi, 2003). Rahat, shown in Table 1 as a centre for in-migration, is in reality the result of forced resettlement; a policy of centralization has transferred the Arabs of the Negev into seven urban centers, of which Rahat is the largest.

The main factor hindering Arab movement is the scarcity of residential land. In some localities, such as Shefar'am and Reine, landowners sell residential land

Table 1: Emigration balance in main* Arab localities, 1999-2001

Localities	Years		
	1999	2000	2001
Abu Sinan	26	47	-48
Umm Al-Fahem	-36	18	-133
Baqa Al-Gharbiyye	38	61	51
Judeide—Maker	27	-76	67
Daliyat Al-Karmel	9	12	23
Tayibe	1	47	51
Tire	35	82	58
Tamra	-5	53	28
Shefar'am	206	154	180
Yafi'	78	54	241
Yarka	-50	16	2
Kafar Kanna	-36	21	-91
Kafar Manda	-92	-103	-39
Kafar Qasem	33	76	54
Kafar Qara	41	39	-1
Mughar	-66	-43	-67
Majd Al-Kurum	-5	-3	33
Nazareth	-490	-208	-549
Sakhnin	-15	-31	-150
Arrabe	-65	54	4
Ar'ara	-12	10	19
Qalansawe	56	64	12
Rahat	-30	82	224
Reine	74	35	68

* Main localities are defined here as those where population in 1999 exceeded 10,000.

Source: Collected from Israeli Central Bureau of Statistics and Ministry of the Interior; *Local Governments in Israel, Physical Data, Special Serials No. 1170, 1186, 1203.*

(land allocated for housing, or land that has the potential to be allocated for housing) to residents of other localities to alleviate the severe housing shortage. Patterns of movement show a tendency for this to be more prevalent among

Christians than Muslims; in general among the Arabs in Israel, Christians tend to be more mobile and more urbanized than Muslims.

Characteristics of Urbanization in Arab Localities

As described above, urbanization among Palestinians began before the establishment of the state of Israel. Urbanization involved the migration from villages in the periphery into Palestinian towns in the center, such as Jaffa, Haifa and Jerusalem. Geographic mobility led to functional mobility and structural changes. Upon the establishment of the state of Israel, these processes of urbanization were reversed. The new state brought not only a western style of development, but also territorial policies. Arabs were subject to land confiscation, spatial control and political domination by the Jewish majority. While they shared somewhat in the growth of the economy, they suffered discrimination and widening inequality.

In the 1950s, economic growth in Israel was partly shared by the Arabs in Israel—although they were not the intended beneficiaries—and led in the 1960s to a slow resumption of urbanization. This new urbanization, however, took different forms and operated in different ways from the past, and involved many physical and functional changes.

Among these changes was the adoption of material and instrumental modernity—as part of adopting a western way of life—while simultaneously preserving traditional customs. Arab localities changed in physical structure and features. The style of housing changed. Their economies became based on nonagricultural activities. Localities' structure shifted from being compact and dense to being dispersed, with lower density areas extending from the dense core. These changes could be seen across localities; similar processes were occurring in all localities and bringing about similar results. In the past 50 years, most localities have doubled in population over six times, and the residential area of each has doubled over 12 times. Yet very limited migration has occurred. The population growth has been absorbed within each locality, leading to expanded residential areas and an increase in housing density—all resulting in a lack of public areas, including roads. The key outcome is that the limited development in Arab localities has not met the needs of the population. In this sense, a large gap can be seen when comparing Arab and Jewish localities.

Before 1948, rural-urban migration ensured a difference between rural and urban areas; villages and towns were distinct from one another. After 1948, the difference between rural and urban areas was diminished. Localities were less distinguishable as villages and towns, not only because of their characteristics as a whole, but also because of the characteristics and behavior of individuals within them.

Researchers have described these processes in various terms. Mear-Brodnes (1969) used "detained urbanization" to describe development in Arab villages. Kipnis (1976) used "latent urbanization" to distinguish between urbanized and urbanizing areas. Khamaisi (2000) used "selective and misshapen urbanization" in a study on the absence of towns' effects on Arab behavior. All these terms refer to the truncation of urbanization that occurred following 1948. After 1948, for example, Nazareth was a small town that had absorbed the refugees of demolished villages in the area. Now, its population is not very different in size from some of the large villages. Previous villages—such as Umm Al-Fahem, Sakhnin, and Tamra—have changed in status to become "municipalities", yet their cultural behavior and infrastructure are reminiscent of villages. This is discussed further below.

Urbanization Through Official Spatial Planning

Central planning and governmental policy has accelerated urbanization among the Arabs, without restructuring the settlement network. It has decreased the number of Arab villages and small localities. Planning and policy has—for the Jewish population only—increased land ownership and control, and dispersed them to all peripheral areas in order to gain a Jewish majority in every region of the new state (Hill, 1980). For the Arabs who remained after 1948, planning and policy has reduced their land ownership and living space, concentrated them in a small area of territory, and rendered them fragmented minorities both geographically and ethnically (Khamaisi, 1990, Falah, 1992). The equation directing Israeli spatial policy has been "maximum territory" and "minimum [Arab] population" (Masalha, 1997). To implement this geopolitical and geo-demographic equation, the Israeli government confiscated land from the indigenous Arabs (Abu-Sitta, 2000). Arab-owned land, especially that of the Palestinians made refugees in 1948, was transferred to the state. All public land was transferred to the state. The landscape was transformed; space was "Judaized" (Falah, 1996). All tiers of planning policy contributed to the urbanization of Arab localities. Through urbanization, successive Israeli governments have achieved Zionist goals and the control of space.

The imposition of Israeli military governors in Arab localities was an effective tool of spatial control. It enclosed areas, limited Arab movement, concentrated them in small territories, confiscated their land, and created economic dependency (Jiryis, 1966, Lustick, 1980). For instance, in 1948, Arab Bedouins in the Negev were concentrated in an area called the "Syage region" in the northeast Negev. In 1964, the government planned to concentrate them in seven new urban localities, including Tel-Shava and the above-mentioned Rahat. Haifa's Arabs (those not made refugees) were concentrated in the Wade Nesnas area. Meanwhile, the military governor prohibited internal refugees from returning to their villages and lands. The government refused to return confiscated lands to their Arab owners. All these limitations—restricting movement of Arab Bedouins and concentrating them in only a small number of villages—comprise a policy of forced urbanization. Such a policy of urbanization concentrates only on physical, territorial and functional aspects, and ignores socio-cultural and behavioral aspects of urbanization. It operates through spatial plans at the central, district and local levels.

Governmental policy to promote urbanization is best illustrated in physical plans. The first physical plan, the Sharon Plan of 1951, envisioned two processes occurring among the Arabs of Israel. First, a reduction of natural population increase. Second, a shift in economic base from agricultural to nonagricultural activities (Sharon, 1951). Another national plan anticipated much migration from Arab villages and the periphery, toward urban centers in the central coastal area (Khamaisi, 1990). The national and regional plans, prepared—top-down—by Jewish planners, presume that the migration patterns among the Arabs in Israel will match those in other countries, including Arab countries. In addition, the plans aim to reduce the number of Arabs living in the periphery, and to weaken their attachment to the land, by promoting migration to towns and by increasing their dependence on non-agricultural and service activities. These aims continue to guide planning and policy toward the Arabs. The two most recent national plans, Number 31 and Number 35, assume accelerated urbanization among Arab localities, and suggest urban centers for implementing a policy of selective urbanization. These national spatial policies guide district-level policies, and thereby impose the policy of urbanization.

National and regional planning policy is implemented through local, highly restrictive planning policy. To limit the development and expansion of Arab villages, a local outline plan is prepared for every recognized village. This leads effectively to rapid urbanization. The explicit goal of local plans is to improve the standard of living among Arabs, by copying and using modern, western, urban planning, and imposing it on traditional, eastern, village communities. The implicit goal, however, is to reduce the territory of Arab localities. Urbanization, because of its positive connotations, is a way to take land from its owners while purporting to help them. Furthermore, in urban localities, the government can concentrate people, reduce its expenditure on developing and maintaining infrastructure, and increase housing density. Finally, urbanization limits population increase, and moves localities closer to the national goal of a Jewish demographic majority.

In 1957, the military government and the Ministry of Interior initiated a project called "Building Area" and began preparing outline plans to restrict the expansion of Arab villages. On the national and regional levels, the government demarcated planning and development policies to disperse the Jewish population to the peripheral regions of the Negev, the Galilee and Jerusalem. The population dispersal policy promoted "ethnic occupation" of the periphery where most Arabs were living. The government set up public committees to examine what it called "illegal housing". These committees recommended preparing outline plans for Arab localities to limit housing expansion, increase housing densities ("fill in" housing areas), and increase urbanization.

A cursory examination of the subsequent outline plans reveals key similarities: all of them pursue a "fill in" policy that increases the density, rather than expanding the area of residential zones. Most of the land in each plan is allocated for housing. Buildings can be up to 400 m^2 in area, four floors high, and are allowed about 144%-164% of building rights. The roads network is oriented in one direction only, and the percentage of land allocated for public use is very small. The majority of the planned area is privately-owned land. The plans appear to have been prepared by a single planner, and copied from village to village with little localization or adaptation.

The reality of community development in Arab villages is far removed from the official plans prepared and approved by the planning institution. The predicted migration, which was to take place from villages in the periphery to cities in the central coastline, did not happen. The government spent little of the allocated resources for improvement of roads and sewage infrastructure. The absence of land for public purposes led to an absence of public facilities in the villages that were growing into towns. Housing was provided through self-housing, meaning that each family built its own house on private land plots. Families in general did not use the full right of building given to them under the official plans. Some land-owners built houses without permits, because their lands had been excluded from the officially planned area and therefore were made ineligible for building permits. Some built housing on areas planned as roads, as resistance against the planned roads—their appeals having been refused by the planning institution. In many cases, only primitive and basic infrastructure was built following housing construction.

These realities, direct results of planning policy, culminated in a severe housing shortage in Arab localities. Infrastructure was weak, very little area was planned for development, homes were demolished because their owners were refused building permits from planning institutions, and entire villages were "unrecognized" by planners. Unrecognized villages, such as those in the Negev and the Galilee, were ignored by national and regional plans, and official policy sought to concentrate their residents in urban centers. In mixed cities (like Lydd) and occupied cities (like East Jerusalem), land use plans were used to achieve national, ethnic demographic goals, by allocating insufficient land—private or public—for development. A second strategy was to reduce the building rights on private lands, thereby making it impossible to obtain a permit for housing, and thus encouraging either a reduction in population or an increase in emigration.

Recently, in the last ten years, the Israeli government has proposed to address this housing shortage by allocating state land for housing. Yet the high-density building permits on such land only increase urbanization, and contradict entirely the current socio-cultural norms regarding housing. The self-housing approach will be rendered impossible. Affected areas include villages in the north (such as the recently "recognized" Kamane, Hosines and Ein Hode villages) and areas in the Negev, where the Bedouin population is largely traditional. The government representative has justified this policy of urbanization—directed exclusively at Arab localities—in terms of sustainability: Israel suffers from a land shortage. Yet most Jewish localities are villages (see Table 2). The number of Jewish localities increased from 771 in 1961 to 941 in 2002. Arab localities increased from 109 to 116, in the same period—and only because some villages gained recognition in the 1990s. . .in fact, no new villages were built. Meanwhile, about 50 Arab villages remain unrecognized.

Thus, the policy of urbanization has two sides, depending on national ethnic

Table 2: Distribution of localities in Israel by type and national affiliation at end of 2002

National Affiliation	Israeli state	Jews	Arabs*
Total	1057 (100%)	941 (89%)	116 (11%)
No. of urban localities	200 (18.9%)	111 (11.8%)	89 (76.7%)
No. of rural localities	857 (81.1%)	830 (88.2%)	27 (23.3%)**

* Arab localities here exclude mixed cities.
** This excludes an estimated 50 unrecognized villages.
Source: Israeli Central Bureau of Statistics (2003) *Statistical Abstract of Israel*, No. 54. Table 2.9 pp. 2-28.

affiliation. For Arab localities, planning institutions and relevant government ministries ask local and national representatives to shrink the allocated land for development, to promote high-rise building, and to place various obstacles in the path of development and expansion. Although national and district level plans suggest slight differences in building densities between small and large Arab localities, nevertheless local outline plans apply the same building densities, which effectively convert the villages into urban localities.

Urban planning policy suggests a transfer from agricultural activities to industry and services. This economic policy, echoed in local outline plans, creates a dependency of the Arab population on the state government, which is controlled by a Jewish majority.

Today, Arab localities resemble one another in the structure of their built environment, their labor force, their primary economic activities, and their social and community interactions. The strength of these similarities and lack of diversity is evidence that the policy of forced urbanization has deeply affected the structure and appearance of Arab localities.

In summary, ideological and geopolitical goals lie behind spatial planning and urbanization policies in Israel (Kipnis, 1987, Gertel and Law Yone, 1991). These policies have developed and crystallized amid a situation of national conflict between Arabs and Jews, which has territorial, geographic, demographic, cultural and political dimensions and implications. The vision of the Zionist movement and Israeli government to transform the demography, geography and culture of the country continues to cope with Arab resistance. The allocation of land and resources is part of this larger conflict (Zureik, 1978, Yiftachel, 1992, Falah, 1989, Yiftachel, 1997).

A clear example is the contrast between Arab and Jewish settlement structure and distribution that is a direct result of official spatial planning and development policy. While official policy enhances and expands the number and distribution of Jewish settlements—including agriculture-based settlements—it reduces the number of Arab localities and urbanizes their villages.

Ruralism Amid Urbanization

The policy of urbanization is accompanied by economic and functional changes. Urbanization changes villages into towns through changes in population size, the provision and distribution of services, the locality's features and fabric, and primary economic activities. Arab localities are no longer based on agriculture; less than 5% of the labor force is employed in agriculture. Although Arab localities are subject to discriminatory government policies and high inequality compared to Jewish localities, they have nevertheless benefited marginally from the economic growth since 1948. Yet this has also generated tendencies toward consumer culture and altered demands for goods and services. The Arabs in Israel, therefore, are resuming the urbanization process after its truncation in 1948, but in different ways and under different circumstances.

One of the distinguishing features of this resuming urbanization is related to the restrictions on geographic and functional mobility. Urbanization is occurring without the creation of new Arab urban centers or cores, which would function as administrative and cultural centers. Nazareth, which was predicted to become the center or "capital" of the Arab population in Israel, has not ended up in this role due to internal factors, governmental restrictions and imposed policy limitations.

Although various Arab villages have grown into towns, none have attracted immigration, and their residents continue to define themselves as villagers and to follow rural codes and norms. The question under discussion in this paper is why individuals and communities prefer to define themselves as rural villagers, despite their urban way of life and consumption patterns. In other words, why is urbanism so limited amid prevailing urbanization? Below are various possible explanations.

1. **The development of rural elites:** Arab communities in 1948 lost their political, cultural and economic elites. Following 1948, the Arab population was mainly village-based. As they worked to form a new upper class, they remained scattered in various regions and localities. The new elites did not concentrate on urban centers and did not trigger community mobilization. They used the traditional social structure in their localities to strengthen their position, and therefore did not develop a civil society that would enable social mobility outside of traditional rural structures.

2. **Forced segregation:** Movement restrictions have led to a segregation of space (including residential space) according to national and religious affiliations. Although no law separates localities by national affiliation, nevertheless, the national conflict and imposed spatial behaviors have enforced spatial segregation. As a result, current geographic patterns are the same as those created by the war of 1948. Arabs are concentrated in the same localities despite

doubling in number over six times since 1948. They continue to consider themselves villagers because they have never left the "village".

3. **Exclusion by the state:** The state of Israel was established by the Zionist movement as a Jewish state. Arabs are given citizenship as native people. The state supports Jewish settlement while restricting Arab functional mobility and participation in government, public service and policy-making circles. Opportunities for Arabs are limited at the local level; chances for integration and participation at the regional and national levels are even less. As a result, loyalty to the village is strengthened. Instead of the state or civil society, it is the *hamula*, or kinship network, that is increasingly seen as providing protection, securing interests, and preserving a feeling of belonging. Amid increasing competition for state and private resources, individuals use the hamula for socio-political and economic development. With constraints on participation at national and regional levels, and increasing competition at local levels, community members therefore rely on traditional, rural social norms and structures. In sum, the absence of national opportunities and functional mobility serves to strengthen localism and traditional behavior according to rural codes.

4. **Land confiscation:** Territory is one of the key sources of conflict between Israeli state institutions and the Arab population. Ruralism (rural culture) and the villager are more connected to the land. To protect their land, Arabs define themselves as villagers, despite the fact that agriculture is usually only a supplementary source of income, if a source at all. Ruralism is a way of coping with the state policy to confine Arab localities' territorial development. Ruralism is an expression of the need to connect to the land, to reduce the threat of leaving the land, and ultimately, to prevent its confiscation.

5. **Economic marginalisation:** Despite the policy to urbanize the Arab population to attain territorial and demographic goals, and despite the assumption that urbanization brings a higher standard of living, in reality, no job creation has been situated in Arab localities. Government and public institutions and industrial zones are not located in Arab localities, which continue to develop according to organic models and processes. Meanwhile, governmental initiatives and support are provided to Jewish "new towns" established between and adjacent to Arab localities such as Nazareth and Carmiel. The central government, therefore, has not given Arab localities the tools and mechanisms to be cities. Arab localities continue to depend upon Jewish localities for employment and governmental and public services—hence Arab localities persist in an organic and rural way of life.

6. **Socio-cultural belonging:** Limited emigration is partly due to the need for a feeling of belonging. Being a stranger in a large city, amid stark inequality, racism and social rejection, is far less preferable to ruralism, where individuals can feel rooted and accepted.

7. **Quality of life:** Most of the land within the official boundaries of outline plans is privately owned. Housing is provided through self-housing. Arabs prefer to live in a house with its own plot of land, where they can build gradually according to their financial capabilities. The cost of living and the cost of providing housing are lower in villages than cities. For financial and socio-

cultural reasons, therefore, people continue to reside in their communities and localities; they would rather preserve such a situation than urbanize.

8. **Fears for the future:** To be wary of unexpected change is normal. Among communities that have suffered in the past and face an uncertain future, such fears are likely to be even stronger. Rural Arab families feel committed to provide their children with land and housing. Thus, parents build homes for their children even while they are young; others purchase or retain land even if they are in financial need. Traditional families prefer to remain in the territory of their hamula, and refuse migration to other villages. The feelings of "small is beautiful" and of aversion to strangers are part of ruralism. Thus, retaining land for inheritance and reluctance to sell to outsiders both lead to a preservation of ruralism. The above observations were the result of experiences in preparing Master Plans for Arab localities.

Conclusion

This paper is a discussion of the anomalous urbanization among the Arabs in Israel. Despite urbanization and material change, mobility among the Arabs remains limited. Arabs prefer ruralism and organic development. Central government policy to urbanize Arab localities has not been supported by tools and mechanisms; instead, the opposite has occurred—Arabs suffer from discrimination and a scarcity of allocated resources, leading to feelings of exclusion.

The Arabs in Israel are undergoing different processes in comparison to other societies. National, regional and local spatial planning in Israel is dualistic, and discriminates on the basis of national and ethnic belonging. With respect to Arab localities, the policy strategy is to reduce the territorial base, increase the population density and concentrate the population, decrease the number and size of localities, and neglect the urban centers. The aim is to accelerate urbanization in order to serve territorial goals. The limited opportunities for rural-urban migration serve to widen inequality between Arab and Jewish localities.

While urbanization has led somewhat to increased development, the gap between Arab and Jewish localities remains large. The institutional and political discrimination causing this gap continues to this day. Thus, Arab localities are made dependent upon Jewish ones economically and for service provision. The policy for the Judaization of space has led to landscape change and has imposed foreign roles on Arab localities. All of the above comprises a policy of forced urbanization of Arab localities, who nevertheless persist in choosing ruralism to provide for their needs and to cope with (and reject) the policies of the central government.

Forced urbanization of Arab localities creates internal social problems, summarized by the gap between (physical) urbanization and (cultural) urbanism. The spatial physical structure is not planned or organized. The infrastructure and lack of services are results of unplanned developments. Finally, the ongoing forced urbanization of the Arab population is gradually forcing people to migrate between Arab localities, and from Arab localities to Jewish ones. While planning at the end of the 1990s was slightly modified to better suit localities, the goal of most outline plans remained to accelerate the urbanization process in Arab localities. What is now needed is a rethinking of planning policy, to make it more diverse, flexible, decentralized, and responsive to the needs of each community. Changes in policy should address the needs of Arab localities, rather than exacerbating them. Currently, the Arabs face new urbanization trends, which may alter the prevailing ruralism and promote mobilization.

Bibliography

Abo Sitts, S. 2000. *Confiscation of Palestinian Refugees Propriety and the Denial of Access to Private Propriety*, submitted to the social, Economic and Cultural Rights Committee, UN October.

Allen, A. and You, N., 2002. *Sustainable Urbanization*, London: DPU, UCL.

Al-Haj, M., 1988. The Arab Internal Refugees in Israel: The Emergence of a Minority within Minority, *Immigrants & Minorities*, 7(2), 149-165

Applebaum, L. and Newman, D., 1989. *Between Village and Suburban; New Settlement Patterns in Israel*. Rehovoth: Settlement Study Center.

Connel, J., 1974. The Metropolitan Village- Spatial and Social Processes in Discontinuous Suburbs. *In* Johanson, J. H. ed.. *Suburban Growth—Geographical Processes at the Edge of the Western City*, pp. 77-100. London: Wiley.

Gertel, S. and Law Yone, H. 1991. Participation Ideologies in Israeli planning, Environment and Planning C, *Government and Policy, 9*, 173-188.

Gonen, A. and Khamaisi, R. 1992. *Trends in the geographical distribution of the Arab population of Israel*. Jerusalem: The Floersheimer Institute for Policy Studies.

Gonen, A. 1995. *Between City and Suburban*. England: Avebury.

Falah, G. 1989. Israeli Judaization Policy in Galilee and its impact on Local Arab Urbanization, *Political Geography Quarterly, 8*, 229-253.

Falah, G. 1992. Land Fragmentation and Spatial Control in Nazareth Metropolitan Area, *Professional Geographer, 44*, 30-44.

Falah, G. 1996. The 1948 Israeli-Palestinian War and Its Aftermath: The Transformation and De-Signification of Palestine's Cultural Landscape, *Annals of the Association of American Geographers, 86*(2), 256-285.

Israeli Central Bureau of Statistics and Ministry of the Interior 2003); *Local Governments in Israel, Physical Data,* Special Serials No. 1170, 1186, 1203.

Israeli Central Bureau of Statistics 2003) *Statistical Abstract of Israel*, No. 54. Table 2.9 pp. 2-28.

Jeruis, S. 1966. *The Arabs In Israel*. Haifa: El-Etehad (in Arabic).

Khamaisi, R., 1990. *Planning and Housing among the Arabs in Israel*. Tel-Aviv: International Center for Peace in the Middle East.

Khamaisi, R. 1996. *New Palestinian cities alongside existing cities.* Jerusalem: The Floersheimer Institute for Policy Studies.

Khamaisi, R., 2000. Where the Town Hidden. *Pnem, 13*, 53-62 in Hebrew).

Khamaisi, R., 2003. *Metropolitan management for Nazareth Area*. Jerusalem: Floersheimer Institute for Policy Studies, p. 64 (in Hebrew).

Kipnis, B. 1987. Geopolitical Ideologies and Regional Strategies in Israel, *Tijdchrift Voor Economishe en Social Geography, 78*, 125-138.

Kipnis, B. 1976. Trends among the minorities population in the Galili and their planning implecation, *City and Region, 3*(3) 54- 68.

Kretzmer, D., 2002. *The Legal Status of the Arabs in Israel*, updated edition. Jerusalem: The Institute for Israeli Arab Studies and The Van Leer Institute.

Hill, M. 1980. Urban and Regional Planing in Israel. *In* Bilski, R. (ed.) *Can Planning Replace Politics? The Israeli Experience.* The Hague: Martinus Highoff, 259-282.

Lewis G. J. and Mound, D.J., 1976. The Urbanization of the Countryside—A Framework for Analysis, *Geografiska Annaler, B, 58,* 17-27.

Lustick, I. 1980. *Arabs in the Jewish State.* Austin: University of Texas Press.

Masalha, N., 1997. *Maximum Land and Minimum Arabs: Israel Transfer and Palestinians. 1949-1996.* Beirut: IPS.

Mear-Brodnes, M., 1969. Latent urbanization in Arabs Villages in Israel, *Environment and Planning Association Quarterly, 8-9,* 4-14 in Hebrew).

Mear-Brodnes, M., 1983. The dynamics of physical changes in Arabs Villages in Israel; in Shmueli, A. Et al., (eds.), *The Land of Galilee* Tel-Aviv: Eretz, pp. 745-762 (in Hebrew).

Palen, J. 1981. *The Urban World.* New York: Mc-Graw Hill Book Co.

Persson, L., 1990. Urbanization Processes in Peripheral Regions in a Welfare State, *Journal of Rural Studies, 6*(4), 437-442.

Rosenfild, H. and Al-Haj, M., 1990. *The Development of Local Government in the Arabs localities in Israel*, Gevat Habeba, (in Hebrew)

Sharon, A. 1951. *Physical Planning in Israel.* Jerusalem: Internal Minister.

Yiftachel, O. 1992. *Planning a Mixed Region in Israel: The Political Geography of Arab-Jewish Relations in the Galilee*, Aldershot: Averbury.

Yiftachel, O. 1997. Israeli Society and Jewish-Palestinian Reconciliation: 'Ethnocracy' and its Territorial Contradictions, *Middle East Journal, 51*(4):505-519.

Zureik, E. 1978. *The Palestinians in Israel: A study in internal Colonialism.* London: PKP.

Suicide Terrorism and America's Mission Impossible

Scott Atran

The past three years saw more suicide attacks than the last quarter century. Most of these were religiously motivated. While most Westerners imagine a tightly coordinated transnational terrorist organization headed by Al Qaeda, it seems more likely that nations under attack face a set of largely autonomous groups and cells pursuing their own regional aims. Repeated suicide actions show that massive counterforce alone does not diminish the frequency or intensity of suicide attack. Like pounding mercury with a hammer, this sort of top-heavy counterstrategy only seems to generate more varied and insidious forms of suicide terrorism. Even with many top Qaeda leaders now dead or in custody, the transnational Jihadist fraternity is transforming into a hydra-headed network more difficult to fight than before.

Poverty and lack of education *per se* are not root causes of suicide terrorism. And Muslims who have expressed support for martyr actions and trust in Osama Bin Laden or the late Hamas leader Sheikh Yassin do not as a rule hate democratic freedoms or Western culture, although many despise American foreign policy, especially in the Middle East. Rising aspirations followed by dwindling expectations – especially regarding civil liberties – are critical factors in generating support for suicide terrorism.

The United States, Israel, Russia and other nations on the frontline in the war on terror need to realize that military and counterinsurgency actions are tactical, not strategic responses to suicide terrorism, the most politically destabilizing and psychologically devastating form of terrorism. When these nations back oppressive and unpopular governments (even those deemed "partners in the war on terror") this only generates popular resentment and support for terrorism against those governments and their backers. To attract potential recruits away from Jihadist martyrdom – suicide terrorism's most virulent strain - and to dry up its popular support, requires addressing basic grievances before a downward spiral sets in where core meaning in life is sought, and found, in religious networks that sanctify vengeance at any cost against stronger powers, even if it kills the avenger.

Growing Threat of Suicide Terrorism

Suicide attacks have become more prevalent globally, gaining in strategic importance with disruptive effects that cascade upon the political, economic and social routines of national life and international relations. The first major contemporary suicide attack was the December 1981 bombing of the Iraqi embassy in Beirut, probably by Iranian agents, that left 27 dead and more than

100 injured. From 1980 to 2001, political scientist Robert Pape observed that 188 suicide attacks took place, most for non-religious motives.[1] According to an August 2003 congressional report "Terrorists and Suicide Attacks" this represented only three percent of terrorist attacks worldwide during this time period but accounted for nearly half of all deaths.[2]

The history of suicide bombings since the early 1980s demonstrates how such attacks have generally achieved attackers' near-term strategic goals, such as forcing withdrawal from areas subject to attack, causing destabilization, and demonstrating vulnerability by radically upsetting life routines. In Lebanon, Hizbollah ("Party of God") initiated the first systematic contemporary suicide attack campaign in 1983, killing hundreds of U.S. and French soldiers in coordinated truck bombings, compelling the United States and France to withdraw their remaining forces. Hizbollah had dramatically lessened its strategic reliance on suicide bombing by 1992, when it decided to participate in parliamentary elections and become a "mainstream" political party, and after achieving its main objective of forcing Israel to abandon most of the territorial and political gains made during Israel's 1982 invasion of Lebanon.

Hamas and Palestine Islamic Jihad used suicide attacks to effectively derail the 1995 Oslo Interim Agreement that was designed to serve as the foundation of a peace process between Palestinians and Israelis. In Sri Lanka, Tamil Eelam ("Tamil Homeland") only recently suspended its suicide squads of Tamil Tigers after wresting control of Tamil areas from the Sinhalese-dominated government and forcing official recognition of some measure of Tamil autonomy. Suicide bombings by Al Qaeda in Saudi Arabia in spring 2003 accompanied a drastic reduction in the U.S. military and civilian presence in the country. Of course, the September 11 attacks themselves were suicide attacks.

Newer trends since the start of the millennium pose distinct challenges, making the threat posed by suicide terrorism not only more prominent in recent years but also more frequently religiously motivated. From 2000 to 2003, more than 300 suicide attacks killed more than 5,300 people in 17 countries and wounded many thousands more.[3] At least 70 percent of these attacks were religiously motivated, with more than 100 attacks by Al Qaeda or affiliates acting in Al-Qaeda's name.

Even more ominous, Islamic Jihadi groups are now networked in ways that permit "swarming" by actors contracted from different groups who home in from scattered locations on multiple targets and then disperse, only to form new swarms. Multiple coordinated suicide attacks across countries and even continents is the adaptive hallmark of Al Qaeda's continued global web-making. The war in Iraq has energized so many disparate groups that the Jihadist network is better prepared than ever to carry on without bin Laden.[4] The International Institute of Strategic Studies in London reports that: "The counter-terrorism effort has perversely impelled an already highly decentralized and evasive transnational terrorist network to become more 'virtual' and protean and, therefore, harder to identify and neutralize."[5]

Table 1. Suicide attacks worldwide, 2000–2003 (author's compilation)

Country	Suicide Attacks Per Year Per Country				Total Attacks	Religious Attacks	Total Dead In all Attacks
	2000	2001	2002	2003			
Afghanistan**				2	2	2	11
Chechnya/Russia**	8	1	1	10	20	20	382
China			2		2	0	5
Indonesia**			1	1	2	2	215
Iraq**				33	33	15	244
Kashmir/Jammu**	17	29	18	11	75	75	409
Kenya*			1		1	1	18
Morocco**				5	5	5	44
Pakistan**			2	2	4	4	84
Palestine/Israel	3	40	64	22	129	78	555
Philippines**			1	1	2	2	24
Saudi Arabia*		1		5	6	6	57
Sri Lanka***	14	4		1	19	0	205
Tunisia**			1		1	1	16
Turkey**		1		5	6	4	64
USA*		4			4	4	3002
Yemen*	1				1	1	19
SUM	43	80	91	98	312	220	5354

*Al Qaeda attacks
** Involving Al Qaeda associates
***LTTE attacks (Tamil Tigers)

Each country in which suicide attack has occurred has seen people become more suspicious and afraid of one another. Emboldened by the strategic successes of suicide-sponsoring terrorist organizations in upsetting the long-term political calculations and daily living routines of its foes, and by increasing support and recruitment among Muslim populations angered by U.S. actions in Iraq, Jihadi groups believe they are proving able to mount a lengthy and costly war of attrition. Even U.S. Secretary of Defense Don Rumsfeld himself lamented: "The cost-benefit ratio is against us! Our cost is billions against the terrorists' cost of millions."[6]

The longer this war of attrition lasts, the greater the long-term strategic risk of radicalizing Muslim sentiment against the United States, of undermining the United States' international alliances, and of causing serious and sustained discontent among the American people. A White House panel reported in October 2003 that Muslim hostility toward the United States "has reached shocking levels" and is growing steadily.[7] In April 2004, Egyptian President Hosni Mubarak warned: "There is hatred of the Americans like never before in the region."[8] Margaret Tutwiler, U.S. Undersecretary of State for diplomacy, bemoaned to a Congressional committee in February 2004 that: "It will take us many years of hard, focused work" to restore U.S. credibility, even among traditional allies.[9] Most Americans today feel no safer from terrorism, more distrustful of many longstanding allies, and increasingly anxious about the future. A survey released in early spring 2004 by the non-partisan Council for Excellence in Government found that fewer than half of all Americans think the country is safer than it was on 9/11, and more than three-quarters expect the U.S. to be the target of a major terrorist attack in the near future.[10]

There is good reason to be anxious. One distinct pattern in the litany of terrorist atrocities is that there has been an increasing interest in well-planned attacks designed to net the highest numbers of civilian casualties. Charting data from the International Policy Institute for Counter-Terrorism, Robert Axelrod, a political scientist at the University of Michigan, observes that a very few terrorist attacks account for a very large percentage of all casualties. Not only does this trend call for anticipating attacks with ever broader political, economic and social effects, it also seems to point to an eventual suicide attack using chemical, biological or nuclear weapons. Although that may take some time to effectively plan, long-term planning has proven to be Al-Qaeda's hallmark.

"God has ordered us to build nuclear weapons," proclaimed Fazlur Rahman Khalil of Pakistan's Harkat ul-Mujahideen on the CBS television news show *60 Minutes II*.[11] A subsequent suicide attack on India's Parliament in December 2001 by Jaish-e-Muhammed, a Pakistani splinter group of the Al-Qaeda affiliate that Khalil heads, perhaps brought nuclear war closer than at any time since the Cuban Missile Crisis.[12] Imagine what these people could do with the non-conventional weapons they actively seek.

In sum, terrorists are becoming increasingly effective by using suicide attacks and the trend points to a catastrophic unconventional terrorist attack that could make the March 11 Madrid or September 11 New York and Washington attacks pale in comparison. The U.S. strategic response relies on overwhelming military force to crush evolving Jihadist swarms, but this inflexible and maladaptive strategy only propagates leaner and meaner mutations of suicide networks and cells.

Suicide Terror Today

Repeated suicide actions in the disputed regions of Palestine, Kashmir, Chechnya, and now in U.S.-occupied Iraq show that military action has not stopped, or even reliably diminished, the incidence of suicide attacks. For example, from 1993 through 2003, 311 Palestinian suicide attackers launched themselves against Israeli targets. In the first 7 years of suicide bombing, 70 percent (43 of 61 attempts) were successful in killing other people. From the start of the Second Intifada in September 2000 through 2003, however, while the success rate declined to 52 percent, the number of attacks increased from 61 to 250, with 129 of those successful (up from 43).[13]

The trend is even more alarming in Iraq and elsewhere. On May 1, 2003, President George W. Bush declared an end to major combat operations in Iraq and "one victory in the war on terror that began on 9/11."[14] Cofer Black, the State Department's coordinator for counterterrorism, declared soon thereafter that Al Qaeda had to "put up or shut up... They had failed. It proves the global war on terrorism is effective."[15] Within just two weeks, a wave of Jihadist suicide bombings hit Saudi Arabia Morocco, Israel, and Chechnya. Collectively, these attacks were more numerous and widespread than any in the preceding 12 months.

In October 2003, five full months after major military operations had been declared over, Iraq suffered its worst spate of suicide bombings to date. White House claims that such attacks only confirmed the "desperation"[16] of terrorists in the face of increasing U.S. progress in the war on terrorism provided little evidence that the military response was working and were ridiculed by Arab commentators.[17] A November 2003 suicide attack on Italian forces in southern Iraq convinced several countries not to participate in the military occupation, and spurred the United States to accelerate its timetable for transferring authority to Iraqis.

Outside Iraq, suicide bombings in Turkey by self-declared friends of Al Qaeda, also in November, sought to undermine the best example of nonsectarian and democratic rule in the Muslim world, and extended the strategic threat to NATO's underbelly. In December 2003, renewed attacks by Chechnya's "black widows" (women allowed by militant Islamic leaders to become martyrs, usually because of what Russian soldiers have done to their husbands, fathers and brothers) brought terror to Russian civilians. During the year-end holidays, alerts for Al Qaeda suicide skyjackings brought continuous air patrols and surface-to-air missiles to major U.S. cities and caused cancellations of several international flights. Pakistan's President Pervez Musharraf barely escaped assassination on Christmas Day when two suicide truck bombers from Jaish-e-Muhammed rammed his motorcade.

And all of this occurred despite the fact that State Department funding for counterstrategies to combat terrorism overseas increased 133 percent from September 11, 2001, through fiscal year 2003, according to the final U.S. Federal Interagency report on *Combating Terrorism*.[18] Including the Iraq theater (originally billed as a war of necessity to deny weapons of mass destruction from Al Qaeda and its associates), U.S. Department of Defense budget increases and emergency supplemental measures, the bill for foreign operations in the war on terrorism into 2004 exceeds $200 billion. Yet the incidence and impact of suicide terrorism have not declined. Of course, not all of this "hard power" spending on terrorism is wasted, but the nearly exclusive reliance on military might has not stifled the martyr's appeal or stalled the threat.

In fact, 2003 witnessed more suicide attacks (98) than any year in contemporary history. A plurality (33) occurred in Iraq, now plagued with suicide terror for the first time since the thirteenth century *hashasheen* ("assassins") slaughtered fellow Muslims and Crusaders to purify Islamic lands (it took the Mongols to stop them). In the first three months of 2004, more than three dozen suicide attackers struck six U.S. allies (2 attackers in Afghanistan, 18 in Iraq, 2 in Pakistan, 8 in Israel, 1 in Turkey, and at least 5 female bombers in Uzbekistan, a first-time target of suicide terror) killing over 600 people and wounding thousands. In Iraq alone (which has so far been budgeted $165 billion as part of the "War on Terror"), from February 1 to March 2, ten suicide bombers killed more than 400 people —a greater number than in any single country for any 31-day period since the attacks of September 11. Even a casual glance at media outlets and websites sympathetic to Al Qaeda reveals a proliferating Jihadist fraternity that is not deterred by Saddam's capture, but rather, takes heart from the fall of Iraq's secularist tyrant.[19]

In short, the record clearly demonstrates that military actions against terrorism and its purported sponsors have not come close to squelching suicide terror. At a minimum, an effective strategy for combating suicide terrorism requires a layered approach that works on three levels in a coordinated way:

- A last line of defense involves the attempt to protect sensitive populations and installations from attack. Mostly through development and use of scientific technology, efforts are made to block suicide terrorists from hitting their targets or to lessen (through preparation) the effects of an attack that has not been prevented.
- A middle line of defense involves preemptively penetrating and destroying terror organizations and networks, mostly through a combination of intelligence and military action.
- A first line of defense involves understanding and acting on the root causes of terrorism so as to drastically reduce the receptivity of potential recruits to the message and methods of terror-sponsoring organizations, mostly through political, economic, and social action programs.

Billions upon billions of dollars have been targeted on countermeasures associated with the last and middle lines of defense (protection, mitigation, preemption). These measures may have helped to thwart a steep rise in suicide attacks; however, they have produced no appreciable decline of suicide terrorism.

Unfortunately, the same U.S. Federal Interagency report on *Combating Terrorism* that documents the significant increase in funding for combating terrorism, and reviews plans and activities by dozens of civil and military agencies, reveals scant evidence of serious effort or funding to understand why individuals become, or to prevent individuals from becoming, terrorists in the first place. Even more serious than the scarce interest and funding on this score thus far, however, is the fact that current U.S. policies that do attempt to address the underlying factors of suicide terrorism are woefully misguided. The record suggests that addressing these root causes might provide a more promising approach.

Misconceiving Root Causes

A common notion in the U.S. administration and media spin on the war against terrorism is that suicide attackers are evil, deluded or homicidal misfits who thrive on poverty, ignorance and anarchy. This portrayal lends a sense of hopelessness to any attempt to address root causes because some individuals will always be desperate or deranged enough to conduct suicide attacks. But as logical as the poverty-breeds-terrorism argument may seem, study after study shows that suicide attackers and their supporters are rarely ignorant or impoverished. Nor are they crazed, cowardly, apathetic or asocial. The common misconception underestimates the central role that organizational factors play in the appeal of terrorist networks. A better understanding of such causes reveals that the challenge is actually manageable: the key is not to profile and target the most despairing or deranged individual but to understand and undermine the organizational and institutional appeal of terrorists' motivations and networks.

The U.S. *National Strategy for Combating Terrorism* highlights the "War of Ideas" and "War on Poverty" as adjunct programs to reduce terrorism's pool of support and recruitment.[20] The war of ideas is based on the premise that terrorists and their supporters "hate our freedoms," a sentiment Bush has expressed both with regard to Al Qaeda and to the Iraqi resistance.[21] Yet survey data reliably show that most Muslims who support suicide terrorism and trust Osama bin Laden favor elected government, personal liberty, educational opportunity, and economic choice.[22] Mark Tessler, who coordinates long-term surveys of Muslim societies from the University of Michigan's Institute for Social Research, finds that Arab attitudes toward American culture are most favorable among young adults—the same population that terrorist recruiters single out—regardless of their religious orientation.[23] Khalil Shikaki, director of the Palestinan Center for Survey and Policy Research, consistently finds that a majority of Palestinians has a favorable impression of U.S. (and Israeli) forms of government, education, economy, and even literature and art, even though nearly three-fourths of the population supports suicide attack.[24]

In sum, there is no evidence that most people who support suicide actions hate Americans' internal cultural freedoms, but rather, every indication that they oppose U.S. foreign policies, particularly regarding the Middle East. After the 1996 suicide attack against U.S. military housing at Khobar Towers in Saudi Arabia, a Defense Department Science Board report stated: "Historical data show a strong correlation between U.S. involvement in international situations and an increase in terrorist attacks against the United States."[25] U.S. intervention in Iraq is but the most recent example. A United Nations report indicated that as soon as the United States began building up for the Iraq invasion, Qaeda recruitment had picked up in 30 to 40 countries.[26] Recruiters for groups sponsoring terrorist acts were telling researchers that volunteers were beating down the doors to join.

Similarly, the war on poverty is based on the premise that impoverishment, lack of education, and social estrangement spawn terrorism. Economist Gary Becker's theory that the greater the amount of human capital (including income and education) a person accumulates, the less likely that person is to commit a crime.[27] The theory is that the greater a person's human capital, the more that person is aware of losing out on substantial future gains if captured or killed. Similar thinking applies to suicide terror: the less promising one's future, the more likely one's choice to end life. Almost all current U.S. foreign aid programs related to terrorism pivot on such assumptions, now generally accepted by the mainstream of both U.S. political parties, but although the theory has proven useful in combating blue-collar crime, no evidence indicates its bearing on terror.

Studies by Princeton economist Alan Krueger and others find no correlation between a nation's per capita income and terrorism,[28] but do find a correlation between a lack of civil liberties, defined by Freedom House,[29] and terrorism. A recent National Research Council report, *Discouraging Terrorism*, finds: "Terrorism and its supporting audiences appear to be fostered by policies of extreme political repression and discouraged by policies of incorporating both dissident and moderate groups responsibly into civil society and the political process."[30] U.S. backing of weak, failed, and corrupt states generates animosity and terrorism against the U.S. There seems to be a direct correlation between U.S. military aid to politically corroded or ethnically divided states,[31] human rights abuses by those regimes,[32] and a rise in terrorism,[33] as initially moderate opposition is pushed into common cause with more radical elements.

Despite these realities, the meager U.S. monies available for non-military foreign aid are far too concentrated in poverty reduction and literacy enhancement. In fact, in Pakistan, literacy and dislike for the United States have increased nonetheless while the number of Islamist *madrassa* schools grew from 3,000 to nearly 40,000 since 1978. According to the U.S. State Department report, *September 11 One Year Later*, development aid is based "on the belief that poverty provides a breeding ground for terrorism. The terrorist attacks of September 11 reaffirmed this conviction,"[34] and Bush declared at a UN conference on poor nations in Monterrey, Mexico: "We fight against poverty because hope is an answer to terror."[35] Yet study after study demonstrates that suicide terrorists and their supporters are not abjectly poor, illiterate, or socially estranged.[36]

Another misconception that implicitly drives current national security policy is that suicide terrorists have no rational political agenda and are not sane. According to General Wesley Clark, unlike nineteenth-century Russian terrorists who wanted to depose the czar, current Islamic terrorists are simply retrograde and nihilist: "They want the destruction of Western civilization and the return to seventh-century Islam."[37] Senator John Warner testified that a new security doctrine of preemption was necessary because "those who would commit suicide in their assaults on the free world are not rational."[38] According to Vice President Dick Cheney, the September 11 plotters and other like-minded terrorists "have no sense of morality."[39]

In truth, suicide terrorists on the whole have no appreciable psychopathology and are often wholly committed to what they believe to be devout moral principles. A report on *The Sociology and Psychology of Terrorism* used by the Central and Defense Intelligence Agencies (CIA and DIA) finds "no psychological attribute or personality distinctive of terrorists."[40] Recruits are generally well adjusted in their families and liked by peers, and often more educated and economically better off than their surrounding population. Researchers Basel Saleh and Claude Berrebi independently find that the majority of Palestinian suicide bombers have a college education (versus 15 percent of the population of comparable age) and that less than 15 percent come from poor families (although about one-third of the population lives in poverty). DIA sources who have interrogated Al Qaeda detainees at Guantanamo note that Saudi-born operatives, especially those in leadership positions, are often "educated above reasonable employment level, a surprising number have graduate degrees and come from high-status families."[41] The general pattern was captured in a Singapore Parliamentary report on prisoners from Jemaah Islamiyah, an ally of Al Qaeda: "These men were not ignorant, destitute or disenfranchised. Like many of their counterparts in militant Islamic organizations in the region, they held normal, respectable jobs. Most detainees regarded religion as their most important personal value."[42]

Except for being mostly young unattached males, suicide attackers differ from members of violent racist organizations to whom they are often compared, such as American white supremacist groups.[43] Overall, suicide terrorists exhibit no socially dysfunctional attributes (fatherless, friendless, jobless) or suicidal symptoms. Inconsistent with economic theories of criminal behavior, they do not kill themselves simply out of hopelessness or a sense of having nothing to lose. Muslim clerics countenance killing oneself for martyrdom in the name of God but curse personal suicide. "He who commits suicide kills himself for his own benefit," warned Sheikh Yussuf Al-Qaradhawi (a spiritual leader of the Muslim Brotherhood), but "he who commits martyrdom sacrifices himself for the sake of his religion and his nation... the Mujahed is full of hope."[44]

Another reason that personal despair or derangement may not be a significant factor in suicide terrorism is that the cultures of the Middle East, Africa and Asia where it thrives tend to be less 'individualistic" than our own, more attuned to the environmental and organizational relationships that shape behavior, and less tolerant of individuals acting independently from a group context.[45] Terrorists in these societies also would be more likely to be seeking a group, or collective, sense of belonging and justification for their actions.

A group struggling to gain power and resources against materially better-endowed enemies must attract able and committed recruits—not loaners—who are willing to give up their lives for a cause. At the same time, the group must prevent uncommitted elements in the population from simply free-riding on the backs of committed fighters, that is, sharing in the fighters' rewards and success without taking the risks or paying the costs of fighting. Insurgent groups manage this by offering potential recruits the promise of great future rewards instead of immediate gain, such as freedom for future generations or eternal bliss in Paradise. Only individuals committed to delayed gratification are then liable to volunteer. Insurgent groups also tend to seek out individuals with better education and economic prospects, because they view a person who invests resources in education and training for a better economic future as signaling willingness to sacrifice today's satisfactions for tomorrow's rewards and able to realize commitments. For this reason, relative level of education and economic status is often higher among insurgent groups that recruit primarily on the basis of promises for the future than among traditional armies that rely more on short-term incentives.[46]

Relative Deprivation and Religious Redemption

The connection between suicide and terrorists and religion might be explained by the role that religious ethnic groups can play. Ethnic groups offer a good foundation for sustaining resource-deficient insurgencies because they provide a social structure that can underpin the maintenance of reputations and the efficient gathering of information about recruits. But ethnicity alone may not be enough; religion may also be needed to cement commitment. A comparison of ethnic Palestinians with ethnic Bosnian Muslims (matched for age, income, education, exposure to violence, etc.) shows the Palestinians much more liable to use religious sentiments to confidently express hope for the future by willingness to die for the group, whereas the Bosnians do not express religious sentiments, hope or willingness to die.[47] Martyrdom, which involves "pure" commitment to promise over payoff, and unconditional sacrifice for fictive "brothers," will more likely endure in religious ethnic groups.

None of this denies that popular support for terrorism is sustained, in part, by economic factors, such as explosive population growth and underemployment, coupled with the failure of rigidly authoritarian governments to provide youth outlets for political and economic advancement. Middle Eastern and more broadly most Muslim societies, whose populations double within one generation or less, have age pyramids with broad bases: each younger age group is substantially larger (more people) than the next older. Even with states that allowed for a modicum of political expression or economic employment, society's structure of opportunities can have trouble keeping pace with population.

Regional governments are increasingly unable to provide these opportunities, enhancing the attractiveness of religious organizations that are able to recruit tomorrow's suicide terrorists. Weak and increasingly corrupt and corroded nationalist regimes in Muslim countries have sought to eliminate all secular opposition. To subdue popular discontent in the post-colonial era, the Ba'athist socialist dictators of Syria and Iraq, the authoritarian prime ministers of Pakistan and Malaysia, the monarchs of Morocco and Jordan, and the imperial presidents of Egypt, Algeria, the Philippines and Indonesia, all initially supported militant Islamic groups. To maintain their bloated bureaucracies and armies, these "failed states" – all poor imitations of Western models with no organic history in the Arab and Muslim world - readily delegated responsibility for the social welfare of their peoples to activist Islamic groups eager to take charge. These groups provided schooling and health services more efficiently and extensively than governments were able to, offering a "desecularized" path to fulfill modernity's universal mission to improve humanity. When radical Islam finally vented political aspirations – beginning with the 1965 "Islamic Manifesto," *Milestones*, written in prison by the Muslim Brotherhood's Sayyid Qutb just before he was hanged for sedition by Egyptian leader Colonel Gamal Abdul Nasser - popular support proved too deep and widespread to extinguish.

Although the process of rising aspirations followed by dwindling expectations that generates terror can be identified, disentangling the relative significance of political and economic factors in the Muslim world is difficult and perhaps even impossible. During the 1990s, momentous political developments in Algeria (multiparty elections, including Islamic groups in 1992), Palestine (Oslo Peace Accords in 1993), Chechnya (dissolution of the Soviet Union and the end of communist control), Indonesia (Suharto's resignation in 1998 and the end of dictatorship), and elsewhere fanned rising aspirations among Muslim peoples for political freedom and economic advancement. In each case, economic stagnation or decline followed as political aspirations were thwarted (the Algerian Army cancelled elections, the Israel-Palestine Camp David negotiations broke down, Russia cracked down on Chechnya's bid for autonomy, and Suharto army loyalists and paramilitary groups fomented interethnic strife and political discord).

Support and recruitment for suicide terrorism occur not under conditions of political repression, poverty, and unemployment or illiteracy as such, but when converging political, economic, and social trends produce diminishing opportunities relative to expectations, thus generating frustrations that radical organizations can exploit. For this purpose, relative deprivation is more significant than absolute deprivation. Unlike poorer, less educated elements of their societies—or equally educated, well-off members of our society—many educated, middle-class Muslims increasingly experience frustration with life as their potential opportunities are less attractive than their prior expectations. Frustrated with their future, the appeal of routine national life declines and suicide terrorism gives some perceived purpose to act altruistically, in the potential terrorist's mind, for the welfare of a future generation.

Revolutionary terror imprints itself into history when corrupt and corroded societies choke rising aspirations into explosive frustration.

Organization and the Banality of Evil

This frustrating confluence of circumstances helps to account for terrorism's popular support and endurance but not the original spark that ignites people's passions and minds. Most people in the world who suffer stifling, even murderous, oppression do not become terrorists. As with nearly all creators and leaders of history's terrorist movements, those who conceive of using suicide terrorism in the first place belong mostly to an intellectual elite possessing sufficient material means for personal advancement but who choose a life of struggle and sacrifice for themselves and who often require even greater commitment from their followers. Their motivations are not personal comfort or immediate material gain. Rather, their motivation is religious or ideological conviction and zeal, whose founding assumptions, like those of *any* religion, cannot be rationally scrutinized, and for which they inspire others to believe in and die. But arational motivations don't preclude rational actions.

Sponsors of martyrdom are not irrational. Using religious sentiments for political or economic purposes can be eminently rational, as when martyrdom or missionary actions gain recognition, recruits, and power in order to increase political "market share"[48] (to gain in the competition for political influence in a regional context, within the larger Muslim community, or with the rest of the world). Dwindling returns on individuals' future prospects in life translate into higher levels of recruitment and prompt returns for terrorist groups and leaders. This degree of manipulation usually works only if the manipulators themselves make costly, hard-to-fake commitments, however.

Through indoctrination of recruits into relatively small and closeted cells— emotionally tightknit brotherhoods—terror organizations create a family of cellmates who are just as willing to sacrifice for one another as a parent for a child. Consider the "Oath to Jihad" taken by recruits to Harkat ul-Mujahedeen, a Pakistani affiliate of the *World Islamic Front for Jihad against the Jews and Crusaders*, the umbrella organization formed by Osama Bin Laden in 1998. The oath affirms that by their sacrifice members help secure the future of their family of fictive kin: "Each [martyr] has a special place—among them are brothers, just as there are sons and those even more dear."[49] These culturally contrived cell loyalties mimic and (at least temporarily) override genetically based fidelities to kin while securing belief in sacrifice to a larger group cause. The mechanism of manipulation resembles that of the U.S. army (and probably most armies), which trains soldiers in small groups of committed buddies who then grow willing to sacrifice for one another, and only derivatively for glory or country (motherland, fatherland).

Key to intercepting that commitment before it solidifies is grasping how, like the best commercial advertisers but to ghastlier effect, charismatic leaders of terrorist groups turn ordinary desires for kinship and religion into cravings for the mission they are pitching, to the benefit of the manipulating organization rather than the individual manipulated. Therefore, understanding and parrying suicide terrorism requires concentrating more on the organizational structure, indoctrination methods, and ideological appeal of recruiting organizations than on personality attributes of the individuals recruited. No doubt individual predispositions render some more susceptible to social factors that leaders use to persuade recruits to die for their cause. But months—sometimes years—of intense indoctrination can lead to blind obedience no matter who the individual.[50]

Part of the answer to what leads a normal person to suicide terror may lie in philosopher Hannah Arendt's notion of the "banality of evil," which she used to describe the recruitment of mostly ordinary Germans, not sadistic lunatics, to man Nazi extermination camps.[51] In the early 1960s, psychologist Stanley Milgram tested her thesis. He recruited Yale students and other U.S. adults to supposedly help others learn better. When the learner, hidden by a screen, failed to memorize arbitrary word pairs fast enough, the helper was instructed to administer an electric shock, and to increase voltage with each erroneous answer (which the learner, actually an actor, deliberately got wrong). Most helpers complied with instructions to give potentially lethal shocks (labeled as 450 volts, but in fact 0) despite victims' screams and pleas. This experiment showed how situations can be staged to elicit blind obedience to authority, and more generally that manipulation of context can trump individual personality and psychology to generate apparently extreme behaviors in ordinary people.[52]

Social psychologists have long documented what they call "the fundamental attribution error," the tendency for people to explain human behavior in terms of individual personality traits, even when significant situational factors in the larger society are at work. This attribution error leads many in the West to focus on the individual suicide terrorists rather than the organizational environment which produces them. If told that someone has been ordered to give a speech supporting a particular political candidate, for example, most people in Western society will still think that the speaker believes what he is saying. This interpretation bias seems to be especially prevalent in individualistic cultures, such as those of the United States and Western Europe, as opposed to collectivist cultures, such as Africa and Asia. Portrayals by the U.S. government and media of suicide bombers as deranged cutthroats may also suffer from a fundamental attribution error: no instance has yet occurred of religious or political suicide terrorism resulting from the lone action of a mentally unstable bomber (e.g., a suicidal Unabomber) or someone acting entirely under his own authority and responsibility (e.g., a suicidal Timothy McVeigh). The key is the organization, not the individual.

For organizations that sponsor suicide attack to thrive—or even survive—against much stronger military foes, they need strong community support. Yet the reasons for that communal support can differ among people. Among

Palestinians, perceptions of historical injustice combine with personal loss and humiliation at the hands of their Israeli occupiers to nurture individual martyrs and general popular support for martyr actions. Palestinian economist Basel Saleh observes that a majority of Palestinian suicide bombers had prior histories of arrest or injury by Israel's army, and many of the youngest suicide shooters had family members or close friends with such a history.[53] Khalil Shikaki, a psychologist and Director of the Palestinian Center for Policy and Survey Research in Ramallah, has preliminary survey data suggesting that popular support for suicide actions may be positively correlated with the number of Israeli checkpoints that Palestinians have to regularly pass through to go about their daily business and the time needed to pass through them (this can involve spending hours at each of several checkpoints, any of which can be arbitrarily closed down any time to prevent through passage). Humiliation and revenge are the most consistent sentiments expressed by not just recruits but also their supporters, though expressed more as community grievances than as personal ones.[54]

Although individual grievances generate support for terrorists and motivate some people to become recruits, debriefings with captured Al Qaeda operatives at Guantánamo and with Jemaah Islamiyah prisoners in Singapore suggest that recruitment to these organizations is more ideologically driven than grievance-driven. Detainees evince little history of personal hardship but frequently cite relatives or respected community members who participated in earlier jihads, or close peers presently engaged, as influencing decisions to join the fight.[55] Of course, ideology and grievance are not mutually exclusive. Jessica Stern's interviews with jihadists and their supporters in Kashmir reveal that both abound.

Despite numerous studies of individual behavior that show situation to be a much better predictor than personality in group contexts, Americans overwhelmingly believe that personal decision, success, and failure depend on individual choice, responsibility, and personality. This perception is plausibly one reason many Americans tend to think of terrorists as homicidal maniacs. "If we have to, we just mow the whole place down," said Senator Trent Lott, exasperated with the situation in Iraq. "You're dealing with insane suicide bombers who are killing our people, and we need to be very aggressive in taking them out."[56] As Timothy Spangler, chairman of Republicans Abroad (a group of Americans living overseas that helps the Republican Party develop policy) recently put it, "We know what the causes of terrorism are—terrorists... It's ultimately about individuals taking individual decisions to kill people."[57] According to last year's Pew survey, most of the world disagrees.[58] Although we cannot do much about personality traits, whether biologically influenced or not, we presumably can think of nonmilitary ways to make terrorist groups less attractive and undermine their effectiveness with recruits. That holds the key to defeating terrorism.

Soft Power Counterstrategy

Whatever the basis of community support for organizations that sponsor terrorism, that support needs to be the prime long-term focus of attention by U.S. policymakers and others who are interested in combating the threat they pose. For without community support, terrorist organizations that depend for information, recruitment and survival on dense networks of ethnic and religious ties can no more thrive than fish out of water. No evidence (historical or otherwise) indicates that popular support for suicide terrorism will evaporate, or that individuals will cease to be persuaded by terrorists' groups promises of future rewards, without complicity in tackling at least some fundamental goals that suicide attackers and supporting communities share, such as denying support to discredited governments and going full press on ending the conflict in the Palestinian territories, whose daily images of violence engender global Muslim resentment.[59] Republicans and Democrats alike clamor for the allocation of billions of dollars to protect innumerable targets from suicide attackers. Guarding sensitive installations is a last line of defense, however, and probably the easiest line to breach because of the abundance of vulnerable targets and would-be attackers.

Preempting and preventing terrorism requires that U.S policymakers make a concerted effort to understand the background conditions as well as the recruitment processes that inspire people to take their own lives in the name of a greater cause. Current political and economic conditions that policymakers currently monitor are important although not necessarily determinant. Rather, what likely matters more is the promise of redeeming real or imagined historical grievances through a religious (or transcendent ideological) mission that empowers the militarily weak with unexpected force against enemies materially much stronger. This was as true for Jewish Zealots who sacrificed themselves to kill Romans two millennia ago as it is for modern Jihadists.

Identifying sacred values in different cultures and how they compete for people's affections is surely a first step in learning how to prevent those values from spiraling into mortal conflict between societies. All religions, and many quasi-religious ideologies that make claims about laws of history or universal missions to reform humanity, are based on sacred values.[60] Such values are linked to emotions that underpin feelings of cultural identity and trust. These emotion-laden sentiments are amplified into moral obligations to strike out against perceived opponents no matter the cost when conditions of relative deprivation get to a point where suicide terrorists actively seek alternatives because of lack of political and economic opportunity.

Such sentiments are characteristic of apparently irrational, emotionally-driven commitments, including heartfelt romantic love and uncontrollable vengeance, which may have emerged under natural selection's influence, to override rational calculations based on seemingly impossible or very long odds of achieving individual goals, such as lasting security.[61] In religiously-inspired suicide terrorism, these sentiments, again, are manipulated by organizational leaders, recruiters and trainers, mostly for the organization's benefit at the expense of the individual. Such manipulation is an extreme form of a common practice, where society's ruling management demands readiness-to-die from its own members – and occasional execution of this demand – as a demonstration of faith in society. In times of crisis, every society routinely calls upon some of its own people to sacrifice their lives for the general good of the body-politic. For militant Jihadists, crisis is constant and unabating, and extreme sacrifice is necessary as long as there are non-believers (*kuffar*) in the world.

Policy may head off this downward spiral towards mortal conflict between incommensurable moral views of the world by helping to provide political and economic opportunity for some. But once that spiral starts for others, the task becomes much more difficult. Once values become sacred, negotiated tradeoffs based on balancing costs and benefits become taboo - much as selling off one's child or selling out one's country is taboo, no matter what the payoff is - and offers of compromise or exchange are met with moral outrage. Counting on military pressure, the economic power of globalization, or the Western media's powers of persuasion to get others to give up such values is probably a vain hope. Policymakers from nations that fight sacred terror and hope to defeat it need to circumscribe the point at which commitment becomes absolute and nonnegotiable and seek to reach people before they come to it.

Traditional top-heavy approaches, such as strategic bombardment, invasion, occupation, and other massive forms of coercion, cannot eliminate tactically innovative and elusive Jihadist swarms nor suppress their popular support. According to a survey by the Pew Research Center released in March 2004, nearly half of Pakistanis and substantial majorities of people in supposedly moderate Muslim countries, such as Morocco and Jordan, now support suicide bombings as a way of countering the application of military might by the United States in Iraq and by Israel in Palestine. [62]

Pinpoint responses may not be the answer either.[63] Kathleen Carley, a professor at Carnegie Mellon University, has used intelligence reports and sophisticated computer modeling to monitor the changes in jihadist networks, including the cell responsible for the suicide bombing of the American embassy in Tanzania. She found that eliminating the ``central actors'' - that is, cell members who have the most ties to other cell members and to other groups - has actually spurred terrorists to adapt more quickly, and has been less effective in the long run than eliminating less-central foot soldiers. Thus targeted assassinations of known leaders (a favorite Israeli tactic) may be counter-productive,[64] in addition to causing public revulsion.

Rather than focusing on hard power as a last defense, the first line of defense should be convincing Muslim communities to stop supporting religious schools and charities that feed terrorist networks. For example, just a small percentage of what the U.S. spends on often ineffective counterinsurgency aid to unpopular governments can help to train teachers and administrators, build schools and dormitories, furnish books and computers, provide fellowships and stipends, and fund local invitations for all willing parties to discuss and debate. Radical Islamic and other terrorist groups often provide more and better educational, medical, and social welfare services than governments do; so democratic nations that fight terrorism must discretely help others in these societies to compete with

– rather than attempt to crush – such programs for the bodies, minds and hearts of people.

Clearly, shows of military strength are not the way to end the growing menace of suicide terrorism: witness the failure of Israel's and Russia's coercive efforts to end strings of Palestinian and Chechnyan suicide bombings. Rather, those nations most threatened by suicide terrorism, in particular the world's democracies, must show people the aspects of democratic cultures they most respect. These nations, should promote democracy, but must be ready to accept "democracy's paradox": if people choose representatives who America and its democratic allies don't like, or who have different values or ways of doing things, still voters' decisions must be accepted as long as this does not generate violence. Democratic self-determination in Palestine, Kashmir and Iraq – or for that matter, Pakistan, Uzbekistan and Saudi Arabia – will more likely reduce terrorism than more military and counterinsurgency aid. At the same time, America and its allies need to establish an intense dialogue with Muslim religious and community leaders to reconcile Islamic custom and religious law (*shari'a*) with internationally recognized standards for crime and punishment and human rights.

To address the problem of relative deprivation, the U.S. and its allies should promote economic choice. But people must be allowed to pick and chose those goods and values that they desire, and must not be forced to privatize their traditional ways of trading and doing business any more than they should be forced to collectivize; neither should they be made to accept goods and values that they may not want in the name of "free markets" or "globalization." Most important, America and its allies should actively seek to redress the denial of civil liberties, by withdrawing military and political support from those of its "partners in the war on terror"[65] who persistently infringe on human rights and deny political expression to their people, and by encouraging moderates to constructively argue for and against alternative visions for their societies. Candor and debate with open dissent instill confidence, but propaganda and manipulative public relations breed disaffection and distrust. As any good scientist or businessman knows, people who acknowledge errors can correct them to perform better, and in performing better they are better able to recognize and correct their errors. Of course, the U.S. can't just unilaterally pull out of places that would then be threatened with collapse or hostile takeover. But long-term planning must not allow America and its allies to become embroiled in maintaining brutal and repressive regimes whose practices generate popular resentment and terrorism.

In addition, because it is the main target and foe of suicide attacks by Jihadists, the United States must work in concert with the international community to address the historical and personal grievances – whether perceived or actual - of people who have been denied the opportunity and power to realize their hopes and aspirations for personal security, collective peace, environmental sustainability and cultural fulfillment. The festering conflicts and killing fields of Israel/Palestine, Pakistan/Kashmir/India, Russia/Chechnya, the Western Sahara, Mindanao, The Moluccas, or Bosnia should be as much of a concern and a prod to action as the current state of the world economy.

Finally, the United States has to stop insisting on planetary rights of interference in the belief that our vision of civilization is humanity's last great hope or that U.S. national security depends on the world accepting "a single sustainable model of national success... right and true for every person, in every society."[66] "America is a nation with a mission," proclaimed President Bush in his 2004 State of the Union address. Yet a key lesson of the Vietnam War, according to former defense secretary Robert McNamara, was the error in thinking "we're on a mission. We weren't then and we aren't today. And we shouldn't act unilaterally militarily under any circumstances. We don't have the God-given right to shape every nation to our own image."[67] The new *National Security Strategy of the United States* frames America's new global mission in words the President first used at Washington's National Cathedral three days after 9/11: "our responsibility to history is... to rid the world of evil." Of course, exorcising the world's evil – or even all forms of terrorism - is as much an impossible mission as forever ending injustice (or earthquakes). More seriously, this publicized mission that pits America's moral world of Good against the Jihadist world of Evil directly parallels the Jihadist division of the world between "The House of Islam" (*Dar al-Islam)* and "The House of War*" (Dar al-Harb*), and feeds Jihadism's religious conviction and zeal as well its power to persuade recruits. This does the U.S. and its allies no good.

Clearly, none of this necessitates negotiating with terrorist groups that sponsor martyrs in the pursuit of goals such as Al Qaeda's quest to replace the Western-inspired system of nation-states with a global caliphate. Osama bin Laden and others affiliated with the mission of the World Islamic Front for the Jihad against the Jews and Crusaders seek no compromise, and will probably fight with hard power to the death. For these groups and already committed individuals, using hard power is necessary. The tens of millions of people who sympathize with bin Laden, however, are likely open to the promise of soft-power[68] alternatives that most Muslims seem to favor—elected government, freedom of expression, educational opportunity, economic choice. The historical precondition for such opportunity, as well as the popular legitimacy of any form of governance, to be effective, however, is to ensure that potential recruits in the Arab and Muslim world feel secure about their personal safety as well as their cultural heritage. Although such soft-power efforts may demand more patience than governments under attack or being pressured to reform typically politically tolerate in times of crisis, forbearance is necessary to avoid increasingly catastrophic devastation to the United States, to its democratic allies, and to the future hopes of peoples who aspire to soft empowerment from a free world.

Epilogue.

"Civilization is intermittent."   Menahem Begin

To capture the hearts and souls of people around them, terrorist groups provoke their enemies into committing atrocities. Two millennia ago, the first

Jewish Revolt against Roman occupation began with youths throwing stones, and Roman commanders telling their soldiers to sheathe their swords and defend themselves with wooden staves. The Jewish Zealots and Sicarii ("daggers") upped the ante – much as Hamas would do later against Israelis and Iraqi insurgents increasingly do against America's coalition - attacking Roman soldiers and their Greek underlings in self-sacrificial acts during public ceremonies. The Sicarii, who claimed to be freedom fighters but whom the Romans deemed terrorists, modeled their mission on Samson, who centuries before had brought down on himself a Philistine temple to help Israel.

The Jewish revolt ended with collective suicide of perhaps hundreds of Sicarii warriors and their families at the desert-fortress of Masada in 73 A.D. But that was hardly the end of the story. This "heroic" death inspired two subsequent revolts, ending with Rome expelling all Jews from Judea, including many Christians who still considered themselves Jews. Judea became "Palaestina," renamed for the Philistines. The Jewish Diaspora spread a universalizing faith to the far corners of the world, eventually converting the Roman emperor Constantine and the Arabian chieftan Mohammed to monotheism.

Ever since the Enlightenment, the modern world's major movements – the big "isms" of recent history - have been on a mission to invent "humanity" by saving it and making it their own. Modernism is the industrial legacy of monotheism (however atheist in appearance), secularized and scientifically applied. No non-monotheistic society (save Buddhism perhaps) ever considered that all people are, or should be, essentially of a kind. To many in our society, the 20th-century demise of colonialism, anarchism, fascism and communism left history's playing field wide open to what Lincoln besought as "the last great hope of mankind," our society's ideal of democratic liberalism (though Lincoln, like Jefferson, foresaw that the U.S. would "meanly lose" this hope if advanced by the sword).[69] Even after 9/11, there is scant recognition that unforseen events of history perpetually transform or destroy the best laid plans for historical engineering. Yet the catastrophic wars and revolutions of the modern era teach us that the more uncompromising the design and the more self-assured the designer, the harder both will fall

If we take an evolutionary perspective on history, which frames success and failure in terms of the growth or decline of traits over populations (and, eventually, in terms of the growth or decline of populations themselves), then current U.S. (or Israeli) antiterrorism policies do not seem adaptive. Support for the U.S. (and Israel) is declining in the world as support for terrorism increases. Moreover, U.S. (and Israeli) procedures to combat terror are often predictable and reactive. Even the "new" security strategy of preemption is preponderantly about maintaining U.S. preponderance (the global status quo) using traditional military means and other Great Power tactics. By contrast, terrorist stratagems are increasingly innovative and proactive. Perhaps more important, increasingly many people in the world perceive the terrorists' anti-American agenda to be turning the tide of history. Such perceptions invariably act upon the future in unpredictable ways that make it folly and hazardous to believe in the constancy "clashing civilizations,"[70] the inevitability of the world's globalization ("Americanization" for some),[71] an overriding "logic of human destiny,"[72] or some guiding spirit that ultimately causes "the end of history" and political struggle in a "fully rational" (secular, democratic, economically liberal) world.[73] Whatever the final outcome, the more fixed that religious fundamentalisms become in their own messianic mission to "desecularize" modernity,[74] the more likely they, too, will miserably fail. The most extreme Jihadists sway between calls for their own Masada and a Holocaust for non-believers. Whereas some saw resistance to the Israeli attack on Jenin in spring 2002 as the "Palestinian Masada,"[75] others, like Islamic Jihad leader Dr. Ramadan Abdallah Shalah, declaimed: "We are not creating a Palestinian Masada, but a Palestinian Karbala'a [speaking of the battle of Karbala'a in AD 680, which established "martyrdom" in Shi'ite tradition], which will hasten the second Jewish Masada … until the Zionist entity ceases to exist."[76] For Abu Shihab al-Kandahari, in his *Fatwah* issued in the name of Al-Qaeda: "Nuclear warfare is the solution for destroying America."[77] Defend against Jihadism we must, and help it to burn itself out. But let's not add life to its forlorn mission by unrelentingly muscling others with our own.

Notes

[1] Robert Pape, 2003. The Strategic Logic of Suicide Terrorism, *American Political Science Review, 97* (August), 434-361.

[2] Terrorists and Suicide Attacks, 2003. Congressional Res. Service Rep., Lib. Congress, Washington, DC, August 28, p. 12), www.fas.org/irp/crs/RL32058.pdf.

[3] See supplementary online materials for Scott Atran, 2004. Individual Factors in Suicide Terrorism, *Science, 304*, April 2, 47-49,
http://www.sciencemag.org/cgi/content/full/304/5667/47/DC1.

[4] Scott Atran, 2004. A Leaner, Meaner Jihad, *New York Times,* March 16, A25.

[5] *The Military Balance 2003–2004*, 2003. International Institute for Strategic Studies, London: Arundel House, October 15.

[6] *The Military Balance 2003–2004*, 2003. International Institute for Strategic Studies, London: Arundel House, October 15.[6] Dave Moniz, Tom Squitieri, 2003. Defense Memo: A Grim Outlook, *USA Today*, October 22, 1.

[7] Changing Minds, Winning Peace: A New Strategic Direction for U.S. Public Diplomacy in the Arab & Muslim world, 2003 (Rep. Advisory Group on Public Diplomacy for the Arab and Muslim World, Comm. On Appropriations, U.S. House of Representatives, Washington, DC, October 1),
http://www.rice.edu/projects/baker/Pubs/testimony/winningpeace/24882.pdf.

[8] Mubarak: Arabs Hate U.S. More than Ever, 2004. *Reuters* news wire, April 20.

[9] Christopher Marquis, 2004. U.S. Image Abroad Will Take Years to Repair, Official Says, *New York Times*, February 5, A5.

[10] Christopher Lee, 2004, Most Say They Are Less Safe since 9/11, *Washington Post*, 1 April, A3.

[11] Fazlur Rahman Khalil interviewed on *60 Minutes II (CBS news)*, October 15, 2000.

[12] Rahul Behdi, 2002. India 'Will Go to War After the Monsoon', *News Telegraph*, May 21, www.telegraph.co.uk/news/main.jhtml?xml=/news/2002/05/21/wkash21.xml;

Rory McCarthy, 2002. Dangerous Game of State-Sponsored Terrorism that Threatens Nuclear Conflict, *The Guardian*, May 25. The danger of nuclear confrontation on a "one-rung" escalation ladder, where any use of nuclear weapons entails massive use, is particularly acute for countries, like Pakistan and Israel, that have practically no territorial depth.

[13] The Middle East Resource Exchange Database, August 14, 2003, www.mered.org/topic.asp?TOPIC_ID=132&FORUM_ID=1&CAT_ID=1&Forum_Title=News&Topic_Title=Data+Shows+Suicide+Bombers+Young%2C+Well+Educated; the MERED data have been updated through 2003. The breakdown of successful attacks is: Hamas = 51, Palestinian Islamic Jihad = 27, Al Aqsa Martyrs Brigades = 31, other Fatah groups = 7, Popular / Democratic Front for the Liberation of Palestine = 3, unknown = 10.

[14] David Sanger, 2003. President Says Military Phase in Iraq Has Ended, *New York Times*, May 2.

[15] Cofer Black, 2003, cited in Walter Pincus and Dana Priest, Spy Agencies' Optimism on Al Qaeda Is Growing: Lack of Attacks Thought to Show Group Is Nearly Crippled, *Washington Post*, May 6, sec. A, p. 16.

[16] President Bush, Ambassador Bremer Discuss Progress in Iraq, 2003. White House release, October 27.

[17] Neil MacFarquhar, 2003. Arab World of Two Minds about U.S. Involvement in Iraq, *New York Times*, October 29, A10.

[18] Combating Terrorism: Interagency Framework and Agency Programs to Address the Overseas Threat, 2003. U.S. General Accounting Office, Washington, DC., May 23, 4, www.gao.gov/new.items/do3165.pdf.

[19] For example: "Saddam Hussein was an evil tyrant who wreaked havoc and abused his people for many decades. As Muslims we believe wholeheartedly in the miserable ending of all tyrants, including the one who parade today as triumphant victors." From: 2003. What after the Capture of Saddam," December 16, www.islamonline.net/livedialogue/english/Browse.asp?hGuestID=mYDRef.

[20] *National Strategy for Combating Terrorism*, 2003. U.S. Department of State, Washington, D.C., February, 13, http://usinfo.state.gov/topical/pol/terror/strategy/.

[21] Address to a Joint Session of Congress and to the American People, 2004. White House news release, September 20, 2001. Bush: 'Al Qaeda Types' Committing Terror in Iraq, 2003. *Fox News*, August 22. "These killers don't have values," President Bush declared in response to the spreading insurgency in Iraq in April 2004, "terrorists can't stand freedom," *The Times and Democrat*, April 19, 2004, http://thetandd.com/articles/2004/04/06/opinion/opinion1.txt.

[22] Views of a Changing World 2003, 2003. Survey Report, Pew Research Center, June 3, http://people-press.org/reports/display.php3?ReportID=185.

[23] Mark Tessler, 2002. Do Islamic Orientations Influence Attitudes toward Democracy in the Arab World: Evidence from Egypt, Jordan, Morocco, and Algeria. *International Journal of Comparative Sociology, 2*, 229-249. Mark Tessler, Dan Corstange, 2002. How should Americans Understand Arab and Muslim political attitudes, *Journal of Social Affairs, 19.*

[24] Khalil Shikaki, 2003. Palestinians Divided, *Foreign Affairs*, January/February; Palestinian Center for Policy and Survey Research, Public Opinion Poll No. 9, October 7-14, 2003, www.pcpsr.org/survey/polls/2003/p9a.html.

[25] DoD Responses to Transnational Threats, Vol. 2: DSB Force Protection Panel Report to DSB, 1997. U.S. Department of Defense, Washington, D.C., December, p. 8, www.acq.osd.mil/dsb/trans2.pdf.

[26] Colum Lynch, 2002. Volunteers Swell a Reviving Qaeda, UN warns, *International Herald Tribune,* December 19, 3.

[27] Gary Becker, 1968. Crime and Punishment: An Economic Approach, *Political Economy, 76,* 169-217.

[28] Alan Krueger, Jitka Malecková, 2003. Seeking the Roots of Terror, *Chronicle of Higher Education,* June 6, http://chronicle.com/free/v49/i39/39b01001.htm

[29] Alan Krueger, 2003. Poverty Doesn't Create Terrorists, *New York Times,* May 29.

[30] *Discouraging Terrorism,* 2002. Washington, D.C.: National Academies Press, p. 2.

[31] The U.S. State Dept. budget (fiscal 2003) for Foreign Military Financing includes as top receivers: Israel ($2.1 billion), Egypt ($1.3 billion), Columbia ($98 million), Pakistan ($50 million). Special Support Funds are also budgeted in emergency supplemental bills: $600 million for Pakistan (half targeted for direct military assistance); $40.5 million in economic and law enforcement assistance for Uzbekistan; $45 million in military financing for Turkey and Uzbekistan; $42.2 million for training and equipment for security forces in Uzbekistan, Tajikistan, Turkmenistan, Turkey, Kyrgyzstan, Azerbaijan, Kazakhstan; and added millions in special Defense Department funds for counterterrorism in Central Asian Republics. Michelle Ciarrocca, William Hartung, 2002. Increases In Military Spending And Security Assistance Since 9/11/01, Arms Trade Resource Center, October 4, www.worldpolicy.org/projects/arms/news/SpendingDOD911.html.

[32] Amnesty International and Human Rights Watch regularly document "horrific" and "massive" humans rights abuses occurring in countries that receive the most U.S. aid in absolute terms (Israel, Egypt, Colombia, Pakistan) and the greatest relative increase in aid (Central Asian Republics, Georgia, Turkey). For details, see supplementary online materials for Scott Atran, "Individual Factors in Suicide Terrorism," *Science,* vol. 304, April 2, 2004, pp. 47-49, http://www.sciencemag.org/cgi/content/full/304/5667/47/DC1.

[33] Global Terrorism Index 2003/4, 2003. World Markets Research Centre, 18 August; available at www.worldmarketsanalysis.com. According to the 2003 World Terrorism Index (compiled primarily for multinational investors), Columbia, Israel and Pakistan top the list of places at risk for terrorist attack (Egypt has been relatively quiet since the late 1990s, when Egypt's Islamic Jihad essentially fused with Al-Qaeda to initiate action on a more global scale). Iraq, not previously a major risk, has leapt to the forefront.

[34] September 11 One Year Later, 2002. U.S. Department of State, Washington, D.C., September, p. 14, usinfo.state.gov/journals/itgic/0902/ijge/ijge0902.htm. According to Secretary of State Colin Powell: "Terrorism really flourishes in areas of poverty, despair and hopelessness," World Economic Forum, Davos, Switzerland, January 26, 2003, www.state.gov/secretary/rm/2003/16869.htm. See also 2002, The Link between Poverty and Terrorism," statement by minister of state for foreign and commonwealth affairs, Baroness Symons, House of Lords, London, February 27, 2002; Interview with Christopher Patten, European Union Foreign Affairs Commissioner, 2004. *United Nations World Chronicle Transcript,* April 7, http://207.36.70.90/pattentrans.html.

[35] White House press release, March 22, 2002. See also comments by Nobel Peace Prize laureates, in J. Jai, 2001. Getting at the Roots of Terrorism, *Christian Science Monitor,* December 10, p. 7.

[36] Scott Atran, 2003. Genesis of Suicide Terrorism, *Science, 299,* March 7, 1534–1539.

[37] Wesley Clark, 2003. Address to Veterans of Foreign Wars, Nashua, N.H., C-Span television, December 20.

[38] David Von Drehle, 2002. Debate over Iraq Focuses on Outcome, *Washington Post, 7* Oct., p. A1.

[39] D. Cheney, interviewed on *Fox News* (with Brit Hume), 17 March 2004.

[40].The Sociology and Psychology of Terrorism, 1999. Federal Research Division, Library of Congress, Washington, D.C., September, p. 40, www.loc.gov/rr/frd/pdf-files/Soc Psych of Terrorism.pdf.

[41] Scott Atran, 2003. Who Wants to Be a Martyr, *New York Times*, May 5, p. A23.

[42] White Paper—The Jemaah Islamiyah Arrests, 2003. Ministry of Home Affairs, Singapore, January 9, http://www2.mha.gov.sg/mha/detailed.jsp?artid=667&type= 4&root=0&parent=0&cat=0&mode=arc.

[43] Raphael Ezekiel, 1995. *The Racist Mind: Portraits of American Neo-Nazis and Klansmen,* New York: Viking.

[44] *Al-Ahram Al-Arabi,* 2001. Cairo, February 3.

[45] Richard Nisbett, 2003. *The Geography of Thought: How Asians and Westerners Think Differently and Why.* New York: Free Press.

[46] Jeremy Weinstein, 2003. Resources and the Information Problem in Rebel Recruitment, Center for Global Development, Working Paper, November.

[47] Brian Barber, 2003. *Heart and Stones: Palestinian Youth from the Intifada.* New York: St. Martin's Press.

[48] Mia Bloom, in press. Devising a Theory of Suicide Terror. In *Dying to Kill: The Global Phenomenon of Suicide Terror.* New York: Columbia Univ. Press. In 2001, militant factions of the main "secular" nationalist groups, Fatah (Al Aqsa Martyrs Brigades) and the Popular Front for the Liberation of Palestine (Abu Ali Mustafa Brigades), began using language and tactics of martyrdom and Jihad to compete with increasingly popular Islamic groups for public support. Al Aqsa' Martyrs Brigades, January 10, 2003, www.idf.il/newsite/english/0112-2.stm; "Communiqués of the Martyr Abu Ali Mustafa Brigades, March 15 - April 25, 2002," www.tao.ca/~solidarity/texts/palestine/PFLPcommuniques.html; cf. Hamas communiqué (Qassem Brigades), August 9, 2001, www.intellnet org/resources/hamas communiques/hamas/comm text/2001/9 aug 01.htm.

[49] David Rhode, and C.J. Chivers, 2002. Qaeda's Grocery Lists and Manuals of Killing, *New York Times*, March 17, A1.

[50] Studies of people who become torturers for their governments demonstrate the eventual power of such blind obedience. See Mika Haritos-Fatouros, 1988. The Official Torturer: A Learning Model for Obedience to the Authority of Violence, *Journal of Applied Social Psychology, 18,* 1107–1120.

[51] Hannah Arendt, 1970. *Eichmann in Jerusalem: A Report on the Banality of Evil.* New York: Viking Press.

[52] Stanley Milgram, 1974. *Obedience to Authority.* New York: Harper & Row.

[53] Basel, Saleh, 2003. Economic conditions and Resistance to occupation in the West Bank and Gaza Strip: There is a causal connection. Paper presented to the Graduate Student forum, Kansas State Univ. April 4, 2003. Saleh compiled information on 171 militants killed in action (nearly all during the Second Intifada, 2000-2003) from Hamas and Palestinian Islamic Jihad (PIJ) news services, including 87 suicide attackers.[1] Majorities of militants were unmarried males (20-29 yrs.), from families with both parents living and 8-15 siblings, and who completed secondary school or attended college. Suicide attackers, which included bombers (29 Hamas, 18 PIJ) and shooters (14 Hamas, 26 PIJ), had more pronounced tendencies in these directions. A majority of Hamas bombers attended college; PIJ had more shooters aged 14-19. Majorities of bombers, but few shooters, had prior histories of arrest or injury by Israel's army; however, most shooters had one or more family members with such histories.

[54] Ariel Merari, in press. Social, Organization, and Psychological Factors in Suicide Terrorism. In *Root Causes of Suicide Terrorism*. London: Routledge.

[55] Scott Atran, 2003. Who Wants to Be a Martyr, *New York Times*, May 5, A23.

[56] Trent Lott, cited in *The Hill,* October 29, 2003.

[57] Timothy Spangler, interviewed on BBC News, January 21, 2003.

[58] Views of a Changing World 2003, Survey Report, Pew Research Center, June 3, 2003, http://people-press.org/reports/display.php3?ReportID=185.

[59] One possibility is to offer and guarantee a clear resolution of "final status" acceptable to majorities of Israelis and Palestinians. Without clear resolution of final status *before* implementation of « confidence building » measures, with an understanding by all parties of what to expect in the end, it is likely that doubts about ultimate intentions will undermine any interim accord – as in every case since 1948. Scott Atran, 1990. Stones Against the Iron Fist, Terror within the Nation, *Politics and Society, 18*, 481-526.

[60] Scott Atran, 2002. *In Gods We Trust: The Evolutionary Landscape of Religion.* New York: Oxford University Press.

[61] Robert Frank, 1988. *Passions Within Reason: The Strategic Role of the Emotions.* New York: Norton.

[62] A Year After Iraq War: Mistrust of America in Europe Ever Higher, Muslim Anger Persists, 2004. Pew Research Center Survey Report, March 16, http://people-press.org/reports/display.php3?ReportID=206.

[63] Kathleen Carley, 2003. Modeling covert networks. Paper presented to the workshop on Culture and Personality in Models of Adversarial Decision-Making, U.S. Air Force Office of Scientific Research, 13 Nov. 2003, Arlington, VA. See K. Carley, 2004. Estimating Vulnerabilities in Large Covert Networks. Carnegie Mellon University: Institute for Softwear research International, April.

[64] When I posed this issue to a representative of the Israeli Security Services (Shin Beit) at an FBI meeting in Charlottesville, VA (April 5, 2004), he responded that assassination of Hizbollah leaders may have helped to make that organization stronger. Concerning targeted assassination of Hamas leaders, he acknowledged that short-term considerations (disrupting the current spate of attempted suicide attacks, then averaging 48 per day) trumped consideration of long-term prospects for Israeli security. "What else can we do?" he concluded.

[65] Combating terrorism: Interagency framework and agency programs to address the overseas threat, 2003. U.S. General Accounting Office, Washington, DC, 23 May, p. 24, www.gao.gov/new.items/do3165.pdf. The "new partners in the war on terrorism" cited are the Eurasian Republics of Kazakhstan, Kyrgystan, Tajikistan, Turkmenistan, Uzbekistan and Georgia. All but Tajikistan – and just recently, Georgia - is run by former Communist Party leaders-turned-nationalists, whose rule – like Saddam's – involves brutal personality cults.

[66] George W. Bush, 2003. Introduction to *National Security Strategy of the United States*, White House, Washington, D.C., September, http://www.whitehouse.gov/nsc/nss.html.

[67] Robert McNamara, 1995. In Retrospect—The Tragedy and Lessons of Vietnam, address to the John F. Kennedy School of Government, Harvard University, April 25, www.ksg.harvard.edu/ifactory/ksgpress/www/ksg_news/transcripts/mcnamara.htm.

[68] Joseph Nye, 2004. *Soft Power: The Means to Success in World Politics.* New York: Public Affairs.

[69] In Jefferson's words: "That ideas should freely spread from one to another over the globe, for the moral and mutual instruction of man, and improvement of his condition." Thomas Jefferson to I. McPherson, August 13, 1813, in *The Founder's Constitution*, 1987, vol. 3, art. 1. sec. 8, clause 8, doc. 12, Chicago: Univ. Chicago Press.http://press-pubs.uchicago.edu/founders/documents/a1_8_8s12.html.

[70] Samuel Huntington, 1996. *The Clash of Civilizations*. New York: Simon & Schuster. If, as Huntington argues, civilizations are cultures writ large, then the same dynamical processes apply to civilizations as to cultures. Cultures, like species have no fixed boundaries or essential structures. Unlike species, they also interchange elements and merge, and split and remarry in ways that are always somewhat unpredictable (Scott Atran, *In Gods We Trust*). There is nothing fixed or inevitable in human history and international relations, no matter how hard people think it so, or try to make it so. There are always contingent and unpredictable events, and there is always an element of uncertainty between expectations and outcomes. In politics, as in economics, the most well-structured policies and practices are the ones that also produce the greatest variety and impact of unintended consequences and cascading effects, which makes them the most liable to revolutionary fall and overthrow. This may be a general characteristic of complex, dynamical systems that have "looping effects" (where agents' actions affect environments that, in turn, affect agents' actions), including systems involved in biological and cultural evolution. See Stuart Kauffman, 1993. *The Origins of Order.* New York: Oxford Univ.

[71] For Thomas Friedman, Pulitzer-prize winning *New York Times* columnist: "The emerging global order needs an enforcer. That's America's new burden." Thomas Friedman, 1999. Manifesto for the Free World, *New York Times Magazine,* March 28, 40. Most critical is American enforcement of open markets - a view that George Soros refers to as "market fundamentalism." For Friedman, "The driving idea behind globalization is free-market capitalism--the more you let market forces rule and the more you open your economy to free trade and competition, the more efficient and flourishing your economy will be. Globalization means the spread of free-market capitalism to virtually every country in the world. "[*ibid.* p. 42]. Those who believe 9/11 shattered the reality or dream of globalization are dead wrong. Thomas Friedman, 2003. Is Google God? *New York Times*, June 29. From this vantage, suicide attacks against the U.S. presence in Iraq "are a fundamental threat to civilization." Thomas Friedman, 2003. Is Peace Possible? *Paula Zahn Now*, CNN television, October 28. Those who sponsor or tolerate suicide attacks "unlike many leftists – they understand exactly what this war is about.... They understand that this is the most radical-liberal revolutionary war the U.S. has ever launched – a war of choice to install some democracy in the heart of the Arab-Muslim world." Thomas Friedman, 2003. It's no Vietnam, *New York Times*, October 30. Iraq is "no Vietnam," because the "real" aim of the war is not "to shore up a corrupt status quo, as in Vietnam." [*ibid.*] Nevertheless, U.S. leaders in the Vietnam era believed that they, too, were on a global mission to save the world from evil (communism) by nurturing democracy far from home (South Vietnam). B. Van De Mark and R. McNamara, 1996. *In Retrospect: The Tragedy and Lessons of Vietnam.* New York: Vintage.

[72] Francis Fukuyama, 1992. *The End of History and the Last Man.* New York: Simon and Schuster. Historically, emergence of liberal democracy of the kind envisaged for Iraq requires a high degree of nationalism as the individuals' primary source of social identity; nationalism, in turn, depends upon a significant degree of social and economic mobility across cultural boundaries that comes with industrialization. Without an overriding sense of nationalism, "Liberal democracy is not very good at adjudicating the claims of longstanding linguistic or ethnic communities living on their traditional territory within multi-ethnic societies." Francis Fukuyama, 1991. Liberal Democracy as a Global Phenomenon, *PS: Politics and Society*, 24, 659-664. There is little indication that Iraqi nationalism – a strategic ploy initiated by the British to help them control the population and the region between Turkey and Persia – overrides ethnic allegiance. But that only makes the nation-building experiment in Iraq more challenging and invigorating for

America's effort to implement its world-historical will. There is no real alternative because: "liberal democracy alone provides the possibility of fully rational recognition of human dignity" and "there is a rational and progressive pattern to world history." (*ibid.*) Using a faith-based logic reminiscent of Marxist-Leninist arguments that the inevitable historical direction of world history may use a helping hand to speed it along, Fukuyama opines: "We are for better or worse in the nation-building business. It indicates an increasing trend in world politics ... for failed states and troubled countries." Francis Fukuyama in A. Stephens, 2003. J. Garners says U.S. action in Iraq will change entire Middle East, *U.N. Wire* (United Nations Foundation), August 1. www.unwire.org/ UNWire/20030801/449_7157.asp. History ends, it appears, only if it can be fixed – but it won't be. Modern history is chock full of revolutionary ideologies that brought about their own destruction in an impossible attempt to realize an end to history (anarchism, Hegelianism, Marxism, Nazism, Pol Potism, Khomeneism, etc.).

[73] Robert Wright, 2000. *Nonzero: The Logic of Human Destiny*. New York: Random House.

[74] According to Sheik Omar Bakri Muhammad, founder of the London branch of Hizb Al-Takhrir ("Islamic Freedom Party") and a supporter of the *World Islamic Front*: "motivating the people to rebel against the regime under which they are living [is] the establishment of Al-Khilafah whose foreign policy is to conquer the whole world by Jihad.... As for secularism, Islam considers anyone adopting this to have committed an act of apostasy." J. Reynalds, 2003. Radical Islamic Cleric Apparently Threatens House of Commons, *American Daily*, 27 July, http://www.americandaily.com/item/1793.

[75] From Masada to Jenin, 2003. *The Palestine Chronicle*, January 10, www.palestinechronicle.com/story.php?sid=20030110102946113.

[76] Interview with Ramadan Abdallah Shalah on *Al Manar* (hizbollah television), cited in Arab accounts back Israeli version of Jenin, 2002. *WorldNetDaily*, April 24, www.worldnetdaily.com/news/article.asp?ARTICLE_ID=27370.

[77] Abu Shihab El-Kandahari, 2002. *Fatwah* on Nuclear warfare as the solution for destroying America, December 26 (reissued, September 16, 2003). Saudi cleric Sheikh Naser al-Fahd also declared in a *fatwah*: "use of WMD's is permissible, even knowing that it will kill every infidel it lands upon, including women and children." See Reuven Paz, 2003. The first Islamist *Fatwah* on the use of Weapons of Mass Destruction, PRISM special dispatches on Global Jihad, no. 1, May, 2003, www.e-prism.org/images/The%20age%20of%20non%20conventional%20terrorism.doc. In the *Ghazwa* of April 6, 2004 (weekly Urdu jihadi publication of *Jammat-ud-Dawa* – formerly *Lashkar-e-Taiba*), Hafez Sayeed, erstwhile leader of *Lashkar-e-Taiba* , declared: "Mass killings of the non-believers is the only solution to international conflicts... in the Muslims' favor."

Some Reflections on Anthropology and Political Economy

Keith Hart

Introduction

This essay attempts to draw together several strands of my work in the context of celebrating Henry Rosenfeld's life. I never managed, as he has, to develop an anthropology rooted in the history of political conflict where I live; but I share with him a commitment to making anthropological writing relevant to understanding the forces that shape contemporary society. In particular, I have been drawn to examine the political economy of state capitalism and its alternatives, and I have found much that is inspirational in his historical political economy of Israel/Palestine during the period of state capitalism's ascendancy. An anthropological approach to these questions must be vivid and particular in its treatment of people's lives, as Henry's invariably is. But, for the purposes of this short essay, I concentrate on outlining the abstract reasons that I have found for juxtaposing anthropology and political economy.

There are five loosely connected sections. In the first I approach anthropology's relationship to political economy through an attempt to define 'the human economy'. I then address the inequality of our world through the idea of *apartheid* as a universal principle of social organization. This is because the dominant social form of the twentieth century, state capitalism, combines the territorial imperative of agrarian civilization with the powers unleashed by the machine revolution. I go on to consider the possibility that the digital revolution in communications has spawned a successor phase, tentatively labeled 'virtual capitalism'. Finally I develop a class analysis aimed at clarifying the issues at stake in the political economy of the internet. These explorations point to an anthropological method for grasping our moment in history on a scale appropriate to the forces transforming it.

The Human Economy

Civilization is conceived of largely as an economy these days. And that is a good thing, since most people care a lot about their own economic circumstances. The days are long gone when politicians could concern themselves with affairs of state and profess ignorance of the livelihoods of the masses. Hence Bill Clinton's famous memo to himself, "It's the economy, stupid!" For millennia, economy was conceived of in domestic terms, as household management. Then, when money, machines and markets began their modern rise to social dominance, a new discipline of political economy was born, being concerned with the public consequence of economic actions. For over a century now, this discipline has called itself economics and its subject matter has been allegedly the economic decisions made by individuals, not primarily in their domestic capacity, but as participants in markets of many kinds. People as such play almost no part in the calculations of economists and find no particular reflection of themselves in the quantities published by the media.

My main aim is to produce an understanding of the economy that has people in it. This makes the approach broadly anthropological, in two senses. First, I am concerned with what people have done by themselves, especially when free of control by large-scale organizations. The ethnographic tradition privileges experience of life over abstract ideas. Second, my interest is in the history of humanity as a whole, our past, present and future; and my examples are drawn from all over the world. Somehow we have to find meaningful ways of bridging the gap between the two. There are of course many economies at every level from the domestic to the global and they are not the same, but I speak of 'the human economy' in the singular because the prevailing approach to economic life is itself universal in pretension and because giving priority to people's lives and purposes lends a certain intellectual unity to my efforts. At the very least, I hope to show that claims for the inevitability of mainstream economic institutions are false.

The twentieth century saw a disastrous experiment in impersonal society. Humanity was everywhere organized by remote abstractions—states, capitalist markets, science. And, as if that were not enough, the main common preoccupation was war. For most people it was impossible to make a meaningful connection with these anonymous institutions and this was reflected in intellectual disciplines whose structures of thought had no room for human beings in them. Whereas once anthropologists studied stateless peoples for lessons about how to construct better forms of society, such an exercise now seemed pointless, since we were all powerless to act. Of course, people everywhere did their best with a bad job, seeking self-expression where they could—in domestic life and informal economic practices. But the gap between individuals and society widened, even as most regimes claimed that they governed in the name of the people.

Part of the problem is intellectual. People's lives do not figure prominently in the theorems of economists. If we are to make a meaningful connection with the economy, we must understand it in more human terms. Economics is also not very good with machines. Yet the world of economic possibility depends on whether we can harness the machine revolution to human ends. Curiously enough, economists are not very good with money either. Traditionally liberal economics considered money to be an insignificant lubricant of exchange; and in any case the dominance of money in contemporary social and spiritual life is a topic too big for the economists to handle. So the three most important components of modern economic life—people, machines and money—are not properly addressed by the academic discipline devoted to its study. This emphasis on people, machines and money echoes Marx's in *Capital* (1867).

There he reflected on humanity's estrangement in the face of the modern economy by putting abstract value (money) in the driving seat, with the industrial revolution (machines) as its instrument and people reduced to the passive anonymity of their labour power. Marx's intellectual effort was aimed at reversing this order and that remains our priority today.

What might be meant by the term 'economy'? English dictionaries reveal that the word and its derivatives (economic, economical, economics, economist) have a number of separate, but overlapping referents. These include:

1. Order
2. Conservation
3. Practical affairs
4. Money, wealth
5. The circulation of goods and services
6. A wide range of social units involved

The word comes from Ancient Greek, *oikonomia*. It literally meant 'household management', the imposition of order on the practical affairs of a house, usually a large manor house in the countryside with its slaves, animals, fields and orchards. Economic theory then aimed at self-sufficiency through careful budgeting and the avoidance of trade, where possible. The market, with its rootless individuals specialized in money-making, was the very antithesis of an economy that aimed to conserve both society and nature. So in origin 'economy' emphasized the first three above while focusing on the house as its location. For Aristotle and thinkers like him, it had nothing to do with markets or money nor with wider notions of society (Polanyi 1957).

This ideal persisted in rural Europe up to the dawn of the modern age. The problem is that the economy has moved on in the last 2,500 years and especially in the last two centuries. In particular, a revolution in ideas led by Adam Smith (1776) switched attention from domestic order to 'political economy' and especially to the functioning of markets using money. Instead of celebrating the wisdom of a few patriarchs, Smith found economic order in the myriad selfish acts of individuals buying and selling commodities, the famous 'hidden hand' of the market.

Two things happened next. First, the market was soon dominated by large businesses commanding more resources than most, a system of making money with money eventually named as 'capitalism'. One of capitalism's chief features is a focus on growth, not on staying the same. Then states claimed the right to manage money, markets and accumulation in the national interest. And this is why for us 'the economy' usually refers to the country we live in. The question of world economy has encroached on public consciousness of late; and almost any aggregate from associations of states like the European Union to localities, firms and households may be said to have an 'economy' too. In the process, 'economy' has come to refer primarily to the money nexus of market exchange, even though we retain the old sense of efficient conservation of resources.

So part of the confusion with the word 'economy' lies in the historical shift from the self-sufficiency of rural households to complex dependence on urban, national and world markets. But that isn't all. It is by no means clear whether the word is primarily subjective or objective. Does it refer to an attitude of mind or to something out there? Is it ideal or material? Does it refer to individuals or to collectivities? Perhaps to all of these—in which case, we should focus on the links between them. If the economists argue that economy is principally a way of reasoning, we can hardly say that all those people who talk of economies as social objects are wrong. Moreover, if the factory revolution shifted the weight of economy from agriculture to industry, mainstream economic life now takes the form of electronic digits whizzing around the ether at the speed of light. The idea of economy as provision of material necessities is still an urgent priority for the world's poor; but for a growing section of humanity it no longer makes sense to focus on economic survival. The confusion at the heart of 'economy' reflects not only an unfinished history, but wide inequalities in contemporary economic experience.

Nor is the matter finished there. This paper is written in English and so have most of the foundational texts of economic theory and method. The term 'economy' is as specific to the English language as *société* is to the French. If the various meanings of the word are obscure in English, their translation into most other languages is even more problematic. In German, for example, the nearest indigenous term is either *Ökonomie*, referring mainly to household budgeting, or *Sozialpolitik*, with a meaning closer to public policy than economy in the English sense. Britain and America have dominated global capitalism in the 19th and 20th centuries respectively and so, gradually, the peoples of the world have come to absorb something of their economic terminology as common usage.

All of these issues and more have to be addressed if 'the human economy' is to be made a meaningful expression, so that we can talk about how world society might be considered as an economy. We must start from our moment in history, the world we live in today. So far, since the millennium, we have witnessed the collapse of the 'dot com' boom and the start of a 'war against terrorism'. September 11th, 2001 was a turning point for sure. The world is in movement, but it is not obvious how we are to understand that. The second half of the 20th century brought the peoples of the world closer together, mainly through an expanded network of markets, transport and communications. We also became much more unequal in this period. We need a vision of world history anchored in the present, so that we might understand where we have come from and where we might be going.

So many of our methods for studying society were formed by the need to understand the new nation-states of the 19th and 20th centuries that it takes a considerable shift in perspective to study world society. I have begun elsewhere (Hart 2003) to explore a 'cubist' approach to the world we live in, based on my own lifetime's experience of movement. It seems as if the world is subject today to a neo-liberal revolution imposed from above. What is the relationship between this and the liberal revolutions that inaugurated the modern age? This in turn requires us to understand how capitalism and the machine revolution were built on the unequal society bequeathed by 5,000 years of agrarian civilization. Our world is older than the ideologues of modernism claim, even as the last few decades have brought humanity into a single interactive network that is entirely new. The key to making sense of this is to see how national monopolies of economy and society were formed 150 years ago and why they may be giving way to larger- and smaller-scale processes now. To be human is to be individual and collective at once; the difficult part is to find social forms that are conducive to both. Following Marx and Engels, our task is to understand how the present phase of the machine revolution might support more democratic economic forms.

Apartheid as a Universal Social Principle

In the Great Depression, Maynard Keynes (1936) offered a solution to national elites concerned that their governments would be overwhelmed by the mass poverty and unemployment generated by the economic collapse. The rich countries today are similarly cast adrift in a sea of human misery which includes most people alive. Marx used to say that the social relations of production act as so many fetters on the development of the productive forces, by which he meant that capitalist markets could not organize machine production for the benefit of society as a whole. At the most inclusive level the main fetter on human development today is the administration of economy by nation-states which prevents the emergence of new forms of economic life more appropriate to the conditions of global integration into which we have so recently stumbled. This also, of course, prevents the implementation of a Keynesian programme aimed at alleviating world poverty by transnational redistribution of purchasing power.
In the film *Annie Hall*, Woody Allen says that he doesn't feel like eating out tonight because of all those starving millions in the Third World (Hart 1995). The audience laughs, uneasily. The gesture rings false: why tonight and not every night? No-one could live consistently with that proposition—could they? We might well ask how people live with economic inequality. And the short answer is that they don't, not if they can help it. Most human beings like to think of themselves as good. This normally involves being compassionate in the face of others' suffering. The worst thing would be to imagine that we are responsible for that suffering in some way. Better to explain it away as having some other cause: perhaps the people deserve to suffer or are just pretending to be poor. Better still not to have to think about it in the first place. In the last resort we can ignore the problem by defining them as less than fully human (not like us). Distance (in every sense—physical, social, intellectual, emotional) is the answer to the unwelcome conflict between inequality and human compassion. And, while each of us engages in thousands of voluntary acts distancing ourselves from the suffering of others, the task is performed more reliably, at the communal level, by institutions.

An *institution* is an established practice in the life of a community or it is the organization that carries it out. (The root *sta-*, to stand or set up, is shared with 'establish' and, of course, with 'state', the institution that secures all others in society). What they have in common is the idea of a place to stay, in opposition to the movement, flux and process of life itself. Institutions and agriculture go together. The conflict between fixing society in the ground and reinventing it on the move underlies our contemporary global crisis. The maintenance of inequality depends on controlling the movement of people. If the poor are to be kept at a proper distance, it would not do to have them invade the protected zones of privilege established by the rich. Better by far that they should know their place and stay there.

The two principal institutions for upholding inequality, therefore, are formal political organization (laws administered by states) and informal customary practices widely shared by members of a community (culture). The most important task of both is to separate and divide people in the interest of maintaining rule by the privileged few. Classifying people is as old as language and society; and, as Durkheim and Mauss (1905) pointed out, it can help to define solidarity within and between groups. But, it is equally well-known that labeling people differently is a means of preventing them from combining. One of the main ways that modern ruling elites everywhere have come to terms with the anonymous masses they govern is to pigeon-hole them through systems of classification. The intellectuals have devoted themselves to devising and maintaining such categories. Social science itself would be impossible if individuals were not subordinated to these impersonal systems of thought and enumeration.

To the extent that society has become a depersonalized interaction between strangers, an important class of categories rests on overt signs which can be recognized without prior knowledge of the persons involved. These are usually visual—physical and cultural characteristics like skin colour or dress; speech styles may also sometimes be taken as revealing social identity. Modern states are, of course, addicted to documentation, identity cards, preferably with a photograph of the bearer. By a standard symbolic logic, these sign systems are often taken to reveal underlying causes of behaviour—trustworthiness, ability and much besides. On this arbitrary basis, personal destinies are decided, people are routinely included and excluded from society's benefits, inequality is made legitimate and policed, the world is divided into an endless series of "us" and "them" and monstrous crimes against humanity (like genocide) are carried out.

After the Second World War, South Africa's ruling National Party set out to institute what they called *apartheid*. Despite the close integration of people of European and African origin in the country's economic system, they decided to separate the 'races', by allocating to 'blacks' a series of homelands (themselves fragmented according to 'tribal' origin) and denying them the right to reside in the cities, where the 'whites' mainly lived, except with a pass (work permit). Within the cities, black and white areas were kept apart and were unequally endowed with resources. Establishing and keeping up such a system required the systematic use of force, although collaborators were, as usual, not hard to find. Internal resistance built up gradually and the rest of the world expressed variable degrees of outrage, eventually translated into an intermittent boycott. The release of Nelson Mandela in 1990 signaled a retreat from this policy which culminated quite soon in African majority rule. But apartheid can't be abolished by the stroke of a pen.

The South African experiment was ugly, but not the most extreme form of inhumanity known to the 20th century. Stalin and Hitler between them were responsible for much worse; and even as the ANC was being peacefully elected, a million people lost their lives in Rwanda, while Bosnia revealed that genocide was alive and kicking in Europe. Yet the Afrikaners managed to provoke the most coordinated international opposition since the second world war. Why? What they did was obnoxious, but was it so exceptional? Perhaps their main crime was to be explicit, even boastful about their method of maintaining inequality. For the same method could be said to operate everywhere, without being acknowledged so openly or practiced so violently. I believe that South Africa became a symbol of a universal institution about which people were feeling generally uneasy. It offered a limited target, outside the societies of its international critics, which could be vilified and rejected as an alternative to more painful introspection. For do not people like to think of themselves as good? Opposing evil elsewhere is a way of displacing our ambivalence over how we handle inequality closer to home. In any case, after the official demise of apartheid in South Africa, something similar to it is the ruling principle everywhere by which the inequalities of world society are managed today.

This principle can be stated briefly as follows. Inequality is intrinsic to the functioning of the modern economy at all levels from the global to the local. The rich and poor are separated physically, kept apart in areas which differ greatly in their standards of living. It is impossible to prevent movement between the two areas in any absolute sense, if only for the fact that the rich need the poor to perform certain tasks for them on the spot (especially personal services and dirty work of all kinds). But movement of this sort is severely restricted, by the use of formal administrative procedures (state law) or by a variety of informal institutions based on cultural prejudice. These rest on systems of classification of which racism is the prototype and still the single most important means of inclusion and exclusion in our world.

There is a great lie at the heart of modern politics. We live in self-proclaimed democracies where all are equally free; and we are committed to these principles on a universal basis. Yet we must justify granting some people inferior rights; otherwise functional economic inequalities would be threatened. This double-think is enshrined at the heart of the modern nation-state. Nationalism is racism without the pretension to being as systematic or global. So-called nations, themselves often the outcome of centuries of unequal struggle, link cultural difference to birth and define citizens' rights in opposition to all-comers. The resulting national consciousness, built on territorial segmentation and regulation of movement across borders, justifies the unfair treatment of non-citizens and makes people blind to the common interests of humanity. As long ago as the Algerian war of independence, Frantz Fanon (1959) identified "the pitfalls of national consciousness" as the main obstacle to political progress in our world.

There are other ways of classifying the poor, of course, besides visible signs of 'natural' difference encoded as race. Nationality, ethnicity, religion, region and class can be signaled in many other ways. But the pervasive dualism of modern economies derives from the need to keep apart people whose life-chances are profoundly unequal. Engels (1887) noticed it when he came to Manchester in the 1840s. In medieval cities, the rich and poor lived together. Here the rich lived in the suburbs and worked in the city centre; and they rode to and from their businesses along avenues whose facade of shops concealed the terrible housing conditions of the slums behind. Post-apartheid Johannesburg takes this to extremes, with its rich white Northern suburbs policed by private security firms and poor blacks still crowded in monochrome townships like Soweto. The apartheid principle is now to be found everywhere in local systems of discrimination, more or less blatant. It is ironic that Israel, a society formed in part by the worst racial attack in history, is seen by many outsiders as the most blatant successor to the social experiment of the Afrikaners. Of course, passage though any of the world's airports today shows how the 'war against terrorism' has universally strengthened state apparatuses in their attempts to control the movement of people.

Between Agrarian Civilization and the Machine Revolution

In the last 200 years, the human population has increased six times and the rate of growth of energy production has been double that of the population. Many human beings work less hard, eat better and live longer today as a result. Whereas about 97% of the world's people lived in rural areas in 1800 and no region could sustain more than a tenth of its people in towns, half of humanity lives in cities today. This hectic disengagement from the soil as the chief object of work and source of life was made possible by harnessing inanimate energy sources to machines used as converters. Before 1800 almost all the energy at our disposal came from animals, plants and human beings themselves. The benefits of this process have been distributed most unequally and the prime beneficiaries have been the pioneers of western imperialism in the nineteenth century.

The 1860s saw a transport and communications revolution (steamships, continental railways and the telegraph) that decisively opened up the world economy. At the same time a series of political revolutions gave the leading powers of the coming century the institutional means of organizing industrial capitalism. These were the American civil war, Italy's *Risorgimento*, the abolition of serfdom in Russia, Britain's democratic reforms, Japan's Meiji Restoration, German unification and the French Third Republic. Karl Marx published *Capital* (1867) and the First International was formed. The concentration of so many epochal events in such a short time would indicate a degree of integration of world society. But in the 1870s, the share of GNP attributable to international trade has been estimated as no more than 1% for most countries (Lewis 1978); and the most reliable indicator of Britain's annual economic performance was still the weather at harvest-time. The 'great depression' beginning in 1873 turned out to be an effect of American and German competition on the rate of return to British capital, while the rest of the world's regions were booming. A century later in 1973, so great was the dependence of all national economies on world trade that the OPEC oil price rise set in train an economic depression from which we have still not recovered. Shortly afterwards, money futures markets were invented and within a quarter-century national governments were mostly adrift in a rising tide of money, known simply as 'the markets', conveyed at the speed of light over telephone wires as so many electronic bits (Hart 2001).

Capitalism has always rested on an unequal contract between owners of large amounts of money and those who make or buy their products. This contract depends on an effective threat of punishment if workers withhold their labour or buyers fail to pay up. The owners cannot make that threat alone: they need the support of governments, laws, prisons, police, even armies. Perhaps Karl Marx's most vivid contribution to our understanding of the modern world was to imply that capitalism was actually feudalism in drag, with the owners of the means of production still extracting surplus labour from workers under threat of coercion. By the mid-nineteenth century it became clear that the machine revolution was pulling unprecedented numbers of people into the cities, where they added a wholly new dimension to traditional problems of crowd control. The revolutions of the 1860s were based on a new and explicit alliance between capitalists and the military landlord class to form states capable of managing industrial workforces, that is, to keep the new urban masses to an unequal labour contract. Germany and Japan were the clearest examples of such an alliance. I call this phase 'state capitalism', the attempt to manage markets and accumulation by means of national bureaucracies. It became general in the first world war and it may or may not be decaying in our day.

Despite a consistent barrage of propaganda telling us that we now live in a modern age of science and democracy, our dominant institutions are still those of agrarian civilization—territorial states, embattled cities, landed property, warfare, racism, bureaucratic administration, literacy, impersonal money, long-distance trade, work as a virtue, world religion and the family. This is because the rebellion of the western middle classes against the old regime that gave us the scientific revolution and the Enlightenment, as well as the English, American and French democratic revolutions, has been co-opted by state capitalism and, as a result, humanity's progressive emancipation from unequal society has been reversed in the last century and a half. Nowhere is this more obvious than when we contemplate the shape of world society as a whole today. A remote elite of white, middle-aged, middle-class men, 'the men in suits', rules masses who are predominantly poor, dark, female and young. The rich countries, who can no longer reproduce themselves, frantically erect barriers to stem the inflow of migrants forced to seek economic improvement in their midst. In most respects our world resembles nothing so much as the old regime in France before the revolution (Hart 2002).

Africa is the most poignant symbol of this unequal world. Having entered the twentieth century with an extremely sparse population and next to no cities, Africans leave it having undergone a population explosion and an urban revolution of unprecedented speed and size. In 1950 Greater Europe (including

Soviet Central Asia) had twice the numbers of Africa. Today Africa has a population 120 millions larger than Europe and Central Asia and is projected to be well on the way to double their size by 2010. Although the conventional image of Africa is of starving peasants ravaged by war and AIDS, the new social reality is burgeoning cities full of young people looking for something to do. Africa largely missed out on the first and second stages of the machine revolution and is far behind in the present one associated with digitalization. Today development there as likely as not consists of irrigation and ox-plough agriculture. In other words, Africa has only now been going through Childe's (1954) urban revolution, erecting state bureaucracies and class society on the basis of surpluses extracted from the countryside. This is not without contradiction, given the pretensions of modern governments, the rapidly expanding population and the widespread failure to mechanize production. (Hart 1982)

This brief sketch throws new light on the relevance of Jack Goody's work (e.g. 1976) to an anthropology of world society (Hart 2004). First, like Bruno Latour (1993), he has been saying that we have never been modern. The modern project of democracy has as its antithesis the unequal society that ruled the Eurasian landmass for 5,000 years. Goody's contrast between Eurasia and Africa reminds us of the durable inequalities of our world and suggests that the reasons for them may be less tractable than we like to think. At the same time the rise of China and India underlines his warning against European complacency. The world is now simultaneously more connected than ever and highly unequal. A recent popular scientific text (Barabasi 2002) helps us to understand why this may be so. Left to their own devices, 'scale-free networks' exhibit a power-rule distribution where a few hubs are highly connected and most nodes are only weakly so. That is, the proliferation of networks, as in world markets today, would normally produce a highly skewed distribution of participants. The reduction of national political controls over global markets in the last two decades seems to have accelerated the gap between the haves and the have-nots everywhere, generating huge regional disparities in the process (Hart 2001). The task of devising institutions capable of redressing this situation seems further away today that it did in 1945.

Virtual Capitalism

The digital revolution (the convergence of telephones, television and computers into a single digital system of communications) is driven by a desire to replicate at distance or by means of computers experiences that we normally associate with face-to-face human encounters. All communication, whether the exchange of words or money, has a virtual aspect in that symbols and their media of circulation stand for what people really do for each other. It usually involves the exercise of imagination, an ability to construct meanings across the gap between symbol and reality. The power of the book depended for so long on sustaining that leap of faith in the possibility of human communication. In that sense, capitalism was always virtual. Indeed Marx's intellectual effort was devoted to revealing how the power of money was mystified through its appearance as things (coins, products, machinery) rather than as relations between living men (Marx 1867: ch 1) Both Marx and Weber (1981) were at pains to show how capitalists sought to detach their money-making activities, as far as possible, from real conditions obstructing their purposes. Money-lending, the practice of charging interest on loans without any intervening act of production or exchange, is one of the oldest forms of capitalism. So the idea of the money circuit becoming separated from reality is hardly new. Yet the changes taking place now deserve a distinctive label and 'virtual capitalism' will have to do.

In 1975, Milton Friedman, favourite economist of Ronald Reagan and Margaret Thatcher, set out, with a partner from the Chicago Mercantile Exchange, to prove that the age of Keynesian macro-economics was over (Hirsch and de Marchi 1990). The instrument he devised was intended to alleviate the uncertainties inflicted on midwestern farmers by wide fluctuations in exchange rates. If a farmer sells his pork bellies to German supermarkets six months ahead of delivery time, the dollar/deutschmark exchange rate may deteriorate and his actual earnings will be less. A futures market in money allows him to determine that exchange rate six months in advance and to stabilize his expectations. Others can buy and sell the piece of paper for the sake of making money; but the farmer gets paid reliably for his pork bellies.

From this unremarkable beginning, a new phase of capitalism emerged. In the mid-70s, almost all international currency exchanges financed the purchase of goods and services (like cocoa or tourist vacations). Today less than 0.1% of international money transactions are for that purpose; the rest is just money being exchanged for money, in a bewildering variety of instruments and forms. It is now possible to buy futures in anything, such as the likely level to be reached by the index of a major stock exchange. This was how a Singapore trader broke the British bank, Barings, by betting on the Tokyo Nikkei Index at a time when an earthquake depressed stock prices unpredictably. The advocates of derivatives claim that they are a powerful force for the integration of markets for diverse commodities. But there is also plenty of scope for 'animal spirits' (Keynes), for speculating on a hunch. There is a magical and a rational side to this development and it is by no means obvious which will win out.

Capitalism has become virtual in two main senses: the shift in emphasis from material production (agriculture and manufacturing) to information services; and the corresponding detachment of the money circuit from production and trade. This in turn is an aspect of the latest stage of mechanization. The same developments that have been responsible for the growing integration of world society are also the cause of its increasing polarization. Long-distance trade in information services requires a substantial technical infrastructure. The internet has its origins in scientific collaboration between America and Europe during the Cold War. Its main language is English. Every stage of the machine revolution has been initially concentrated in a small part of world society; and this one is no different. Equally, diffusion of the new techniques has been quite rapid. Satellite and cellular telephony, as well as videotape, have brought telecommunications to many parts of the world where the old infrastructure of electricity grids was underdeveloped. But many poorer regions appear to be stuck in phases of production that have been marginalized by this latest round of uneven development.

The most problematic issue concerns the explosive markets for money that have injected a new instability into global capitalism. After the East Asian crisis of the late 90s, the dot com bubble burst soon after the millennium. Billions of paper assets were wiped out overnight. Mismanagement by the banks has reached colossal proportions. (Crédit Lyonnais made "errors of judgment" that amounted to losses equal to the debt accumulated by the French social security fund!) This apotheosis of capital, its effective detachment from what real people do, has made many huge fortunes, often for individuals controlling sums more than the annual budgets of Third World countries.

The situation is comparable to the interwar period when a stock market boom ended with the Wall Street crash of 1929. The resulting depression lasted over a decade. This was the opportunity for states to assert their own dominance over a capitalism that was then still more national than international. The subsequent period of about four decades was the heyday of state capitalism. What political forces are adequate to regulate the present money system in the interest of people in general? The world organization of money has now reached a social scale and technical form which make it impossible for states to control it. This may be good news for democrats and anarchists in the long run; but in the meantime Hegel's (1821) recipe for state moderation of capitalism has been subverted, with inevitable results: rampant inequality at all levels and appalling human distress without any apparent remedy.

Virtual capitalism is built on abstraction and this is largely a function of ever more inclusive levels of exchange, as the world market becomes the principal point of reference for economic activity, rather than the nation-state. If we would make a better world, rather than just contemplate it, one prerequisite is to learn to think creatively in terms that both reflect reality and reach out for imagined possibilities. This in turn depends on capturing what is essential about the world we live in, its movement and direction, not just its stable forms. The idea of *virtual reality* goes to the heart of the matter. It expresses a particular form of movement—*extension from the actual to the possible.* 'Virtual' means existing in the mind, but not in fact. When combined with 'reality', it means a product of the imagination that is almost but not quite real. In technical terms, 'virtual reality' is a computer simulation that enables the effects of operations to be shown in real time. The word 'real' connotes something genuine, authentic, serious. In philosophy it means existing objectively in the world; in economics it is actual purchasing power; in law it is fixed, landed property; in optics it is an image formed by the convergence of light rays in space; and in mathematics, real numbers are, of course, not imaginary ones. 'Reality' is present, in terms of both time and space (seeing is believing); and its opposite is imagined connection at distance, something as old as story-telling and books, but now given a new impetus by the internet. Already the experience of near synchrony at distance, the compression of time and space, is altering our conceptions of social relationships, of position and movement.

I am less interested in the digital divide between people with and without access to the internet, the 'wired' elite versus the 'unwired' masses, than in how what we do off-line influences what we do on it and *vice versa*. In this, I have taken some inspiration from Martin Heidegger's *The Fundamental Concepts of Metaphysics: World, Finitude, Solitude* (1930). He says there that 'world' is an abstract metaphysical category for each of us (all that relates to or affects the life of a person) and its dialectical counterpart is 'solitude', the idea of the isolated individual. Every human subject makes a world of his or her own whose centre is the self.. The world opens up only to the extent that we recognize ourselves as finite, as individual, and this should lead us to 'finitude', the concrete specifics of time and place in which we necessarily live. So 'world' is relative both to an abstract version of subjectivity and, more important, to our particularity in the world (seen as position and movement in time and space).

The internet is often represented as a self-sufficient universe with its own distinctive characteristics, as when Castells (1996) writes of the rise of a new ideal type, 'network society'. The idea that each of us lives alone (solitude) in a world largely of our own making seems to be more real when we go online. But both terms are imagined as well as being reciprocal; they are equally abstract and untenable as an object of inquiry. We approach them from a relative location in society where we actually live. Therefore it cannot be satisfactory to study the social forms of the internet independently of what people bring to it from elsewhere in their lives. This social life of people off-line is an invisible presence when they are on it. It would be wrong, however, to deny any autonomy at all to 'virtual reality'. Would we dream of reducing literature to the circumstances of readers? And this too is Heidegger's point. 'World' and 'solitude' may be artificial abstractions, but they do affect how we behave in 'finitude'. The dialectical triad forms an interactive set:

Diagram 1. Heidegger's dialectical metaphysics

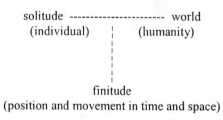

solitude ------------------------ world
(individual)   (humanity)

finitude
(position and movement in time and space)

The Political Economy of the Internet

If we are to grasp the political potential of the current world crisis, we should step back and revisit classical political economy, the discipline that was formed to make sense of the first machine revolution's economic consequences. Modern knowledge, as organized by the universities, falls into three broad classes: the natural sciences, the social sciences and the humanities. The academic division of labour in our day is concerned with nature, society and humanity, of which the first two are thought to be governed by objective laws, but knowledge of the last requires the exercise of subjectivity or critical judgment. Nature and humanity are represented conventionally through science and art respectively, but the best way of approaching society is moot, since social science is a recent and questionable attempt to bring the methods of the natural sciences to bear on a task that previously had fallen to religion. If science is the commitment to know the world objectively and art the means of expressing oneself subjectively, religion was and is a bridge between subject and object, a way of making meaningful connection between something inside oneself and the world outside. Now that science has driven religion from the government of modern societies, we must find new forms of religion capable of reconciling scientific law with personal experience.

The onset of the age of machines coincided with various attempts to develop a science of society, of which British political economy (Ricardo 1817), French sociology (Comte 1832-40) and German philosophy (Hegel 1821) all achieved a high level of definition in the years following the end of the Napoleonic wars. Political economy was concerned with how the distribution of the value generated by an expanding market economy might best be deployed in the interest of economic growth. Smith, Ricardo and their followers identified three types of resources, each thought to be endowed with the power of increase: the environment (land), money (capital) and human creativity (labour). These in turn were represented by their respective owners: landlords, capitalists and workers. Their concern was with the distribution of the specific source of income—rent, profit and wages—which between them contained the key to the laws of political economy. The conflict was then between landlords and capitalists; and the policy was to ensure that the value of market sales was not diverted from the capital fund to high rents. Only later did the main issue lie between capitalists and workers.

Political economy held that competitive markets lowered the margins available to distributive agents and forced capitalists to reduce their production costs through innovations aimed at improving efficiency. This was achieved through economies of scale, division of labour and ultimately the introduction of machines to factories (Marx 1867). The productivity of labour was thereby raised, allowing the resulting profits to be ploughed back into an expanded level of activity. Society's manpower was thereby freed up for more elaborate forms of commercial production. The only threat to this upward spiral was if landowners raised their rents to take advantage of these newly profitable industries, diverting value into wasteful consumption. Worse, whereas the capital fund was inherently limitless, land was definitely in limited supply. Economic expansion meant population growth, thereby driving up food prices and squeezing the capital fund on the other side through wages. The solution was to expose Britain's landowners to competition with cheap overseas suppliers; and this made free trade the great political issue of the mid-19th century.

The basic division between classes possessing the environment, money and human creativity persists today. Indeed, writers as diverse as Locke (1690) and Marx (1867) had visions of history in which a state of nature or society based on the land gives way to an age of money (our own) whose contradictions should lead to a just society based on fair reward for human creativity. So how are these broad classes of interest manifested in the struggle for the value generated by electronic commerce? If the owners of money and labour were first allied against the landlords (industrial capitalism) and then landlords and capitalists united to control the workers (state capitalism), how are the classes aligned in the present phase of virtual capitalism?

The landlord class has by no means rolled over and died; but the internet offers a means of escape from land shortage, indeed from spatial constraints of all kinds. The territorial controls once exercised by the landed aristocracy have largely now passed to national governments. Territorial states seek to extract taxes and rents from all money transactions taking place inside or across the boundaries of their jurisdiction. This has been greatly facilitated by the advances in bureaucracy made over the last 150 years; but it becomes more difficult when the source of value shifts from car factories and downtown shopping centres to commodity exchange conducted at the speed of light across borders. The system of involuntary transfers (taxation and rents on physical assets) could once be justified in terms of economic security for all. But that principle has been under attack by the neo-liberal consensus for over two decades now.

The capitalists have come a long way too. Having formed an alliance with the traditional rulers from the 1860s onwards, they absorbed and ultimately defeated the challenge posed by the workers. The recent revival of free market liberalism provides triumphal evidence of that victory. But the relationship of capital to the state has become increasingly moot. Money has always had an international dimension and the corporations that dominate world capitalism today are less obviously tied to their nations of origin than before. There are now some three dozen firms with an annual turnover of $30-50 billions, larger than the GDP of all but eight countries. Moreover, half of the world's 500 largest firms are American and a third European. So the world economy is controlled today by a few firms of western origin, but with dubious national loyalties. Capital and the nation-state have always had a relationship of conflict and co-operation. The wave of anti-trust legislation that accompanied the rise of monopolists like John D. Rockefeller in the early 20th century is matched today by the feebler efforts of governments to contain the economic power of Microsoft and a few companies like it. The idea of profit as a form of rent (income from property) has been confirmed, even if the burden has shifted from workers to consumers. The state competes for a share of the value of commodities in the form of taxes. But both rent and tax depend on a system of legal coercion, on a realistic threat of punishment, to make people pay up. This remains a shared concern of governments and corporations alike.

So where does that leave the rest of us? If Marx and Engels (1848) could identify the general interest with a growing body of factory workers tied to machines owned by capitalists, the majority of us now enter the economic process primarily as consumers. Economic agency is largely a matter of spending money. Despite the collapse of traditional industries in recent decades, there are still those who argue that workers associations, unions, remain the best hope for organized resistance to big business. State capitalism once made people believe in society as a place with one fixed point. But now the internet points to a more plural version of society composed of mobile networks. The mass of its ordinary users have a common interest, as individuals and pressure groups, in avoiding unreasonable regulation and retaining the economic benefits of their equal exchanges. So we may provisionally accord to the 'wired' a class identity in opposition to governments and corporations.

Table 1. The three classes of political economy

World	**Nature**	**Society**	**Humanity**
Knowledge	Science	Religion / Science	Art
Resources	Environment	Money	Human creativity
Factors	Land	Capital	Labour
Classes 1	Landlords	Capitalists	Workers
Income	Rent	Profit	Wages
Classes 2	Governments	Corporations	Persons
Income	Tax / Rent	Profit /Rent	Exchange

The main players in the political economy of the internet are thus governments, corporations and the rest of us, the people (the minority who are wired). The landed interest, following a class alliance between landlords and capitalists forged in the mid-19th century, now takes the principal form of territorial power, the coercive capacity of states to extract taxes and rents on threat of punishment or by right of eminent domain. Capitalist profit is now concentrated in a handful of huge transnational corporations whose interest is to keep up the price of commodities and to guarantee income from property (rent) in the face of resistance to payment. On an analogy with the workers who tended the factory machines (themselves initially a very small minority), we could start by looking at the wired, the ordinary people who exchange services as equals on the internet, as representatives of the general human interest. Governments and corporations need each other, for sure, but their interests are far from coincident. Both may be vulnerable to self-conscious use of internet resources by democratic movements. The main threat to us all is the jealous concentration of state and corporate power to block our collective potential to build a just society with shared responsibility for life on this planet. We could do worse then than return to Ricardo's focus on how wealth is distributed in human society and, in particular, on the contradiction between coercive demands for tax and rent and the formation of a world market where people freely exchange services as equals, using money instruments of their own devising (Greco 2001).

This rather abstract formulation can be seen at work concretely in current conflicts over intellectual property rights. The fight is on to save the commons of human culture, society and environment from the encroachments of corporate private property (Lessig 2001). This is no longer mainly a question of conserving the earth's natural resources, although it is definitely that too, nor of the deterioration of public services left to the mercies of privatized agencies. The internet has raised the significance of intangible commodities. Increasingly we buy and sell ideas; and their reproduction is made infinitely easier by digital technologies. Accordingly, the large corporations have launched a campaign to assert their exclusive ownership of what until recently was considered shared culture to which all had free and equal access. Across the board, separate battles are being fought, without any real sense of the common cause that they embody. The 'napsterization' of popular music, harbinger of peer-to-peer exchange between individual computers, is one such battle pitting the feudal barons of the music business against our common right to transmit songs as we wish. The world of the moving image, film, television and video, is likewise a site of struggle sharpened by fast-breaking technologies affecting their distribution and use. In numerous subtle and not-so-subtle ways, our ability to draw freely on a common heritage of language, literature and law is being undermined by the aggressive assertion of copyright. People who never knew they shared a common infrastructure of culture are now being forced to acknowledge it by aggressive policies of corporate privatization. And these policies are being promoted at the international level by the same American government whose armed forces now seem free to run amok in the world.

In the case of the internet, what began as a free communications network for a scientific minority is now the contested domain of giant corporations and governments. The open source software movement, setting Linux and an army of hackers against Microsoft's monopoly, has opened up fissures within corporate capitalism itself. The shift to manufacturing food varieties has introduced a similar struggle to agriculture, amplified by a revival of 'organic' farming in the context of growing public concern about genetic modification. The pharmaceutical companies try to ward off the threat posed to their lucrative monopolies by cheap generics aimed at the Third World populations who need them most. The buzzword is 'intellectual property rights', slogan of a corporate capitalism determined to impose antiquated 'command and control' methods on world markets whose constitutive governments have been cowed into passivity. The largest demonstrations against the neo-liberal world order, from Seattle to Genoa, have been mobilized to a significant degree by the need to oppose this particular version of global private property. The events of September 11th 2001 have temporarily diminished this movement, especially in North America, just as they have added to the powers of coercion at the disposal of governments everywhere. In this sense, the global movement for greater democracy and less inequality has suffered a reverse.

It is a widely shared and justified belief that the age of money, whose culmination we are witnessing today, is not in the interest of most human beings, that the American government and giant corporations are indifferent to that common interest of humanity. The rest of the world needs Americans to join them in the struggle for decent human standards in social life. They bring tremendous resources of technology, education and economic power to that struggle, but above all they bring their country's liberal political traditions. It would be a pity if the effect of September 11th was to obscure that possibility of global democratic solidarity, leaving the world stage to Texas oilmen and Muslim fanatics, with their mutual conspiracy to divide and rule.

References

Barabasi, A-L. 2002. *Linked: The New Science of Networks.* Cambridge MA: Perseus Publishing.

Castells, M. 1996. *The Information Age: Economy, Society and Culture. Vol. 1: The Rise of Network Society.* Oxford: Blackwell.

Childe, V.G. 1954. *What Happened in History.* Harmondsworth: Penguin.

Comte, A. 1975 (1832-40). *Cours de la Philosophie Positive.* Paris: Hermann.

Durkheim, E. and M. Mauss 1970 (1905). *Primitive Classification.* London: Cohen and West.

Engels, F. 1887. *The Condition of the Working Classes in England in 1844.* New York: Lovell.

Fanon, F. 1968 (1959). *The Wretched of the Earth.* New York: Grove Press.

Goody, J. 1976. *Production and Reproduction: A Comparative Study of the Domestic Domain.* Cambridge: Cambridge U.P.

Greco, T. 2001. *Money: Understanding and Making Alternatives to Legal Tender.* Burlington VT: Chelsea Green

Hart, K. 1982. *The Political Economy of West African Agriculture.* Cambridge: Cambridge U.P.

_____ 1995. Angola and the World Order: The Political Economy of Integration and Division. *In* K. Hart and J. Lewis (eds) *Why Angola Matters.* London: James Currey.

_____ 2001 (2000). *Money in an Unequal World.* London and New York: Texere. First published as *The Memory Bank.* London: Profile. (See www.thememorybank.co.uk)

_____ 2002. World Society as an Old Regime. In C. Shore and S. Nugent (eds.) *Elite Cultures: Anthropological Approaches.* London: Routledge.

_____ 2003. *Studying World Society as a Vocation*. Goldsmiths Anthropology Research Papers No.9. London: Anthropology Department, Goldsmiths College.

_____ 2004. Agrarian Civilization and World Society. In D. Olson and M. Cole (eds) *Technology, Literacy and the Evolution of Society: Implications of the work of Jack Goody*. Los Angeles: Lawrence Erlbaum.

Hegel, G.W.F. 1952 (1821). *The Philosophy of Right*. London: Oxford U.P.

Heidegger, M. 2001 (1930). *The Fundamental Concepts of Metaphysics: World, Finitude, Solitude*. Bloomington: Indiana U.P.

Hirsch, A. and N. de Marchi 1990. *Milton Friedman: Economics in Theory and Practice*. London: Harvester Wheatsheaf.

Keynes, J.M. 1936. *The General Theory of Employment, Interest and Money*. London: Macmillan.

Latour, B. 1993. *We Have Never Been Modern*. Amsterdam: Harvester.

Lessig, L. 2001. *The Future of Ideas: The Fate of the Commons in a Connected World*. New York: Random House.

Lewis, W. A. 1978. *The Evolution of the International Economic Order*. Princeton: Princeton U.P.

Locke, J. 1960 (1690). *Two Treatises of Government*. Cambridge: Cambridge U.P.

Marx, K. 1970 (1867). *Capital: A Critique of Political Economy. Vol.1* London: Lawrence and Wishart.

Marx. K. and F. Engels 1968 (1848). The Manifesto of the Communist Party. In *Marx-Engels Selected Works*. London: Lawrence and Wishart

Polanyi, K. 1957. Aristotle Discovers the Economy. In K. Polanyi, C. Arensberg and H. Pearson (eds.) Trade and Market in the Early Empires. Glencoe IL: Free Press.

Ricardo, D. 1971 (1817). *Principles of Political Economy and Taxation*. London: Penguin.

Smith, A. 1961 (1776). *An Enquiry into the Nature and Causes of the Wealth of Nations*. London: Methuen.

Weber, M. 1981 (1922). *General Economic History*. New Brunswick NJ: Transaction Books.

The Globalization of Spirit Possession

Herbert S. Lewis

When Henry Rosenfeld and his cohort committed themselves to live in Israel at the time of the establishment of the state, it seemed as though they were going to a society that would be predominantly secular and based on modern principles of reason and scientific understanding.[1] They could not have foreseen the degree to which their country, a half century later, would contain such a wealth of dreams, miracle cures, and belief in and pilgrimages to dead saints, and what might be called (by some) "superstitions," and "obscurantism." (See Beit-Hallahmi, Bilu, Edelstein, Weingrod, for some cases from contemporary Israel.) In this paper I want to address the question of why there has been such a growth of belief in and practices relating to certain forms of supernatural in the "modern world" in general. In doing so I shall also try to address part of the question of why this is happening in Israel as well.[2]

I. M. Lewis begins the Preface to the second edition of his influential Ecstatic Religion (1989) by noting that "Since the first edition of this book (1971) there has been a remarkable growth of interest in, and research on, spirit possession and shamanism." Without wanting to detract from Ioan Lewis's achievement in alerting anthropologists to the significance of ecstatic religion, I shall argue that the major cause of this remarkable growth of interest and research is due to the remarkable growth and spread of the phenomenon of spirit possession itself. The major reason that anthropologists are reporting spirit possession more and more is because they are encountering it more and more.

To our evolutionist forerunners, notably E. B. Tylor and J. G. Frazer, spirit possession represented one of those forms of superstition (animism) against which they had set themselves.[3] To them it seemed only a matter of time before "the army of spirits, once so near," would be "banished by the magic wand of science from hearth and home, from ruined cell and ivied tower, from haunted glade and lonely mere..." (Frazer 1922:546). According to Tylor, "Where the world-wide doctrine of disease-demons has held sway, men's minds, full of spells and ceremonies, have scarce had room for thought of drugs and regimen" (1920:ii, 131 [orig. 1871]). It is ironic that more than a century later spirit possession is not only alive and well but is spreading rapidly and growing in popularity all around the world, together with "drugs and regimen."

As I. M. Lewis's book makes clear, spirit possession is old, widespread, and well recognized.[4] But, as Lewis also notes, it has frequently played a peripheral role in many societies, and a survey of texts and treatises on religion reveals that until relatively recently anthropologists gave spirit possession little more than a nod, whereas today our colleagues are busy organizing symposia and volumes and writing articles and books about spirit possession in most parts of the world. The literature is growing at a extraordinary rate.

The common response to this observation, that it is only because anthropologists have chosen to focus on spirit possession at this time, is too facile. Where spirit possession and its attendant behaviors and ceremonies, including music, dance, and other arts flourish, it is not easy to miss. Had these phenomena been as much in evidence fifty years ago as they are today there would have been no reason for anthropologists to have ignored them. [5] Although we have certainly become far more alert and attuned to the topic today, there is so much more research and writing on it because spirit possession itself is becoming less peripheral and more salient in the lives of the people we study.

While a variety of manifestations of spirit possession flourish in the contemporary world, I am particularly interested in one form that I shall call, for the sake of exposition, "oracular spirit possession."

Types of Spirit Possession

Given the underlying belief that powerful incorporeal spirits exist and are capable of seizing and possessing human beings, there are a number of ways that people can attempt to deal with these supernatural beings. Ioan Lewis writes of two main types of ecstatic religion in his book, and I attempted a rough categorization of spirit possession manifestations in Ethiopia, finding at least five distinct approaches to the reciprocal relations between spirits and humans in that culture area alone (1983). (Cf. M. Spiro's types of possession in Burma [1967:157ff.]) In this paper I want to focus on one sort, *oracular* spirit possession, which is essentially what Raymond Firth calls "spirit mediumship." (Firth 1967b: 296; cf. Gilbert Rouget.)

In oracular spirit possession, believers understand that the spirits who possess particular individuals either have direct power over the lives of human beings (and not merely the medium being possessed) or that they have special information about the supernatural forces that do have such power. Therefore, rather than trying to exorcise the spirits—as people do in cases where the spirits are seen as mostly malevolent--they need to cultivate them in order to make use of their knowledge and to try to derive the most benefit from these powers. Believers want information in order be restored to health, bear children, seek protection, and perhaps remedy a variety of life problems.[6]

In contrast to spirits that are seen as trouble-makers, such as the *zar* of Northeast Africa (and contemporary Israel [Edelstein]) or those difficult Moroccan *jnun* Crapanzano reports on, these powerful and potentially benevolent spirits are invited, pleaded with, cajoled, to come and take hold of the medium. The spirits are urged to speak and to respond to the questions and petitions of the faithful who have come to have their problems solved through communication with them. They are sung to, prayed to, praised, thanked, and given presents. (I. M. Lewis calls this "accommodation" or, after Luc de Heusch, "adorcism.") The spirits are asked questions about the causes of ills and the course of action to take for better fortune. They are begged for forgiveness and understanding. Because they have a hand in human destiny, the spirits are approached for their aid in the affairs of men and women.[7]

As the missionary Henri Junod put it in *Les Ba-Ronga* (1898),

> They strive to establish intercourse with the Beyond in which they firmly believe. They are not concerned with driving out spirits as were those who expelled demons in the middle ages and in apostolic times, but with getting into touch with them, knowing their name, their history, and ensuring by expiation, by blood, that these mysterious beings will no longer torture the sick by bodily afflictions, but will speak [to] them gently and rather become their protectors.
>
> (Quoted in Oesterreich 1966:377.)

An Ethiopian Case

The following example of oracular spirit possession is based on fieldwork in Ethiopia. In 1965-66 I carried out research in a rural area of west central Ethiopia which at that time had experienced virtually no "development" and no disturbance or dislocation. Outside of the very few small towns strung along the one east-west road there were no schools, clinics, running water, secondary roads, wage labor; there was no "capitalism," no industrialization, no urbanization. The Oromo people of the rural areas, almost everyone, that is, were subsistence farmers, eating the food they produced from their fields and their livestock, and selling what they could spare of their grain crop to buy salt, coffee, an occasional item of clothing, and other small items from the periodic markets. I revisited these people briefly in 1991 and 1993 and found the belief in and activities associated with the spirits very much as it had been earlier, so I shall use the present tense when describing it. (For fuller accounts see Knutsson 1967, H. S. Lewis 1990.)

The Oromo believe in a powerful supernatural being called *wak'a,* which is also the word for "sky." But between this remote god and living men and women there are the *ayana,* incorporeal and invisible spirits that are closely involved with humans.

The *ayana* care about human morality, and while they punish bad conduct they may also alleviate the sufferings of the good, the penitent, and the faithful. They are capable of affecting human lives immediately and directly, for good or ill. They can cause the barren woman to bear children, the herder to find lost animals, and the weak to combat more powerful opponents--if the person is in the right. They can punish the wicked with illness, madness, death, or the loss of animals, crops, or anything at all.

The spirits are capable of possessing individual men and women, taking hold of their bodies, making them do their bidding, and speaking and acting through the medium of the possessed person. When possessing mediums (who are called *k'allu*) the *ayana* manifest themselves through the movements they force upon the *k'allu,* and by the words they speak and sounds they make through them. On these occasions living women and men have the opportunity to address the spirits, directly or through other human intermediaries, and receive responses in return.

People gather periodically at the temples of these *ayana* and by drumming, singing, and imploring, induce the spirits to possess the *k'allu*. The mediums are impressively dressed in the trappings and regalia appropriate to the particular *ayana* they call upon, and they lead the rituals of propitiation. After the appropriate singing, drumming, and movements, the spirit is expected to seize the *k'allu* and make its presence known by various signs, including the frenzied movements of the host. This sort of performance is reported over and over again from all over the world.

People come before the *ayana* and give thanks to them, ask for blessings, tell the stories of their (often terrible) troubles and ask for relief and well-being. Not infrequently the *ayana* themselves have caused these troubles as retribution for the sufferer's wrongdoing. Many hundreds of people come to present their petitions at the temples of the greatest of the *k'allu* and *ayana,* sometimes staying at the temples for several days. They bring offerings to fulfill their vows or show their fealty. Some *k'allu* are possessed by relatively unimportant *ayana* and have small followings. Others are possessed by a number of very powerful spirits, and these men and women may influence the lives of thousands, even tens of thousands, of believers. As a result, the *k'allu* themselves may become powerful and wealthy figures, maintaining large ritual centers, supporting many servants, functionaries, and their own families from the resources generated from the offerings of the faithful.

Through the mediumship of the *k'allu* ordinary humans are enabled to communicate directly with the spirits in order to learn why they are suffering. They can find out what spirit is punishing them (has "caught" them), and why, and learn what to do to make amends with the spirits and with their fellows whom they have wronged. They receive diagnoses and directions for action: to reconcile with others, to pay indemnification, to carry out rituals, and so on.

Some people attend just to watch and listen and be part of the crowd and the excitement, or to support their needy friends and relatives. They meet other people, join in the singing, and listen to the narratives of pain and loss--some of which serve as powerful cautionary tales to the listeners who may react as one would to horror stories.

The *k'allu* had moved to the center of western Oromo life in the countryside by the mid-1975s. They supported and organized an important developing rural "court" system for major conflict resolution and they underwrote the largest public celebrations in that part of Ethiopia. In 1975 the country was taken over by the soi-disant Marxist-Leninist "Derg" regime and many mediums were forced into hiding, but immediately after the downfall of the "revolutionary" regime in 1991 many emerged to restore their institutions.[8]

In summary, this is a typical case of spirit mediumship, people in which people believe in and relate to spirits that are to be feared, but also cultivated, propitiated, prayed to, communicated with, brought offerings, and served, in the search for health and security. This is different in principle (though not always in practice) from the way *zar* spirits are understood and treated, and it is different also from the phenomenon of mass possession that sometimes takes hold of Oromo women and male transvestites and drives them to run around the countryside in groups, from one ritual center to another.[9] "Ayana" possession can also be distinguished from forms of individual possession that make some people "insane," but, as noted in footnote 6, a person who appears to be sick or mad as a result of possession by a spirit may be going through episodes which will eventually lead to a career as a medium.

The origins of this institution among the Oromo are not lost in the primordial mists. It evidently developed over the past 70 or 80 years. Both Knutsson's informants and mine claimed that the first *k'allu*, those who created the institutions and rituals that exist today, were the grandfathers of the *k'allu* who flourished in the mid-1960s, at the time of our fieldwork. And in fact the literature on the Oromo before this time (meagre as it is) contains no mention whatever of powerful spirits and mediums--something that could not be missed in the 1960s. (As Natvig remarks on a similar case, "It would be difficult to perform zar ceremonies without anyone noticing" [1991: 180]. I was told about the *k'allu* and *ayana* on my first day in the area during a casual meeting with schoolboys.) It seems clear that mediumship among the Oromo was a new phenomenon developing and spreading rather than an ancient or "traditional" one persisting.

Other contemporary cases of oracular spirit possession

Despite the antiquity and near worldwide distribution of oracular spirit possession, there is considerable evidence that it is currently being adopted by more peoples, or at least becoming more popular and becoming more acceptable among a wider range of socio-economic and religious groups throughout the world. In the following section I can do no more than hint at the wealth of evidence.[10]

The occurrence of oracular spirit possession would seem to be pan-African in its distribution, from the northwest to the southeast, from the Atlantic to the Indian Ocean and its islands. The literature is so vast and ubiquitous that it would be pointless to try to survey it, but I shall cite only a very few exemplars that point to the growth of the phenomenon.[11]

In Ethiopia alone, before the revolution in the mid-1970s, there was a great efflorescence of different types of spirit possession. (See Knutsson 1975; H.S. Lewis 1983.) Oracular possession was flourishing among the Oromo of central and western Ethiopia, among the Guji Oromo of southern Ethiopia, and in northern Kenya where Somali, Boran, and other Oromo groups lived together. (Paul Baxter [personal communication] reports an increase among the Borana between the 1950s and the 1980s.) For a while it had a vogue among the Sidamo (J. & I. Hamer). I.M. Lewis discussed a similar phenomenon among the people of Kafa (based on Amnon Orent's dissertation).[12]

M.J. Field, working among the Akan of Ghana in the 1950s (then the Gold Coast) found many flourishing shrines at which oracular spirit possession took place that had been established only in the 1940s and 1950s. What is more, she reports that they were rapidly growing in number; in her area alone the shrines had increased from three to twenty-nine (1960:87). In 1921 Oesterreich wrote, "It is a very remarkable fact that possession in Egypt is not a survival of the old manifestations, but appears to have been introduced from Abyssinia a few decades ago..." (1966:230), and Natvig (1991) presents evidence that validates this contention. Even if, as Natvig suspects, it was introduced by slaves from the Sudan and Ethiopia, today many middle class and wealthy men and women in Egypt may participate in possession ceremonies regularly (e.g. Saunders 1977).

Lesley Sharp writes, "Within the last fifty years...there has been a virtual explosion in the incidence of tromba possession" in northwest Madagascar, producing a great number of women mediums "who are respected by both commoner Sakalava and non-Sakalava as powerful healers and as advisers on personal affairs" (1993: 2). Sue Kenyon reports that *zar* possession is "a phenomenon that has expanded rapidly in recent years" in the Sudan, and "is becoming both more popular and more acceptable"—in the context of modernizing processes (1995: 107, 118). One of the most talked-about ethnographic accounts of recent years is *Guns and Rain: Guerillas and Spirit Mediums in Zimbabwe*, by David Lan (1985). The works on possession and mediumship by Paul Stoller among the Songhay (1989b), Susan Rasmussen among the Tuareg (2001, e.g.), Janice Boddy (1989) and Susan Kenyon 1991) in the Sudan, and Michael Lambek (1981) on the Indian Ocean island of Mayotte add to our growing awareness of these phenomena. (Also see the volumes edited by I. M. Lewis 1991, and Behrend and Luig 1999.)

Oracular spirit possession appears to be flourishing throughout South Asia from Nepal to Sri Lanka. To give just a few examples, in one recent account, Mary Hancock (1995) tells of a woman medium in urban South India among Smartha Tamil Brahmans. This woman has built up a congregation of devotees who come to her home for the same sorts of reasons that people attend the temples of the k'allu of the western Oromo. A goddess possesses this medium, speaking through her, as she "advised and counseled an ever-increasing population of devotees." Here, too, people bring offerings that help support the institution at the same time as they add to the display and to the status of the medium. Isabelle Nabokov who worked among Tamil villagers in the late 1980s found spirits and possession inescapable (personal communication; 2000). Kathleen Erndl has described something similar among women in North India (1993) while J. McDaniel discusses ecstatic religion in Bengal (1989) and William Fisher writes of the profusion of spirits and possession in Nepal (1988). And these are only a few examples of the very many that could be cited from South Asia. At the annual meetings of the South Asianists at Madison, Wisconsin in 1984 a full day was devoted to sessions on spirit possession. In 1988 one session was devoted to Nepal alone. This would not have happened 30 years earlier. Surely it is a measure of the increase in the incidence of the phenomenon, not just of scholarly interest in it. Nor is there any lack of literature on spirit possession in Malaysia (e.g., R. Firth 1967a; C. Kessler 1977; M. Roseman 1991), Borneo, or Thailand.

Over and over one hears that spirit possession is becoming more popular than it had been, often replacing other religious manifestations. Walter Irvine writes of "the growth of professional spirit mediumship in the recent past" in Northern Thailand, to some extent displacing ancestor spirit cults. He estimates that there was an increase of practitioners in the city of Chiang Mai from about 30 in the late 1950s to between 250-300 in 1977. These mediums and their spirits can help explain or cure illnesses, protect members of one's family, aid in the search for a better job, influence a superior, or "discover the winning number of a lottery draw"(1984:315). (Irvine's article appears in a special issue of *Mankind* that contains 11 papers on spirit cults and the position of women in Northern Thailand.) Elizabeth Collins (1997) claims there has been a notable steady increase in the popularity of *bhakti* devotionalism and possession trance among Hindu Tamils in Malaysia.

In Brazil, where it has been said that over 95% of the people believe in spirits of one sort or another, Umbanda, Macumba, and Candomble, seems to follow the same general pattern as that described for the Oromo *k'allu*: the adept or medium maintains a ritual center to which others come for possession ceremonies. They sing and drum and bring the spirits down upon the medium, whose voices then relays messages to the believers who gather for solace, information and help. (See E. Pressel, e.g. on Umbanda.) But in Brazil some people turn to healers who work with a more distinct "medical model," operating on patients or writing prescriptions or healing through the laying on of hands while possessed by spirits of long-dead doctors. (Greenfield 1987.) This form of *espiritismo, kardecismo*, is based on the ideas of Allan Kardec, the influential nineteenth century French writer who established this version of belief in spirits and reincarnation.[13]

There are said to be hundreds of thousands of Cuban immigrants in Florida who are turning to Santeria, among whom are gamblers who are trying to improve their odds, just as Brazilian devotees of Macumba seek good fortune in soccer games, and as Akan lorry drivers resorted to mediums for protection on the roads (Field 1960: 122-123). (On Santeria see Gonzalez-Wippler 1992; Murphy 1988.)[14]

There is hardly an area in the world for which we cannot find recent accounts of spirit possession and accompanying practices and beliefs. Michael Kearney describes a system for healing through *espiritualismo* in northwest Mexico that fits the profile exactly. "Each temple is founded by a spirit medium, known as a *materia*, who has done so at the command of a spirit-being which appeared to her during the course of an illness" (1979:20). The afflicted come to the temple at scheduled sessions, at which times the mediums become possessed and the spirits can attend to the needs of their clients. (Kaja Finkler has written extensively about possession and healing in other areas of Mexico [e.g. 1986].)

Nor is spirit mediumship lacking in modern East Asia. For Japan see, for example, Takie S. Lebra's account of spirit possession in a Japanese healing cult (1976), Laurel Kendall's extensive writings on Korean shamanism and possession, Melford Spiro on Burmese supernaturalism, and David Sutton on Taiwanese spirit mediums.

In the United States and England it is not only "new agers" who turn toward "channeling" and the spirits. Once again, as in the Victorian era of E. B. Tylor, spirit possession is undergoing a revival in England and America. (For Victorian England see, for example, A. Owen, 1989. No less a man of the socialist left than James Kier Hardie was a firm believer in spirits.) A quick check of the internet reveals a very wide range of concern with spirits, and the religion pages of the weekend editions of the Madison, Wisconsin newspapers (for example) carry numerous notices of charismatic and Pentecostal church services that feature healing services, speaking in tongues, and possession by the Holy Spirit. And along with the resurrection of the Orthodox Christian faith in Russia there is apparently an efflorescence of belief in spirits and many other supernatural phenomena. My colleague Anatoly Khazanov reports that shamanism has become very important among peoples in Siberia, only partly as a symbol of ethnic revival and nationalism. (Alexander S. Mikovsky gives a vivid picture of a contemporary Siberian shaman [1992]).

Spirits and Saints in Contemporary Israel

In Ethiopia, in early 1965, a woman living to the east of the town of Ambo sent word to the prominent *k'allu*, Fayisa Innika, saying that the *ayana*, Abba Fit'al, had appeared to her in a dream, saying that he would soon come to possess Fayisa, but first there had to be a temple built for him. Accordingly, Fayisa obtained use of an appropriate piece of land, not far from the road and near a small Tuesday market, and sent out word for people to bring wood for the walls and the posts, vines and split saplings for binding the uprights, and grass to thatch the roof. When these were collected he called upon the people to come to work on the temple. On the appointed day many came to work on the structures while others brought food and drink. The temple and a smaller structure for the *k'allu* and for storage were soon built. Then the spirit came to possess the *k'allu* and people began to attend sessions at the temple by mid-1966.

In Israel, "In 1973 a forty-year-old man named Avraham dedicated a small room in his modest apartment to Rabbi David u-Moshe, following a dream series in which the saint had appeared to him and indicated his wish to reside with him. In so doing Avraham claimed to have transferred the saint from the Atlas Mountains to Israel" (Bilu 1987:289). And thus this apartment in the city of Safad became the center of a saint, a *tsadik*, and another destination for pilgrimage. On Lag b'Omer in 1977 I found myself among the many thousands of Israelis, most of Moroccan origin, who streamed through that apartment on that day. They were following the particular *hillula* (pilgrimage) that runs from Tiberius and the tomb of Meir Baal Ha-Nes, through Hatzor and the shrine of Honi Ha-Me'agal, via Rabbi David u'Moshe's shrine in Safad, and ends the day in Meron at the tomb of Rabbi Shimon Bar Yohai.

In January 1984, Harvey Goldberg, Yoram Bilu, and I visited the day-old grave of Baba Sali (Rabbi Yisrael Abuhatsera) in the small city of Netivot, and congregated with some of the many mourners as they arrived from as far away as London and Lyons. We talked with the people on the long line waiting to enter the house to express condolences to the Abuhatsera family. We listened to the stories of the miracle cures worked by Baba Sali, "when all others had assured us there was no hope." Within a few years his small grave in the cemetery was replaced by a great tomb in a magnificent domed stone building that also contains a fine synagogue. This building is surrounded by numerous vendors selling posters, tapes, videocassettes, key chains, and all manner of religious articles, trinkets, and souvenirs to the thousands upon thousands of visitors who come to visit the saint's shrine each year. One can buy bottles of water thought to have curative properties because they are supposed to have been blessed by the *tsadik*. A new *yeshiva* (school for higher Jewish study) has been erected nearby.

Over the past 40 years, Israelis of North African origin, especially from Morocco, have revived and elaborated the institution of saint worship right in the heart of a state whose foremost theoreticians and political leaders were determined rationalists who had turned their backs on religious belief and practice, let alone anything as "primitive" and "backward" as saint worship. Nor are these hidden institutions, involving a small minority of new immigrants just off the boat. People from Morocco and Tunisia account for more than 10% of the Jewish population of Israel and the institution is being spread and further institutionalized and elaborated by veteran Israelis, people whose families have been resident in Israel for half a century in many cases.

Spirit possession is not a prominent part of the adoration of these saints but there are points of similarity between this growing institution and oracular spirit mediumship. In each case the primary motivation for people to flock to these centers of supernatural power is the hope that they will benefit from this association, above all in their quest for cures, health, and well-being.[15] (It is not the only motivation, of course.)

Alex Weingrod asks of the followers of another saint, "why do they come? What impels or motivates these crowds of persons to take part in Hillulat Ha'Rav Chayim Chouri, Rabbi Chouri's memorial celebration?" (1990:39ff.). The key is their belief "that the rabbi, now dead, possesses magical or mystical powers and that taking part in the pilgrimage and prayer at his grave is both rewarding in itself and may also have certain beneficial consequences" (40). It is said that the tsadik "is able to perform miraculous acts..." and people come with "specific prayers or requests in mind. These typically refer to a range of personal as well as family problems and quandaries: illness, female barrenness, the inability to resolve some vexing problems, or prayers for good luck in a new venture that the celebrant is about to begin." (40)

Joel Greenberg of the New York Times offers the following description of activities at the annual pilgrimage to the tomb of Baba Sali.

> But the center of activity was inside the shrine, where crowds of men and women...surged against the velvet-covered tomb of the saint. Straining to touch his last resting place, they placed on the grave bottles of water that they would later drink, believing that the liquid had been blessed.
>
> "Baba Sali, help me," some women cried out, while others leaned against the tomb, whispering prayers and requests. Some asked for children, others for

protection from road accidents, still others for a safe return of sons from the army. A bachelor asked for a wife. (2/14/93)

And all around there will be people speaking of miraculous cures that happened to them, their family members, people they know, and those they have just heard about. (See footnote 19.) With some variations, I believe that the discussion of "causes" and processes that follows is relevant for hillula and attendance upon the saints in Israel as well as the spread of oracular spirit mediumship elsewhere.

The Problem of Explanation

It is not uncommon for authors of works on spirit possession and mediumship to offer explanations of the causes of these striking phenomena. (See Boddy 1995 for a relatively recent survey of some of these.) Some years ago, when researchers speculated on the origins and *raison d'etre* for possession in the particular societies they studied, they tended to offer answers in social-psychological terms specific to each society, perhaps as the result of some sort of "problem" in each case. These are often social psychological in nature, stressing the functions of possession for those suffering status deprivation or requiring an outlet for or respite from troubles inherent in their culture and society. I.M. Lewis's influential writings (1966, 1971) stressed the importance of *zar*-type spirit possession for women enduring the hardships and afflictions of "the subordinate female sub-culture" (1971:99; cf. Messing 1958). [16] Both Simon Messing (1958) and John and Irene Hamer (1966) consider the importance of possession to status-deprived men, with Messing calling possession "group therapy." (See H. S. Lewis 1983 for a discussion of a variety of explanations in the Ethiopian context.)

Benjamin Beit-Hallahmi's *Despair and Deliverance: Private Salvation in Contemporary Israel* (1992) is an excellent example of an attempt to explain the roots of magical thinking and action as the result of personal insecurity in a crisis-filled society. Although he doesn't deal with manifestations of spirit possession or with the development of saints and pilgrimages, Professor Beit-Hallahmi discusses such manifestations of the turn to the irrational as the "return" to orthodox—even ultra-orthodox-- Judaism; the development of new religions, sects, and cults; the search for self-improvement through Alcoholics Anonymous, the cult of dieting, or good sex); interest in and involvement with the occult as well as with "psychotherapy subculture." The author contends that these deviations from the expected rationality of modernity are expressions of the despair of those who cannot adjust to the malaise and the crises in Israeli society, of which there have been so many. [17]

In the era of "the posts" another type of explanation has became widespread. These days spirit possession is as likely to be seen as resistance, a response to oppression and domination and to the confusions and losses people suffer through urbanization, capitalism, and globalization. It can be seen as another "weapon of the weak," growing in reaction to negative experiences of deprivation. (See, e.g., Boddy 1989, Collins 1997, Jean Comaroff 1985, Ong 1987, Stoller 1989a.)

Where once social scientists who were surprised (perhaps appalled) at the persistence of the irrational in the face of "modernization" had recourse to something like "anomie" as an explanation, today "resistance" strikes the right chord. But it seems a little too easy for an investigator to explain away occurrences undreamt of in our philosophy or social science with reference to the assumed difficulties that others have coping with change, urban life, industrialization, capitalism, racism, or patriarchalism.

I do not want to deny or make light of the extent of the difficulties accompanying change, or the dislocations of "modernity," or the injustices and indignities of colonialism, racism, and patriarchalism, or to deny that people will resist indignity, injustice, and oppression. And it is clear that spirit mediumship, *zar*, or shamanism may become prized symbols of group identity and culture for Oromo in Ethiopia, Ethiopians in Israel (Edelstein 2002), Songhay in Niger (Stoller 1989), or Siberian peoples, Cuban-Americans, or any other group striving to distinguish itself and improve its status. It is also certain that individuals may improve their social, economic, and political positions by becoming mediums or by associating themselves with the spirits and the institutions surrounding them. But this does not explain the existence of these beliefs and institutions in the first place. It only speaks to some of their uses.

I contend that oracular spirit possession is growing in popularity around the world for different reasons than those so often cited and I shall suggest some different perspective on the problem. [18] To begin with, I believe that scholars too often prefer to impute unseen "deeper" social and social-psychological causes of these phenomena while ignoring the most obvious and fundamental fact: people actually *believe* that these powers exist and can affect their lives. If they did not believe, none of this would be possible.

Second, writers on this topic rarely look beyond the single case that they have studied in depth; absorbed in the unique features of a single case they ignore the parallels that exist elsewhere.[19] We get another perspective by considering this phenomenon in the light of its worldwide distribution.

Another Approach

It goes without saying that people, as individuals and as members of groups, will adopt beliefs and practices of spirit possession and mediumship for their own reasons, and they will shape it in their own ways, adapt it to their own needs, produce new combinations of elements, and imagine and create new ways to do things. Thus each local situation may have *additional* particular reasons for being and benefits for individuals and the group. But I suggest that, when seen in worldwide perspective, oracular spirit possession offers people a general set of productive ideas to use in the pursuit of physical wellbeing and security. It is worth attending to this aspect of "globalization" as well as to the internet, the cell-phone, multinational capitalism, and "neo-liberalism."

The principal elements in the argument:

1. The spread and/or the increase in popularity of spirit possession is occurring on such a scale at present that it should not be looked at, in the first instance, as outgrowths of particular local causes but as the result of a great wave of *diffusion*, or the spreading of ideas and practices from one group to another, adopted and adapted for local use.

"Diffusion" has long been out of fashion as explanation in anthropology for a number of reasons—both right and wrong. For those whose anthropology derives from ancestors who fought against the *Kulturkreislehre* of Germany and Vienna and the "extreme diffusionists" of Britain, the very term is anathema, for good reason. For those of a neo-evolutionist bent who associate it with the attack on evolutionism and with "particularism," it fares little better. But for those who appreciate Franz Boas's insistence on the necessity to try to work out the "actual" histories of cultures and cultural growth in order to understand the processes of culture, diffusion has a very different meaning. In the tradition of Boas, A. L. Kroeber, Melville Herskovits, Alexander Lesser, Ralph Linton, and others, diffusion is one of those fundamental processes by which cultures change, through learning from others, through the processes of emulation, through borrowing. Innovation, or invention, and diffusion, and the consequences (often unanticipated) of these, are the basic processes of change and culture growth. (Cf. Barnett 1953; E. M. Rogers 1971; Tarde 1903.)

Those favoring the perspectives of structural-functionalism, neo-evolutionism, and Marxism, look for explanations in terms of internal, system-based causes and repeated independent inventions due to like causes. The first two ignore or deny history, and all three favor the discovery of "laws;" they privilege "society" or "culture" over the individual. (For a relevant recent statement of British anthropological antipathy to the word see I.M. Lewis 1989b: 187.) But today another turn is discernible, to a consideration of the agency of individuals, and of groups making choices in the light of both received ideas ("culture") and their existential circumstances. In this view, the choices that individuals make, given their interests, situations, knowledge, and perceptions, are seen as significant. There are also signs of a new openness to the idea of cultural transmission from one group to another. (See, e.g., Appadurai 1990; Fox 1992.) And I argue that in the case of spirit mediumship, the process of emulation, borrowing, and diffusion is currently going on apace.

Probably no one would seriously contend that spirit mediumship is invented independently and anew each time it appears somewhere; the evidence of borrowing is often obvious. Generally, adjacent peoples, and even peoples at considerable distance from one another, share similar linguistic usages, operate with recurrent images, ideas, and "scripts." There are similarities of decoration and regalia from people to people, and it is not uncommon for one group to entertain spirits that represent dead historical figures or spirits from neighboring groups. According to Katherine Bowie, in northern Thailand women are often possessed by the spirits of Burmese war leaders. (Kearney [1979], Sharp [1993], and Giles [1995] offer examples from their areas. H. S. Lewis [1983] and

Kenyon [1991b] discuss the diffusion of possession throughout Ethiopia and the Sudan, respectively.) That borrowing is involved is clear; the question is why is so much being borrowed so widely and developed so rapidly at this time?

2. In the case of oracular spirit possession we are dealing with what David Hume, speaking of religion in general, called "the irresistible contagion of opinion" (1956: 76). Social science explanations in terms of social status, psychological disorientation, or resistance may tell us a great deal about the uses and the dynamics of spirit possession and mediumship in particular contexts, but we should not lose sight of the fundamental basis on which the phenomenon stands: people believe in these beings and their powers. If they didn't there could be no such institution.

The growing popularity of oracular spirit possession should be seen much the same way as we used to view the major functions of "religion" in general. With Melford Spiro, I see religion in part as an institutionalized means to satisfy the need "to know, to understand, to find meaning.... Religious belief systems provide the members of society with meaning and explanation for otherwise meaningless and inexplicable phenomena" (1966:109-110). In addition to explanation, however, religious beliefs and practices may also aid humans in coping with and trying to control the unknown forces that affect them, and in their "attempts to overcome or transcend suffering." As Spiro puts it,

> *The most obvious basis for religious behavior is the one which any religious actor tells us about when we ask him - and, unlike some anthropologists, I believe him.* He believes in superhuman beings and he performs religious ritual in order that he may satisfy, what I am calling, substantive desires: desires for rain, nirvana, crops, heaven, victory in war, recovery from illness, and countless others (1966:112; my emphasis).[20]

Oracular spirit possession is probably spreading as rapidly as it is because it carries the promise to help human beings in the struggles of their lives. The problem of health always takes first place, but the spirits' writ will usually be broadened to deal with the full range of human problems. People turn to these spirits and the mediums in search of better health, children, protection, and for explanations of why they are suffering.

If one wants to control one's fate in an uncertain world, what is more auspicious than to actually speak to the beings that either control that destiny or are in a position to give information and advice about it? Oesterreich (349) offers the following account from a missionary among the Tamils. "The worshippers of the village gods...believe that through their priests they are in direct communication with their gods--through these very utterances of the priest when in a state of possession. They sometimes point to a frank contrast with the Christians: 'Your God never talks to you, but we have a god who converses with us.'" And M. A. Muecke, who writes, "Spirit mediumship has enjoyed a rising tide of popularity in urban areas of northern Thailand" (1992: 97) concludes that "The mediums...offer far more than predictability to their clients. They offer knowledge of the supernatural, and ...moral power" (102). These would seem to be powerful attractions indeed.

During the era when modernization theory was fashionable it was common for social scientists to accept the idea that urbanization itself might cause disorientation and sufficient normlessness for newcomers to the city to cling to the supernatural during a period of transition to true "modernity." This attitude may still be influencing the tendency to attribute the growing popularity of spirit possession in cities to moral dislocation. But a wider comparative view indicates it has been spreading in rural areas as well, and among people of many different social and economic statuses. Besides, can we demonstrate that there is more need for supernatural aid when one lives in Sao Paulo or Chiang Mai than when one lives in the countryside? There is at least as much illness, and certainly poorer medical care, in the rural areas, and plenty of other sources of uncertainty. What are our measures of relative insecurity? [21]

Explanations that depend upon the presumed disorientation of urban life smack of "Tylorism" or non-believer's ethnocentrism. It suggests that people will accept something that is as irrational, as "primitive," as spirit possession only because they are in psychological trouble. We should be careful of this sort of assumption.

3. In order for people to turn to the spirits and the medium they must be convinced of the reality of the spirits and of the efficacy of turning to them and it appears that more and more people are becoming convinced. Through the testimonies of others and their own experiences, millions seem to believe that these spirits exist, can affect human destinies, and can be approached via the mediums. Those who have witnessed the impressive rituals and demonstrations of the spirits may testify to the great power of these to impress even casual observers, let alone those wanting to believe. Spirit possession performances are usually accompanied by exciting music, drumming, hyperventilation, frenzied dance and movement, costuming, stagecraft, showomanship and showmanship. (See E. Bourguignon's vivid presentation of "trance dance," for example [1968], or M. Leiris (1958) on theatre in *zar* possession, R. Firth on "ritual and drama in Malay spirit mediumship," John Beattie's "spirit mediumship as theatre" [1977].)

The spirits often reveal what seems to be remarkable knowledge of the secret troubles and concerns of the petitioners. Sometimes possessed individuals demonstrate imperviousness to pain. With their words of explanation, hope, or threat, the spirits can inspire trust or fear, even terror. But most important of all are the testimonies regarding all the "cures"—the miracles--that the spirits are said to have wrought, which are a regular accompaniment to these institutions. To cite just one example, on the day after Baba Sali's burial we heard many stories of the miraculous cures that he had effected through his power. These tales were not from official spokesmen but from "ordinary people" who said they knew of these from personal experience. Among them was an orthodox Ashkenazi man from London, the father of a boy who had been cured after "all the doctors and all the rabbis" had assured him that his son would die. He and his family were now Baba Sali's devotees. Is it any wonder that such a powerful way to influence, the unseen world is growing in popularity?

This growth has been occurring among rural and urban peoples, those undergoing rapid change and those not, among the middle class and among workers, among Muslims and Christians, both Catholic and Protestant, Buddhists, Hindus, and those without affiliation to the "world religions." This is not to say that everyone in a community believes in and attends to the spirits, but to argue there are sufficient examples of many categories of people believing in and becoming involved with spirits to question the standard recourse to explanations in terms of oppression, deprivation, loss of status, etc. Indeed, people with wealth who have resources to expend on these institutions may play important roles.[22]

There is a general, worldwide increase in "faith" as people look for both explanation and for aid. Recent trends in Catholicism include increasing attendance at pilgrimage shrines, and the development of the "Charismatic Renewal" as a religious movement (Bord and Faulkner 1983). Like the rapidly growing and spreading Protestant Pentecostal movement, Charismatic Renewal in Roman Catholicism is another case of "ecstatic religion," characterized by healing ceremonies, speaking in tongues, the casting out of demons, and possession by "The Holy Spirit."

There is a great upsurge in attendance at the shrines of Our Lady of Fatima in Portugal, Lourdes in France, Sainte-Anne-de- Beaupre in Quebec, the tomb of St. James the Apostle in Santiago de Compostela in Spain, often by middle class and well-educated Catholics from all over the world, who come in hopes of a cure for their illnesses. A major pilgrimage center for worship of the Virgin Mary has developed at Medjugorje in Herzegovina since the first apparitions were reported there in 1981 (Bax 1991)! Tens of thousands of Venezuelans and people from various countries around the Caribbean flock to the shrine of Maria Lionza, where many spirits possess many mediums, and people come for solutions to their problems, bringing offerings and leaving letters with their prayers and requests. These examples could be multiplied many times over, and the remarkable growth of *hillula* in Israel is just one more such case.[23]

4. The spirits are unseen, unknown, mysterious, and thus susceptible to elaboration according to the imagination of their mediums and their followers. There is great creativity involved in these institutions. Despite the constant reoccurrence of certain themes and the element of emulation, there is great scope for invention of all sorts. Thus local traditions, conditions, and problems find their way into the rituals, costumes, poetry, and music, and are built upon. As the rich and growing ethnographic literature attests, spirit mediumship and possession offer a wonderful domain for cultural production--for symbolic, artistic, psychological, and socio-political elaboration.[24]

5. To return to the matter of diffusion, it seems ironic that some of the very forces that were supposed to bring about the end of "animism" are acting to spread it. Knowledge of the spirits and how to deal with them is diffused by the increasing mobility of people as they travel and migrate for work, for education, for asylum, or for pleasure. Cubans bring Santeria to Florida, and Haitians bring *vodun* to New York, while Hmong and Koreans introduce new shamans to various parts of the United States (Thao 1989). (Koss and Garrison discuss the transmission of *espiritismo* to Puerto Rico and thence to New York [Garrison

1977].) Kardec's *spiritisme* originally traveled from France to Brazil, but today French people in Paris, Marseilles, and Lyons can learn new ways to health and fertility from their Algerian and Moroccan neighbors.[25]

Just as the mass media heighten the awareness of ethnicity and sub-nationalism, so do they help to spread the news of various belief systems and of the prospects for cures through them, even as they also spread word of the limitations or the failures of technology, medicine, and secularism. Oracular spirit possession, as well as other forms of mystical healing and aid, is spreading both among millions of people who never doubted the reality of the spirits and the supernatural, and among millions who are no longer sure that the supernatural may not be more important than their rationalist teachers and elders had led them to believe. Modern medicine and science have their limits and will never be able to fully and satisfactorily answer the question, "why me?" or to tell you what to do once the doctors have said there is no hope. It is worth noting that in July 1992 the World AIDS Conference officially agreed to consider alternative therapies for HIV/AIDS. Among these were acupuncture, shamanism, and *spiritism*. In the 21st century, increasing numbers of people in the United States are turning to all manner of "alternative" prophylaxis and therapies that depart from the "rational" and experimental medical and scientific model.

Conclusions

Spirit possession has been looked at from a number of distinctive perspectives: sociological, social psychological, Freudian, Marxian, feminist, hermeneutic, post-colonial, among them. (Cf. Bourguignan 1965, 1983.) The point of this paper is not necessarily to deny the applicability of any particular analysis done from these other perspectives as applied to particular cases. Like any complex cultural phenomenon, these have many dimensions and can mean different things to different people and peoples. Oppression or domination, rapid urbanization, status loss, mental illness might well be implicated in particular manifestations of spirit possession. But these are probably secondary aspects, not the primary causes or raisons d'etre of the institutions.

The Main Points of the Argument:

1. Spirit possession, in all of its manifestations, is presently undergoing a notable expansion and elaboration in most parts of the world and can be seen as another product of "globalization." The *spread* of these beliefs and practices is due, in the first instance, to processes of emulation and borrowing that were called "diffusion" in modern American anthropology.

2. The explanation of the popularity of spirit possession must begin with the fact of belief. People believe that these spirits exist, that they can affect their lives for good or ill, and that they can be communicated with directly. In the

case of oracular spirit mediumship they believe that they may be able to gain some control over their fates through this interaction. Believers and congregants generally show the greatest concern about health, but all other aspects of their wellbeing, security, and fortune may be involved in their adoration and solicitation of these spirits.

3. Oracular spirit possession is spreading among peoples of many different backgrounds and classes, rural and urban, in many different social situations, and is probably not, in the first instance, caused by deprivation, oppression, neo-colonialism or the traumas of urbanization and capitalism.

4. Spirit possession and mediumship are diffused both by local connections and through more extensive movements of people, as well as through the mass media and other modern forms of communication. Like other fashions, this one may not last, but for the moment it appears to be a productive idea that is finding favor all over the world.

Acknowledgments

I want to thank the following for reading earlier drafts of this paper or giving me information over the years. These include: Sue Kenyon, Kaja Finkler, Mary Grow, Marta F. Topel, Henry Rosenfeld, Judah Matras, Harvey Goldberg and Yoram Bilu (fellow pilgrims), the late Morton Klass, Sidney Greenfield, Lourdes Giordani, Linda Giles, Joanna Harris, Tijani Eltahir, J. H. Preston, Katherine A. Bowie, Michael Schatzberg, Paul Stoller, I. M. Lewis, and, as always, Marcia Lewis.

Notes

[1] Even Martin Buber wrote, "The typical individual of our time is no longer capable of believing in God..." (in Glatzer 1967, from Leslie 1971:5).

[2] Although the focus of my paper is on spirit possession, which is not that prominent in Israel (yet), I believe that the case I am making applies equally well to the growing phenomenon of the adoration of "saints" (*tsadikim*), the most prominent of these institutions.

[3] It should be unnecessary to point to all the other significant thinkers of the past 250 years who believed that religion and other manifestations of unreason and belief in the supernatural were bound to decline, if not disappear altogether.

[4] See, e.g., T. K. Oesterreich's *Possession, Demoniacal & Other among Primitive Races, in Antiquity, the Middle Ages, and Modern Times* (1966 [orig. 1921]). For recent works on possession in Judaism and Jewish life see Goldish et al (2003) and Chajes (2003).

[5] In his astringent and fashionable way Vincent Crapanzano (1977:33) writes, "For the Westerner, the spirit possessed representative of 'another cultural tradition,' embodies the Other in its most extreme, most exotic, most alien form." Without agreeing with the author's critical tone, his comment makes the point that it is not likely that earlier anthropologists would have passed up the chance to discuss this phenomenon had it been in evidence.

[6] All typologies divide up the flow of reality and are feeble, and it is obvious in this case, too, that there are no "pure types." For example, it regularly happens that troublesome spirits can be cultivated, "tamed," and thus converted into oracular spirits. See, e.g., S. Kenyon (1991), Finkler on Mexican spiritualist healers (1986), McDaniel's portrayal of the experiences of "ecstatics" in Bengal (1989), and Van Binsbergen's portrayal of a "standard biographical pattern for Central African Religious innovators" (1977).

[7] I.M. Lewis might consider these to be "cults of affliction," but they may go beyond concern with suffering to deal with other aspects of life and social relations, as he also notes (1971:128).

[8] In 2002, the French anthropologist Thomas Osmond filmed ceremonies involving the spirits that seem almost exactly like ones I witnessed in the same area 40 years earlier.

[9] This "infectious" possession seems to be similar to that reported by Lesley Sharp (1995) for Madagascar, Ong (1987) for Penang, Malaysia, and Felicity S. Edwards (1984) for South Africa. But these Oromo are rural farming women, without schooling and with no knowledge of factory labor or capitalism, the factors to which Sharp and Ong attribute the manifestations of possession they studied.

[10] Some earlier readers questioned how I knew that spirit possession is on the rise. I think I provide enough information, enough cases, enough testimonies, enough bibliography, and enough reasons, with reference to enough parts of the world, to turn the burden of proof back on those who doubt that there has been a great growth of these phenomena.

[11] Janice Boddy writes, "As Karp has noted, 'a single researcher would have difficulty in reviewing the literature on spirit possession in Africa alone'" (1995:409). The bibliography for her article is a good place to start, but cf. The annotated bibliography in I. M. Lewis et al (1991) which contains 106 entries for *zar*, *tumbura*, and *bori* in Northern Africa and Arabia alone. For an older collection see Beattie & Middleton 1969.

[12] There is no connection between this efflorescence of spirit possession and the revolution. There was no political or economic unrest connected with spirits and the mediums, and the revolution was carried out by military officers, generally from other ethnic groups and backgrounds, who had very different agendas.

[13] Kardec's tomb is in Paris in the great Père-Lachaise cemetery, where loyal followers of his *spiritisme* can be seen worshiping any day. Indeed, members of "un groupe de 'combattants pour la suprématie de la Raison'" were so disturbed by this irrationality that they blew up the dolmen at the shrine with plastic explosives in July 1989. Kardec was not without visitors very long, however (Soutigny 1989: 141).

[14] In 1990 a Scot anthropologist of my acquaintance reports that his yuppie brother and sister-in-law belong to a group that believes that the spirits can guide them in their investments.

[15] Issacher Ben Ami (1981), Alex Weingrod (1990), and Yoram Bilu (1987, 2000) provide rich discussions of the growth of the adoration of the saints, of their shrines, and the great pilgrimages to them. Bilu and Hasan-Rokem (1989) present a portrait and analysis of the life and work of a woman healer whose career also began with a visitation in a dream by a saint from Morocco.

[16] These manifestations may be distinguished, theoretically or typologically, at least, from cases where possession appears to be a patterned form that "madness" takes in individuals with deep psychological and mental troubles.

[17] In the same spirit, here are the words of another Israeli social scientist (who shall remain anonymous [Henry Rosenfeld], personal e-communication):

> ...I do not have the slightest doubt that the last 50+ years of militarism, ultra-nationalism, racism, organized religiosity, occupation, great economic disparity, and all the rationalizations that have entertained the total transformation in life here (if you wish, from

extensive rationality to overwhelming irrationality) must be taken into account, some more some less if you wish to consider 'the increasing recourse to spirits'

I suggest that there are reasons to doubt that these are major factors.

[18] I am concerned primarily with oracular possession, rather than *zar*-type possession or similar manifestations that are found primarily among women and seem so clearly related to problems of status, relations with spouses, rebellions against male authorities, etc. (I. M. Lewis, various works.)

[19] I. M. Lewis is an outstanding exception, having been determinedly comparative from the very beginning.

[20] It was Malinowksi, of course, who first presented this idea so well in his essay, "Magic, Science and Religion" (1925).

[21] Linda Giles (1995: 93) suggests that possession groups are "more active and elaborate in Mombasa than in the more isolated rural area" because people "have better access to cash and other resources," have more opportunity to meet and organize in a densely populated area.

[22] According to Mary Grow, who carried out research in Thailand in the 1980s and 1990s, "The rising middle class is very much associated with spirit mediumship. Their outstanding and rapid economic success has contributed greatly to the popularity of particular cults" (personal communication). (See also Saunders 1977.)

[23] Even as I write, the New York Times this day has an article about pilgrimages of thousands of Israelis to the tomb of the long-dead rabbi, Yonatan ben Uziel in order to find wives and husbands for themselves and their children ("Ancient Rabbi Becomes a Modern Israeli Matchmaker," June 22, 2004: 4). According to Joseph Berger, Yoram Bilu said, "forces like the turmoil set off by the Palestinian uprising and disillusionment with once popular movements like socialism had led many ordinary Israelis to latch on to a folk mysticism and New Age spirituality." But since when did peaceful Palestinians or socialism promise to find wives and husbands for Israelis? Are there similar political events to account for all those millions in many other countries who are also undertaking religious pilgrimages?

[24] We should not ignore the fact that these activities are a source of entertainment, pleasure, fun, as well as an opportunity to gather with friends and meet other people. These motivations undoubtedly add to their popularity. (Cf. Finkler)

[25] Of course this sort of transmission is not new. Snouck Hurgronje speaks of the meeting in Mecca of many peoples from all over who practice their zar exorcisms in their own way there – and learn from others. "There are, for example, exorcisms of the Zar in the Maghrib, Soudanese, Abyssinian, and Turkish manner..." (quoted in Oesterreich 1966: 232-233).

References

Appadurai, A., 1990. Disjuncture and Difference in the Global Cultural Economy, *Public Culture*, 2:1-24.

Barnett, H. G., 1953. *Innovation: The Basis of Cultural Change.* New York: McGraw-Hill.

Bax, M., 1991. Patronage in a Holy Place: Preliminary Research Notes on a 'Parallel Structure' in a Yugoslav Pilgrimage Centre, *Ethnos*, 56: 41-55.

Beattie, J., 1977. Spirit Mediumship as Theatre. *RAIN*, #20: 1-6, June.

Beattie, J. and J. Middleton (eds.), 1969. *Spirit Mediumship and Society in Africa.* London: Routledge & Kegan Paul.

Behrend, H. and U. Luig (eds), 1999. *Spirit Possession, Modernity, and Power in Africa*. Madison: University of Wisconsin.

Beit-Hallahmi, B., 1992. *Despair and Deliverance: Private Salvation in Contemporary Israel*. Albany, N.Y.: SUNY.

Bilu, Y., 1987. Dreams and the Wishes of the Saint. In H. Goldberg (ed), *Judaism: Viewed from Within and Without*. (pp. 285-313. Albany: SUNY.

Bilu, Y., 2000. *Without Bounds: The Life and Death of Rabbi Ya'aqov Wazana*. Detroit: Wayne State University.

Bilu, Y. and G. Hasan-Rokem, 1989. Cinderella and the Saint. Psychoanalytic Study of Society 14: 227-59.

Boddy, J., 1989. *Wombs and Alien Spirits: Women, Men and the Zar Cult in Northern Sudan*. Madison: U. of Wisconsin Press.

Boddy, J., 1994. Spirit Possession Revisited: Beyond Instrumentality. *Annual Review of Anthropology*, 23: 407-434.

Bord, R. J. and J. E. Faulkner, 1983. *The Catholic Charismatics: The Anatomy of a Modern Religious Movement*. University Park: Pennsylvania State University Press.

Bourguignon, E., 1965. The Self, the Behavioral Environment, and the Theory of Spirit Possession. In M. E. Spiro (ed), *Context and Meaning in Cultural Anthropology*. N.Y.: Free Press.

Bourguignan, E., 1968. *TranceDance*. Dance Perspectives 35.

Bourguignan, E., 1976. *Possession*. (Reissued: Chicago: Waveland, 1991).

Bourguignon, E. (ed.), 1983. *Religion, Altered States of Consciousness, and Social Change*. Columbus: Ohio State University Press,.

Buber, M.,

Chajes, J.H., 2003. *Between Worlds: Dybbuks, Exorcists, and Early Modern Judaism*. Philadelphia: University of Pennsylvania.

Collins, E. F., 1997. *Pierced by Murugan's Lance: Ritual, Power, and Moral Redemption Among the Malaysian Hindus*. DeKalb: Northern Illinois University Press.

Comaroff, Jean, 1985. *Body of Power, Spirit of Resistance: The Culture and History of a South Africa People*. Chicago: University of Chicago.

Crapanzano, V., 1977. Introduction. In V. Crapanzano and V. Garrison (eds). *Case Studies in Spirit Possession*. N.Y.: John Wiley.

Crapanzano, V., 1977. Mohammed and Dawia: Possession in Morocco. In V. Crapanzano and V. Garrison (eds.). *Case Studies in Spirit Possession*. N.Y.: John Wiley,

Edwards, F. S., 1984. Amafufunyana Spirit Possession: A Report on Some Current Developments, *Religion in Southern Africa*, 5:3-16, 1984.

Erndl, K. M., 1993. *Victory to the Mother: The Hindu Goddess of Northwest India in Myth, Ritual and Symbol*. New York: Oxford University Press.

Field, M.J., 1961. *The Search for Security*. Evanston: Northwestern U. Press.

Finkler, K., 1986. The Social Consequences of Wellness: A View of Healing Outcomes from Micro and Macro Perspectives, *International Journal of Health Services*, 16: 627-42.

Firth, R., 1967a. Ritual and Drama in Malay Spirit Mediumship, *Comparative Studies in Society and History*, 9(2):190-207.

Firth, R., 1967b, *Tikopia Ritual and Belief*. London: Allen and Unwin.

Fisher, W. F., 1988. Re-Told Tales: Towards an Understanding of Spirit Possession in Central Nepal. Revision of paper presented at the 17th Annual Conference for South Asian Studies, Madison, WI.

Fox, R. G., 1991. For a Nearly New Culture History. In R. G. Fox (ed), *Recapturing Anthropology: Working in the Present*. Santa Fe, N.M.: School of American

Research.

Garrison, V., 1977. The 'Puerto Rican Syndrome' in Psychiatry and *Espiritismo*. In V. Crapanzano and V. Garrison (eds.). *Case Studies in Spirit Possession*. N.Y.: John Wiley.

Giles, L., 1987. Possession Cults of the Swahili Coast: A Re-examination of the Theories of Marginality. *Africa*, 57(2).

Giles, L., 1995. Sociocultural Change and Spirit Possession on the Swahili Coast of East Africa. *Anthropological Quarterly* 68 (2): 89-106.

Goldish, M. 2003. *Spirit Possession in Judaism: Cases and Contexts from the Middle Ages to the Present*. Detroit: Wayne State University.

Gonzalez-Wippler, M., 1992. *The Santeria Experience: A Journey into the Miraculous*. St. Paul: Llewellyn Publications.

Goodman, F., 1988. *How About Demons? Possession and Exorcism in the Modern World*. Bloomington: Indiana U. Press.

Greenfield, S.M., 1987. The Return of Dr. Fritz: Spiritist Healing and Patronage Networks in Urban, Industrial Brazil. *Social Science and Medicine*, 24(12):1095-1108.

Hancock, M. E., 1995. Dilemmas of Domesticity: Possession and Devotional Experience among Urban Smarta Women. In L. Harlan and P. Courtright (eds.) From the Margins of Hindu Marriage (pp. 60-91). New York: Oxford University Press.

Hume, David, 1956. *The Natural History of Religion*. Stanford: Stanford U. Press (Original 1757).

Irvine, W., 1984.   Decline of Village Spirit Cults and Growth of Urban Spirit Mediumship: the Persistence of Spirit Beliefs, the Position of Women and Modernization. *Mankind*, 14(4).

Kearney, M., 1979. Spiritualist Healing in Mexico. In P. Morley and R. Wallis (eds.) *Culture and Curing: Anthropological Perspectives on Traditional Medical Beliefs and Practices*. Pittsburgh: University of Pittsburgh.

Kendall, L., 1985. *Shamans, Housewives, and Other Restless Spirits: Women in Korean Ritual Life*. Honolulu: University of Hawaii.

Kenyon, S. M., 1991a. *Five Women of Sennar: Culture and Change in Central Sudan*. Oxford: Clarendon.

Kenyon, S. M., 1991b. The Story of a Tin Box: *Zar* in the Sudanese Town of Sennar. In I. M. Lewis, A. Al-Saf, S. Hurrer (eds.) *Women's Medicine: The Zar-Bori Cult in Africa and Beyond*. Edinburgh: Edinburgh University.

Kenyon, S. M., 1995. Zar as Modernization in Contemporary Sudan. *Anthropological Quarterly* 68 (107-120).

Kessler, C.S., 1977. Conflict and Sovereignty in Kelantanese Malay Malay Spirit Seances. In V. Crapanzano and V. Garrison (eds.) *Case Studies in Spirit Possession*. New York: John Wiley.

Kim Harvey, Y., 1979. *Six Korean Women: The Socialization of Shamans*. West.

Klass, M. 2003. *Mind Over Mind: The Anthropology and Psychology of Spirit Possession*. Lanham, MD: Rowman and Littlefield.

Knutsson, K.E., 1967. *Authority and Change: A Study of the Kallu Institution Among the Macha Galla of Ethiopia*. Goteborg: Etnografiska Museet.

Knutsson, K.E., 1975. Possession and Extra-Institutional Behaviour: An Essay on Anthropological Micro-Analysis. *Ethnos*, 40:244-272.

Lambek, M., 1981. *Human Spirits: A Cultural Account of Trance in Mayotte*. New York: Cambridge University.

Lan, D., 1985. *Guns and Rain: Guerillas and Spirit Mediums in Zimbabwe*. Berkeley: University of California.

Lebra, T. S., 1976. Taking the Role of Supernatural 'Other': Spirit Possession in a

Japanese Healing Cult. In W. P. Lebra (ed.) *Culture-Bound Syndromes, Ethnopsychiatry, and Alternate Therapies.* Honolulu: University of Hawaii.

Leiris, M. 1958. *La Possession et ses aspects aspects theatraux chez les Ethiopiens de Gondar.* Paris: L'Homme.

Lewis, H. S., 1983. Spirit Possession in Ethiopia: An Essay in Interpretation. In S. Segert (ed.) *Ethiopian Studies, Dedicated to Wolf Leslau.* Wiesbaden: Harrassowitz.

Lewis, H.S., 1991. Gada, Big Man, K'allu: Political Succession Among the Eastern Mech'a. *Northeast African Studies.*

Lewis, I. M., 1966. Spirit Possession and Deprivation Cults, *Man,* 1:307-329.

Lewis, I.M., 1989a. *Ecstatic Religion: An Anthropological Study of Spirit Possession and Shamanism.* New York: Penguin, 1971 (1st ed.); London: Routledge (2nd ed.).

Lewis, I. M., 1989b. South of North: Shamanism in Africa: A Neglected Theme, *Paideuma,* 35:181-88.

Lewis, I. M., 1990. Gender and Religious Pluralism: Exorcism and inspiration in the family. In I. Hamnett (ed.) *Religious Pluralism and Unbelief.* London: Routledge.

Lewis, I. M., A. Al-Safi, and S. Hurreiz (eds.), 1991. *Women's Medicine: The Zar-Bori Cult in Africa and Beyond.* Edinburgh: Edinburgh University Press.

Malinowski, B. 1925. Magic, Science, and Religion' in J. Needham (ed.) Science, Religion and Reality. London (?): Macmillan.

McDaniel, J., 1989. *The Madness of the Saints: Ecstatic Religion in Bengal.* Chicago: University of Chicago.

Messing, S. D., 1958. Group Therapy and Social Status in the Zar Cult of Ethiopia, *American Anthropologist,* 60:1120-1125.

Milovsky, A. S., 1992. Tubiakou's Spirit Flight. *Natural History,* July (35-41).

Muecke, M. A., 1992. Monks and Mediums: Religious Syncretism in Northern Thailand. *The Journal of the Siam Society,* 80 (2): 97-104.

Murphy, J., 1988. *Santeria: An African Religion in America.* Boston: Beacon.

Nabokov, I. 2000. *Religion Against the Self: An Ethnography of Tamil Rituals.* New York: Oxford University Press.

Natvig, R. 1991. Some Notes on the History of the *Zar* Cult in Egypt. In I. M. Lewis, A. Al-Safi, and S. Hurreiz (eds.), *Women's Medicine: The Zar-Bori Cult in Africa and Beyond.* Edinburgh: Edinburgh University Press.

Obeyesekere, G., 1970. The Idiom of Demonic Possession: A Case Study. *Social Science and Medicine,* 4:97-111.

Obeyesekere, G., 1977. Social Change and the Deities: Rise of the Kataragama Cult in Modern Sri Lanka, *Man* (N.S.) 12:377-96.

Oesterreich, T. K., 1966. *Possession, Demoniacal* and *Other among Primitive Races, in Antiquity, the Middle Ages, and Modern Times.* New Hyde Park, N.Y.: University Books. (Orig. 1921.)

Ong, A, 1987. *Spirits of Resistance and Capitalist Discipline: Factory Women in Malaysia.* Albany: SUNY.

Owen, A., 1989. *The darkened Room: Women, Power, and Spiritualism in Late Nineteenth Century England.* London: Virago.

Pressel, E., 1974. Umbanda Trance and Possession in Sao Paulo, Brazil. In F. Goodman et al (eds.), *Trance, Healing, and Hallucination.* N.Y.: John Wiley.

Rasmussen, S. J., 2001. *Healing in community: medicine, contested terrains, and cultural encounters among the Tuareg.* Westport: Bergin and Garvey.

Rogers, E. M., 1971. *Communication of Innovations.* New York: Free Press.

Roseman, M., 1991. *Healing Sounds from the Malaysian Rainforest.* Berkeley: University of California.

Rouget, G., 1985. *Music and Trance: A Theory of the Relations between Music and*

Possession. Chicago: Chicago University.

Saunders, L. W., 1977. Variants in Zar Experience in an Egyptian Village. In V. Crapanzano and V. Garrison (eds.). *Case Studies in Spirit Possession*. N.Y.: John Wiley.

Schieffelin, E. L., 1976. *The Sorrow of the Lonely and the Burning of the Dancers*. New York: St. Martin's.

Shack, W. A., 1971. Hunger, Anxiety, and Ritual: Deprivation and Spirit Possession in Ethiopia, *Man*, 6:30-43.

Sharp, L. A., 1990. *The Possessed and the Dispossessed: Spirits, Identity, and Power in a Madagascan Migrant Town*. Berkeley: University of California Press.

Sharp, L. A. 1995. Playboy Princely Spirits of Madagascar: Possession as Youthful Commentary and Social Critique. *Anthropological Quarterly* 68: 75-88.

Soutigny [Maurice Soutif, Alain Guigny], 1989. Quand Frappent les Esprits. *Geo*, September, 132-155.

Spiro, M., 1966. Religion: Problems of Definition and Explanation. In M. Banton (ed.) *Anthropological Approaches to the Study of Religion*. London: Tavistock.

Spiro, M., 1967. *Burmese Supernaturalism*. Englewood Cliffs, N.J.: Prentice-Hall, 1967.

Stoller, P., 1989a. Stressing Social Change and Songhay Possession. In C. Ward (ed.) *Altered States of Consciousness and Mental Health*. Newbury Park: SAGE.

Stoller, P., 1989b. Fusion of the Worlds: An Ethnography of Possession among the Songhay of Niger. Chicago: University of Chicago Press.

Sutton, D.S., 1990. Rituals of Self-mortification: Taiwanese Spirit-mediums in Comparative Perspective. *Journal of Ritual Studies*, 4(99-125).

Tarde, G., 1903. *The Laws of Imitation*. New York: Henry Holt.

Thao, Paja, 1989. *I Am a Shaman: a Hmong Life Story with Ethnographic Commentary* (by Dwight Conquergood). Minneapolis: University of Minnesota Press.

Tylor, E.B., *Primitive Culture*. London: J. Murray, 1920. (Orig. 1871)

Van Binsbergen, W. M. J., 1977. Regional and Non-regional Cults of Affliction. In R. Werbner (ed.) *Regional Cults*.

Weingrod, A., 1990. The Saint of Beersheba. Albany, N.Y.: SUNY.

THE BEDOUIN'S LIFELINE:
ROVING TRADERS IN SOUTH SINAI

Emanuel Marx

Introduction

Traders play a vital role among the Bedouin in South Sinai, for they supply them with most of the essential food and consumer goods. The most crucial imported commodity is grain, as the limited availability of soil and water has never permitted local grain production. Without a steady supply of wheat and corn, the staple foods, neither man nor flock could survive in this arid region. Most other foods and condiments, clothing, tools and technological appliances and building materials are also imported. Documents of the Santa Katarina monastery, some of which go back to the 11th century, and the reports of travelers through the ages, indicate that the trade was usually in the hands of the Bedouin themselves. But from the early 1970s until the mid-1980s it was taken over by roving merchants from the town of al-'Arish in Northern Sinai. This essay explores the relations of these strangers with their Bedouin customers and attempts to explain why the merchants from al-'Arish supplanted the Bedouin traders at that particular juncture. This will require another look at Simmel's concept of the stranger. I argue that in his *Soziologie* (1908) Simmel used the word in two distinct senses, only one of which, namely that 'the stranger [is] the outsider who has come to stay' (Simmel 1950a: 403)[1], has been adopted by anthropologists, but is not especially relevant to our case. The other one is that in the modern cosmopolitan world every individual becomes a stranger (1950b: 409), an idea that re-emerges in the work of Lofland (1973), Bauman (1995), Lipman (1997) and others. This idea neatly fits the case of the traders from al-'Arish and their Bedouin customers, being as they are members of a complex modern civilization.

As the preceding sentence may surprise some readers, let me reiterate a proposition that has in recent years become widely accepted, namely that Bedouin everywhere are citizens of the modern world, that they are integrated in urban civilization and participate in the market economy in numerous ways (Marx 1995). That applies in even greater degree to the Bedouin of South Sinai, whose sheer survival depends on urban markets. The men are either migrant laborers working mostly outside the region, or horticulturalists and herders, smugglers, drivers, storekeepers, artisans, such as traders, builders, well-diggers and basket-weavers, healers, employees of the monastery and the administration, tourist guides, etc., all of whom make a living locally. The smuggling of narcotics, in particular, has often been an important branch of the economy, second only to migrant labor. During my fieldwork smuggling was at low ebb, but continued to play an important role in the thoughts and actions of the

Bedouin, who knew that it would sooner or later re-emerge as a major source of income. Only a handful of Bedouin engage in fulltime animal husbandry, and as they cannot easily leave the flock they sell goats and sheep and the occasional camel to the roving traders. Most Bedouin households raise small flocks of eight to ten sheep and goats and a camel or two and maintain orchards in the mountains. Bedouin consider this to be a reserve economy, to take care of the expected contingency if the labor migrants should lose their employment. During the long absences of the men, this segment of the economy is run by the women and girls who remain at home. Whenever there is a political or economic upheaval, the men return home and take over the management of this economy. They then try to increase the yields of the flocks and orchards, and to sell the produce in the cities. The animals and fruit generally fetch good prices in the market, and with the proceeds they buy all the grain they need as well as the other necessities of life.

All the Bedouin's economic transactions are made in cash. Those who are involved in the drug traffic, a large-scale international operation, are involved in complex financial transactions and stay abreast of the exact exchange rates of several currencies. Those who become migrant laborers know the rates of pay in various jobs and the current market prices of the commodities they consume. They receive their wages and other types of income in cash, and the people at home spend the money on imported goods. Most values are translated into terms of money. Even the bride-price is, in contrast to Bedouin practice elsewhere, quoted in cash and not in numbers of animals, although here too it is mostly paid off in several instalments.

South Sinai

The southern half of the Sinai Peninsula, Egypt, is a huge triangle whose tip points south, lapped by the deep waters of the Gulf of Suez and the Gulf of Aqaba. It covers an area of 17,000 square kilometers. The only paved highway hugs the seashore. The mountainous interior, with pinnacles rising to a height of 2,600 meters, is reached by rough motor tracks and one asphalted road leading from a point on the main road from Taba to Sharm al-Sheikh up to Santa Katarina and down to Wadi Firan. These tracks generally run on an east-west axis. Rainfall is very low and irregular, with an annual average of only 10 millimeters in the low-lying areas, and about 60 millimeters in the mountains (Greenwood 1997: 58). Summer temperatures are high in the low-lying areas, reaching daily maxima of over 40°C, but are milder in the mountains. Winters can be quite cold; I experienced temperatures as low as -15°C in the Santa Katarina area. As radiation and evaporation are very high, the climate of the region ranges from arid to hyperarid (Greenwood 1997: 61). Horticulture is therefore confined to the elevated main valleys where ground water can be tapped, while the erratic and scattered rains shift the pastures unpredictably from one area to another.

Between 1972 and 1982 I spent altogether over a year in South Sinai. My fieldwork period coincided with the Israeli occupation which lasted from 1967 to 1982. (The Santa Katarina region reverted to Egyptian rule in 1979). The indigenous civilian population of South Sinai consisted of about 10,000 Bedouin. Many of the men were labor migrants, who spent months on end away from home. The Israelis set up army camps, and established new towns and villages for Jewish colonists, thus more than doubling the population. The administration developed new oil fields in the region, built roads and settlements, providing employment for menial and semi-skilled workers. Although the Israeli authorities tried to keep down the wages of Bedouin workers, they were higher than those paid by the Egyptian administration and the monks of Santa Katarina. Work opportunities increased constantly and wages rose accordingly, so that in the end most men became migrant laborers. The trend was temporarily interrupted by the 1973 war between Egypt and Israel, but it resumed and even accelerated from 1974 onwards, only to be disturbed once again in 1976 when US Secretary of State Kissinger tried to negotiate a peace agreement between Egypt and Israel and the Bedouin feared that the Egyptians would soon return and employment opportunities decline.

Due to the unsettled political and economic conditions and a harsh and fickle climate, the South Sinai Bedouin alternate between two types of market economy, both of which comprise nomadic and sedentary activities. When employment is scarce, the men stay at home and become pastoralists and gardeners. At such times the search for water and pasture through the cycle of seasons and the necessity to irrigate the orchards and oases in which they grow fruit and vegetables, compels the Bedouin households to move between the desert pastures and the mountain valleys. In the decades before the Israeli occupation, there were times when jobs in the cities were not always available, and many Bedouin remained in Sinai, living in tents and moving around with their flocks. Flock-owners with grown up sons would adopt this nomadic way of life routinely. The herders' itineraries varied according to the availability of pastures, but the annual movement cycle generally culminated in one or more visits to the city markets in al-Tur, Suez and even distant Cairo. There they sold their animals and fruits and bought grain and other foods, tools and clothing. Many Bedouin owned only small flocks, and resided during the long summer months in their orchards in the mountains and consumed some of their own produce. But even they made at least one annual journey to al-Tur or Suez to sell their apples, quinces and almonds, for which there was a ready demand. These visits did not exhaust the Bedouin's contacts with markets. Throughout their annual movement cycle, and even while camping out in the desert, they relied on the services of itinerant traders and artisans.

During the greater part of the twentieth century, however, labor migration was the Bedouin's chief source of income. Every able-bodied Bedouin male in South Sinai spends the best years of manhood as a migrant laborer, starting as a young unmarried adult and continuing for many years after marriage, expecting eventually to send out his teenage sons to take their turn as labor migrants. At that stage, he returns home to become a fulltime petty pastoralist and horticulturalist, and if his ambitions run high he might join a smuggling gang.

He could also engage in one of the many occupations available to the Bedouin.

During the Israeli occupation of Sinai the pattern of labor migration changed. Due to Israeli colonization and Israel's intensive exploitation of Sinai's oil reserves, work opportunities in the region and its periphery multiplied. Now every man, whether young or old, had access to regular work in Eilat or in the new town of Sharm al-Sheikh (Ofira) and the colonies set up by Israelis on the Gulf of Aqaba and in the Santa Katarina area. The workers in the large Israeli towns and colonies did not settle their families near their place of work, mainly because they knew from experience that they might lose their jobs almost overnight, and partly because the Israeli administration segregated the Bedouin in the places of work and caused them many bureaucratic inconveniences. Therefore the Bedouin families remained at home in the mountains, to maintain the reserve economy. There they soon began to congregate in villages. The foundations of the villages were laid by enterprising Bedouin, who established transport terminals and trading posts for the labor migrants and their families. The health clinics and employment services of the Israeli administration also gravitated to these locations which gradually turned into service centers. Around these centers more and more Bedouin households settled, to make use of the shops, schools, medical services and transportation, and where relatives who could lend a helping hand were within easy reach. Soon people began to build solid houses around the service centers. At Milqa and Abu Silla near Santa Katarina monastery houses were constructed of local stone, and at Dahab and Nuweb´a on the Gulf of Aqaba – of reeds, or of concrete, mud bricks and slabs of coral. These settlements rapidly grew into regular villages. The Bedouin houses, in contrast to those built by the Jewish colonists, fitted so snugly into the landscape that one was tempted to believe they had been there since time immemorial. Yet aerial photographs of the early 1960s show no permanent houses in those locations.

The women ran the households, raised the families and maintained relationships with neighbors and kin. They also made weekly trips into the mountains to cultivate and irrigate the orchards. They put limited efforts into the orchards, watering the trees and vegetable patches only in order to just keep them alive. Herding practices also changed. The Bedouin tended to raise fewer animals, to replace camels with sheep and goats, and instead of moving between pastures they now sent young women and girls to graze the small flocks of eight to ten animals on the periphery of the village. The animals rapidly devoured all the available vegetation, and when they returned to the village in the evening had to be given supplementary feed. It was also up to the women to maintain the vital networks of relations with kin, friends and neighbors, and in the settlements they could meet and entertain them at leisure.

The rising standard of living was expressed in new consumption patterns. In each village there were several stores which stocked not only the traditional staples, such as wheat and corn, sugar, oil and tea, but also tinned foods, biscuits, sweets, dresses, shoes, knives, electric torches, plastic piping, baby foods and medicines. The labor migrants brought home a taste for fresh vegetables and spices that they had acquired in town. The new needs made the

Bedouin even more dependent on the external world than before. The traders thus did more than simply provide an essential link between the village and the urban supply centers. They were the Bedouin's lifeline; without their services the Bedouin would not survive for long.

Transportation became almost neatly segmented: a fleet of over a hundred American and Russian light army vehicles and assorted pick-ups, mostly in run-down condition, and owned by individual Bedouin, transported passengers to areas of employment in Israeli settlements in Sinai, such as Sharm al-Sheikh (Ofira), Dahab (Di Zahav) and Nuweb'a (Neviot), and towns in southern Israel, especially Eilat. A dozen or so well-maintained heavy trucks owned by entrepreneurs from the town of al-'Arish in northern Sinai carried the bulky commercial goods. They traveled all over the mountain ranges and supplied both the Bedouin stores and the camps encountered along the route. The division of tasks was caused by the market conditions. The Bedouin labor migrants found employment in centers of economic growth, where wages were decent, but the price of goods was high. Therefore they brought home only small gifts for friends and relatives, but did not buy great quantities of food and everyday clothing, whereas the roving traders from al-'Arish obtained their merchandise in the economically depressed Israeli occupied Gaza strip, and were therefore able to sell it relatively cheaply. They also had access to garages and spare parts, which did not exist in South Sinai.

The Traders

As the old market town of al-Tur was deserted, and Suez and Cairo were no longer accessible, most goods were now supplied by roving traders from the town of al-'Arish in Northern Sinai, whose trucks called on the new villages and the scattered nomadic camps. These traders supplied both the village stores and the mobile camps with grains and other staples, as well as with a rapidly growing range of groceries, clothing, household goods, and agricultural implements. They also took orders for special deliveries, such as spare parts for water-pumps or motorcars, for plastic pipes, which revolutionized gardening practice (Katz 1983: 39 ff.), and even brought in circumcisers for the boys. These traders provided the Bedouin with basic foods and essential goods and services, which enabled the women, children and flocks to survive while their men worked outside the region. But the Israeli authorities, unlike the preceding colonial and Egyptian governments which had adopted a laissez-faire attitude, never saw eye to eye with the traders. As they did not realize how crucial they were for the Bedouin's existence, they frequently sought to curb their activities or to dispense with their services altogether. As far as they were concerned, they were strangers who could not be trusted: they overcharged the Bedouin, their activities and movements were not easily regulated and, furthermore, they opened a window to the wider Arab world and that could be dangerous.

In my field trips to South Sinai I observed how the changing political and economic conditions affected the Bedouin's economic pursuits, gender relations and patterns of consumption. At first, I did not pay much attention to the 'Arishi traders, who appeared at roughly monthly intervals in the Santa Katarina area. They usually arrived in the afternoon, transacted business with the storekeepers and with other persons and left early the following morning. They were not very friendly and talkative, and kept their own counsel. They did not stay overnight with shopkeepers, but slept on or under the trucks. Only when I realized how precarious the local economy was, and how much people relied on goods brought in from outside the region did I begin to appreciate the central role of the traders.

Wheat and corn are the staple foods of the inhabitants, but are not grown in Sinai. From the documents preserved in Santa Katarina monastery we learn that grain has always been imported (Humbsch 1976, documents 29, 41, 46, 66 and 69). The documents, dated between 1567 and 1790, show that the monks regularly imported large quantities of wheat from the Egyptian Delta to Sinai. More recently, Shuqair (1916: 127) reported that in the beginning of the 20th century, the South Sinai Bedouin (*Tawara*) bought from traders in Suez some 4,500 ardeb (an ardeb contains 198 liters) of grain annually, amounting to two thirds of their food consumption

Labor migration led to a strict sexual division of labor: most adult men left to work away from home, while the women remained behind and maintained the household and the gardens and small flocks which served as an economic security net. There was no need for them to move around with flocks or to spend long periods in their orchards up in the mountains. All they had to do was to keep these economic ventures going. The men were earning good wages, which they remitted to their wives' care. The women controlled the spending of these relatively large amounts of money. They used the money mainly for daily consumption, but also managed to put aside savings. Women never went to the stores in person. Instead, they used to send children with instructions what to buy. For while women acquired much power, they knew it was temporary. Sooner or later the men would return home and take over the management of the household. Even during the height of the migrant labor market, most men interrupted work every six to eight weeks to return home for short visits, during which they maintained and strengthened their social networks.

The advent of the al-'Arish traders was a relatively recent development. In colonial Egypt, in the early 20th century, Bedouin obtained most of their grain from one or two wholesalers in Suez (Shuqair 1916: 127). But some Muzena tribesmen brought their grain from the Negev, where they hired themselves out as reapers. Those Bedouin who owned orchards in the mountains sold apples, pears and quinces in al-Tur or Suez, and bought grain with the proceeds. Some informants claimed that with the money they could acquire enough grain to last them through a year. Under Egyptian rule, before 1967, Bedouin had operated some 26 trucks. Qararsha tribesmen of Wadi Firan owned 21 of these; it appears that they had specialized in this business. Three trucks were owned by Sawalha and two by Jabaliya men. They had hauled minerals from the Umm Bogma and Abu Zneima mines, which employed over 2,000 workers brought in from mainland Egypt but only a handful of Bedouin, and they also carried food and supplies for the Bedouin and the mineworkers. Their supply base had been in Suez, and most of the business had been conducted with one storeowner, Mahmud al-Masri. "We used to sit and drink a cup of coffee, while he took care of our list of requirements", recounted one Qararsha chief. Al-Masri extended credit to his customers, and also obtained for them the shop licenses required to get through 'customs' (jumruk). In order to combat smuggling, the Egyptian police had set up a check point on the road from Abu Zneima to Suez, where all cars were searched for contraband and travelers questioned about their destination. This procedure was popularly called 'customs'. The Bedouin truck-owners and the merchant from Suez jointly almost monopolized the wholesale trade.. The truck-owners acted as wholesalers for practically the whole of South Sinai and also acted as agents for the government's food aid to the Bedouin (sadaqa) periodical rations of wheat flour, sugar and oil. They set up a commercial center in Faranja, an exposed hilltop on the main east-west thoroughfare, near Nabi Saleh, the central pilgrimage site of the Muzena. This supply center served the Bedouin living in the mountains and the eastern reaches of South Sinai. The truck-owners owned or controlled the sixteen stores. They sold their wares on the spot to individual customers and distributed them by truck all over the region. Jum'a Ghanem, a public-spirited truck-owner who was also one of the biggest smugglers in Sinai, dug a well on the site, which permitted the storekeepers to live comfortably in the place. Soon tracks and footpaths branched out in every direction.

This arrangement broke down immediately after the Israeli occupation. By the time I worked in Sinai, there were no stores left in Faranja. The occupation cut off Sinai from its regular sources of supply in Egypt, and all commodities had to be brought from Israel and the Israeli-occupied Gaza Strip. Mining operations and industrial production in the occupied areas ceased entirely, so that truckers had to look for alternative employment. While the Bedouin population still depended on imported grains and other foods and goods, the Bedouin truckers could no longer supply them at competitive prices. The merchants from al-'Arish were in a much better position: they could obtain goods at the lowest prices in the Gaza area, close to home, where the rate of taxation and the cost of labor were lower than in Israel. There were other reasons why the merchandise had to be cheap: the wages of the Bedouin workers within the borders of Sinai were controlled and kept low by the military authorities, and transportation costs were high. Goods had to travel over a long distance and rough terrain. The traders from al-'Arish drove new and powerful trucks, but the rocky mountain tracks took a heavy toll on them. However, they had at their disposal an infrastructure of garages, spare parts and trained mechanics, all of which were lacking in Sinai. The military administration was concerned about the displacement of the Bedouin truckers. It worked out a solution that would, so it hoped, gradually phase out the 'Arishi traders: they would be allowed to proceed as far as Gharandal, a crossroads located some 30 kilometers north of Abu Zneima, on the boundary between the military districts of North Sinai and South Sinai. From there the Bedouin truck-owners would take over and distribute the goods among the tribes. The Bedouin truck owners were subsidized, so that they would be able to compete with the 'Arishi traders. The administration also sought, unsuccessfully, to re-open a garage in Abu Zneima. One major element in this arrangement worked for approximately five years: from 1968 until 1973 Gharandal became the exclusive supply center for South Sinai.[2] But the Bedouin truck-owners never stood a chance. Having no sources of supply, lacking garages and spare parts, and saddled with an incompetent administration located in distant Tel-Aviv that attended to their affairs only sporadically, they were no match for the 'Arishi traders.

When I visited Gharandal in August 1972, there were five stores and a coffeehouse, all of which were branches of al-'Arish firms. Each store consisted of a booth, which remained open day and night, and a locked storeroom just behind it. The stores were owned by two or three partners, each of whom stayed about fourteen days and nights in Gharandal and was then relieved by another partner. The traders worked, ate and slept in their booths. The biggest trader was Matar, who claimed that his partnership owned eleven trucks, all working in Sinai. Another trader, Suliman Musallam, had formerly owned a store in Qusema, now a deserted town on the route to Gharandal. They all belonged to the large Fawakhriya clan of al-'Arish.

The traders sold wheat, corn, rice, lentils and sugar by the bag, paraffin by the barrel, and cooking oil in tin cans. They also stocked potatoes, tea, coffee, cigarettes and rice paper for homemade cigarettes, bottled soft drinks and chewing gum. Although the transportation costs were quite high, prices seemed to be similar to those charged elsewhere in Israel, and lower than the prices in the village stores of Sinai. The traders made a profit by buying goods in the cheap markets of the Gaza strip, as well as by supplying inferior quality goods, such as substituting rigid plastic pipes for electric wiring for elastic irrigation pipes demanded by the Bedouin, and by adulterating goods, such as adding water to sugar, and mixing corn and wheat flour. They also bought animals for slaughter. I was told that an average of twenty camels changed hands monthly in Gharandal.

At that time most of the trade of South Sinai passed through the hands of the traders of Gharandal, so that the figures obtained from them allow us to make a rough estimate of the Bedouin's 'national accounts', i.e. of the total imports, which equal the total consumption of the Bedouin population less small quantities of home-produced fruit and vegetables. Every month some thirty trucks left al-'Arish for Gharandal, carrying a payload of approximately 6,000 Israeli Pounds. Assuming that most of the supplies passed through Gharandal, the annual imports amounted to 2,160,000 Israeli Pounds, or 216 Israeli Pounds per capita. In addition, the traders distributed on behalf of the Israeli authorities, who carried over a practice from the Egyptian administration, monthly food rations (*sadaqa*) of flour, oil, and sugar. The total annual value of this assistance was 372,000 Israeli Pounds, or 37.2 Israeli Pounds per capita. Each Bedouin then spent on food annually 253.2 Israeli Pounds, which indicates that in 1972 the standard of living was very low (at the time the Israeli Pound was worth some thirty American cents). The number of jobs in Sinai was still limited, and smuggling had ceased altogether in 1970, as the smugglers were finding it too dangerous to cross the lines between two powerful armies facing each other. The Bedouin were tending their orchards in the mountains in order to increase their food supply. However, they could no longer sell their fruit in town: al-Tur was deserted and Suez had become inaccessible. They also tried to develop their herds of camels and their flocks, as animals could be sold to the traders in Gharandal. One sheikh described the situation in these terms: "Today there is no income from smuggling or from trade [which is controlled by the traders from al-'Arish]; there is only employment for menial workers. The days of Gamal ['Abd al-Nasser] were much better."

The Bedouin truck-owners of Wadi Firan were in no position to compete with the al-'Arish traders. The mines that had provided a large part of their business had closed down. In addition, they were cut off both from sources of supply and from maintenance facilities. There was not even one car repair shop or trained mechanic in South Sinai. The trucks were turning into scrap metal before their very eyes. The trade had moved to the eastern reaches of Sinai, where the owners of pick-ups served not only the migrant workers, but also the international tourists who flocked to the beaches and coral reefs of the Gulf of Aqaba in large numbers. These car-owners had access to garages in Eilat and elsewhere.

All that changed abruptly in October 1973, when Egyptian and Syrian armies carried out a coordinated attack on Israel. The Israeli positions on the Suez Canal succumbed to the first onslaught, and the Israeli army was hard pressed to repel the attack. Israeli government and civilian activities in Sinai stopped completely, and were not resumed for about six months. There was not even enough transport to take the Bedouin migrant workers back to their homes. Most of them walked two-three days over the mountains. As all sources of employment had dried up, the Bedouin made great efforts to develop their gardens and build up their flocks, but in the meantime they dug into their hoards of food. Every Bedouin household maintains a storehouse (*qerie*), usually a cave secured by a door and a heavy padlock, or a small building, for just such an expected eventuality. They lay in a food stock that should suffice for some three months. The first supplies of grain and other foods were brought in by the al-'Arish traders two months later, when food stocks had already become low. If they had not arrived in time, the Bedouin population would have starved. The traders retained their near-monopoly on supplying South Sinai after the Israelis returned to the region, and in return for providing an essential service they made a good profit.

That is not how the officials of the Israeli Sinai Development Authority in Tel-Aviv viewed the situation. Just a month before the war broke out, in September 1973, the councilor for trade demanded in a memoir that "The traders from al-'Arish must be restricted. In this critical civilian matter the Police must be involved..." (Fish to Aloni, 6.9.1973). The same official pursued this idea after the war, and again claimed that the traders overcharged the Bedouin and demanded, this time explicitly, that they should be banned. These recommendations were not implemented, as Egypt and Israel began negotiations for the restoration of Sinai to Egypt.

The traders from al-'Arish carved out a new, but probably temporary economic niche, which helped them to survive the loss of work caused by the Israeli occupation. They managed to achieve this, because they provided a vital service to the Bedouin of South Sinai, just at a time when the latter could no longer supply their own food.

The literature on Middle Eastern pastoralists is very extensive, but only a handful of authors pay much attention to the traders (Ferdinand 1962; Lancaster and Lancaster 1987; Musil 1928; Stein 1967). Khazanov (1984:212) discusses the role of traders among nomads through the ages in some detail, and reaches the seemingly paradoxical conclusion that "as a whole trade with the sedentary agricultural and urban world was not something from which the nomads profited, but it was vitally necessary from the economic point of view". He may imply that the nomads viewed the merchants as unscrupulous exploiters, but could not survive without them. The salient point to emerge from the literature and from experience in the field is that most traders are based in cities, and that only they have the funds to finance the buying up of large numbers of animals. They maintain long-term links with the potential consumers. A famous example is the house of Ibn Bassam, which had by the beginning of the twentieth century established branches in Basra, Bombay, Cairo, Damascus and Taif (Musil 1928: 278-9). Its agents, the so-called 'Aqelis, went out to the nomads' camps, bought the animals with money advanced by the Ibn Bassam, and were responsible for driving the animals to the market at the right times (see also Stein 1967: 84-89). These dealers released the Bedouin from making frequent visits to the market and permitted them to devote themselves to the demanding routine of nomadic animal husbandry. Other traders, also based in cities, supplied the Bedouin with the necessities of daily life. They would move from one camp to the next, selling goods mostly on credit. As they were providing a vital service to the Bedouin, their safe passage and the payment of debts was assured (Musil 1928: 269).

This trade could become the mainstay of the ephemeral states set up by Bedouin chiefs in the Arabian Peninsula. It could even, as Rosenfeld (1965: 80-85) has shown, become the reason for Bedouin chiefs to impose their rule on desert cities, such as Hail. The ruler made it his aim to provide safe passage for traders. Safe trading provided him with a steady source of income, and the Bedouin – with a secure market town.

Trade among the Bedouin of South Sinai followed a dynamic pattern: prior to the Israeli occupation of Sinai in 1967 the traders came from their midst. There was no need for big animal buyers, as the Sinai Bedouin raised sheep and goats only as an economic reserve and consequently kept only small flocks. The Bedouin truckers could fulfill both the functions of animal dealers and of itinerant traders. Their limited capital sufficed for local needs. Only the new conditions created by the Israeli occupation cut off the Bedouin truckers from their sources of supply and from their regular animal markets, and ruined their livelihood. This vacuum was filled, very efficiently, by the traders from al-'Arish who in turn, were after 1982 once more replaced by roving Bedouin traders.

There was yet another reason for the displacement of the Bedouin traders.

Members of tribes could engage in mobile trade during periods of intensive smuggling, for smuggling caravans crossed all tribal boundaries and the big smugglers saw to it that the roads remained open and that peace reigned between the tribes. When smuggling was no longer possible on a large scale, labor migration became the only important source of income. Most of the men stayed for months on end at their work-places outside the tribe, and worried about maintaining links with home. Therefore most men made a point of returning periodically to their homes. They also became concerned for the tribe, and returned home especially for the annual tribal pilgrimage, a main purpose of which was to reaffirm the tribe as a living reality. In this manner they wished to remind themselves and others of their exclusive rights to tribal resources, such as the trade routes crossing tribal territory and sites suitable for the development of orchards. Inter-tribal trade therefore became problematic and the Bedouin traders' business declined in volume. They could no longer maintain lorries which have high overhead costs. Therefore each Bedouin trader now sought to monopolize business in his own tribe. This was the time for the traders from al-'Arish to appear on the scene. As strangers who supplied a basic service they could freely cross tribal boundaries and move among the tribes. Soon they became wholesalers for the entire Bedouin population.

Traders as Strangers

While the traders from al-'Arish are strangers, they are unlike the 'stranger' described in much of the anthropological literature. The anthropological concept is derived from Simmel (1950a: 408), who taught us to perceive the stranger "not as the wanderer who comes today and stays tomorrow, but rather as the *person* who comes today and stays tomorrow." He is both integrated in his adopted community and knowledgable about it, and at liberty to act and move around. As Bodemann (1998: 126) has pointed out, he is an integral functioning element of the community, and only conceived by other members as external to it. Because of his ambiguous position in society, conventions and social pressures are less binding on him than on ordinary members. Simmel's insight has influenced several generations of social scientists. In anthropology, the stranger first appeared as the Nuer 'leopard skin chief' (Evans-Pritchard 1940), the archetypal mediator and peacemaker. Almost forty years later, Shack and Skinner (1979), still relying on Simmel's famous essay, sought to apply the concept to groups of strangers in the new African nations, such as white colonialists, Lebanese traders and groups of labor migrants from neighboring countries. A generation later, Berland and Rao (2004) offer another crop of essays based on Simmel's fertile idea. Clearly, Simmel suggested a most interesting way to look at the stranger. But the popularity of this idea has obscured Simmel's other contribution to the understanding of the stranger, namely that modern man, overburdened as he is with sensual stimulations, reduces them to the minimum by eliminating all individuality, all relationships which "cannot be exhausted with logical operations" (Simmel 1950b: 411).

Therefore "metropolitan man reckons with his merchants ... and often even with persons with whom he is obliged to have social intercourse" (*ibid.*). In this formulation, everyone who is beyond the small circle of a person's intimate relationships becomes a stranger. In the city, he argues, people depend on one another to the extent   that "without the strictest punctuality in promises and services the whole structure would break down into an inextricable chaos" (Simmel 1950b.: 412).

The Bedouin in South Sinai are willy-nilly integrated in a cosmopolitan world, on which they rely both for most of their income as well as their supply of food and other goods. Their dependence on a regular food supply is so great that the relations with the traders of al-'Arish must be rational and regulated, based on the commercial interest of both sides, and not on friendship or other diffuse ties.

Bauman argues that "the movements of the [strangers] being not fully predictable ... navigating contains always an element of risk and adventure and is always plagued by the paucity of reliable signposts and in need of more routine" (1995: 126). One way of coping with this contingency is to ignore it: by blending "the movement of strangers into the background one need neither notice nor care about [them]" (1995: 128). This common, but self-defeating, tactic appears to be the one adopted by the Bedouin. Now we can better understand why traders were not invited into Bedouin homes, and why some Bedouin even spoke of getting rid of the rapacious traders, words that could never be translated into action.

Acknowledgments

Field-work in South Sinai was made possible by the financial assistance of the Wenner-Gren Foundation, and the Ford Foundation through the Israel Foundation Trustees. I gratefully acknowledge the generous support of these institutions. I presented an early, perhaps premature, paper on traders at the IUAES Inter-Congress in Lucca, April 1995 organized by Aparna Rao and Michael Casimir, and benefited greatly from the discussions there. In 1997 I wrote a first version of the article at the Institute of Anthropology in Copenhagen (Marx 2004), and am deeply grateful for all the help I received there. I thank Joseph Berland, Ann Gardner, Ida Nicolaisen, Aparna Rao and Shelagh Weir for their detailed comments.

Notes

[1] In Simmel 1950, Wolff translates a selection from Simmel 1908. Fortunately it contains the two discourses on the Stranger.
[2] Gharandal was visited by Niebuhr (1968: 227) in 1762 and Burckhardt (1992: 473) in 1816. Both travelers describe it as a way-station on the trail from Suez to Mount Sinai, where palm groves and a copious supply of water and are found.

References

Bauman, Zygmunt, 1995. *Life in Fragments: Essays in Postmodern Morality*. Oxford: Blackwell.

Berland, Joseph C. and Aparna Rao (eds.), 2004. *Customary Strangers: New Perspectives on Peripatetic Peoples in the Middle East, Africa, and Asia*. Westport, Connecticut: Praeger.

Bodemann, Y. Michal, 1998. Von Berlin nach Chicago und weiter. Georg Simmel und die Reise seines "Fremden". *Berliner Journal für Soziologie* 1: 125-142.

Burckhardt, Johann Ludwig, 1992 (1822). *Travels in Syria and the Holy Land*. London: Darf.

Fabietti, Ugo, 1984. *Il popolo del deserto; I beduini Shammar del Gran Nefud Arabia Saudita*. Roma, Laterza.

Ferdinand, Klaus, 1962. Nomad expansion and commerce in Central Afghanistan. *Folk* 4: 123-59.

Greenwood, Ned, 1997. *The Sinai: A Physical Geography*. Austin: University of Texas Press.

Humbsch, Robert, 1976. *Beiträge zur Geschichte des osmanischen Ägyptens: nach arabischen Sultans- und Statthalterurkunden des Sinai-Klosters*. Freiburg: Schwarz.

Katz, Shaul, 1983. Ginot meromei Sinai (Gardens in the Sinai Mountains). *Nofim* 17: 1-54.

Khazanov, Anatoli M., 1984. *Nomads and the Outside World*. Cambridge: Cambridge University Press.

Lancaster, William, 1981. *The Rwala Bedouin Today*. Cambridge: Cambridge University Press.

Lancaster, William and Fidelity Lancaster, 1987. The Function of Peripatetics in Rwala Bedouin society. In *The Other Nomads: Peripatetic Minorities in Cross-Cultural Perspective*, A. Rao (ed.). Köln: Böhlau.

Lipman, Jonathan N. 1997. *Familiar Strangers: A History of Muslims in Northwest China*. Seattle: University of Washington Press.

Lofland, Lyn, 1973. *A World of Strangers: Order and Action in Urban Public Space*. New York: Basic Books.

Marx, Emanuel, 1995. Are There Pastoral Nomads in the Arab Middle East? Pp. 71-85 in *The Anthropology of Tribal and Peasant Pastoral Societies*, U. Fabietti and P.C. Salzman (eds.). Pavia: Collegio Ghislieri.

Marx, Emanuel, 2004. Roving traders among the Bedouin of South Sinai. Pp. 58-69 in *Customary Strangers: New Perspectives on Peripatetic Peoples in the Middle East, Africa and Asia*, J.C. Berland and A. Rao (eds.). Westport, Connecticut: Praeger.

Musil, Alois, 1928. *The Manners and Customs of the Rwala Bedouins*. New York: American Geographical Society.

Niebuhr, Carsten, 1968 (1774). *Reisebeschreibung nach Arabien und den umliegenden Ländern*, 3 vol. Graz: Akademische Druck- und Verlagsanstalt.

Rosenfeld, Henry, 1965. The Social Composition of the Military in the Process of State Formation in the Arabian Desert. *Journal of the Royal Anthropological Institute* 95: 75-86 and 174-194.

Shack, William A. and E.P. Skinner (eds.), 1979. *Strangers in African Societies*. Berkeley: University of California Press.

Shuqair, Na'um, 1916. *Ta'arikh sina al-qadim wal-hadith wa-jighrafiatiha* (The History and Geography of Ancient and Modern Sinai). Cairo: Ma'arif Press.

Simmel, Georg, 1908. *Soziologie: Untersuchungen über die Formen der Vergesellschaftung*. Leipzig: Duncker und Humblot.

Simmel, Georg, 1950a. The Stranger. Pp. 402-8 in *The Sociology of Georg Simmel*, Kurt H. Wolff (transl. and ed.). New York: Free Press of Glencoe.
Simmel, Georg, 1950b. The Metropolis and Mental Life. Pp. 409-24 in *The Sociology of Georg Simmel*, Kurt H. Wolff (transl. and ed.). New York: Free Press of Glencoe.
Stein, Lothar, 1967. *Die Šammar-Ǧerba: Beduinen im Übergang vom Nomadismus zur Sesshaftigkeit*. Berlin: Akademie-Verlag.

"Pleasures of Duty" of the Occupiers, "Duty of Sumud" of the Besieged: The Israeli Imposed Closure Regime in the Occupied West Bank[*]

Maya Rosenfeld

Introduction

More than half a million people live in the Khalil (Hebron) governorate, the largest of all West Bank districts in terms of both population and territory; approximately 150,000 of them are residents of the urban complex of Khalil (Hebron), and the remainder inhabit dozens of smaller towns, villages and refugee camps. An estimated 170,000 live in the urban, rural and refugee locales of the adjacent Bethlehem district. Together the inhabitants of the Khalil and Bethlehem districts form nearly 30% of the West Bank population (including Arab Jerusalem).

Yet, traveling by car on the main route connecting Jerusalem with Khalil – starting with the tunnel road (south-east of the Gilo settlement), continuing along the western outskirts of Beit Jala and al-Khader, the Etzion junction, al-Arroub refugee camp, Beit Omar municipality, up to the town of Halhul that borders on Khalil (Hebron) – one is unlikely to encounter evidence of the hundreds of thousands of Palestinians who populate the region; an impression that remains intact when switching from the longitudinal route to the main transverse roads. Most conspicuous is the total absence of Palestinian private cars; virtually none can be detected. Occasionally an older peasant women or man riding a donkey or mule appears on the scene; tractors and pick-up trucks are nowhere in sight. No less salient is the rarity of public transportation: there are days, at times weeks, during which not a single bus comes, no minibus or service cab with Palestinian license plates is to be seen; at other times the number of vehicles – almost all outmoded - does not exceed several dozens.

The mystery of the absent Palestinians is not solved once one stops at Etzion checkpoint, located on a central intersection where the Bethlehem district (north of the checkpoint) and Khalil (Hebron) district (south of the checkpoint) meet. Even when the site is relatively more crowded, it is rare to observe a gathering of more than two hundred people at a time. At checkpoint 300, on the northern entrance to Bethlehem, Palestinian presence is even scarcer, no more than several dozens at one time.

On the other hand, those traveling along the above described route, especially during the morning and early afternoon hours – times when people leave for and return from school and work- may easily come to the conclusion that Jewish settlers and the army are the majority population in the region.

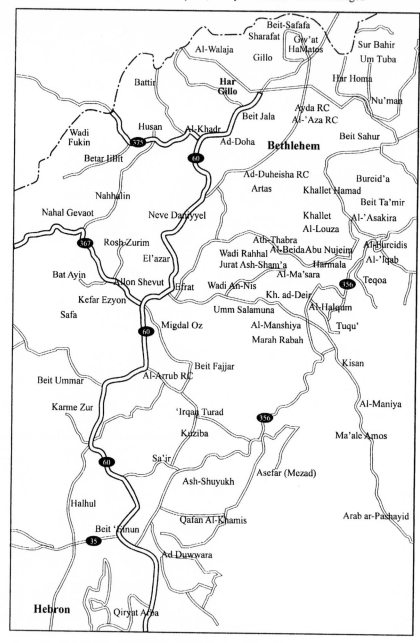

Map of roads in the West Bank
Source: Btselem 2004, adapted with Permission.

Thousands of their private cars and vans, and hundreds of busses and other service cars – almost all brand new –are on their way to and from Jerusalem. Dozens of army jeeps, patrol cars and armored carriers move back and forth along the major routes and dozens more are stationed at main and side junctions at any given moment. Hundreds of soldiers and border-policemen staff permanent and mobile checkpoints, watchtowers and roadblocks, and hundreds more are deployed in the open areas between these barriers. However, a quick data search will suffice to show that the entire Jewish settler population in the southern West Bank, that is the combined number of settlers in the Khalil and Bethlehem districts, does not exceed 50,000: approximately 7% of the region's population.

Persistent searchers, those who remain determined – previous failures notwithstanding - to follow the tracks of the hidden nation, have no choice but to leave their car near one of the hardly noticeable signposts leading to a Palestinian locale and to start walking. Soon enough they will be faced with a strange mound, its width equal to that of the road, its height ranging between one and two and a half meters, and its texture, a mixture of rocks, earth, waste and trash, often reinforced with concrete blocks. Closer examination of the mound will reveal what appear like carved grooves; these are well-compressed layers of earth and stone, eroded by the continuous clambering of peoples' feet. Those among the observers who take an interest in local flora will not be able to ignore the stubbornness of wild flowers and thorns that - in the course of four winters and three summers - have struck root in the mound and adapted to its clods of refuse and dirt.

Provided that their tour does not coincide with the imposition of curfew, our observers will now be able to view the hitherto invisible people as they climb up and carve their way through the barrier: old people leaning on their canes, traditionally dressed peasant women carrying heavy baskets on their heads, school children with schoolbags mounted on shoulders, clerks and professionals in suits and ties, laborers holding to their bread and cheese lunch in tightly fastened nylon bags, disabled men and women on crutches or wheelchairs.

A surprise awaits the more daring among the trackers who cross the barrier and proceed walking in the direction of the Palestinian locale, still concealed from sight: a second mound with a consistency similar to that of the first one, though often higher and steeper. And it is not unlikely that a third mound will confront them as they continue walking. Having ascended this last barrier, their eyes will be flooded by an orange-yellowish brightness, the color legally assigned (by the Palestinian Authority) to Palestinian service cabs. Dozens of these vehicles, Mercedeses and Ford Transits, are parked at the "internal" side of the (last) mound that demarcates the boundary beyond which driving is prohibited. The drivers, who up until the end of September 2000 carried passengers throughout the West Bank, nowadays sit idly at the mound waiting for their turn: a curtailed ride within the confinements of the "Pale". Peddlers move between the "grounded" cabs in the improvised parking lot offering coffee, falafel and cigarettes, ushers take care that culminating distress and frustration do not explode into open fights between fellow drivers. There, at a distance from the roads for Jews only, the checkpoints, barriers, and trapped taxis, a handsbreadth of beseiged Palestine is finally exposed.

*

The above description illustrates some of the visible manifestations of the closure regime – a scheme of Israeli imposed military measures and orders that prevent, prohibit and/or restrict Palestinian movement between and within locales and districts inside the Palestinian territory as well as between the Palestinian territory and Israel proper. Since the outbreak of the second Intifada in late September 2000, and for nearly four years now, tens of thousands of soldiers and border-policemen, equipped with a threatening arsenal of arms and vehicles enforce the closure policy upon the residents of towns, villages, and refugee camps throughout the West Bank. Much of their activity takes place at dozens of permanent and "flying" (mobile) checkpoints and at hundreds of roadblocks[1]. At the same time, millions of Palestinians confront the increasingly devastating impact of closure on their employment situation, family welfare, health condition, educational achievements, community life and personal security. While the overwhelming majority of the population struggles to hold out within the besieged communities, a very large portion – all those who work, study or seek services outside their immediate place of residence – confront the closure also at major sites of its enforcement; i.e.; the checkpoints and roadblocks. Checkpoints are, therefore, arenas of an ongoing confrontation between the Israeli armed forces engaged in the imposition of the closure regime and a besieged Palestinian civilian population struggling to survive.

I became intensively exposed to this confrontation through activism with "Machsom Watch" (Checkpoint Watch), an Israeli women's anti-occupation and human rights action group, whose member "Watchers" monitor the violations of Palestinians' rights at checkpoints and roadblocks around Jerusalem and inside the West Bank, intervene on behalf of the abused when possible, and document the occurrences and developments in daily reports[2]. My documentation, covering a two-year and three-month period of "watching" – divided between a central "border checkpoint" north of Bethlehem and internal roadblocks and checkpoints in the Bethlehem and Khalil (Hebron) districts – served as the major primary source for this paper. Following a short historical background on Israel's closure policy, the paper traces the implementation and identifies stages in the enforcement of a closure regime in the southern districts of the occupied West Bank since the outbreak of the second Intifada and through July 2003. The sequence of detailed reports is then used to underscore and interpret developments and changes over time in the conduct and attitude of the closure-enforcing Israeli military on the one hand, and in modes of coping and steadfastness among Palestinian civilians on the other hand. Throughout, the paper endeavors to point to the connection between the specific occurrences and developments, as recorded at particular sites of closure enforcement, and the overall Israeli military policy in the Occupied Palestinian Territories.

Spring 2001 – Spring 2002: The Closure at Bethlehem Checkpoint

Bethlehem checkpoint (also known by the military name of checkpoint 300) is located at the northern exist of Bethlehem on the southern border of "Metropolitan Jerusalem", some 300 meters south of the Gilo - Beit Safafa junction and approximately 500 meters north of the Tomb of Rachel[3]. The area between the Tomb, where an immense, well fortified military base was set up, and the checkpoint was designated in the Oslo accords as "Area C", that is, it remained under full Israeli military and administrative control (supposedly until future negotiations). To the west of the checkpoint is the Tantur Ecumenical Institute, encompassed by a well-tended garden and a large olive orchard and surrounded by a high stone wall. To the east of the checkpoint is a broad, fairly deep valley (hereafter 'the wadi'), reaching to the disputed Jewish settlement of Har Homa (Jabel Abu Ghneim) to the east, the monastery of Mar Elias to the north and the main road into Jerusalem (Hebron Road) to the west. The checkpoint compound stretches over an area of road some 60 meters long with manned guard-posts at each end, and includes an improvised "terminal"; a very narrow single lane corridor, through which pedestrians must pass on their way to a manned booth where IDs are checked.

Contrary to a prevailing notion, the Bethlehem checkpoint, like all other checkpoints between the West Bank and Israel, is a fairly recent phenomenon in the history of the Israeli occupation. Until the latter years of the first Intifada (1992-1993) Palestinians moved more or less freely from all parts of the West Bank into Jerusalem, the Arab (commonly known as East) part of which constituted the commercial, institutional and cultural center of the West Bank throughout the first 25 years of occupation. The imposition of periodic closures and the accompanying erection of checkpoints along the green line and around the municipal borders of 'greater Jerusalem' became a central component of the Israeli policy in 1993, and increasingly so following the establishment of the Palestinian National Authority (PNA) in 1994 and throughout the subsequent Oslo years (1994-2000). During the latter time period the military and administrative control over most of the Palestinian territory as well as over all border crossings remained in Israeli hands. The closure policy was employed in conjunction with the partial and intermitent Israeli implementation of the interim agreements, specifically the withdrawal from "Area A" and redeployment in "Area B". Closure implied the sealing off of Israel proper and of Arab Jerusalem to residents of the Occupied Territories, including heavy restrictions on (at times total prohibition of) the entrance of Palestinian workers into Israel for the purpose of day wage labor, the encirclement of the Gaza strip and its effective disconnecting/isolation from the West Bank, and the imposition of a host of obstacles and limitations on the exporting, importing and trafficking of goods and services. Shifting between "total" and "partial" or "relaxed" (depending upon changing decisions of the military government and the subsequent enforced measures), closures of varying intensity were employed as means of collective punishment (e.g. in the wake of Hamas terrorist attacks), and as a main instrument of exerting political and economic pressure upon the PNA in the context of the lingering negotiations between the extremely un-balanced parties. The detrimental impact of the closure policy on Palestinian economy and society received wide attention, especially given the direct negative consequences for the viability of a future Palestinian state[4].

During the Oslo years the Bethlehem checkpoint functioned more or less as a border crossing, entrance to Israel and Jerusalem through which passage was contingent upon specified temporary permits - to enter, work, receive medical treatment , etc. - issued by the Israeli Civil Administration and approved by the shabak (General Security Service). Entry of Palestinian private cars was forbidden. The heavy restrictions on movement and the obstacle-ridden procedure for obtaining permits significantly reduced the number of south West Bankers (residents of the Khalil and Bethlehem districts) who crossed to Jerusalem/Israel on a regular basis, particularly the number of day-wage laborers, which saw a sharp decline, reaching an unprecedented low in 1994-1996[5]. Nonetheless, during most of the Oslo period, and especially throughout its latter years (1998- Sept. 2000), the checkpoint was bustling with activity, including a constant stream of transitees, a regular service-taxi line, and petty-trade (peddlers and small food stalls). Among those who made their way through the checkpoint on a regular basis were day wage laborers, employees at Palestinian institutions in Arab Jerusaelm, school and university students, merchants, those seeking medical care, and visitors. All were to disappear soon after the outbreak of the second Intifada in late September 2000.

The Checkpoint as a Manhunt Terrain

From checkpoint to barrier: the early months

The term "closure" remained part of the occupation lexicon, but ever since the eruption of the second Intifada its meaning became increasingly identified with the total war Israel waged against the Palestinian Authority and Palestinian civil society in general. Starting in October 2000, the Bethlehem checkpoint ceased to operate as a crossing zone and a "check –point"; rather it now functioned as a barrier, a formidable means of preventing all residents of the Ocuuppied Territories that hold Palestinian identity cards from entering Jerusalem. To this end, entire battalions, including artillerymen, paratroopers, armored forces, and border police, were sent to replace the handful of soldiers who manned the post in the bygone Oslo years. Only a small fraction guarded the checkpoint compound itself, however; most forces – armed to the teeth and reinforced by jeeps and field cars, and at times by police or army helicopters as well - were deployed in the fields, orchards, and valley that surround it, their major mission consisting of preventing "closure breakers" from what was now dubbed "infiltration".

All formerly valid entry permits were suspended and the civil administration ceased issuing new ones. In their absence, crossing through the checkpoint facilities was rendered a non-option, leaving the Palestinians no choice but to resort to the paths and byways that bypass it from east and west. From March through most of August 2001 Machsom-Watch activists reported that the number of people who attempted to cross the "seam" each morning via the grounds of the Tantur Ecumenical Institute and via the eastern wadi was as high as several thousands. The majority were day-wage laborers from all over the southern West Bank, including townships and villages as far from the checkpoint as Yatta (south-east of Khalil/Hebron) and Dura (south-west of Khalil/Hebron), and as close to it as Beit Jala and 'Aida refugee camp (bordering on Rachel's Tomb). Conversations with them revealed that almost all laborers had lost their former workplaces immediately following the outbreak of the Intifada. Most remained without regular work since, except for short stints here and there, and there were those whose days of work since October 2000 could be counted on the fingers of one hand. The ranks of the "illegals" also included students (at Jerusalem-based Palestinian institutions of higher education), teachers (including many who for years/decades were employed by the Jerusalem municipality), peasant-women with their produce, men and women seeking medical care in Jerusalem clinics and hospitals, and others. In short, a representative sample of an entire public that prior to October 2000 was dependent on jobs, casual work opportunities, services and facilities in west and east Jerusalem. Of the thousands who tried their luck, many hundreds would eventually be caught, detained, and brought to the checkpoint compound, where they would be held for hours before their confiscated documents were returned to them. Luckier ones - numbering several hundreds on better days and several dozens on bad ones - succeeded in evading the troops and patrols and make their way into Jerusalem (where they faced high risk of being caught by police patrols). Although referring to a single individual, the following case - described in a Machsom Watch report dated August 26th - was typical (at that time) of veteran, self-employed skilled laborers in the building sector whose work history in Jerusalem spanned several decades:

> Between 8.20 and 9.00 a.m., we waited within the checkpoint forecourt for identity cards to be returned to detainees that were caught earlier that morning. Among them was Faisal, a builder-plasterer-painter in his late fifties from Beit Jala, who carried a ladder and a set of heavy tools on his shoulders. He had gone to work in a Jerusalem apartment, with all his equipment on his back. A border policeman caught him while he attempted to cross through the Tantur garden. Leaning heavily on his yellow ladder, with sweat dripping down his forehead and temples, Faisal told us that he was doing his current job especially cheaply, "half free". The owners of the apartment he was painting were "new immigrants that have no money" he explained, conveying his sympathy, as though it were they that should be pitied. He then called them on his cell phone and said he'd been "delayed", without saying why.... In the meantime, documents that had been confiscated by Border Police in the very early hours of the morning (people said around 5 a.m.) were returned. Identity papers taken later on, including Faisal's, were not returned. The burning August sun was already high in the sky, adding to the distress of the detained laborers, who saw their work day slip away. Faisal did not lose his temper, neither did the thought of giving up cross his mind. He said he'd try his luck again as soon as he is released and entertained the idea of

appealing to the hearts of the police: "but surely I would find at least one person willing to listen". At 10.30 we contacted Faisal by phone. He had been released a short while before, had manged to sneak through Tantur, and was on his way to the apartment.

Ongoing escalation

The months that followed – from August 2001 through February 2002 - saw an ever expanding scope of Israeli military aggression in the areas that were then still under full or partial Palestinian control and the stepping up of terrorist attacks (particularly suicide bombing) inside Israel by several Palestinian organizations. The unfolding of events showed a spiral pattern: international pressure – albeit very moderate, or rather, U.S.-cushioned – to implement the recomendations of the Mitchell Report[6] was met with an Israeli refusal to undertake the recommended measures for the "rebuilding of confidence", first and foremost, the IDF withdrawal to pre Sept 28th 2000 positions and a total freeze of settlement building. Rather, Israel demanded that the Palestinians satisfy its definition of "complete cessation of violence" followed by a six week cooling-off period as a precondition for implementing the redeployment and/or any other significant measures. This Israeli strategy, of imposing conditions that could not be accepted by the Palestinian side - a strategy which, to a large extent, won the support of the U.S. diplomacy via envoys George Tenet (CIA director at the time) and later Anthony Zinni[7] – repeatedly defered the "threat" of the Mitchel Report and finally removed it from the agenda. At the same time, as violence and counter violence continued, Israel advanced its by then established policy of extrajudicial executions, that is, the assassinations/ "liquidations" of Palestinian leaders, activists and militants deep in the areas under Palestinian control. In turn, the assassinations – which more often than not claimed the lives of the non- targetted as well – provoked retaliation on the part of the Palestinian organizations, including terrorist attacks within Israel proper. These provided pretexts, or rather, opened additional "windows of opportunities" for renewed Israeli strikes inside the Palestinian territory, mainly in the form of large scale incursions into Palestinian population centers within "Area A", during which an arsenal of heavy and sophisticated weaponry - including tanks, bulldozers, F-16s, attack helicopters, air to surface missiles – was put to use. Alongside the incursions, Israel further stepped up its assassination campaign, expanded the scale of house demolitions, (particularly in the Gaza Strip) and conducted frequent F-16 raids against PNA security (police, preventive security, intelligence) facilities and personnel.

This intensification of the use of military force continued almost uninterruptedly throughout the period under review - including during intervals of varying length in which the Palestinian factions observed a unilateral, PNA-negotiated "cease-fire", that is, a halt of terrorist attacks within Israel proper. It culminated with the extensive IDF operation ("Operation Colorful Journey") in major West- Bank and Gaza Strip refugee camps (February 29th –March 19th 2002), and finally with the subsequent full reoccupation of the West Bank towns

(Area A) in what was termed "Operation Defensive Shield" (March 29th- May 10th 2002). More than 550 Palestinians were killed, thousands were wounded, and thousands more were imprisoned in the course of these operations, which took place inside population centers. The invading forces caused unprecedented destruction of private and public property and of physical infrastructure, looted and wrought heavy damage upon government institutions and facilities, all but destroyed the presidential headquarters (the Muqata'ah) in Rammallah and further tightened the blockade around President Arafat, and rendered what remained of the West Bank-based PNA security forces inoperative[8]. That hardly any limits were set on the level of Israeli violence should be attributed, first and foremost, to the obstructive mediation on the part of the most-favorable-ever Administration in the White House, which not only showed a remarkable "understanding" vis a vis the Israeli military policies and measures, but also repeatedly adopted the official Israeli positions and interpretations.

It is in the context of this escalating military aggression that the Bethlehem checkpoint was turned into a full fledged man-hunt terrain. Each morning the army and border police would conduct exacting and prolonged pursuit of laborers crossing the valley to the east of the checkpoint (the wadi) and within the precinct of Tantur Institute[9] and the area around its northern gate, which borders on the Gilo junction. The following illustration, extracted from a report dated September 9th 2001, should be placed in the setting of the immediate circumstances that prevailed in the Bethlehem region at the time: On August 27th the IDF assassinated (by Apache-launched missiles) Abu-Ali Mustafa, the secretary general of the Popular Front for the Liberation of Palestine (PFLP) in his al-Bireh office – the highest ranking political leader on Israel's assassination list at the time. His "liquidation" set off a wave of popular protest that swept through the Palestinian territories, including renewed incidents of shooting (light weapons) from Beit Jala on the adjacent Gilo settlement. These provided the "excuse" for a massive Israeli machine gunning and tank shelling of Beit Jala and subsequently for a three day invasion and re-occupation of the town, causing casualities among civilians and considerable damage to homes and infrastructure.

September 9th 2001: the manhunt in the wadi

Until today we have never witnessed such an extensive hunt here. Hardly anyone managed to bypass the checkpoint and enter Jerusalem. The general picture was clear from the start of our watch: hundreds of laborers were trapped in the wadi to the east. Some of them were spread out in the area between the terraces, among piles of garbage, bushes, rocks and other obstacles. Other concentrated in three groups – on the northwest side of the wadi, in the centre of the wadi and to the south, close to the checkpoint itself. The soldiers moved between these three groups and every ten minutes or so would renew the chase and drive the men back towards the checkpoint. Each time, the men would move a few paces back, and would then rally and once again advance to the spot from which they had been driven. We were in the wadi between 7:00-8:00 a.m. in the company of laborers who already know us and even wait for us to appear. Some of them told us they had reached the wadi at 5:00 a.m. and were trapped there since. The troop deployment was so extensive that it formed a solid wall that no one could penetrate.

In one of the "pockets", dozens of men were huddled surrounded by three soldiers. The workers, some of whom had left home at 4:00 a.m (mainly those from the Khalil (Hebron) region), had not lost their sense of humour. One of them turned to a soldier and said: "Soldier, you probably didn't sleep all night did you?" The soldier concurred. "No, I didn't sleep". "So get some sleep now" said the laborer, "its better you should sleep." And another scene from the wadi experience: The moment the soldiers start up and begin the chase, the wadi is filled with voices and echoes of voices of the laborers. Some imitate sheep, others crows, some whistle while others "Indian call". The tension and despair gnaw at them. The daily manhunts force them to return home, often without having managed to earn a penny, at the same time having paid the costs of the long journey to the checkpoint.

The First Large-Scale Invasion of Bethlehem and Its Aftermath

The situation was further aggrevated by the first large-scale IDF invasion of the Bethlehem region since the outbreak of the second Intifada, which began on October 19th – supposedly in retaliation for the assassination two days earlier of the Isaerli tourism Minister, Rehavam Ze'evi, which itself was a retaliation for the above mentioned assassination of the PFLP Secretary General[10] – and lasted until October 28th. Army forces entered deep into Zone A and took up positions in the heart of the civilian population in the center of Bethlehem, Beit Jala, the 'Aida refugee camp, and Beit Sahour. During the week of 19-25 October 2001, IDF soldiers shot to death fifteen Palestinians, eleven of them civilians. Two minors and three women were among the dead. The other four killed were members of the Palestinian security apparatus. IDF gunfire caused widespread damage to residences and shops, as well as to Bethlehem's two major hospitals. No IDF casualties were reported in the Bethlehem region during that week.[11] During the invasion of Bethlehem, the checkpoint became a fortified military post, as described in a Machsom Watch report dated October 23rd 2001:

The place looked like a war zone. The checkpoint was closed off with cement blocks and sandbags, and in the center of the compound there were tanks, command cars, and a huge bulldozer. A strong military presence, with no civilians present except for TV crews from all over the world. In short, no rights and no humans...We couldn't figure out what we were doing alongside the parked tanks.

Following the IDF withdrawal from Bethlehem (October 29th 2001) the checkpoint zone did not return to the pre-invasion "routine" of summer 2001. The main thrust of police-military activity moved to locations away from the immediate vicinities of the checkpoint, including the Tantur garden and orchards, the eastern wadi up to "Har Homa", the main road up to the Gilo Junction, and sometimes also north of it, and the village of Beit Safafa. The number of border police, regular (blue) police and soldiers spread around the area in the mornings, on foot and in cars, rose substantially as did the violent means deployed: tear-gas, firing in the air, armed chases, hauling people out of service taxis, ambushes from between the trees, ambushes within the village of Beit Safafa, and use of undercover police. Correspondingly, the number of laborers trying to get into Jerusalem decreased further and stood at no more than 200 to 300 people, with only a minimal number managing to successfully bypass. Some of these developments were vividly captured in the report below dated November 4th, 2001:

> A mobile military checkpoint was set up on a side road at the northern edge of the wadi, not far from the Mar Elias monastery, that is, well inside the municipal boundaries of Jerusalem. When we arrived there we encountered a group of reserve soldiers armed from head to foot and a number of jeeps. In the wadi that stretches below we could see several dozens of workers who managed to get as far as the northern edge of the road and were forced to halt there. As we climbed down, they immediately gathered around us - about forty men, mainly villagers from Sa'ir, Shuyukh, Yatta, Taqo'a, Beit Fajar, some of them very young, 16 and 17-year-olds, others much older, in their 40s and over – and pleaded for some intervention on their behalf. In the meantime, the reservists spread out across part of the road, moving along it with their rifles aimed towards the wadi. Suddenly, there was the sound of a gunshot. The laborers fled for their lives into the depths of the wadi, and we began shouting and chasing after the gunman (the commander of the group). The commander made sure he didn't respond by so much as one word, but one of the soldiers approached and quietly thanked us for being there.
>
> In the meantime, the laborers who had been chased away climbed back and patiently waited for the right moment [to try to pass]. But the reservists would not ease up. Later, they called in reinforcements - a Border Police jeep, and police vans. The Border Police fired tear-gas in the direction of the valley, while the police tried unsuccessfully to get rid of us. At around 8.30, a reservist fired another shot into the air and the workers fled into the valley. At around 9.00 a.m. it became clear that the laborers had been worn down by the struggle. Most of them began to abandon the place and turn back.

While the months that elapsed between the above November report and the large scale invasion of the Bethlehem refugee camps ('Aida and Dheisheh) in early March 2002 were marked by further escalation in all components of Israel's military aggression, the situation in the Bethlehem checkpoint and its vicinities as recorded by Machsom Watch reports remained more or less unchanged. In other words, one may say that by that stage of the conflict, all available means of imposing the closure policy short of the reoccupation of the entire Palestinian territory (and/or the erection of an insurmountable barrier) had been exhausted by the Israeli military and police.

The *Sumud* for a Day's Work in Jerusalem

By October 2001, a year into the "re-modeled" closure, the number of Palestinians who attempted to enter Jerusalem was as low as a few hundred a day, this in comparison with the many thousands who were prepared to take the risk and endure the consequences when the policy was first imposed. The dwindling lines of those who stayed put included mainly veteran laborers, men in their late thirties, forties and fifties, fathers of six to ten children on average, most of them residents of villages and townships in the Khalil/Hebron district. Like their many counterparts who were defeated at the manhunt terrain, these veterans too had lost their jobs sometime in October 2000 or shortly after. A year or so later, they no longer fitted the definition of day-wage, casual laborers, nor were they part of a reserve army of the unemployed. Rather, they could now be described as long-time "discharged" laborers seeking a day's work. Correspondingly, their *sumud* – literally: staying power, here connoting holding out, perseverance, persistence - no longer consisted of trying to hold on to an existing job, or trying to get back to a former workplace, but rather of seizing upon and materializing a day's work in Jerusalem, at times one or two work days a week, at times as few as one work-day in two or three weeks. On top of the daily exposure to manhunts, detention, harassment and humiliation, the "*sumud* for a day's work in Jerusalem" entailed bearing the burden of the journey from their home villages to the checkpoint vicinity and back. The trip, which once took no more than a 30 minute drive at a minimum fare, now required at least two hours of carving one's way around and through barriers and roadblocks that the army had set up in the midst of the Palestinian heartland, and cost approximately seven times that of pre-October 2000. The following instance and testimony, extracted from a report dated October 14th 2001, brings home some of the above:

At the checkpoint compound, we met some 60 people who had been detained earlier that morning, all of them laborers, the majority coming from villages and towns in the Hebron district. They were now waiting – sitting on the ground - for their confiscated documents to be returned. One detainee, a laborer from Yatta (a township south-east of Hebron) and father of ten, told us: "I left home at 3.30 AM , and was caught at the olive grove of Tantur around 5.30 AM. On my way from home to here I had to cross 5 roadblocks and to change three service cabs. Because of all this, the cost of the trip from Yatta to the checkpoint and back is now 70 shekels. Before the closure we used to pay 5 shekels for each direction, that is 10 shekels all in all. For a day's work I would get 130 shekels, from which only 50 is left after we take off travel costs.

He had intended to get to the Makhane Yehuda market, where he worked in construction for several days during the previous week. According to him, if he didn't get there by 7.30 a.m., the contractor would go to the "slave market" in East Jerusalem and pick other workers:"How can they continue to so abuse other human beings, when they all know and see that we are laborers. They should look at our trousers and our shoes, if they are in doubt....

We asked the soldiers in the booth and at the checkpoint what was happening with the identity papers. The answer we received: "The detainees will wait until 9 AM, at the earliest, because if we return the documents earlier, they will infiltrate again, and get to work." In other words, the job of the soldiers was to ensure that the laborers would lose a day's work, and they knew it.

A short elaboration on the changing content and multiple meanings of *sumud* in the context of Palestinian life and struggle under Israeli occupation is in place here. When first introduced to the Palestinian popular lexicon in the mid 1970s, less than a decade into the occupation, *sumud* was employed to state: "we will not give up", "we will stay put", and "we shall prevail". Back in those days, commitment to steadfastness implied, first and foremost, not to abandon the homeland (emigrate) despite the deliberate Israeli policies of non-development, wholesale land-grab, ongoing persecution of leaders, banning of national institutions; holding on to what remained of the land, investing in education as the major future resource (human capital), cherishing the Palestinian culture and heritage and rooting them in the young generations, and so forth[12]. The early and mid 1980s saw a sharp shift in the public attitude toward the concept, with the term *sumud* becoming an object of criticism and ridicule. The reversal came about in the wake of the setting up in 1979 by the Jordanian-Palestinian Joint Committee of the "*sumud* funds", which extended financial support to various institutions in the occupied territories in an attempt to enable their holding out vis a vis the policies of the occupation. The criteria employed in the distribution and allocations of the "*sumud* money" gave rise to widespread resentment and critique, particularly among the Palestinian left, which portrayed "institution-alized *sumud*" as an incentive for political corruption, moral decadence, and withdrawal to passivity.[13]

During the first Intifada, *sumud* and the *samidun* (those who stay put) were pushed aside in favor of *nidal* (struggle) and the *munadilun* (those who struggle), that is, in favor of the intensive and highly demanding collective struggle for liberation from occupation and those who make the sacrifice. At times, though, *sumud* and *nidal* were alternately used to connote various forms of popular and individual resistance, e.g. the proven steadfastness of a community subjected to a prolonged curfew regime, or the holding out of a detainee under Shabak interrogation. While *sumud* did not resurface as a widespread idiomatic expression during the Oslo years, it is possible to point to at least two major spheres with respect to which the term was applicable. One was associated with the building of national institutions – nation-wide and local, governmental and non-governmental, political and socio-cultural – in the absence of national sovereignty and under the political uncertainty that prevailed. The other could be referred to as the "Oslo-closure *sumud*" of the remainder of the day-wage laborers' class, that is, of the tens of thousands of day wage laborers who struggled to hold on to jobs inside Israel despite the Israeli closure policy that attempted to remove and replace them. This latter *sumud* was finally defeated at the border checkpoints under the post Sept 2000 closure. What was left of it was the "*sumud* for a day's work in Jerusalem" that we observed among the persistent laborers who returned each morning to the Bethlehem checkpoint arena.[14]

The "*sumud* for a day's work in Jerusalem" was all but defeated in the aftermath of the invasion of the refugee camps in the Bethlehem urban complex and the reoccupation of the West Bank towns that followed shortly after (March-

April 2002). The months-long curfew regime that the army imposed on all urban and most rural locales of the Bethlehem region, and the thick deployment of troops and tanks around population centers and throughout the Bethlehem and Khalil (Hebron) districts, rendered the journey to the Bethlehem checkpoint, let alone the attempt to bypass and enter Jerusalem, almost impossible.

Impact of the Closure Policy on the Conduct of Soldiers' Imposing it

The first seventeen months of total closure also saw some shift in the conduct and behavior of the soldiers at the checkpoints. Six or seven months into the closure it was still not uncommon to identify vague signs of embarrassment or discontent. Here and there one would hear a paratrooper or artilleryman complain that the "duty at the checkpoint" as he would put it, deprives him from fulfilling his military training as combat soldier. Although a pale version, this discontent echoed the resentment that gained some ground among soldiers who took part in the suppression of the first Intifada and who claimed, at the time, that they were trained to fight against armies, tanks and war planes, not against women, children and civilians. However, the tension between the alleged "calling" and the actual realization was soon to be bridged and smoothed away. A year into the closure the utmost reservation one might have come across was confined to: "It is not me who makes the decisions. I only carry out orders".

The convergence of several interelated factors went far to disguise and mask the essence of the orders from those who carried them out, and contributed to the cultivation of what I refer to as "a false consciousness of participation in combat missions" in their midst. There were the rules and regulations that enabled the soldier not to see the construction laborers, housemaids, teachers, students, or the ill, despite their appearance, clothes, shoes, documents, and despite the fluent Hebrew that many of them spoke. After all, according to orders, all are prohibited from entrance, and, post factum, all are "illegal arrivals", trespassers, infiltrators, criminals. And then there was the great abundance of arms: rifles, sub-machine guns, personal guns, tear gas canisters and grenades, not to speak of the Hummer jeeps, brand new Land Rovers, and the more conventional vans and jeeps - all imploring to be put to use. Not only did the build-up of forces create an internal, "structural" pressure for their potential to be exercised, but also it reinforced the soldiers' false consciousness of participation in combat missions. Yet an even more crucial impact can be attributed to the ongoing escalation in the Israeli aggression against the Palestinian civilian population during the lengthy time period that preceded the full re-occupation of "Area A" – an escalation that provided the setting for intensifying the violence at the checkpoints and facilitated its legitimation. Credit should also be given to the official, as well as to most of the commercial Israeli media, at the service of State power, consistently ready to justify crimes of the military in the name of "security", rarely courageous enough to ask "whose security?" "whose interests?" Needless to say,   the terminology employed in news briefings and reportage was adjusted accordingly: armored incursions into crowded neighborhoods were now "heavy battles", and border policemen engaged in hunting laborers at the checkpoints were re-ranked as "fighters", a title previously reserved to members of the "exclusive elite units".

Summer 2002 - Summer 2003: Siege as the Higher Stage of Closure

From Closure to Siege

As mentioned, the reoccupation of the Palestinian towns / "Area A" in March-April 2002 signaled the defeat of the "*sumud* for a day's work in Jerusalem" at the Bethlehem checkpoint. The major arenas of confrontation between those imposing the closure regime and those hit by it were now transferred to the checkpoints and roadblocks at the heart of the Palestinian territory, and in our case, to the heart of the Bethlehem and Khalil (Hebron) districts. While a substantial number of these barriers were set up there shortly after the outbreak of the second Intifada in the wake of the renewed deployment of Israeli troops and tanks throughout the Palestinian rural zone (Areas B and C), dozens of additional ones were erected in the aftermath of the full reoccupation of the West Bank. At the same time, "post "Defensive Shield" closure" implied a significant increase in the forces deployed, further tightening of the blockade around all Palestinian locales, and an expanding list of prohibitions and restrictions on Palestinian movement within Palestinian land. Palestinian vehicular traffic outside the immediate residential centers was nearly brought to a halt: private cars were forbidden to move on all interurban roads; the routes of service taxis were confined to rural back roads within bounded zones; the Khalil (Hebron)-Bethlehem bus-line was banned: a handful of bus-drivers and busses (numbers ranged between a low of three and a high of thirty) were issued temporary permits – that could be withheld at any given moment - to move on a mere seventeen-kilometer section of road 60, between the blocked northern entrance to the town of Halhul and the blocked western entrance to al Khader village. On top of this came the restrictions on the movement of people: Throughout the period under review "legal" movement between the Khalil and the Bethlehem districts was possible only through the Etzion checkpoint, which was set up on a central junction (Etzion junction) at the interface of the two districts. However, Palestinian men under 45 (at times, under 40) – in other words, the overwhelming majority of the male population - were prohibited from crossing through the checkpoint unless they held valid permits to work in Jewish settlements (within the West Bank, on Palestinian territory). Moreover, on numerous occasions the prohibition on inter-district crossing was extended to include the entire population regardless of age, gender and permits. Extreme measures of this kind, subsumed under the title of "tightened closure", were imposed during and following IDF assaults and assassination campaigns in the Khalil and Bethlehem regions and elsewhere in the West Bank, during and following Jewish holidays, in the wake of Palestinian terrorist attacks inside

Israel proper, and at times with out a declared or apparent reason. Furthermore, movement between adjacent locales within a single district was also frequently prohibited and forcefully prevented, not to mention repeated occasions when a 24-hour curfew was imposed on localities.

Taken together, the enforcement of the above measures effectively disconnected the Khalil district from the Bethlehem district and sealed off the overwhelming majority of the population within its places of residence. In other words, we are speaking of the imposition of siege as the higher stage of the closure regime.

Sights of Siege at Internal Roadblocks and Checkpoints

Our Machsom Watch team was first introduced to the realities of siege in the summer of 2002. In mid-June Israel launched another major offensive throughout the West Bank -"re-reoccupation" of the occupied Palestinian population centers, entitled "Operation Determined Path" - which lasted through July and most of August. Consecutive weeks of 24-hour imposed curfew brought everyday life in the Bethlehem region to a standstill, leaving border and internal checkpoints alike beyond the reach of the besieged residents. It was following this deterioration that we took the decision to "relinquish" the Bethlehem checkpoint – where a handful of Palestinians maintained their relentless *sumud* for a day's work and where our intervention on their behalf became increasingly hopeless - in favor of internal roadblocks and checkpoints in the Bethlehem and Khalil districts.

Al-Khader western roadblocks

Starting in August 2002 and over a three-month period, the major part of our weekly shifts was spent at a battery of four roadblocks that were set up by IDF bulldozers on the western access road and entrance to al-Khader - a medium-size Palestinian village (local municipality) that lies to the southwest of Bethlehem and neighbors on the southern outskirts of Beit Jala[15]. The most western of "al-Khader western roadblocks"[16] borders on a main intersection on road 60 (al-Khader-Husan junction) and blocks vehicular passage from this main route into al-Khader and Bethlehem. It is "reinforced" by a second, usually unmanned roadblock that was erected on the same access road, approximately 100 meters to the east of the junction, very close to the village homes (hereafter the internal roadblock). Two additional barriers were piled up near the entrance to the adjacent al-Khader Government Boys' School, which stands on a slightly elevated plain that overlooks the junction. The latter is part of a complex of buildings that host four schools - two for boys, two for girls (elementary and secondary for each) – serving al-Khader children. Complementing the array of barriers is a 24-hour-manned watchtower, which was erected at the rear of the girls' secondary school, no more than 25 meters away from the classrooms.

The following report - dated September 22nd 2002 – captures a facet of the violent military intrusion into everyday school-life at the al-Khader boys' school:

September 22nd 2002: The Headmaster protects his students from the soldiers

We arrived in al-Khader western roadblocks at around 7:20 a.m. to find the al-Khader –Husan junction all but empty of Palestinians, two army jeeps, and some eight soldiers commanded by two low-ranking officers: a woman and a man.

The movement of residents in and out of al-Khader was completely forbidden today. To assure that the order is obeyed the soldiers positioned themselves in the narrow vineyard strip that overlooks the most western roadblock and the junction, pointing their guns at every moving object. Two soldiers then turned to the shortcut path that leads from the "inner" (most eastern) roadblocks to the gate of Al-Khader Government Boys' School. Dozens of school-children who had just crossed the inner (unmanned) roadblock were advancing along the path. One soldier stood at a distance of no more than 10 meters from the children pointing his gun at them as they climbed through a barrier of dirt and rocks that the army had piled across the path. The other soldiers "covered" from behind. At some stage a third soldier (perhaps the officer) shouted from his slightly distanced position : "If anyone crosses the line, shoot him in the knee..". We couldn't figure out which line, and who precisely was being addressed.

In the midst of all this stood the headmaster of the boys' secondary school, who was watching over his students, seeing that each and every one of them arrives safely at the school's gates, where they were welcomed by two male teachers. Calm, patient, very humble, the headmaster told us that he stands at this barrier every day between 6.45 and 7.45 in the morning to protect the children from further harassment by the military, and to prevent them from responding to the ongoing provocation. "A single stone aimed at the soldiers' direction, is all the army needs as pretext to shut down the school", he explained. The headmaster has been doing his "guard-duty" for over a year and a half now, ever since he enterd his position in 2001. He mentioned repeated incidents of abuse of his students as well as of teachers (including himself) by soldiers and spoke of anxiety, trauma and a sense of loss and disorientation among the children. It is almost impossible to discipline them under the current circumstances, he said. The soldier continued to point his gun all along.
By 7:55 all children were inside, and the national anthem (a recording) could be heard from a distance.

The soldiers now descended from the vineyard to the western roadblock to stop a group of approximately fifteen men who gathered there and asked to be allowed to continue their journey. No, not to Jerusalem, not even to Hebron, they only wanted to get to the neighboring village of Husan, on the other side of road 60. The woman officer who appeared to be having much fun that morning approached the Palestinians and ordered them to disperse and go home. "And have a good day", she added. The group stepped back and then stopped to consult on their next move.

Continuous Machsom Watch reports from al-Khader western roadblocks underscored further aspects of the violation of school-life by the military, including repeated hours-long detention of students and teachers at the roadblocks, incidents of beatings of students by soldiers, frequent break-ins of troops into the school compound, the sealing-off of window-shutters on the first floor of the secondary boys' school, occasional shooting of tear-gas in the close vicinity of the school, and several incidents when the school was shut down following an order by the military commander. On top of these, during the 2002-3 school year students lost almost two months of schooling as a consequence of curfews imposed on the region. The follow-up visits to al-Khader schools continued until the end of the school year (June 2003) and commenced again in September. Yet, starting from mid-November 2002, the main thrust of our Watch activity was moved to checkpoints and roadblocks further inside the Palestinian heartland.

The enforcement of siege at Etzion checkpoint

Approximately thiteen kilometers south of al-Khader western roadblocks, on the intersection of road 60 with the transverse road leading to the Gush Etzion settlement bloc, one finds the Etzion checkpoint. Set up mid-way between Bethlehem and Khalil/Hebron, this checkpoint was designated as having a "strategic role" in the layout of internal barriers serving the closure policy; that of cutting off the Bethlehem district (north of checkpoint) from the Khalil district (south of checkpoint). At the same time, the checkpoint ensures the safe and uninterrupted vehicular passage and movement of settlers from the Gush Etzion settlement bloc and elsewhere. During the time period under review here, the checkpoint compound –stretching over an approximately 100-meter-long section of road 60 – was manned by eight to twelve soldiers on average. These were reinforced by troops and jeeps thickly spread along the road and in the immediate and outlying surroundings of the checkpoint compound, including a thin forest to its east, and the orchards and vineyards (property of Beit Omar residents) to its south-west .

The following selection of extracts from reports provides a representative sample of the scenes, situations and experiences that were documented at Etzion checkpoint from mid November 2002 through July 2003. While the excerpts are chronologically ordered, they are not supplemented with references to the wider context, specifically the overall trends of Israel's military aggression in the Palestinian occupied territory. This omisson is justified by the fact that throughout the reviewed period the siege regime remained a constant factor, the intensity ("tightness") of which was affected only marginally, at times even accidentally, by developments on a wider scale.

December 15th 2002: Crossing from Khalil to Bethlehem conditioned upon permit to work in Jewish settlements
The same scene repeated itself over and over during our morning shift at Etzion checkpoint: a bus coming from the direction of Hebron (departing from

roadblocks at the northern entrance to Halhul, approximately 5 km south of Etzion checkpoint) arrives at the checkpoint, where it is ordered to stop. The driver then collects IDs from all passengers and hands them over to a soldier - one of five or six manning the post - who soon afterwards orders passengers to climb down. Following a lengthy ID inspection, the officer in charge orders all men under 45 who do not carry permits to work in Jewish settlements to leave and turn back: "ruh" (go away, and in certain intonation: "get lost") is about the single Arabic word that this young man has mastered so far during his service. Some passengers then plead with the officer to "review" their cases, only to be faced with a louder "ruh"-roar. Eventually the bus is allowed to continue with less than half the original passengers on board, most of them elderly men and women. We learn that none of the few who carry valid permits work in Israel proper; rather most work in major Jewish settlements in the Bethlehem region: Efrat and Beitar Illit, and others in the more distant Maale Adumim (near Abu-Dis) and Kochav Yaacov (near Ramallah) settlements, to which they travel (after this first ordeal is over) through checkpoint-sown Wad- a-Nar. In short, in order to enter Bethlehem, a Palestinian from Hebron needs a permit to work in an Israeli settlement.

One passenger, dressed in fancy clothes, is a manager at the Bethlehem branch of the Arab Bank who lives in Idna village (West of Hebron). In the (now distant) past the journey from home to work took him 25 minutes, he says. Now it's been more than three weeks since he last entered Bethlehem, and he does not know whether today's journey that began before 6 AM will bring him to his workplace, or end in vain. Another man is on his way for a medical check at a Bethlehem clinic. The officer wouldn't listen: "ruh", he tells the man, "get your treatment in Hebron". A young guy with a permit to work in Kochav Yaacov is also prevented from re-boarding the bus. True that he holds a permit, the officer explains, but the man in the attached photo is wearing sun-glasses. There is a chance that the permit is forged, making the permit holder a potential suspect.

A second bus arrives, followed by a third one. The well trained drivers collect the IDs in no time; searching for ways to make life a little easier for the passengers, they approach the soldiers in the kindest, most pleasing manner. Some soldiers are about to comply and let the bus move on, but the officer intervenes demanding that a thorough check be carried out. He is a Kibbutznik, he tells us, "and in civil life my opinions are not much different from yours...", he tries. "But this is war, and I am in charge of a particularly dangerous zone".

March 02 2003: The joys of manhunt in the forest
At some stage a group numbering fifteen young detainees, all in their twenties and early thirties, was brought to the checkpoint compound. Walking at some distance behind the fresh detainees (IDs confiscated of course) were six soldier including a woman soldier - or rather, in the spirit of the day, combatant - their faces glowing with joy and satisfaction. "What were you doing up there in the bush?" one of the guards at the post asked the woman soldier, not trying to conceal his envy. Turning to us he said: "they caught mekhablim (terrorists) ...yesh matzav!"[17]

We were soon to learn that all fifteen men were construction workers from Yatta (south-east of Hebron) who work at a building site in Bethlehem. They started their journey around 5 AM, advancing in the direction of Bethlehem through back roads and side paths (changing local service cabs and covering long distances on foot). Since none of them holds a permit to work in a Jewish settlement, crossing through Etzion checkpoint is a non-option. The only alternative to bypass Etzion is to walk on a side path that goes through a thin forest to the east of the checkpoint. It was there that they fell into the "ambush" set by the soldiers.

April 13th 2003: Sergeant Shabi teaches the Open University student a lesson

Policy remains unchanged: only holders of permits to work in the settlements or in Israel proper are allowed to cross to the Bethlehem district; the rest, regardless of their condition, need, and purpose of journey are sent back. In the absence of an officer the ten soldiers manning the checkpoint today are headed by a sergeant named Shabi. Shabi does not listen to Palestinians; neither does he talk with them. The only communication he engages in consists of orders, shouts, threats and chasing after those who dare not to obey. "Yallah Habaita", he roars, with a grin of self satisfaction smeared over his whole face and his arm lifted in the direction of where he imagines "home" to stand.

Grasping very quickly in front of whom they stand, the lined-up Palestinians refrain from any attempts: almost no one bothers to argue with Shabi and company about the right to complete one's journey, almost no one waves a medical prescription, a hospital appointment, a student card, etc., (as is usually the case at this stage of the ordeal). The few who fail to estimate Shabi's might are punished on the spot. These are very young, inexperienced, restless and extremely talkative men from the village of Beit Omar, who are fed up with sitting at home with no work. By approaching Shabi and team they lose hold of their IDs, which are immediately confiscated. Understanding that now they are doomed (who knows how long they will be held), one of the boys starts walking away from the checkpoint, in an attempt to start his day afresh without the ID...

By that stage, some of the men who were ordered to get lost and have distanced themselves from the checkpoint, make an attempt to bypass the soldiers through the thin forest to the east of the compound. Spotting them in no time, mighty Shabi is now chasing the men, gun pointed in their direction. He catches the slowest among them, takes his ID and orders him to sit outside the fence. The detainee is a fourth-year student at the Open University (the Bethlehem branch) on his way to take an exam scheduled for 10.00 AM. We intervene on his behalf but to no avail. Shabi is determined to teach the student a lesson.

April 20th 2003: The social worker is refused crossing at gunpoint

All men heading to Bethlehem who arrived at the checkpoint with the Halhul-al-Khader- roadblocks bus were ordered to line-up at the fence (to the east of central post). Three soldiers positioned themselves behind a concrete block, one of them pointing his gun in the direction of the Palestinians. The men were then orderd to approach the soldiers, one at a time. One after the other they stepped forward, one after another they were rejected. The "procedure" was very short: the Palestinian advances slowly showing his ID, the soldier takes a short glance and nods to his fellow mates: "this man is going home," followed by a "yallah, habaita, piss off".

While all in the crowd know that they are about to lose a workday, scheduled appointment, medical treatment, etc., no one raises his voice, no one complains about being forced to stand in the cold (comeback of winter today) in vain, no one loses his nerve at the sight of the pointed gun, no one makes a move. One man, a forty something (not yet 45 though...) plasterer from Halhul who was trying to reach his workplace in Bethlehem, comments that more than 80% of the Palestinian people are under 45 years of age... others respond with a weary smile. Shortly after this worker is prevented from continuing his journey, another man is refused. He is a 43 year old senior employee at the Bethlehem branch of the Ministry of Social Affairs. As he turns back and starts walking in the direction of Hebron, this social worker recounts memories of a joint seminar for Israeli and Palestinian social workers he once attended at Ben-Gurion University (mind that this "once" was not once upon a time, but less than 3 years ago (2000)).

Yet another man from Hebron, also forty something, is on his way to Ramallah, where his wife is due to undergo a serious operation today at the government hospital. He holds all the necessary documents specifying the date and kind of operation, yet the soldiers laugh in his face and send him away: "there are hospitals in Hebron too", one of them shouts as the man pleads again.

April 27th 2003: What does it take to be counted as a "humanitarian case"?
Arriving at Etzion checkpoint at 7.20 we noticed a very meager Palestinian presence, even in comparison with previous weeks. There were no busses at the main compound, and no more than two dozen people were waiting behind and near the fence. We were soon to learn of today's tightened, total closure, though none of the soldiers had the slightest idea why it was imposed.

The major difference between the by-now routine, 'standard' closure and today's is that under 'tightened' closure the prohibition on inter-district crossing is extended also to permit holders and to the elderly. Orders in force notwithstanding, the few who did manage to arrive at the checkpoint, cultivated some hope that their perseverance will finally win them a soldier's OK nod. These included two laborers from Halhul who on regular closure days expand the nearby Neve-Daniel settlement and to that end are equipped with precious permits, and three brothers from Yatta, also permit holders, who on regular closure days make the Har Homa settlement bloom. All five approached the soldiers showing the neatly folded document, but to no avail.

The remainder of the small crowd included mainly sick people who were on their way for medical checks in Bethlehem clinics or hospitals. None of them, however, attested to the army criteria of a"humanitarian case", that is, none was considered to be in a situation serious enough to justify the violation of the closure regime. It appears that to fall into the "humanitarian" category a Palestinian must be half dead (or better, dead...). Thus, a forty-year-old man suffering from a (highly visible) acute skin disease, was not allowed to complete the journey to his doctor: "This is not an emergency," one soldier said assertively. "He might be fooling us all, who can guarantee that he is not a mekhabel (terrorist)," suggested his mate. Our intervention did not irritate them, yet it by no means pushed them in the direction of second thought, reconsideration, let alone a sign of compassion.

This was most evident when a young man who had been ill with hepatitis approached the soldiers. He was on his way to an appointment at a medical clinic in Bethlehem, the man said, trying to explain his situation, pointing at his liver, then at his skin color, then at eyes. The soldiers wanted to see a referral and the man did not have one. He suggested that they call his doctor (offering his cellular) and check for themselves whether or not he had a scheduled appointment. They said he should go home and bring documents. He explained that he lives in far away Dura (south west of Hebron) and that there are no busses on the road. We intervened. The man withdrew and then reappeared, again pointing at various organs of his body. One soldier lost patience and shouted at the man to get lost. He withdrew again to behind the fence and collected new energies only to re-emerge on the scene and start his pleading afresh. The more determined he grew the more the soldiers turned hostile and obnoxious. Finally we succeeded in locating their commander – who all along was absorbed in the erection of a "surprise" mobile roadblock some 200 meters to the north of the junction – and persuaded him to do us a great favor and let the man pass.

June 29th 2003: Marching alongside the Arab-free road

June 29th 2003: Marching alongside the Arab-free road

Upon arrival at Etzion junction, we were approached by three bus drivers, all of them long time acquaintances: Over the last three weeks, all drivers on the Halhul –al-Khader roadblocks line were banned from carrying passengers, except for yesterday and the day before yesterday, during which the ban was partially lifted. This morning, when the drivers arrived at Etzion soldiers once again prevented them from continuing the journey in both directions (al-Khader and Halhul) and confiscated their IDs.

Indeed, when we approached the checkpoint compound we learned that the prohibition on the movement of busses remains in force. In the absence of transportation, the total number of people at the compound was very small. These included a few men who were caught while trying to cross through the forest (punished harshly- made to wait for over three hours, from 5AM until 8.30 AM), a handful of permit holders, and stubborn walkers, who managed to reach this location on foot. The soldiers arogantly dismissed the bus-drivers, not bothering even to listen to their claims: "They are trespassing into my territory, as if it were theirs..." an officer who referred to himself as the commander in charge said. They then conditioned giving back the IDs upon the drivers' immediate withdrawal from the zone.

At some stage a family of seven, including mother, father, four young kids and a baby, arrived at the checkpoint from the direction of Bethlehem. They came all the way from their home in Jalazun refugee camp, north of Ramallah, to visit the wife's parents and family in al-Fawwar refugee camp, south of Hebron. How they managed to get as far as Etzion with no busses on the roads remained a riddle, but now they faced the soldiers' order: wife (originally a Khalil/Hebron district resident) and kids allowed to continue to destination, husband refused. When all pleas failed we offered the couple to take the woman and kids to Halhul (where she will be able to catch a service taxi) while the husband will manage somehow. After some persuasion on our part the husband gave his consent. It turned out that this is the first time in two and a half years that the woman is paying a visit to her family and home camp (combination of closure/siege and lack of means).

The distance between Etzion checkpoint and the nothern entrance to Halhul is approximately 5 kilometers. With not a single Palestinian car, bus or cab on the road, we watched women and men of all ages walking and walking and walking along the margin. Dropping our passengers at Halhul junction we followed the woman and five children as they climbed over the first roadblock and walked to the next one, behind which they could find a service taxi that would take them to the next roadblock, and so on. In the meantime the husband called and was relieved to gain a renewed measure of control over his wife's unexpected (checkpoint-bounded) independence. We turned back taking new passengers - two women and a man from al-Arroub refugee camp, who had been waiting for hours (together with dozens of others) for a bus that never came. Letting them off at their destination we turned back again in the direction of Halhul, this time giving a lift to a woman in her late seventies and another with two small children, both from al-Arroub, who were walking up-hill struggling with the heat and exhaustion. At Halhul roadblocks we were approached by a desperate bus driver. He was caught by soldiers when attempting to load passengers and bring them closer to their destination. His ID and bus-keys were confiscated. Unable to help we loaded new passengers - this time two women engineers from villages in the Hebron district, and a librarian. All three women work at the al-Arroub agricultural college and have been waiting at the junction/roadblock since 6 AM (three hours) for a bus that failed to arrive.

July 20th 2003: The aborted mini- rebellion
When we arrived at Etzion checkpoint at 7:15 this morning, we were immediately drawn into the eye of the storm. At the fence and behind it were approximately 70 men: some 40 of them were standing near the gate, all enraged, all exhausted from the endless nightmare. Another 30 or so were scattered on the rocks and between the low bushes to the east of fence, searching for some shade. The IDs of all had been confiscated earlier, in some cases as early as 5 a.m.

We approached the soldiers and inquired about the harsh measures. "As far as I am concerned," one of them replied, "whatever is to the south of this checkpoint is the Territories, and whatever is to its north is Israel". Soldiers manning an internal checkpoint (approximately 20 km to the south of Jerusalem) are entertaining the false idea that they are guarding the border between Palestine and Israel proper...

Dozens of furious laborers – all villagers from the Khalil/Hebron region gathered around us, each telling his story, or repeating parts of what he had already recounted before. One was beaten by a soldier in the forest earlier that morning, another has been "sitting at home" (that is, has not been working) for more than six months and today was his first attempt to search for work since, a third is working at a stone-cutting workshop in Nahalin village (Bethlehem region) and hasn't been able to reach his workplace for over a week ("each day of work is offset by six days spent at the checkpoint"), a fourth went on mourning the devastating situation of all laborers in his village, Beit Omar ("we spend more money on transportation than we earn from work, because we never get to our workplaces"). And the stream of words kept pouring out.

At 8 a.m. the sun was already high in the sky and not a single shady spot could be found near the fence (32 degrees today). Suddenly, ten of the laborers - some of whom had just retrieved their IDs, others with IDs still confiscated - made a move and started walking together in the direction of the forest. A soldier immediately chased them with a pointed M-16. We ran after the soldier. The mini-rebellion was aborted, collapsing into a heated verbal exchange. Soldier screamed at laborers: "are you out of your minds?" One laborer shouted back (in Hebrew): "I want you to know that i was prepared to continue walking, knowing that you may shoot me in the head. You should be ashamed of yourself". Another added: "All of you know well enough that we are heading to Bethlehem, not to Jerusalem." And a third one joined: "This is your government's deliberate plan to drive us all crazy, step by step". The soldier finally retreated to the compound.

The "Pleasures of Duty" and the "Duty of *Sumud*"

The cumulative impact of the Israeli closure policy on entire spheres of social and economic life in the Occupied Palestinian Territories – in particular the impact on employment, household income, standards of living, health, education, the functioning and performance of social institutions - have been subject to extensive and comprehensive documentation by a host of international and local organizations and humanitarian agencies[18]. Various reports published over the last three years pointed at the closure and siege as the ultimate direct cause for the loss of hundreds of thousands of jobs, and consequently for soaring rates of unemployment (reaching 60% in the Gaza Strip and 40% in the West Bank at various points in time, compared with approximately 20% and 10% respectively in Sept. 2000); an unprecedented decline in the standard of living (between 60% and 70% of Palestinian households currently live below the poverty line, compared with 20% in Sept. 2000); a twenty-fold increase in the number of families that seek emergency relief assistance; the high prevalence of malnutrition and anemia among Palestinian children and nursing mothers; a steep retrogression in the achievements of school children in general and those taking the matriculation examinations in particular. And this is a very partial list indeed.

Life under siege necessarily gave rise to varied forms and manifestations of steadfastness and solidarity, that is, of *sumud*. Providers that did not lose their jobs – first and foremost, employees of the Palestinian National Authority (PNA) and of the United Nations Relief and Works Agency for Palestine Refugees (UNRWA), the first and second largest employers in Palestine – shared their wages with unemployed kin and their families; housewives sustained the upkeep of households with hardly any income at hand; community-based institutions, committees and NGOs organized emergency job-creation projects for the unemployed and special recreational activities for youths and children; schools introduced emergency regulations and remedial programs; medical committees operated emergency health centers and mobile clinics, charitable societies expanded food distribution campaigns to the ever-increasing list of the needy. The manifestations of *sumud* at internal checkpoints, which loom large in the above Machsom Watch reports, are therefore only one prototype of a much wider social and political reaction, all components of which deserve and await proper research. The absence of such broader contextualization notwithstanding, some concluding commentary is in place.

Unlike the *sumud* at the Bethlehem checkpoint, which centered on the attempt to realize a day's work in Jerusalem, the manifestations of *sumud* at internal checkpoints and roadblocks revolve around attempts to reach workplaces, medical care, schools, universities, etc., within people's homeland districts, at times within one's hometown or village. A student from Beit Omar must either cross or bypass the Etzion checkpoint and the al-Khader western roadblocks in order to reach his university in Bethlehem; a stone-cutter from Dura or Yatta who works in Nahalin or Husan is forced to bypass no less than five barriers before reaching work; a sick man from Halhul is unlikely to make it to a medical check in a Beit Jala clinic, unless he is prepared to take the risk of being detained by chancing the forest route; teachers and pupils of al-Khader Government School have no choice but to cope with the presence of military violence in their midst.   The persistence, the restraint, the willingness to endanger oneself, the power to withstand the physical effort, to endure abuse, harassment, insults and humiliation each morning and afternoon – all of these became a necessary condition for survival, for keeping life going, and hence the expression "duty of *sumud*"; *sumud* is obligatory because people can not survive without it, and this is the source and secret of its strength.

Neither is the mission of enforcing siege similar to that of enforcing closure at border checkpoints, like the Bethlehem one. The means employed by the military at the latter prevent Palestinians from working, obtaining services and visiting in Jerusalem. The means employed at internal checkpoints deny Palestinians work, education, medical care, regular services, etc., inside the Palestinian homeland. On the face of it, a mission of this kind should have given rise to strain, reservations, and mounting doubts among those who carry it out, if not for any better reason, then at least because it is difficult to justify the policy in terms of defending the state's borders. As we have seen, however, there is no evidence that such a process has struck root in the rank and file of the military. To the contrary, we found that the previously entertained rationalizations and justifications, centering on one's duty to obey the commands/orders of one's superiors, were now replaced with a growing indulgence in "the pleasures of duty", an expression I borrowed from Sigfried Lenz's renowned novel *The German Lesson.*[19] The distance between the two cognitive states and behavioral patterns observed among soldiers – i.e., between the mere identification with one's role, associated with the earlier phases of the closure policy, and the manifestations of hyper-devotion, associated with the imposition of siege - is not large. Unlike a common assumption, neither should be attributed to "attrition on the job", that is, to some kind of mental and moral fatigue that overcomes soldiers after spending a time period policing a civilian population. Rather, both are rooted in the above-mentioned "false consciousness of participation in a combat mission" that denies the essence, meaning and outcome of the actual deeds that the soldiers are engaged in, a denial which inevitably leads to the dehumanization of the Palestinian "other".

The drift towards addiction to the "pleasures of duty" should be traced to the impact of the continuous escalation in the use of military force against the Palestinian civilian population. One should bear in mind that the violence entailed in the imposition of the siege regime is only one component in the overall Israeli military policy, and a far less lethal and destructive one when measured against its other major "cornerstones", i.e., incursions, air strikes, tank shelling, serial assassinations, house demolitions, and mass imprisonment. The daily killing of civilians, the wholesale demolition of entire neighborhoods (particularly in the Gaza Strip), the mass destruction of infrastructure and of agricultural lands, all signal to the soldiers, as well as to citizens of Israel in general, that Palestinian lives, property, and collective assets are infinitesimally cheap. From here derives the complete devaluation of Palestinians' work, health, education, time, and all other essential human needs, as put into practice by the siege-imposing soldiers.

However, unlike the "*sumud* for a day's work in Jerusalem" that was put down in the aftermath of the reoccupation of the Palestinian territory, the "*sumud* of the besieged" can not be defeated by force. Even if a soldier is sent hunting after every worker, a border policeman after every sick person, and an officer after every teacher, and even if a jeep or an armored personnel carrier stands in the way of every peasant and every student – and this is by no means an imaginary scenario, but rather one that is not at all far from current reality - as long as Palestinians continue to live on their land the duty of *sumud* will prevail.

Notes

* This is an expanded and revised version of an earlier paper that appeared in Hebrew in *Politika: The Israeli Journal of Political Science & International Relations* issue 11-12, Summer 2003-Winter 2004, under the title: "Sunday Mornings at the Checkpoint: Pleasures of Duty of the Rulers, Duty of *Sumud* of the Ruled" (pp. 41-57).

[1] Throughout the text a distinction is made between what I refer to as "border checkpoints", that is, checkpoints that were erected on or at the vicinity of the "green-line", and "internal checkpoints", that is, checkpoints that were erected inside the Occupied Palestinian Territory. "Border checkpoints" were enforced in the latter years of the first Intifada and during the Oslo years (1994-2000), in the framework of the then Israeli policy to seal off Israel proper and Arab Jerusalem to Palestinian residents of the Occupied Territories, with the exception of permit holders; i.e. those Palestinians who obtained permits via the Israeli Civil Administration (and the authorization of the Shabak (GSS)). Internal checkpoints were all erected after the inception of the second Intifada in late September 2000, in the framework of the current Israeli closure/siege policy. They are located on the major longitudinal road that runs from the southern to the northern end of the West Bank (known as road 60), as well as on transverse roads (east- west), on major road intersections, and at the entrances to larger and smaller Palestinian locales; in short, on Palestinian territory between and within Palestinian districts/governorates. In addition to dozens of internal checkpoints that are permanently manned by IDF soldiers and border policeman, the army also employs dozens of "flying checkpoints", that is, checkpoints "on the move", that are constantly relocated. On top and above the permanent and "flying" internal checkpoints, the army has sealed off hundreds of villages

and towns throughout the West Bank with barriers, or roadblocks – often a mixture of rubble, rocks, concrete-blocks, trash and the like – that were erected with the aid of bulldozers at the major entrances to the Palestinian locales. Many locales have been sealed off from all directions, implying that vehicles can not enter and exit; in order to get in or out people are forced to climb up and down the barrier. While the military or border-police does not permanently man roadblocks, part-time manning is a common, and often a daily occurrence. Presence of troops at the roadblocks implies that all pedestrians who wish to enter and exit their hometown or village are forced to undergo checks and are frequently prevented/prohibited from continuing their journey.

[2] "Machsom Watch" was set up by a small group of Jerusalem-based women activists in February 2001, some five months after the outbreak of the second Intifada, following the mounting evidence on IDF violence and gross violations of Palestinian human rights at military checkpoints. The group – which soon after was to be joined by approximately 70 members, at first all from Jerusalem - identified itself as one composed of "Israeli women who oppose the occupation and the closure policy", and decided to focus on direct activism at military checkpoints. Members committed themselves to regular "shifts", during which they observed and documented the conduct of the military at the checkpoints and intervened on behalf of harassed and abused Palestinians. Activism was confined at first to checkpoints around and in the vicinity of Jerusalem. However, in the wake of the escalation of Israeli military aggression in the Occupied Palestinian Territory, and following an influx (during the second and third years) of new volunteers from the Tel Aviv and Beer-Sheva regions, Machsom Watch was able to extend activity and to send its teams to internal checkpoints throughout the West Bank. As of 2004, Machsom Watch numbers more than 300 active members, who operate in teams (3-5 members each on average) that carry out weekly shifts at border checkpoints and at internal checkpoints in the southern (Hebron, and Bethlehem regions), central (Ramallah), western (Tulkarem region) and northern (Nablus region) West Bank. Membership in Machsom Watch is completely voluntary (no paid members), the group activities and internal coordination are managed on a democratic, non-hierarchical basis through an organizing committee (open to all members), with assumption of representative, organizational and administrative roles requiring the approval of members.

This is an opportunity to thank Chaya Ofek and Lauren Erdrich, my Machsom Watch team members from spring 2001 through fall 2003, for their extraordinary comradeship.

[3] The Bethlehem checkpoint is discussed here as an example of what I refer to above (see footnote 1) as "border checkpoints", many of which are located on the pre-1967-war borders (the "green line") between Israel and the West Bank. This particular checkpoint, however, stands further south of the green line, on the southern boundaries of the Jerusalem municipality, or what is referred to as metropolitan Jerusalem. The latter currently includes vast areas of Palestinian land that were confiscated by consecutive Israeli governments in the aftermath of the 1967 war (ever since the late 1960s and throughout the 1970s, 1980s, and 1990s) and officially annexed to the Jerusalem municipality. So that the Bethlehem checkpoint is located on the "de-facto" borders between "greater Jerusalem" (an ever-expanding territorial entity) and the town of Bethlehem.

[4] See, for example: Diwan, I., and R. Shaban, eds. 1999. *Development under Adversity: The Palestinian Economy in Transition.* Washington D.C.: The World Bank and Palestine Economic Policy Research Institute. See, also: Roy, Sarah. 1999. "De-Development Revisited: Palestinian Economy and Society since Oslo." *Journal of Palestine Studies* 28, no.3: 64-42.

[5] Some historical background is in place here. From 1974 through 1987 Palestinian day-wage laborers that were employed in Israel accounted for approximately 35% of the labor force in the Occupied West Bank and Gaza Strip. In absolute figures, their number in 1987 was estimated at 110,000. In retrospect the above years could be described as the era of "classical" Israeli colonial control over the economy of the Palestinian Territories. During the first Intifada (end of 1987-mid-1993) the employment of Palestinian day wage laborers in Israel was directly affected by Israel's policy of collective punishment, e.g. the employment of such measures as the imposition of weeks- long curfews on localities and regions, mass imprisonment of young people (affecting entire generations), and the enforcement of sweeping restrictions on the movement of released prisoners – all of which measures sealed off the Israeli labor market to various populations for shorter and longer time periods. As mentioned, the Oslo years (1994- Sept 2000) saw the imposition of closure(s) as policy (element in a system of control), in the wake of which entry to Israel became contingent upon special security permits. Over these years the number of (permit holding) laborers employed in Israel saw many fluctuations, and ranged between an unprecedented low of several thousands during most of 1994 through 1996, and a high of approximately 40,000 during most of 1998-Sept 2000. Alongside the "authorized" permit-holders, it was estimated that each day between 40,000 and 60,000 workers on average crossed the green line illegally, bringing the total of those employed in Israel on the eve of the second Intifada to approximately 100,000. The same Oslo years, however, also saw the consolidation of the Palestinian National Authority, the public sector of which became the largest employer in the Palestinian "market", with approximately 120,000 employees on its payroll. A detailed discussion of the history, structure and conditions of Palestinian employment in the Israeli labor market can be found in my *Confronting the Occupation: Work, Education and Political Activism of Palestinian Families in a Refugee Camp*", Stanford University Press, 2004.

[6] Publicly released on May 20th 2001,"The Mitchell Report" is the product of the investigation carried out by "The Sharm al-Shaykh Fact-Finding Committee" (headed by former U.S. senator George Mitchell) that was appointed by President Clinton in November 2000, following the October 2000 Sharm al-Shaykh summit. The recommendations of the report focused on the steps that should be taken by the Government of Israel and the Palestinian Authority in attempting to "End the Violence" and to "Rebuild Confidence". The parties were called upon to "reaffirm their commitment to existing agreements and undertakings", to "implement an unconditional cessation of violence" and to "immediately resume security cooperation". Most importantly, the recommendations regarding the rebuilding of confidence stipulated that the Government of Israel "should lift closures, transfer to the PA all tax revenues owed and permit Palestinians who had been employed in Israel to return to their jobs..." and "should freeze all settlement activity, including the "natural growth" of existing settlements." The PA was called upon "to make a 100 percent effort to prevent terrorist operations and to punish perpetrators." (The Summary of the Recommendations of the Mitchell Report as well as excerpts from the report can be found in *Journal of Palestine Studies*, 30, no. 4 (Summer 2001), pp. 147- 151. Also available in the same issue of JPS are the official PLO response to the Mitchell Report, ibid. pp. 152-156, and the official response of the government of Israel, ibid. pp. 160-162.)

[7] Illuminating concise summaries of the U.S. diplomacy vis-à-vis the parties and its affect on events in the months following the release of the Mitchell Report can be found in *Journal of Palestine Studies* 31 no. 1, pp. 103-114 ("Peace Monitor"), *Journal of Palestine Studies* 31, no. 2, pp. 101-111 ("Peace Monitor"), and *Journal of Palestine Studies* 31 no. 3, pp. 118-128 ("Quarterly Update on Conflict and Diplomacy").

[8] For an excellent concise overview and summary of "Operation Colorful Journey" and "Operation Defensive Shield", see Journal of Palestine Studies 31, no. 4, pp. 140-151 ("Quarterly Update on Conflict and Diplomacy"). For detailed information on the humanitarian catastrophe in West Bank refugee camps caused by "Defensive Shield", see the *UNRWA Emergency Appeal 2002: Fifteenth progress report covering March and April 2002*, and *UNRWA Emergency Appeal 2002: Supplementary Appeal.* For one assessment of the damage caused to Palestinian infrastructure and institutions, see the World Bank 2003 publication, entitled: *Twenty-Seven Months - Intifada Closures and Palestinian Economic Crisis: An Assessment,* pp. 17-20. For data on deaths and injuries see the widely quoted web page of Palestine Red Crescent Society: www.palestinercs.org.

[9] In principle, Tantur has extra-territorial status and military personnel may not enter without permission. In practice, IDF, Border Police, and regular police personnel daily violated this rule.

[10] The military wing of the PFLP declared that the assassination of Ze'evi came as retaliation for the liquidation of the PFLP Secretary General, Abu-Ali Mustafa on August 27th 2001.

[11] Data from B'Tselem, Information Sheet, December 2001. For full details, see the B'Tselem report entitled: Excessive Force: Human Rights Violations during IDF Actions in Area A, December 2001.

[12] For an original and highly individualistic articulation of *sumud* as a kind of mid-way strategy between outright struggle and submission, see Raja Shehadeh's early memoir: *The Third Way: A Journal of Life in the West Bank* (1982).

[13] Further elaboration on the critique of *sumud* during the 1980s can be found in Salim Tamari's "The Palestinian Movement in Transition: Historical Reversals and the Uprising" *Journal of Palestine Studies* 20, no.2 (Winter1991).

[14] Both terms – "Oslo-closure *sumud*" and "the *sumud* for a day's work in Jerusalem" – are mine. Elaboration on the situation of Palestinian day wage laborers during the Oslo years and the related "Oslo-closure *sumud*" is beyond the scope of this paper. I have dealt with this topic extensively in my *Confronting the Occupation: Work, Education and Political Activism of Palestinian Families in a Refugee Camp*, Stanford University Press, 2004.

[15] To the south-east of al-Khader is the urban settlement of Efrat, the second largest Jewish settlement in the Bethlehem region (6,400 inhabitants in 2000). Efrat was built on vast areas of agricultural and pasture lands that belonged to villagers of al-Khader and the adjacent village of Irtas, and which were confiscated over the years to that end. More of al-Khader's lands were confiscated for the sake of the building and expansion of settlements in the Gush Etzion settlement bloc. Yet additional lands were confiscated in the 1990s for the sake of the construction of the major bypass roads that were built to the west of al-Khader in the wake of the Oslo Accords. The extensive confiscations left the village with a minute fraction of its former agricultural lands, and with hardly any un-built land reserves.

[16] It should be noted that similar series of roadblocks seal off the southern and north-western entrances to al-Khader. The "al-Khader southern roadblocks" are located on a road intersection, further south on road 60; the north-western roadblocks are located on intersections with the access road to Beit Jala. The only unsealed entrance is the eastern one, which lies inside the Bethlehem urban complex, further away from the route of the currently all but Palestinian-free road 60.

[17] The expression "yesh matzav" resembles "that's cool" or "awesome".

[18] See, for example: The World Bank. 2002 (March). *Fifteen Months – Intifada, Closures and Palestinian Economic Crisis: An Assessment;* The World Bank. 2003 (July). *Twenty-Seven Months – Intifada, Closures and Palestinian Economic Crisis: An Assessment;* UNSCO. 2002 (October). *The Impact of Closure and other Mobility Restrictions on Palestinian Productive Abilities: 1 January 2002 – 30 June 2002;* The Palestinian Central Bureau of Statistics (PCBS). *The Labor Force Survey* (quarterly results); PCBS. *Impact of the Israeli Measures on the Economic Conditions of Palestinian Households,* 4th round, 5th round, 9th round; PCBS. *Main Findings of the Access to Health Services Survey – 2003;* UNRWA. 2003 (June*). UNRWA Sixth Emergency Appeal (July – December 2003)*; Johns Hopkins University and al-Quds University. 2002 (August). *Nutritional Assessment and Sentinel Surveillance System for the West Bank and Gaza.*

[19] "The Pleasures of Duty" is the title of an essay assigned to Sigie Yepzen, a German youth held in a "rehabilitation" institution/prison for juvenile delinquents in the Germany of the 1950s, and the major protagonist of *The German Lesson.* The title floods Sigie with memories centering on the image of his father, a policeman at a remote town in the north of Germany, who –during the World War II years – was assigned a special mission: the enforcement of a Nazi order that prohibited a famous local painter from practicing his art. While the policeman's initial reaction was that of some embarrassment, especially since the painter was an old acquaintance, inhibitions soon gave way to growing identification with the prohibition order followed by the policeman's enthusiastic devotion to his role. The addiction to his mission reaches its climax when, in the wake of the removal of the banning order, the policeman burns and destroys the artist's paintings out of his own initiative.

The Dispersal, Ethnic Cleansing and Return of the Tatar People

Baruch Kimmerling

The Crimean peninsula has been, and remains, a disputed territory frought with inter-ethnic friction and witness to a cruel history of ethnic cleansing and genocide. Russian armies first invaded the Crimean peninsula in 1736, and in 1783 Catherine II annexed the peninsula. This was the beginning of a period of Russian and Slavic immigration to the peninsula as well as of Tatar emigration from the peninsula. Following the October Revolution, Crimea briefly became an independent state, but was soon occupied by German forces. In 1921, it was annexed to the Soviet Union as the Crimean Autonomous Soviet Socialist Republic. Presently, the largest section of the population is Russian – about 1.2 million. Ukrainians number about 500,000 and Tartars – who consider themselves to be the native population of the land – number about 300,000. Large populations of Crimean Tatars can also be found in Turkey, where they number over 5 million, Bulgaria (10,000), Romania (40,000) and the United States (6,000) (Uehling, 2002).

After independence, Ukraine perceived itself as a model of inter-ethnic peace. Nonetheless, from the spring of 1994 onwards, Max van der Stoel, the High Commissioner on National Minorities for the Organization for Security and Co-operation in Europe (OSCE) has been deeply involved in issues in the Ukraine. The inter-ethnic tensions which the Ukraine has been forced to overcome, have been, in part, rooted in policies and decisions taken during the Soviet area, and partly in choices made and developments that occurred after the Ukraine broke away from the USSR.

A significant part of the Russian population resents being part of the Ukraine and support Russian nationalist calls for the peninsula to be annexed by Moscow. They also resent the return of the Tatars, who have been trying to acquire land for homes, farms, mosques, schools, and other buildings.

The history of the Tatars is little known in the West. This may be attributed to a lack in adequate published material about them, their small numbers and their contemporary low profile of non-violent political behavior and culture, which may be contrasted, for example, with those of the Chechens.[1] At the same time, Fisher's assertion that "...there is no account in any language of the history of Crimean Tatars from their first appearance in Crimea until today" (Fisher, 1978:xii) is not precise. Western scholarship relating to the Crimean Tatars is, in fact, not a *tabula rasa*. This can be said to be true mainly as a result of the attention they attracted, consequent to being completely uprooted from their homeland in 1944.

Mythology or History?

The origin of the Crimean Tatar people is an issue of controversy. This controversy reflects a theoretical debate. On the one hand, we find Smith's (1972) approach to ethno-nationalism as an "ancient" and primordial entity. On the other hand, and at same time, we find it to be explained as a modern manifestation (created by the French Revolution) as well as a continuously invented and reinvented entity (Hobsbawm and Ranger, 1983 or Gellner, 1983). Thus Greenfeld perceived nationalism as a tool for political modernization, while Gellner, for example, viewed nationalism as an outcome of modernity. First, it is the privilege of the elite to be "sovereign" within the framework of the nation-state and only later is this privilege extended to the entire people (Greenfeld, 1992). Moreover, it seems that a considerable portion of Tatar history was invented by Tsarist Russia's ethnographers, followed by Soviet historiography, thereafter to be incorporated into Western standard history.

In brief, the sequence of historical events is as follows: For centuries, the Crimean peninsula had been the subject of a tug of war between the Byzantine and Khazar empires, Kievan Rus - the forerunner of modern Russia – and various nomadic tribes. Then, in 1223, a new force appeared on the scene. Chingiz Khan's Golden Horde entered Crimea, conquering and restructuring all that lay within its path. The peninsula was incorporated into the Golden Horde (the western part of the Mongol Empire) as a province. Because the overwhelming majority of the conquerors came from the Turkic peoples of Central Asia, who had been conquered by the Mongols prior to the invasion of the Crimea, the Mongolians can be said to have changed the ethnic composition of the Crimean population. Furthermore, a considerable number of Turkics settled in Crimea and intermarried with the local peoples. The above narrative can be seen as a mixture of real and forgotten selective historical events, aimed at denying the indigenous status of the Crimean Tatars so as to present them as a more recent "invader." But many contemporary scholars have rejected this 'historical' account and have asserted that the ethnos of the Crimean Tatars actually originates among numerous mountainous, coastal and steppe tribes of Crimea. In addition, these native groups were further hybridized with several other peoples and ethnic groups at different historical times, including Europeans, and only later those belonging to the Golden Horde warriors. As a result of this assimilation, a Crimean version of the Tatar ethnic group developed, quite distinct from the Kazan, Astrakhan, and other Tatars. (Williams, 2001:7-27).

Crimea became part of a huge Tatar empire, stretching from China in the east to beyond Kiev and Moscow in the west. Because of its sheer size, it was impossible for Chingiz Khan to govern his empire from Mongolia, and thus, the Crimean Khans enjoyed a considerable amount of autonomy. The magnitude of the Tatar empire, and the power of the Great Khan, meant that certainly for a while, merchants and other travelers under his protection could journey east and west in relative safety. The Tatars concluded trading agreements with the Genoese and the Venetians, and Kaffa (Feodosia) and prospered in spite of the taxes levied on them. Marco Polo apparently landed at Sudak on his way to the court of Kublai Khan in 1275.

The Tatar Empire was influenced by the cultures it encountered during its expansionary expeditions. According to legend, in 1262, the Egyptian Mamluk Sultan Baybars wrote to one of the Tatar Khans suggesting that the Tatars should convert to Sunni Islam. The oldest mosque in Crimea, built in 1314 by Tatar Khan Uzbek, still stands in Stary Krim. Before their collective conversion to Islam, the Tatars worshipped *Mongke Koko Tengre,* ("The Eternal Blue Sky"), the almighty spirit controlling the forces of good and evil, and believed that powerful spirits lived in fire, running water and the wind.

In 1475, the Ottoman Turks conquered Crimea, taking the Khan Mengli Girei prisoner, but after a while released him to rule Crimea as their representative. Thereafter, the Crimean Khans were mostly appointed by Constantinople, although they still maintained considerable autonomy in terms of domestic rule. Over the next three hundred years, the Tatars remained the dominant population of the peninsula, and a thorn in the side of the developing Russian empire. The Tatar Khans began building their center around the "Grand Palace," which stands at Bakhchisarai, in the 15th century.

Since the end of the 14th century a special ethnos – the Crimean Tatars – had already started to form in the Crimea as a result of assimilation. The Crimean Tatar ethnos increased at the expense of Turkic immigrants from the Lower Volga region and of Crimean highlanders, part of whom accepted the language and religion of the Turkic people.[2] Today, the differences among the Crimean Tatar sub-ethnoses have disappeared, even though some vernacular differences do persist.

The oldest Crimean Tatar texts date back to the 13th century. A reform of the high-literary language began in the 19th century. Until 1927, the literary tradition was based on a Southern dialect after which it was replaced by the central one. Until the end of the 1920s, the Tatars used Arabic letters. Then, until 1938, they used the Latin alphabet, until they were forced to use Cyrillic letters. This was part of a wider policy, begun by the Tsarist regime to be followed by Soviet Russia, of using Russian settlers to Russify and settle non-Russian territories and at the same time to transport and "re-settle" other ethnic groups from their land. According to a 1989 census, more than 73 million Soviet citizens (a quarter of the total population of the Soviet Union) lived outside of their "national territories" (Brubaker, 1996:36).

The Crimean Tatars created and invented their territorial ethnic identity on the Crimean peninsula, and the Khanate of the Crimea was founded in 1443 as a remnant of the Golden Horde. As military allies of the Ottoman Empire, the Crimean Khanate possessed considerable power in Eastern Europe from the beginning of the 16th century and up until the end of the 17th century. In 1783, following a series of wars between Russia and Turkey over control of the Black Sea, the Khanate was annexed by Russia.[3] The Crimean peninsula provided Russia with an important strategic asset - warm water ports that could enhance Russia's economic, political, and cultural ties with Europe; fertile soils capable of growing products for export as well as feeding Russians in the interior, and a secured southern border that would consolidate Russia's military potential when facing the Ottoman Empire. During that time, the Crimean Tatars constituted 90 percent of the peninsula's population (Fisher, 1970). In the 19th century, the Crimea became the Russian's Black Sea naval basis and a bridgehead to the Mediterranean. The expropriation of land and deportations, especially in the 1850s and 60s, forced a large number of Crimean Tatars to emigrate to Turkey (Karpat, 1986:127-12) and present-day Bulgaria (Pinson, 1972-3). At the same time, an influx of Russian settlers began. By the end of the 19th century, the Crimean Tatars constituted a minority in their historic homeland.

Fueled by the rise of Pan-Islamic and the Pan-Turkish movements, the national awakening of the Crimean Tatars began in the last quarter of the 19th century. By 1905, for example, 350 national schools had been established in the Crimea. Following the Russian February Revolution, the Crimean Tatars began to demand cultural autonomy. Later, this was expanded to include territorial autonomy (Kirimli, 1996).

From Russification to Ethnic Cleansing

In 1921, the Crimean Autonomous Republic was established within the Russian Federation and by 1930 more than a fifth of the population (about 200,000) were Crimean Tatars.[4] In the first years of the Soviet regime, the development of Crimean Tatar national culture was tolerated: national schools were re-opened, the Tatars founded national research centers, museums, libraries and theatres, and Tatar place-names were restored to use. The Tauria University opened in Simferopol in 1925 and schools were permitted to use Tatar language and to teach Tatar literature.

However, this liberal policy came to an end in 1928 (Nahaylo and Swoboda, 1990:209). That year marked the beginning of oppression, Sovietization, collectivization and Russification. Between the years 1928 to 1939, about 40,000 people were imprisoned or deported (Conquest, 2003). The intellectual and the educated class were almost completely annihilated. The study of the Crimean Tatar language and literature was outlawed and its teaching was forbidden. All Crimean Tatar publications and press were banned. The core of the Russification was the coerced substitution of Arabic, Turkish or Persian expressions by Russian ones and the substitution of Latin script by Cyrillic. When the Germans occupied the region in 1941, they were welcomed as liberators from the Communist and Russian regime.

The post-war Soviet rule used the Crimean Tatars alleged collaboration with the Nazis as a pretext for the definite solution of a "demographic problem" in the peninsula.[5] The deportation of all Crimean Tatars, about 180 thousand people, occurred on May 18 1944. The majority were deported to the Uzbekistan, Molotov (Perm district), and Sverdlovsk regions. About 45 percent of the Crimean Tatars died on the way, many in the concentration camps of Sverdlovsk. Two years later, Soviet newspapers proclaimed two Moslem peoples – the Chechens and Crimean Tatars -- as traitors, and accordingly denied their right to autonomy (Nekrich, 1978).

The cleansed territories were colonized with ethnic-Russians and the central state propaganda machine developed a total hatred campaign against the Tatars. In 1945, the Crimean "Autonomous Soviet Socialist Republic" was downgraded to an autonomous region and, finally, in 1954 it was incorporated into the Ukraine (Fisher, 1978). Until 1956, the Tatars were deprived of all civil rights and freedom to travel. At the same time some concessions were made to the partisans and soldiers who served in the Red Army (Bohdan and Victor, 1990). The mass deportation of 1944 paralyzed the Tatar culture. Far from home, scattered among foreigners, a whole generation of uneducated or ill-educated Crimean Tatars has grown up. Only in 1957, after thirteen years, were the Crimean Tatars allowed to publish their own newspaper *Lenin Bayragi* ("Lenin's Banner") in Tashkent. In recent years, some other periodicals have appeared, including, since 1989, a weekly in Simferopol. In 1957, the Tatars began a campaign to collect signatures among prominent Soviet intellectuals petitioning to be allowed to return to their homeland. The leaders of this movement were arrested, confined to mental hospitals or assassinated.

In 1967, the Presidium of the Supreme Soviet issued a decree of 'Rehabilitation of the Tatars of Crimea'. Under its terms the Crimean Tatars were still not recognized as an ethnic group and were not allowed to return home. A supposed autonomous district was created in Uzbekistan, with the aim of making the Tatar settlement there permanent. The Tatars rejected the plan.

Revival and Return to Homeland?

The Tatar demand for repatriation to their historic territory was renewed in 1987 using petitions and demonstrations. The central government acted promptly and with brutality, reaffirming the justifications for the deportations and violently suppressing the demonstrations. Nonetheless, in 1989, the Supreme Soviet of the Soviet Union adopted a formal decision which allowed the Crimean Tatars and the Volga ethnic Germans to return to their homelands and to re-establish a local administration without detailing any timetable or concrete plan for the implementation of the resolution.[6]

The Organization of the Crimean-Tatar Ethnic Movement was founded in order to lead the struggle. The return home has been little more than nominal. In a 1992 referendum among the Tatars, over 61% of the voters supported a "sovereign" Tatarstan. During the mid-1990s, about 90,000 Crimean Tatars had returned to the Crimea. By the summer of 1991, the number had increased to 150,000.[7] Ukrainian official figures show that up until 2004, about 244,000 have returned. Tatar leaders say another 200,000 want to come back. The Crimean Tatar Congress (*Kurultai*) has demanded privileges for the Tatars in the Crimea and the right to self-determination and access to the use of natural resources and resort areas. These demands have been made because the Tatars have been allocated eight defined areas for settlement, all of which are considered unsuitable for settlement and lack any natural resources. Prior to the deportations, these lands were almost completely unpopulated. Now, they host about 65 percent of the people. The Russian-ethnic population of the peninsula – settling the vast majority of the area and possessing hegemonic political power, including military personnel and their families – strongly oppose the creation of an independent or even a federal Crimean Tatar state.

The Crimean Tatars have begun to organize themselves in order to achieve some autonomy and influence, and also to improve the deplorable living conditions facing them. The most influential among several nascent political movements within the Crimean Tatar community, "The Organization of Crimean Tatar National Movement" (OKND), founded in 1986, leads the movement. In June 1991, i.e. prior to Ukrainian independence, a National Assembly (*Kurultai)* was convened by the OKND and a national flag and anthem were adopted. Furthermore, a "Declaration of National Sovereignty of the Crimean Tatar People" was issued. It demanded control over all land and natural resources of Crimea and stated that the only subjects of self-determination within the territory of Crimea were the Crimean Tatar people, whose "political, economic, spiritual, and cultural rebirth is possible only in its national sovereign state."[8] However, the Crimean Tatar leaders were in general not as radical as this quotation might lead one to assume. The declaration also stated that this state would be based on "mutual respect between Crimean Tatars and all other national and ethnic groups" and proclaimed a strict observance of the rights of "all people irrespective of their ethnic origin."

Natalya Belitser (2002a:7) tells us that "today, it can only be speculated how much the events of February 1991[9] affected [the] general mood of the Crimean Tatar returnees and in particular, stimulated their political mobilization under the guidance of the OKND. But it seemed plausible that the traumatic experience of not being allowed, in any capacity, to have a voice in a political decision-making process that would have been of paramount importance to their future, as well as the quite unfavorable outcome of this process, had an impact on further developments."

In 1993, the Assembly elected the *Mejlis*, a representative political body of the Crimean Tatars between the periodical sessions of the *Kurultai*. Since then, the Crimean Tatars have consistently tried to officially integrate these organs into an institutionalized decision-making structure of the Crimea and Ukraine. Their position, however, within the peninsula is paradoxical – they claim sovereignty as being the indigenous people but at the same time they constitute an ethnic minority in the peninsula, without the hope of becoming a majority at any time. At the same time, the Ukrainians themselves are a minority in the peninsula and feel like victims who desire to return to their native language and culture, or to "de-Russify" themselves. The Ukrainian laws now limit the official use of Russian in both cultural events and in the media in those regions where Russian constitutes the language of the majority. In 1992-1993, the Ukrainian Ministry of Education initiated a multi-lingual program aimed at bringing the percentage of first-graders taught in various languages in accord with the ethnic composition of the population of every region.

Diaspora and Internet Nationalism

In all probability, the several hundred thousand Crimean Tatars were not, and are not, perceived as a "demographic threat" for the Russian settler community and the Ukrainian minority. The anxiety was, and probably still is, the potential mass-return of additional several hundred-thousands, perhaps even millions of Tatars from diasporas of Crimean Tatars, primarily from Turkey. This fear is not totally groundless. Recently, there has been a move to create unity among the dispersed Crimean Tatars who also lack any worldwide organization. This has been done predominantly through the Internet, with the aim of recruiting political and financial support, and of creating an imaginary transnational community. According to Aydin (2002:29) "the Crimean Tatars in Turkey 'remember' the Crimea, even though they are very much involved in the political agenda of Turkey. At the same time more and more people are regarding themselves as 'Crimean Tatars' and are discovering their migrant origins. They are striving to remember or learn the language, culture and traditions, and by uniting their "cultural survivals" with the knowledge of other Crimean Tatars in the homeland or around the world they seek to re/create their nation."

Today, the Crimean Tatar diaspora, mainly in Turkey and the United States, is involved in the political, economic and social problems of their co-ethnics, and has been providing considerable support for them to rebuild Crimean Tatar institutions in the Crimea. With all their involvement, "the idea of return" is presently not an integral part of their ethnic identity, save for some very small nationalist groups who have adopted this idea. Nonetheless, the Crimean Tatars still constitute an identifiable community within the societies in which they live today, even in the Turkish society in which they are considered to be totally assimilated. The Crimean Tatars have formed social organizations in the countries where they live and they are aware of the threats of assimilation over time. For this reason, they search for proper ways to continue the preservation of their identity. Their present move to create a unity among Crimean Tatars spread all over the world through the Internet, probably constitutes the first case of "internet nationalism" in history.

The Struggle over the Citizenship

Many of the returnees found that they were not able to acquire Ukrainian citizenship, a situation that has caused legal and economic problems for the returned Crimean Tatars. The Citizenship Law meant that all the then current residents were automatically granted citizenship. However, a considerable number of Tatars arrived after this date, and thus some 100,000 returnees (around 40%) were obliged to fulfill requirements such as a five-year period or residence prior to obtaining Ukrainian citizenship. Amendments were subsequently introduced to this law, such as a short procedure whereby one only had to submit a formal application and evidence of residence. However, the

Crimean Tatar returnees were not among those who were eligible for this process. They did, in fact, receive a different "simplified procedure", but this still involved a declaration of respect for the Ukrainian Constitution (thereby questioning their loyalty), renouncing any former citizenship (the Ukrainian law only allowed the possession of single citizenship), possession of legal sources of existence (which most Tatars did not have), and knowledge of the Ukrainian language (which most of them do not command). These procedural requirements in fact made it very difficult for the remaining Crimean Tatars to become Ukrainian citizens.

On 16 April 1997 a new citizenship law was legislated and entered into force on 20 May 1997. The law apparently solved the citizenship problem for those returnees who until now had been stateless. These people numbered some 23,000, i.e. a quarter of those who had not been granted citizenship on 13 November 1991 and somehow had not been able to acquire it in the meantime. To solve the problem for the remaining 82,000, those who still were citizens of another state, the Ukrainian government began negotiations with Uzbekistan in October 1997. The Uzbek government was at first reluctant to cooperate, but its desire to establish a strategic partnership with the Ukraine made it change its mind in the long run.

On 31 July 1998, a decree was issued by the Uzbek government that provided for a temporary procedure for registering the cancellation of the citizenship of former Tatar deportees. In August, the final agreement was concluded, and it came into force on 4 September 1998. It introduced a procedure that enabled the returnees to obtain a free proof of cancellation in no less than six months by the authorities in Crimea, thereby freeing them of the obligation to travel to Uzbekistan. Furthermore, the date of cancellation of the former citizenship and of acquisition of the new one would coincide, avoiding any period of statelessness.

This new arrangement can be considered a substantial advance from a Tatar point of view. By the beginning of 2002, 98% of returned Crimean Tatars had acquired Ukrainian citizenship. It also prompted the European High Commissioner to make his only public statement concerning his involvement in the Ukraine. He accepted the agreement with "great satisfaction" and judged it an "excellent example of the co-operation between the two governments and some international organs" (Kulyk, 2002:94-97). The agreement was subsequently prolonged, and Kiev has also undertaken to conclude similar treaties with other states.

Moreover, on 18 January 2001, a new Citizenship Law entered into force. It is much more liberal than the previous one and does not exclusively insist on a single (Ukrainian) citizenship. Rather, it is more occupied with avoiding statelessness. Also, if a person is unable to acquire a document of cancellation, a personal declaration of renunciation is now sufficient. The new law thereby follows one of the recommendations of the High Commissioner (Kulyk, 2002:95).

The Failed Struggle over Representation

In October 1993, the parliament of Ukraine adopted an Electoral Law that did not provide for any special Crimean Tatar representation. Since under Ukraine's resettlement policy, Crimean Tatars are not allowed to make up more than 27% of the total population in any one administrative unit, and since the electoral system was purely majoritarian, the returnees stood almost no chance of having any of their representatives elected into parliament. It was only after vehement protests by the Crimean Tatars that the law was amended and a 14-seat quota was allocated for them, but this law was used only for the election held in 1994. On 18 May 1999, the anniversary of the deportation, the Ukrainian President Kuchma issued a decree "On the Council of Representatives of Crimean Tatar People," in which the members of the current *Mejlis* would participate but without the recognition of the *Mejlis* itself by the Ukrainians (Kulyk, 2002:98; Belitser, 2002:11).

The Ukrainian Constitution of 1996 does not recognize the existence of indigenous peoples in its territory[10]. Neither does the Crimean Constitution, adopted in 1998, mention such a concept but is rather based on an exclusively individual concept of human rights.[11] On 8 September 1994, the parliament of Crimea amended the law on the Presidency removing the President from the post of head of government and establishing a post of Prime Minister. This signaled the end of the separatist monopoly in Crimea. Previously, in the summer and autumn of 1994, the Ukrainian legislature took measures to synchronize the Crimean legislation with that of the Ukraine. The autonomy was from now on to be called the Autonomous Republic of Crimea (ARC). On 17 November 1994, the Ukrainian parliament used its new powers and annulled some 40 acts of the autonomy. The beginning of Russian military operations in Chechnya in December 1994 further reduced pro-Russian sentiments among the Crimean Ukrainian and Tatar population (Flückiger, 2003).

On 21 October 1998, a draft of a new Constitution was passed by the Crimean parliament. It had pragmatic priorities and it was a new text instead of an amendment to the November 1995 Constitution (which had been invalidated in June 1996). There was no struggle for symbolic assets and no insistence on the autonomy's powers regarding the appointment of security officials or the deployment of Russian troops. The text also recognized the priority of the Ukrainian language and provided broad powers for autonomy, i.e. for the Crimean elites and authorities. Although this draft still contradicted the Ukrainian Constitution on more than 50 issues, it obtained a thin majority of anti-centrists in the Ukrainian parliament. The pro-Ukrainians were able to insert a provision which would declare any Crimean acts that ran counter to Ukrainian legislation (i.e. not only to the Constitution) as invalid. However, that was considered a poor achievement. On 12 January 1999, the Constitution of the Autonomous Republic of Crimea eventually took force. The new Constitution was a modest victory for the Ukrainians over the Russian majority, but completely ignored the demands and the interests of the Crimean Tatars (Flückiger, 2003).[12]

In April of 2000, a parliamentary hearing on the issue of Tatars was finally placed on the agenda. The recommendations that followed called for the implementation of the Constitutional provisions regarding indigenous peoples and national minorities and for the protection of deportees' rights. It also recommended the adoption of a law on the status of the Crimean Tatars in the Ukraine. However, the recommendations of the parliamentary hearing were not implemented owing to strong Ukrainian resistance.

The Russian majority perception of Tatars is in large measure racist and anxious, believing that they act as a fifth column for Turkey, and also inspired by fears of losing their political and demographic supremacy.[13] This last point is often based on misperceptions and myths, such as that of an allegedly exploding birth rate among Crimean Tatars. In reality, however, their birth rate hardly outnumbers their death rate. Furthermore, even if all deportees returned, they would only make up 17% of the peninsula's population (Ozcelik, 2001:41-42). Because of these anxieties, the local authorities are often hostile towards the Crimean Tatars. Thus, even if they practically gain legal rights, they are seldom implemented.

In 1999, for example, there were several attacks against Crimean Tatars: the building of the *Mejlis* was attacked, the office of the Chairman burned and destroyed. Several mosques were also burned, and graveyards and a monument to the deportation were profaned. The local mass media deliberately and openly disseminate hate against Tatars and Moslems. The authorities are also often hostile and discriminate against the Tatars: the land they were given upon return was in no way fit for either agriculture or housing. Funds allocated for resettlement often "disappear" or are misused by hostile and corrupted state and local bureaucracy. In 2002, the unemployment rate among the Tatars was about 55%, which was at least twice as high as that of the peninsula as a whole. They are also aware that any resort to violence would only worsen their situation and status in the peninsula, as indeed some limited local riots in 1996 and the Chechnyan experience demonstrate.[14]

In August 1995, a presidential decree was issued to establish a committee of inquiry into the causes of riots by Crimean Tatars. The commission pointed to the high levels of unemployment, unsatisfactory housing conditions and the lack of social and cultural infrastructure as the main causes of the riots (Kulyk, 2002:78-79). Following the committee findings, a resolution was achieved that included an ambitious project aimed at solving the Tatar problem. In addition to allocating funds (including assistance from foreign sources) for return and resettlement and ordering an investigation into the spending of previous funds by the Crimean authorities, the resolution also included the setting up of a working group which was authorized to determine the status of the *Mejlis* in order to match it with Ukraine's political and legal system. However, raising the money for these projects turned out to be more difficult than expected. The law on the deportees' rights was never adopted, and the legal recognition of the *Mejlis* was merely symbolic and did not really empower the Tatars. In the meantime conflicts between Tatars and non-Tatars had increased in frequency, and Tatars often complained of police harassment. The 1st of February 2004 saw one of the most serious incidents so far. Police in the Sudak area fired shots over the heads of hundreds of Tatar demonstrators who were trying to free a local leader - who had been arrested for allegedly attacking and injuring a local man - from police custody. The crowd finally dispersed with no injuries on either side. The arrested leader has since been released but may yet face court proceedings (Reuters, 11 February 2004).

Currently, the Crimean Tatars' major goals are a government sponsored return of the Crimean Tatar people to Crimea; full restoration of their rights and property; recognition of the *Mejlis* as the official representative body; and representation of the Crimean Tatars in the Crimean Parliament. In addition to a full political rehabilitation and repatriation to the homeland, the Crimean Tatars are engaged in revitalizing their religion, language, and culture. However, at least until now, the whole initiative of returning to the homeland should be seen as a human tragedy and a political failure. The Crimean Tatars have no real possibility of achieving any genuine self-determination in what they see as their ethnic homeland despite their glorious past and the very low level of violence which they have displayed.

Those who do demonstrate tendencies to employ violence are the Crimean ethnic Russians. Their high levels of cohesion and organization and consistent protest are contributory factors. However, these levels of protest have been slowly declining. In addition, the high degree of autonomy granted to the Crimean local government by the Ukraine, at the Tatars expense, has alleviated some of their grievances. Given that during the 2000s there has been an increasing popular sentiment in Russia for the annexation of the Crimea, it is unlikely that the central government will implement such an act This might mean entering into a possible armed conflict with Ukraine, as well as incurring a political crisis with the European Union. Crimean Russians are subject to very little governmental repression and to less societal discrimination (due to their being a majority) than their ethnic kin elsewhere in the Ukraine (D'Anieri, Kravchuk, and Taras. 1999:104-117).

Ethnic Russians will probably continue to protest at moderate levels but there is little indication that the central Ukrainian government is going to change its policies (e.g. state-level language laws and policies regarding Tatar immigration) in the near future. The highest risk for violence in the Crimea is between ethnic Russian and Tatar groups. Political agitation on the part of both groups has been sustained in recent years. However, only limited scale incidents of violence have occurred, and these only sporadically. With the increase of the Tatar population (and hence increased pressure on the Russian population and on economic resources), these incidents are likely to increase, barring more vigorous intervention by the central government or other actors.

Some Intermediate Conclusions

It has become almost trivial or self-evident to state that all the "scientific," political or ideological expectations and predictions about the "end of nationalism" or ethnicism as a universal phenomenon were premature, much like the presupposed "end of history." Such theories were presented as a kind of historical determinism, without the necessity to explain how this process would occur and under which conditions and circumstances. Of course, over history many specific ethnic or proto-national identities have disappeared, but we have very little knowledge of how this has happened. We do, however, know much more about building, inventing and re-inventing "imagined communities" (Anderson, 1983; Hobsbawm, 1991 or Gellner, 1989), than about their dissolution in the modern era.[15] The same failure of prediction can be ascribed to the disappearance or decrease of religious and other primordial sentiments. All these modern and pre-modern sentiments and loyalties, together with their highly institutionalized structures (like nation states and churches), have found a way to be incorporated and adapted into the new postmodern world order. Moreover, these sentiments and structures have found ways to exploit globalization and transnationalization processes for their strengthening, fortification and expression.[16]

The Tatar case, despite its complexity, only very partially covers the issues related to diverse approaches related to the contemporary manifestations of ethnicity and nationalism. At the same time, the case includes some important elements that are worthy of generalization, subject to the necessary skepticism that accompanies any generalization and extrapolation from a single case study. The Tsarist and the Soviet Empire builders did almost everything to "dissolve" any "small" ethnic or national loyalties, especially those linked to specific territories (Kolarz, 1952). They used three major tools to achieve this goal: (a) Deterritorialization of those ethnoses by removing them from the lands they considered as their homelands and the resettlement of those territories with other ethnic groups, mainly Russians.[17] (b) Dissolution of their ethnic identities by cultural oppression, banning the teaching and printing of ethnic languages, destroying museums, libraries, churches and mosques as well any other cultural institutions, and changing geographical and local names. Some of their culture was "folklorized" and defined as "low culture." (c) Annihilating elite groups and sometimes groups of ordinary people.

The long-term result of this policy has been the creation of a complex and insolvable situation where two ethnic groups, in addition to the Ukrainians and Ukrainian state, have claims for the same territory. The Russian ethnic group not only makes up the majority of the population, but after already being there for several generations, they consider the peninsula to be a part of the Russian Motherland. They not only regard the return of the Tatars as a direct threat to their political and economic status, as an ethnic minority in Ukraine, but also as expressing a false and unjust historical logic because a reversal process in time and history is perceived as impossible. Moreover, according to their historiography, Slavic people preceded the Mongol conquest, and the deportation of the Tatars, especially following their collaboration with the Nazis, was seen as poetic justice. They propose that even if a great crime was committed against the Tatars in the past, it is not justifiable that they, who were also victims of the same demographic-spatial policy, have to pay the price. The

Crimean ethnic Russian's enmity and hatred toward the Tatar returnees seems inevitable.

The cry of justice for the Crimean Tatar people and the demand to allow their return to the Crimean homeland has been recognized by the sovereign Ukrainian state without opposition by the Russian Federal government. Most probably, the Ukrainian minority of the peninsula has perceived the Tatars as some counter-balance to the Russian majority. The central government presents this as a humanitarian gesture toward the European Union which they want to join, and from whom they wish to acquire financial aid.[18]

The Tatars are aware of these achievements but, at the same time, have not lost sight of their weakness and vulnerability. Their success has included the repatriation of about half of their people, who had lived in former Soviet territory, to their own homeland within a relatively short period of time. Furthermore, they have proved to themselves and to the world that their ethnic entity has been preserved and is capable of being activated when politically opportune. Their short-term goal is to accomplish their return to the geographical, economic, political and social borders of Crimea, without raising too much antagonism from the Russian majority, and without losing their symbolic status as the native people of the peninsula. From the outset, they aspired towards large-scale cultural autonomy, where they can rebuild their schools, academic centers and mosques, since religion is considered to be a part of their ethnic identity. Certain groups of Tatar nationalists aspire towards more than cultural autonomy and revival. They remember and cultivate the glorious past of the Tatar Empire. On the other hand, most of the Tatars in the Diaspora desire to rebuild their ethno-national identity not on a territorial basis but as a virtual Internet community based on culture and kinship. One may hazard a guess that this is probably not the end of the Tatar Odyssey.

Notes

[1] Chechnya was incorporated into the Russian Empire in 1859. The Chechnya-Ingushetia region was incorporated as the Checheno-Ingushkaja Autonomous Soviet-Socialist Republic during the establishment of the Soviet Union. During WWII, the Chechens endured a forced deportation of the entire population to the Kazakhstan. After the Soviet Union was dismantled, an independence movement emerged in Chechnya as a strong forceful opposition to the federal government. As a result, Chechnya has undergone two civil wars which have left most of Chechnya under the control of the federal military. Chechen separatists still claim an independent Chechnya and have initiated sporadic guerilla warfare within Chechnya and other regions of Russia, including Moscow.

[2] Turkic-speaking peoples live primarily in Russia. They number about 5.5 million and are largely Sunni Muslims. Their name is derived from Tata or Dada, a Mongolian tribe that inhabited present Mongolia in the 5th century. First used to describe the peoples that overran parts of Asia and Europe under Mongol leadership in the 13th century, it was later extended to include almost any Asian nomadic people. The Crimean Tatars are only a small fragment of this ethnic group and are divided into three subethnoses. The Northern (Nogay) one lived on plains. They had numerous remnants of nomadic traditions. The Middle (Orta yolaq) one inhabited the region of foothills and low

mountains. Their dialect became the base for the Crimean Tatar cultural language. The South (Yali boylu) one settled in the mountains and on the South seashore representing the Mediterranean type and speaking a dialect close to the Turkish language.

[3] It must be mentioned that the Tatar intellectual life during the period immediately after the annexation of 1783 and prior to the emergence of Ismail Bey Gaspirali and his newspaper *Terjuman* in 1883 was not generally apparent. Thus the cultural life of that period was not written, or documented, by the Crimean Tatars themselves. As such, scholars do not have enough sources to evaluate the Crimean society from the end of the eighteenth and through most of the nineteenth centuries.

[4] An interesting side story was a trial, during the 1920s, where leading Russian Jews attempted to secure a Jewish homeland in the framework of the Soviet Union in Crimea. They were assisted by a strange alliance of Bolshevik revolutionaries and New York Jewish philanthropists. The attempt to remake a portion of Soviet Jewry into a prosperous peasant farmer class - and to construct a nationality-based republic similar to other Soviet creations – drew the attention of many Jews everywhere as an alternative to Zionism and emigration to North America. The scheme failed, but ultimately led to the creation of the "Jewish Autonomous Region" of Birobidzhan. The Tatar resistance to the program was just a small additional obstacle to the implementation of the project (see Kagedan, 1994).

[5] As a matter of fact, initially many of the peoples of the Soviet Union, including the Belarusians and Ukrainians, welcomed the Wehrmacht as liberators from Russian oppression as well as from the Communist regime. During and after the war, discussing this issue regarding major nationalities became a taboo in the Soviet Union. However, some small racial and ethnic groups were singled out and accused of treason. The accusations against "many Crimean Tatars" for treason, desertion from military units of the Red Army, going over to the enemy, forming "voluntary Tatar military units," "brutal carnage of Soviet partisans," creation of "Tatar national committees," assistance to "German occupants in the organization of forced deportation of Soviet citizens into German slavery" and so on, were formulated in the "Resolution of State Defense Committee #5859" dated 11th May of 1944. In addition, it must be noted that Tatars also joined both the Soviet partisans fighting in the Crimean forests and the Red Army sent to the front. Official sources suggest 20,000 Crimean Tatars fought in the Red Army.

[6] For good sources on the contemporary struggles of the Tatars, written by dissidents living the US, see the collection edited by Edward Allworth (1988).

[7] Recently, many of the returnees have found that they could not acquire Ukrainian citizenship. Non-citizens, besides not being able to vote and stand for elections, cannot participate in the privatization of land and state assets. They have no right to a place of residence, which means that they cannot register at the workplace and as a consequence do not receive free medical care and other services.

[8] See, http://www.iccrimea.org/scholarly/nbelitser.html, accessed 17/04/03, p.4. They also tried to restore other cultural traditions. A primary focus of concern and activity is language. Music and dance have also received attention. After over fifty years of exile, programs to renew the arts, including embroidery with gold and silver thread, fine jewelry making in the filigreed Tatar style, and the weaving of *kilims* or carpets, have begun.

[9] The issue of special rights for the Crimean Tatars, who were returning to Crimea after their forcible mass deportation of 1944 and almost half a century of living in exile, first surfaced as an important political issue during the debates in the national legislature of the Ukraine on 12 February 1991. That whole day, the Supreme Council of the Ukrainian Soviet Socialist Republic discussed the then hottest issue of raising the status of the Crimean region (then, an ordinary enclave of Ukraine) to the level of Crimean

Autonomous Republic without giving any voice to the Tatars themselves. The Russian separatists attempted at the same time to establish an independent Soviet Socialist Crimean Republic.

[10] Ukraine at least declaratively desires to be a multi-racial, multi-ethnic and multi-cultural nation. According to the Ukrainian Constitution of 1996, indigenous peoples, together with the titular ethnos and national minorities, constitute the people of Ukraine, or Ukrainian *political nation*.

[11] The criteria for identifying an indigenous people were: descent from traditional inhabitants of a certain geographical region within current Ukrainian borders; preservation of and wish to further maintain and develop a cultural, linguistic and/or religious group identity different from that of the titular ethos or national minorities; distinct historical traditions, social institutions, self-governance institutions; absence of an ethnically related national state or motherland outside Ukraine (Belitser, 2002: 7).

[12] The Russian majority of the peninsula expected a strong Russian political intervention in order to preserve their hegemony, but such an intervention has never come. In general there was no opposition against the Ukrainisation policies since the population was above all preoccupied with the harsh economic situation. But in the East and South of Ukraine, where the percentage of Russian-speakers is highest, some parents were reluctant to let their children be taught in Ukrainian. Self-evidently, the Russophone elites even felt like victims when they started to lose their privileged positions. Later, the Russophones made an important achievement, succeeding in having the Council of Europe Charter for Regional or Minority Languages ratify a decree which makes Russian an official language in around 50% of the territory of the Ukraine.

[13] They are labeled as "Barbarians", as violent and as a people who lack culture. This image is deeply rooted in folk songs, tales, children stories and proverbs.

[14] Local Crimean authorities erect bureaucratic hurdles for the Tatars. Russian nationalist groups accuse the Tatars of using violence against locals and of nurturing Islamic militants, including supporters of Al-Qaeda. Tensions have increased because 2004 is supposed to be the last year that land can be disbursed free by the government. From 2005 land will be sold, and Tatars fear that it will go to rich Russian and Ukrainian businessmen instead of being allocated for the needs of the existing Tatar population on the peninsula and for those who have not yet returned.

[15] A great exception is the genocide of the native and aboriginal peoples of the immigrant-settlement lands, such as North-America, Australia and New Zealand (Hartz, 1970). However in the contemporary era even genocides (like the Turkish of the Armenians, Nazis of the Jewish and Romany people or the civil-war techniques of the Khmer Rouge militia in Cambodia), did not succeed in annihilating these people and their collective identities. More successful were the politicide processes of different minority groups, that is, a process that has, as its ultimate goal, the dissolution of a people's ethnic group existence as a legitimate social, political and economic entity. This process may also, but not necessarily, include their partial or complete ethnic cleansing from the territory known as their homeland (Kimmerling, 2003).

[16] One exceptionally interesting case, that so far has not been analyzed in these terms, was the explosion of an American "nationalism-of hurt" following the 9/11 attacks. The over-reaction of the Americans was exploited for a new Crusade (expressed not only by the military invasion of Afghanistan and Iraq but also by a cultural war against Continental Europe) and the quest for a worldwide hegemony (Chomsky, 2003).

[17] The Soviet regime also restricted them to a specific territory, by using a complex system of internal passports, that paradoxically also contained the rubric of "nationality",

1 The Dispersal, Ethnic Cleansing and Return of the Tatar People

for the bureaucratic need of control and surveillance (Torpey, 1999). Ironically, these "passports" helped the preservation of ethnic identities in the Soviet Union.
[18] EU relations with the Ukraine are to a large extent based on the "Partnership and Co-operation Agreement" (PCA), which came into force in 1998. The PCA highlights respect for shared fundamental values as an essential element for the relationship. It furthermore provides an appropriate framework for political dialogue; sets the principal common objectives in terms of harmonious economic relations, sustainable development, co-operation in a number of areas, and support of the Ukraine's efforts towards democracy; as well as creating an institutional framework for pursuing these goals. For the Ukraine, the President's Strategy for European Integration of 1998 has repeatedly been endorsed by President Kuchma and received support from the Parliament. A number of specific agreements in the fields of trade, science and technology, and nuclear energy are also in place. Technical assistance has been provided since the early 1990s in support of the transition process towards democracy and market economy. The EU is the largest donor to the Ukraine; over the last 10 years, total assistance amounted to €1.072 billion from the EC, while the Member States disbursed around €15 million in the period 1996 – 1999. This consists of technical assistance, macro-financial assistance, and humanitarian assistance.

References

Allworth, Edward, (ed.). 1988. *Tatars of the Crimea: Their Struggle for Survival.* Durham and London: Duke University Press.

Anderson, Benedict . 1983.*Imagined Communities: Reflections on the Origin and Spread of Nationalism.* revised edition. London: Verso.

Aydin, Filiz Tutku. 2002. "Crimean Turk-Tatars: Crimean Tatar Diaspora Nationalism in Turkey. Working paper. Washington, D.C.: International Committee for Crimea. http://www.iccrimea.org/scholarly/aydin.html

Belitser, Natalya. 2002. "Indigenous Status for the Crimean Tatars in Ukraine: A History of a Political Debate." Paper prepared for the ESRC funded project "Fuzzy Statehood" and European Integration in Central and Eastern Europe (ref. L213252001), Birmingham: The University of Birmingham.

_____. 2002a. "Indigenous Status" for the Crimean Tatars in Ukraine: A History of a Political Debate. Working Paper. Kyiv, Ukraine: Pylyp Orlyk Institute for Democracy.

Brubaker, Rogers. 1996. *Nationalism Reframed: Nationhood and the national question in the new Europe.* Cambridge: Cambridge University Press.

Chomsky, Noam. 2003. *Hegemony or Survival: America's Quest for Global Dominance.* New York: Metropolitan Books.

Conquest, Robert. 2003. *Soviet Deportation of Nationalities.* New York: Textbook Publishers.

D'Anieri, Paul, Robert Kravchuk, Kuzio Taras. 1999. *Politics and Society in Ukraine.* Boulder: Westview Press.

Fisher, Alan W. 1978. *The Crimean Tatars.* Stanford, CA: Hoover Institution Press.

_____. 1970. *The Russian Annexation of the Crimea, 1772-1783.* Cambridge: Cambridge University Press.

Flückiger, Katya. 2003. "The role of the OSCE High Commissioner on National Minorities in Ukraine." Working paper submitted to Séminaire "La gestion multilaterale de la question des minorités nationales" http://www.clients.ch/hei/ghebali/OSCE%2OUkraine%20paper.doc.

Gellner, Ernest .1989. *Nations and Nationalism.* Oxford: Basil Blackwell.

Greenfeld, Liah .1992. *Nationalism: Five Roads to Modernity.* Cambridge, Mass: Harvard University Press.

Hartz, Luis (ed.). 1970. *The Founding of New Societies: Studies in the History of the United States, Latin America, South Africa, Canada, and Australia.* New York: Harcourt, Brace and World.

Hobsbawm, Eric .1991.*Nations and Nationalism Since 1780: Programme, Myth, Reality.* Cambridge: Cambridge University Press.

_____ and Terence Ranger (eds.). 1983. *The Invention of Tradition.* Cambridge: Cambridge University Press.

Kagedan, Allan L. 1994. *Soviet Zion: The Quest for a Russian Jewish Homeland.* New York: St. Martin's Press.

Karpat, Kemal H.. 1986. *Ottoman Population, 1830-1914: Demographic and Social Characteristics.* Wisconsin: The University of Wisconsin Press.

Kedourie, Elie .1961. *Nationalism.* London: Hutchinson University Library.

Kimmerling, Baruch. 2003. *Politicide: Ariel Sharon's War against the Palestinians.* London: Verso.

Kirimli, Hakan. 1996. *National Movements and National Identity among Crimean Tatars (1905-1916).* Leiden: Brill Academic Publishers.

Kolarz, Walter. 1952. *Russia and Her Colonies.* London: George Phillip and Son..

Kulyk, Volodymyr. 2002. "Revisiting A Success Story: Implementation of the Recommendations of the OSCE High Commissioner of National Minorities to Ukraine, 1994 – 2001." In: Wolfgang Zellner, Randolf Oberschmidt and Claus Neukirch (eds.) *Comparative Case Studies on the Effectiveness of the OSCE High Commissioner on National Minorities.* Hamburg: Institute for Peace Research and Security Policy at the University of Hamburg.

Lazzerini, Edward James. 1988. "Ethnicity and the Uses of History: the Case of Volga Tatars and Jadidism," *Central Asian Survey,* I, # 2-3: 61-69.

Nahaylo, Bohdan and Victor Swoboda. 1990. *Soviet Disunion: A History of the Nationalities Problem in the USSR.* New York: Simon & Schuster Adult Publishing Group.

Nekrich, Alexander M. 1978. *The Punished People.* New York: W. W. Norton & Company Inc.

Ozcelik, Sezai. 2001. "The Conflict Resolution Approach in Analysis of the Crimean Tatars Case: The Preventive Diplomacy, the Role of Non-Governmental Organizations (NGOs), the High Commissioner of the National Minorities (HCNM) and the Problem-Solving Workshop." George Mason University, Institute for Conflict Analysis and Resolution. http://www.geocities.com/tatarkirim/ct.html, accessed 11/04/03

Pinson, Mark. 1972-3. "Russian Policy and the Emigration of the Crimean Tatars to the Ottoman Empire, 1854-1862," *Guney Dogu Avrupa Arastirmalari Dergisi.* Istambul: Istanbul University, part I and II.

Smith, Anthony. 1972. *Theories of Nationalism.* New York: Harper and Row.

Torpey, John. 1999. *The Invention of the Passport: Surveillance, Citizenship and the State.* Cambridge: Cambridge University Press.

Uehling, Greta Lynn. 2002. "The Crimean Tatars" Encyclopedia of Minorities," Chicago:Fitzroy Dearborn Publishers.

Williams, Brian Glyn. 2001. *The Crimean Tatars. The Diaspora Experience and the Forging of a Nation.* Leiden: E. J. Brill.

Why It's So Hard to Teach Radical Ideas: Some Reflections on the Sociology of (Radical) (Sociology) Teaching

Yuval Yonay

This is a confession of a failure: written words cannot demonstrate for Israelis the full horror of the Gaza Strip occupation. . . . The failure does not stem from the weakness of the word or the paucity of pictures. It is the outcome of the Israeli society's ability to live peacefully with the [information about the occupation].
Amira Hess, *Haaretz*, 3.3.04[1]

Introduction

Strange encounters occur at interviews for MA candidates in the Department of Sociology and Anthropology at the University of Haifa. Two professors, most likely Ashkenazi Jews, interview young candidates who have just finished or are about to finish their BA studies. Our interviewing strategy is to ask the candidates about an assigned article; last year's choice was an article by two Israeli researchers on the paradox of illegal foreign workers turning into political players in the Israeli public arena in spite of their precarious legal status (Kemp and Raijman 2000). Not unexpectedly, the article frequently refers to the numerous injustices those workers suffer from; while written in the detached scientific style of value neutrality, the authors' sympathy with the plight of the workers is unmistakable.

Or so I thought until the encounters with our MA candidates. We asked them to criticize the article—not because it is bad, but in order to examine their critical faculty. One student labors hard but then does find a flaw: the article, God-forbid, claims that there is racism in Israel! Another does not understand what we want from him and rather than criticizing the authors, condemns the foreign workers: they cynically exploit their skin color to advance an illegal struggle. Nobody among the entire group of candidates is bothered by the way these workers' status is taken advantage of, and when we ask them what interests may be at play that thwart all attempts to protect these workers' social rights, the ultimate scapegoat of secular Jews in Israel is offered as an answer—the ultra-orthodox.

This was a strange experience, not only because of our candidates' obvious failure to internalize what they had studied, but also because of the paradox of relatively affluent Ashkenazi professors trying but not succeeding to "milk" some critical assessment from students, who all came from Israel's economic and geographic periphery (we asked) and all belonged to the disadvantaged Mizrahi group. That is, we failed them—i.e., did not recommend their acceptance—because we thought they had not understood their own marginal position: they did not realize they had to protest *against us.*

This experience—the more frustrating the longer I think about it—is not exceptional. In many other cases our efforts to teach sociology seem to shipwreck on our students' deepest personal convictions. In this essay I would like to use such frustrating experiences as a platform for discussing the nature of ideology and our role as social science teachers in the wider ideological apparatus. I will first exemplify the ideological differences that seem to separate student from lecturer in three domains and then add an introspective look at the way my own ideology developed. I will conclude with some reflections on the relationships between the teaching we do and the ideology that surrounds us.

Postcolonial Experience I: Mizrahi Jews' Denial of Racism

I will start with perceptions of the differences between Mizrahi and Ashkenazi Jews and the relations between these two groups. Sociologists routinely debate the significance, intensity, and especially trend of this cleavage: has it become a stable feature of Israeli society today, or is it a relic of the past that is gradually waning. Signs of integration and fusion are abundant: intermarriage rates are rising, individuals of Middle Eastern origins hold top positions in the Israeli economy, polity and army, and many Mizrahim belong to the middle class. On the other hand, Israel's proletariat and underclass are overwhelmingly of Middle Eastern origin (and include the country's Palestinians, of course),[2] and every few months expressions of racism, hostility, even hatred come into the open and via the media generate a public storm.

The *adati* (ethnic in the context of inner-Jewish distinctions) conflict has been the pivot of Israeli sociology since its inception. Students of stratification, mobility, and education have documented the continuing significance of *eda* (Jewish origin) in educational and socio-economic achievements. Although firm conclusions regarding third-generation Israelis are still lacking, there are many indications that the gaps persist (e.g., Kraus and Yonay 2000; Cohen 1998; Cohen and Haberfeld 1998). Students of Israeli culture claim that those Mizrahim who have entered the middle class have done so mostly by adopting the mainstream culture as that has been shaped by the European Jews—have become *Ashkenized,* so to speak. Lately Mizrahi researchers themselves have built upon postcolonial theories to shed light on their parents' and their own experiences (e.g., Hever et al. 2002; Shenhav 2003; Shohat 1988).

Our students want nothing of it! When I teach Weber's "Class, Status and Party" and use European and Middle Eastern Jews as local examples of status groups, I see the disbelief in their eyes. Every year a new cohort raises the same doubts about the relevance of the *adati* divide. Anticipating such objections, I make sure to come to class equipped with the findings of a recent experiment that involved students at Tel Aviv University and the University of Haifa, showing that students (including Mizrahim) have less trust in students with Mizrahi names (Fershtman and Gneezy 2001).

Obviously, it is hard for students to accept this claim as it contradicts their notion of Jewish Israeli solidarity. I would like to give two additional illustrations. The first is from interviews with educated young Mizrahi women and men on the significance of their ethnic origin conducted by participants in my In-Depth Interviewing Workshop. The majority of interviewees sternly denied the relevance of *adatiyut* (ethnicity) both for themselves personally and for Israeli society as a whole.[3] One example is specifically pertinent for my discussion here.

The interviewee, a woman of Egyptian-Turkish origin who was in her early 30s at the time, doggedly denied any exposure to *adati* discrimination and even said she doubted stories of discrimination her own relatives sometimes would come up with. When asked for a third time whether she really never witnessed a case of discrimination, she suddenly remembers an incident that bothered her a lot when it happened:

> Once I encountered something like that personally. It occurred when I was already . . . at the university; at the university of all places! . . . It upset me greatly . . .; a professor of education at the U of Haifa for some reason . . . asked the Mizrahim to raise their hands, then the Arabs, and then *Ashkenazim*. . . [Q: How did you feel?] . . . I felt she was making distinctions among us. . . I felt very strange . . . Perhaps she wanted to demonstrate something, but still, it was very disturbing.

Those who believe ethnic differences are no longer all that important among Jews may cite this incident as an example of how likely social scientists are to create something that is not there. For me this excerpt is a trenchant example of the very opposite. Although I have no psychoanalytic training, I find it hard to avoid the feeling that the interviewee has repressed an unresolved tension regarding her ethnic origin. The level of anxiety the professor's didactic experiment caused her indicates that the interviewee is uncomfortable with her Mizrahi origin. Stories like this one abound.[4]

When I lecture about ethnic distinctions and prejudices among Jews in Israel I raise similar anxieties. It is not something about distant countries and faraway experiences but something nearby that resounds in their minds and awakens dormant fears. Ashkenazi students are less involved emotionally—members of dominant groups can always pretend that racist prejudices are part of others, not themselves. Mizrahi students, on the other hand, cannot be indifferent. Being depicted as victims of their own society inevitably affects the way they conceive of their belonging to that society, it affects their sense of identity (cf. Khazoom 2003).

Not all Mizrahi students, of course, have deep-seated anxieties. On my last military reserve duty I witnessed at close hand another strategy of coping with the subordinate status of Mizrahi Jews. It was while I was patrolling at a distant base in the Negev together with a combat woman soldier, a Beer-Shevaite of North African origin. Although I was off my academic duties, the sociologist inside me never takes a break, and I used the opportunity to learn from her "how the younger generation looks at things." Naturally I asked her, why she had chosen tough combat training and not something less demanding. "But of course, to serve the country," she avowed spontaneously without a trace of pompousness, reminding me of bygone days when such talk was commonplace in my own social circles. It no longer is. Many middle class draftees do volunteer for risky and demanding combat units, but they usually justify their action by giving it rationalizations of an individual nature ("I want to be the best I can") or by making a cynical reservation that serves almost as an apology for their idealistic declaration (cf. Sasson-Levy 2002).[5] *Mizrahiyot* and *Mizrahim* (i.e., Mizrahi women and men, respectively), like my combat soldier, do not suppress unresolved tensions; they have adopted the official hegemonic identity—one based on the unity of Jews and the exclusion of Arabs—to the degree that it has become so much part of them that they live with it peacefully. Such students resist the "news" about discrimination, including their identity as victims, and choose instead to reaffirm the Jewish unity of all *edot* (Ben-Rafael and Sharot 1991; Herzog 1986; Regev 2000). They do so not because such a narrative is liable to open more or less closed personal wounds but because it threatens to destabilize a healthy ego and encumber it with a collective wound (cf. Nagar-Ron 2004).

We teach sociology and anthropology as scientific disciplines: theories, concepts, data, sources, methods, reasoning, and so forth. But the substance of what we teach touches their most basic convictions. One reason they fail to listen to what we have to say is that the power of reason proves powerless in the face of strongly-held sentiments, which leads me to my first proposition.

Proposition I: Scientific theories cannot overcome convictions in which students are emotionally involved.[6]

Students do not live, of course, in a vaccum; their self-identities are created from the materials handed to them by their social surrounding. That many students espouse an all-Jewish identity is due to the fact that this identity formation is propagated by powerful social agents. It is reaffirmed by school and military ceremonies; it is implied in many curriculum materials (e.g., Ben-Amos 1994; Piterberg 1996); it occurs again and again in the mass media (e.g., Avraham 2002). A frequent cliché used in Israel to calm down heated arguments is the phrase, "after all, we are all Jews," namely, despite our differences, we are all sisters and brothers. The irony is that Jewish students and lecturers use this phrase—thoughtlessly—even when Palestinian students are present.[7] In other words, the Jewish collective identity and unity are so natural for, have been so inculcated in, Israeli Jews, myself included, that we use it instinctively even when it is obviously out of place. The second proposition is therefore the following:

Proposition II: Radical theories have to compete with hegemonic ideologies that are supported by powerful institutions and agencies and are deeply

couched in the available cultural repertoire.

The second proposition may sound as if there is a conflict between "science" and "ideology": our scientific teachings reveal the Truth, but ideological forces prevent our students from grasping it. This is not what I argue; science is always part of society, and therefore science and ideology are inextricably intertwined. While the critical views about *adatiyut* are shared by many, if not most, sociologists today, not too long ago the official ideology was also part of the sociological teaching that went on at our universities, and even now eminent sociologists insist that the importance of *adatiyut* is declining and believe that those who claim otherwise interrupt the natural process of developing inter-Jewish solidarity (e.g., Lisak 1996). These sociologists are likely to have connections to the Establishment, will often be elected to government committees and invited to official ceremonies, and are routinely interviewed as authorities by the mass media.[8] Thus:

Proposition III: Radical theories must compete with hegemony-supporting theories that are kept in place by established powers.

Postcolonial Encounter II (the Jewish Palestinian Conflict)

In the spring term of 2003 I taught a class on the "Sociology of Occupation" (i.e., military, not job). I felt that it was my social as well as professional duty to use the tools available to me through my academic discipline to try and shed light on what is the most pressing question on the agenda of each and every Israeli citizen. I was afraid of the students' responses to what I was going to tell them, and I feared the ferocious arguments liable to erupt among them, but was convinced it was important to look at the occupation in sociological terms and resolved to allow the students broad latitude to express their interpretations and attitudes.

The actual experience went quite differently from what I imagined. On the day of the first class I chose to open with a newspaper clip about the intentional poisoning of crops grown by Bedouin in the Negev. It was a short and matter-of-fact report, but it was useful to help me demonstrate the routinization of the power relations within Israel between the Jewish majority and the Palestinian minority. As the story was unrelated to the Intifada, I expected the students to be more sympathetic towards the Bedouins, many of whom serve in the Israeli army. I also expected to be asked why I had brought an example from the Negev to a class about occupation. I wanted to raise the disturbing claim that sociologically one could analyze Palestinian-Jewish relations *inside* Israel as a case of occupation as well.[9]

None of these expectations came true. The students showed little interest in the plight of the Bedouin, and none brought up the question whether the Negev was occupied territory as well. In following weeks I continued to bring more shocking testimonies of Israeli violence in the occupied territories. I thought that it was important to start from factual realities.[10] The case of a father who had lost his two sons because Israeli soldiers forgot to inform them that their workshop had been booby-trapped was especially shocking, I thought. Not for my students. My idea of shocking them in order to create an interest in analyzing the underlying causes failed, as they were more likely to counter by explaining to me the necessity of whatever the IDF was doing.

This response could be expected based on our first three propositions: the students, who as soldiers will have participated in the daily policing of Palestinians under Israeli occupation or know personally soldiers who have, find it hard to acknowledge a perspective that undermines their sense of the morality of such practices. Their resistance is supported by the ideological apparatuses around them, including the teaching of many university professors.

Another interesting dynamic perpetuated this situation. At the beginning of the semester the students actually argued with me quite fervently, but after a few classes I noticed that they became less "belligerent." The reason, however, was not that they had been won over, but that they had lost interest and reverted to their routine apathy. From conversations with some of them during and after class I got the impression that they understood I belonged to the "extreme Left," which for them undermined my credibility as a teacher.[11] Rather than asking what was it in the sociological perspective that had prompted me to hold "unorthodox" views, the students assumed that my ideology had taken over my scientific wisdom, and thus felt it was okay for them to ignore the evidence I supplied.

Proposition IV: The hegemonic discourse positions radical speakers as partisan and unreliable in contrast to "neutral" speakers.

Of course, mainstream theories and views are no less ideological than radical ones, but as it is the dominant ideology that constructs the boundary of the discourse, it is able to delineate the boundaries of reasonable controversies and to define those that deviate from these boundaries as "extreme," and hence, unworthy of serious consideration.

One class was supposed to start less than two hours after a Palestinian suicide bomber had blown up a bus en route to the university. One student, I later found out, had "missed" that bus.[12] Naturally, I could not conduct a regular class and instead started a discussion about the reasons behind the wave of suicide bombers. At the very beginning one student passionately declared: "I don't care why; such a horror can't be justified, and nothing else should be said." I took issue with this statement, arguing that as social scientists, it is our task to try to understand the phenomenon if we want to prevent further tragedies. The ability and need to understand Palestinian "terrorism" became the main question debated; clichés from the mass media were more often used than sociological arguments. Only one student mentioned that a few days earlier, IDF soldiers had killed three Palestinian children. After 40 minutes of heated discussion, one student asked to stop the debate and to return to the academic subject of the class; he wanted "theory" not "ideology," and was joined in this by a large number of his peers. This response is typical of the way many Israelis deal with the political frustration: avoidance, which leads me to my fifth proposition:

Proposition V: Radical views are not welcomed by students who wish to avoid politics altogether.

Over the past few years I have had the opportunity to talk with many of our graduate students about "the situation." I am quite active on campus, and various testimonies of what is happening are always posted on my door. Students who feel uneasy about the events thus come to and talk with me about it. They listen with much curiosity to my stories about my activities against the occupation and in support of Palestinian-Jewish solidarity inside Israel with much curiosity; they may even express some agreement. But rarely does one of them consider taking part in these activities. They have some reservations; they do not like collective action; they feel strange about identifying with (what they consider) extreme views; they lack faith in their ability to change things. The arguments are numerous, but behind them, I feel, there is always the same fear that makes adopting a radical view psychologically hard for many people.

Proposition VI: Adopting radical views may put students on a collision course with family and with close friends and with their own beliefs. Avoiding politics helps them to steer away from hard conflicts.[13]

At the end of the course I distributed a feed-back questionnaire to find out what my students felt about it. Out of 30, 25 said that they had learned new things about the situation;[14] only 5 said they had learned nothing new. Nevertheless, 24 said that they have not changed their political views about the conflict. Only five testified that it had affected their views, with three expressing confusion and uncertainty.[15] Several remarks added to the negative answers and were indicative of many students' mood. One woman said she had not changed her views and added "luckily!" Another bothered to add combatively that the course had not changed her views "not even an inch." Two said they now were even more Right-wing than they had already been.

These responses demonstrate that the students are emotionally invested in the information they gained from the class. They are frank enough to admit they learn new things, but they make efforts *not* to let this influence their opinion, reinforcing our first proposition. A class on the sociology of military occupation (colonialism) is not like a math class, nor even like a history class on racism in, say, America. Students may memorize and repeat what they are told about the Protestant ethic; they have no stake in it.[16] But when they run across issues relevant to their own lives, their resistance is up. It is all very different with Palestinian students, to whom I turn now.

Postcolonial Encounter III (Teaching Palestinian Students)

The University of Haifa has the highest proportion of Arab-speaking students in the country.[17] Our administration deftly plays this card when seeking donations from liberal-thinking millionaires, but hides it under the table when wanting to attract Jewish students. Recent attempts to strengthen the presence of Arabs on campus symbolically—e.g., by adding signs in Arabic, including Arab music and literature at official ceremonies, having official days-off during Christian and Muslim holidays—have failed miserably due to disinterest among the faculty (only 0.1 percent of which is Arab) and a mixture of suspicion and wariness among the administration. Social ties between Arab and Jewish students are the exception rather than the norm, and the student organization has been known to spread virulent propaganda against the Arab students, unaware how similar their rhetoric is to that of anti-Semitic students used in darker periods not to long ago.[18]

The position of Palestinian-Arab students is thus a delicate one. In my political activities on campus I have met and talked to many Palestinian students with strong convictions about their rights as Palestinians and a clear determination to fight for them. Some of them were brought up in politically active families, while others are being socialized into political life through their activities on campus. Most of the Palestinian students in my classes, however, are careful to shun politics, and therefore I often find myself teaching them radical views about the Palestinian-Jewish conflict that they themselves are afraid to express in public, perhaps too afraid even to think.

Unlike the case of Mizrahi students who fervently hold on to the official ideology of Jewish solidarity, most Palestinian Arabs are not influenced by the state ideological apparatuses. Though they read and listen to the Jewish controlled mass media and their history and social-science curriculum is based on Jewish narratives, they are educated on local narratives (e.g., Maget 2000; Frisch 2003) and exposed to TV channels and written media from neighboring Arab countries, and are immune to the Israeli official ideology (Smooha 1992).[19] Thus they tend to appreciate it when their point of view is acknowledged in class. Often simply writing sociological concepts on the board in Arabic brings a sparkle to their eyes. Sometimes they will come to me after class and thank me for acknowledging—not necessarily accepting—the Palestinian perspective. Yet when I expect them to study the theoretical material and to turn their political grievances into sociological language, I am usually disappointed. Again, there are several reasons for this situation.

In another class on the sociology of occupation one third of the students were Palestinians but they remained mostly silent throughout. When I asked one student after class why he had not participated in class discussion, he said he had been afraid to and explained that there were rumors that people who expressed subversive ideas in class might be rejected when they applied for fellowships and jobs. My instinctive response was to assure him that such rumors were unfounded, but something stopped me: could I be wrong? Could I really promise this student that he had nothing to fear? How could I be so sure?

It is impossible to gauge to what extent secretive repression inhibits the expression of radical views, but it is there. Jews who belong to the hegemonic class can express their opinions more freely, but even they have to become more mindful of what they say if they aspire to positions of power. Similarly, many of my colleagues—Jewish men and women from middle class background—are afraid to even sign petitions against human rights violations by Israel, and if this is the case for lecturers from socially advantaged strata, can one blame Palestinian students, whose future prospects depend largely on employment in state-controlled schools?[20]

Proposition VII: Radical views are less represented in class due to sheer fear of repercussions, real or imagined.

One of the Arab students I worked with to advance equality between Jews and Palestinians on campus became a friend, and I was able to meet and talk with his parents. His father is what one may call a "self-made" person, someone who for years had worked very hard in construction and then became self-employed. He is proud of his achievement but wants to see his children in more rewarding jobs; my friend's younger sister finished law school, but he himself is still in school, being too committed to his political work (not to mention the three disciplinary hearings he had to go through because the University of Haifa's administration resolved to curb Palestinian activity on campus). On my visits to his house I witnessed several heated discussions between the father and the son over the latter's intensive political work. The father thought his son ought to finish his studies first. He was paying for them and wanted to know that his son has gained the tools with which to secure his future. This pressure is typical. Many Arab-Palestinian students—and of course, many Jewish students as well—come from working class families; often they are selected by the family as best suitable for higher education. In a sense, they are representatives of their families, and their success is important for the prospect of the whole family. They cannot afford to take risks.

Proposition VIII: Some students avoid politics so as not to jeopardize their studies as these are essential to their families' prospects.

But it would be naïve to say that fear and responsibility are the main reason for Palestinian students' failure to grasp, let alone adopt, radical sociological theories. Like their Jewish peers, most of the Palestinian students simply do not think radically, not even on the plight of their own people.[21] A major reason is that abstract theories are often alien to their way of thinking: it is one thing to have a different narrative than the state-sanctioned Zionist one; it's another thing to understand and adopt a theoretical paradigm that supports multiple narratives and doubts the epistemic status of social "truths." Moreover, given the social oppression they live under, Palestinian students can ill afford to do so.

Theoretical discourse is the result of detached reflection and abstract reasoning, practices that are more likely to arise in the leisure classes and are less immediately relevant for those who suffer from oppression and who need to act rather than reflect on it.[22] Of course, there are radical discourses that emerge from the experiences of disadvantaged classes and as a response to their oppression. Such ideas, which are developed "in the field" by people who lack formal education, are often not sophisticated enough to attract the intellectuals, who are interested in finding "the Truth" rather than in responding to a specific condition (Foucault 1996). Sometimes interesting cross-fertilization occurs between academia and social movements—the Israeli *Pantherim Shhorim* (Black Panthers) is a good example—but the very moment a discourse becomes intellectualized and the object of reflection and refinement by academics, it becomes less accessible to "simple" people not cut out for intellectual work. This gap of perspective and interest underlies many of the controversies that have hindered the cooperation between the intelligentsia and disadvantaged classes. It also accounts for a gap between radical professors, whose interest in social change is more theoretical, and students with revolutionary visions, whose interest lies in *doing* rather than in *thinking* (cf. Gramsci 1971).[23] Hence:

Proposition IX: Abstract radical theories do not appeal to disadvantaged students whose needs for action run counter to detached reflection.

Introspective Look

Asking why students have difficulties in understanding and adopting radical views sounds paternalistic. It assumes one occupies a superior position from which one can see the "Light" that students refuse to see. Modesty of course, suggests that we acknowledge that we might be wrong. But leaving aside this troubling possibility, there is another pretension I would like to clear myself of. Pretending to understand better other people's social conditions and problems and the ways to solve them ignores the fact that not too many years ago my views and attitudes were similar to those pervasive among my students today.

As a Sabra brought up on the myths of 1948 and 1967 I thought of Israel as a state that had always aspired to peace and as doing all it could to achieve it. Had I been in a class on the sociology of occupation as an undergraduate in the late 1970s—it is hard to think, however, that such a class could be offered then[24]—I would have responded probably in much the same way my students respond to me. My current views are the outcome of a process I have undergone over many years, starting—admittedly—with my studies at a relatively radical department at Tel-Aviv University. It continued with Ph.D. studies far away from Israel (at Northwestern) where I was exposed to other perspectives that allowed me to start seeing things in ways it would have been impossible to do here.

A trivial anecdote may exemplify this process. Once a class mate, an activist in a Quaker group that regularly visited Hebron, asked me whether it was true that all people in Israel who sported a mustache (but no beard) were

Palestinians. My first thought was "what nonsense," but in my mind going over the people I knew, I could not find a single Jew to fit the description (except of a picture of my dad in his early 20s, taken sometime in the 1950s). Thus, I learned an intimate lesson about my own society in faraway Evanston, Illinois.

The change in my views did not come from the American media, whose general perceptions are close to those pervasive in the Israeli public, nor from the America-oriented curriculum. But in the States I had access to other sources of information like my good Quaker class mate. It was in the States that I learned that according to Islam Jesus was one of the prophets. First I argued with the friend who told me this, assuming that coming from the Middle-East I knew better than she. But, of course, she was right, and I realized how little we, Israeli Jews, know about our fellow Arab citizens. One eye-opening lesson was my friend's report of how the African-American students, in their dorm club, had applauded the missiles hitting Tel Aviv in the Gulf War of 1991. It was a troubling tale; I was angry at their reaction, but it made me think, and it gave me a wider perspective to reflect on similar cheering in Israeli occupied Palestinian territories.

There are of course the theories I picked up in the courses I took and in academic reading: Althusser and Foucault on the nature of ideology; Anderson on the emergence of nationalist consciousness; Said on how the "Occident" constructs the "Orient" (and, thus, constructs itself). These classes and readings taught me many new things about Israel as well: I read Shafir (1989) on the class structure of the first Jewish colonies in the late nineteenth century; Swirski and Bernstein (1993) on how the new immigrants from the Middle East and North Africa were treated in the 1950s; and I read Carmi and Rosenfeld (1974, 1989, 1992; Rosenfeld 1978, 1981) on the proletarianization of the Israeli Palestinians and Israeli political economy.

In sum, I changed and adopted new attitudes as a consequence of what I experienced and of the social networks of which I have become a part. Few of my students as yet have had these kinds of opportunities to see the situation from afar and to be exposed to alternative sources of information.[25] They were exposed to the same ideological apparatuses we talk about in our sociology courses. At this point I would like to move to some concluding comments about ideology.

Conclusion

The conventional model of teaching is that of a teacher with a certain kind of knowledge and pupils who are supposed to absorb that knowledge, whether it is multiplication tables in elementary-school algebra or the nature of social change in sociological theory for graduate students. This is similar to the basic model of communication engineering: a transmitter emits information, a receiver picks it up, and the quality of the broadcast, the communication, is measured by comparing the information the receiver obtains with that issued by the source. This model is problematic even in engineering and in simple cases of human communication. It is naïve to think it can work in the classroom. By reflexively contemplating my own anecdotal experiences my goal was to identify the main reasons teaching does not work this way. If we look at the above propositions and generalize them, the following are the main reasons many students pass our classes, and even our exams, without grasping our theoretical perspectives, especially the radical ones.

First, many things we wish our students to study contradict what they have learned from many other sources. As Ulrich Beck argues, in the age of reflexive modernity (1994), various discourses are developed simultaneously in a rational manner, and yet, since they start from different assumptions and look at different aspects of life, they reach contradictory conclusions. The radical teachings of sociology appear to us as solid conclusions of decades of sociological (as well as anthropological, historical and so forth) studies and deliberations, but they have to compete with discourses developed by alternative theoretical approaches and competing disciplinary bodies.

Moreover, we should not forget that the university is part of society. We cannot expect, and do not want, society to stay indifferent to what academics say, and we cannot expect, and do not want, social scientists to be immune to thought currents that flow outside our ivory tower. If radical theories are truly radical they are bound to threaten powerful institutions, and the latter have the resources to sideline us and our teachings even inside our tower and support academics who accept the hegemonic ideology and develop conservative approaches.

Second, our teaching also has to compete, of course, with all other sources of socialization: with the novels our students read and the movies they watch; with the Zionist meta-narratives they imbibe at school and in the army; and with the news commentaries they hear on radio and TV channels (Bourdieu 1998).

Third, and perhaps most importantly, knowledge is often related to personal experiences. How students respond to our teachings depends on what they have experienced, or, if they do not have direct experience, on stories and interpretations of close family members and intimate friends.

Fourth, students generally have goals that differ from ours. Regardless of our political convictions, we, as teachers, are engaged in a scholastic practice; we want to understand, explain, and win intellectual battles. Some of our students share, of course, these goals, but most of them have more pressing tasks: to obtain a degree, find a job, and provide for themselves and for their existing or planned families.

Here we have to acknowledge cultural differences between classes. Bookish perspectives and intellectual speculations are part of middle class culture. Playing with radical ideas is part of the normal training expected of its young women and men who are then supposed to "grow out" of it later (Berger 1967).[26]

Historians of medieval times tell us about the complete academic freedom that reigned in the original universities established by the Church. But this freedom had a price: knowledge and thought had to be confined to the university grounds. Our modern ideal is different. We aspire for campuses integrated with the surrounding community and serving its needs, in exchange, of course, for the material resources drawn from that surrounding. We want to have an impact, and we therefore cannot expect outsiders to remain indifferent to what we say and write. If we threaten powerful factors, we should expect to be restrained by them. If we teach what our students and their future employers deem redundant, we will end up without students. If we can get away with saying "scandalous" things, it is often because we are a negligible minority, but also because as a whole we are of some service to the Establishment.

So are we merely puppets or extras in the grand show of society? Such a pessimistic view is also unwarranted. The greatest economist of the 20 century, John Maynard Keynes, wrote at the end of his most famous book that intellectuals have more power than we think. "Madmen in power," he wrote, "who hear voices in the air, are distilling their frenzy from some academic scribbler of a few years back." And: "The power of vested interests is vastly exaggerated compared with the gradual encroachment of ideas. Not, indeed, immediately, but after a certain interval" (1964, 383). Universities are places where new ideas are played out. The academic arena is neither a place where reason surpasses ideology nor a tool in the hand of rulers to control society. Like the mass media, the church, and the arts, it is another arena where social, cultural, and ideological forces compete. It is neither free nor fair play, but it has the potential that under certain circumstances, it will help advance equality and justice.

That the glass is nine-tenths empty should not blind us to the one tenth that is full. After all, some students are affected by our teachings. The students in my "Sociology of Occupation" course, who held fast to their views, still acknowledged that they learned new things about a topic they had heard so much about in the mass media, and a few of them said it made them more confused; for others it might be one more drop of information that together with other drops may finally change their views. As I myself changed, I have encountered during my work many students, who told me how other lecturers and I have helped them to better understand important facets of our social life.[27]

One should wonder not that society does not hear the voice of reason, as shaped by researchers, but that once in a blue moon new and radical views get a chance to be heard and disseminated in academic establishments, paid for by tax payers' money and populated by social dignitaries. Academics play their role in distributing hegemonic ideas. It cannot be otherwise. Israeli academia has played and still plays a pivotal role in instilling the Zionist discourse, the same way academics elsewhere propagate the ideas that are hegemonic where they are located. Some people criticize Israeli academia, because it is not particularly radical. They compare Israeli universities with the image they have in their mind of what universities ought to look like. One should instead ask what society would look like without universities. What material infrastructure would be there to support radical thinking?

This does not mean one has to be complacent about the current situation and accept ideological pressures from the outside as legitimate. Neither is there room to be grateful to the powers that be for allowing academic freedom. If universities have developed in such a way as to allow *limited* freedom, this is due to the fact that they either support the major interests of those in power, or because in certain circumstances it proves impossible to stifle bourgeoning egalitarian ideas. In any case, whatever we think about our own power, we have no other choice but to use the freedom we have to advance the values we believe in. "The only thing necessary for the triumph of evil," Edmund Burke wrote, "is for good men to do nothing." We cannot afford to do so.

Notes

[1] Hess gives the following data: 8,000 Jews live today in the Gaza Strip alongside 1.4 millions of Palestinians; out of the 365 square kms of the Gaza Strip, 20% is used by Israeli settlers and army; 1,231 Palestinians, including 81 women and 344 children below 18, were killed from September 2000 until mid-February 2004.

[2] With the entrance of immigrants from the former USSR and of foreign workers this has changed to some extent, but among veteran Israelis this ethnic stratification still holds.

[3] A few interviewees spoke about a clear sense of ethnic divisions among Jews with which they have grown up; a few others recounted stories of "awakening" and discovery; they had assumed that inter-ethnic tensions were all long gone but something happened to them and they understood they were wrong.

[4] In a recent interview to Haaretz, the novelist A. B. Yehoshua says: "The fact that my grandfather came 30 years earlier [than those who came during the mass immigration] from Morocco has not made me into a Moroccan. . . . Morocco that my mother knew was Morocco of elites, and suddenly much more common groups arrived that she had no connection to. She was afraid to be identified with that group; that my sister and I would be identified with that group. She was terrified. . . . The discrimination was generated then; the Mizrahim were branded; I did not want to be branded as Mizrahi" (Haaretz magazine, March 19, 2004). Yehoshua's confession raised angry responses and a heated debate in the following issues of the magazine.

[5] Unfortunately most of them have the bravery to join combat units but not the courage needed to resist the continuing occupation, refusing to enlist or fighting to prevent the cruelty of their comrades.

[6] This limitation, however, also indicates the importance of our teaching: while it threatens the identities of some people, it offers guidance and help to those who have suffered from the hegemonic ideology and look for alternative views. There are many examples of this, but within the confines of this essay I cannot deal with the matter here.

[7] In one of the last graduation ceremonies at the University of Haifa the then Minister of Science and Culture, ex-General Matan Vilnai, talked about the hard times Israel was facing two years into the Al-Aksa Intifada. Vilnai wanted to cheer up the audience—almost half of it Arab-Palestinians, who are more likely to attend these ceremonies than Jews—by assuring them unthinkingly that "the Jewish genius would find a solution, as it has always done."

[8] Anti-Establishment sociologists are also courted by sensation-seeking journalists but are usually positioned as outsiders and as extremists. Outside sociology, in such fields as Jewish History, Political Science, Hebrew Literature etc. the hegemonic ideology is even more powerful.

[9] Radical, and not so radical, Palestinians talk about the "occupation of 1948" and the "occupation of 1967," but it is rare to find Israeli Jews, including sturdy leftists, who see the 1948-49 war, their "War of Independence" as a war of occupation.

[10] When asked by students why I had not brought evidence about the Palestinian attacks on Jews and their dreadful outcomes, I answered that those outcomes were well known. Indeed, I saw no reason to use the scarce time of the class to retell these facts. I wonder whether this decision was a mistake, both pedagogic and psychological.

[11] In my view, my position is quite moderate but within the Israeli political discourse, I must agree that my views are quite marginal and therefore are categorized as "extreme Left."

[12] A Palestinian sociology student was injured and for a few days his life was in danger but he recovered; two Palestinian women were killed in that explosion in addition to more than a dozen Jews, demonstrating the indiscriminate nature of terror.

[13] This tendency might also hinder the identification of women with the feminist movement even when they benefit from its achievements and actually share many of its tenets (Friedman 1999).

[14] A few qualified this: they had learned "a little more," or had learned "the leftist point of view," or "more about the Palestinians."

[15] One student said that following the course she had started to ask questions; a second said the course had made her already-confused opinions even more confused; and a third said that her previously held views had been undermined, but she had not been able to form new ones. A fourth student wrote that the course had helped her shift from the right-wing to the middle of the political map.

[16] At least no stakes they are aware of!

[17] The percentage is around 20; even this simple figure is the subject of political struggle. Arab students have claimed that the university underestimates their number to avoid being stigmatized as an "Arab" institution. Unfortunately, it indeed happens that prospective students and their parents express concern about the presence of so large a number of Arabs at the university. The label "the Jewish Bir Zeit" (after the most prestigious university in the Occupied Territories) is an indication of this attitude. On the other hand, given the demographic fact that the majority of Palestinians in Israel live in the north of the country, the percentage ought to have been much higher, all other things being equal – which they are not, of course.

[18] As someone fully engaged in political activities on campus since October 2000, I can personally vouch for and corroborate each of these claims.

[19] If we would like to be more precise theoretically, we would not be able to say that they are not influenced at all. Even if they end up believing in other values and narratives, it is possible to conceptualize their differences as part of the overall ideological configuration; see Althusser 1971.

[20] Those who rush to discount my student's fear as unfounded, should also reflect for a moment on the fact that the Ministry of Education in Jerusalem employs a high-ranking official of the General Security Services (Shabak) whose approval is needed for the appointment of every Arab school principal. The previous Minister of Education, Yossi Sarid, said that he ignored the official's recommendations but was powerless to cancel the position. Before the publication of this issue in Haaretz, well-intentioned Israeli Jews – for Palestinians the report was old hat – may have been able to discard rumors on political considerations in the nominations of Arab school principals as baseless and exaggerated.

[21] This is a speculative conclusion on my part based on eleven years of teaching dozens of Palestinian students.

[22] Of course, different levels of schooling and dissimilar styles of teaching are other factors involved in creating and reproducing gaps in way of thinking between middle-class and working-class children and among ethnic groups. Less qualified teachers, less

funding, more authoritarian teachers, less parent involvement, and more disciplinary problems usually suppress the development of critical thinking in schools. This, however, is a topic for another essay.

[23] In addition, economically disadvantaged students—Jewish as well as Palestinian—often come from traditional families. Their direct access to poverty and to its structural causes may make them aware of economic injustices but it is not an environment that encourages subversive thinking about gender and sexuality. Therefore, even those who develop radical thinking are often less sensitive to the needs of women and of sexual minorities, further thwarting possibilities of cooperation with middle-class women, gays, and Lesbians.

[24] Henry Rosenfeld was among the very few who taught an heterodox perspective at the time I was an undergraduate (late 70s and early 80s), but he was at Haifa, whereas I studied at Tel Aviv University, where Avishai Ehrlich and Gershon Shafir started teaching radical theories about Palestinian-Jewish relations only in the mid 80s.

[25] Students growing up outside Israel but amidst tight Jewish communities may have been exposed to other socializing forces, but probably in the same direction regarding Jewish solidarity and the exclusion of Arabs.

[26] While some may view this statement as paternalistic, it is also paternalistic to expect the working class to have the same evaluation of intellectual discourses as the middle class. Of course, this does not mean that working class people are less intelligent, although it might be interpreted this way by middle class people.

[27] We are inclined to call those students "bright" but perhaps they are bright because they think like us?

Bibliography

Althusser, Louis. 1971. "Ideology and Ideological State Apparatuses." In his *Lenin and Philosophy and Other Essays.* NY: Monthly Review Press.

Avraham, E. (2002). "Social-Political Environment, Journalism Practice and Coverage of Minorities: The Case of the Marginal Cities in Israel." *Media, Culture, and Society* 24(1): 69-86.

Beck, Ulrich. 1994. "The Reinvention of Politics: Towards a Theory of Reflexive Modernization." In Ulrich Beck, Anthony Giddens, and Scott Lash (eds.,), *Reflexive Modernization: Politics, Tradition and Aesthetics in the Modern Social Order,* 1-55. Stanford: Stanford University Press.

Ben-Amos, Avner. 1994. "An Impossible Pluralism: European Jews and Oriental Jews in the Israeli History Curriculum." *History of European Ideas* 18: 41-51.

Ben-Rafael, Eliezer and Stephen Sharot. 1991. *Ethnicity, Religion, and Class in Israeli Society.* Cambridge: Cambridge University Press.

Berger, Peter L. 1967. *Invitation to Sociology: A Humanistic Perspective.* Harmondworth: Pinguin.

Bourdieu, Pierre. 1998. *On Television.* Tran. Priscilla Parkhurst Fergusun. New York: Free Press.

Carmi, Shulamit and Henry Rosenfeld. 1974. "The Origins of the Process of Proletarianization and Urbanization of Arab Peasants in Palestine." *Annals of the New York Academy of Sciences* 220: 470-85.

-----. 1989. "The Emergence of Militaristic Nationalism in Israel." *International Journal of Politics, Culture, and Society* 3(1).

-----. 1992. "Israel's Political Economy and the Widening Class Gap Between Its Two National Groups." *Asian and African Studies* 26: 15-62.

Cohen, Yinon. 1998. "Socioeconomic Gaps Between Mizrachim and Ashkenazim, 1975-1995." *Israeli Sociology* 1(1): 115-134. (Hebrew).

Cohen, Yinon and Yitchak Haberfeld. 1998. "Second Generation Immigrants in Israel: Have the Ethnic Gaps in Schooling and Earnings Declined?" *Ethnic and Racial Studies* 21(3): 507-28.

Fershtman, Chaim and Uri Gneezy. 2001. "Discrimination in a Segmented Society: An Experimental Approach". *Quarterly Journal of Economics* 116: 351-377.

Foucault, Michel. 1996. "Nietzsche, Geneology, History." In Lawrence E. Cahoone (ed.), *From Modernism to Post-Modernism,* 360-381. Oxford: Blackwell.

Friedman, Ariella. 1999. "On Feminism, Femininity, and Women's Power in Israel." In Dafna N. Izraeli et al., *Sex Gender Politics: Women in Israel.* Tel Aviv: Hakibbutz Haneuchad. (Hebrew)

Gramsci, Antonio. 1971. *Selections from the Prison Notebooks.* New York: International Publishers.

Herzog, Hanna. 1986. *Political Adatiyut – Imagery v. Reality.* Tel-Aviv: Hakibbutz Hameuhad. (Hebrew).

Hever, Hannan, Yehouda Shenhav, and Pnina Motzafi-Haller. 2002. *Mizrahim in Israel:A Critical Observation into Israel's Ethnicity.* Jerusalem and Tel-Aviv: Van Leer Jerusalem Institute and Hakibbutz Hamechad. (Hebrew).

Frisch, Hillel. 2003. "Ethnicity or Nationalism? Comparing the Nakba Narrative among Israeli Arabs and Palestinians in the West Bank and Gaza." *Israel Affairs* 9(1-2): 165-84.

Kemp, Adriana and Rivka Raijman. 2000. "Foreigners in the Jewish State: The New Politics of Migrant-Labor in Israel." *Israeli Sociology* 3(1): 79-110. (Hebrew)

Keynes, John Maynard. 1964[1936]. *The General Theory of Employment, Interest, and Money.* San Diego: First Harvest/HBJ.

Khazoom, Aziza. 2003. "The Great Chain of Orientalism: Jewish Identity, Stigma Management, and Ethnic Exclusion in Israel." *American Sociological Review* 68(4): 481-510.

Kraus, Vered, and Yuval Yonay. 2000. "The Power and Limits of Ethnocentrism: Palestinians and Eastern Jews in Israel, 1974-1991." *British Journal of Sociology* 51(3): 525-51.

Lissak, Moshe. 1996. "Critical 'Sociologists' and 'Establishment' Sociologists in the Israeli Academic Community: Ideological Conflicts or an Appropriate Academic Discourse." In *Zionism: A Contemporary Controversy, ed. Pinhas Genosar and Avi Bareli,* 60-99. Sede Boker: Ben Gurion Heritage Center. (Hebrew)

Meget, Ilan. 2000. *Biram: A Mobilized Memory Community.* Givat Haviva: Peace Research Institute. (Hebrew)

Nagar-Ron, Sigal. 2004. "When Periphery Turns Center: On Zionism and Israeliness in the Discourse of Mizrahi Women in Ofakim." Paper presented in the 35th Annual Meeting of the Israeli Sociological Association, Be'er Sheva, 25-26.2.2004.

Piterberg, Gavriel. 1996. "Domestic Orientalism: The representation of Oriental Jews in Zionist/Israeli Historiography." *British Journal of Middle Eastern Studies* 23:125-45.

Rabinowitz, Dani. 1993a. "Oriental Nostalgia: The Transformation of the Palestinians into 'Israeli Arabs.'" *Theoria Uvikoret* (Theory and Criticism) 4: 141-52. (Hebrew)

-----. 1993b. *Overlooking Nazareth: The Ethnography of Exclusion in Galilee.* Cambridge: Cambridge University Press.

Regev, Motti. 2000. "To Have a Culture of Our Own: On Israeliness and Its Variants." *Ethnic and Racial Studies* 23(2): 223-47.

Rosenfeld, Henry. 1978. "The Class Situation of the Arab National Minority in Israel."
     Comparative Studies in Society and History 20: 374-407.
-----. 1981. "Change and Contradiction in the Rural Family." In A. Layish, ed., *The Arabs
     in Israel: Continuity and Change*. Jerusalem: Magnes. (Hebrew)
Sasson-Levy, Orna. 2002. "Constructing Identities at the Margins: Masculinities and
     Citizenship in the Israeli Army." *The Sociological Quarterly* 43(3): 357-83.
-----. 1992. *Arabs and Jews in Israel. Vol. 2: Change and Continuity in Mutual
     Intolerance*. Boulder: Westview Press.
Shafir, Gershon. 1989. *Land, Labor and the Origins of the Israeli-Palestinian Conflict,
     1882-1914*. Cambridge: Cambridge University Press.
Shenhav, Yehouda. 2003. *The Arab Jews: Nationalism, Religion and Ethnicity*. Tel-Aviv:
     Am Oved. (Hebrew)
Shohat, Ella. 1988. "Sephardim in Israel: Zionism from the Standpoint of its Jewish
     Victims." *Social Text* 19-20: 1-35.
Swirski, Shlomo and Deborah S. 1980. "Who Works in What, for Whom, and for What?
     Economic Development in Israel and Ethnic Division of Labor." *Mahbarot Lemehkar
     Ulefituach* 4: 5-66.

What Went Wrong?[1]

Alex Weingrod

Not long ago, in what began as a casual conversation with new acquaintances in a Central European capital, the conversation moved to the topic of Israel. Yes, I am from Israel, I confirmed, and the others nodded their heads and voiced sympathetic remarks: "It must be hard with the terror and all", "Will it ever end?", "What do you think about Sharon?". And then one of the assembled, a man in his mid-fifties, looked straight at me and said something like the following: "You know, we always looked up to you. For us, Israel was something special—perhaps it was the kibbutz, socialism in a young state that seemed very open and alive, some kind of spirit that gave us hope. We used to say, "Yes, but in Israel…" meaning that things were different there, better then most. So what happened to you? How did you get into this mess?"

I do not recall what I said in reply: probably mumbled something of a general kind, and then the conversation turned to other topics. Yet this wistful disappointment with my country caught me short, mainly, I suppose, since it came from an unexpected direction. After all, Israelis (or at least some Israelis) know and often experience disappointment with our national life; we are used to the daily loud critique in the newspapers, accustomed to the outbursts of anger when events that we oppose seem to overwhelm us, apparently out of control. But this critique came from an outsider—even more, from a former admirer— and it therefore was even more cutting and powerful, and I suppose that is why it remained with me.

How did we get into this mess? What went wrong?

Let me clarify my intentions: that is, explain what I hope to do in this essay. Whether voiced from inside or out, a certain sense of Israeli national unhappiness is widespread. This is not the usual whining about not having enough money to "finish the month", or disapproval of the sad state of the schools or roads; nor is it the traditional Israeli Friday evening gathering during which one vents complaints about "the government" and "the bureaucracy". The current state-of-unhappiness is far more basic, wide-ranging, and systemic. There is an uncomfortable feeling that things have just gone wrong ("this is not the child that we prayed for"), and that Israel at the beginning of the twenty- first century is a less humane, creative and forward-looking society. The critique ranges over diverse and yet inter-connected topics— most emphatically, the endless violence and war, the future of the West Bank settlements and foiled attempts to reach agreements with the Palestinians, the War of the Jews between secular and religious Jews, a kind of unbridled nationalism heavily mixed with religious Jewish themes, what is perceived to be a lowering of personal and national moral standards, the widening gulf of economic inequalities and concomitant drive towards personal profit and unconcern with others, the Americanization of daily life and culture--and the list could be expanded. These are sobering, real concerns, and they have brought about this nagging mood of national despair.

Now, if this is an accurate assessment, it is important to locate and understand the sources of this discontent. Once again: what went wrong? To be sure, phrasing the topic in this way implies that "once-upon-a-time life was better"--that the Israeli past was markedly better then the present. This is an important issue--and although I will consider it, this is not the major theme of this presentation. Rather, I wish to locate the constellations of social-economic-political factors that may have brought us to this downturn in national life. More particularly, I propose to explore these issues by first turning to two recent sociological studies of contemporary Israeli society. The two studies, the first by Baruch Kimmerling, titled *The Invention and Decline of Israeliness: State, Society and the Military*, and the second, *Being Israeli: The Dynamics of Multiple Citizenship*, by Gershon Shafir and Yoav Peled, are ambitious attempts to present a wide-ranging analysis of the shape and content of Israeli society at the beginning of this century. In addition, as a second step I also discuss a number of other factors that have driven the society into its current impasse. In brief, my presumption is that these two recent sociologies of Israel may serve as beginning guides for comprehending today's state-of-affairs, and that by considering them we are able to better understand "what went wrong". [2]

The New Israeli Sociologies

The two new sociological studies have a great deal in common. Both books were published almost at the same time—Kimmerling in 2001, and Shafir-Peled a year later in 2002. The authors identify themselves as "political sociologists"—Kimmerling and Shafir are members of sociology departments, and Peled is situated in a department of political science—and their previous publications consider a wide range of historical and contemporary topics. Moreover, the three authors have a central place in the roster of "new" or "critical" Israeli sociologists: together with other younger scholars, they have been especially active in defining a fresh agenda and radically different perspectives in the study of Israeli society. [3]

This is an important point. Early in their books, both Kimmerling and Shafir-Peled tell the reader that their study breaks away from previous ones and represents a new conceptualization of Israeli society: thus Kimmerling writes in his Introduction "the present volume is a third-generation sociohistorical analysis of Israel" (page 7), and, even more pointedly, Shafir-Peled claim that their book "is the first attempt to present a comprehensive analysis of Israeli society from the "new" or "critical" perspective" (page 32). These books are, in other words, conscious attempts on the part of the authors to chart out some different perspectives and understandings. Their scope is equally ambitious-- these are not intensive studies of one topic or another (say, religious Israeli Jews, or relationships between Israeli Jews and Arabs), but rather broad-scaled attempts to conceptualize and explain the internal dynamics of the society as a whole. What is more, following Kimmerling, they are "third-generation" Israeli sociologies. As anyone familiar with Israeli sociology will know, the "first generation" refers to the work of Shmuel Eisenstadt at the Hebrew University; from the 1950s through the 1980s Eisenstadt's many publications presented a theoretically-informed and relatively comprehensive interpretation of Israeli society and institutions. The "second generation" in the 1970s and 1980s was made up of his disciples (such as Moshe Lissak, Dan Horowitz and others) as well as his critics (notably Yonatan Shapiro, Sammy Smooha, Shlomo Swirski, and Henry Rosenfeld and Shula Carmi) who, moving out from different theoretical premises and perspectives, developed contrasting interpretations of Israeli society.[4] According to their own account, the two books considered here are the "third generation": they not only refer to events in the 1990s and the turn of the century, they also aspire to present a different interpretation of Israel's past and the present. For this reason too they are particularly relevant for my purposes.

Israeli History Reconsidered: Kimmerling's Account

Kimmerling's book seems ideal for anyone interested in understanding "what went wrong": the title—"The Invention and Decline of Israeliness"—immediately intimates that things have gone awry. While selective, he presents a systematic account of persistent and changing features—and the downhill course—of present-day Israeli culture and society.

The "Israeli story", as he tells it, has its opening in the late-nineteenth and early twentieth centuries, and while it begins with European Jews and Zionism, it soon becomes a tale of Jews and Arabs, and then of Israelis and Palestinians. "In the beginning" the Jewish settlers created bridgeheads in Palestine by purchasing land from Arabs and establishing their own separate settlements; indeed, just as in other European settler societies (South Africa, Algeria, Australia, Ireland) they too built their own separate economic and political institutions. According to Kimmerling's reading, the British, the colonial power from 1918 to 1947, instituted what he calls a "minimalist state" that was mainly pro-Jewish, and as a result the Zionist settlers were able to build their own "state in the making" that was, although small in size and numbers, increasingly resilient and strong. The relative power of the state is one of the key ingredients in his analysis, and these developments foreshadowed the emergence of Israel as a "strong state" with its "tremendous capacity to mobilize its citizens" (p. 56).

Israeliness is a clumsy term—hard to pronounce and always looking as if it were misspelled —and it also has an overly general, spongy meaning. Yet it is central to Kimmerling's thesis, and therefore needs to be explained. Israeliness is a mixture of interlocked institutions plus cultural codes, symbols, and "rules of the game"—the quintessence of what it means (or better, meant) to be "an Israeli". Putting it differently, it is the particular form of political-cultural hegemony that was fashioned by the European Jewish elites who controlled the society and state practically from its inception. Surprisingly, although the verbiage is different and his admiration more restrained, Kimmerling's depiction does not differ much from the canonical understandings introduced by the first and second-generation sociologists. The pre-1948 state-in-the- making was the product of both the imagination and the tough realities faced by the small, self-selected activist members of the East European pioneering Zionist settlement movement. The boundaries between "state" and "society" were "completely blurred", and the leading socialist parties dominated practically all features of everyday life. In addition, "an entire subculture based on symbols—a (red) flag, anthems, ceremonies, parades, festivals and holidays (May Day)—was also developed" (p. 65-66). The revival of the Hebrew language was crucial to their endeavor. And, in addition, they were "enlightened" Jews, and while mandatory Palestine included several small orthodox Jewish religious as well as other enclaves, the dominant socialist- Zionists were overwhelmingly secular in outlook and behavior.

This complex of institutions, values and ideologies subsequently blossomed and also gained new dimensions in the first two decades following Israel's establishment. It is in this context that Kimmerling sees the full emergence of "Israeliness" as the hegemonic regime. The veteran socialist elites quickly took over the new, all-powerful state; indeed, they prospered in the process and soon became the Ashkenazi middle and upper-middle classes. Beyond political dominance, the established elites also spearheaded the creation of new Israeli cultural formats—that is, the emergent version of the hegemonic "Israeliness". What was new in this post-state "Israeliness" was its emphasis upon nationalism, and, in obvious tandem, the celebration of "the military" (p. 101). "The state developed its own cults and civil religion", and an ideology of statism (mamlachtiut in Hebrew) "was located at the center of personal and collective existence and essence" (101). The state's task was not only to provide political order and security, but also to re-socialize the large numbers of Middle Eastern and European Holocaust survivors then pouring into the country. Here the tones of Kimmerling's prose, usually restrained and matter-of-fact, go up several notches: "The melting pot, a giant mincing machine, was supposed to incorporate most of the newly immigrated Jews, but not the Arabs" (p. 97) This meant forging the "new Jew", a muscular Hebrew speaking hero who was to be "a warrior, industrious, hard-working, rational, modern, Western or "Westernized", secular...educated (but not an intellectual), and obedient to authorities (that is, to the state and its representatives)"(p. 101).

Although their hegemony was at times challenged (for example, in the Wadi Salib protests in 1959), the ruling Ashkenazi elites were remarkably successful in maintaining their rule: "secular nationalist Zionist culture was strong and flexible enough to include under its umbrella other varieties of Jewishness, reinterpreted as "Israeliness (p.128). These first two decades—from 1948 until 1967—were consequently challenging and creative, representing Zionism's triumph: they were, in fact, "the good times" (my interpretation, not Kimmerlings), and, inevitably, after them came "the fall".

The watershed, of course, was the Six Day War and Israel's expansion into the West Bank, Gaza, the Golan Heights and Sinai. The Israeli mood was ecstatic (a "euphoric power trip")—and yet, ironically, "the big social and cultural transformation in Israeli society occurred as a result of the 1967 war" (p. 109). Why? Analyzing this "transformation" and its outcomes is Kimmerling's major theme. He argues that Israel's post-1967 conquest brought about a situation in which alternative elites, already poised to challenge the old hegemony, quickly hoisted their newly-fashioned, activist settlement ideology. The religious-nationalist Gush Emunim movement claimed historic Jewish right to the West Bank, and they not only established new settlements in the midst of Palestinian centers, but also developed their version of Zionist ideology with its own symbols ("the knitted skull-cap"), political power centers and rules-of-the-game. In this new alliance "between secular chauvinism and religious ethnocentrism", the old secular Israeliness was challenged by an assertive, at times mystical "religious interpretation of "Judaism" (p. 110-111). Even though the religious-nationalists were a small minority, once the old dominant system had been cracked, other groups began to establish their legitimacy as Israelis. Thus, as Israeli nationalism became "more Judaic and religious", the ultra-orthodox non-Zionist Jewish minority, the <u>haredim</u>, also began to spin their own versions of "what- it- is- to- be- an Israeli", and acted to assert their growing power. Given this turn of events, the old secular-socialist order failed to maintain its centrality since, among other things, it was caught within its own internal contradictions. "Israeliness" thereby became only one identity among many—there were other models and possibilities, and this spelled "the end of hegemony".

This process of "cultural plurality" (or, alternatively, "cultural decomposition") accelerated throughout the 1980s and 1990s. In a long chapter called "The Newcomers", Kimmerling describes additional sub-cultures: the "traditionalist counterculture" of the Mizrahim, the Jews from Middle Eastern countries, many of whom became allied to the highly successful Shas movement that mixes traditional Jewish themes with strong anti-establishment messages; the "Arab citizens of Israel", who grew to almost twenty percent of the Israeli population, and, while on the one hand becoming "more Israeli", also became increasingly alienated as the overall society grew more nationalistic and "Jewish"; what he calls "the Russian speaking immigrants", practically a million persons who maintained a certain cultural separation as well as close nostalgic and other ties to "Mother Russia"; the Ethiopians who for other reasons, including racialism and prejudice, have been relegated to lower socio-economic ranks and retain their own distinct, separate community; and finally, the "noncitizen workers", a variety of presumably temporary guest-workers mainly from Eastern Europe, Thailand and the Philippines who, just as in other industrialized states, immigrate in search of temporary work and are exploited by the native population. According to Kimmerling's count there consequently are seven different "sub-cultures" that together make-up "Israeli society": the unifying features of a single dominant hegemony are gone, and in their place one finds a variety of sub-cultures that compete, often aggressively, and march in different directions to their own separate drummers.

Is this "what went wrong": that the society lost its previous concensus and became much more fractured and conflictual? Not necessarily. Kimmerling exhibits little nostalgia for the previous Labor- dominated hegemony, and besides, "cultural plurality" in which sub-cultures compete might provide a fresh, more open and even more creative society. Instead, the deeper problem lies not in what separates Israelis, but rather in what keeps them (or most of them) together. Paradoxically, some of the basic assumptions that are shared by Israelis may be the root of the problem.

Kimmerling argues that there are two "common meta-cultural codes or narratives" that are shared by nearly all Israeli Jews: the first of these he calls "Jewishness", and the second the "code of security". To be sure, they exclude Israeli Arabs, but, on the other hand, "these codes are common to both the (Jewish) right and left, to Ashkenazim and Mizrahim, to the poor and the rich, to women and men, and to the religious...as well as the secular" P. 173). The two codes have a kind of "functional purpose"—they are so "primordial" that they are able to keep the deeply split society together. Kimmerling goes on to use these codes as a platform for dissecting a number of basic contradictions in the society—contradictions that became more apparent after 1967, but that he believes to be inherent in the structure of the Israeli state. Regarding "Jewishness", he argues that Israel cannot be both "Jewish and democratic", and as a result "the Israeli state fluctuates between secular liberal democracy and nationalist theocracy" (174). Indeed, while Israel appears to be a Western-styled democracy, since it cannot "separate religion from nationalism and nationality" it is basically undemocratic in its relationships with the non-Jewish Arab minority (p.181). Israel consequently has become an "ethnocracy" in which one "ethnos", the Jews, maintain exclusive control of their strong state while depriving the other "ethnos", the Arabs, of basic civil rights.

This is a dismal situation, and when coupled with "the code of security"— the second meta-cultural code presumably shared by all Israelis—the picture becomes even darker. The origins of this code reach back to the pre-state period, and it has been strengthened in the endless violence, conflict and war between Arabs and Jews, and between Israel and the neighboring Arab states. While he cites different Israeli approaches to "the conflict", Kimmerling's point is that Israeli culture itself is deeply militarized: "this is expressed mainly by the use of excessive power in solving social and political problems, by the "military-mindedness" of large parts of the civilian population and political leadership, and by the high expectancy that the military will solve nonmilitary problems" (p. 226). Thus, at its core, Israel is merely (as Time magazine once put it) "an ugly little Spartan state" in which the military will "continue to dominate...both in political and symbolic terms" (p. 237). The present, and presumably the future too, are consequently depressingly grim.

Kimmerling's conclusions have obvious implications for understanding "what went wrong". However, before pursuing that set of issues, I want to turn next to the second recent full-length Israeli sociology—Shafir and Peled's *Being Israeli: The Dynamics of Multiple Citizenship*. Not surprisingly, even though their conclusions are different, there are both similarities and differences between the two studies.

"Being Israeli": The View from Tel Aviv

Shafir and Peled also review and interpret the last one-hundred- plus years of Jewish settlement in Palestine-Israel, and they too state that the "transformation of Israeli society" is the central focus of their book (p. 109). However, the prism that guides their analysis is considerably different. As the title of their book suggests, the focus is on "citizenship". But this is not "citizenship" as it is usually understood: the issue is not how a state decides to grant passports or voting rights to its citizens, but rather (following Soysal and others) a consideration of how, over time, a particular "incorporation regime" allocates basic rights and privileges to persons living within its domain. The "citizenship discourse" ranges over a broad array of political, social and legal rights—access to good jobs as well as voting rights or the possibility of being elected to office. In brief, whereas Kimmerling places the changing face of "Israeliness" at the center of his analysis, these authors focus more upon "equality", or better, "inequality, and they draw upon an impressive battery of recent studies of Israeli society to present a historical review of social, political and economic stratification and change as these pertain to Jews and Arabs in Palestine-Israel.

This is a long journey with a surprising outcome, and the authors tell their story in a professional, business-like manner. Moving out from contemporary political theory, they argue that three different "citizenship-discourses...are currently predominant—liberal, republican, and ethno-nationalist" (p. 3). Moreover, these three compete and co-exist, and, in fact, they can be seen to have contested with one another throughout the last century of Zionist settlement and subsequent state-formation. The republican view, in which rights are granted by virtue of "active participation in the pursuit of a common good" (p.5), dominated the heroic pre-state period and continued into the 1970s. Gershon Shafir's previous book, "Land, Labor and the Origins of the Israeli-Palestinian Conflict, 1882-1914", presented a critical de-bunking of earlier interpretations of the origins of Israeli institutions, and the authors present an up-dated version in the first section of this book. In what has since become the new canon, the argument is that nineteenth century socialist and other ideologies played a secondary role in the formation of the kibbutz, the Histadruth, the moshav, and other major Labor Zionist-settler institutions. Instead, the unique societal structure that evolved was a consequence of the Jewish-Arab struggle over the control of land and labor: the "split-labor market", access to the national funds raised by Zionists in the diaspora, and the material conditions of everyday life in Palestine, better explain the activist, communitarian and ultimately successful regime that emerged. For example, according to this reading the radically-egalitarian kibbutz was not so much "socialist", but rather was an ideal vehicle for gaining control over land. The "incorporation regime" emphasized commitment and personal involvement, and consequently the Labor

Settlement Movement "pioneers" were the first-among-equals in the pre-state regime that was more autocratic then democratic ("democracy never appeared in its liberal version", p. 53). In brief, during the pre-state period the dominant ideological rhetoric emphasized "equality", while, in fact, significant groups were excluded (the entire Arab population, orthodox Jews, members of competing Zionist ideological groups on the Right and Left, and others) and the existing inequalities were hidden from view.

Having established its hegemony, this regime controlled the state and dominated the society through the 1970s. The economy continued to be highly centralized as the state was the recipient of huge capital inflows ("Together with Taiwan and South Korea, Israel... was the major beneficiary of unilateral capital transfers", p. 56). Various state-funded industrial and agricultural projects were initiated, including a significant "military-industrial complex" that subsequently became "the engine of growth...for advanced high-technology industries and the primary influence on the modernization of (Israeli) industry" (p. 59). In later chapters Shafir and Peled go on to analyze how the regime sought (and failed) to accommodate other large groups—new immigrants from Middle Eastern countries, women, Israeli Arabs, and orthodox religious Jews. They also broach the question of why, given the socialist rhetoric of the powerful Histadruth and other major institutions, the economy and society that developed in the 1950s and 1960s did not become "socialist"? Their reply is clear and expected: "socialism was no more than the handmaiden of the (Labor elites') national-colonial aims"(p. 55). Grasping land and establishing the state were their basic goals, and consequently a kind of "plural economy" that included a growing private sector was set in motion.

We might ask at this point: Is this what went wrong? Was the initial excitement and promise of an "idealistic" Jewish State lost or plain worn-out by the practical exigencies of state-building, mass-immigration, hostility and war? Like Kimmerling and other critics, Shafir and Peled punch holes in any remaining idealization of the pre-state period and tend to emphasize its darker sides. More important, the question itself is premature: as they see it, Israeli society has recently taken several unexpected twists, and questions of evaluation had best be deferred until one views the entire historic process.

Shafir and Peled then take the reader through the changing dynamics of Israeli citizenship. Their emphasis is upon inequalities and, consequently, the focus is on stratification. The old Ashkenazi-dominated Israeli "incorporation regime" is shown to have failed to grant equal citizenship status to major social groups and categories. For example, in a chapter titled "Mizrachim and Women", the authors show how both have been discriminated against and marginalized. The large waves of post-state Mizrachi immigrants were "orientalized" by the dominant Ashkenazim, and many were thrust into peripheral development towns where housing was inadequate, incomes low, and their childrens' education inferior. As a consequence, they were attracted to an "ethno-nationalist" citizenship discourse that emphasized nationalist Jewish themes; at first drawn to the Likud, they later supported Shas, the ultra-orthodox ethnic party that championed a "return to Mizrachi glory". The Israeli women's story is different. Although they partake in each of the three citizenship discourses, they also are unequal in each: for example, since they cannot fully serve as soldiers they are unable to fulfill the republican ideal; they are discriminated against with regard to occupation, making them unequal in the liberal citizenship discourse; and they are inferior to men according to Jewish halakhic law, and consequently the ethno-nationalist discourse also pushes them to the margins. Moreover, "the record of feminism in Israel has been disappointing", and in the absence of a sustained gender protest these inequalities are likely to persist (p. 108).

As these brief summary remarks should indicate, Shafir and Peled's presentation is smart, up-to-date and informative. They continue their analysis of major groups by discussing Israeli Arabs ("The Frontier Within") and Zionist and non-Zionist Orthodox Jews ("The Wages of Legitimation"). Here too the "citizenship discourses" indicate gross inequalities, and the authors' also raise new questions regarding "cultural autonomy" for Israeli Arabs and the impact of the "liberal citizenship discourse" upon the relationships between religious and secular Jews. In a later chapter they also consider the new groups that entered the society during the 1980s and 1990s: Russian immigrants, the Ethiopians, and what they call" overseas labor immigrants". However, in contrast with Kimmerling, they do not emphasize the schism that divides between the various Israeli groups and their ideologies: on the contrary, "multiple citizenship" means that there is an "internally connected regime of groups", rather then deep cleavages that divide "the society into distinct and separate groups". Conflicts, yes, and yet the society has been moving in a direction. The central question, then, is not what holds the society together, but rather the overall trajectory that it may be following.

The directions in which Israeli society is moving—or, in their terms, which of the "citizenship discourses" has gained in strength—is closely related to the main events that shaped the society since the 1970s: namely, Jewish colonization in the West Bank territories, and the Palestinian resistance that ultimately resulted in the two intifadas. The authors' argue that Labor, still in power in 1967, could not resist the opportunity to continue its old colonization practices. However, their "republican discourse" was soon overtaken by the "messianic version of a new, synthetic, religious-republican discourse" promoted by Gush Emunim (p.162). Then, in 1977, when the Likud party won the election that ended Labor's hegemony, the triumphant new government opened the "sluice gates" to settlement on the West Bank. For their part, "Palestinian opposition to each additional phase of settlement was more intense than to the earlier, more modest, phase. Each additional stage of expansion intensified the frontier conflict" (p. 183). Moreover, the Palestinians have been living under an Israeli military colonial "control system" in which they were not only exploited economically, but also "deprived of all political and most civil rights" (p. 185). Shafir and Peled go on to present, in broad but clear strokes, the awesome, see-saw march of events from 1990 almost to the present-- the Oslo Accords, subsequent Israel- PLO negotiations, Rabin's assassination by a religious Israeli Jew, the failure of the Taba negotiations, and the outbreak of the second intifada in late 2000. How have these events influenced the Israeli "citizenship discourses"?

This brings us back to the question of "trajectory". Writing from the perspective of the late 1990s, the authors argue that a majority of Israelis have begun to realize that "the benefits of colonial control were outweighed by its cost" (p. 201), and consequently, the possibility of ending "the conflict" with the Palestinians has become attainable. Shafir-Peled allocate the key role in this major shift to the Israeli business community: as they put it, "the conflict "became 'solvable' when it was reconceptualized as an obstacle to the integration of Israeli business into the global economy" (p. 251) And, in addition, they also claim that Israeli society has been moving in the direction of the "liberal discourse" and "the emergence of civil society". Why this major shift has taken place, and what its implications may be, is the central "up-beat" theme of the book's final chapters.

In brief, not only was the old Ashkenazi Labor hegemony trapped in a "malaise", among its younger elite the concept of a market-economy became increasingly attractive. Other political-social groups, such as Shinui and Meretz, also championed a "free economy" and "civil rights". Moreover, the swift growth and power of the "global economy" was a key factor in the liberalization of the Israeli economy— opening the economy to foreign investment, and doing away with government control over currency, were necessary steps in joining the world economic system. The central, totalistic reign of government control weakened; for example, the authors interpret the Likud policy of settling the West Bank with suburban-styled private homes rather then communal villages as another indication of the growing popularity of the "liberal discourse". They go on to cite other kinds of evidence; for example, the central bank (Bank of Israel) took on new strength as an independent agency of economic policy, and the Supreme Court enacted a series of Basic Laws that were to guarantee civil rights. On the other hand, they also criticize the ways in which the reigning "market mentality" has lead to "shrinking social rights": while Israeli GNP and personal incomes rose spectacularly during the 1990s, social services (such as health and education) tended to decline, and the income and other inequalities between the disadvantaged (meaning Israeli Arabs, religious Jews, and Mizrahi Jews) and the high-tech managers and professionals also grew. Liberalism's "success" has meant the demise of the Israeli version of the Welfare State.

Finally, given the success of this liberal discourse, Shafir and Peled also see the possible successful emergence of an Israeli version of a "civil society"— that is, a multiculturalist vision in which Israel would no longer be a "Jewish State", but instead will evolve into a "state of all its citizens", Jews and Arabs, Christians as well as Reform-Jews. This is, of course, the current left-radical slogan, and even though the ethno-nationalist and republican discourses continue to have wide support, their argument is that this may be the path of the future, the trajectory that the society is following.

Contrasting Visions?

My interest in the two new sociologies of Israel is not to critique their overall agendas or question the theory that each has adopted. Rather, I turn to them as a vehicle for examining the widespread feeling that "something has gone wrong" in contemporary Israeli society. What do they tell us about the present maladies?

Before that, though, we might rightfully ask: Would any Israeli, or anyone familiar with Israeli society, actually recognize Israel in the analyses presented in these two studies? For example, is the emphasis upon Israeli militarism as widespread as Kimmerling claims? Palestinians, who certainly are familiar with Israeli society, would undoubtedly agree, and not a few Israelis would also concur. But does this emphasis not reduce the greater social and cultural complexity to one or two presumed primordial fixations? Just as in a functional theory, in which everything can be "explained" once one accepts the basic assumptions, so too putting "militarism" at the core too easily "explains" anything that is not patently militaristic.[5] Similarly, how widespread is the kind of "cool liberalism" that Shafir and Peled attribute to the present-day scene? Those familiar with Israeli life will recognize the daily "hot" melodrama of unfolding public events: where exactly are these reasoned, dispassionate sensibilities located? Are the frail liberal institutions not in danger of being overwhelmed by a growing nationalist-religious-mystical chauvinism? These emphases, as expressed in both studies, may be overstated. Nonetheless, both studies succeed in presenting original, broad-scaled and reliable analyses of the current shape of the society and its internal dynamics.

While each of these books begins at the same point and follows a similar overall scenario, at the end they arrive at significantly different conclusions. There are no big differences in their representation of the Jewish pre-1948 society—in both studies the Zionist Ashkenazi pioneers are seen to be intrusive colonists on the way to forming a settler state that excluded Palestinians, and while there are nuances of difference both also trace the ways in which Labor forged its long-lasting hegemony. Similarly, Kimmerling and Shafir-Peled shed no tears over Labor's subsequent demise. They also devote chapters to the same major Israeli social groups—Mizrahim, Arabs, orthodox religious Jews, the recent waves of Russian and Ethiopian immigrants, foreign workers—and while their terms of analysis are different, in general they tell much the same story about each of the groups.

What is more, they both claim that Israel's 1967 territorial expansion was the big event that initiated "the society's transformation". Both studies emphasize the "transformation" that took place in the 1970s, and each traces the changes that subsequently took place as a result of colonization of the West Bank and the continuing violence between Israel and the Palestinians. However, what is different is their interpretation of the directions, or the implications, of this transformation. These differences are crucial, and they bring us directly to this essay's core issues: how do Kimmerling and Shafir-Peled explain the sources of Israel's present discontent?

If I read him correctly, Kimmerling's thesis is that Israel's expansion into the West Bank and Gaza brought about a deep cultural transformation in which the state became ever-more splintered, and increasingly nationalistic, militarist and fundamentalist. But this is only the "immediate cause": the major flaw is much deeper and extends back a century earlier to the origins of Zionism, Jewish settlement in Palestine, and the original "invention of Israeliness". From the very beginning, planting a Jewish immigrant- colonist society in Palestine could only result in bloody Jewish-Arab conflicts, deep internal divisions between opposed ideological and other camps, and as a result the inability to successfully resolve fundamental issues. The post-1967 occupation simply intensified the internal divisions and brought them to the surface. What is more, settler states such as Israel are inevitably nationalist and militaristic, and the particular notion of a state that is "Jewish and democratic" is false since these are inherently contradictory terms.

In addition, there does not appear to be any way to genuinely alter these circumstances—the mutual nationalist and religious-fed hate is too deeply rooted—and consequently there is not much to be done. Kimmerling leaves little room for different choices or different leaderships—what in the current jargon is sometimes called "human agency"—that might influence and alter the tragic course of events. New political constellations may come and go, new leaders on both sides may adopt different policies, economies expand and undergo crises—but the fundamental dilemma remains unchanged. Indeed, the sins are original, and, sadly perhaps, Israel's cultural transformations and present-day character are the result of inevitable historic processes and circumstances.The conclusion is therefore inescapable: *nothing went wrong, since nothing was ever right.*

Shafir-Peled's interpretation is considerably different. As we know, they do not argue that the Israeli past was better or held greater promise then the present. The "fatal error"(my term, not theirs) occurred in 1967 with the occupation of the West Bank and Gaza, the subsequent establishment of Jewish settlements there, and the formation of an exploitative Israeli regime that imposed military control over the Palestinian population. This is "what went wrong"—and yet, these events and others are part of broad historical processes that are influenced from both within and without. As seen from the late 1990s, they argue that "the conflict" is in the process of becoming resolved, and, partly as a result, that the society is evolving in the direction of greater "liberalism" and openness. In other words, Shafir-Peled's position is that societal structures and historical circumstances are not fixed and final, but rather more open and changing: different choices have been made, "human agency" has (for many different reasons) selected new policies and directions, and consequently the third or fourth generation of Jewish settler-colonists, and the Palestinian minority in Israel together with Palestinians on the West Bank, need not endlessly be locked into violence. Their conclusion therefore is that while the occupation was a "fatal error", Israeli society may be moving towards rectifying it. Israel is fast becoming a "nation like other nations", part of the contemporary global economic and international political system, and therefore influenced by the forces that the global world is uncertainly traveling along.

Both of these interpretations are problematic. Looking back, there are too many paths not taken, too many opportunities missed by both Palestinians and Israelis, that might have reduced if not resolved our conflict. Surely this is tragic (an understatement!)—but neither fated nor inevitable. In this regard I find Kimmerling's conclusions unconvincing. On the other hand, the terrible, useless cycle of mutual violence and killing continues, and Shafir-Peled's claim that it was about to be reduced or ended is, unfortunately, overly optimistic. Writing in the midst of fast-changing events is obviously perilous, and they are not to be faulted for building upon events and decisions that subsequently crumbled (the Oslo accords, Taba negotiations, al-aksa intifada, and more). Their contention that the "Israeli business community" took the lead in pressing for peace is questionable. It is not clear that this group (whoever they may be) has much influence over the really major issues of peace and war. But this is a relatively minor matter, and their overall tracing of trends seems closer to the mark.[6]

Looking Back—and Ahead

So, what did go wrong? Having made use of the two new sociologies of Israel as a springboard, what conclusions can be drawn?

To put it simply, my own sense is that "the transformation" derives from Israel's occupation of the West Bank and Gaza, and that the corrupting processes that were then set-off have inevitably produced destructive changes within Israeli society itself. There is no such thing as a "humane occupation", as many Israelis once mistakenly referred to the conquest of the Palestinian territories, and violence over the Green Line inevitably has the result of encouraging violence (plus a great deal more) within Israel itself. It is idle to conjecture what Israel would be like today had the West Bank and other territories not been colonized; but different chains of events would have been set-off, and we would have missed being entrapped, as we continue to be, in downward spirals of violence that lead nowhere. For example, the huge expenditures (lasting a third of a century!) that have been wasted in security fences and endless West Bank "by-pass roads" might better have been invested in improving all levels of education and building a decent infrastructure. We might have been spared the kind of crooked nationalism, confounding so-called patriotism with mystical religious symbols, that periodically engulfs us.

It seems to me too, that the continuation of "the conflict" is not inevitable, and that, to the contrary, Palestinians and Israelis may one day agree to scale down the current terrible hostilities. When that day will finally come is hard to know, and, writing in the summer of 2004, it is all too clear that it has not yet arrived. To be sure, it will require deep compromises on both sides, as well as the understanding that pushing one side into a corner will only prolong the agonies. Paradoxically, while the violence has increased the mutual hate and suspicion, both Palestinians and Israelis have moved closer to a more realistic recognition and understanding of each other. Not that they have come to admire or empathize with "the other": the opposite is undoubtedly true. But many have concluded that they will not be able to "get on with it" until the conflict is finally controlled or ended. The issues are hugely complex and entangled, but the "sins are not original", and, as in other recent seemingly insoluble problem-areas (South Africa, Ireland and even Bosnia come to mind) it may be possible to achieve some measure of mutually agreed upon resolution. If Israeli colonization is at the heart of "what went wrong", then, with all of the difficulties involved, an agreement that would remove the settlements, deal with the refugee issues, establish a Palestinian state and draw borders between it and Israel, may still be possible. Such an agreement would not spell the end of hostilities "for all time", but it obviously would have an enormous positive effect.

This does not mean, of course, that other aspects of the current malaise—for example, the emphasis upon power in a wide range of issues and encounters, widening economic and social inequalities, growing evidence of corruption in public affairs-- would then automatically disappear. These and other maladies are undoubtedly connected to "the conflict", but they also have their own separate sources. For example, the turn to a more market-oriented economy may have strengthened "the liberal discourse", but it also has led to significantly greater inequality and to an oligarchy composed of super-wealthy families and their political cronies. On the other hand, without an understanding or agreement with the Palestinians none of the other afflictions will be repaired.

There is another piece in this puzzle that should be added. Let me put it this way: In analyzing the contemporary Israeli scene, where is the Likud political party to be located? Historically nationalist, expansionist and anti-Labor--the party of Begin, Shamir, Netanyahu, Sharon and their many supporters--the Likud has been the dominant Israeli political party during the past quarter-century. How does this enter into an understanding of "what went wrong"?

Surprisingly, the change in regime that began in 1977 is not critically acknowledged or addressed in recent social science research. The two new Israeli sociologies well-illustrate this point. For example, it is hard to know where to place the Likud and its supporters in Kimmerling's division of contemporary Israeli society into "seven cultures". These include "the previously hegemonic secular Ashkenazi upper middle class, the national religious... the traditionalist Mizrahim", and several others. While it is clear that Labor and other "Left" adherents belong to the first culture, where do the Likud leadership, activists and their supporters belong? In effect, their role and influence as the dominant party is given little significance in his analysis. Even though they are more explicit, the same can be said regarding Shafir-Peled's presentation. They relate the facts and some of the implications of the Likud's coming to power—and yet they devote much more space and energy to the analysis of Labor's demise and the subsequent emergence of competing "citizenship discourses". For example, in a chapter titled "Agents of Political Change", they present a lengthy, detailed description of "new liberal circles" within the Labor Party-- but at no point is there a parallel consideration of shifting ideologies and group formations within the Likud Party. It is as if the post- 1977 Likud regime were a phantom, hardly existing, and that (as the old

Israeli saying goes), for many Israelis "Labor is still in power", and, if anything goes wrong, "Shimon Peres is probably to blame"!

Let me be clear: I am not arguing that the Likud party's ascent to power is "what went wrong". That is much too simplistic. And yet, it does seem to me that the growth of a nationalist, populist and "Jewish" political-cultural viewpoint is closely connected with the Likud's by now lengthy reign. To be sure, Labor and Likud have joined together in several "National Unity Governments", and they share, among other things, an emphasis upon the use of military power as a means to "solve the conflict". Nevertheless, the Likud Party and its political allies have maintained the policies of continued occupation, and, at the least, an analysis of their policies and organization is a requirement for understanding present-day Israel.

Is there any way out of the present impasse? Has Israeli society--tired, confused and deeply divided-- the inner resources required to reconstruct itself? There can be no certainty that the malaise will not simply continue. However, there are instances in which societies worn down by violence and division are able to reconstruct themselves. Ireland, which seems to be blooming, may be such an instance, and some of the post-Communist Central European states may be another. There surely are many signs of renewed energy in present day Israel; the arts appear to be flourishing (either because or despite "the situation"), for example, and there are many instances of creative local initiatives. Hopefully, we may yet arrive at the moment when we can sit back and consider "what went right".

Notes

[1] My thanks to several persons who commented on previous versions of this article.

[2] The problem of "what went wrong" is examined , or alluded to, in a number of earlier studies. For example, in his 1985 *The Transformation of Israeli Society: An Essay in Interpretation*, Eisenstadt argues that "the disintegration of initial institutional molds" (p. 401), and the exhaustion of the "regnant ideology", brought about deep changes in the society. This view is expanded in greater detail in Horowitz and Lissak's 1989 *Trouble in Utopia: The Overburdened Polity of Israel*. Writing after the ascendance of the Likud Party to power, and in the midst of the Palestinian intifada, they make the case that Israel became a "multi-cleavage society" in which the "social system is overburdened" and unable to resolve basic issues ("The story of Israeli society is flawed fulfillment") (p. 231). Taking a much different view, Carmi and Rosenfeld have also sought to explain the society's transformation. Their argument, detailed in a series of lengthy articles, is that the establishment of the state in 1948 was the "critical moment", and that the long-reigning Mapai regime deliberately turned away from forming what might have been a socialist state and society. In their view the turn towards "statism" set-off the processes of nationalism and militarism that continue to the present.

[3] There is by now an entire literature written by the "new sociologists", and also rejoinders by their critics. These include, for example, Uri Ram's *The Changing Agenda of Israeli Sociology: Theory, Ideology and Identity* ; Laurence Silberstein , *The Post Zionism Debate: Knowledge and Power in Israeli Culture;* and Moshe Lissak, " 'Critical Sociology' and 'Establishment Sociology' in the Israeli Academic Community: Ideological Struggles or Academic Discourse?".

[4] Several important sociological studies of Israel do not fall into this "generational" grouping. For example, Judith Shuval's early work on immigrant absorption, and her later studies of social medicine, provide a different, more empirically grounded analysis. Eva Etzioni-Halevy has also written broad- scaled analyses of Israeli political culture. Elia Zureik's studies of Israeli society, especially with reference to Arab-Jewish relations, develops an analysis mainly from the theoretical perspective of "internal colonialism".

[5] One example is the apparent interest on the part of many Israelis in "Eastern cultures". This takes the form of repeated trips to India, Thailand and Nepal, as well as a concern with Eastern music, dance and religious "mysticism". Many of those who take part are youngsters after their army service, but this "discovery of the East" also includes middle aged and older Israelis. The question is, how should this "cultural fact" or phenomenon be interpreted? Following Kimmerling, the answer would be that this is a reaction or counter to local Israeli "militarism". And yet it undoubtedly is much more complex, including the appeal of "the exotic", a search for other understandings, and considerably more.

[6] The two studies also differ with regard to their wider contexts: Kimmerling focuses entirely upon events as they unfold in Palestine-Israel, while Shafir-Peled occasionally place local events into a wider "world-system" focus. The latters'argument regarding the strengthening of the "liberal discourse" rests heavily upon the intrusive power of world-wide processes, and, in particular, economic globalization. For example, their claim that the "opening" or liberalization of the Israeli economy came about since it was a requirement for taking part in the world economy, is undoubtedly correct. More questionable is the contention that the 1980s emergence to political prominence of Shas was linked to the worsening situation of Israeli low-income groups resulting from globalization, and, as noted, that the Israeli interest in the 1990s "Oslo peace process" came about as a result of the Israeli business community's conclusion that peace was a prerequisite for taking part in the new high-tech global economy. Shas's great success during the 1980s and later has much more to do with latent ethnic tensions and clever leadership then with sudden economic deprivation. Regarding the "business community" and the peace process, were they such a powerful force, then why did these "economic elites" not exercise greater pressures as the conflict grew in intensity following 2001? In these instances, the analysis may conform with the authors' theory or perspective, but their explanation is not convincing.

References

Carmi, Shulamit, and Henry Rosenfeld. 1989. "The Emergence of Militaristic National-ism in Israel", *The International Journal of Politics, Culture and Society*, Vol. 3, pp. 5-49.

Eisenstadt, S.N. 1985. *The Transformation of Israeli Society: An Essay in Interpretation.* Boulder: Westview Press.

Etzioni-Halevy, Eva, with Rina Shapira. 1977. *Political Culture in Israel: Cleavage and Integration among Israeli Jews.* New York: Praeger.

Horowitz, Dan and Lissak, Moshe. 1989. *Trouble in Utopia: The Overburdened Polity of Israel.* Albany: State University of New York Press.

Kimmerling, Baruch. 2001. *The Invention and Decline of Israeliness: State, Society and the Military.* Berkeley: University of California Press.

Lissak, Moshe. 1996. "Critical Sociology" and "Establishment Sociology" in the Israeli Academic Community: Ideological Struggles or Academic Discourse", *Israel Studies* *1*, 247-294.

Ram, Uri. 1995. *The Changing Agenda of Israeli Sociology: Theory, Ideology, and Identity.* Albany: State University of New York Press.

Rosenfeld, Henry and Carmi, Shulamit. 1976. The Privatization of Public Means, The State-Made Middle Class, and the Realization of Family Value in Israel, in: J.G. Istiany, Ed. *Kinship and Modernization in Mediterranean Societies.* Rome: American Universities Field Staff.

Shafir, Gershon. 1996. *Land, Labor and the Origins of the Israeli-Palestinian Conflict, 1882-1914.* Berkeley: University of California Press.

Shafir, Gershon, and Peled, Yoav. 2002. *Being Israeli: The Dynamics of Multiple Citizenship.* New York: Cambridge University Press.

Shuval, Judith. 1963. *Immigrants on the Threshold* New York: Atherton Press.

Silberstein, Laurence. 1998. *The Post-Zionism Debate: Knowledge and Power in Israeli Culture.* New York: Routledge.

Zureik, Elias. 1979. *The Palestinians in Israel, A Study in Internal Colonialism.* London: Routledge

A Talk with Henry

Zvi Sobel

As Henry Rosenfeld enters his ninth decade, it is clear that a radical critique of what has emerged here in Israel in societal and political terms lies at the core of his life's work. His writing revolves almost exclusively around issues such as the 1948 refugees, Arab-Jewish relationships, Palestinian society, political economy in Israel, and the struggle over the identity of the State with regard to the place of socialism as against capitalism. His interest in these questions did not derive from a series of dusty propositions accumulated through gaps in the literature produced by predecessors or colleagues in the discipline, but from life lived among real people with real fates. It is work, which above all, is characterized by a deep commitment to an overarching humanism, and a sense of certainty that things could and should be "made right"; that equality and justice should be sought, that history is not blind determinism but rather a work in progress – the creation of thinking men and women rather than uncontrolled forces. To those who know him, as well as to those who are familiar with his work it is evident that Henry Rosenfeld has a guiding impulse, a world view and it is that of a socialist and a humanist who has managed to achieve a striking and superb degree of balance and integration between the two. His socialism places him in a Marxist materialist tradition which is framed always against a matrix of deep sympathy for the wounded and ill-dealt with of this world.

The fact that it was Israel which became the theatre and the subject of his life's work was, if one is to accept Rosenfeld's own explanation, an accident. As he tells it, he came to Palestine in 1946 nine months after his discharge from the U.S. Army for which he had volunteered in 1942. He left University (NYU) about a year before finishing his degree managing to complete his studies at the end of the war after which he boarded ship for Palestine. Why Palestine? Was Rosenfeld a Zionist? An adventurer? A lost soul finding it difficult to re-adjust to civilian life? I can assert with a certain amount of surety and after some thirty years of friendship with the man that none of the possibilities alluded to above provide an answer. He is not and was not a Zionist in any conventional sense of the term: neither a political Zionist nor a cultural Zionist. Neither was he an adventurer, nor was he troubled by a renewal of his civilian status. About the best that can be ascertained regarding his coming to Palestine is that somehow the fact that Palestine was becoming perhaps *the* singular place of refuge for the survivors of the holocaust focused both his sympathy and his interest.

While much that happens to all of us in life can be attributed to "accident", or was unintended, or poorly thought out beforehand, one could nonetheless assert that even accidents have reasons, though often not understood.

Rosenfeld's life in the United States as the younger of two sons in a fairly assimilated middle class family did not in any way suggest pre-state Palestine as a likely destination or goal. His home was not Zionist, or for that matter particularly "Jewish" in orientation and to this day Rosenfeld's ties to Judaism are, at best, tenuous, although a similar distance can be discerned with respect to all manifestations of religion of whatever type or persuasion. In this he shares the self-description of Max Weber, who describes himself as "religiously unmusical", notwithstanding, at least in Weber's case, a life-long involvement with the phenomenon. Retaining a kind of religious virginity or at least innocence while growing up on the Upper West Side of Manhattan, though easier in the 1930s and 40s than it would be today, represented nonetheless something of a victory of will over presumed destiny. Henry has managed to hold aloft the banner of this victory in a wry and thoroughly combative fashion till this very day.

These two questions of how and why a young man with only the most conventional and un-self selected ties to Judaism and the Jewish community, a thorough-going ignorance of and non-commitment to Zionism, a budding and growing involvement with socialism – and specifically its universalist dimensions – not only decided to come to Palestine but also to volunteer and participte in Israel's War of Independence, holds a certain fascination. Perhaps it was as with Freud who when asked what part being Jewish played in his life is reputed to have answered – "Very little – just the most important part". Or perhaps, as suggested earlier, it can be explained as a visceral response to the near-victory of fascism and the horrors of the holocaust, with Palestine-Israel being viewed not only as a refuge for the survivors, but as a victory, a poetic *and* practical victory against the forces of powerful evil.

Ultimately, however, one must accept the subjective perception that a strong element of "the accidental" played a role in what was to become a key life decision for Henry Rosenfeld when he boarded ship for Palestine in 1946 – even if the accidental had, in the final analysis, "legs".

It is here in Israel that Henry Rosenfeld married, became the father of four children, built his life both inside and outside the academy and made, as many others can attest – a difference. He made a difference in two ways which in the final analysis must be seen as being deeply connected. The first is his contribution as a scholar and teacher who has addressed in both his writing *and* teaching some of the most significant issues confronting Israeli society. Most of this body of work holds existential implications for those of us who live here and are part of this society, but in addition his work provides a number of intellectual signposts bearing a more universal dimension. It can safely be said that none of his work can be viewed as "filler", as academic muscle-flexing or as being in anyway trivial. Secondly, he has given us an example in his life as lived of what being a humanist is about, of what it means in the most grounded sense. It is not, in Henry's way, an ontological system nor any other formalistic undertaking where A leads to B resulting in a mechanistically derived C. It involves always, again following Weber, "a sympathetic understanding" of that which is being studied or observed. Probably a simpler and more accurate way of putting it would be to say that Rosenfeld follows and is committed both in his life and his work to a concept of some antiquity and very little academic cachet known as Menshlichkeit – or being a "mentsch".

What follows in "A Talk with Henry" is essentially a conversation, or more correctly a series of conversations we conducted over the period of a few months. The aim was to "cover" some of the recurrent themes in both his life and his work, which as it turns out, are interlinked and largely inseparable. Our conversation includes bits and pieces of biography as well as observations about the development of Anthropology as a discipline here in Israel, the kibbutz, socialism and inescapably – the Arabs. In our talks we have chosen (or perhaps just found ourselves doing this) to move in and out of areas of interest so that while talking about kibbutz, for example, some observations might be made about communism and the fate of the Soviet Union, or even the study of Anthropology. No attempt was made to compartmentalize the material or to encapsulate the discussion in a systematic way. Certain themes are returned to over and over again – occasionally because we two old-timers forgot that we had already dealt with them and at other times because we felt that a second (or third) go-around was warranted.

It is, when all is said and done, largely a conversation (sometimes contentious) between two old friends and colleagues, who often don't see eye to eye but who hopefully share not only a universe of discourse but a high degree of mutual respect and affection.

Zvi: I would like to begin by asking you to try to place yourself somehow in terms of your early concerns and the major influences in your life. Who, for example, were your early intellectual mentors?

Henry: [In college]... I was reading literature, mainly literature. I can't say that I was firmly into history or political works. I considered myself a socialist, I considered myself maybe even someone who was close to Marxism, but I don't think I knew very much. I was young. But I can say there were people, probably people I have forgotten about, who had an impact and I had a number of teachers who certainly impressed me. One of these was Sidney Hook.

Zvi: I take it Hook did not please you.

Henry: No, that isn't true. I was absolutely impressed, but I wasn't knowledgeable enough to fully benefit from the experience. It's nothing that at that time I could come to grips with, that I could entertain arguments let's say with someone at the level of Hook. I also had a very fine history teacher, who taught ancient history, a fine workshop in writing, and others. And there were people like that who certainly impressed me, educated me.... But clearly in terms of your question, there were a number of men and women, who had this kind of personal impact, and probably gave me a certain kind of direction. A young person going to college in the Greenwich Village area learns quickly. At the time I thought I was going into a writing career. I think mainly I thought about journalism, and actually worked on a newspaper in Bayonne, New Jersey for a period of time.

Zvi: Did the Jewish question concern you in any way at that time?

Henry: No, no. The Jewish question didn't concern me. It only concerned me, later, in terms of what happened to the Jews. This certainly had an impact on me, but I should think that there are other things that had an impact on me just at the same time. For example, the dropping of the atom bomb on Hiroshima and Nagasaki certainly had a tremendous impact on me.

Zvi: You were aghast.

Henry: Of course.

Zvi: Not so "of course". Remember at that time where we were and who we were.

Henry: Okay, I was knowledgeable enough at least to think that the reason that the bomb was dropped was not simply to terminate the war as quickly as possible; that was certainly a justification that was used, but among other things, I should think that the idea of forestalling the Russians from entering the war against Japan was a much sharper reason. And perhaps worse, the U.S. government was making a statement that it held this awful power and could use it.

Zvi: But the Russians did enter the war against Japan.

Henry: Yes, but not really, not in the full sense. They just terminated the war and placed the United States Government in the controlling position in Japan, and not Russia. One of the things I think that affected me was John Hersey's book, *Hiroshima*, and I won't say that I shuddered or trembled, but certainly it's one of the things that definitely educated me, educated me at that point in time. Speaking about the Jewish question, I became, let's say, alert as to what happened to the Jews through reading I.F. Stone, and reading other things which were contemporary, which weren't involved in understanding Jewry as an ongoing historical development, but rather what it meant to be a Jew, and why it meant something to be a Jew in contemporary terms. Personally, I had two things in mind. I wanted to help bring Jewish refugees to Palestine (and here the I.F. Stone influence), and I wanted to see socialism in action, which was my understanding of the kibbutz.

Zvi: I didn't understand what you said a moment ago. Did you say that you *were* beginning to think about what it means to be a Jew, and the nature of being a Jew?

Henry: Yes, I did. As things became clear to me, I had to think about choices and what I wanted and what I wanted to do. I was looking for something active. I wanted to play some kind of part. Maybe that's one of the reasons that brought me to Palestine. There were other factors, personal, and individual ....

Zvi: Was there any element of accident involved in your decision to go to Palestine?

Henry: Only in a sense. Equally, I could have remained in New York with friends, study, and so on. The opportunity turned up, and the possibility of using the G.I. Bill to study in Palestine was a formal link. It wasn't only an opportunity for me. There were others who opted for this course, even though I didn't know it at the time. I went by myself. On the boat I made friends with David Brodsky, a man with fluent Hebrew, who had gotten out of Warsaw and reached the States before the outbreak of the war with Japan. We went from kibbutz to kibbutz for about six weeks and then to Jerusalem where, with about fifteen other ex-G.I.s on the G.I. bill, we were quartered, through the Hebrew University, at a pension. Most of us studied Hebrew – of which I didn't now a word – and joined the Haganah.

Zvi: Let me jump back for a minute and ask a hypothetical question that probably is unanswerable, but maybe you've played with it once or twice: Had you stayed in America, what would have been your relationship to being Jewish to being in the Jewish Community, or identifying as a Jew. Do you have any idea how this would have played out?

Henry: It would have played out certainly in reference to what had taken place with the Jews – what was taking place in Palestine. It's difficult for me to think back in terms of how alert I was prior to that; let's say, during the period of time that I was in college. You have to understand that going to college and also at my age – I was sixteen when I entered – also meant this constant involvement with other people, generally older people. You go around, you share thoughts but not in the Jewish community as such although most of my friends were Jewish. I doubt if I would have taken part in the Jewish community in any formal sense. I was a political young person and I've remained on the radical left. I'm an atheist who was always alert to being a Jew and acting on it. I would have fitted in as probably many of my later-to-be buddies fitted in, and that is to say, I began a program of studies. I became an anthropologist which involved many different things. So let's say when I went to study anthropology, I had a focus, a different kind of involvement, and I had to invest my time and my effort in learning. This would have taken me away, if I had remained in the States, certainly, from things that I got involved with when I came to Palestine, and then my future in Palestine and Israel.

Zvi: You think your Jewish connection would have been that of an enlightened third-generation American, academic...?

Henry: It would have depended on what kind of work I did, what kind of research I did.... I could have gone to dozens of different places, and might well have.

Zvi: You mean other than America and Palestine?

Henry: Other than to Palestine, and then to Israel. In September-October 1947, that is, after a year in Palestine, I returned to the States, and I returned to the States with a wife, my then wife. And I began to study anthropology, probably through the influence of a boyhood buddy of mine.

Zvi: Who was this?

Henry: This was Stan Diamond. Stan wanted me to study anthropology. He had already begun anthropology. That is, my age group all began their anthropology studies in 1946 when I went to Palestine. People like Stan, Eric Wolf, Mort Fried, who became dear friends – began their studies then. (By the way, no one called me Henry. I was Hank, not only to my friends, but even to my parents). Then when I came back, in 1947 I started studying anthropology

Zvi: Where did you start studying anthropology?

Henry: At Columbia.   Stan introduced me to Gene Weltfish, and Gene
encouraged me. Stan then dropped out for two years because he was married
and had a kid, and he wasn't on the G.I. Bill. I started studying, then the war
broke out in Palestine, and so I dropped my studies and I returned to
Palestine, Palestine which then became Israel.   So I only studied
anthropology for a month or two…

Zvi: During the war here did you have any engagements that you were involved
in?

Henry: Nothing really serious. I started in Machal (foreign volunteers), enlisted
in the Palmach and was then switched to the Air Force as were most U.S.
citizens who volunteered. This came from above. I became the Signals
Officer for Squadron 101, after a couple of months in the Negev. I returned
to the States in 1949 to continue my studies. I studied from 1949 till 1951,
essentially for two years, during which time I got my doctorate. I did a
library research project; that is, I didn't do field work as most
anthropologists and many of my peers did to get their degree. Among my
classmates are friends I can mention: Zachary Gussow, Vera Rubin, Bob
Stigler, Jules Rabin, Bob Murphy, Sally Falk, Eleanor Leacock and many
others.

Zvi: What did you do your thesis on?

Henry: On the caste system in the Arabian Desert which was sort of an original
piece of research. That is, other people had drawn attention to the fact that
there were caste-like groups in the Arabian Desert, but I think I gave it its
explanation, an analysis of the internal processes involved, and distinguished
the different groups within the Arabian Desert.

Zvi: Did you come right back to Palestine-Israel, or Israel at this stage?
Immediately following your degree?

Henry: After my degree I came back immediately.

Zvi: And what was bringing you back. What did you intend doing here? The
war was over.

Henry: The war was over. I had a wife, and by that time a child – Ron was born
at that time. I suppose there were a couple of things. I had never really lived
on a kibbutz for a long period of time. And I thought of going back to doing
research on the kibbutz. Of course my wife wanted to return to her family
there, and she was very happy with the idea. I got a grant from the Social
Science Research Council. I got a joint grant with Stan Diamond, and we
even bought a car together, and we got on the boat with our families. This
was in the summer of 1951. I should think it was in the late summer… Stan
went to Kiryat Anavim – that's where he worked, and I shopped around for
awhile but ended up at Ein Harod. For the first several months, I worked on
the kibbutz and this was very tough. It was tougher working for weeks on
end, and after a period of time, I saw that a participant-observer was one
thing, but the business of being a full time participant was out of the
question. I couldn't do it. If by that time I weighed 140, I went down to 130
pounds, something like that. It was exhausting. It was terribly difficult, but

I began to appreciate Ein Harod, and I began to appreciate the people at Ein Harod, the level of the place. From almost every stand point I was totally impressed – from child care to dining rooms, to the level of the cow sheds, the level of industrial plants, to the art museum, to the nature museum, the very high intellectual level of many many people.

Zvi: What about interrelationships?

Henry: I became dear friends with many people. Friendships that have lasted more or less to this day taking into consideration that many in my age group, and those who were older are no longer around. I was particularly attached to the older generation – I mean there's a generation my age, but the older generation was particularly impressive. Ein Harod is the oldest big kibbutz in the country – 1920-21 was when it was founded so there were people who came to Ein Harod who brought children with them, people who were born there – they were my age, or a couple of years older.

Zvi: And this is the generation that you found most contact with? The ones of your age, or their parents?

Henry: With both.

Zvi: Were they all auto-didacts?

Henry: Several of course were a combination. There were people – dozens and dozens who finished secondary school or its equivalent. You have to understand that it was a much higher level than our high schools in the States, and they maybe had a year or two of university, but their intellectual involvement flourished also because of belonging to youth and political movements, and also because of a deep sense of mission that they were imbued with. I found among them a great deal of sophistication of thought. When I have to consider a span of life that involved let's say, two key generations – that is the parental generation and their children, certainly the interaction, the purposeful interaction between the parental generation and their children was tremendous.

Zvi: I'm not sure I follow what you mean by "purposeful interaction". Everybody has purposeful interaction.

Henry: No. There's a difference. I think I stated it correctly. While parents all over the world are concerned about their children, I think, generally speaking, in the immigrant society, or the modern society in which we grew up – you and I – there was a separation between the parental generation and our generation. I don't know about you but my parents, for example, had a couple of years of high school at best. I know other people whose parents were lawyers and doctors. But, generally speaking, middle class Jews in America wanted successful careers for their children, careers that moved them beyond their parents. But here, in Ein Harod, let's say there was a totally joint enterprise. The involvement was a mutual involvement of growing up in order to achieve certain purposes, in order to see that there would be a continuity in the kibbutz, and therefore the input of the parental generation towards their children was different.

Zvi: That the parental generation would have provided this kind of input makes sense to me. How do you explain the response of the receiving generation?

It seems to be a widespread phenomenon, certainly in Western civilization, that there is dissonance between children and their parents, either on a psychological Freudian level, or on an existential level. How do you explain this business of the children buying in so solidly to the vision of the fathers?

Henry: I have to sort of bring it back to facts on the ground – that is, many many different things were happening just at this time which maybe in part speaks to the question you raise. First of all, when I got to Ein Harod in 1951, this was only 2 years after the 1948-49 war. Several young men from Ein Harod were killed in the war.   And this is not only simply a heart-breaking situation which exists all over the world where there is war, but on top of what happened to Jewry under Nazism, on top of that the 1948 war was fought in Israel – on these grounds, and there were those who were killed in the valley, some in Emek Yisrael, others around Jerusalem and elsewhere.   So what I'm also trying to say is that in terms of the fact that there's one generation that's trying to raise another generation, to something which is novel, which raises questions such as how to develop a commune and how to live communally? How to do it? And as I say, the material at Ein Harod was extraordinary in certain respects, human and ordinary in others, but nevertheless there was no pattern from which to take direction.   There was nothing really to copy from, nothing really to guide them.   There's a certain logic in life and the commune is an idea, it's an ideal.   Where you raise your children [you have to think about] how they're going to sleep, where you're going to eat... All these things. You see the end product, but how you get from the beginning to the end, you don't see until you do some history, or you live the thing through by yourself. Most important, two generations of active people, the sons and daughters often with greater local skills, but both generations of educated workers.

Zvi: It's interesting. It sounds like you're describing a pattern that could have resulted in mass desertion on the part of the second generation, but it didn't, it did the opposite.

Henry: Yes and no. You have to think of the thousands – I don't know what the numbers are; at one time I tried to work this out, but maybe even tens of thousands of people went through kibbutzim, who went *through* kibbutzim, so you have to figure that also happened in Ein Harod.   And you have to remember that in Ein Harod there was a split that resulted in numbers going to Tel Yosef, and then there was this whole group that returned to Russia, a group which lost faith in the enterprise here. Moreover, when I came to Ein Harod, it was in the throes of a split, a division within Ein Harod. Ein Harod belonged to the Kibbutz Hameuchad, and after the split there were two Ein Harods – Ein Harod Hameuchad, and Ein Harod Ichud.   They split in half totally.   And in some cases parents on one side and children on the other. The split, basically, was over differences on socialism and differences in political party positions that then reverberated into all spheres of life. And this went through the entire kibbutz movement bringing us to one Ein Harod on top of the hill, and one below – two separate places; you can understand something about the despair which set in.

Zvi: Perhaps here we see the seeds of disorganization and the unraveling process: a breach between the generations.

Henry: No, I don't think so. It was a complex political situation. Think of the situation as it exists today where the kibbutz is in shreds and a younger generation has defected.

Zvi: It's not only the kibbutz.

Henry: Exactly. And these are the things that have to be explained, but it's not a thing between parents and children – it's what happens to parents and children under certain circumstances. The unraveling is a total historic, fifty-year, Israeli process.

Zvi: You clearly see in the kibbutz a really great success story of human interaction, this business of parents and children as it were, all on the same wave length. A sense of continuity developing between them.

Henry: I don't have the slightest doubt about it.

Zvi: We talked about Spiro, who in his books on the kibbutz had developed a conflict model as a backdrop for the development of certain aspects of the kibbutz.

Henry: Conflict between the generations?

Zvi: Yes, and what you suggested as a fascinating dimension of the kibbutz story was the sense of continuity between parents and children, and of the carrying forward by the second generation of the visions and dreams that almost seem to be co-developed with the younger generation.

Henry: Okay, listen, you comment also about the fact that there's something haphazard in life in the sense that people don't always know what they're doing, and there is some sense of confusion. The thing I wanted to say is that there were so many other things going on at the same time; that is, the kibbutz was so involved in the political situation and the political situation was so dominant within every form of life within the country, and it had an immense effect on the kibbutz. And the split within Ein Harod – and the split within Kibbutz Hameuchad itself, which led to dozens of kibbutzim splitting down the middle – whole groups of people moving from one kibbutz to another. And as we said previously, so many people coming to kibbutzim, going through kibbutzim, some staying, some leaving kibbutzim. And the thing that I wanted to get to really, is that the new State from 1948 on had a tremendous impact on the kibbutz. The statism that was put into practice had a tremendous impact on the kibbutz. The State as being primary and above everything else as if the State itself had economic and social and intellectual meaning in every sense of the word, as if the State explained itself. All this gave rise to tremendous internal divisions. The main effect, destructive in my opinion, was in the attack on socialism, on the socialist potential that existed in the kibbutz movements, the Histadruth, the left-wing leadership and the public it represented. The way this was intertwined with a vibrant political and intellectual culture is complex.

Zvi: You think that the State, and certainly statism, was a bad thing for the kibbutz idea? You think it's part of the root causes for the unraveling of the kibbutz or is it in the nature of things?

Henry: No, I don't think it's in the nature of things to unravel if you mean to
deteriorate. I don't think that this statism is the only factor, certainly not,
there were other prominent factors at the same time. It's a certain kind of
state dominance, which, in the process also meant the defeat of other
political and social movements.

Zvi: I think that's a very interesting observation. One of the dimensions of the
kibbutz movement is that it's very much turned in upon itself in terms of
developing the new man, in terms of pioneering visions, in terms of ethics
that were undergoing change as to the relationships between the sexes, (even
though that element is open to contention), whereas the state demanded a
loyalty that took you out of the narrow community and expanded it and
broadened it. And it could have had consequences that weren't all that
happy to the idea of kibbutz.

Henry: With kibbutzim, it's not simply a social experiment. Kibbutz is also
politics; there never was a time when kibbutz people weren't involved in the
total political context of Palestine and the kind of future they wanted in
Palestine, and therefore there were different denominations of socialism –
radical socialism, the socialism of the kibbutzim on the Left, of Mapam as a
political party, and also the so-called social democracy of Mapai, but as
these things came together under the State, Mapai, and Ben Gurion became
the dominant factors in Israeli life and of course this meant transformations.

Zvi: On the personal level were you favorably impressed by what you saw on
the kibbutz?

Henry: Very much. These were highly developed social groups, spread
throughout the country, practicing a form of socialism. People similar to me
in many respects. There were highly skilled people, men and women, who
were acquainted with the most recent advances in agriculture, who ran
factories, tractor stations, first-rate school systems, large-scale kitchens and
dining rooms, nurseries, and were key people in party politics, publishing
houses – the list goes on and on; simply running a kibbutz was a major
intellectual and physical project. Let's be clear. NOT everybody wanted to
lead a kibbutz life. Urban living represents a different life style. The thread
that linked the two was in joint political movements and in 1946-47 of
course, the underground. Almost all of them whom I met had made a
tremendous transition in their lives, and they had developed routines which
seemed to them to be, and seemed to me as well, highly worth while.

Zvi: You were a Marxist and a non-Zionist and here in the kibbutz were two
ideologically vigorous movements, or vigorous strands, Marxism and
Zionism. You were cast into this ideological cauldron – Did others try to
convince you, or you others about the merits of your respective views?

Henry: Yes and no. I very very quickly learned that there were people in
Palestine who belonged to social movements which were absolutely radical,
absolutely advanced. And actually it was people from Achdut Avodah to
whom I was more attracted. Strangely enough at the time in 1946-47 and
then through the '48 war, because I didn't really – I think I really wasn't into
'the Arab question' deeply enough. Achdut Avodah was really pointed in the

direction of delaying any idea of statehood until socialism could be developed, while people from Hashomer HaTsair emphasized bi-nationalism, and I was a bit closer to the activism of the former.

Zvi: You had this relatively rare thing, at least rare in our circles; you were in Palestine when there was no Jewish state, when it was being contended for by Arabs and Jews. Do you remember, and are you aware of a real shift in the attitude, or in the way that Arabs behaved in this period as opposed to your contacts with Arabs in the post-State period when they were a subjugated minority? In other words, was there a sense of minority that came through then.

Henry: It's clear that I didn't know enough. Probably, it's true that in one circle of friends where I had developed contacts, friends that I had made, there were people who were very active in the Jewish underground, mainly in the Palmach. And, this may have warped my vision to a certain extent. Even though I began reading whatever I could lay my hands on – I didn't search out Arabs, on a personal or an intellectual level in 1946-47. The aftermath of the 1948 war brought me to other understandings.

Zvi: Basically, you seem to have known and been in contact only with Jews at the time!

Henry: I did not have, as far as I recall, any Arab friends in any real sense of the word. Though through Arabs that I had met who had worked around Pension Pax in Jerusalem, I made some visits to Arab villages. I traveled on Arab buses, traveled to Nablus, and don't forget Jerusalem and Haifa, where I spent a lot of time, were mixed cities. And no, the Jews were the minority population.

Zvi: During this initial phase of introduction to Palestine in 1946-7, was there any figure or person that seemed to figure very prominently in terms of an influence on you? Either intellectual or social or political?

Henry: I don't think so. I mean – not at this time. True enough, through a young friend, who I was later to marry, and was an officer in the Palmach, I met and became good friends with people like Itshak Sadeh and Israel Baer; I quickly became involved in underground and political affairs. This was the way of life of an entire public. One of the things that I did learn and I can't link it to any specific person, was that there were Jewish intellectuals in the country who were at the same time activists, and this means that they were activists generally speaking either in the Underground or people who lived and worked in kibbutzim.   And this kind of combination, that is the combination of people who were either politically and militarily active, or people who were activists in a socialist sense – I think this kind of combination had a deep impact on me. I also developed a kind of a sense of people who came from European backgrounds that I really didn't know previously. That is, people who came either from Russia, from Poland, from Germany. What can I say? We were similar, and they were different at one and the same time.

Zvi: Can you characterize the difference in some way?

Henry: Well, look, the main difference was that certainly I had a place to return
to, and I was going to return to the States; and the other thing which I think
was different was that I had never really been an activist in the same sense
that they were. They were actively confronting the British, the Arabs, and
they belonged to active political circles and parties. In a small way, I became
part of that. That is, I was active, perhaps, intellectually, mentally but not in
practice as they were.

Zvi: Did you ever have a 'Eureka' experience in terms of your political,
intellectual outlook, a type of experience where somehow your eyes were
opened and you said this is the direction, this is where I'm heading, and this
is what I believe. Or was it more gradual...

Henry: I can probably say there were moments of awareness that were also a
process. I think I told you one of them was much later on when I went to
live and work in kibbutzim, and since I went to the kibbutz at the time, as a
non-Zionist, the whole experience, was once again, a built-up experience in
terms of the people I met, and the fact that somehow I grasped the
tremendous transformation that took part in their lives. That is people from
the older generation, people who came from eastern Europe, for which I had
no deep sentiment or understanding until I got to the Kibbutz, and I saw that
here these were people who left Europe in their late teens or early 20's and
went to live and work in kibbutzim in Palestine. People apparently whose
education and attempts to revolutionize their lives was also expressed in a
great change in their own personal development in the way that they saw
themselves, the way they saw their children, work and a joint enterprise, the
way they viewed the future or hoped for the future. And this kind of
combination of work – and the idea of the socialist labor movement —
people who were participating on a personal level and also within a
movement was impressive. What I want to say is that one of the things I
learned on the kibbutz was that it had many, many different facets and it was
not simply a place for drudgery – and this maybe was expressed in a place
like Ein Harod. But really I believe that it went through the entire
movement, through town and country, a concern with politics, ideas, world
relations, colonial rule, the Arabs – there was very little that was left out.
And the kibbutz in Palestine and then later on in Israel was in the forefront of
everything or at least seemed to be. However, it was not a question of
Eureka. All along, I must admit, albeit an enriching experience, I thought my
place was where I grew up.

Zvi: Aside from your description of the kibbutz and the personal influences of
people in your life, was there any critical event that determined your political
orientation at this point? World War II? The State? The depression?

Henry: These are all critical events for everybody, not only for me. It's the way
you interpret these events. That I lived through the Depression, this is a fact.
The fact that my parents were upper middle-class people, and their downfall
was immediate, practically total, this is also a fact. I think I once told you
my father was saving nickels and dimes in order to exist. The Depression
only ended with World War II and once again everybody, most middle-class

people, had a resurgence in their lives, but I don't think my parents returned to the level of the late 1920s. As to the war – everybody went through the war...

Zvi: Yes, but not everybody was seminally affected by these events.

Henry: This is quite clear. What brought me to Palestine was immediate events in terms of the fact that I was a Jew and the fact of this grotesque murder of the Jews tied as it was to fascism.

Zvi: But that didn't make you a socialist.

Henry: Socialism is also a learning process. I read a great deal in college and I had a group of radical friends, mostly older, several with political party experience. Part of it could be as emotional and as simple as people who want to find social equality which can only be arrived at, I would say in a socialist world, and a socialist society – I don't have any doubt about that at all. These are both emotional and intellectual things. The older I become, and I'm old, the more secure I've become in this kind of belief that only some form of socialism can answer the world's problems.

Zvi: Is there a model abroad that you would point to?

Henry: I don't think we need a model. What we learned for one thing is what happened with the destruction and the downfall of the Soviet Union. I certainly thought of total change in the world. I don't think that we would have anything like this Bush madness in Iraq if the Soviet Union still existed.

Zvi: So you saw the Soviet Union as a positive experiment in Socialism.

Henry: Absolutely. The fact that other things were also taking place in Soviet Russia, there was nonetheless no doubt about the fact that I was a supporter of the Soviet Union, and that I remain a supporter in the sense that this kind of historic attempt was central – there's no doubt about it. The downfall of Soviet Russia and the downfall of socialism within Russia is a tragedy. It's a worldwide tragedy.

Zvi: Who's at fault.

Henry: I think that there are two factors here. I think that the United States is probably the main factor for the downfall, and the other side is Soviet Russia itself which acquiesced in this downfall. We have to put up a struggle, in the sense of not letting something like this happen, and not only is there an internal responsibility, but the responsibility to the people of the world. How you go about something like this is beyond my capacity to answer, but there is no doubt that this is a loss. Today there is no counter to the reckless dominance of the U.S. in the world.

Zvi: Do you think that the well-documented excesses of Soviet Communism in terms of its killing of vast numbers of its opponents, the Gulag, the type of repression which existed, played a role?

Henry: Nobody who is sane can condone brutality.

Zvi: Let's talk a bit about anthropology. As you noted earlier getting into anthropology was not so much accidental as it was a group of people that you were in contact with and respected and who thought that it was a good idea and you thought maybe it wasn't a bad idea either. But were you perhaps thinking of it as a social tool or as a device for social change.

Henry: Please understand, until I entered graduate school I hadn't taken a
course in anthropology or sociology. I wanted a broad, historical perspective
and that's what I received.

Zvi: An intellectual world, not a practical political world.

Henry: An intellectual world for sure. I saw a possible future in it. Exactly
how, I didn't know, probably in teaching and research, and even though my
whole experience in studying anthropology was over a mere two year period,
during which time I also wrote my doctorate and did all my studying, it was
a clear choice. It was pretty encapsulated, and pretty intense, and maybe that
also was a factor which bound me to the discipline.

Zvi: Many of the people with whom you studied were members or close to the
communist party. Did you ever join the Party?

Henry: No

Zvi: What was the reason?

Henry: What was the reason? I was too young, I suppose, when I was a college
undergraduate. And by the time I went into the Army, got out of the Army,
went to Palestine, got back from Palestine – it's true, during that period there
were people I knew who were in the Party, and people who lost their jobs
because of it. That's also true. Nobody represented a force or a personality
that was pushing me in that direction. I'm not saying I avoided it, but I can't
answer it beyond the fact that there were other things that were happening.

Zvi: Why didn't you join the party in Israel?

Henry: I think there were probably two reasons, immediate reasons, let's say, in
1948. By the way, during the time that I was in Palestine in '46-'47, I had
already spoken to people who were in the Communist Party, and they were
people who were my age and students at the Hebrew University. Two
things: one is that during the first period of time in 1946-1947, fairly quickly
I came to the conclusion which later became firmed up for me, that the
Zionist socialist groups in Palestine at the time were certainly no less
advanced in theoretical terms; their activities were more central to what was
going on, and as I said, I had this kind of personal attraction even then for
the kibbutz. The activists, let's say in terms of people who were bringing
Jews into Palestine were in the Socialist Zionist movements, and these
people – were involved in what I wanted to be involved with – bringing
Jewish refugees to Palestine. Nevertheless, whatever role I could play along
these lines was important to me. We (the ex-G.I.s) were in the Haganah, and
among other tasks we were given, we took part in helping set up kibbutzim
in different places. For example in Gush Etzion, what is today Revidim—we
were the people who set up the perimeter fences, and that was in 1947. Then
later on when I returned during the war, I was certainly concerned about
taking part in the war. I wasn't a pacifist. For people who were in the
Communist Party this was a problem. I know people in the Party, I know the
role they played, and I have nothing against that role. I'm just talking about
myself. I also thought that the 1948 war was, on the part of the Jews, a just
war. There's this kind of combination. I also had friends who were

pacifists, and didn't take part. To be a conscientious objector is a tough road to take – they have all my respect.

Zvi: And later on, after your political views of the conflict as well as your socialist views developed, you also saw no reason to join the party – probably the only Marxist party in the country – the Communist Party?

Henry: You have to look at things in terms of the time bands – in terms of the changes that took place over time. One of the main changes and I come back to this all the time, is that the Jewish socialist parties in Israel have more or less collapsed over time, and collapsed in the sense that they don't represent true opposition forces in terms of what's been going on in the country. So to answer your question, over time I think I would say that I have supported the Communist Party on many issues. That doesn't mean that I joined. I suppose that I could very well have joined or even could join now. I can only reply to that question in that maybe I've always been pushing for some kind of a resurgence that hasn't happened. Over recent years I give my support to groups that are active against the Israeli occupation. That's what we have.

Zvi: About the party, is there anything Communist left about it, or is it only an expression of the Arab nationalist voice in the country?

Henry: I think people within the Communist Party in Israel are not extreme nationalists; probably their views in terms of nationalism are no different than mine. Right now the project is a joint project between Israeli Jews and Israeli Arabs, faced with an internal rightist movement that's taken over in Israel. The right wing has become more and more ultra nationalist, more and more racist, and militarist; let's give it the not so quaint sobriquet proto-fascist.

Zvi: Could you say, and I don't want to put words in your mouth clearly (which you would reject in any case), that the factor of discipline – the political discipline, the intellectual discipline, someone might call it rigidity, or the demands for toeing the line – is this something that prevented you from joining the Communist Party?

Henry: I don't know, and I'm not really clear on why you press in that direction. I don't really have an answer to that. The only thing I can say is that it's in terms of a process and what I want to say once again is that the Jewish socialist movement in Palestine and early Israel, was probably more advanced at all levels in its marxism than the Communist Party in Israel. Everything has fractured over time, including the Communist Party. What I do now, what I support now, I think more or less is in terms of ad hoc things. I was one of the founder members of the Committee in Support of Beir Zeit, the Committee with Solidarity for Beir Zeit, and one of its transformations, the Committee Against the Occupation, and the Committee against the War in Lebanon, and this brought me into contact with people in the occupied territories, and we used to operate within the occupied territories. These activities we took on mainly as Jews who did everything that they could in order to show solidarity, to take on different tasks which would help the Palestinians. This was in terms of direct action, of going to Beir Zeit and putting ourselves on the line. But these ad hoc situations come and go. By the way, I must put in that part of my intellectual and personal development has been together with my wife, of some fifty years, Shula, and in the familial context, this is an ongoing thing. All my children have taken stands, some of which have been personally costly for them. As I become older, my own physical capacity has become much less – there are things that I cannot do. So, some of these things we try to pass on. Some of these things, as I said, are ad hoc.

Zvi: In hearing you talk about these issues, I get the impression that in terms of political affiliation, somehow or other you missed the boat. Something was happening, always, which prevented you from finally deciding to come down as a member of this or a member or that. You found various groupings in change or in transformation, or the situation didn't allow for it, and you couldn't join up, you couldn't jump in, and I think you find yourself in the same situation today. Are you perhaps becoming less radical than in the past?

Henry: No. Absolutely not. Not less radical, if anything, *more* radical. Absolutely. I know that I'm not alone. I'm absolutely sure that my personal situation is not too different from that of many other people who are my age and have gone through fairly similar experiences. The differences between me and lots of other people, lots of other Jews, let's say, in Israel, is that I came from the U.S., and I came when I was already an adult of 22. But, to make the jump – what has gone on in Palestine-Israel is something that I've gone through with lots of other people whether I know them or not – a number of these people had personal backgrounds in movements which maybe even tied them to these movements for longer time periods. You push, and I think wrongly so, in the direction of the Communist party; as if, as a confirmed leftist, why did you avoid the Communist party? Don't forget there have been different parties that have developed through the years. Mainly they had minor inputs, maybe they got one or two people into the Knesset, but they were not going any place. The fact that they were not going any place reflects on the fact that other so-called major parties like MAPAM (which I was a member of – I mean in distinction to what you said previously) failed, I joined MAPAM, and I certainly had great hopes for MAPAM.

Zvi: When did MAPAM stop being an effective instrument?

Henry: By, oh, certainly less and less by the 60s; then everything – everything was wiped away by the 1967 War.

Zvi: By the way you said the '48 war was a just war. And the '67 War?

Henry: There are two ways of looking at it. There were certain things that took place in the 1948 War and certain things that took place in the 1967 War – one thing, for example, and I don't know if I've said it previously in terms of the 1948 War, which I think is an absolutely just war – I've never been able to accept the fact that no attempt was made to answer the refugee problem of the Arabs.

Zvi: How do you mean answer?

Henry: Answer, and this is a terrible thing, and I've said this previously. What happens in war, during war, when a war is going on, terrible things happen; not only do people get killed, there are foul deeds all over the place. But after the war the Palestinians had to be returned to their homes.

Zvi: But then there wouldn't be a Jewish State.

Henry: I've always believed in a homeland, a state, for the Jews. A Jewish state, baldly defined as such, gives free rein to ultra-nationalists and is too exclusivist. Some kind of an understanding between the State of Israel and the Palestinian refugees had to be reached. This means that people have to work at it. People have to reach some kind of an understanding that for other people to lose their homes, to lose their land, to lose their homeland, is out of the question. And this has to be faced and dealt with. What their numbers had to be – it's not a question of token things – it's beyond token. It has to be a kind of mutuality where people work together to find some kind of mutual adjustment. Also in terms of what you just responded with – this would have been the end of the Jewish state or something like that – this I doubt very much. Nobody is going to terminate the Jewish state although it is rapidly becoming a place we ourselves will not wish to live in. We had to reach an understanding that this terrible tragedy has taken place, and we have to resolve it in some intelligent humane fashion.

The other thing in terms of the 1967 War is quite clearly the fact that what took place after the 1967 War is the Occupation, and we're living the occupation, and the extremes of the Occupation, the takeover of racism, of driving other people from their homes, taking over their lands, and trying to make this a permanent fixture of Israeli life. This has altered everything that we know in terms of the way we lead our lives today. We've reached the higher militarism of Israeli statism; Israel is now a colonial power.

Zvi: You seem to think, and I believe it is one of the major thrusts in your article on the refugee problem that many wars involved the creation of this type of thing, of people being displaced. But you indicate in the article that after war correctives are made. But this isn't necessarily the case historically. For example the Sudetanland where the Germans of the Sudetanland of Czechoslovakia were kicked out unceremoniously, lock stock and barrel – I think there were between 1.2 million - 2,000,000 of them and they're in Germany now and not in the Czech Republic. There are examples from Transylvania with the Hungarian-Rumanian population. You have the example of Poland having taken over a significant chunk of East Germany and removing the population. With respect to the Palestinians and the Jews here, you think there has to be a re-exchange, that they have to come back. Why here and not these other places?

Henry: First of all I didn't say that. I said this had to transpire immediately. And if not immediately, sooner. And this meant that something that had to take place within the internal Jewish leadership in Israel from 1949 and 1950 and from then on. This is not what happened, and as time goes on, quite clearly, we're five decades and more after this – now compounded by the

Occupation – we have to quite clearly look for other kinds of solutions, of reconciliation at all levels.

Zvi: What do you have in mind?

Henry: First of all, all of these things go back to the fact that yes, people have to recognize mistakes that have been made, and they have to make this kind of statement.

Zvi: The interesting thing is, that maybe it wasn't a mistake; perhaps an injustice to all intents and purposes, but not a mistake.

Henry: You're getting on to something now that we spoke about when we last met and I said that Benny Morris was disgraceful for now saying in a recent interview that it was a mistake not to get rid of all the Arabs in 1948, and you didn't like the stronger word I actually used. But it fits a different definition, and I'm saying that it's bordering on corruption of the self which we see here. What do I mean by that? I mean that he's not only relating to the past in terms of his understanding of the present and the future, that is, he thinks it would have terminated the problem, but he's also relating to *people* in the past and in the present, and he has no problem with that. As if he is simply being practical and pragmatic and thereby honest. I hope we don't entertain these terrible kinds of evaluations. Look what is going on in our university. We have a professor who has made an academic career out of justifying the idea of transfer of Arabs from Israel. Another, presently on leave, a philosopher I believe, who announced today from the Knesset, after justifying the deed, that Israel has the right to kill its enemies living outside of Israel and the occupied territories as well. Speak about terminating problems. I suppose he'll return one day to teach ethics. To return to your point, I think that first of all, we have to come together with the Palestinian people and say that this terrible thing has happened. (Don't forget the Arab states attacked us in 1948 – we don't know what would have happened if they would have stayed out – so all of these things are true, all these things are true.) Nevertheless, we have to find our way to some kind of common understanding and common sense of guilt that we each feel as both Jews and Arabs, in order to say, "What can we do? You want me to say we have to take back 100,000 Palestinians; hopefully, the people will say "Yes, let's take back 100,000 Palestinians." What can I say about the 1967 war? You see what's happened yourself. Has anybody, anyone who is sane, anybody that is rational, who has some kind of sense of social justice – is he going to accept the idea of this conquest state? Is he going to accept the occupation. You don't accept it either do you?

Zvi: No I don't.

Henry: Okay, for all the reasons that have developed and are further developing, and all the reasons that have brought about this development of a proto-fascist state – and the disappearance of anything sane and rational, we have to seek a way out!

Zvi: But the causes of this disappearance are rather complex and involve a lot of forces that we're not going into. We're talking about what would have happened if the refugees came back immediately following the 1948 War –

the War of Independence, and I had maintained, Henry, that if the refugees had come back, if justice so to speak, had been done, then the possibility of a Jewish State, of a Jewish ethos, of a dominant Jewish symbolic framework, being in place in this country certainly at this stage in the game, would have been close to zero.

Henry: Okay, the first thing I said and you agreed, is that the Jewish ethos as we see it right now, in Israel, is not a Jewish ethos that we respect. The other thing I think, is more or less what I've been saying all the time – but sort of push it in a slightly different direction. The U.N. resolution in terms of the division of Palestine, that is the 1947 Partition Plan, gave Jewish Palestine or Israel a certain territory and within this territory 60% were Jews and 40% were Arabs. That meant that the majority were the Jews – It was a percent that we had to deal with – the Jewish population and the Arab population – we would have had to reach some kind of a *modus vivendi*. This is not what happened because the war broke out. Now let's say that war had not broken out. We would have had to reach some kind of a solution and this kind of solution would have been a different kind of solution. I don't know what the Jewish ethos would have been. I'm not so sure I really care what the Jewish ethos would have been as long as the two peoples worked at living together.

Zvi: You don't really care, but many others do care.

Henry: Okay, but I'm not saying to anybody not to live your Jewish ethos as you see it. My Jewish ethos combines this deep socialist element of whatever is both humanist and socialist, and I cannot see anything that's worthwhile in a Jewish ethos that doesn't combine this kind of socialism, that doesn't combine an understanding of the fact that another people are living together with me, and that I don't have an objection to another people, and I cannot understand how we should live in a society where there are only Jews. I don't accept it. I can accept and understand the fact that people, Jews, want to live with other Jews. This is a sentiment, this is a feeling, and is also something realistic and has historic justification. But do people want to live with Jews only? This is out of the question. What for? What for? You have to reach an adjustment so that Arabs could live with their ethos and then there would be another kind of Arab ethos, a different kind of a Jewish ethos, and it might be a very very reasonable, very understanding, very heartfelt kind of ethos, and there might be all kinds of combinations. I don't know, and you can't know, but the two of us are disgusted with the kind of ethos that's developed here. We're trying to think of what we can do to overturn this whole business. It stinks to high heaven.

Zvi: You're making an assumption here when you say – in some ways, forgive me, but as a Marxist and materialist you don't want to be labeled with this, – but it's sort of an utopian assumption. When you speak of what would have happened if the 60/40 division had played out, if there hadn't been a war in 1948, we both know that the differing population situation would have brought about at least parity if not an Arab majority in this territory. Clearly the country had limited absorption capabilities for the large number of Jews who could have come into this very small area that was assigned to the

Jewish state. But we also know something else, and that is that the two peoples were not at similar stages of political development, political consciousness, economic development, institutional development, and what have you. Would it have been useful, and do you think you would have come to this grand utopian, *modus vivendi* where each would follow its own ethos, where each man would be under his fig tree and vine? Under this situation of vast differentials between the population to say nothing of the fact that they represent very different cultures in terms of Islam and the dominance of Islam vs. Judaism, or different cultures in terms of history, in historical memory and so on. Was this not doomed? Wasn't it sort of an invitation to constant struggle and dominance on the part of one and subjection on the part of the other? Was this not an almost inevitable outcome?

Henry: What do you have today? You don't have subjection today?

Zvi: You do, you do, and the situation is far from ideal.

Henry: I'm speaking about a different situation in any case. Don't forget that part of the 60/40 arrangement included areas that are in today's Palestine as well. Let me just answer in a few words because you're raising a situation which is quite clearly almost unanswerable. The only thing that I would say is that without both nations, without each nation being sensitive to the demands and the claims of the other nation, nothing is really going to succeed. I mean if you're going to educate people to extreme nationalism, you're not going to succeed; something's going to erupt and I can only think that it's worthwhile that faced with this kind of a situation where two people have to live together, they have to work something out, and I think that's a life worth living for. I have nothing against people enhancing their particular ethos. And we all think that our life ways are most precious and they are, and I don't suggest that we make light of our lives. But I think certain lives are more worth living, and I think that this kind of attempt of coming together, working things out together was and is possible. By the way, you speak about Islam as a problem, but the Palestinians who would have lived with the Jews were also educated people who were living both in an agricultural and an urban context. Heartland both for Jews and for Arabs, in many many different fields, although I don't say that these matters were absolutely parallel. Also you're getting into this dangerous kind of area entering this kind of mystique about the great differences between Islam and the West, equating an Islamic type with the Palestinians both in Israel and in Occupied Palestine, as if everything is insoluble, insurmountable, and this is not so.

Zvi: I don't know if everything is insoluble. I don't know if I would take that point of view, but I certainly would take the view that there are differences – considerable ones, fateful ones.

Henry: I just have one more point, and we're speaking, we're also speaking in Israel today about our situation as middle-class Jews who are reasonably well off, and we've had this certain kind of academic success – security, and this academic 'success' has had its economic payoff. We live well. There are things that we wouldn't want to forego, and I think we're liable to think in these kinds of terms – – what I'm saying is that we're not only speaking in some kind of abstract intellectual vein. We also live a certain kind of material life, and most people we know live this kind of life. And when you're speaking about a Jewish ethos, you're also speaking about this kind of ethos which has its material aspect. And there are things about our lives today, which could be very different if in 1949 things had turned out differently. We would have lived a different kind of life, so maybe our material situation wouldn't be a replica of what it is today.

Zvi: You mean it would be a tougher situation – more difficult: prosperity corrupts?

Henry: I don't know what kind of situation it would be, but certainly we isolate ourselves to a high degree. We have something here which I see that people are defending – quite clearly people (Jews) in the occupied territories are defending it. They're defending a certain kind of standard of living and they wrap it in a Jewish 'ethos' envelope, and to a high degree this pervades Israeli society.

Zvi: That could be … it may very well be correct. I can only say that in any conscious sense, it plays no role in the thrust of my questions or my position. That's for sure.

Henry: No, I'm not claiming something about you personally. How we're looking at the situation – if we can even use Benny Morris as an example once again – I'm quite sure that he's not aware of the fact that he speaks from a certain kind of defensiveness which he wrongly equates with an intellectual position.

Zvi: In defense of a class interest is what you're saying. I'm saying – if it exists, it's completely unconscious. It's much more obscure, much less apprehensible. But I have one final question along these lines to ask you. I was trying to draw a picture of what I consider to be a type of an extensive pattern of asymmetry between the Palestinian population in 1948-1949 and the Jewish population, something which I think continues today in any number of areas. There's another one that might be of some importance here, but maybe more symbolic than anything else. You're making a demand which I think is just – that we recognize the injustice that was done vis-à-vis the refugees, in moving people from their land, their livelihoods, their roots, their physical roots certainly, etc. And I understand this argument. And I think tens of thousands of us, if not more, recognize the justice of this argument. Are there tens of thousands of Arabs who would accept your position that the 1948 war was anything but the Naqba, that it was a just war; that it was a war for the independence of the state that was attacked? Again, I'm on this point of asymmetry. It has some importance, I think.

Henry: The answer is yes. I'll just try to answer it with one statement. I believe sincerely that the present Palestinian leadership – could reach an understanding that the attack on the Jews in 1948 was wrong, and they would state this. Certainly they would do so within the context of a negotiated settlement.

Zvi: I wonder! I would like to move our conversation in another direction for a
bit, and talk a little about your professional life as one of the early
practitioners of Anthropology as a discipline in this country. You were one
of the first teachers of the subject here in Israel. How did it begin?

Henry: First of all I had gotten a couple of research grants from the Social
Science Research Council, and later on from the Ford Foundation, and I
started working, living, and also doing field work and research in kibbutzim,
mainly in kibbutz Ein Harod where I lived with my family. This was mainly
between the years 1951-1953. And then I started working in an Arab village
in the lower Galilee. Actually in a number of Arab villages, but then I
settled on Tur'an in the Lower Galilee.

Zvi: What year?

Henry: 1953, 1954, and I continued living in Ein Harod, and I continued living
and working in Tur'an as well. Of course I collected an immense amount of
data, a great deal of which I still have, and which will remain, I suppose,
unpublished, which is a pity. And then I started teaching for a number of
reasons, one of which was certainly financial. I had a number of thoughts by
then about returning to the States, but I also had two young children, Ron
and Tamar (Tami) from my first marriage, and there was no way that I would
separate myself from them. And by that time Shula Carmi and I were
together. It's now some fifty years, and we have two children, Maya and
Dana. In any case I started teaching anthropology from 1956, if I'm not
mistaken, and I taught at the Hebrew University, and I taught at one of its
adjuncts in Haifa at the same time. Later on, when Tel Aviv was set up as an
adjunct of the Hebrew University, I taught there as well. I used to combine
these – because I didn't have a full time job at the Hebrew University where
I taught two courses. Therefore it was necessary for me to teach both in
Haifa and in Tel Aviv. At the end of the 1950s, I'm not sure of the date,
maybe 1960 through 1961, I managed to get a grant – $10,000 which at the
time was a lot of money – in order to set up an anthropological research
center in Jerusalem. Here I also got some personal, not financial, support
from the Sociology Department, and especially from Prof. Ya'akov Katz.

I set up the Israeli Center for Anthropological Research, and I invited all
the anthropologists – but not only anthropologists because there were very
few professional anthropologists around at the time – to join with us.
Nevertheless, people who joined hands with me in this were Helen
Antonovsky, Phyllis Palgi, Dov Noy, Dina Feitelson, Alex Weingrod and
others. For the moment I'm only mentioning people who at the time had
Ph.D.s in anthropology or something close to it. Dov Noy was a folklorist,
and there were other folklorists who also pitched up as well. In any case it
was a focal point for all the anthropologists in the country, and the idea was
that it would be run democratically, and that we would try to the best of our
ability to do anthropological research and train students. At the time, to no
small extent it represented a home for a good number of people who were
also jobless, but nevertheless wanted to work in anthropology. Don't forget
at the time there were no departments of anthropology, and sociology was

strictly at Jerusalem. Tel Aviv was not yet established. At the time the anthropologists who eventually studied at Manchester were still students in sociology at the Hebrew University. Nevertheless, as I said, it was a point of focus, and it was an attraction for people, and people used to come there, and talk anthropology.

Zvi: Did the center sponsor research projects?

Henry: Exactly – mainly – aside from the fact that it was a place that brought anthropologists and people who were on the periphery of anthropology together. We gave small grants for different projects, and a number of people published under the name of the Center. No one received a salary at any time.

Zvi: Did it assume anything of an Israeli coloration, something that would distinguish it as Israeli? Did it represent any school? That sounds unlikely because you're talking about the eclecticism of the people who were involved which would mean that the idea of a school emerging from this, or a point of view of a particularly Israeli nature, was probably a difficult hook to have developed; but did it?

Henry: I think that if you're looking for something in terms of a theoretical stream or something like that, I rather doubt it. Once again, this was in the beginning of the 60s, and if you want to look back you have to understand that the majority of people who were around this center hadn't really gotten their full training yet. And also, because of their jobless situation, they were also people who were searching for avenues to get the necessary training. My own training at Columbia was in an historical, probably Boasian tradition more than anything else, in addition to my theoretical position relating to political economy. And this wasn't in keeping with the existing dominant (Israeli sociology) understanding of what Sociology and Anthropology were supposed to be. As people came into anthropology, they went into anthropology in terms of functionalism and structuralism in one form or another. Well, I saw this as an avenue, as something you worked with, but, for me, in a political economy, a historical context; that is, I thought in terms of things that were coming into being, and transformations.

Zvi: Was this shared by many in the group?

Henry: I can't say – I don't know. I mean, the group as a group didn't gel as such. It was too much in flux in terms of its membership.

Zvi: Was the work that most of them engaged in focused on one or another aspect of Israeli society?

Henry: They were focusing exactly on things Israeli. Israeli society. Michael Saltman, who didn't have a degree at the time, worked on Djerban Jews in Israel – that was his field research. Helen and Dina were trying to work on comparisons between Ashkenazi and Sephardic youth in different kinds of contexts; Phyllis worked on magic among Moroccan Jews, and the money eventually went – even $10,000 eventually runs out after a few years. By the way, I have to tell you something about where I got the money from because the money came from a dear friend of mine with whom I studied anthropology at Columbia – Vera Rubin and Vera had her own anthropology institute in New York. She was of an older generation, and she and her then husband supported many different projects, social and educational projects; in the States the anthropology department at Brandeis University, music academies in Jerusalem, Tel Aviv and Haifa as well. Vera and I studied for our comprehensives together with a number of other people, and the Rubins also had a deep emotional interest in Israel. In any case this grant came through Vera's help and a deep willingness and desire to advance anthropology in Israel. Eventually, as I said, after a few years, the money ran out. I kept the office working as long as I could, mainly trying to help young people – whoever showed up, whoever wanted help – and when we ran out of money, wanted advice. And shortly after, in the late 1960s, I went on a sabbatical year, and taught at Brooklyn College. Following this I received a senior research fellowship at Manchester for a year.

Zvi: Was Gluckman in anyway involved in your development?

Henry: In my development, no. Max set up his own research project and trained a number of young Israeli sociologists at Manchester through to their Ph.D.s. Among them were Emmanuel Marx, Shlomo Deshen, Moshe Shokeid, Israel Shepher and several others who became anthropologists. Max and I became friends, but when I came to Manchester, he went to Jerusalem. We were friends, but our anthropological perspectives were different. He viewed history like most of the functionalists at the time, more or less as unknowable. Need I say Max is rightly recognized as a foremost anthropologist, and I go along with that.

I think maybe two or three other anthropological-sociological ventures of mine are worth mentioning because of their broader contexts, including joint effort. One of them was when I came to the University of Haifa and got a job at Haifa (1968-69) where I tried setting up an anthropological program, in which anthropologists would do not only social-cultural anthropology, but also include pre-history, physical anthropology and linguistics. I think it was a good attempt, and I managed to set it up with the help of other anthropologists, including Michael Saltman. The teaching staff included a first-rate physical anthropologist (Nikko Haas) and linguist (Nira Reiss), eventually a fine prehistorian (Mila Ohel), as well as anthropologists who were social cultural anthropologists – that is mainly me, Michael and Jonathan Oppenheimer (and over the years many others). Don't forget that this rather ambitious program was within the context of the joint department that was the anthropology and sociology department at Haifa (and we were the first department in the country with anthropology in its title), meaning that the number of slots open to us was limited; something between 4 and 5. This also meant that people who were either linguists or physical anthropologists could not be full-time teachers, and had to find other means of financial support. In general it meant working on other projects or teaching in other places and generally and especially it meant that it took them away from Haifa. The other side of it was that we were in tension and sometimes open conflict with the other part of the department – sociology – which also wanted to grow and which also had its sub-fields: criminology, organizational sociology, statistics, and so on.   One must also take into consideration that there was the university itself which ultimately determines how many positions it allots to this or that discipline. I probably should have tried to push harder for, at least at that time, the setting up of a department, separate from sociology. I attempted to achieve this, but among other things, at that time in other parts of the country new joint departments were being set up: At the Hebrew University, at Tel Aviv University – and many years after at Beer Sheva and Bar Ilan – which all combined sociology and anthropology. So this became sort of a fixed format as if sociology and anthropology necessarily had to be under one roof. Can be, doesn't have to be.

Zvi: Do you think that there's any intellectual justification for the separation or was it purely in terms of the ability to grow at a pace of your own choice.

Henry: I think the two possibilities clearly exist, but when there are a limited number of teaching positions, it becomes a situation that generally leads to aggravation and generally, the field that is negatively affected is anthropology. First of all, you require the funding for a separate department, especially when the plan aims for a four-field department. It depends also on personalities and other factors, and the personnel that you manage to get together. However, the case still should be made, can be made, for the old-time four-field anthropology viewpoint. That is, there's no reason not to look at humankind's condition as a totality, to be viewed in terms of its total history, meaning its prehistory, and major developmental aspects which have to do with the human biology of mankind. And of course, look at linguistics – perhaps each of these disciplines developed singly, and their coming together sometimes looks as if it's artificial, but when you put them all together, you get a much larger intellectual perspective. You make students aware of a different perspective, and it makes much larger demands on students (not to speak of yourself), even if they only get a fraction of training in each of the sub-disciplines. If they adopt one or the other as a major, they perhaps only get a touch of something else, but that touch is everlasting; and it comes together as the sum of this total complexity of our past, present and future. But that's not what happened, and I'm most sorry for it because one of the things is that if it happened here, it would have influenced other places in the country.

In 1978 Shlomo Swirski, Debby Bernstein, Dvorah Kalekin and I started, at Haifa, to put out the journal *Critical Notebooks*. It was a joint venture. It was a breakthrough in terms of its content, that it presented a different and radical conceptualization and analyses of Israeli society and certainly in terms of what Israelis were publishing here and elsewhere at least at the time. I think it had an impact both within the universities, probably mainly on students, and outside as well. We had our differences, and for a number of reasons the journal was relatively short-lived. But people still turn to it, refer to articles that were published there. Shlomo and Barbara Swirski and Shula and I remain dear friends to this day for both personal reasons and in our political solidarity. I can add, I think it was in

1980, I resigned my position as chairman of the Department of Sociology and Anthropology in protest when Shlomo and Charles Kamen didn't receive tenure. Two of the finest sociologists! Each went on to outstanding careers mainly outside the academy with its security and perks. Two persons of character, and great friends.

Zvi: You said you had another major venture.

Henry: In terms of a major project that I was instrumental in setting up and then directing, was one that began in the 1980s when The International Center for Peace in the Middle East turned to me and asked if I would formulate a research project for the study of Arabs in Israel. I wrote a research proposal – I wrote up (I don't really remember) something between a 50-70 page research proposal for which they didn't have any money – no money at all, but I wrote a formal research proposal, and they gave it to the Ford Foundation which gave financial support while setting certain limitations in terms of the subject matter. I didn't like these limitations, but nevertheless, I thought there were ways of overcoming it in the best sense of the word.

Zvi: What sort of limitations?

Henry: Well, the limitations were that they weren't interested in political matters. They wanted the subject matter to concentrate on practical aspects of the condition of the Arab population in Israel. And therefore the subject matter was in terms of subjects like social welfare, local government, crime and delinquency, the legal situation, health, economy. You can't go into a formal investigation in terms of the social situation of the Arabs within the Israeli state and not deal with things like discrimination and the political context of health and so on. You can't set it up that way. But when you research with integrity and in depth, the political is part and parcel of it. And that's the way we worked it out. I made it a joint Jewish-Arab project, that is, half of the researchers were Arabs, and half were Jewish (Majid Al-Haj, Stanley Cohen, Aziz Haidar, Raasem Khamaisi, David Kretzmer and Nira Reiss). This was a highly successful project, despite the fact that I, together with the other researchers, were under great pressure by the administration of the Center to turn out the work quickly in order to get more money.

Zvi: What resulted from this in terms of publication?

Henry: In the first phase we got four volumes out which were published first by the International Center for Peace, and then I wrote up an additional research project and all-in-all a quarter of a million dollars was raised (and by the way, people only got money for their research). And of course the Center got what centers get, 15% or something like that, and that kept the Center going, and it kept the administrative part of the center going. Eventually, 8 volumes were published – 8 of which came out of the center; 6 of these were later published by commercial presses also; that is 4 of them came out in a set in Westview, and two others came out under the auspices of good commercial publishers, and there was no reason for the other two not coming out by commercial presses as well. In any case, this was a major piece of work – it was a joint piece of work.

Zvi: You imply that you put the political dimension in through the back door.

Do you think that anthropology must have a political purpose?, a political dimension?

Henry: You have to put it a different way. I don't think that there is any anthropology that is worth its salt which in one way or another isn't political. I'll put it differently. In the modern situation, that is, *the* existing situation, no matter where you study it involves people within a political context. It cannot be otherwise. It doesn't make any difference what aspect of life that you take, whether it's health, urban conditions –the status and condition of women – name it, whatever it is it has a political context. That doesn't mean reducing research to politics.

Zvi: Does that mean that the researcher must have a political agenda?

Henry: Not necessarily a political agenda since not every researcher is a political person. However, political awareness must exist. In order for a person to manage humanness, consciousness and conscience, there is no avoiding the political if you want to study.

Zvi: What I'm really asking is is whether you can visualize the situation of a person who in his personal life and the way he looks at the world, his *weltanschauung*, is truly conservative: Who has adopted all the verities of late 20th-early 21st century capitalism and free enterprise. I ask simply, could this person do good anthropology?

Henry: I say it's like many other things. A person can do good anthropology, but one has to pit oneself against other ideas, and other ways of approaching the world. What you describe is clearly a person with a political viewpoint, 'conservative' in this case. Reality, at least since the time of early states, is a situation of power. Social scientists who are concerned, read, translate, and interpret power; they cannot avoid the political, dominant, context of life. Clearly we pit interpretations one against the other. What you seem to be driving at is that a free-enterprise, etc., researcher arrives at his-her explanations by the same, or an equal, road as that taken by one from the political left, and that the explanations will be of equal value. I say, we judge them, relativism is not an option for educated people. Personal integrity is an issue and it is a long-term, a life's term, project. Both conservatism and radicalism have roots, that is, each is linked to other viewpoints regarding the human situation. We judge work over the long run, conservative or radical.

Zvi: Let me put it another way. Do you know of any politically conservative, or let me go one step further, politically reactionary, anthropologists who have done work of substance and of worth as anthropologists?

Henry: Look, there are quite clearly tens of key figures in anthropology as in sociology, in all fields, who are people who avoided politics, stayed far away from politics, and insisted that their students also stay far away from politics, a so-called liberal, so-called objective, way of looking at life. There is always work that can avoid political assessment. There are formal things that people work at like technical linguistics, like counting culture traits, and so on. But even in fields like these, there is a social medicine, social welfare. Why not a social botany, a social astronomy? Of course, there are aesthetics in life, a certain routine involved, a certain kind of effort involved, and a person doesn't only deal with 'free' intellectual work; there are hands, bellies and emotions involved. Nonetheless, what you might call intellectual satisfaction often guides a person. There are always inspirational factors that bring a person to intellectual and scientific work – romantic, family socialization, aesthetic, teachers – that are enough in themselves; these are joined to building on the work of others, the opening-up of new avenues of study, and so on. Simply objective input as it were, getting the facts straight in something you enjoy doing. All this is so. But, as you enter a field of work, you begin to understand its complexities, perhaps the positions taken on problems by its protagonists, historic, institutional, ideological – political, that is, an awareness is present, you should not avoid.

So there are different kinds of investments in life, but when somebody starts thinking seriously, and that's his life's work, and he wants to know why mankind is exploring the universe; why certain kind of flowers go into certain kinds of pharmaceuticals, and how pharmaceutical companies deal with this, and what kind of profits derive from this – all of a sudden the fields expand. And when we go into something like space ships, and space exploration – there are different concerns, different ideas of why man should or should not explore the universe. Oceanography, quickly involves claims on oil reserves, planting the flag in the Antarctic has little to do with pure exploration, no matter the adventurism or the esthetics of the explorer. And if we explore the universe, and we think of settling people on other stars or planets – for what purpose? To what end? Jointly or secretly? What kind of a society will be set up? What to publish, what to deny? All different kinds of questions such as these must be posited.

Zvi: In other words, you think it's not serious to go out there and collect, and not serious just as it were to present. What you must do is draw conclusions backwards and forwards, backward to the roots, and forward to the implications.

Henry: One of the problems of people working in science is that they're faced with other people who are working in science. No matter what they say it has to affect their hearts and heads when they see that other people make common cause with helping mankind lead a happier, fuller life. Most simply, I assume that every social scientist has studied racism, class, gender – what they mean in daily life. If they can't apply them in their work life, at least after work.

Zvi: We keep coming back to the kibbutz – clearly a central passion of your life. What was your approach to its understanding on a scholarly level?

Henry: The direction that I think that I went to was to the history of the kibbutz, the origins of the kibbutz, generally. But what I did especially at Ein Harod was to try to understand how the different communal or collective enterprises, things like collective sleeping for the children, the collective/communal dining room, work routines, the division of labor, management roles, the role and condition of women, the place of intellectual work, and so on – how they came into being. Why and how did they develop the way they did? Getting hundreds of people into a communal cooperative organization, and to set up, as I say, these communal institutions which seem to be clearly functional, as if they were the normal development of a commune or a collective settlement, is not necessarily true. The input is something different, and the formation of these groups, how people who themselves were only then in their late teens or early twenties – managed it – is worth thinking about. Nevertheless, as I say, what is the idea of input and what is the actual expression and the contradictions that developed within the input in the growth of these institutions is something that interested me, and when I got to Ein Harod there was already this generation that had its own children that were born in the kibbutz or came to the kibbutz (Ein Harod) when they were a year or two old, and of course they had a lot to tell me. I learned a great deal from many people.

Zvi: To what extent do you think that a place like Ein Harod developed its institutions as a result of pragmatic considerations, and to what extent do you think it was ideological?

Henry: It's difficult to answer because quite clearly it's a combination of both, and if you mean by pragmatic developments on the ground, it's also a working out of institutions over time. That seems to be to me, more to the point. That is, the refining of these institutions took time. It's still not over with. Different formats will develop as times change, but the idea of communal life will remain. Don't forget, we are in a downswing in Israel and the world as a whole mainly due to U.S. empire proclivities. You asked me previously, in a part that is not included here, about 'human nature', and I recall that I said that it was too big a topic to handle briefly and intelligently. The material and idea factors that enter, in addition to the time factor, that is historical complexity, cultural complexity, the dimension of change, are all part of the totality, and, of course, in most interpretations, 'human nature' is explained in terms of a biological base, needs, underlying determinism, usually to rationalize aggression, social or personal, in action. In any case, I believe that 'human nature' will return again and again to equity, people won't give up the struggle for equity. It's the idea, returning to Jews in Palestine and your question, the ideological part, which I think is much older – it begins from what Shula and I have called political idea groups, and these political idea groups have their formation in and prior to the Second Aliyah. That is, there are also political idea groups that begin in Russia, in Poland, and in other areas. They are political idea groups in terms of people representing themselves to the political and Zionist ideas that were forming in the late nineteenth century. And don't forget, what we're speaking about in terms of their definitiveness are people who are radical, people who are socialists of one kind or another, and people who combine in one form or another within this emerging national movement of Zionism. That is, here there is a specific history in respect to the work-idea groups that developed into communes.

Zvi: Which makes it a rather unique form of community.

Henry: It makes it unique in the sense that I think I like unique. It's as if there's almost a contradiction between something which is national or nationalist and something which is socialist or radical – more universal. The Bund might provide another example.

Zvi: The Bund was not nationalist in any conventional sense. It was ethnic, but certainly not nationalist.

Henry: In terms of its particular ideology, of course you're correct, but it also was Jewish. What I really want to emphasize, what I wanted to say, is I believe, and I do think I believed then (I told you that I was a non-Zionist, but never an anti-Zionist), that there are such things as progressive nationalisms. And it's within this kind of national movement, Zionist movement, that I think people worked things out through political idea groups, and these early groups became work-idea groups leading to the establishment of the kibbutzim. Their socialist movements, their socialist agenda, and the way they viewed the world, the way they also viewed their program for Palestine, made the national movement and even the nationalist movements, legitimate in my eyes.

Zvi: Could you say a word about what you think is a progressive nationalist movement.

Henry: I think there have been numerous examples in the world. You have to consider that almost any national movement that works against oppression, discrimination, frees itself or attempts to free itself from colonialism, has a progressive element. What makes it really progressive is the extent to which it is truly social in content, hopefully socialist in its ideology, and I think that this happens and has happened throughout the world.

Zvi: Then the Palestinian National movement is not a progressive movement?

Henry: First of all the Palestinian National movement is progressive in the sense that it tried to free itself from something total – there's this element of getting free from the British regime in Palestine, and now of course freeing itself of the Israeli occupation. And this certainly makes it progressive. At one and the same time there are also socialist and communist movements within the Palestine National movement. There are also right-wing movements, and people; Palestinians, quite clearly have choices to make. I mean I can, in regard to the Palestinian situation today give my support to Fatah. It's certainly progressive in the sense that it attempts to combine the different social political groups in Palestine and it tries to carry out activities to free itself from the occupation, and I support it. Of course, I abhor terrorism in any form including Israeli state military terror.

Zvi: I sort of sidetracked you by asking what a progressive nationalist movement is. I'd like to go back to the kibbutz. Do you think that the kibbutz movement somewhere along the line stopped being a progressive force?

Henry: No, I don't think so. First of all, the kibbutz movement was never solely a kibbutz movement, it was part and parcel of other things. Part and parcel of the Histadrut, part and parcel of workers movements, and political parties. And I think that they were more or less the avant-garde of a totality, the dominant (not the sole element, that's for sure), but the dominant element politically in a workers' movement that was involved in every facet of life. And this continued without doubt until statehood in 1948. And if you're asking about today, I think there's still certainly residual, more than residual elements, of an advanced workers movement there. The kibbutz movement still has the potential for being a force. I mean it still exists. However, other things have happened, and of course the main thing that has happened has been the kind of state that Israel became.

Zvi: Clearly, there were things that happened in society that ran quite counter to everything that the kibbutz stood for – individualism, globalization, materialism which has something to do with the State for sure, but other forces were at work as well. One, that I would like to just throw out to you is the kibbutz movement as a communal undertaking, as an intentional community, had an extremely long run for a non-religiously oriented intentional community. The only ones that have had longer runs have been those that were based on a religious idea. So could it simply be that its time has come in historical terms? Historically, all the intentional communities that were not religiously based, as well as many that were religiously based, had a two-generation run, maybe three, but mostly two generations. Could it be, that simply put the forces or the dynamics that were at work in this type of enterprise took their toll rather than the State or other forces?

Henry: You're starting more or less from the premise that the developments that have taken place were internal to the kibbutz itself.

Zvi: To some extent, yes.

Henry: And this is more or less this kind of Weberian routinization understanding. I think that a number of things took place and they took place because of political acts, and the political acts didn't stem from the kibbutzim or the kibbutz movement, but stemmed from the internal struggle between the social democrats under Ben Gurion and the middle-class and religious parties that joined with them, and the socialist parties on the left. This happened within the context of statehood, the war victory, the non-return of the Arab refugees, the mass immigration of Jews to Israel, and the world-wide support for the new State.

Zvi: You mean you're of the opinion that had the political leadership of the country – the party and the leadership of the country – been supportive of the kibbutz idea and its playing out over the 30-40 year period when it was developing when there was more and more communalism, you think that the kibbutz would be alive and well today?

Henry: I've tried to put it in the context of what took place in the decade following statehood.

Zvi: So you think that people who largely attributed the change to the opening up of Israel after the Six Day War – travel abroad, recognizing that everybody out there was getting richer and fatter, and having more cars and things – this wasn't a factor in turning the heads of the youth of the kibbutz, and making possible, or likely, the tremendous outflow of the young generation since 1967?

Henry: You've jumped to 1967. Let me get to that eventually, since there's no
possibility of answering every kind of question, and all the kinds of
possibilities that develop over time. Certainly Palestine wasn't isolated, and
Israel when it became a state wasn't isolated. Quite clearly it became a state
due to many kinds of international factors and not only because of its own
development. However, The British didn't have to forego their mandate as
they did in 1947. The U.S. and the Soviet Union could have intervened in
terms of the war. The Arab states invaded Palestine and attacked Israel ---
all these things happened, and they changed the immediate history, and out
of that immediate history, the Israelis won the war, and a state emerged.
Speaking to its aftermath, there are things that I don't hold true, don't accept,
and I also think they had a definitive effect on what happened to us, and I'm
not only speaking about the kibbutz. It's not the kibbutz. It's the whole
socialist potential, communal, cooperative, potential in its various forms.
This potential affected people, affected Jews from top to bottom in every
area of life. Every Jew in Palestine in every aspect of life, no matter what it
was – you name it – workers institutions, health, education, welfare,
buildling, transport, agriculture, industry, and workers dominance and even
workers hegemony, had an effect on everybody. And what I'm saying is that
things could have been otherwise, but what they would have become
otherwise, I can't say. What they became I see, and two main things were of
particular importance at the time. First of all, the denial of socialism by the
Social Democratic Party, Mapai and especially its leader, Ben Gurion, and
the denial of socialism and its replacement with statism, a sharp turn to the
right, to deny the past, to turn to privatization, to ally itself to the U.S. and so
on. And that had a total disastrous effect – Mapai sought to establish
connections with the right-wing parties in the country, and the religious
parties and so on.   Look where we are now with our former health,
education, welfare institutions in total disarray. Privatization and manpower
firms have taken over and the people who once ran their own institutions are
on the outside looking in. Political parties on the left tried to maintain
themselves within the State, but for many different kinds of reasons, they
failed.

The second thing that I think that happened that was more or less a total
expression, a terrible expression of this kind of statism, was the non-return of
the Palestinian refugees. And this represented a totally different direction in
the life of the country. Not only through the refusal to allow people to return
to their homes and lands after the war, but also the takeover of their property
and villages, and all that it meant. And one of the things that it definitely
meant was the rise of a new kind of nationalism. It was the expression of a
new kind of nationalism because alongside the obverse of the return coin, the
open return of Jews to Israel, is the non-return of the Palestinian refugees.
And this meant a different kind of goal from what had existed previously
during the Mandate Period where an attempt at coexistence was made
between Jews and Arabs, true enough, coexistence within conflict, but this
was the direction taken. And also understanding that there is another people

here and an understanding that the other people were once the majority and that we Jews were the minority.

Zvi: That would have remained the case had the refugees returned.

Henry: This is something else. Why is it something else? First of all, we don't know because there are other possibilities. There is a different kind of division of the land between Palestine and Israel. Nobody says that 700,000 or 750,000 Palestinians, would have returned, and that isn't really the main point. Within the context of returning people, another modus vivendi would have developed, there would have been another way of solving problems. Other things could have developed. What the other things would have been, who knows; nevertheless, this is what happened, and this is something that shouldn't have happened. I just want to go back to a point made earlier – when I said that I supported the war (1948); I became a soldier in the war; I'm not a pacifist, though sometimes I think there is something to be said for pacifism. What I wanted to say is that the Jews were attacked –in 1948, there was a threat against Israel's existence which, I think, was real and evident.

Zvi: The revisionist historians are saying now that it was not true.

Henry: I don't buy that. A time came when it was clear that there was going to be a Jewish victory. But until that time came, it was only after thousands of Jews had been killed, and thousands of Arabs had been killed, and there had been an exodus of Arabs, who not only fled the country, but also had been pushed out. All these things happened, and they happen in war time, and this is not the only place that they happened. With its socialist, humanist underpinnings, Israel should not have reached that kind of a policy, the policy of not returning the refugees.

Zvi: As we said previously, there are so-called socialist states in Europe that had reached exactly that policy after World War II.

Henry: Okay, I'm not responsible for other places. I'm responsible for what I'm saying here in the sense that I also have and I have still to this day, a tremendous amount of respect for the pre-State socialist movement, and the possibility of a social alternative that existed then, and as I said, it should have expressed itself otherwise. And one of the ways it should have expressed itself is in terms of trying to seek some kind of a solution to the circumstance of the Palestinian refugees. Of course other things then took place – politically and materially. And I'm not saying that there weren't other factors. There were hundreds of thousands of Jewish immigrants that came into the country between 1949-53, giving rise to all kinds of explanations and rationalizations, as if there was a population exchange, as if there was a place where the new Jewish refugees had to be housed, had to work the land, had to be turned into pioneers.

Zvi: We talk about these things as if they take place in a vacuum; in other words, that nothing else is happening. There's the refugee problem, the refugees were booted out or fled or both. And then the war ended, and what should have happened is that the refugees be brought back, or allowed back. But wasn't it really a situation of, if not utter chaos – if not a void, certainly a dynamic situation in which the surrounding Arab states at any rate, did not make their peace with the idea of Israel. The rhetoric that we heard and the writings that we saw, suggested that another round was not only conceivable, but in store. Against that matrix, could it be that that was a very important factor in the non-return of the refugees.

Henry: I'm not denying that there wasn't an on-going threat from surrounding Arab states. I don't know if the threat would have been the same kind of threat if there had been some kind of a return of refugees. It's a problem, but that's life and the question is how you seek your solutions to problems. If you always give militaristic answers, then you're going to arrive...

Zvi: A militaristic answer, or an answer that is based on military considerations.

Henry: Military considerations, o.k., but not militaristic expediency. And that's the direction that I think that Israel has taken. Just look at six or seven years later in the 1956 War, where we found ourselves (and I found myself with the 9th Brigade en route to the capture of Sharm el-Sheikh) in partnership (what a scandal) with the two colonial powers – the English and the French against a Nasserist attempt to take over their own Egyptian Suez Canal. And of course we joined forces with gusto, and then just think of what happened. Two superpowers (the U.S. and the U.S.S.R.) at the time put the English and the French and Israel quite simply, with a wave of the hand, in their place. And they retreated. I'm not saying that Israel doesn't have to protect itself. But by providing its own kinds of military explanations of the world, with militaristic necessity out of its militarism as a policy, then that's something else.

Zvi: Aside from and in addition to the refugee problem you also did a lot of work on the subject of the Arab village population in Israel. Could you talk a little about this work?

Henry: I think in 1953, 1954, I started working in an Arab village. I worked and lived in an Arab village in the Lower Galilee, Tur'an. It represented more or less a springboard for different directions. I think that if political processes and how specific communal practices came into being were my main focus when I thought about the kibbutz, they weren't really my main focus when I started working on the Arab villages.

Zvi: What was?

Henry: I mean the Arabs then were a fragmented community – a fragment of a fragment of a fragment. There were only about 120,000 Arabs ...

Zvi: The figure generally given after 1948 is that there were 150,000.

Henry: That's so – What remained was something like 110,000-120,000 and then there was what they euphemistically called family return and by 1953, it came to 150,000, or so. Nevertheless, these were fragmented communities. The villagers were the majority of the remnant population. They no longer had a periphery of other villages. All these other villages disappeared as such.

Zvi: No national institutions...

Henry: No institutions. And therefore I think, since it didn't seem to have its own political structure, I looked at it more or less locally. I worked mainly in trying to see if, for a residual population, there were also residual life ways within the radical change that had taken place. And I did this in terms of an occupational structure and within this family, lineage, marriage, women. I tried to see how people worked, how they worked in the past and how they worked in the present, because I knew that by the end of the Mandate, while the majority was rural, they had begun this kind of proletarianization process by seeking work in the towns. This was mainly through the impetus of the Mandatory Government and the World War II situation where certainly half and more than half in certain instances of the male population, was working outside the villages. I wanted to know if these processes continued.

Zvi: Isn't there a claim among many Arab leaders and scholars of this period, that it was Jewish land confiscation that moved Arabs into the city? But you're saying that it was a process that had already begun in the Mandate Period when more than half were working in the city.

Henry: Yes, I think that the business of Jewish land takeover prior to 1948 is exaggerated. Don't forget that by the end of the Mandate, Jews owned – I don't remember the exact number – 11 or 12 percent of the land in Palestine, and the number of expropriated Arab peasants, was relatively small. I don't mean that it doesn't mean anything – it certainly means something to the people so affected. The problem of land loss by peasants was their eviction by Arab landowners as an ongoing historic process.

Zvi: In other words it's the continuation of a process that had begun some time before. I have a question here that you just started to answer. I notice that many of your articles are about marriage and family in the Arab sector. Why this issue, and not, let's say, religion or culture?

Henry: I can't deny that. I've never worked on religion. I mean, it's something that I have some kind of a difficulty with. In Tur'an though I worked a great deal on trends in Muslim-Christian relations in the village.

Zvi: Okay, to get back to the subject of your dealing with marriage and the family... Did you see marriage and family as the key element or paradigm for understanding questions such as change, stability, etc.?

Henry: It's not only marriage and the family. Perhaps the greatest emphasis was on work, on how people made their livelihoods, and what changes had taken place in the past, and what changes were taking place in the present. Again, the context was now a small Arab population under a military government. And this you have to put together with family, family life, family structure, marriage patterns, and let's say, the whole environmental political situation in terms of marriage and the family. For example, certain clans and families had made the majority of their marriages in neighboring villages. A number of these neighboring villages were no longer in existence. How did this affect the entire marriage system, taking into consideration the marriage system in Palestinian Arab villages involves both internal clan *hamula* marriages, then marriages perhaps between in-laws from different clans as well as external marriages – marriages from other villages.

Such things also affect the internal structure of the village, that is factions are developed in order to make political statements, in other words, to get together groups to represent political force, consequential in broad terms, and consequential in local terms since these political forces gained recognition from the government. Thus, here the internal dynamic interested me.

Zvi: In general we think of marriage as being contracted for family status reasons, for honor, for wealth, the sharing of wealth rather than the division of wealth. Are you suggesting that in the Arab village, post-1948, marriage took place against this new dimension? That is the creation of political federations, as it were, in order to exercise some influence.

Henry: The answer is "yes", but the answer also requires further elaboration, and that is that there was always a political dimension vis-à-vis state power, be it the Mandatory power or be it the Ottoman power. What I'm trying to say is that Israeli state power, for all its differences, from let's say the earlier feudal type Ottoman system and the previous Mandatory control government after it, the Israeli Government treated the Arab villages as fiefdoms: sort of like feudal entities in the sense that they had their "men". The men were picked to become the muhtars of the villages to the degree that they would keep their kinsmen and related kinsmen in order.

Zvi: You're suggesting a much higher level of interference on the part of Israelis in these matters than was true of the Ottomans or the English.

Henry: A different kind, I mean the Ottoman feudal forces were interested mainly in taxes, almost exclusively, in taxes and order. Getting people on the land for economic-tax ends. I don't think taxes had to do much either with the Mandatory Government, and not too much to do with the Israeli government. Here the priority was order and police order, spying and informers, for the sake of internal order. It is the same kind of informers which were required not only in terms of external Arab forces, but in terms of political internal politics, like the Communist Party apparatus and matters of that kind. That's what the military government was interested in. And by the way, you know this business of military governments and what they're interested in -- sometimes they don't know what they're interested in – any kind of information that sort of delves into people's 'secrets'. Whether these secrets are important or not is not necessarily the way intelligence bureaucrats operate.

Zvi: They had to keep their knives sharp...

Henry: Exactly. Generally, it's dirty work, and it's not simply a fear of a fifth column and the like. Secrets for the sake of secrets and then spin. Most of all that someone is watching you.

Zvi: You seem to feel, at least in the study of Arabs in Palestine, which comes through in your published work, that it's not structure or culture that brings about social change or which hampers social change. What is central has to do with the peculiar position of the Arabs vis-à-vis the dominant Jewish population. Is this a correct understanding?

Henry: I think that's so. You know that they have this kind of perception which has turned up of late suggesting the growth of Israeliness among the Arabs. This is so, but it's only so in a sense that certain attributes in common can be described, but the main thing is missing. That is, if you describe it, you better describe its barriers and its limitations, where it stops, and where it stops is really the heart of the matter. I mean if it were "Israeliness", then it would mean that the country would be wide open in a different sense, not only in the sense that Arabs work all over the country from Eilat to Metulla, in Haifa and in Tel Aviv. But that's not where they live. They still don't live there, and the villages have become specific to and particular to Arabs. That is, they continue to live in communities that are separate from Jews, and taking into consideration that people who work all over the country but don't live all over the country, neither do they marry all over the country, neither do they marry Jewish women, and Jewish women don't marry Arab men – barely; maybe even less so than they did during the Mandate Period when there was a certain kind of community sense within the Communist Party and there was a certain degree of intermarriage in the upper echelons.

Zvi: That wasn't the thrust of my question... When I said that culture matters, I think that you, in contrast just don't think the culture of the Arab villager was a barrier to social change. You think it was external factors and political factors, the political economy if you will. And it wasn't about structural and cultural things that had to do with Islam – that had to do with a peasant society, that had to do with a family structure that was peculiar to the village.

Henry: I don't think so at all, but what I said before is a partial answer and I think it may be the key answer, and that is that Arab social life has been kept separate from Jewish social life. All of which means that some of the main things that bring people together, create an openness, not simply free movement in the sense that you can get into your car and travel all over the country, but in the sense that you have people who you can visit, and they come from the other nation. And when the other nation visits you, works alongside you, studies with you, and so on, little by little there is a breakdown of this kind of insular Arab village life. No new Arab town has been set up. No new movement of Arabs into a place like Haifa has taken place.

Zvi: Is that to be attributed only to the reluctance of the majority community – or does it have something to do with cultural factors?

Henry: Look, cultural factors as such, do develop, if you keep this kind of isolation syndrome in effect; this is what happens. In great part this is a class matter. Overwhelmingly, male Arabs are manual laborers and not in managerial positions, high-tech positions, government offices and so on. There are separate schools, you know, and it's not the same when you go down to the wadi, and you buy some vegetables there, or you have a better falafel, or better shwarma, or you go to visit Jaffa for an exotic experience.

Zvi: This is true even in a neutral environment where you have vastly different cultures. For example, ultra-orthodox Jews and I don't meet very often, unless it's a research situation.

Henry: Yes, but you're asking about this business, for example, of the
fundamentalism that's developed among the Arabs, the exaggerated number.
Why? Because people turn inward. People say we're not on political terms
with the Jews, the Jews regard us as second class citizens, and now
especially, as dangerous, even 'inscrutable'. We don't work in all the
different fields available to Jews.

Zvi: That's seeing the matter in a very limited way. I think you are viewing it
non-historically and non-dynamically, because the same things seem to be
happening in many societies in the world. In Moslem nations as well we see
the same thing, and it's not because of a conquest and it's not because of
isolation. It's because of other factors including a cyclic factor that we've
seen in history of the ups and downs of religious fundamentalism and indeed
of religious renewal generally.

Henry: Is that what you see all over the world? No! I don't see that all over the
world.

Zvi: You don't see it in Egypt? You don't see it in Syria? You don't see it in
any number of other countries where the pace of modernization has been
slow?

Henry: This is certainly so, but this is exactly a class problem in other places.
Here it's a class and national problem.

Zvi: That may be. It may be a class and national problem. But what I'm
suggesting may help us to explain something with regard to the lack of
progress towards modernization or the slowness of the process. Of course
modernization has taken place. I'm suggesting that it doesn't answer the
question of the return to religion and religious fundamentalism. This seems
to be a phenomenon that has many many other factors related to it.

Henry: There are other factors, including, quite clearly, the on-going conquest-
occupation situation. All this eats into the hearts of everybody. All this
creates further kinds of separation.

Zvi: It's [fundamentalist growth] happening all over the Arab world, the
Moslem world.

Henry: What you're looking for is something that says that culture explains
itself, as if it's fundamental to a mind set.

Zvi: I think what I *am* looking for is a way in which we might identify the
mechanisms which may help to explain why some societies move forward
more rapidly towards modernization and others, perhaps even in the other
direction, away from modernization.

Henry: You press in a direction of a Western modernity, an Islamic failure to
enter the world of modernization and, thus, an internalized, basic, Arab
cultural defect, if to speak to the local scene. I don't want to exaggerate your
position, but it's implicit. True, the historical development is western, it is
part of the Enlightenment, it is linked to scientific developments, the struggle
against monarchism, and despotism, the rise of a public spirit, the inroads
made against church and state. And among much else, fundamentalism has
increased in Arab Israeli society (encouraged at one time by the Israeli
government, by the way) and it is quite fundamental today to Jewish Israeli

society, by the way. The Enlightenment also gave rise to our two disciplines among much else. People are socialized into life, that is they learn and pass on cultural practices. I spoke before about how and why in 1953-54 I began my work in an Arab village on work, the family, marriage, etc., internal processes. But within a decade or two, through the work process mainly, the same Arabs remade themselves, through their perseverance, under the most difficult conditions. They became skilled workers throughout the country, became *the* manual and skilled workers. They built modern homes, equipped them with modern fixtures, turned their children into university students, turned to party politics, established country-wide roof organizations, demonstrated against inequality. This is change, modernity as you understand it, and as I do. And I wrote about politics then.

Nevertheless, in Israel if you are an Arab, you bring up your children within a village environment, even though the agriculture has disappeared, or maybe 1% of the population is involved in working in agriculture; it may be pastoral to the eye, but it is backward in terms of what it could enjoy. You have this kind of village environment with people on people, and all clumped together within a certain kind of a perimeter. I think this boundedness has to be changed. It hasn't undergone a total change in all the different areas such as in infrastructure, in education, in health care, in establishing an Arab university with half the students Jews, in Arab-Jewish industrial and high-tech centers. It is this kind of modernity that is lacking for them. People don't dodge modernity, at least not the modernity which clearly benefits their values. It's true that generally speaking there's a problem in the manner that many Arab men regard Arab women. But even with the great success of feminism in the West, it is an ongoing struggle throughout the world. This is a problem, but even if people would want to work out this problem they would have to do so under different kinds of circumstances, and these kinds of circumstances have not been provided. Nevertheless, I think many things have changed for Arabs, some of their own doing, some due to welfare and life in Israel in general. But even with the great success of feminism in the West, it is an ongoing struggle throughout the world.

Zvi: I have to ask, do we see similar lack of change and development in Moslem Arab societies in other places, where the reality of conquest and the reality of suppression and repression is not the key element? There may be political lack of freedom, but not exactly what we have in Israel: Non-integration, marginalization, and so on. I have to ask the question: Do certain fixed, or relatively fixed, cultural factors, help to explain the lack of rapid modernization or rapid change among the Arab population? And this inevitably gives rise to questions. Could it be that a shared culture, a shared religious culture, for example, a shared memory culture, can be such that it stymies modernization and development, as much, if not more, then external pressure?

Henry: The Middle East is certainly a backward and depressed area because of its political and economic structures. And the thing that I was saying was that we don't know what happens to people when new and other opportunities are provided. But this kind of investment in the Arab community in Israel has not really taken place. I'm not saying that welfare circumstances in Israel for Arabs aren't better than they are for Arabs in Egypt, Iraq, and elsewhere. Perhaps better, but it's not like what the Jewish population in Israel enjoys. This has been due to local Jewish history and to state input. The demeaned status of the Arabs, and they also remain controlled, is a barrier to their making their own history. By now it should be a joint Jewish-Arab process, to modernity, if you so wish to phrase it. If we want to understand culture not as a static entity, but something that is constantly changing, constantly being developed by the people whose culture it is, it means that this culture takes on new styles, and new approaches, even if it works against the matrix of the existing culture, meaning the existing culture has to change. Until we make a radical change in a so-called cultural baseline, we don't know what is the potential, and what input the Arabs in Israel can bring to it. When there is no political-religious repression people adopt the modernity that enhances their existing culture.

Zvi: But there are things that *are* seemingly static and which do come under the general rubric of culture. For example, the position of women. Now, it has been pointed out that one of the reasons for a lower rate of income in the Arab community can be attributed to the reluctance to accept the idea of women working outside of the village. Now, had there been more flexibility, cultural-religious flexibility, in this area could not other breakthroughs on the road to modernization have taken place?

Henry: Absolutely. What you say is half true. Half true for the reasons that I stated before. The other side of it is that there has to be input on people's part at the same time. It's not only something for the state to deal with. It's also for the Arabs, for the Palestinian Arabs in Israel also to do something about it. And quite clearly people have to free themselves. As I think I pointed out before, to a great extent they have done so. There are hundreds and hundreds of women in Arab villages who are teachers and lawyers and people with B.A.s and M.A.s and doctorates, but this is only really a very very small minority. There must be a realization that people have to do a number of things before change can occur. They have to make sure that women are educated. They have to make sure that women don't marry at 16, 17, 18, and for that matter not necessarily at 20, 21. The emphasis doesn't have to be on children. And there are certainly other factors. There are no Arab colleges, or maybe one, there's no Arab university. I'm not saying that this is an absolute necessity, but nevertheless, this would go a long way towards getting women into higher education.

Zvi: It's interesting that you're supportive of or in favor of a move in the direction of Arab higher education in the country which reinforces one of the problems that we discussed previously, namely the mutually agreed upon segregation between Arabs and Jews in the educational structure up to the university level. If they don't meet at the University level, where are they going to meet?

Henry: This kind of question of sort of imposing isolation – it's only one thing. The other universities exist. Jerusalem, Haifa, Tel Aviv, Beer Sheva – they all exist; it doesn't mean that all the Arabs in the country are going to university. People are realistic; people understand the fact that the universities in Israel, are at a relatively high level, and that kind of investment in the physical or natural sciences and in medical schools which would be required is questionable. It's okay. A central Arab university perhaps in Nazareth would point-up the problem of isolation. But Arabs would then have a choice of going to one or another university, but it would be a choice, and Jews would choose as well.

Zvi: One notices, walking around Haifa University, a tremendous growth of Arab women wearing traditional religious garb. Something that didn't exist five, seven, ten years ago. What does this represent, this seeming return to religion? Is it a response to the objective condition of the Arabs in Israel, who are looking to God to improve their situation? Or is it part of a worldwide trend, within Islamic culture?

Henry: Part of the answer is quite clear and to a degree it's a Middle Eastern Arab phenomenon. Things simply diffuse and they end up here as well. But, I mean I look at Israel also in terms of its particularity, and this didn't have to be. If you recall, 20-25 years ago there was a strong joint Arab-Jewish student organization in Haifa. Like I said before, I think there's been a destructive regression in Israeli society; society has gone into reverse. Not only has it become ten times more nationalistic and militaristic but additionally this arrogant religiosity has become a strong element in Jewish Israeli society, and for different reasons in Arab-Israeli life. The fact that the kinds of developments that should have taken place among the Arab community have not taken place, has allowed for inroads as well in terms of, what I believe are certainly not progressive elements. I don't regard a return to religion or a movement toward religion as a positive development. I personally think it's something which is irrational, even if we can provide explanations. My response is that it is something that the Arabs themselves have to struggle against. An atmosphere has been created which doesn't represent new openings for people. It's a retreat, and it comes in place of going into open politics and the development of political activity with Jewish political groups. Arabs are liable to find themselves in the same camp with the Jewish fundamentalists, even if for exact opposite national aims. That is, nationalism if it has any positive side to it has to be a progressive kind of nationalism, that is, it has to emphasize international solidarity at one and the same time. It has to look for something that leads to joining between people – that leads to working together with other people – not only within your own community, but with other communities as well. It means a new and different kind of openness, and as I say, this present fundamentalism is retrograde evolution. It's regression, it's everything that the Arabs in Israel don't require. And I think that the Israeli government just loves this kind of a situation, where they have Arab fundamentalists to point to. It allows for this kind of Jewish-Israeli paternalism.

Zvi: In an area different from the position and status of Arabs, you argue in one of your papers that the state encouraged the development of the middle class. What model for the growth and allocation of capital would have been more useful than the creation of a middle class by the State in a situation where the middle class was weak and small and the state was centralized? Did you have a model in mind, or are you merely observing that the state was the initiator of this middle class development and gave it shape and form?

Henry: I think that in regard to your question, that there were two things involved. A comment – I don't think we, since this also involves Shula, I don't think we had a model in mind. We apply what we know about power, the state, history, classes; you don't analyze if you don't have the intellectual tools for it Of the two points, the first one I think, would have to be that people, anthropologists, sociologists, people who study life, the life we lead in the place we live in, have to make evaluations. Secondly, how come it developed the way it did, or how come things happen in a certain fashion? As social historians, you have to find out what the reasons are, what the causes are; that's basic, right?

Zvi: The piece was rather descriptive of how things develop rather than programmatic in how they could have or should have developed.

Henry: I think that the other side of it comes out in most of our papers, and that is that because of the nature of Israeli society, not only should things have been different, but that they could have been different; in our essays on 'militaristic nationalism', 'the socialist alternative', 'the non-return of the Arab refugees' and others. That's the point, meaning that in this respect, steps were taken by the political forces that were present and they explicitly turned things around. Israel was not a socialist society, but the potential for a socialist society, an alternative society, existed. It existed in terms of the input that had been made previously, by the political movements which were there. The political groupings to a degree fought among themselves, but they were also in conflict – not only in intellectual conflict, but in political conflict as well – with bourgeois forces, and class forces. We're speaking here about a workers' society that had the potential to become a socialist society but the forces in power opted for a different direction and they carried the disaffected, the right, and the new immigrants with them.

Zvi: Let me take that a bit further. I think we agree that the truly socialist or collective dimensions of the society were limited to the relatively few even in the early years – those who lived in the kibbutzim, to some extent in the moshavim, perhaps certain forces within the Histadrut. Essentially, an urban society was evolving here based on a European model. Maybe a model of social democracy or a liberal bourgeois model, but not a model of socialism. Was there ever really a chance that this society, other than in revolutionary circumstances, would develop into a socialist entity?

Henry: First of all, I think certain revolutionary conditions had already been met. While this was predominantly an urban society, it was also an organized society. And the Histadrut wasn't small potatoes – it was a strong organized force and people were committed to it. No, you are wrong, these weren't small numbers, this current represented a majority in the Yishuv. And the fact that the numbers in kibbutzim were relatively small, (some 7%, 8 % at maximum) it was living a communal life; I mean the kind of life that we've often spoken about was the kind of life that we wanted to live, in one form or another, a life of implicit equality. I'm speaking of people with a political, social and ethical sense of life. This sense of what is worthwhile was shared by most. These were certainly people who had transformed their way of life, and it wasn't only people who worked on the land and in industry, and who fundamentally controlled a life situation within the kibbutz and within cooperative villages. And by themselves, these social formats were revolutionary and certainly revolutionary for Jews, but also, the socialist and the social democratic parties were dominant in pre-state Israel throughout the mandatory period until 1948. There wasn't an area of life – be it in terms of medicine, welfare, the land, transport, industry, even in banking – there wasn't an area of life in which people who belonged to the Histadrut and the left-wing political parties which directed it, weren't dominant. This came about even though a middle class was always present in Israel. There were capitalists who always existed in Israel. There were 'bourgeois', and perhaps a bourgeois mentality present and whatever derives from that. But these weren't the people who dominated society. And even if you want to speak of a certain sense of – I think we've mentioned this previously – even if you want to speak of a certain kind of hegemony, a certain kind of total control, not only in terms of the political, but in all areas, and in almost everything – in poetry, in literature, in cultural life in general – you name it, people who were represented in the workers' parties, had a strong influence on institutionalized life and on a general life style. Look nothing was final, absolutely crystallized, a struggle was going on between forces and classes. It's the struggle that is missing today.

Zvi: Wouldn't you say that the nature of the immigration that followed the creation of the state inevitably would have doomed such an idyll?

Henry: I don't know what's inevitable. This sense of the possibility of statehood on the horizon was certainly fairly well developed by the early 1940s and this was the direction that Mapai certainly was considering. There are clearly dozens of other factors involved, such as the support that the US gave the fledgling state which certainly was not meant to aid in the development of a socialist state, but rather of something that would move in a direction more amenable to the understanding of the United States. Not incidentally, there hasn't been a radical political-social situation in the world where the United States did not intervene. Additionally, the Arabs fled the country and were pushed out more or less simultaneously, but all of a sudden there was booty to be had. Land was open in all the Arab villages. All the Arabs were gone. All the Arab property was now in the hands of the new Jewish State, and this was enticing. When you take into consideration that at one and the same time, there was a so-called replacement of the Arabs who were no longer present by a mass Jewish immigration, there was this interlocking interrelationship that for one thing, was a fact, and for another thing could be exploited for whatever reasons the state deemed necessary. Soon the massive reparations from Germany would flow in. A social democratic party that was now going in the direction of statism, and statism here meant not socialism but putting to work forces under a bureaucracy that was little by little beginning to enjoy extensive external means.

Zvi: The question we're trying to pursue is why the socialist ethos that had been so dominant, as you maintained, in Israel, and pre-Israel began to disintegrate and unravel. And you are suggesting that one of the issues was the replacement of the Arabs which lead to the accumulation of great wealth and land by the State and the development of statism. Also America which was giving so much aid (although the aid from America in the early years was not that great). However, there's another issue here that might have been more influential: The state had to develop capital for industrialization, for supporting the masses of immigrants who arrived in the early years. I don't know what methods existed for the creation of capital from a starting base of zero other than inflicting great suffering as we saw in the Soviet Union, after the revolution and during the twenties, or to try to garner capital through reparations, and through the support of world Jewry which raised other questions. World Jewry was not keyed into the idea of the socialist state any more than the American government was. So the question becomes, was there another way of doing it? Maybe you can say yes, maybe it would have taken longer, but it would have come through the development of wealth using the methods that the kibbutz used to develop wealth, that the moshav used to develop wealth. But maybe the time needed was an untenable luxury for such a fragile national enterprise as this was.

Henry: What you're saying is that, here look, this is what happened, and to a large degree it has proved itself successful, depending upon how you mean "successful." Certainly Israel became viable fairly rapidly, and it became a Middle East force for dozens of different reasons. It became a bright light that got support from throughout the world, and particularly American Jewry, the German reparations, and it also became a military force in the area. All these things began to dovetail also in terms of U.S. – Israeli military relations – you know – a new tier with Turkey, Iran and Israel, and all these things began to work out. It took years, Israel pleading to become an ally and when Israel developed militarily it was taken aboard. But to answer your question, you can only know if you try to solve the problem of getting capital and attaining massive amounts of capital by a socialist society. Since it wasn't really undertaken, I don't have a real answer. If I have to fall back on anything, it would be to assert that the groundwork existed here – the possibility existed. Part of the thing is if we like the path that we've taken when we look at developments within Israel, and we want to judge them, what do we say? We look around and we see all the modern universities, we see all the modern industry, we see all the high tech, the great accumulation of wealth, a real capitalist class, and so on and so forth. We see "modernity" at large in Israel – and what do we do, we pat ourselves on the back and we say we're satisfied. And others, I think, say things quite the opposite. We're trying to say, how can we turn things around? We like to see the industry, we like to see the fine universities, and we like to see nice housing sections in Haifa and Tel Aviv and other places, and I'm not making light of it. I mean all of these things have taken place, and brought a good deal of satisfaction at the same time. What do we also see? We also see at the same time this massive segment of wealth that is in the hands of a very few people, together with an expanded middle class and a greatly expanded lower class. A true class society, with totally changed values. We see a militaristic society in Israel; we see the occupation; Israel a colonial state; we see people who no longer really live in a welfare state, and even if during the 50s and the early 60s, they could combine warfare and welfare more or less at the same time, or at least to a high degree, this is very rapidly disappearing. People can no longer rely on the Histadrut. People can no longer rely on health care. There are people who are, I won't say absolutely poverty stricken, but who are close. And certainly people suffer. And we're making another people suffer, that is the Palestinians, at the same time. And if we look at our place in the world, we enjoy being the allies of the U.S., and at the same time I think we're judged by the majority of the world as an oppressor state. So what do you say? You're not satisfied, I know. I know lots of people who at least talk in these terms. We no longer have socialist parties in this country. No longer. We don't have a socialist opposition to what's going on. Left-wing, opposition newspapers no longer exist. We barely have an organized opposition in any radical sense of the word. Once upon a time, this was the majority of the population. We don't want a world where Israel also represents the Atom Bomb, threatens world stability, and threatens itself.

Zvi: You think Israel threatens its neighbors with an Atom Bomb?

Henry: This kind of threat exists, Zvi. It exists. What? Do you think the people who live around Dimona don't feel threatened? What do they know about the air they breathe. All these things of course are touch and go. But it's not the kind of thoughts that people want floating around in their heads. And if the nuclear scientists tell us, nah what are you speaking about; who knows? Who really knows? And this is only one facet of what's going on. The other facets are also the fact that we're committed to warfare, while everybody knows that the solutions lie someplace between Oslo and the Geneva Accords, some form of reconciliation with the Palestinians. This is the kind of arena in which our children and our grandchildren are educated, and we say, well, this is not the way we think; this is not the way we feel. We have to do more; otherwise, vulgarity will overwhelm us. People will leave, and apparently great numbers are already doing so.

Zvi: But the reasons for emigration from this country are more than the sum total of the nature of life in this country. It has to do with size, it has to do with history, it has to do with culture.

Henry: Exactly, what are we speaking about?! We're speaking about history, culture, science – we're speaking about all these things.

Zvi: The history and culture of the Jews is one of movement and migration.

Henry: I'm sorry – if you want to speak about movement as mechanical
   movement and ...

Zvi: Here's another word: "rootlessness".

Henry: ...migration or the "rootlessness" of mankind...?

Zvi: Not of mankind – of Jews!

Henry: Or of Jews -- whatever. If I understand, my sense of Zionism is such
   that one of the things that Zionism is supposed to have overcome, and rightly
   so, is the sense of rootlessness.

Zvi: And it didn't – among the other things that it didn't do.

Henry: Okay, but it's not something due to the nature of the Jews. It is also the
   sense of dissatisfaction and also the sense that if you want greater
   satisfaction, you might well achieve greater satisfaction in New York,
   London, and Toronto. Or wherever.

Zvi: This is open to disagreement, debate. Why and how the whole business of
   emigration, the whole business of ties, of rootedness, the lack of rootedness,
   and what have you. But to come back, you and Shula have spoken of Israel
   as a militaristic society. Could you sum up very succinctly what you mean
   by a militaristic society. Is it a society in which the army takes center stage
   in terms of decision making; the use of the national treasure, or in the sense
   that the country is militarily organized, as it were, militarily determined in
   what should be civilian enterprises: its teaching, its learning, its culture, its
   economy? Why is this a militaristic society is what I'm asking.

Henry: This is, like everything else in life, an historical development. This
   means that there are multiple things involved. First of all, I have to say that I
   don't doubt that Israel from the very start had to defend itself, and I also
   believe that there's no way, knowing the world as we do – it can defend
   itself if weak. Meaning as far as we can see in general terms, there has to be
   a military. But I'm speaking about something else. I think more or less that
   the seeds of the militaristic nationalism that developed in Israel began very
   close to 1948 and the fallout from the war. I'm not saying that this fallout
   was due to Israeli evil or anything like that, but part of the fruits of this war
   were, of course, the Arab refugees. And when 150,000 remain and 750,000
   are outside, and Israel begins a policy where it is definitely against any
   return of the Arab refugees, it also represents a certain stance, a position, a
   certain kind of a regard (or disregard) for Palestinian Arabs, and also for
   surrounding Arab states. It means that there's something that's already
   developed in Israel. I mean along with it we create rationalizations. We
   regard other people in a certain way, and this becomes problematic, for
   example, the ultra-nationalistic element in militarism. It also became a
   military supporter of the United States, and over time a military ally of the
   United States in almost every capacity. We've also always considered the
   local Arab population as a potential fifth column, and we've inculcated this
   kind of idea into Israeli Jewish society. That is, we regard the others, local
   Arabs, surrounding people, either as our enemies or our potential enemies.
   And meanwhile we've also built up this military force which is second to
   none in the Middle East (and as the Israeli military and the Israeli state like

to claim, maybe not secondary to any other except the U.S.). And we are preoccupied, of course, with the military and our number one industry is the military industry, and it's a military industry which is prepared to sell throughout the world and works in cohorts with the United States. It's what we are – what we are is military, what we are, what we represent to ourselves, what we represent to Jews, and to the surrounding neighborhood and to the world as a whole. And we flaunt the atom bomb. We are powerful and we use our military force to take over land, to occupy. We do not negotiate for peace; rather, we use our force to threaten, to say we gain our ends by military means. Both our means and our ends are destructive and our government, our military, our religious leaders, and a large segment of our population lend support. It's a military society, and it's certainly more complex than being solely a military society, but if you want to define it, if you want to look for its overarching elements, we can say that it's become a militaristic-nationalistic society.

Zvi: I'm afraid I still don't really understand the militaristic part of it. If you want to say that the society has an inordinate amount of influence filtering into it from perceived military needs or the nature of how the military is built here, I would agree. But if you walk the streets of this country, and review the nature of its institutions you might, with a certain degree of justice, arrive at another position.

Henry: No, I would not. It also puts it to use. Day in and day out, look at the way we regard the larger Palestinian population. I mean what kind of a society can keep an occupation going for almost four decades. What kind of a society can keep an occupation going for this amount of time. We are a militaristic society. What are we using our military for? For land aggrandizement; to prove our value to our ally; to threaten, and more.

Zvi: Is America a militaristic society?

Henry: Yes. To a great extent yes. It's the most powerful and wealthy society in the world, and it uses its power to gain its ends, and nobody can stand against the United States. Everybody collapses before the United States. It's a terrible situation, especially with the downfall of the Soviet Union, people don't have any other place to turn for support. They can't utilize even the Soviet Union – if they want to become allies or not, they can't utilize the Soviet Union as a counter force. America controls the world – goes to war, practically speaking, whenever it wants to go to war, and it can rely on Israel to do whatever it says... And as for us locally, simply the idea of containing, of controlling another people – it's disgusting. Now, this is the military. We have so many patriotic children who want to go into the toughest kinds of combat units – it speaks to a certain kind of problem. I think it's a problem worth studying because many of these young people come from families who know better, and nevertheless allow their children to make this kind of step and go into these kind of units under these kinds of circumstances. It's a problem. It remains a kind of dominant ethos in Israel – perhaps because of its history. But it is totally different from Jewish heroism during world War II and during and prior to the 1948 war.

Zvi: It's a country full of paradoxes, but that's a paradox which I think we can understand.

Henry: I'm not so sure we can understand it. We're liable to put it into words, but we're also liable to make a mistake. There are many ways of rationalizing things, and there have always been kids from the 12th grade who have organized letters to the Prime Minister and refused to serve in the occupied territories. And you know, they are 17 and 18 years old, but their numbers are small.

Zvi: Towards the end of your article on "Israel's Political Economy and the Widening Class Gap", you posit that the regime is equalizing the status of Arabs on both sides of the Green Line, downgrading the local Arabs to those of the West Bank. Do you still think the facts justify this, that we're downgrading the local Arabs to the status of those in the West Bank? Also, is there any fault to be found with local Israeli Arab leadership which may be working towards blurring the line between the two groups?

Henry: I think that the starting points are different for the Palestinian Arabs in Israel, and the Palestinian Arabs in the occupied territories. The main difference having been that for long periods of time after the end of military government, the Palestinian Arabs in Israel traveled all over the country, moved all over the country, worked all over the country, and their economic situation, and therefore their general social situation improved greatly. Now, there was a very brief period of time when 100,000 Palestinians from the occupied territories were working in Israel, and then these two groups were to a degree, intermingled. However, two things of a different nature apparently happened. One thing is that for the Palestinians in the occupied territories, this period ended fairly quickly. The sources of income for the occupied Palestinians were cut off, and total, full occupation descended upon them, and they entered into a period which constitutes a poverty situation. Meanwhile, the Palestinian Arabs in Israel move freely, and work wherever they want to work within Israel. Of course no longer within the occupied territories, and very little with Palestinians from the occupied territories. These kinds of connections have been truncated and almost done away with completely. At the same time, meanwhile, the unemployed among the Arabs in Israel has skyrocketed. There are villages where 15, 20, 25% of the working population is unemployed, and this means a disastrous situation. There are other factors that were also involved. The numbers of educated Arabs in Israel has grown greatly – the numbers of professionals, skilled people – there are people entering different lines of work, and even a certain kind of a middle class – lawyers, doctors and others as well – has developed among them. But this educated stratum can't easily find employment either.

Zvi: In other words, you don't think the situation is equal, as between the Arabs in Israel and the Arabs in the West Bank, in terms of their economic standing, their educational standing, and other factors. The Arabs of Israel still enjoy a higher standard of life than the Arabs in the West Bank.

Henry: For sure, in terms of their work and welfare situation. There's nothing like what is still present in Israel in terms of national insurance, old age

pensions, family supplements. And also compulsory education. Even with
all the inroads that are being made by the neo-conservatives, it's something
that starkly differentiates between the two.

Zvi: In recent articles on the refugees, you note that expulsions happen in war,
but non-return, you say, is a new position. My point is, as I noted to you
earlier in our conversation, that history is replete with other examples where
in fact it's not the case that return is inevitable even though there are
expulsions in many places.

Henry: I don't think that's what appeared – I don't think it goes that way. What
we wrote, if I remember correctly, is that there is also after the war, that
while there are horrendous situations, and they happen all over the world,
there is an "after".

Zvi: That's exactly what I'm referring to...

Henry: I understand – but with differences in extent, of course, that are most
meaningful and different all over the world. Generally speaking, after the
war, people do return to their homes. They get back to their homes. I'm not
saying that there aren't situations where their homes are closed off to them or
that they've lost their homes or that their states are corrupt and they don't
allow them back. This also happens. What we were trying to say, I'm quite
sure, in this essay, is two things: that in general, there is also after the war,
and there's this kind of sense, there *was* this kind of sense, at least, that after
the war, people would return to their homes. I think the Arabs certainly
thought so, and I think that the Jews thought so as well. It doesn't mean that
every Jew thought so, especially as Arabs fled and other people took their
property and took over their homes. But the main point was that, prior to
1948, and prior to statism, and prior to these first signs of militaristic
nationalism, values were different. Although there was not a socialist regime,
the socialist and socialist democratic parties that were dominant in the
Yishuv, the Yishuv in general, represented people of high social conscience.
People knew better, the Yishuv leadership knew better; the war victory
following a bitter war, the nationalist spirit that separated between Jews and
Arabs, opportunism and the glory of the new Jewish state took over. The
people of the Yishuv were socialized for co-existence, the statist leadership
failed to make a case for the return of the Arab refugees – to the contrary, it
pressured for 'they will not return'. The left-wing in the government, both
from Achdut Ha'avodah and Hashomer Hatzair, did make a case; it should
have been consistent and without respite. This socialist input existed, and
was present. Could it have been otherwise? It could have been otherwise.
And, the Arabs should have been returned. It's not a question Zvi. That's
not what happened. That's exactly what we tried to explain; that the return
could have happened and why it didn't happen.

Zvi: Why it didn't happen I think is complicated, and yet fairly obvious.

Henry: The difference being is that, as we've tried to show again and again, in
that article and in other articles, that this socialist potential is a fact. It
existed, it was deeply entrenched in pre-State Israel, and if history has any
importance in terms of what goes into making a person, making a politically

and socially conscious human being, then socialism had everything going for it, and something of that should have come out and could have, as I said. And by the way, like other things in life, it's not all over. It's not all finished. They're trying to wipe out history by taking over Palestinian territory, by degrading the Israeli Arabs and the Palestinians. Somehow, people don't necessarily forget. New generations come to the fore.

Zvi: What exactly can be done with respect to the refugee problem?

Henry: I don't think that you have to reach any real form of exactness. It's like other things in life. First of all I think you have to recognize overwhelming errors. And one of the things which will change the total complexion of the Israeli State will be this kind of recognition.

Zvi: What is the nature of recognition?

Henry: The nature of recognition is exactly what I said. We have to reach some kind of a common understanding, a reconciliation, in terms of what happened. What form this understanding takes, is something we have to work out with the people who were affected. That is, when Jews and Palestinians will begin to negotiate to speak about this problem in the same way that was done, let's say, in South Africa, and I think there are signs elsewhere as well. It's not only that. This is what has to be done for the sake of intelligence and integrity, and for one's understanding that you can't behave as racists and extreme nationalists, and that people have to work out their problems here. What I'm saying holds for both Jews and Arabs. I'm not a moralist. It's not a matter of mea culpa, but of how to live side by side, and then together if possible.

Zvi: I don't contest what you say about recognition on the part of the majority here of the nature of what happened, and the suffering that was caused, and how this can be a cleansing factor – perhaps a healthy notion. There does exist here a series of sociological political problems that are rather unique. One of them being that if we speak in terms of a refugee return, and if it is a massive refugee return, the nature of the society does a complete flip-flop. With a massive refugee return, it's conceivable that there would also be a complete, population or demographic reversal, which in a democratic context means suicide.

Henry: Zvi, you know we're not speaking of these matters in terms of numbers and a mass return of refugees. That isn't the thing. First of all, just think what would happen if Israel first of all would return to the '67 borders – first step – Israelis would look at one another differently. Secondly, take down this disgusting fence that they're putting up – you know, it's a separation fence that's separating between people. It's also an Israeli statement that "We consider you a dangerous people, you're terrorists." Of course, Israel fails to mention that it wants to rewrite the boundaries, that the occupation has a pay-off. The whole idea is repulsive, but that is the way of the Israeli state, which has rapidly developed into a racist state. I'm sorry, but it's a fact, and that's what we do to ourselves, and what we do to other people, and so people lose recognition of how they could possibly live. And I want a strong Israeli opposition to form which in total will go against what the present Israeli state has stood for. And until something like this happens, then the situation will continue to be intolerable. I mean it smells bad, and in every sense of the word.

Zvi: Is every ethnically-based state, by definition, a racist state?

Henry: First of all, states are as they are, as we find them, and you have to start from there. In Germany today, for example, the starting point is giving the Turks their full citizen rights. That's part of it – opening it up, not setting up boundaries between people. Even if people decide they don't want to live close to their neighbors, let it be, but let them enjoy every possible social benefit that exists. I mean, again as in Germany, you invited them there, you let them come in, as cheap labor, and all of a sudden, they invite their cousins to come in – okay, that is life, if the cousins get in, it is as it should be. The United States has worked it out to a certain extent. Immigrant countries are open, and we both know all the black marks that have existed in this immigration process; the cut-offs, the people that were accepted, the people that were rejected. But nevertheless, that's what exists in America. It constitutes a multi-cultural country. Okay, let them work it out.

Zvi: They [the U.S.] have worked it out. They've worked it out in a very interesting way which other countries are apparently not able to do. One of them is that this vast, diverse immigrant population has assimilated itself to an essentially WASP pattern of dominance. And as long as this is in place, America is satisfied to let it go. You can speak Spanish, you can still have a dark skin, you can still do this, that and the other thing, but you must accept a certain base line cultural identity which has roots and recognizable origins.

Henry: I don't know about that. This is a Huntington sociological answer which assumes that the United States has settled on some kind of a format which it tries to sell. It doesn't necessarily hold water. In fact, I find this WASP theory funny, but funny not to my liking.

Zvi: It has held water up until now.

Henry: People don't accept it. It's very difficult, when 10% of the population is Black, it's very difficult to say that it's White Protestant. It's not that way at all. I don't know what the percentage of Hispanics are, but here too I don't think the demand is that they become WASPs. I think it's some kind of sociological fiction. And I think it works out some other way, but not the creation of a device where this White Protestant element will be the adhesive factor. Hopefully not.

Zvi: It's a matter of a deal that America made with its immigrants. And it was this: The gates are open as long as you, over the course of time, come to look more and more like we do and sound more and more like we do. If you insist on a dominant separative ethnic policy, then you're outside the consensus. And this has been the deal that America has won with. I think they've done remarkably well. But I don't think it's something that Israeli Jews can do vis-à-vis the Arab population, for example, or that the Poles can do vis-à-vis the Germans in their midst, or Transylvanian Rumanians can do with respect to Hungarians. These are ethnic entities that have a self consciousness and a self awareness and a demand for remaining who they were. Now what's going to happen with the Hispanics in America may complicate this. I don't know.

Henry: The price, and it's a good price, of democracy and openness is that people like it, and people take advantage of it as they should, and they don't stick to one neighborhood. And all of a sudden, places get mixed, and all of a sudden there's intermarriage, and you know much better than I do that today the Jews find it tough to intermarry among Jews in the States. I don't find any problem with intermarrying.

Zvi: But isn't it interesting that this is happening at the same time as Jews are becoming so heavily integrated. What does it mean? It means that the price that was paid was the elimination of dissonance, like *intra*marriage. Intramarriage, of course, means you only married among yourselves, which to some extent meant you basically socialized among yourselves. That stopped, and the integration rose (or vice versa). The same is true of any number of other groups in America.

Zvi: In conclusion, I have just two more questions that I want to put to you. You've had a partnership throughout your career with Shula Carmi, your wife of many years. How did this work; how did you work it out?

Henry: What am I going to tell you? We don't speak to one another?

Zvi: Do you split up sections, do you separate research for articles. Do you fight about the articles and about the ideas that are being raised. What's the nature of the partnership?

Henry: How it works out is something I find very difficult myself to totally understand. Some things about it I do understand. Whatever the division of labor is, important or not important, one of the main problems in our collaboration is that it takes us a very very long time to finally finish something.

Zvi: Why? Is it because of the partnership?

Henry: No, I don't think so. Maybe. But sometimes we simply go on to other things because we find them important. I don't know when it started. Whenever it started it was very soon after we met. And we've been together for almost 50 years. I quickly learned to value, as do many others, Shula's intellectual originality and an intellectual independence and intelligence that is rare. I have great respect for her ideas, and I found no problem, absolutely no problem following her lead in many matters. And that's been I think more or less the saving grace. I could say a great deal more, but Shula would never forgive me. She won't forgive me for the little I've said. What do we each contribute? Sometimes it works out, and sometimes it doesn't work out.

Zvi: Do you think it takes longer simply because there are two of you?

Henry: For sure. We work at different times. Until we work together and start organizing and polishing a lot of time passes. And then this whole formalization is always problematic. How and when to finish something! We have published seven or eight essays and have a couple more which together we should put out in book form. We have three manuscripts, each some 300 pages long – one on the kibbutz, one on class-national developments in Palestine and Israel, one on late Ottoman Palestine – that we should do something about.

Zvi: I want to come back to one line of thought you have returned to, perhaps more than once in the course of our talk; it can be summed up as "We had so much going for us, more than other countries, but we killed it."

Henry: Okay, we've gone into this several times in our discussion. I think and I know that other people have thought this as well – and I know for sure, there are thousands who believe that socialism is worth struggling for and living for, and more. It stands for the equality that human beings deserve, and it means above all, struggle. And it is a struggle; I say it's not a struggle without humor, without art, without love. It's with all these things. Nevertheless, there are always these other groups, there are always other ideas; there are always those who contest it. I think that this kind of attempt at socialism was being put into practice in the thirty or forty years prior to the State of Israel, prior to the statehood of Israel. The lexicon of human agency is in place here. People were attempting, and with all their human failures, and with all their mistakes; this is what was going on. And there's no sense in painting an over-glorified picture of what was taking place, but it's very important also to recognize what was going on. And this present-day putdown of this attempt at working for socialism as if it was a passing fancy, as if it were some kind of temporary stage, or some kind of momentary mechanism deriving from the situation, is simple rubbish. It's not true. I believe the Jewish public as a whole had a more sophisticated understanding of the situation of pre-state Israel together with a much greater personal involvement in what was taking place, than do most academics with hindsight have today. And as I say, if there's anything that I find ridiculous, it's people who refer to this as merely nostalgia for the past.

Zvi: Your analysis differs from most working in Israeli social history.

Henry: In a few words, Shula and I took the position that socialist potential, a socialist alternative, was present and we explained why. We went on to explain the great transformation that went into the deliberate undercutting of this alternative with statism; we explained its components and the active forces, such as political parties, economic class, ideology. In different papers we emphasized the processes, the radical changes, involved as the state 'made' a middle class, through privatization of public means, creating sharp class differences within Israeli society and especially with the depressed Arab minority, fostering the rise of militaristic nationalism, and then with the occupation the move to higher militarism, ultra-nationalism, colonial rule. I think in these respects and others we differed fundamentally from those, let us say 'old-historians or old sociologists' who offered their linear interpretation of an implicit development from a simple, but organized state-in-the-making Yishuv Jewish society, to a more complex, more highly organized state society – in which things happen, but for them they fall into place functionally-structurally. And we differed from the 'new-historians, new sociologists' who began with something on the order of 'original sin', whereby the Zionist project was, from the beginning, colonialist-capitalist in deed and in concept, that the second aliyah proto-settlements and then early communes and cooperatives, and then later ones of the Third Aliyah, were mechanical expressions of Zionist institutional bodies finding settlement in groups as being little more than economically expedient. The colonialist-capitalist theorizing is dead wrong, as is the total lack of understanding of what human agency is all about. The input of the socialist-oriented pioneers on the surroundings, on the Zionist settlement institutions, on the groups that followed, the movements, the political parties, the Histadruth, and the combined force this creates – this lack of understanding that passes for critique, is, I believe, misguided. Just think, their critical input in their linear schema today is at the level where the neo-conservative economy of the present day right wing Israeli government is the policy which will terminate the occupation in order to insure Israel's place within the globalized world economy.

Zvi: In a couple of sentences, and this is the last question, do you have any dream or conception or fantasy about what things should or could look like here come ten-fifteen-twenty years from now? Do you think for example that a bi-national state is still a possibility?

Henry: Under current circumstances, no. I think that the best we can achieve, and that's the thing that we have to work for, is a two-state solution with the 1967 boundaries as our reference point. Here I mean with absolutely negotiated boundaries. The sooner that takes place, the sooner other things will possibly work out. Then, how we can cross boundaries and live together. How they work out will perhaps take years.

On Friday my daughter Dana and her children came to visit and Dana has a baby boy whose name is Lenny named after my brother, who is the same age as Adam who is Maya's son. They are the smallest of my twelve grandchildren, each two years old, with only a couple of months between them. And Adam walked into this room of, oh, I don't know, eight to ten people, most being strange to him, and he stood there. And he stood there for maybe five minutes, and he looked around. He just looked around, since Dana and her family live in the Galilee he rarely met with them.. He didn't say a word. Not that he has too many words, but he just looked, looked, and after about five minutes – and he always carries two or three little cars in his hands – he walked over to Lenny who was sitting in his mother's lap and he gave him a little truck. And everybody broke out laughing. Adam hadn't said a word. I mean he was trying to decide what this whole situation meant for him. What was he going to do? Who were these people? I suppose a little truck goes a long way.

Zvi: An example of socialism in action?

Henry: What I wanted to say, of course, in a sentimental foolish vein, is that we pass what we pass on to them and then we'll have to leave it up to them – brothers and sisters, everybody else's brothers and sisters, their cousins and friends, their children.

Zvi: It's neither foolish nor overly sentimental. Thank you.

Henry Rosenfeld
Some Signposts and Bibliography

Date of Birth: Dec. 30, 1922
Place of Birth: New York, New York
Residence: Jerusalem, Israel
Army: U.S. Army 1942-45
      Israeli Army 1948-49 (volunteer)

New York University, B.A. 1939-42; 1946 (Spring) (B.A. 1946).
Columbia University, Ph.D. (Anthropology) 1947 (Fall); 1949-1951 (Ph.D. 1951).

1951	*The Military Occupational Specialization of the Kin: A Key to the Understanding of the Process of Caste Formation in the Arabian Desert* (Columbia University), unpublished. Supervisors: Prof. Gene Weltfish, Prof. Julian Steward, Prof. Joseph Greenberg
1951-1952	Social Science Research Council, Area Research Post Graduate Fellowship - (Development Processes of the Kibbutz)
1952-1953	Ford Foundation Fellowship - (Arab Village Social Structure)
1955-61	Hebrew University - External Lecturer
1956-1960	Social Anthropological Field Research Projects: At request of Department of Health, Israel - (Social Conditions of an Immigrant Town); (Health and Social Conditions of an Arab Village). At request of Prime Minister's Office - (Economic Conditions of Arab Villages). At request of Israel-American Fund (Perspectives for Cultural-Economic Development). At request of Hadassah Medical School - (Social Factors Governing Tension and Heart Disease).
1956	*Taiybe: An Analysis of Patterns of Authority and an Investigation of Basic Health Conditions and Attitudes* (Ministry of Health, Govt. of Israel: 80 pp.).
1957	"An Analysis of Marriage and Marriage Statistics in a Moslem-Christian Arab Village". *International Archives of Ethnography*, 48: 1, pp. 32-62.
1957	"Processes of Structural Change Within the Arab Village Extended Family". *American Anthropologist* 60, 1958. (pp. 1127-1139) (Also in Hebrew - *Megamot* 8: 4).
1957-61	Haifa Extension - External Lecturer
1958	"Kiryat Shmona: A Jewish Immigrant Town". (*Mibiphnim*, Vol. 20, arts 1,2,3 (Hebrew).
1959	"Changes in the Occupational Structure of an Arab Village" *Mibiphnim* 22: 71-83 (Hebrew).

1961-1963	Articles for *New Outlook*: "A Cultural Program for the Arab Village" IV: 3, 1961; (also in Hebrew *Megamot* 11: 3, 1961); "The Arab Village Proletariat", V: 3, 1962; "Wage Labour and Status in the Arab Village", VI: 1, 1963.
1961-66	Hebrew University - Teaching Associate; Haifa College – Teaching Associate; (also Tel-Aviv Extension) - Teaching Associate
1962	Iroquois, Pastoral Nomadism (Encyclopedia of Social Sciences – Hebrew, D. Knaani, ed.); Matriarchate, Morgan, Maori, Mead, Bachofen (Hebrew).
1962-1967	Scientific Director, Israel Center for Anthropological Research.
1963	Review: Murdock, G.P., Africa, Its Peoples and Their Culture History in *Hamizrah Hehadash* (The New East), pp. 173-178 (Hebrew).
1964	Review: Diamond, S. (ed.), Culture in History, in *Megamot*, pp. 285-288 (Hebrew).
1964	"From Rural Peasantry to Rural Proletariat and Residual Peasantry: The Transformation of an Arab Village" in *Process and Pattern in Culture: Essays in Honor of Julian N. Steward*, R.A. Manners (ed.). (Aldine, Chicago: 1964); also in *Peoples and Cultures of the Middle East*. L.E. Sweet (ed.). (Natural History Press, N.Y.: 1970); also in Israel: *A Local Anthropology*, Abuhav, Hertzog, Goldberg, Marx, eds. Tel-Aviv, Tscherikover, 1998 (Hebrew).
1964	*They Were Peasants* (Hem Hayu Falachim) Hakibbutz Hameuchad Publishers, Tel Aviv, 221 pp.
	Papers delivered in Israel include those at the Israel Sociological Association, several at the Israel Anthropological Association, papers at the Israel Oriental Society, Truman, etc., as well as papers at conferences and departmental seinars at Haifa University, The Hebrew Unviersity, Manchester University, Brooklyn College, The New School for Social Research, Rutgers University, Cambridge University, London University, London School of Economics, University of Mexico, University of Lucknow, India, Zaragossa, Spain, Athens, Nicosia, Rome, New Delhi, Marseilles, and papers delivered through the years at AAA conferences.
1965	Ruppin Prize of Haifa City for book: *They Were Peasants*.
1965	"The Social Composition of the Military in the Process of State Formation in the Arabian Desert". *Journal of the Royal Anthropological Institute* Vol. 95: Parts I and II (pp. 75-86), (174-194).
1966	Review: Cohen, Abner, Arab Border Villages in Israel, in *MAN*, March, pp. 272-73.

1966   Review: Fraenkel, Merran, Tribe and Class in Monrovia in *Hamizrah Hehadash.*

1966   "Social Change in an Arab Village", in *The Social Structure of Israel.* Eisenstadt, Adler, Bar Yosef (eds.), Akademon, Jerusalem.

1966   Wenner-Gren Foundation Fellowship, Grant-in-Aid

1966-1968   Member of Advisory Committee to Ministry of Housing - For Housing for Minority Groups.

1966-71   Haifa University College - Senior Lecturer

1967   Review: Matras, J., Social Change in Israel, in *New Outlook,* January 1967, pp. 60-61.

1967:   Review: Weingrod, Alex, Israel: Group Relations in a New Society, in *American Anthropologist,* 69, p. 244.

1967   'On the Council's Anti-War Resolution' in AAA *Fellow Newsletter,* Vol. 8, No 4, April, pp. 9-10.

1968; 1973   Grants from Research Institute for the Study of Man

1968   Review: Marx, Emanuel, Bedouin of the Negev, in *MAN,* pp. 339-40.

1968   "Change, Barriers to Change, and Contradictions in the Arab Village Family" *American Anthropologist,* 70; also in *The Arabs in Israel: Continuity and Change,* A. Layish (ed.), The Magnes Press, The Hebrew University, Jerusalem 1981. (Hebrew).

1968   "The Contradictions Between Property, Kinship and Power as Reflected in the Marriage System of an Arab Village" in *Contributions to Mediterranean Sociology.* Ed. J.G. Persitiany (Mouton, Paris); also in *Les societes rurales mediterraneenees,* B. Kayser and J. Pitt-Rivers (eds.), Edisud, Aix-en-Provence, 1986).

1970   Review: Shiloh, Alon (ed.), Peoples and Cultures of the Middle East, in *New Outlook,* November, pp. 53-54.

1970   Fellow – American Anthropological Association

1970   "The Culture of Kibbutz Ein Harod: An Anthropological Perspective", *Ariel* No. 28; also in *The Kibbutz* (Sadan Publishing House, Tel Aviv, 1973-1977); German and Dutch editions 1975, 1976, Zonig and Keuning: Wageningher; Finnish Edition.

1970-1973   Member of Advisory Committee to Ministry of Education - For Introducing Anthropology into Primary Schools.

1970-1973   Executive Board - Israel Sociological Association

1971   Grant-in-Aid: Jewish Memorial Foundation.

1971   "Immigration, Urbanization and Crisis: The Process of Jewish Colonization in Palestine During the 1920's" *International Journal of Comparative Sociology* XII: 1971 (with Shulamit Carmi). (Also in Hebrew - *Mibiphnim,* 33: 3, 1971).

1972   Visiting Professor, Brooklyn College, CUNY, Dept. of Anthropology.

1972   University of Haifa - Associate Professor.

1972   "An Overview and Critique of the Literature on Rural Politics and Social Change", in *Rural Politics and Social Change in the*

	Middle East, R. Antoun and I. Harik (eds.), (Indiana University Press, Bloomington/London (pp. 45-74).
1972-76	Hebrew University - Visiting Professor
1973	Review: Segre, V.D., Israel, A Society in Transition. In *American Anthropologist*, 75, pp. 861-62.
1973	'Forever' (Poem), *New Outlook,* July-August.
1974	Review: Deshen, S., Immigrant Voters in Israel, in *Megamot*, pp. 467-469 (Hebrew).
1974	'Learning By Rote' (Poem), *New Outlook*, August-September.
1974	"Hamula" -- *The Journal of Peasant Studies* 1: 2.
1974	"Non-Hierarchical, Hierarchical and Masked Reciprocity in the Arab Village" in *Visiting Patterns and Social Dynamics in Eastern Mediterranean Communities. Anthropological Quarterly: Special Issue.* L.W. Sweet, ed., 47:1, pp. 139-166. also in *Studies in Marriage Customs*, Eds. Ben-Ami and Noy, Folklore Research Center Studies, 4, (The Magnes Press, Jerusalem; 1974); also in *Being Female: Reproduction, Power and Change*, D. Raphael (ed.), (Mouton Publishers, The Hague: 1975).
1974	"The Origins of the Process of Proletarianization and Urbanization of Arab Peasants in Palestine" in *City and Peasant: A Study in Social-Cultural Dynamics*, Vol. 220 art. 6 of the Annals of the New York Academy of Sciences (pp. 470-485). Editors: La Ruffa, Freed, Saunders, Hansen and Benet (paper written with S. Carmi). (Also in *Studies of Israeli Society: Migration, Ethnicity and Community* (Vol. I), ed. E. Krausz (Transaction Books, New Brunswick, N.J.: 1981).
1974-75	Simon Senior Research Fellow, The University of Manchester, England.
1975	'The Picnic in the Shaikh's House on the Hill' (Poem), *New Outlook*, May-June.
1975-77, 82-83, 85-91:	Chairman, Committee for M.A. Studies Anthropology, Department of Sociology and Anthropology, University of Haifa.
1976	'At Least Two Viewpoints' (Poem-Satire), *New Outlook*, July-August.
1976	"Social and Economic Factors in Explanation of the Increased Rate of Patrilinial Endogamy in the Arab Village" in *Family Structures in the Middle East*, J.G. Peristiany (ed.). (Cambridge U.P., Cambridge); also in *Society and Development*, D. Soen Ed. ITGG, Tel-Aviv, May 1974 (also in Hebrew - *Social Research Review*, No. 1, 1972).
1976	"The Privatization of Public Means, the State-Made Middle-Class and the Realization of Family Value in Israel", in *Kinship and Modernization*, J.G. Peristiany ed. The American Field Staff, Rome, 1976 (with S. Carmi) (pp. 131-159).
1977	Review: Layish, Aharon, Women and Islamic Law in a Non-Muslim State, in *Hamizrah Hehadash*, pp. 119-120.

1978	Review: Blackman, W.S., The Fellahim of Upper Egypt, in *Hamizrah Hehadash* (The New East), pp. 321-322.

1978 "The Class Situation of the Arab National Minority in Israel" *Comparative Studies in Society and History* 20: 3, July (pp. 374-407).

1978-80 Co-editor, *Critical Notebooks* (Hebrew).

1979- University of Haifa – Professor

1979 Review: Kay, Shirley, The Bedouins, in *American Anthropologist*, p. 729.

1979 "On Determinants of the Status of Arab Village Women" *Man*, LX, 1960; also in *Integration and Development in Israel*. S. Eisenstadt, R. Bar Yosef, C. Adler (Eds.), Israel Universities Press, Jerusalem (also in Hebrew - *The New East* 9: 1-2, 1959).

1980 "Men and Women in Arab Peasant to Proletariat Transformation" in *Theory and Practice*, S. Diamond ed. Mouton, The Hague; also in *Date y matrimonio en los paises mediterraneos*, J.G. Peristiany (ed.), Centro de Investigaciones Sociologicas: Madrid, 1987.

1981 Review: Smooha, S., Israel: Pluralism and Conflict, in *American Anthropologist*, 83, pp. 157-159.

1981 Grant - Israel Academy of Sciences (Basic Research Foundation) - (Social Relations between Nazareth and Upper Nazareth).

1981-1982 Distinguished Visiting Professor, Department of Anthropology, Rutgers University

1981-1983 President - Israel Anthropological Association.

1982 'A Nation at War', *Haaretz*, June 10 (Hebrew).

1982 'Col. Geva—A True Man of Conscience', *Ha'aretz* July 28 (Hebrew).

1983 'On the Lacunae in the "Unnecessary War", *Davar*, 18 July, (Hebrew); also in Al Fajar; also abbreviated in *New Outlook* as 'A Challenge to Peace Now'.

1983 *Arab Society in Israel: A Reader* (editor with A. Haider and R. Kahane), The Hebrew University of Jerusalem, Jerusalem, 508 pp.

1983 "History, Political Action and Change as 'Aberrations' and Zionism as an Irremediable 'Contradiction'". Review Essay of I. Lustick, Arabs in the Jewish State: A Study in the Control of a National Minority, *Israel Social Science Research*, I: 2: pp. 69-76.

1983 The Problem of Arab Peasant Kinship: Superimposed, Structured Collectivity and Descent, Politicized Marriage and Patriarchal Property Control", in *Social Anthropology of Peasantry*, J. Mencher, (ed.), Somaya: Bombay. Madras. New Delhi, 1983.

1983 'As Co-sponsor of the Motion on Lebanon and the Motion on Academic Freedom in Israeli-Occupied West Bank' in *AAA Anthropology Newsletter*, Vol. 24, No 6, September, pp. 6-7.

1985-1986 Grant - Social Science Research Council - (Social Relations between Nazareth and Upper Nazareth).

1985-1990   Director of Project on Status and Condition of the Arabs in Israel
             (Grant from Ford Foundation through International Center for
             Peace in the Middle East).

1985-1990   Director of Research Project: *The Condition and the Status of the
             Arabs in Israel*. 8 monographs published by the ICPME four of
             which published by Westview Press:
             (1) The Legal Status of Arabs in Israel (Prof. D. Kretzmer) 1987;
             (2) Social Welfare Services for Israel's Arab Population (Dr. Aziz
             Haidar) 1987; (3) Health Services to the Arab Population in Israel
             (Dr. Nira Reiss) 1988; (4) Arab Local Government in Israel (Dr.
             M. Al-Haj and H. Rosenfeld) 1988.
             Four additional monographs published in 1990-1991:
             (5) Planning and Housing for Israeli Arabs (Dr. Rassem
             Khamaisi); (6) Crime and Delinquincy among Arabs of Israel
             (Prof. Stanley Cohen); (7) Arab Education in Israel (Dr. M. Al-
             Haj); also as: *Education, Empowerment and Control*, SUNY
             Press, 1995. (8) Arab Occupational Structure and Economy in
             Israel (Dr. A. Haidar); also as: *On The Margins*, London: Hurst,
             1995.

1986   'Obstacles to Peace' in Confronting the Middle East Conflict,
             IDOC INTERNAZIONALE, 86/4, July-August, pp. 62-68.

1987   "Where Who Stands?" (Reply to Boaz Evron), *New Outlook*,
             Sept/Oct, pp. 28-31 (with Shula Carmi).

1988   "Changes in Class – National Relations in Palestine-Israel", in *The
             Condition and Status of the Arabs in Israel*. ICPME, Tel-Aviv,
             (with S. Carmi).

1988   "Nazareth and Upper Nazareth in the Political Economy of
             Israel", in *Arab-Jewish Relations in Israel*, Y. Hofman (ed.),
             (Wyndham Hall, Bristol, Indiana) pp. 45-66.

1988-1990   Member of Social Science Committee (Histadruth) for
             Encouragement of Research.

1989   Review: Lewis, Norman N., Nomads and Settlers in Syria and
             Jordan, 1800-1980, in *Asian and African Studies*, 23: 2/3, pp. 294-
             295.

1989   Review: Khalidi, Raja, The Arab Economy in Israel: The
             Dynamics of a Region's Development, in *Asian and African
             Studies*, 23: 2/3, pp. 303-305.

1989   "The Emergence of an Indigenous Political Framework in Israel:
             The National Committee of Chairmen of Arab Local Authorities"
             (with M. Al-Haj) *Asian and African Studies* 23: 2/3, pp. 205-244.

1989   "The Emergence of Militaristic Nationalism in Israel"(with S.
             Carmi) *in International Journal of Politics Culture and Society*
             3:1, pp. 5-49; Expanded version in *The Anthropology of Peace*, M.
             Zamora, ed. College of William and Mary, 1992, pp. 191-249;
             also in *Israeli Society: Critical Perspectives*, Uri Ram, ed., 1993,
             Tel-Aviv, Breirot (Hebrew). pp. 275-327.

1990   *Arab Local Government in Israel.* (Westview, Boulder, Co.) (with M. Al-Haj). Also in Hebrew (Givat Haviva, 1990).

1990   "The Radical Change: From a Socialist Perspective to Militarism" (with S. Carmi) in *International Journal of Politics, Culture and Society* 4:4.

1990   "Rule of Law Versus Political Interest" (with M. Saltman) *Contemporary Crises* 14.

1991   Professor Emeritus

1991   Review: Peretz, Don, Intifada, in *New Outlook*, April/May, 34:3, p. 39.

1992   Review: Zleibo, Ali H., Before the Mountains Disappear: An Ethnographic Chronicle of the Modern Palestinians, in *New Outlook*, July/August, 35:4, p. 45.

1992   Review: Romann, M. and A. Weingrod, Living Together Separately: Arabs and Jews in Contemporary Jerusalem, in *New Outlook*, September/October, 35:5, p. 42.

1992   Review: Shehadeh, Raja, The Sealed Room, in *New Outlook*, Jan.-Feb.

1992   "Israeli Political Economy and the Widening Class Gap Between its Two National Groups" (with S. Carmi) in *Asian and African Studies* 26, 15-61; also in Israel: *A Local Anthruoplogy*, Abuhav et al, eds. Wayne State Press (forthcoming).

1993   RISM Landes Senior Fellowship.

1994   "A Partial Reply to Elia Zureik", *Journal of Palestine Studies*, XXIII, no 2, pp. 201-203.

1995   Review: Pappe, Ilan, The Making of the Arab-Israeli Conflict 1947-1951, *Palestine-Israel*, No. 5, Winter, pp. 107-111.

2000   Review: Kimmerling, B. and J. Migdal, "The Palestinians: The Making of a People, *Zmanim*, 71.

2002   'Leaving While Remaining', *Haaretz*, March 28, (with Shula Carmi), (Hebrew).

2002   "The Idea is to Change the State, Not the 'Conceptual' Terminology". *Ethnic and Racial Studies*, 25:6, 2002, Pp. 1083-1095

2002   "The Time When the Majority in the Early Israeli State 'Cabinet' Decided Not to Block the Possibility of the Return of the Arab Refugees and that 'There was Enough Land for All' and How and Why the Policy was Defeated in *Land and Territoriality*, M. Saltman, ed. (Berg, Oxford) pp. 37-69 (with S. Carmi); also in Hebrew in *State and Society* 3:2, 371-399, 2003.

2003   'Going Native' in AAA *Anthropology News,* Vol. 4, No 8, November, pp. 6-7.

"Work-Idea Groups as a Phase in the Evolution of the Kibbutz", (unpublished paper, written with S. Carmi).

Many Letters to the Editor (Ha'aretz, Al Hamishmar, Davar).

Work in progress. *The Rise of Urban Life in Ottoman Palestine*: 1850-1917.
Neither Capitalism, Colonialism, Dependence or Dominance as Definitive Factors: Jews and Arabs in Palstine 1880-1947, A Critique.
The Great Retreat from a Mixed Economy to a Version of Late Capitalism and Militaristic-Naitonalism: The Transformation of Social Forces.

Contributors

Majid Al-Haj is a member of the Department of Sociology and Anthropology and head of the Center for Multiculturalism and Educational Research at the University of Haifa. His areas of interest include education, ethnicity and political sociology. His books include *Social Change and Family Processes* and *Immigration and Ethnic Formation in a Deeply Divided Society: The Case of the 1990s Immigration from the former Soviet Union*.

Scott Atran is director of research at the Centre National de la Recherche Scientifique, Institut Jean Nicod (Paris) and is affiliated as well with the Institute for social research at the University of Michigan. His work focuses on Middle East ethnography and political economy and cognitive and linguistic anthropology. Among his books are *Cognitive Foundations of Natural History: Towards an Anthropology of Science* and *In Gods we Trust: The Evolutionary Landscape of Religion*.

Daphna Birenbaum-Carmeli teaches in the department of Nursing at the University of Haifa. Her main areas of interest are medical technologies and women's health and lately procreative medicine and genetic screening. She has published in addition to numerous articles a book (in Hebrew) entitled: *Tel Aviv North: The Making of a New Israeli Middle Class*.

Yoram S. Carmeli teaches in the Department of Sociology and Anthropology at the University of Haifa. His main interest is the rise and crisis of modernity. In this context, he has published extensively on the British traveling circus. He has also researched and co-authored articles with Daphna Birenbaum-Carmeli on social and cultural aspects of new reproductive technologies. He has edited a volume entitled *Consumption and Market Society in Israel* (together with Kalman Applbaum)

Keith Hart teaches Anthropology at Goldsmiths College, London. His work emphasizes economic anthropology, Africa and the African Diaspora and the history of social theory. His books include: *The Political Economy of West Africa Agriculture* and *Money in an Unequal World*.

Rassem Khamaisi teaches in the department of Geography at the University of Haifa. His major areas of research interest are urban planning and urban Geography. In addition to journal publications he is the author of a book entitled *The Jerusalem Urban Fabric*.

Baruch Kimmerling teaches sociology at the Hebrew University in Jerusalem. His areas of specialization include Israeli and Palestinian society, inter-ethnic conflicts and the sociology of the military and war. Among his books are

Zionism and Economy, and Palestinians: the Making of a People (with Joel S. Migdal).

Herbert S. Lewis before his retirement taught Anthropology at the University of Wisconsin, Madison. His areas of concentration are cultural (social) anthropology, political anthropology and ethnicity. He has written: *After the Eagles Landed: The Yemenites of Israel* and edited the forthcoming *Oneida Lives: Long lost Narratives of Wisconsin Oneida.*

Emanuel Marx is a retired member of The Department of Sociology and Anthropology at the University of Tel Aviv. His areas of interest include Bureaucracy, pastoral nomads and forced migration. His books include *The Social Context of Violent Behavior: A social Anthropological Study in an Israeli Immigrant Town* and *Bedouin of the Negev.*

Nira Reiss teaches anthropology at the Gordon College of Education in Haifa and at Columbia University in New York. She specializes in culture, language and communication and medical anthropology. She has published *Speech Act Taxonomy as a means of Ethnographic Description* and *Health Care to the Arab Population of Israel.*

Maya Rosenfeld teaches at the Hebrew University and Sapir Academic College. She is also a research fellow at the Harry S. Truman Research institute. Her primary area of interest is the social and political history of the Palestinians. Her book : *Confronting the Occupation: Work, Education and Political Activism of Palestinian Families in a Refugee Camp* was published in 2004.

Michael Saltman teaches in the Department of Sociology and Anthropology at The University of Haifa. His research is concentrated in the areas of Ethnography of Sub-Saharan Africa and the Caribbean as well as the anthropology of law. His books include *The Demise of the Reasonable Man* and *Land and Territoriality.*

Zvi Sobel was before his retirement a member of the Department of Sociology and Anthropology at the University of Haifa. His areas of specialization are migration and the sociology of religion. Among his books are *Migrants from the promised land* and *A Small Place in Galilee: Religion and Social Conflict in an Israeli Village.*

Shlomo Swirsky is academic director of the Adva Center for the Study of Israeli Society. His areas of specialization include political sociology and the political economy of fiscal policy. Among his books are *The Politics of Education in Israel: Comparisons with the United State*s and *Israel: The Oriental Majority.*

Alex Weingrod before his retirement taught anthropology in the Department of anthropology in the Department of Behavioral Sciences at Ben Gurion University of the Negev. His major research interests include ethnicity, diasporas and the Jews of Morocco. Among his books are *Homelands and Diasporas: Holy Lands and other Places* (with Andre Levy) and *The Saint of Beersheba*.

Yuval Yonay is a member of the department of Sociology and Anthropology at the University of Haifa. He specializes in the Sociology of Science and knowledge, the sociology of culture and gay and lesbian studies. In addition to numerous articles in his areas of specialization he has published a volume entitled *The Struggle over the Soul of Economics*.